The Lynde and Harry Bradley Foundation is the philanthropic legacy of two brothers, Lynde and Harry Bradley. It is a private, independent grant-making organization based in Milwaukee with programs that support human dignity and the value of intellectual and artistic freedom. The Foundation has long underwritten a wide range of cultural and artistic endeavors as a natural extension of its mission to encourage education and scholarship. The Foundation's directors believe that the preservation and understanding of the human artistic heritage is as essential to an enlightened society as the study of history; that in order to remain free, a society must be culturally vibrant and intellectually vigorous.

It is because this transmission of enduring principles from one generation to the next is so much a part of our work that the Lynde and Harry Bradley Foundation is pleased to support the exhibition *Jan Lievens: A Dutch Master Rediscovered.* We hope that it will bring new appreciation for Lievens' genius, a deeper understanding of his place in the history of art, and most important, a renewed sense of the transcendence of beauty and of the human spirit.

The Foundation is grateful to the trustees and directors of both the National Gallery of Art and the Milwaukee Art Museum, and especially to Laurie Winters, curator of Earlier European Art at Milwaukee Art Museum, and Arthur K. Wheelock Jr., curator of northern baroque painting at the National Gallery of Art, for their splendid work in presenting this new perspective on the art of Jan Lievens. We are privileged to be able to assist in their efforts.

Michael W. Grebe
President
Lynde and Harry Bradley Foundation

I must study politics and war that my sons may have liberty to study mathematics and philosophy. My sons ought to study mathematics and philosophy, geography, natural history, naval architecture, navigation, commerce, and agriculture, in order to give their children a right to study painting, poetry, music, architecture, statuary, tapestry, and porcelain.

JOHN ADAMS

Jan Lievens

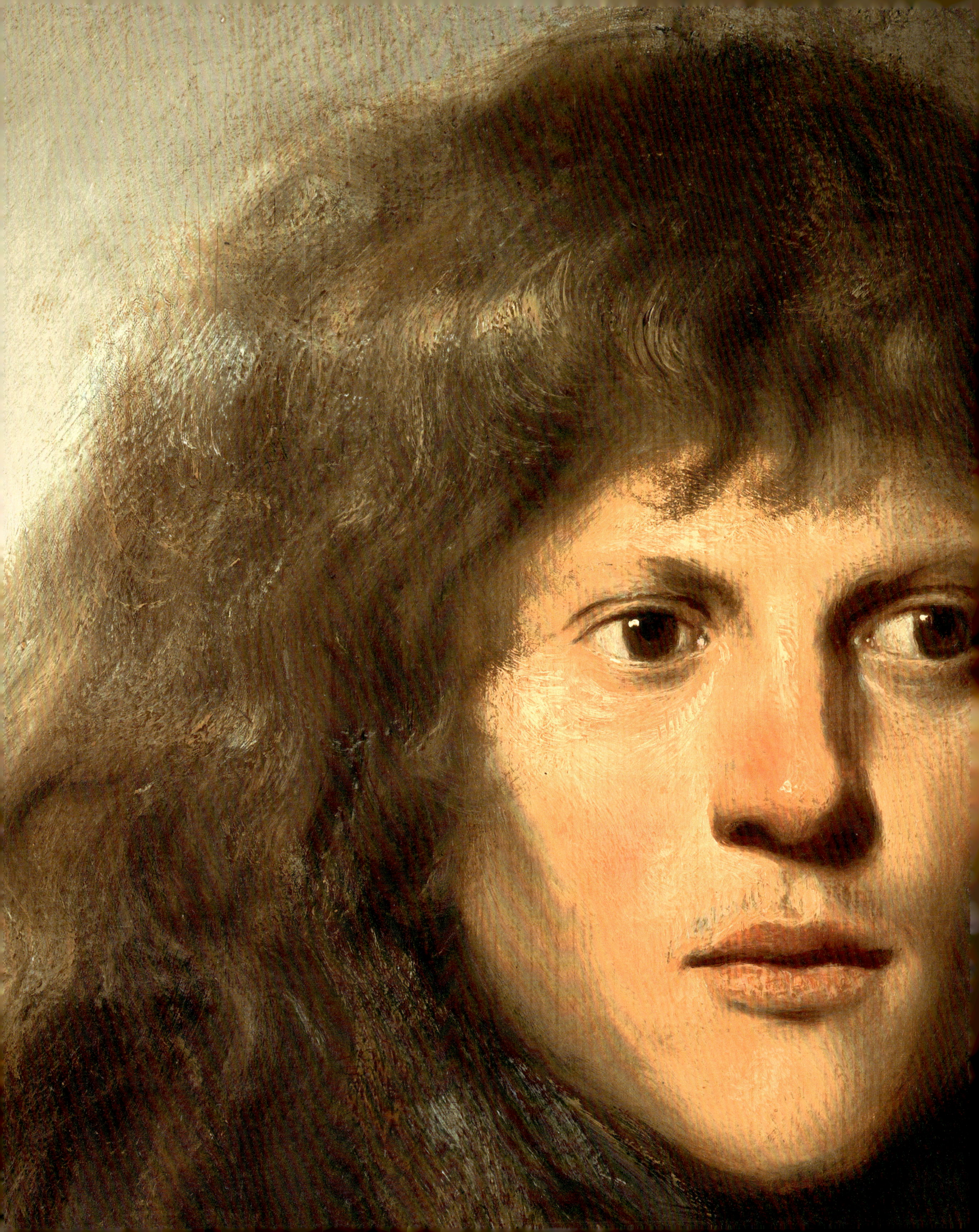

Jan Lievens

A Dutch Master Rediscovered

Arthur K. Wheelock Jr.

WITH

Stephanie S. Dickey

E. Melanie Gifford

Gregory Rubinstein

Jaap van der Veen

Lloyd DeWitt

NATIONAL GALLERY OF ART, WASHINGTON

MILWAUKEE ART MUSEUM

REMBRANDTHUIS, AMSTERDAM

The exhibition is organized by the National Gallery of Art, Washington, in association with the Milwaukee Art Museum and the Rembrandthuis, Amsterdam

The Lynde and Harry Bradley Foundation is the national sponsor of the exhibition

The exhibition is made possible by the generous support of Isabel and Alfred Bader and anonymous donors in honor of George M. Kaufman

Early support for curatorial and conservation research was provided by Mrs. George M. Kaufman and the Joseph F. McCrindle Foundation

The exhibition is supported by an indemnity from the Federal Council on the Arts and the Humanities

EXHIBITION DATES

National Gallery of Art, Washington
October 26, 2008–January 11, 2009

Milwaukee Art Museum
February 7–April 26, 2009

Rembrandthuis, Amsterdam
May 17–August 9, 2009

LIBRARY OF CONGRESS
CATALOGING-IN-PUBLICATION DATA

Lievens, Jan, 1607–1674.
Jan Lievens : a Dutch master rediscovered / Arthur K. Wheelock Jr., with Stephanie S. Dickey... [et al.].
p. cm.

Catalog of an exhibition held at the National Gallery of Art, Washington, DC, Oct. 26, 2008–Jan. 11, 2009, the Milwaukee Art Museum, Feb. 7–Apr. 26, 2009, and the Rembrandthuis, Amsterdam, May 17–Aug. 9, 2009.

Includes bibliographical references and index.

ISBN 978-0-300-14213-6 (hardcover : alk. paper)
ISBN 978-0-89468-355-8 (softcover : alk. paper)

1. Lievens, Jan, 1607–1674 — Exhibitions.
I. Wheelock, Arthur K. II. Dickey, Stephanie.
III. National Gallery of Art (U.S.)
IV. Milwaukee Art Museum. V. Museum Het Rembrandthuis (Amsterdam, Netherlands)
VI. Title.

N6953.L53A4 2008
760.092 — dc22

2008023911

COVER ILLUSTRATIONS

FRONT: Jan Lievens, *Pilate Washing His Hands* (detail), c. 1625–1626, oil on panel (cat. 7). Stedelijk Museum De Lakenhal, Leiden, The Netherlands

BACK: Jan Lievens, *Decaying Pollard Willow* (detail), c. 1655–1665, pen and brown ink on oriental paper (cat. 134). Kupferstich-Kabinett, Staatliche Kunstsammlungen Dresden

Produced by the Publishing Office, National Gallery of Art, Washington
www.nga.gov

Judy Metro, editor in chief
Chris Vogel, production manager and designer
Tam Curry Bryfogle, senior editor
Rio DeNaro, production assistant
Mariah Shay, production editor

Typeset at the National Gallery of Art in Arno Pro and Scala Sans Pro

Printed on Gardapat Kiara by Waanders, Zwolle, The Netherlands.

Published in 2008 by the National Gallery of Art, Washington, in association with Yale University Press, New Haven and London

Yale University Press
P.O. Box 209040
New Haven, CT 06520-9040
www.yalebooks.com

10 9 8 7 6 5 4 3 2 1

Contents

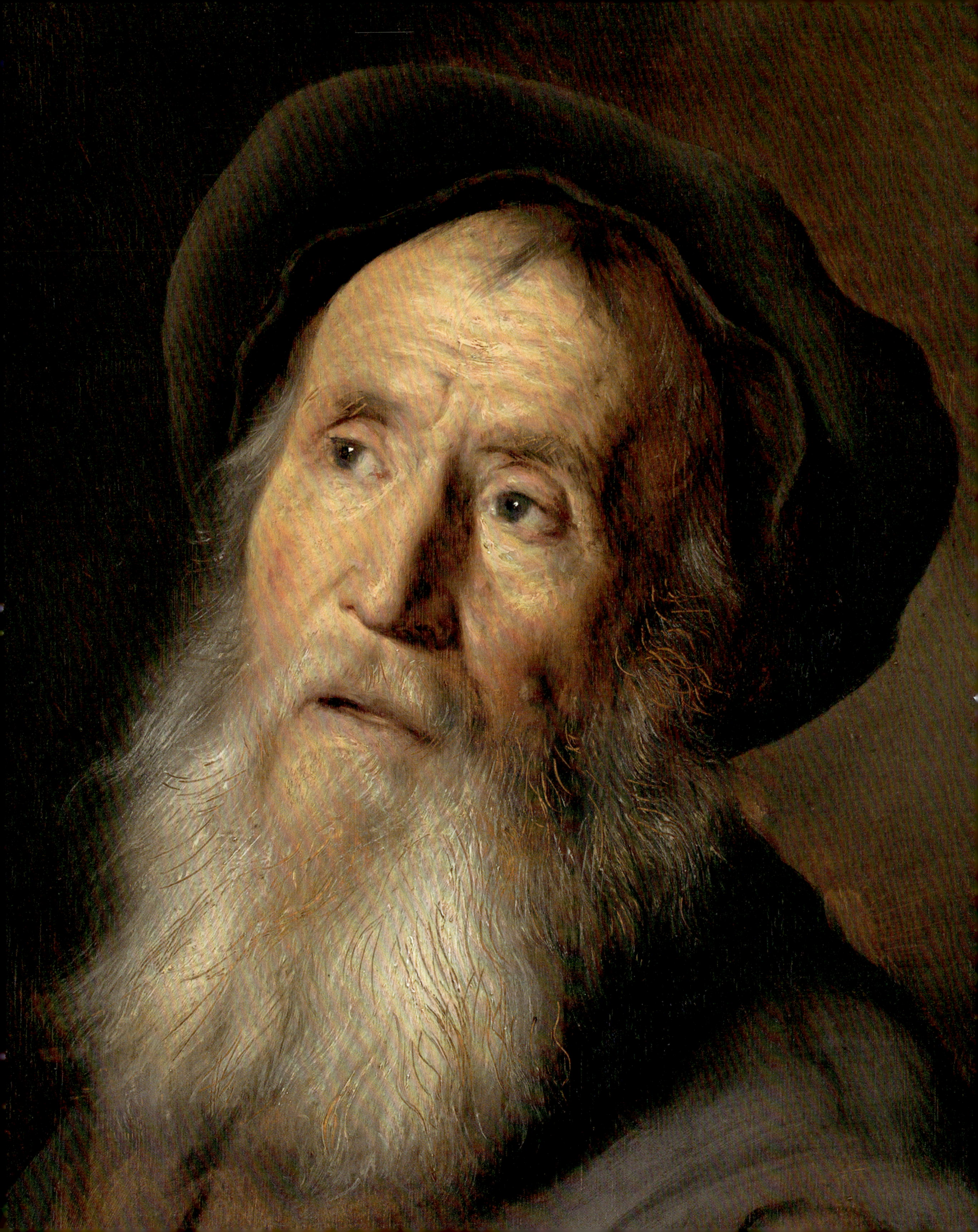

Directors' Foreword

JAN LIEVENS REMAINS ONE OF the most fascinating and enigmatic Dutch artists of the seventeenth century. Daring and innovative as a painter, printmaker, and draftsman, Lievens created memorable portraits, character studies, landscapes, and religious and allegorical images that were not only widely praised during his lifetime but are also highly valued today. Yet his posthumous reputation has never risen to a level commensurate with the quality of his individual works. This is partly due to the peripatetic character of his career, which began in his native Leiden and included extended stays in London, Antwerp, and Amsterdam as well as shorter periods in Berlin and The Hague. But it can also be explained by the variety of styles in which he worked during his career.

Lievens embarked on his career in Leiden in the 1620s after studying with Pieter Lastman in Amsterdam. His bold, early style was influenced by the Utrecht Caravaggisti, in particular by Gerrit van Honthorst. At this point in his life Lievens worked alongside his Leiden compatriot Rembrandt van Rijn. The two artists had a close, symbiotic relationship, in terms of both style and subject matter. Some scholars have argued that they may even have shared a studio. Contemporary critics recognized their precocious abilities, and their paintings were prized by patrons in the Dutch court in The Hague.

Lievens aspired to be an internationally renowned court artist, and in 1632 he left Leiden for London to paint at the court of King Charles I. In London he came under the influence of Anthony van Dyck and developed a more elegant, refined manner of painting, etching, and drawing. In 1635 he moved to Antwerp, where he married into a Catholic family and began to paint landscapes and large-scale religious images. In 1644 he moved to Amsterdam, where his international Flemish style of painting was greatly admired. He painted portraits of prominent members of Dutch society, including political, cultural, and business leaders. In his later years Lievens also received commissions from the municipalities of Amsterdam and Leiden, the States General in The Hague, and the House of Orange. His landscapes were collected by Rembrandt and others.

This exhibition presents an overview of the full range of Lievens' career and provides a needed reassessment of his artistic contribution. It explores Lievens' relationship to Rembrandt but also considers the importance of his later career, which is largely unknown, even to scholars. It includes more than fifty of his finest paintings, borrowed from collections in Great Britain, Europe, Israel, and America. A number of these works were formerly attributed to other artists, often Rembrandt; some have been recently rediscovered; and others have undergone conservation treatment in preparation for the exhibition. Several of Lievens' large-scale in-situ commissions are represented here by oil sketches. The exhibition also features a remarkable group of prints and drawings from all phases of his career.

We are delighted to be working with the Milwaukee Art Museum, which came to us with the idea for the exhibition, and with the Rembrandthuis in Amsterdam. The exhibition has been organized by Arthur Wheelock, curator of northern baroque paintings at the National Gallery of Art, in conjunction with Laurie Winters, curator of Earlier European Art, Milwaukee Art Museum; Bob van den Boogert and Jaap van der Veen of the Rembrandthuis; and Lloyd DeWitt, assistant curator of the John G. Johnson Collection at the Philadelphia Museum of Art. Stephanie Dickey, Bader Chair in northern baroque art at Queen's University, Canada, has overseen the selection of Lievens' prints; and Gregory Rubenstein, head of old master drawings at Sotheby's, London, has guided our selection of drawings. A fully illustrated catalogue contains essays and entries by an international team of experts that expand our understanding of Lievens' work and its artistic significance.

In Washington and Milwaukee we are enormously grateful for the financial support of the Lynde and Harry Bradley Foundation, national sponsor of *Jan Lievens: A Dutch Master Rediscovered.* In Washington we also owe great thanks to a number of private donors, in particular Isabel and Alfred Bader as well as anonymous donors in honor of George M. Kaufman. Other financial contributions have come from Mrs. George M. Kaufman and the Joseph F. McCrindle Foundation. The exhibition in Washington and Milwaukee is also supported by an indemnity from the Federal Council on the Arts and the Humanities.

Earl A. Powell III, *National Gallery of Art, Washington*

Daniel T. Keegan, *Milwaukee Art Museum*

Ed de Heer, *Museum Het Rembrandthuis, Amsterdam*

Acknowledgments

JAN LIEVENS: A DUTCH MASTER REDISCOVERED could only have come about through the generosity of private collectors and museums and the dedication and expertise of many friends and colleagues. The germ of the idea for this exhibition came from Laurie Winters, curator of Earlier European Art at the Milwaukee Art Museum, who asked some years ago if I would like to organize a show on Jan Lievens for our two institutions. This idea was particularly appealing, as I had been rethinking what I knew of the artist because Lloyd DeWitt, a doctoral student of mine at the University of Maryland, was then writing his dissertation on Lievens' life and artistic career. DeWitt, who had assumed his curatorial position at the Philadelphia Museum of Art, kindly agreed to serve as an advisor for the selection of works and to participate in the catalogue by writing entries and an essay focusing on Lievens' complex personality. His essay examines ideas contained in seventeenth-century accounts of the artist by Constantijn Huygens and Jan Orlers, texts that are included in the Appendix.

I am delighted that the Rembrandthuis in Amsterdam is a partner for this monographic exhibition, not only because Lievens was a friend and colleague of Rembrandt in Leiden but also because he produced outstanding prints and drawings as well as paintings. Ed de Heer, director of the Rembrandthuis, and curators Bob van den Boogert and Jaap van der Veen have helped refine the exhibition content and have facilitated loans of works of art. Van der Veen has done valuable archival research on Lievens' patronage, which is presented in his thoughtful essay for the catalogue as well as in entries he wrote on individual paintings. The team of authors who wrote about Lievens' paintings for the catalogue also includes David De Witt, Bader Curator of European art at the Agnes Etherington Art Centre, Queen's University; Meredith Hale, independent scholar; Volker Manuth, professor of art history at the University of Nijmegen; and Virginia Treanor and Molli Kuenstner in the department of northern baroque paintings at the National Gallery of Art.

An important contribution of this exhibition is the presentation of Lievens' remarkable career as a graphic artist, and we would like to thank the many private collectors and museums that have made this possible with their generous loans of Lievens' prints and drawings. Stephanie Dickey, Bader Chair in northern baroque art at Queen's University, who guided the selection of prints, has written a compelling essay about Lievens' prints as well as the entries on individual works. Gregory Rubinstein, head of old master drawings at Sotheby's in London, who oversaw the selection of the drawings, also wrote an essay and individual entries on this complex aspect of Lievens' production. To both of them I extend my thanks and appreciation.

The excellent exhibition on Lievens that Rüdiger Klessmann and Sabine Jacob organized for the Herzog Anton Ulrich-Museum in Braunschweig in 1979 has served as the framework for our efforts to revisit the career of this fascinating artist. Nevertheless, since that time much has changed in the scholarship of seventeenth-century Dutch art, developments that are reflected in the catalogue, particularly our increased understanding of the complex artistic environment in Leiden during the 1620s and early 1630s when Lievens and Rembrandt were in close communication. Also better understood is the broader, international character of Dutch art, particularly as the result of Dutch artists like the Utrecht Caravaggisti returning from distant lands or Flemish artists like Peter Paul Rubens and Anthony van Dyck traveling to the Netherlands, an issue that is especially relevant to an understanding of Lievens' career.

Our image of Lievens' artistic career has also been enhanced by a number of recent discoveries of lost paintings and by a number of works that have undergone conservation treatment for the exhibition. We are grateful to Nancy Krieg, a private conservator in New York, and Maya Dresner, senior conservator at the Tel Aviv Museum of Art, for their generosity in sharing the results of their work. We have been fortunate that Melanie Gifford, conservation scientist at the National Gallery of Art, has been able to examine a great many of Lievens' paintings. The discoveries she has made about Lievens' painting techniques form the basis of her essay in this catalogue but also inform a number of the entries on individual paintings.

In our reassessments of Lievens we are greatly indebted to the research of a number of distinguished scholars, whose publications are listed in the bibliography. Of particular importance have been Rudolf E. O. Ekkart's thoughtful revisions of Hans Schneider's important monograph on the artist, first published in 1932; Werner Sumowski's catalogues of Lievens' paintings and drawings; and Peter Schatborn's exhibition of Lievens prints and drawings at the Rembrandthuis in 1988. Also essential for our considerations have been the writings of Christopher Brown, Edwin Buijsen, Ger Luijten, Doron J. Lurie, Martin Royalton-Kisch, Bernhard Schnackenburg, Gary Schwartz, J. Douglas Stewart, Roelof van Straten, Christiaan Vogelaar, Arie Wallert, Gregor J. M. Weber, and Ernst van de Wetering. In addition to these scholars, I would like to thank Cliff Ackley, Reinhold Baumstark, David Beevers, Mária van Berghe-Gerbaud, Holm Bevers, Nancy Bialler, Marion Bolten, H. Perry Chapman, Marcus Dekiert, Taco Dibbits, Jeroen Giltaij, Emilie Gordenker, Franziska Gottwald, Wolfgang Holler, J. Richard Judson, Thomas Ketelsen, Friso Lammertse, Bernd Lindemann, Norbert Middelkoop, Otto Naumann, Peter Parshall, Andrew Robison, Francis Russell, Scott Schaeffer, Marijn Schapelhouman, Joaneath A. Spicer, Dominique Surh, Pierre Théberge, C. van Tuyl van Serooskerken, Martin Sonnabend, Dennis Weller, Anneke Wertheim, Betsy Wieseman, and Marieke de Winkel, for their interest and support of this exhibition.

In each of the three participating institutions many individuals worked tirelessly to ensure the exhibition's success, and I would like to thank our colleagues at the Milwaukee Art Museum and the Rembrandthuis for their efforts. In Washington we have received outstanding support from D. Dodge Thompson, Jennifer Cipriano, and Jennifer Henel in the department of exhibitions; Julian Saenz in the office of the secretary and general counsel; Nancy Yeide in curatorial records; Sally Freitag and Melissa Stegeman in the registrar's office; Mervin Richard in the department of loans and exhibitions conservation; Mark Leithauser and his talented team in the department of installation and design, especially Elma Hajric, Debbie Kirkpatrick, and John Olson; Susan Arensberg and Margaret Doyle in the department of exhibition programs; Neil Turtell, executive librarian, and members of his staff; Christine Myers and Patricia Donovan in the development office; and Deborah Ziska and Steven Konick in the press office.

My colleagues in the publishing office, under the supervision of Judy Metro, contributed enormously to the preparation of the catalogue. My special thanks go to Tam Curry Bryfogle, who shaped and edited texts with great skill and dedication, and to Chris Vogel, who created the handsome design and oversaw production, with assistance from Rio Denaro and from Mariah Shay, the latter also coordinating comparative images gathered by Ira Bartfield in the department of imaging and visual services. Sara Sanders-Buell secured color transparencies for works in the exhibition. Joanna Champagne and Guillermo Saenz, with the assistance of Margaret Ferris in exhibition programs, prepared the Web feature.

Finally, to my staff in the department of northern baroque painting at the National Gallery of Art, I am extremely grateful. Virginia Treanor, curatorial fellow from the University of Maryland, and Molli Kuenstner, my curatorial assistant, have worked unceasingly to bring logic and order to this complex project. Not only have they been my conduit to and from colleagues both within and outside the institution, they have brought their own insights and judgments to the study of Lievens. Three other members of the team who have worked extensively on the catalogue are Brighton Hanson, University of Maryland museum fellow, Henriette de Bruyn Kops, exhibitions research assistant, and Matthew Lincoln, from Williams College, who spent his winter semester with the department.

To all of those who have helped bring this project to its successful conclusion, I extend my deepest gratitude.

Arthur K. Wheelock Jr.

Lenders to the Exhibition

Maida and George Abrams Collection

Agnes Etherington Art Centre, Kingston

Katrine Ames

Amsterdams Historisch Museum

Alfred and Isabel Bader

Bayerisches Staatsgemäldesammlungen, Munich — Alte Pinakothek

The British Museum, London

The Cooney Collection, Studio City, California

Fogg Art Museum, Harvard University

Frits Lugt Collection, Institut Néerlandais, Paris

The J. Paul Getty Museum, Los Angeles

Joseph and Lieve Guttmann

Hoogheemraadschap van Rijnland, Leiden

House of Lords, London

Johnny Van Haeften, Ltd.

Kaufman Americana Foundation

Kremer Collection

Musée de la Chartreuse, Douai

Musée des Beaux-Arts, Nancy

Musée du Louvre, Paris

Museen der Stadt Bamberg, Historisches Museum Bamberg

Museum Boijmans Van Beuningen, Rotterdam

Museum Het Rembrandthuis, Amsterdam

Museum of Fine Arts, Boston

Museum voor Stade en Lande, Groningen

The National Gallery, London

National Gallery of Art, Washington

National Gallery of Canada, Ottawa

National Gallery of Scotland, Edinburgh

New Orleans Museum of Art

Noro Foundation

North Carolina Museum of Art, Raleigh

Peck Collection, Boston

Philadelphia Museum of Art

The Pierpont Morgan Library, New York

Prentenkabinet der Rijksuniversiteit, Leiden

Private collections

Thomas Rassieur

Rijksmuseum, Amsterdam

Charles Roelofsz

Royal Pavilion and Museums, Brighton and Hove

Staatliche Kunstsammlungen Dresden

Staatliche Museen zu Berlin, Gemäldegalerie

Staatliche Museen zu Berlin, Kupferstichkabinett

Städel Museum, Frankfurt am Main

Statens Museum for Kunst, Copenhagen

Stedelijk Museum De Lakenhal, Leiden

Stiftung Preussische Schlösser und Gärten Berlin-Brandenburg

Teylers Museum, Haarlem

Eijk and Rose-Marie Van Otterloo Collection

The Walters Art Museum, Baltimore

Notes to the Reader

Entries are signed by their authors as follows:

SSD	Stephanie S. Dickey
EMG	E. Melanie Gifford
MH	Meredith Hale
MEK	Molli E. Kuenstner
VM	Volker Manuth
GMGR	Gregory Rubinstein
VCT	Virginia C. Treanor
JVDV	Jaap van der Veen
DDW	David De Witt
LDW	Lloyd DeWitt
AKW	Arthur K. Wheelock Jr.

Dimensions for works in the exhibition are given in centimeters followed by inches, height before width.

Entries for works in the exhibition feature a section of "Selected References" that includes both exhibitions and publications.

In the notes to the print entries we have used abbreviations for standard references that appear in full in the bibliography — B. (Bartsch), D. (Dutuit), Holl. (Hollstein), M.-H. (Mauquoy-Hendrickx), Rov. (Rovinski). If the same catalogue number is assigned to a print in several references, the number is given only once (as, for example, D., Rov., B. 4).

The Appendix to this catalogue includes English translations of two seventeenth-century documents that record first-hand impressions of Lievens and Rembrandt by Constantijn Huygens and Jan Jansz Orlers, previously published — in both Dutch and English — in Christiaan Vogelaar et al., *Rembrandt and Lievens in Leiden* [exh. cat., Stedelijk Museum De Lakenhal] (Leiden, 1991), 128–134, and 135–139. The essays and entries quote extensively from these texts.

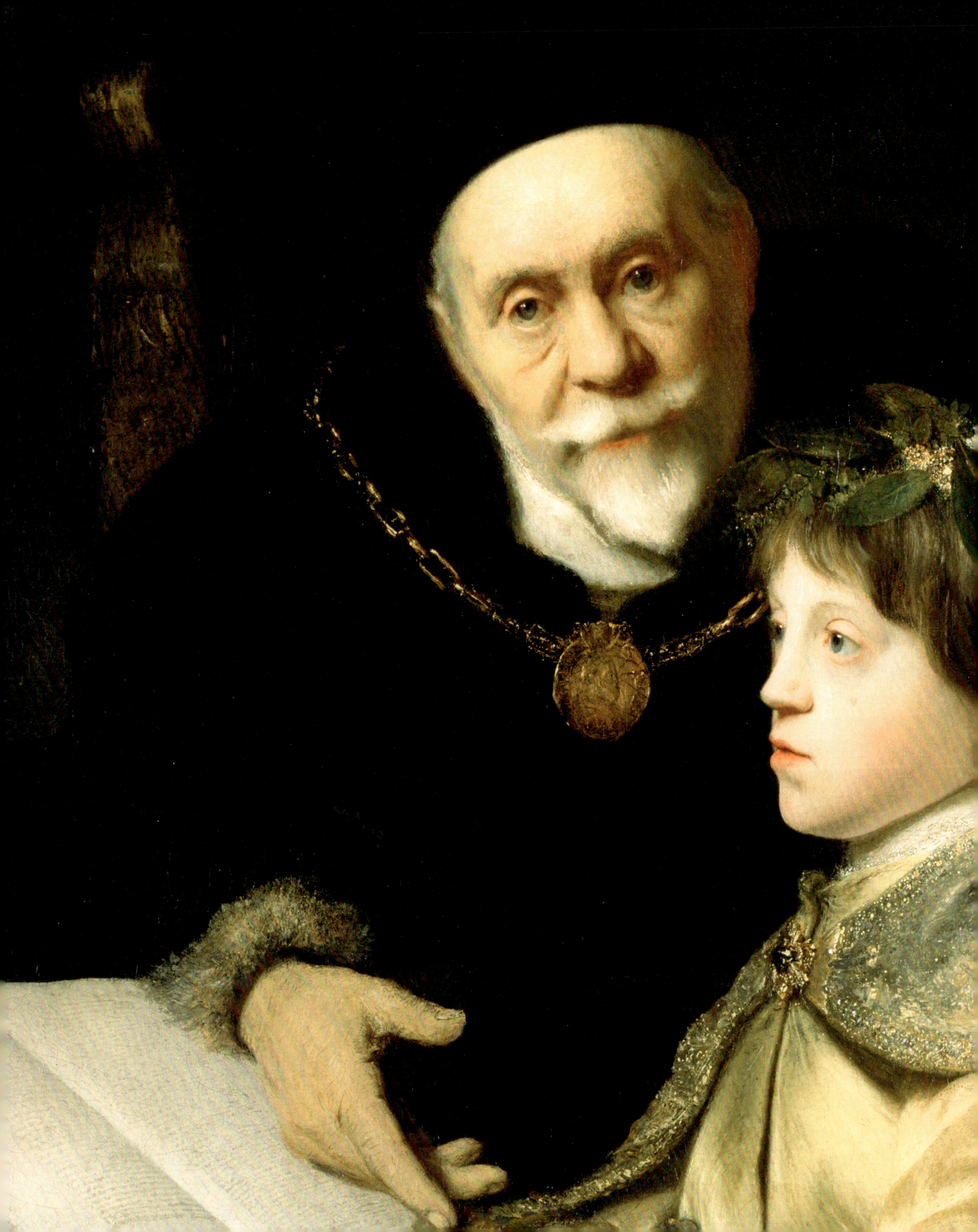

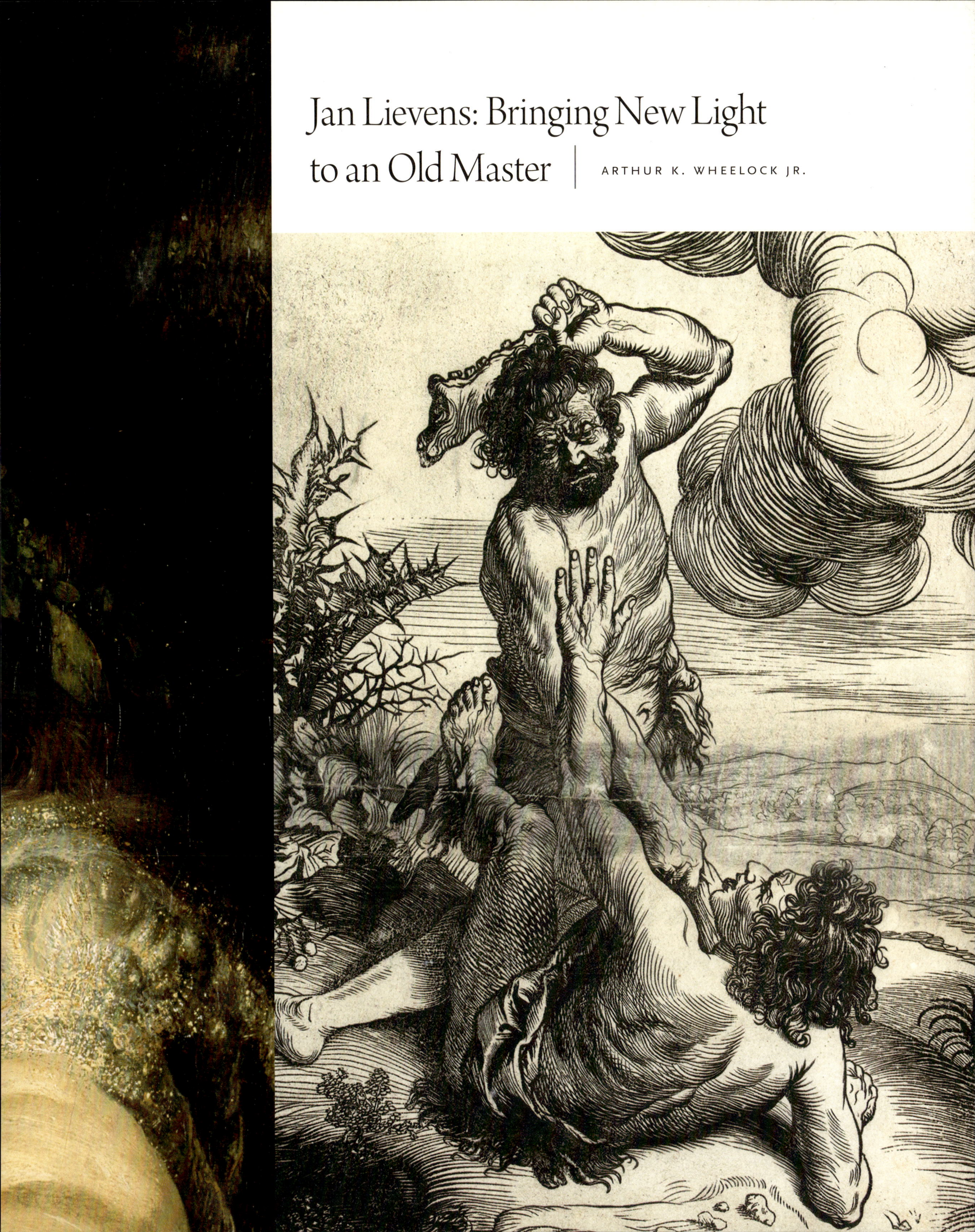
Jan Lievens: Bringing New Light to an Old Master
ARTHUR K. WHEELOCK JR.

HISTORY HAS NOT BEEN KIND to Jan Lievens (1607–1674). A child prodigy — whose talent was prized by connoisseurs and collectors in his native Leiden during his teenage years, whose services were sought by princely patrons in The Hague and London before he reached age twenty-five, and who later in life continued to receive important religious, civic, and portrait commissions in Antwerp, Amsterdam, and Berlin — Lievens barely registers today in the public consciousness. The rise and fall of artistic celebrity is a fascinating phenomenon, with story lines as varied as the personalities involved. Lievens' narrative, however, is more complex than most. It involves an array of issues, including career choices, personality, accidents of history, and the changing assessment of artistic style over the centuries. It also involves a unique complication of time and place: Lievens' close associations with Rembrandt van Rijn, a childhood companion in Leiden, whose status as the greatest artist of the Dutch golden age eventually had a profoundly negative impact on Lievens' own artistic reputation. This essay examines these issues while providing a general overview of Lievens' life and art.

Because Lievens and Rembrandt (1606–1669) were born in Leiden just over a year apart, studied with the same master, and lived near one another, their names are forever conjoined. Many parallels exist between works that each produced in Leiden in the 1620s and early 1630s, and it is evident that as aspiring artists they developed a symbiotic relationship that benefited them both. Nevertheless, owing to the enormity of Rembrandt's subsequent fame, Lievens has often been described as a follower or student, even though he began his career some years before his compatriot.[1] As a result, a number of Lievens' best early works were later attributed to Rembrandt, as well as to other artists, which further raised Rembrandt's standing, at Lievens' expense.[2] Fortunately, this perception has been changing in recent decades, and Lievens' early paintings are now better known, with the brashness of his vision and the boldness of his brushwork seen as rivaling Rembrandt's during the formative period of their careers. It is argued here that in many respects Lievens was the initiator of the stylistic and thematic developments that characterized both artists' work in the late 1620s.

Even if Lievens' early years in Leiden have fallen under the shadow of Rembrandt, at least they have been discussed. Not so his late work, which has been consistently neglected. Lievens, it is alleged, lost his way after having left Rembrandt's orbit, something that is said to have happened when he succumbed to the countervailing influence of the great Flemish master Anthony van Dyck and moved to London in 1632 in search of courtly success. Yet Lievens' career did not end when he moved to London, but continued on in Antwerp, Amsterdam, Berlin, and The Hague. By transforming his style to respond to the evolving taste for Flemish and Venetian modes of painting, Lievens achieved the international renown he so desperately sought, even in Amsterdam, where Rembrandt had moved in the early 1630s.

Lievens' later years have been overlooked for several reasons. Because this fascinating and confounding artist moved frequently in the years after he left Leiden, he does not fit comfortably into historical assessments of the period, which generally focus on the stylistic character of artistic traditions in individual cities. His decision to paint in an international style also proved to be a major liability for his subsequent reputation. Nineteenth- and twentieth-century Dutch historians privileged artists who painted in a "Dutch" style over those who incorporated Flemish and Venetian ideals into their art; their opinion was that while Rembrandt remained true to himself and to Dutch ideals, Lievens did not. Finally, although the broad outlines of Lievens' life are rather clear, the full range of his artistic successes and failures is not easy to judge because of crucial gaps in our knowledge of his art.[3] Many of his important documented works are lost, and those large-scale commissions that have survived are all but inaccessible to most visitors. As a consequence, it is challenging to reconstruct the evolution of his painting style and the radical decisions he made over the course of his career.

The inexorable decline of Lievens' critical fortunes is vividly clear in the art historical literature. Arnold Houbraken, in his lexicon of seventeenth-century Dutch artists, *De Groote Schouburgh der Nederlantsche Konstschilders en Schilderessen* (1718), wrote about Lievens far less extensively than about Rembrandt. He did, however, piece together a positive account of Lievens' life as a history and portrait painter, based on a number of sources from the artist's lifetime — including Jan Jansz Orlers' history of Leiden, *Beschrijvinge der Stadt Leyden* (1641); Philips Angel's celebration of the arts in Leiden, *Lof der Schilderkonst* (1642); and poems by Joost van den Vondel and Jan Vos honoring Lievens' paintings of the 1650s and 1660s.[4] Houbraken highlighted Lievens' early career in Leiden; his departure for London, where he portrayed Charles I; his move to Antwerp, where he worked for the Jesuits and married; his major commissions for the Leiden and Amsterdam town halls; and numerous Amsterdam burghers he portrayed later in his life.

Houbraken's text served as the basis for the biographical account by Jacob Campo Weyerman in 1729, which Jean-Baptiste Descamps repeated in 1753.[5] Weyerman added one

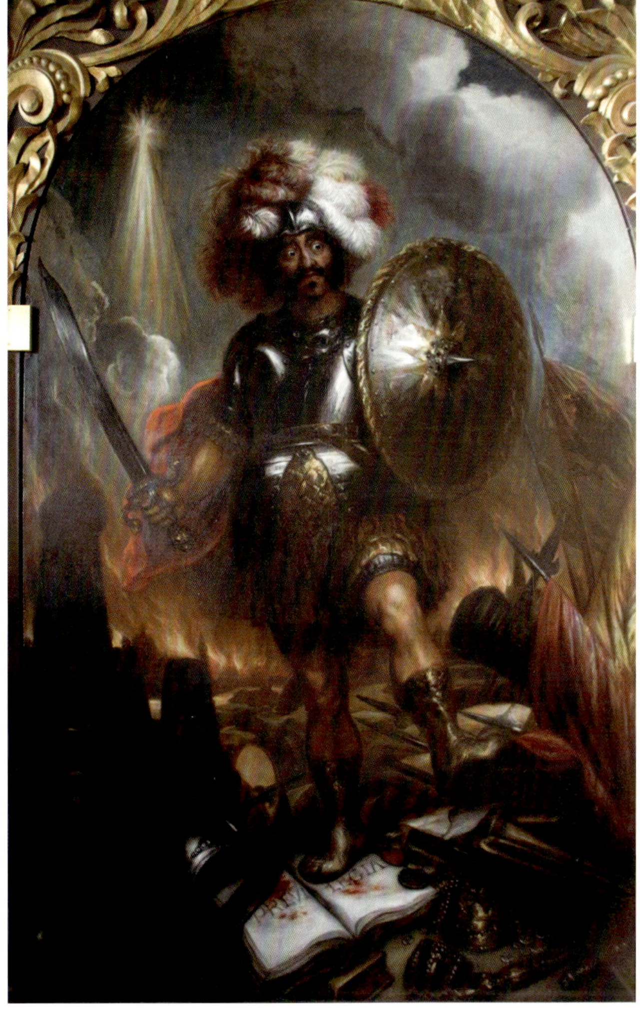

1 | Jan Lievens, *Mars (The Allegory of War)*, 1664, oil on canvas, 340 × 215 cm. Eerste Kamer der Staten-Generaal, The Hague

significant commission to those Houbraken mentioned: the large overmantel painting *Mars (The Allegory of War)* that Lievens executed in 1663–1664 for the Staatenzaal, the assembly room of the States of Holland and West Friesland in the Binnenhof, The Hague (fig. 1). As Weyerman described it, "the Mars is so naturally painted that war officers upon viewing it begin to glow, while burghers and farmers stand before it shaking and shivering."[6]

In 1816 Roeland van Eijnden and Adriaan van der Willigen added further information, noting (incorrectly) that when Lievens was brought from Antwerp to Leiden in 1639 to paint *The Magnanimity of Scipio* for the town hall (fig. 19), he was paid 150 guilders and presented with a gold medal worth 99 guilders and 17 stuivers.[7] They also observed that Lievens was a celebrated graphic artist and that his etched prints "in Rembrandt's manner" (*in Rembrandts smaak*) were greatly valued by art lovers, including the famous Parisian collector Pierre Mariette.

Soon, however, references to Lievens and his work all but disappear. He was omitted from John Smith's early nineteenth-century multivolume catalogue raisonné of Dutch and Flemish painters and was virtually ignored in Cornelis Hofstede de Groot's eight-volume revision of Smith's publication.[8] It is not clear why Lievens' name faded from view, but it surely relates to the continued rise in Rembrandt's fame. Rembrandt's expressive art not only appealed to the nineteenth-century romantics, it also fed the interests of Dutch nationalism, which found its artistic heroes, including Rembrandt and Jan Steen, among those seen as recording the essence of Dutch life and culture. Lievens, who had left Leiden for foreign courts and developed an international style of painting, did not satisfy those requirements.

The few mid-nineteenth-century references that appear inevitably compare Lievens' oeuvre unfavorably to Rembrandt's. Gustav Waagen calls *Job in His Misery* (cat. 25) "a capital work in the taste of Rembrandt, though far less powerful in colouring"; a portrait of a young man in Lord Caledon's collection is "a picture of merit, but too tame for [Rembrandt], and rather to be considered as the work of Jan Lievens"; and a landscape sketch of a drawbridge, houses, and trees creates "an effect of chiaroscuro... with sepia, bistre, and a little colour, worthy of Rembrandt."[9] The natural culmination is Wilhelm von Bode's listing of Lievens among Rembrandt's most prominent pupils and followers in his seminal study of Dutch art (1883).[10]

At the same time, Lievens' monumental *Mars* for the Binnenhof in The Hague suffered such lack of regard in the nineteenth century that a balcony was built in front of it that largely obscured

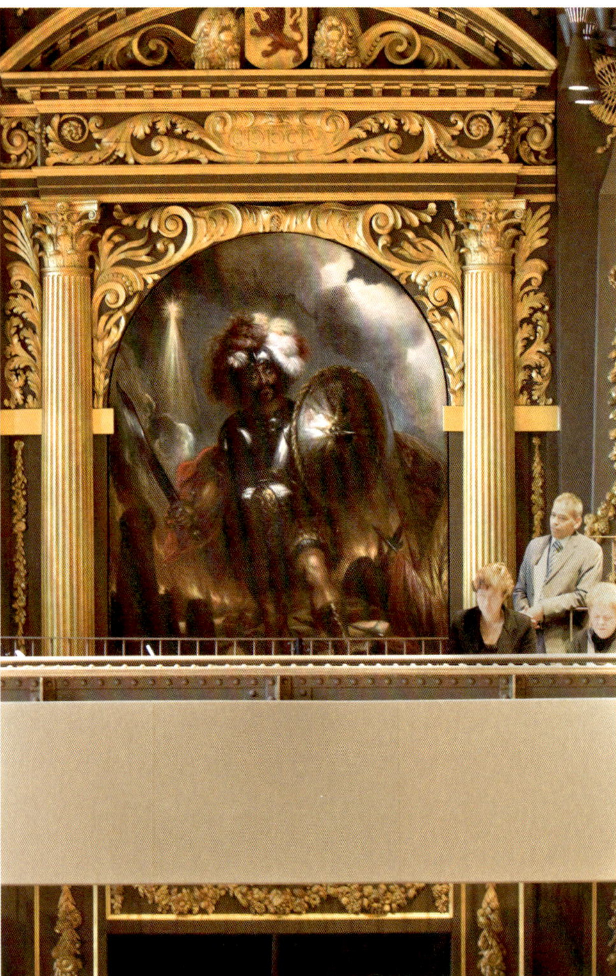

2 | Eerste Kamer der Staten-Generaal, The Hague, with balcony obscuring Lievens' *Mars (The Allegory of War)*

it (fig. 2). Similarly, his enormous *Visitation* (fig. 18), once exhibited in a position of honor in the Rubens gallery of the Louvre, was relegated to a side baffle in a small transition area between galleries.

Lievens regained notice only at the beginning of the twentieth century, perhaps owing to the 1897 publication of an autobiography by Constantijn Huygens written in 1629–1631.[11] That text provided striking insights into the character of Lievens' and Rembrandt's early oeuvres, encouraging a new look at this phase of Leiden painting. Several German scholars, particularly E. W. Moes and Hans Schneider, began to focus on Lievens' work. Indeed, Schneider's 1932 monograph has formed the basis of all subsequent research.[12] Nevertheless, despite their groundbreaking efforts, as well as those of Kurt Bauch, Rudolf E. O. Ekkart (who published a revised edition of Schneider's book in 1973), and Horst Gerson, the artist's star never rose very high, outshone by the glories of Rembrandt.[13]

The most explicit acknowledgment of this also-ran status was the title of Lievens' first monographic exhibition: *Jan Lievens: A Painter in the Shadow of Rembrandt*, which Rüdiger Klessmann organized for the Herzog Anton Ulrich-Museum Braunschweig in 1979.[14] That exhibition, which included an excellent selection of paintings, prints, and drawings, revealed misperceptions in historical assessments of Lievens and Rembrandt. For the first time, the visual power of Lievens' early works received concentrated attention, making possible a broader appreciation of his dynamic and innovative artistic personality. One could see that his Leiden style took inspiration not only from his teacher Pieter Lastman (and from Rembrandt) but also from the Utrecht Caravaggisti — particularly Hendrick ter Brugghen, Dirck van Baburen, and Gerrit van Honthorst — as well as Peter Paul Rubens.[15]

In recent years scholars such as Christiaan Vogelaar, Gary Schwartz, Helga Gutbrod, Ernst van de Wetering, Bernhard Schnackenburg, and Roelof van Straten have continued to explore the complex relationship between Rembrandt and Lievens in Leiden,[16] even proposing that the two may have shared a workshop in the late 1620s.[17] Recent discoveries of a number of Lievens' early paintings, several of them included in this exhibition, have reinforced the sense that Lievens played a more vital role in determining the character of art produced in Leiden at this time than was apparent earlier. Although a more nuanced understanding of the ways in which the two artists interacted is now possible, Rembrandt still looms over Lievens in the literature, even with respect to the Leiden years. As late as 1991 the subtitle of an exhibition devoted to Pieter Lastman identified him as "the man who taught Rembrandt" — not "Rembrandt and Lievens."[18]

While the major emphasis in recent scholarship has been on Lievens' early life, Peter Schatborn, Stephanie Dickey, and Lloyd DeWitt have undertaken studies of his later artistic development.[19] To comprehend the full significance of Lievens' career, one must recognize that he went on to win acclaim for another forty years after leaving Leiden in 1632. He was in the vanguard of Dutch artists who adapted the elegant manner of Van Dyck and helped satisfy the demand for such paintings, prints, and drawings in the Netherlands during the 1640s, 1650s, and 1660s. Just how Lievens came to work in this style and how he managed to reinstate himself among the Dutch political, artistic, and local elites after he had left the Netherlands for London and Antwerp is a story that the present publication hopes to tell.

THE LEIDEN YEARS, 1620–1632

Through the Eyes of Jan Jansz Orlers Lievens' early life is remarkably well documented, thanks to the writings of the Leiden burgomaster, historian, and art lover Jan Jansz Orlers (a source familiar to Houbraken) and the personal reflections of Constantijn Huygens, secretary to Frederik Hendrik, the Prince of Orange (whose autobiography Houbraken did not know).[20] Orlers and Huygens were personally acquainted with Rembrandt and Lievens, and their comments about the two at the onset of their careers are extraordinarily revealing.

Orlers records the birth dates of both artists — July 15, 1606, for Rembrandt; October 24, 1607, for Lievens — in biographies he included in his history of Leiden (1641). He writes compellingly about the two even though both had left Leiden: Rembrandt for Amsterdam around 1631; Lievens for London in 1632. The fame of these native sons was such that even in absentia they warranted extended discussion in his celebratory history of the city. His sense of each artist's potential was strongly positive: regarding Rembrandt, "it was clearly evident that he would one day become an exceptional painter"; as for Lievens, "anyone with an understanding of art can expect him to paint many more fine pictures."

Orlers describes Lievens as having been a precocious child, whose father — identified as "Lieven Hendricxcz., a skilled embroiderer" — observed his "son's great love of painting" and apprenticed him at age eight to Joris van Schooten, "from whom he learned the principles of both drawing and painting."[21] According to Orlers, who lived near the Lievens family and may have seen them almost daily, the boy had such a passionate interest in his studies that he remained at home drawing after prints by Willem Buytewech even as riots raged in Leiden between the Remonstrants and Counter-Remonstrants on October 4, 1617, for "he regarded the love of art as more important than all the upheaval in the world."[22]

After two years with Van Schooten, Lievens was eager to continue his training, and his father sent him to Amsterdam to study with the renowned history painter Pieter Lastman. The boy stayed with Lastman for two years, probably from the winter of 1617/1618 to the winter of 1619/1620. He returned to Leiden by age twelve and, reportedly without further instruction, set up a studio in his family home, "spending all of his time diligently and industriously painting many and varied subjects from life." He also learned by copying other masters, painting remarkably accurate replicas, for example, of a Democritus and a Heraclites by Cornelis Ketel, which were later sold from the estate of a Mr. Boudewijns as originals by Ketel.

Lievens' commitment to his art paid off handsomely, and his talents were soon recognized by a wide circle of admirers in Leiden — including Orlers, who became one of his primary patrons (see cats. 9, 10, 22). Orlers recounts that the young artist's "consummate skill astounded numerous connoisseurs of art who found it hard to believe that a mere stripling of twelve or scarcely older could produce such work — usually his own compositions and ideas to boot." The range of subject matter was exceptional in such youthful works: biblical and genre scenes, allegorical compositions, still lifes, and a portrait that Lievens painted of his mother when he was about fourteen.

Testament that Lievens' early fame extended beyond Leiden's borders is found in Orlers' description of a life-size painting of "a person wearing a round cap, studying near a turf fire." This now-lost work was "painted with such spirit that His Highness the Prince of Orange caused it to be purchased and presented to the ambassador of the king of England who in turn gave it to his master the King; it can still be seen at Westminster."

Comparing Orlers' detailed account of Lievens with his comments about Rembrandt, one gleans the clear impression that Lievens was the more illustrious and advanced of the two. Rembrandt is said to have studied with Lastman for only about six months before returning to Leiden in 1625. Orlers makes no mention of Leiden patrons seeking out Rembrandt's works, let alone appreciation of his genius by the noble and royal clients who sought out Lievens. And Lievens' motivation for leaving Leiden is attributed to the artist's ambitions to expand his horizons, "to see another land and its opportunities."[23]

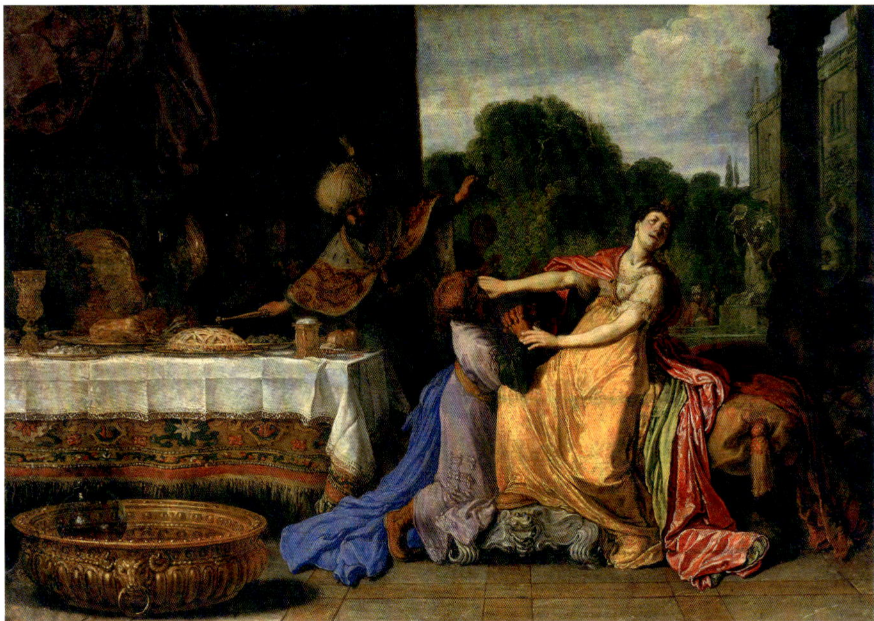

3 | Pieter Lastman, *Esther and Ahasuerus*, 161–, oil on panel, 52 × 78 cm. Museum Narodowe w Warszawie, Warsaw

Traveling to England, Lievens soon met tremendous success, with the king commissioning a portrait of himself, the queen, their son (the Prince of Wales) and daughter, and several great lords.[24] But three years later Lievens "returned to Calais and thence to Antwerp, where he settled." Orlers gives no explanation for this move but notes that Lievens' work, which included paintings for the Jesuit church and for private individuals, was highly regarded in Antwerp. These commissions and his marriage to Susanna Colijns de Nole, daughter of the deceased sculptor Andries Colijns de Nole, in a Catholic ceremony in 1638 have led to speculation that the artist must have converted to Catholicism by that time.[25] Orlers ends by relating how Lievens made two "extraordinarily beautiful pieces of painting for his highness the Prince of Orange and for the Burgomasters of the city of Leiden" (the latter referring to *The Magnanimity of Scipio*; see fig. 19).[26]

Although the broad outline of Orlers' discussion accords well with the documentation subsequently discovered about this period in Lievens' life, it leaves many questions unanswered. For example, how was the decision made to send a ten-year-old lad to study in Amsterdam with Pieter Lastman after a local apprenticeship with Joris van Schooten? Perhaps the family (at Orlers' recommendation?) believed that Lastman, who had traveled to Italy and was internationally known, was a better teacher and more important history painter than Van Schooten. Certainly Lastman could provide Lievens with contacts that might prove valuable for his subsequent career.

Orlers does not tell us what Lievens learned from Lastman, but judging from the young artist's early biblical paintings, such as *The Feast of Esther* (cat. 6), he took inspiration from his teacher's emphasis on dramatic gesture to convey psychological transformation (fig. 3). He also admired the vigor of Lastman's colors and brushwork as well as the variety of exotic costumes. Yet with the exception of a few early drawings (see cat. 90), the broad flow of Lastman's narratives, with their small-scale figures in expansive spaces, is not found in Lievens' early works. Instead, one finds focused compositions, often with an over-life-size, half-length figure illuminated with strong chiaroscuro contrasts. Lievens had probably already begun working in this manner by 1621 (cat. 1).[27]

Despite Orlers' statement that Lievens had no teachers after Lastman, the pronounced shift away from Lastman's style in the early 1620s makes this implausible. It seems equally unlikely that a father who took the initiative to send his son away to study with a prominent artist like Lastman would have been content to let him proceed entirely on his own at the tender age of twelve. Possibly Orlers exaggerated his account to emphasize the young artist's prodigious talents or perhaps Lievens never officially served as an apprentice to another master, but he must have had further direction in developing his personal style.

Northern Caravaggist Traditions: Utrecht and Rubens The most probable destination for Lievens' subsequent training would have been Utrecht, an important artistic center near Leiden that was home to the most successful teacher of his generation, Abraham Bloemaert.[28] No document places Lievens in Utrecht around 1620–1621, the most likely time for this additional study, but none places him in Leiden either. Orlers records that Lievens painted his mother in Leiden in 1621, but there is no evidence that he was there between 1622 and 1624, when his paintings consistently reflect the latest artistic achievements by the Utrecht Caravaggisti, particularly Honthorst and Baburen, who had returned from Rome in 1620, prior to the end of the Twelve Years' Truce.[29] The work of Ter Brugghen also influenced the young Lievens (see cats. 7, 9, 10).[30] Finally, Bloemaert's depictions of saints in prayer and contemplation inspired a number of Lievens' prints and drawings in the mid-1620s (see cats. 71, 72, 92).

Baburen and especially Honthorst had achieved resounding success during their years abroad. Their expressive adaptations of Caravaggio's revolutionary style — Honthorst's dramatic chiaroscuro effects and ability to evoke the enveloping darkness of night; Baburen's broad, almost coarse manner of execution and the stark presence of his unidealized figures — held enormous appeal for major Roman patrons, and the artists' fame preceded them upon their return (figs. 4, 5). The fete organized in honor of Honthorst's homecoming in July 1620 was of such consequence that the Utrecht humanist Arnout van Buchell

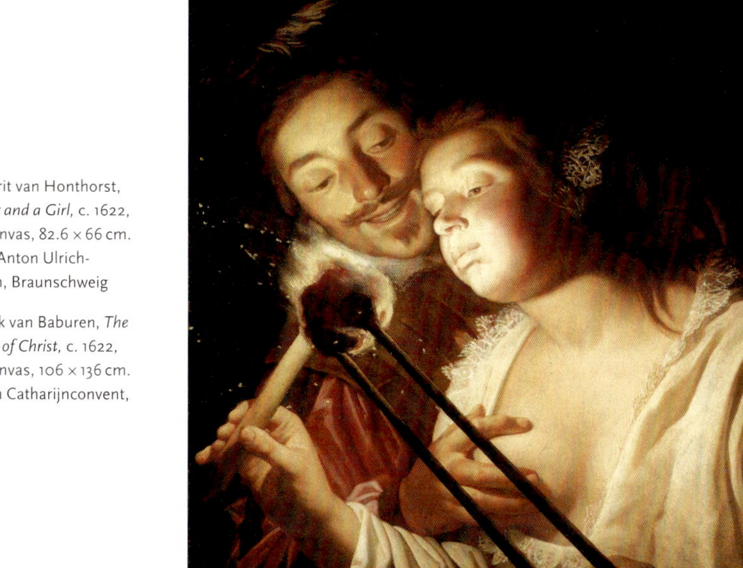

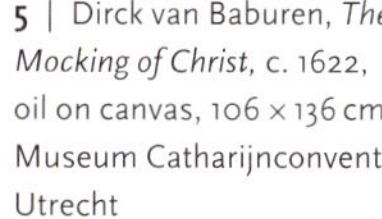

4 | Gerrit van Honthorst, *A Soldier and a Girl*, c. 1622, oil on canvas, 82.6 × 66 cm. Herzog Anton Ulrich-Museum, Braunschweig

5 | Dirck van Baburen, *The Mocking of Christ*, c. 1622, oil on canvas, 106 × 136 cm. Museum Catharijnconvent, Utrecht

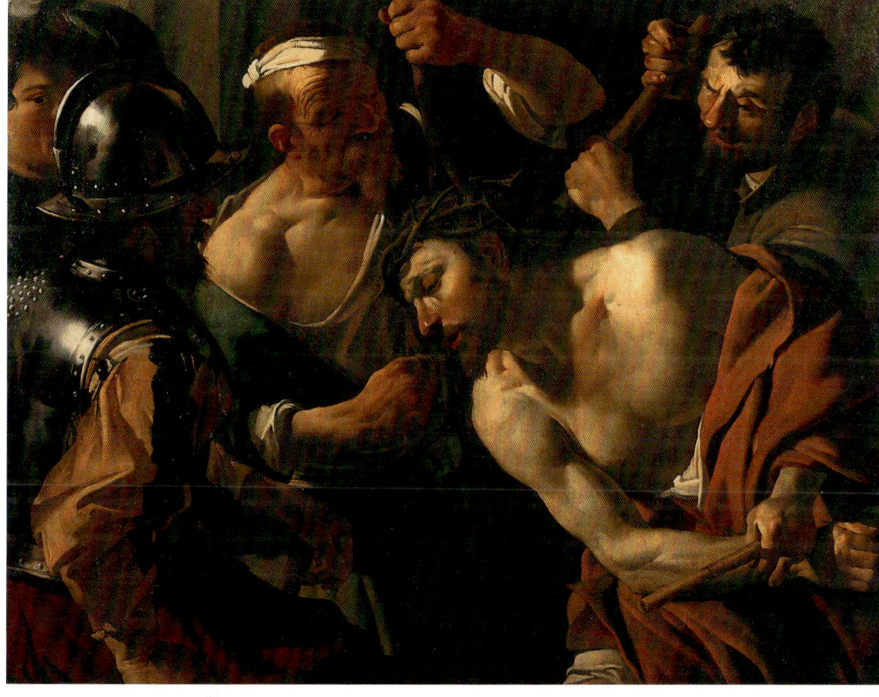

described it in his diary.[31] Lievens, at age twelve, would not have attended, but Buchell does note that among the guests were the Antwerp sculptors Jan and Robrecht Colijns de Nole and one of their sons — probably Andries, whose daughter Susanna married Lievens in 1638.[32]

The paintings of Honthorst, Baburen, and Ter Brugghen in the early 1620s had momentous implications for Dutch art, including that of Rembrandt. But no artist responded as quickly and incisively to their stylistic innovations as Lievens. The fullness of his adaptation of their visual imagery to his own style does not suggest a neophyte studying at some remove, dependent on random work that might pass his way, but rather an eager acolyte witnessing these masters firsthand. Lievens was well prepared for this moment, for in his earlier copies of works by Ketel, he would have understood the power of single-figure compositions like those of the Utrecht Caravaggisti.

Defining a chronology of Lievens' early oeuvre requires guesswork, as no dated paintings from the early to mid-1620s have survived. Traditionally, his youthful paintings, prints, and drawings have been seen through the lens of Rembrandt's artistic evolution, the belief being that Lievens could only have developed his distinctive style after Rembrandt had returned to Leiden from Lastman's studio around 1625. Thus most of Lievens' early paintings have been arbitrarily dated around 1625–1626 to coincide with the beginning of Rembrandt's career in Leiden. Yet it is highly likely that Lievens was already actively producing art in the early 1620s and that his early works should be dated accordingly.

At this time, and in painting after painting, Lievens drew upon the inspiration of Honthorst and Baburen, not only for execution but also for color, chiaroscuro effects, composition, and subject matter. The bold and weighty realism of his figures, made more tangible by their large scale and nearness to the picture plane, left little to the imagination. Their presence feels so real that a series of Four Evangelists he painted in these years was described in Orlers' inventory of 1640 as being "from life" (*naar het leven*) (cats. 9, 10).[33]

These qualities were already evident in the Four Elements, a series that Lievens painted c. 1624–1625 (figs. 6, 7).[34] He greatly enhanced the earthy realism of these allegorical figures with tightly cropped compositions and vigorous painting techniques. The figures have an easy naturalism as they engage in the activities that give them their allegorical identities. Lievens' brushwork is remarkable for its surety, whether in blending his paints to create smooth passages in the flesh tones, or in juxtaposing vigorous, unmodulated brushstrokes.

One of Lievens' earliest paintings depicted the Five Senses, a subject that involved a fascinating range of activity and expression. The theme allowed Lievens to enhance the lifelike quality of his images, with figures engaged in such momentary actions as raising a glass or strumming a lute (cats. 2, 3). Two paintings in Warsaw dating from the mid-1620s, *Allegory of Sight* and *Allegory of Smell*, which probably belonged to such a series, also demonstrate his command of the visual potency of night scenes. Lievens signed both of the latter works "J. Livius," and as Białostocki has emphasized, the decision to sign the Latinized form of his name suggests his desire to associate himself with that proud tradition of artists, reaching back to antiquity, who had captured naturalistic light effects in their representations of daily life.[35] For example, as Pliny noted in *Naturalis Historia* 35.138, Antiphilus was "praised for his *Boy Blowing a Fire*, and for the apartment, beautiful in itself, lit by the reflection from the fire and the light thrown on the boy's face."[36] A classical lineage reinforced an artist's worth as well as helping to validate the pictorial significance of figures participating in everyday activities.

Honthorst, Baburen, and Ter Brugghen were not the only Northern artists to depict figures in dramatic candlelit scenes. One of Rubens' masterpieces, *Judith with the Head of Holofernes* (fig. 8), was in Leiden in 1621, owned by Theodorus Schrevelius, rector of the Latin School.[37] Rubens, epitomizing the heroic stature to which a court artist could rise, inspired many seventeenth-century Dutch artists, including Lievens and Rembrandt. With his firm foundations in classical art, his expressive handling of the brush, and his control over compositional ideas, Rubens established a large workshop in Antwerp that created paintings sought by private patrons, religious communities, and the nobility. It is not impossible that Lievens met the great man. In 1627 Rubens traveled to the Netherlands on a secret diplomatic mission, at which time he visited Utrecht to meet with Honthorst. Though Honthorst was ill, Rubens was feted by local artists. Lievens, who had contacts within that community, may have been there.

Rubens' compositions, widely disseminated through prints, served as models for both Rembrandt and Lievens (cat. 15), but the young Leiden artists would also have known the power of the paintings themselves. In addition to *Judith with the Head of Holofernes*, other paintings by Rubens were in the Netherlands, including those the artist had sent to Sir Dudley Carleton, English ambassador in The Hague, in 1618.[38] Even if Lievens had not actually seen those works, he would have known of their visual impact through Carleton's good friend Constantijn Huygens, a patron of Lievens, for Huygens described Rubens in 1629 as one of the "seven wonders of the world... the prince, the Apelles among painters."[39]

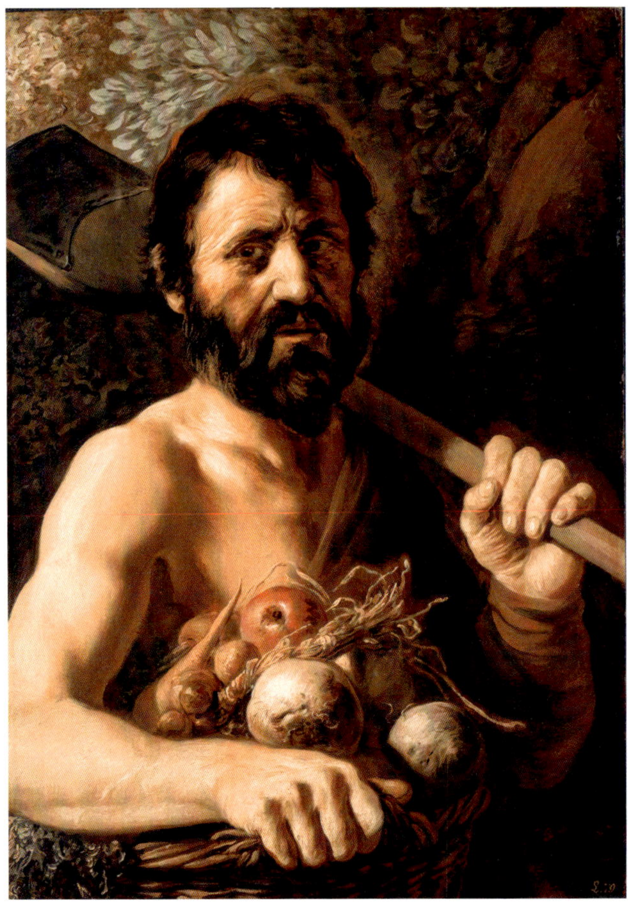

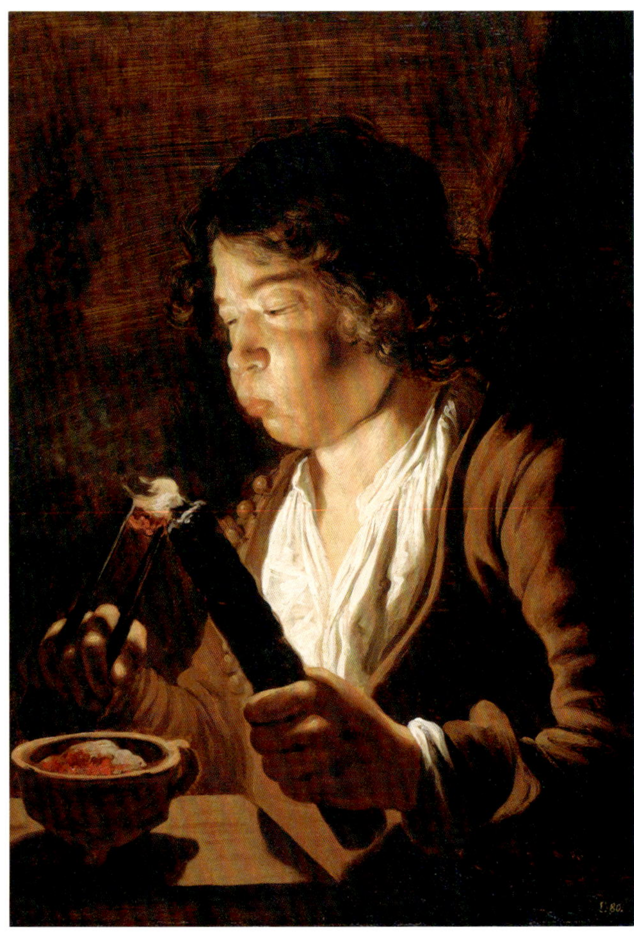

6, 7 | Jan Lievens, *Earth* and *Fire*, from the Four Elements, c. 1624–1625, oil on panel, 83.5 × 60 cm. Staatliche Museen Kassel, Gemäldegalerie Alte Meister

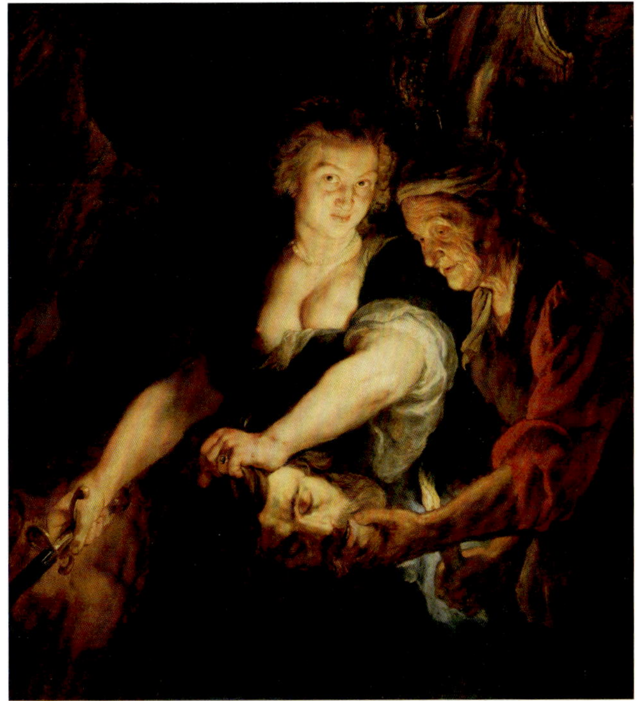

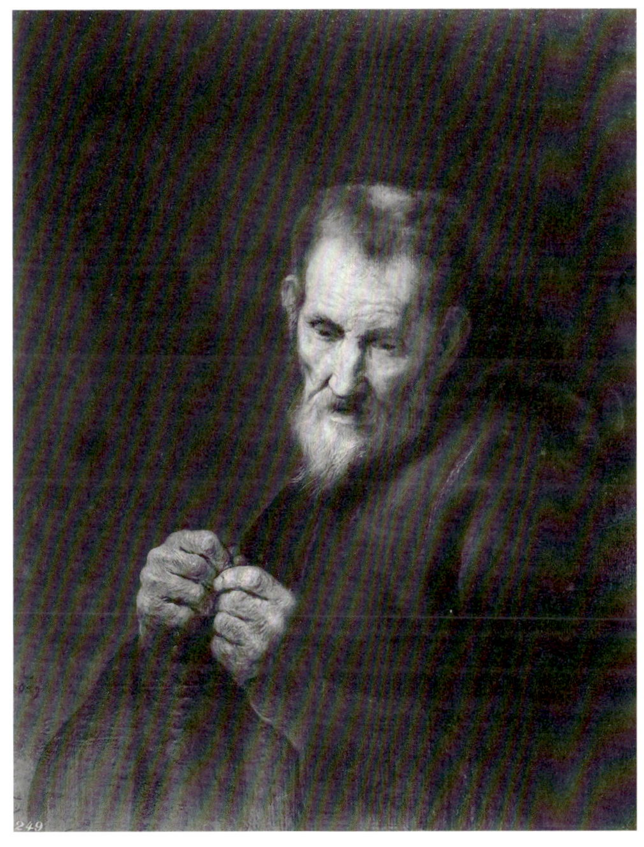

8 | Sir Peter Paul Rubens, *Judith with the Head of Holofernes*, c. 1616, oil on canvas, 120 × 111 cm. Herzog Ulrich Anton-Museum, Braunschweig

9 | Jan Lievens, *Capuchin Monk Praying*, 1629, oil on panel, 96.5 × 86.5 cm. Private collection

The Confidence of Constantijn Huygens When Lievens first met Huygens in 1628, the latter had established himself as the quintessential Renaissance man. Beyond serving as secretary to the Prince of Orange, he was a man of letters with interests in science as well as art and music. He liked to visit artists' studios and promote Dutch artists by arranging for commissions from the court in The Hague. When Orlers notes that the Prince of Orange had purchased a life-size painting by Lievens of a boy studying by a turf fire to present to the ambassador of the king of England, one can be sure that Huygens had recommended the painting as a diplomatic gift.

Huygens had apparently heard of Lievens before meeting the young Leiden artist, for when he and his brother Maurits made a trip to Leiden in October 1628,[40] he was clearly interested enough to stop and see Lievens in his studio. As Huygens describes the encounter, the two struck an immediate accord:

> [Lievens] was seized by the desire to paint my portrait. I assured him that I should be only too pleased to grant him the opportunity if he would come to The Hague and stay at my house for a while. So ardent was his desire that he arrived within a few days, explaining that since seeing me his nights had been restless and his days so troubled that he had been unable to work. My face had lodged so firmly in his mind that he could not wait any longer. This effect on his imaginative powers was all the more remarkable in view of his customary aversion to being persuaded to portray a person.

Huygens deemed the portrait (cat. 16) a triumph and allotted it "a permanent place amongst my most treasured possessions." He recounts that it was admired by many who saw it, including the preeminent court portraitist of the day, Michiel van Mierevelt.

The close relationship that developed between patron and artist had life-changing consequences for Lievens, for his paintings were soon finding their place in princely collections. The now-lost work of the boy beside the turf fire may be one that Huygens saw in the studio, for it was a night scene like those Lievens was painting in the mid-1620s under the influence of Rubens and Honthorst. Almost certainly this work was offered by Huygens to Robert Kerr (cat. 51), representative of the English crown, when he came to the Netherlands in the spring of 1629 to attend the funeral of Charles I's nephew, Frederick Henry, who had drowned in the River IJ.[41]

Kerr, who also took back to England Lievens' *Capuchin Monk Praying* (fig. 9), may have encouraged the artist to return with him to the court of Charles I. But a document dated April 10, 1629, notes that Lievens was at work on a commission for the Prince of Orange that would occupy him for at least three months and require him to postpone an intended departure for England.[42]

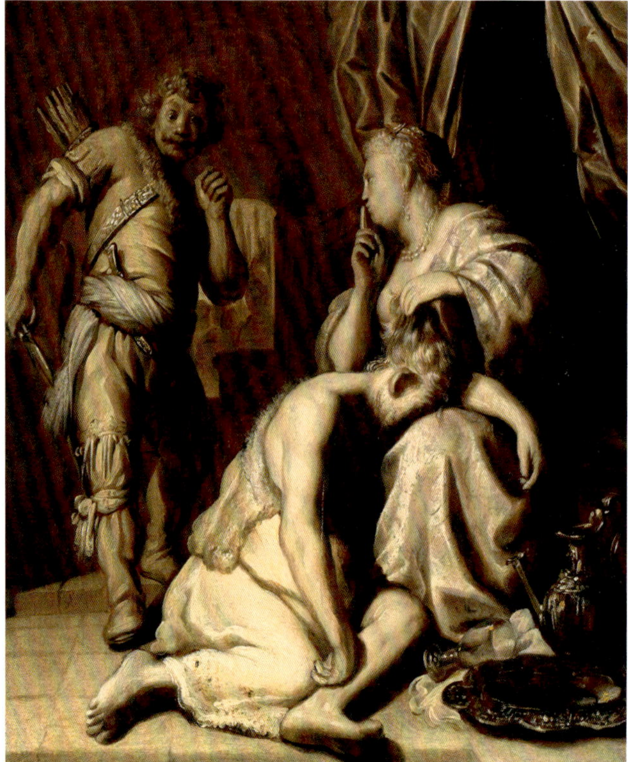

10 | Jan Lievens, *Samson and Delilah*, c. 1627–1628, oil on panel, 27.5 × 23.7 cm. Rijksmuseum, Amsterdam

Lievens does not identify the painting on which he was working, but it was probably the imposing *Sultan Soliman* or the large allegorical *Soothsayer* (cats. 19, 26).[43] Interestingly, given Huygens' predilection for Rubens, Lievens based his *Sultan Soliman* and a grisaille oil sketch of *Samson and Delilah* (see fig. 10), which also entered the Prince of Orange's collection around this time, on prints after Rubens.[44]

Lievens received another significant court commission before he left for England that testifies to the esteem in which he was held in court circles. In 1631 Charles I's sister Elizabeth and her husband, Frederick V, the queen and king of Bohemia, whose exiled court was in The Hague, invited Lievens to paint a portrait of their son, Prince Charles Louis, who was studying in Leiden with his tutor, Wolrad von Plessen (cat. 29). This commission most likely came through the good graces of Huygens.

The story of Lievens' career until 1632 is thus one of mounting success, with his work admired by connoisseurs and collectors at the highest levels of Dutch and English society. So meteoric was his rise that when Van Dyck visited The Hague in the winter of 1631/1632 he painted a now-lost portrait of the young master, which Lucas Vosterman later engraved for inclusion in the *Iconography* (fig. 11), a volume of images of famous artists, collectors, patrons, and art lovers that Van Dyck was beginning to compile. Huygens predicted the young artist would surpass the "absolute genius" of the great masters of the previous generation, including Rubens, Mierevelt, and Hendrick Goltzius. Huygens admired Lievens' diligence as well as the inventiveness and audacity of his themes and forms, noting that everything his "young spirit endeavours to capture must be magnificent and lofty."

Despite the young man's "astonishing talent as a history painter," Huygens most highly praised his ability to render the human countenance. There, he wrote, Lievens "wreaks miracles." Huygens' advice to Lievens would have been to focus on portraiture, to "curb this vigorous, untamable spirit whose bold ambition is to embrace all of nature… [and] concentrate on that physical part which miraculously combines the essence of the human spirit and body." But Lievens would not have welcomed such counsel. Huygens recognized that despite Lievens' "acute and profound insight into all manner of things," his "excess of self-confidence" was a stumbling block: he "either roundly rejects all criticism or, if he acknowledges its validity, takes it in bad spirit. This bad habit, harmful at any age, is absolutely pernicious in youth." One can almost see Huygens shaking his head in disapproval of the twenty-two-year-old prodigy while reflecting on how one should properly behave: "all men, whoever they be, should be approached with a well-disposed heart and an inquisitive mind, in the belief that there is always something to be learned from everyone."

Lievens and Rembrandt Lievens, of course, was not the only gifted and overly self-confident young artist that Huygens knew in Leiden.[45] Rembrandt's rising star had a similar story line, and like any good writer, Huygens used it to enhance his narrative. He saw both artists coming from modest backgrounds and owing "nothing to their teachers but everything to their own aptitude." Their gifts, however, were quite different, and Huygens proceeded to assess their artistic strengths and weaknesses, the first time a connoisseur had directly compared the two. He noted that Lievens painted audaciously on a large scale but felt that Rembrandt "was superior… in his sure touch and liveliness of emotions." Taking as an example *Judas, Repentant, Returning the Pieces of Silver* (fig. 13), he wrote that Rembrandt "devotes all his loving concentration to a small painting, achieving on that modest scale a result which one would seek in vain in the largest pieces of others." Implicit in this statement is the belief that Rembrandt painted more expressive history scenes than Lievens did, a judgment reiterated when recommending that Lievens focus on portraiture, because he "is unlikely to match Rembrandt's vivid invention."

The nature of Rembrandt's artistic evolution is outside the scope of this essay except as it impacts on Lievens' own development and artistic approach during his Leiden years. The two aspiring young artists would surely have known each other growing up,

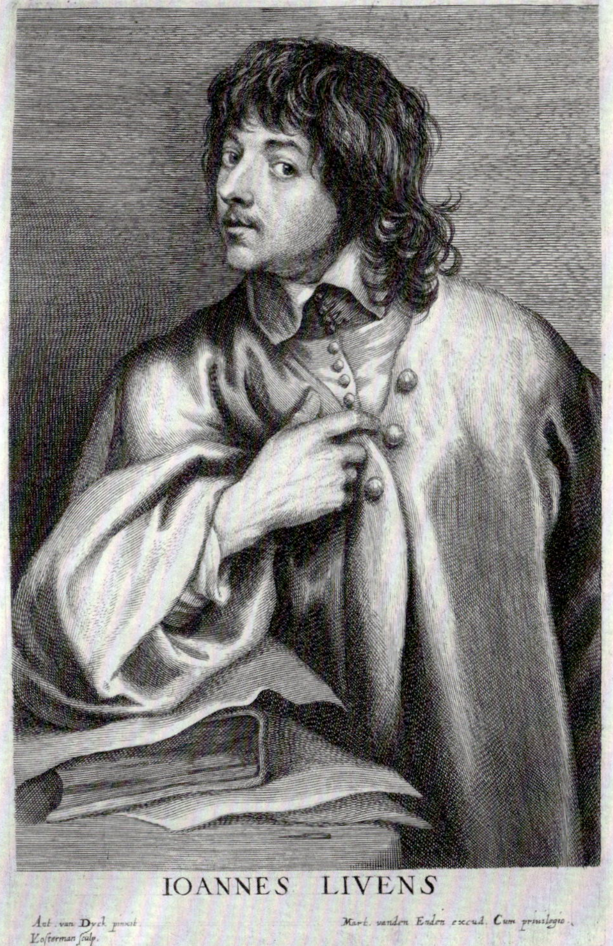

11 | Lucas Vorsterman after Sir Anthony van Dyck, *Portrait of Jan Lievens*, c. 1632, engraving, from the *Iconography*, National Gallery of Art, Washington

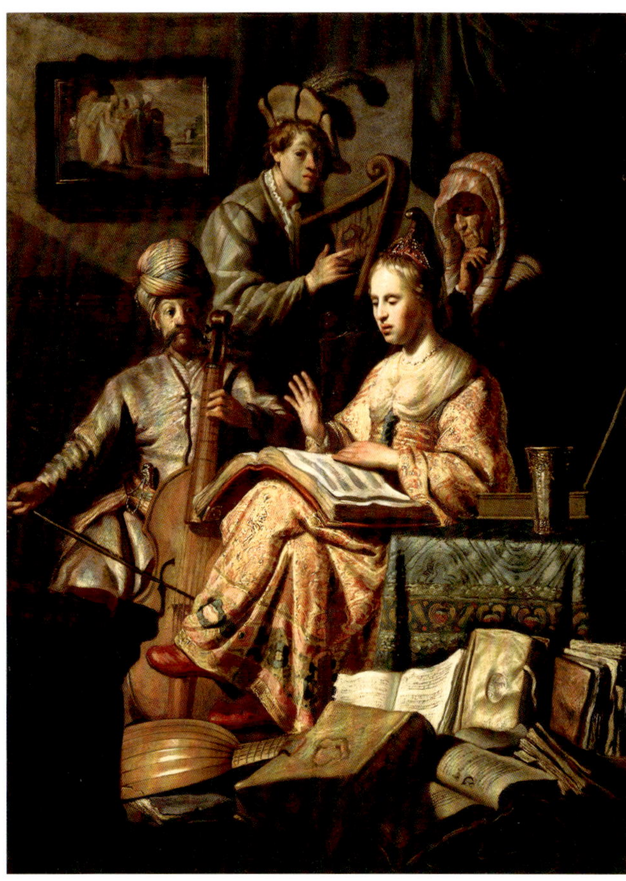

12 | Rembrandt van Rijn, *Music Lesson*, 1626, oil on panel, 63.4 × 47.6 cm. Rijksmuseum, Amsterdam

with Leiden being no more than a modest-sized city and the two families living relatively close to one another. The connections would have grown stronger through their mutual experiences of traveling to Amsterdam at an early age to study with Pieter Lastman. When Rembrandt returned to Leiden in 1625 after a six-month apprenticeship with Lastman, however, Lievens was already a practicing artist with a flourishing trade.

Absolutely no evidence indicates that Lievens invited Rembrandt to share his studio, as is sometimes assumed. In fact, the narrative structures of both Orlers' and Huygens' accounts strongly suggest that the two artists worked independently, though they must have visited the other's studio, discussed artistic issues, and even posed for one another. Some of Lievens' earliest genre scenes include a broad-faced young man with a bulbous nose that must be the young Rembrandt (cat. 3), while Lievens served as a model for a background figure in Rembrandt's *Allegory of Hearing*, c. 1625 (private collection), and *Music Lesson* (fig. 12). Lievens, with his extraordinary talent, industry, and brash self-confidence, initially seems to have taken little notice of the Lastman-inspired style that Rembrandt practiced between 1625 and 1628. He continued to create large-scale paintings with dramatic chiaroscuro effects that had stronger ties to Honthorst, Baburen, Ter Brugghen, and Rubens. Yet as is inevitable in such situations, even with ambitious and overly self-confident individuals, Lievens and Rembrandt learned from each other, developing styles and themes that responded to what the other was doing.

During the late 1620s their manner of painting drew so much closer together that contemporaries were sometimes uncertain as to the attribution of their works.[46] Both artists broadened their styles, learned to create textures by applying paint in various ways — thickly in some instances, thinly in others — and even wiped and scratched their paint to increase the pictorial effects they could achieve. They also expanded their subject matter beyond history, genre, and still-life painting[47] to include *tronies*, or head-and-shoulder studies of young and old — particularly old, for in age they found "character," whether in the creases that lined a wizened face or in the wisdom that radiated from those who have experienced the vagaries of life.

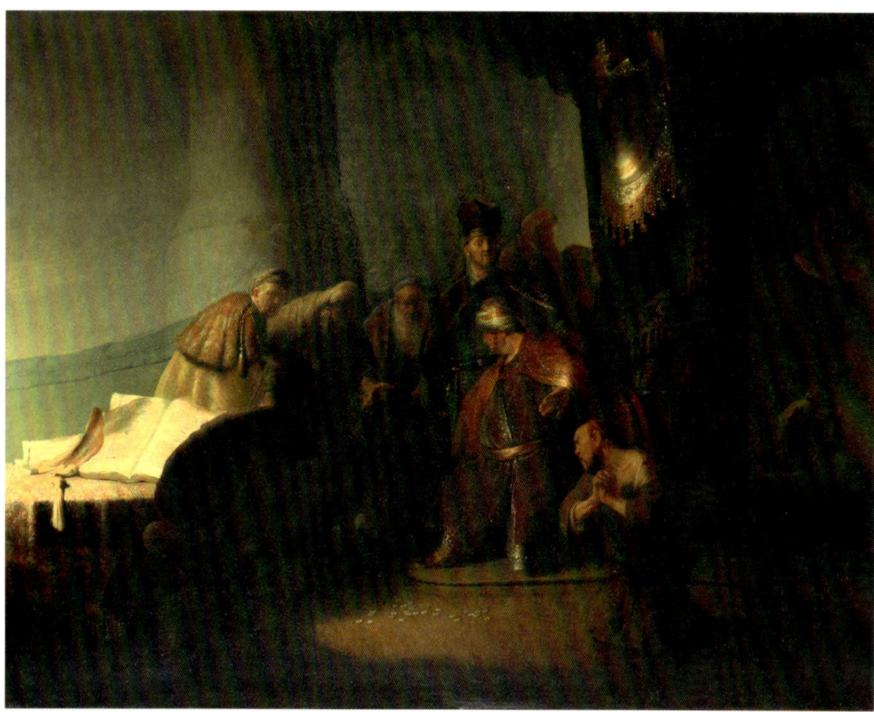

13 | Rembrandt van Rijn, *Judas, Repentant, Returning the Pieces of Silver*, 1629, oil on panel, 79 × 102.3 cm. Private collection

Lievens and Rembrandt often rendered similar themes in their drawings as well, exploring the expressive possibilities available in pen and ink or in black and red chalk. They also pursued similar interests in printmaking, which offered great potential for developing chiaroscuro effects. In their religious images they drew inspiration from the prints of other masters, among them Lucas van Leyden and Willem Buytewech. They looked carefully at depictions of the Dutch underclass, outcasts whose rugged features they etched with passion and sensitivity (cats. 63–70).

As the two artists benefited from their association, so too they felt the pressure of a growing competition for patronage and prestige. This rivalry came to a head when Huygens, the only man in the Dutch Republic who could provide entrée to the House of Orange, first visited their studios. Lievens, with guidance from Orlers, was initially savvier about ingratiating himself with Huygens and leapt at the opportunity to paint the great man's portrait. He also recognized Huygens' delight in Rubens and astutely began to base his own history paintings on Rubens' compositions long before Rembrandt did. Even so, Huygens found the expressiveness of Rembrandt's small history paintings enormously compelling (fig. 13) and, perhaps supposing that competition would spur both to even greater achievements, may have challenged the two young masters to portray the same subjects, each in his own manner. No other hypothesis seems to satisfactorily explain how it was that between 1628 and 1631 Rembrandt and Lievens produced so many parallel works: *Samson and Delilah*, *The Raising of Lazarus*, *Christ on the Cross* (cats. 15, 31, 32), and an old man sitting alone in mournful contemplation — Rembrandt's *Jeremiah Lamenting the Destruction of Jerusalem* and Lievens' *Job in His Misery* (cat. 25) — or why Rembrandt seems to have backdated some paintings, making it appear that he was the initiator rather than the follower.[48]

Among these paired works, the relationship between Lievens' and Rembrandt's depictions of the Crucifixion is illuminating. The compositions are quite similar, so much so that it is possible the artists were working within a defined program, perhaps based on contemporaneous engravings after what may have been two paintings by Rubens (see cat. 32). Their individual responses to the subject, however, underscore how accurately Huygens had judged the distinctions in their artistic personalities. Lievens' work is larger, while Rembrandt's is more poignant. Rembrandt's Christ, strongly lit from the upper right, peers up in anguish. His face resembles the artist's own likeness more than Rubens' heroic visage, a visual association that brings an intensely personal dimension to the image.[49] Lievens' Christ, starkly lit from the front, is more iconic, an object of contemplation rather than empathy. His Christ hangs lifeless, with eyes closed, as blood flows from the sword wound opened in his side.[50]

The probability is strong, although it cannot be proven, that Huygens viewed these paintings as a test to see which artist would best fill a commission for a Passion series coming from the Prince of Orange.[51] Rembrandt eventually won this commission in 1632/1633, perhaps because his *Crucifixion* was deemed more suitable than that of Lievens, but perhaps because Lievens had already left Leiden for London in February 1632.

THE LURE OF ENGLAND, 1632–1635

Lievens seems to have been motivated to move to London by the possibility of working for King Charles I, one of the most eminent art patrons of the day. Other Dutch artists had enjoyed considerable success there, including Honthorst, who had been invited to England in 1626 at the recommendation of Sir Dudley Carleton and painted not only for George Villiers, the Duke of Buckingham, but also for Charles I. Lievens, likewise, would have had an excellent introduction. He enjoyed the support of Huygens, who had twice traveled to London and was on close terms with the English court; and he had just fulfilled an important portrait commission from Charles' sister, Elizabeth, the exiled queen of Bohemia (cat. 29).

Just what precipitated Lievens' decision in February 1632 to pursue a dream he had had since 1629 is not known. Perhaps he realized that opportunities in The Hague would not be forthcoming, with Mierevelt and Honthorst already ensconced as court painters, their smooth classicism being highly favored by the Prince of Orange. When Van Dyck accepted Huygens' invitation to come to The Hague in the winter of 1631/1632, Lievens must have seen his chances at the Dutch court grow even more remote. Van Dyck's refined portraits of Frederik Hendrik and Amalia van Solms brought a sense of elegance as well as gravitas to the prince and princess, and the two elaborate history scenes about the life of Achilles that he painted for the prince's private quarters bespoke an intimate knowledge of Venetian painting in which Lievens was unversed.[52]

Suddenly in the winter of 1632 Van Dyck's Flemish style of painting thus overwhelmed all allegiances Huygens had felt for the boldly expressive works of the young Leiden artists. It even seems likely that Huygens was hoping Van Dyck would agree to become court painter to Frederik Hendrik. As fate would have it, however, Van Dyck had a better offer. On April 1, 1632, less than a month after Lievens left Leiden to seek his fortunes in a new land, Van Dyck took up residence in London as court painter to Charles I, king of England.

It is not known where Lievens lived while in London, nor is it clear what kind of relationship he had with Van Dyck as he sought to develop his career on English soil. He had never traveled far from home and did not know the language, so he must have seemed quite inexperienced and provincial to the English aristocracy, despite his self-assurance and the strength of his recommendations from The Hague. One would hope that the somewhat older and more cosmopolitan Van Dyck helped guide the young Lievens (whom he respected sufficiently to include in his *Iconography*). It is even possible that Lievens served as one of Van Dyck's assistants. Given the convincing way in which Lievens was able to emulate Van Dyck's style of painting, drawing, and etching, he seems to have been able to study the master close at hand.

In any event, whether through the auspices of Huygens, Van Dyck, or Charles I's sister, Lievens gained entrance to the English court. Orlers relates that he painted portraits of the king, the queen, their children, and various lords, although all of these paintings are now lost. Two of Lievens' portraits appear in inventories of the royal collection made in the late 1640s by Abraham van der Doort: his portrayal of the king, and his depiction of Prince Charles and Princess Mary "hand in hand." One supposes that Lievens undertook these works in 1634, after Van Dyck had left the English court for the Southern Netherlands.[53]

Lievens' English-period portraits included not only paintings but prints and drawings as well. One of his most remarkable prints, presumably made soon after he arrived, is a frighteningly direct rendering of a coarse-featured man who stares unrelentingly at the viewer (cat. 74), the type of rough character Lievens depicted frequently in his Leiden years.[54] It was probably this image that inspired Huygens on February 24, 1633, to write: "On the portrait of the giant Porter of the King of England by the hand of J. Livij. Horrible huge hideous monster, deprived of sight he would be the current Polyphemus of the English, if there were one."[55]

While in London, Lievens' style of portraiture began to reflect Van Dyck's pervasive influence. Evidence can be seen in Lievens' elegant etched likeness of the French lutenist Jacques Gaultier (cat. 75). In pose as well as technique, these images owe much to the prints Van Dyck was then making for his *Iconography*. Of equal note is the atmospheric landscape in the background of Gaultier's portrait, suggesting that Lievens had already discovered an interest in landscape that would engage him for the rest of his career. Once again, the source of inspiration was Van Dyck. In two landscape drawings from this period, one depicting London and one Westminster Abbey (see cat. 101), the young master adopted the light-filled, atmospheric quality of Van Dyck's pen and wash landscapes.[56] Lievens' ability to emulate the Flemish master's means of rendering landscape forms, particularly foliage, with long, diagonal hatchings, grew over time as he began, with ever increasing energy, to devote himself to the exploration of nature.

PURSUING AN INTERNATIONAL STYLE: ANTWERP, 1635–1644

Little documentation remains of Lievens' life and work in London, so it is impossible to know why he decided to leave in 1635. Orlers' chronicle is frustratingly terse: "After he had spent some three years in England, he returned to Calais and thence to Antwerp, where he settled." The move probably had something to do with the comings and goings of Van Dyck, who returned to England in the spring of 1635 after having left for Flanders in the winter of 1634. Almost certainly any hope Lievens harbored of becoming court painter to Charles I immediately vanished. In fact, it is striking that one of the first works the king commissioned from Van Dyck upon his return was a group portrait of his three eldest children, whom Lievens had purportedly depicted.[57]

While Lievens may have felt displaced by Van Dyck in England, it seems surprising that he chose Antwerp as his destination. Yet returning to Leiden would have been psychologically difficult for such an ambitious artist, a return to a smaller world rather than a step forward into a grander future. The Hague would also have had negative associations, for despite early successes, he had turned away from the Dutch court in 1632, either on his

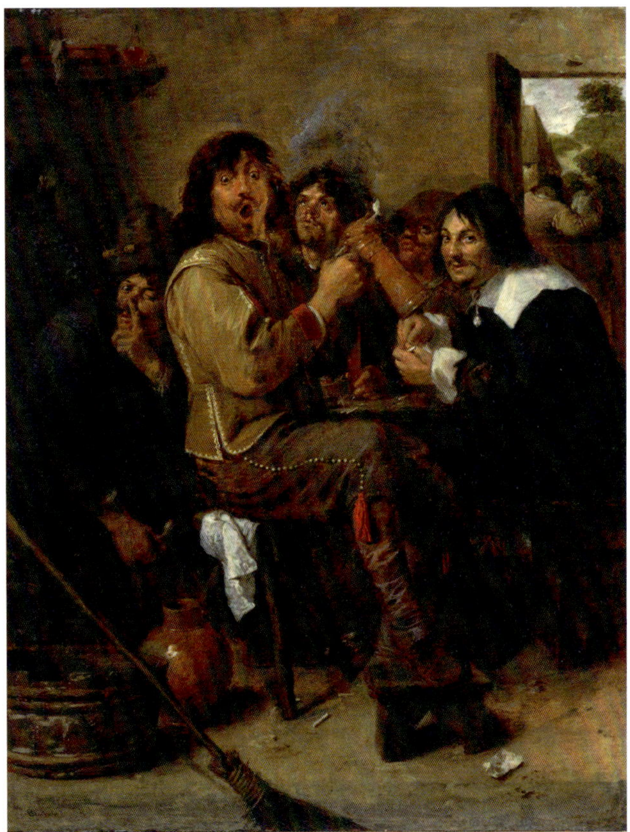

14 | Adriaen Brouwer, *The Smokers*, c. 1636, oil on panel, 46.4 × 36.8 cm. The Metropolitan Museum of Art, The Friedsam Collection, Bequest of Michael Friedsam, 1931

own initiative or because his services were no longer desired. As for the exiled court of Bohemia in The Hague, Frederick v had died in 1632, and Elizabeth was in financial straits.[58] Meanwhile, Amsterdam was the most problematic option of all, owing to Rembrandt's overwhelming fame and success there. Recently married, Rembrandt was now a wealthy man, well connected in society, and head of a large workshop that was poised to dominate artistic production in the city for the foreseeable future.

Antwerp, on the other hand, was entering a period of political stability in 1635 that brought hope and optimism to the people. In November 1634 Cardinal-Infante Ferdinand had arrived in Brussels as the new governor-general of the Southern Netherlands. In the following year, the very year that Lievens arrived, the Cardinal-Infante made his triumphal entry into Antwerp, where his arrival and the era of peace and prosperity expected to derive from it were celebrated with great fanfare, including floats and triumphal arches designed by Rubens. It is not known whether Lievens was present for the occasion or whether he had the chance to meet Rubens, one of his early heroes, but the sense of excitement and expanded possibilities generated by this event must have remained long after the festivities had ended.

Undoubtedly, Antwerp appealed to Lievens as a dynamic artistic center where he anticipated finding a sympathetic environment in which to further his career. He would be able to paint expressive tronies and genre scenes like those he had in Leiden. He would learn to paint large-scale biblical and mythological works in the Flemish manner, a style that Huygens clearly admired and that he had been constrained from painting in England because of the political and religious climate. In Antwerp he could study history paintings and altarpieces by Rubens, Van Dyck, and Jacob Jordaens, some of which he knew from reproductive prints. He would have been eager to examine paintings by Titian, whose impact on Rubens and Van Dyck had been enormous and was growing more so in the mid-1630s. Both Flemish masters had amassed major collections of Titian's paintings, which would have been accessible to Lievens.[59] Thus, in many respects, Lievens' decision to relocate to Antwerp should be viewed as a temporary career move, intended to help him expand his worldly and artistic experiences and develop a painting style that would enable him to procure important commissions when he eventually returned to the Northern Netherlands.

Once in Antwerp, Lievens quickly joined the local painters' guild and settled into a community of artists who specialized in low-life genre scenes, landscapes, and still lifes. Members included Adriaen Brouwer, Jan Davidsz de Heem, David Teniers the Younger, and Jan Cossiers,[60] and judging from Brouwer's wonderfully irreverent portrayal of the group (fig. 14), Lievens was warmly accepted by his new colleagues.[61] Among these artists the one whom Lievens knew best was the still-life painter De Heem, who had lived in Leiden in the late 1620s, having moved there from his native Utrecht. De Heem was probably already living in Antwerp when Lievens arrived, but the two both joined the Guild of Saint Luke in 1635.[62] On May 1, 1636, De Heem along with Brouwer witnessed a contract registering Hans van den Wijngaerde as Lievens' pupil. At about this time Lievens made a black chalk drawing of De Heem posing as a refined gentleman. The half-length format of that drawing, which served as a model for an engraved likeness of the sitter (see Dickey fig. 9), resembles that of other portraits of artists that Lievens created during his Antwerp years, perhaps with some thought of producing a series of portrait prints comparable to Van Dyck's *Iconography*.[63]

The greatest artistic inspiration in this group came from Adriaen Brouwer, whom Lievens portrayed in a delicate chalk drawing with an almost angelic expression, eyes cast upward (cat. 102). Brouwer, who is said to have lived a dissolute life (drinking, smoking, and fighting like the peasants that populate his small panel paintings), was one of the most innovative artists of his day, both in genre scenes and in landscapes, and Lievens seems to have been influenced by his painterly freedom.

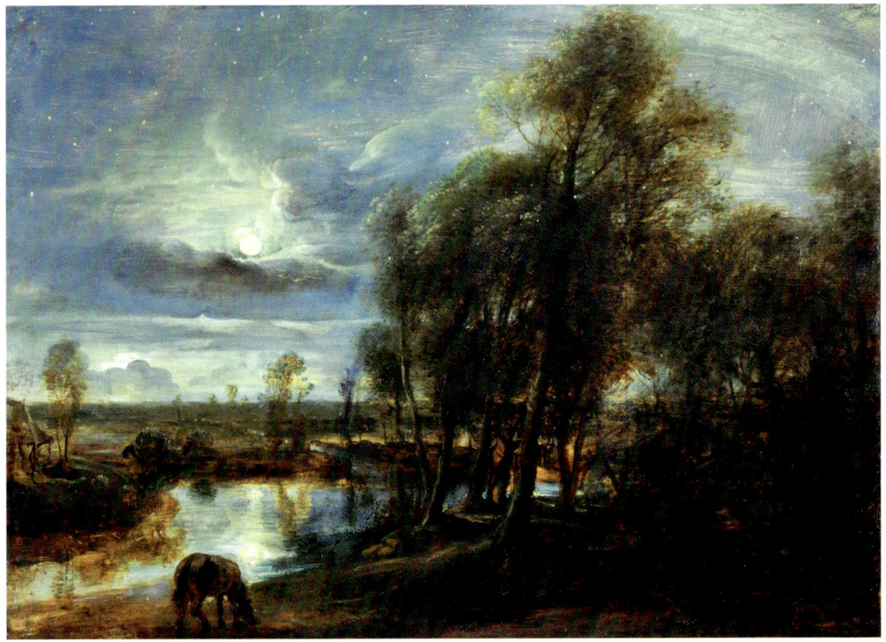

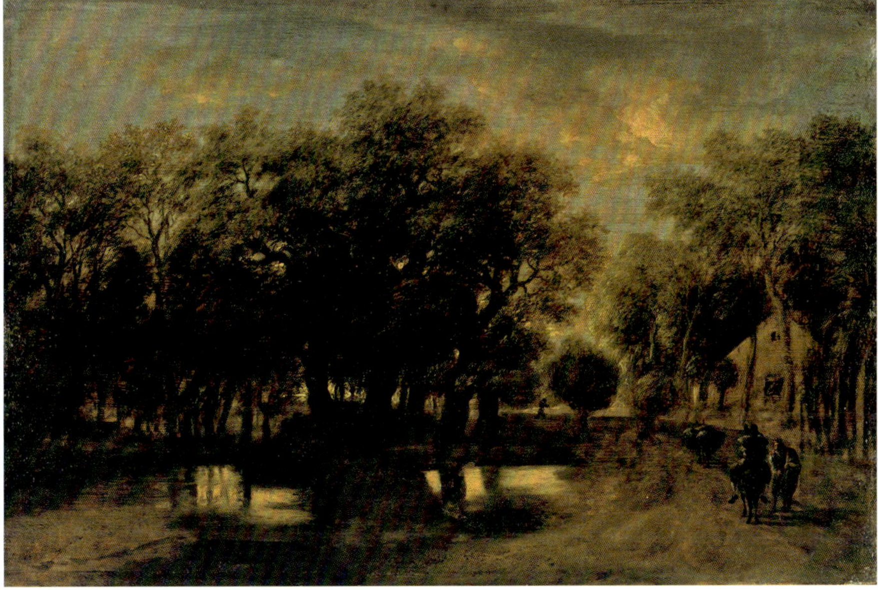

15 | Peter Paul Rubens, *Landscape with Moon and Stars*, c. 1637–1638, oil on panel, 64 × 90 cm. Courtauld Institute Galleries, London, Princes Gate Collection

16 | Jan Lievens, *Evening Landscape*, early 1640s, oil on panel, 28 × 48 cm. Staatliche Museen Preussischer Kulturbesitz, Berlin, Gemäldegalerie

Brouwer's most direct impact on Lievens may have been to encourage him to return to depicting tronies of rough-hewn peasant types, in both his paintings and his etchings. Working with a variety of Antwerp publishers, Lievens published individual prints of tronies that he had originally made in Leiden as well as series of tronies that also consist partly of images from his Leiden years.[64] In 1638, the year of Brouwer's death, Lievens also made two fascinating genre paintings of peasants confronting death, images that capture the gruesome struggle for survival that had given Brouwer's paintings such force (cats. 35, 36). Lievens' etching after one of his paintings (cat. 78) was distributed by two publishers, indicating that his prints had broad appeal.[65]

Lievens began painting landscapes, often of a wooded terrain at sunset, that fully embrace the brooding atmospheric qualities found in Brouwer's work.[66] Interestingly, Lievens asked Teniers, another member of this group of friends, to paint the staffage in some of these scenes (cat. 37). Equally if not more important for Lievens' approach to landscape was Rubens, who was also influenced by Brouwer's evocative handling. In *Landscape with Moon and Stars* (fig. 15), Rubens, who built upon Brouwer's imagery, rendered the light of the setting sun as it passes through a copse of trees and reflections in a calm body of water in a manner that clearly inspired Lievens (fig. 16). The main difference between their two approaches was that Lievens preferred a more restricted landscape vista than Rubens did. He also applied his paints with a thicker range of impastos, which give his work a heavier, denser character than that found in Rubens' light-filled panoramic evening landscape. Lievens' interest in both the painted and drawn landscape continued throughout his life and would ultimately become one of the most important aspects of his oeuvre.

Entering fully into the artistic spirit of Antwerp, Lievens also enthusiastically embraced the medium of woodcut, a graphic technique that had largely gone out of fashion since the Haarlem artist Hendrick Goltzius had exploited the medium for mythological images and landscapes in the mid-1590s. Lievens was clearly inspired by the greatest seventeenth-century master of the woodcut, Christoffel Jegher, who had begun making reproductive woodcuts of some of Rubens' compositions in the mid-1630s. Unlike Jegher, however, Lievens designed his own images for woodblock prints, not only biblical scenes, portraits, and tronies but also a landscape (cat. 80). This landscape is particularly interesting, for its visual progenitor is a woodcut by none other than Titian.[67]

Rubens' legacy, of course, dominated Antwerp's artistic culture, and Lievens' keenest aspirations remained focused on becoming a great history painter in the manner of Rubens. It must have thrilled him to stand before paintings by this preeminent master, who epitomized the ideals of capturing the "magnificent and lofty" on a larger-than-life scale, which Huygens had perceptively noted in Lievens' own artistic personality. Rubens' compositions of the 1630s challenged Lievens to paint much larger works than he had previously attempted, and the older artist's melding of Titian's gentle spirit with a broadness of handling and boldness of color inspired Lievens to loosen his brushwork and emphasize quiet moments of human exchange. Unlike the scenes of height-

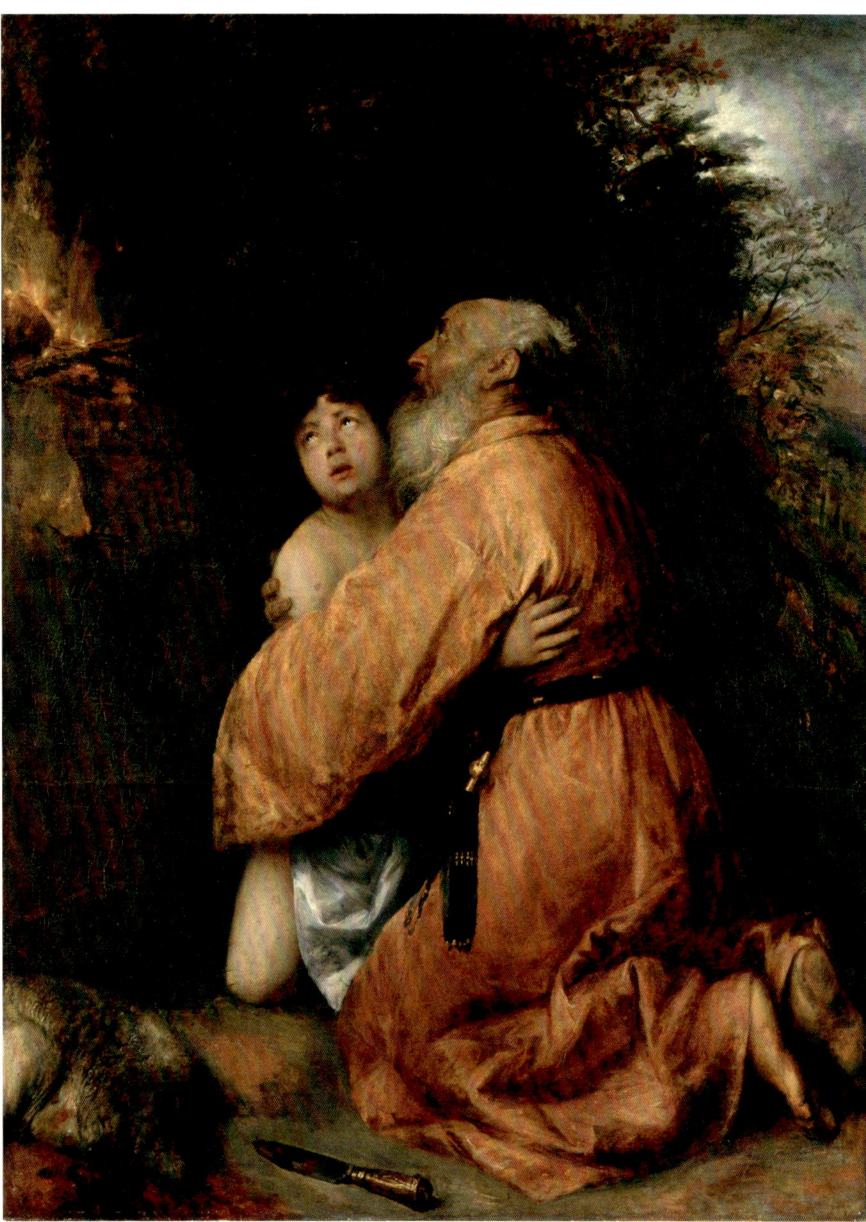

17 | Jan Lievens, *Abraham and Isaac*, c. 1637, oil on canvas, 180 × 136 cm. Herzog Anton Ulrich-Museum, Braunschweig

ened drama that Lievens had painted in Leiden, such as *Samson and Delilah* or *The Raising of Lazarus*, his finest religious paintings executed in Antwerp feature such intimate exchanges as the tender embrace of Abraham and Isaac as they gratefully contemplate the blaze that consumes the sacrificial ram (fig. 17) or the greeting of the Virgin and the aged Elizabeth as they joyfully celebrate the unexpected news that both are with child (fig. 18).

Despite Rubens' compelling influence, Lievens remained surprisingly independent in his interpretation of subject matter and in his style of painting. His brushwork is softer and more modulated than that of Rubens, while his figures have an emotive character closer to the spirituality of Van Dyck than of Rubens. At the same time, Lievens never generalized his forms to the same degree as did Rubens or Van Dyck. His strong Dutch roots emphasized the specifics of nature rather than idealized form. In the graphic arts Lievens' style is quite distinct from Rubens' as well, but connections do exist: Lievens based his allegorical drawing of a river god on an image by Rubens (cat. 104). Meanwhile, the composition of his woodcut *Cain Slaying Abel* demonstrates his awareness of both Goltzius' *Hercules Slaying Cacus* and Jegher's *Hercules Fighting Furing and Discord* (cat. 81).[68]

While in Antwerp, Lievens dated few paintings, hence the chronology of the works he produced here is a matter of conjecture. Information is also lacking about how he secured commissions for the large-scale altarpieces he made for the Jesuit churches in Antwerp and Brussels.[69] It is possible that his future father-in-law, Andries Colijns de Nole — an important sculptor working for the Jesuits in Antwerp in the mid-1630s — made contacts with religious leaders that led to these commissions.[70] Prestigious commissions may also have been more forthcoming after December 1640, when Lievens acquired Antwerp citizenship.[71]

The only commission for which we have documentation during Lievens' Antwerp period came from Leiden, where the artist agreed to produce the monumental painting *The Magnanimity of Scipio* for the council chamber (Vroedschapkamer) of the town hall. In conjunction with this project Lievens visited Leiden in 1639, returning to Antwerp in June 1640 to execute the painting.[72] He was paid the large sum of 1,500 guilders for the work the following November and was awarded a gold medal.[73] Jan Orlers, who described this painting in glowing terms in 1641, must have helped persuade the burgomasters that the power of Lievens' brush would bring added distinction to the city.

The subject, featuring an example of Scipio's judicious rule, was a story from Roman history that the Dutch favored for public buildings because it symbolized good government. Although

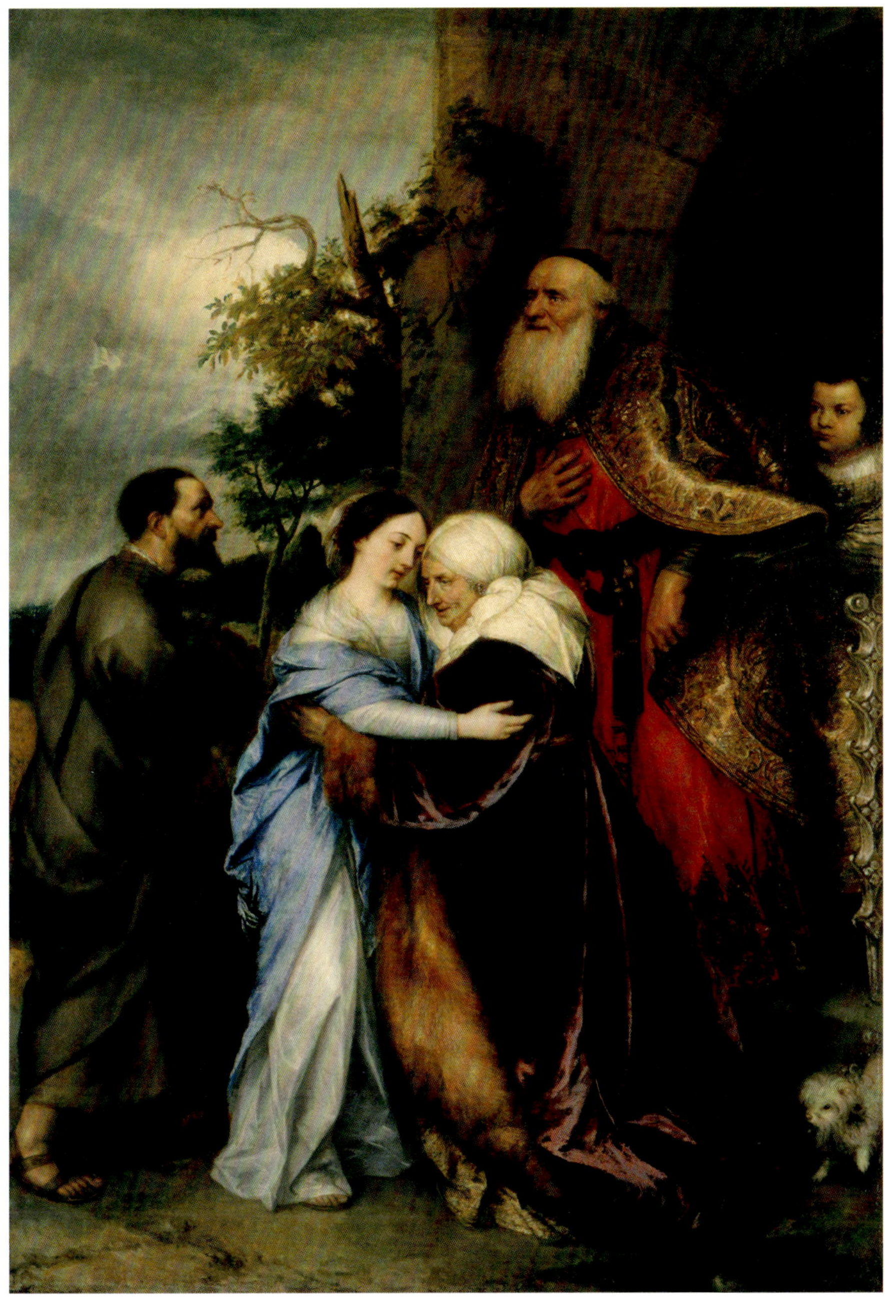

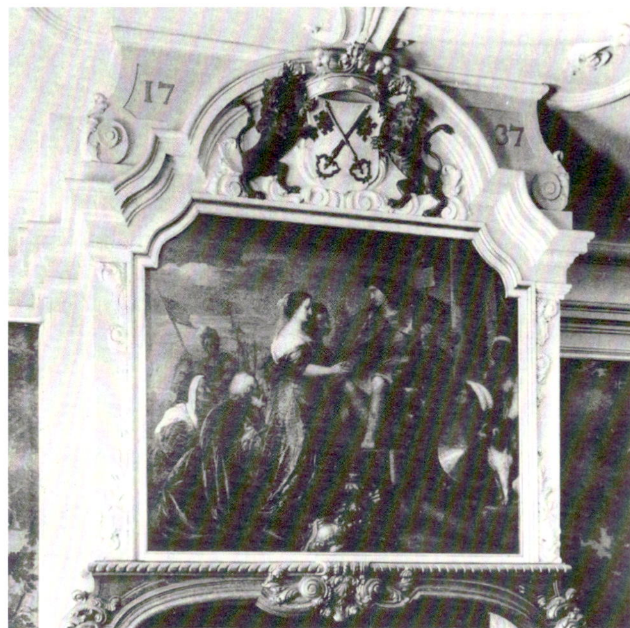

18 | Jan Lievens, *The Visitation*, c. 1638, oil on panel, 280 x 183 cm. Musée du Louvre, Paris

19 | Jan Lievens, *The Magnanimity of Scipio*, 1639–1641, Leiden Town Hall (original destroyed 1929)

the original painting was destroyed in a fire in 1929, a photograph (fig. 19) suggests that Lievens took as his model Rubens' *Judgment of Solomon*, depicting another exemplar of wisdom, which would have been known to Leiden authorities through a workshop version in the town hall in Delft.[74] Both works showed the wise ruler sitting in strict profile on a raised dais before his supplicants.

Orlers mentions another work that Lievens painted around this time for the Prince of Orange, but no further information is known. One can be sure the commission came through Huygens, and there is a possibility it was related to a chimneypiece Rubens had undertaken in July 1639 but had not finished at his death on May 30, 1640.[75] Shortly thereafter, Lievens contacted Huygens through David de Wilhem (who was occasionally Huygens' intermediary) and offered to complete the work himself.[76] It should perhaps be mentioned that while in the Netherlands in 1639–1640 Lievens visited Huygens and portrayed his former patron once again, this time in a direct yet sensitive black chalk drawing (cat. 103).

While Lievens may have left England in 1635 intending to return to the Northern Netherlands eventually, it seems likely that by the early 1640s he had come to think of Antwerp as home. He was comfortably married with a wife who had brought a handsome dowry. Although their first son died in infancy, their second, Jan Andrea, was healthy. Lievens had good relationships within a close community of artists and patrons, many of whom had posed for him, including the Earl of Arundel, then living in exile there (cat. 109). He also succeeded in landing several major commissions for religious institutions in Antwerp and Brussels. Yet despite these successes, Lievens appears to have had problems managing money, and on October 9, 1643, he was forced to turn

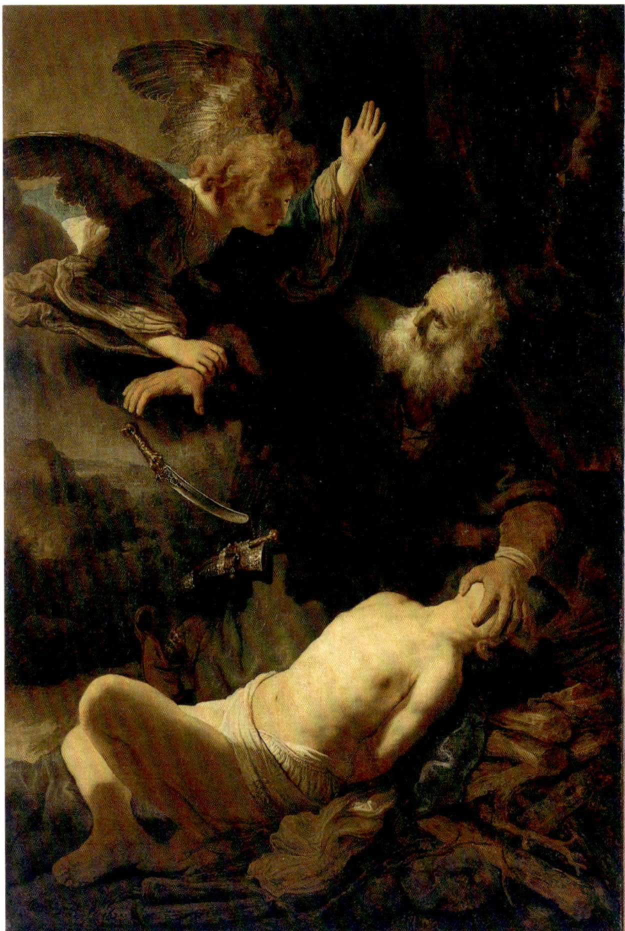

20 | Rembrandt van Rijn, *Sacrifice of Isaac*, 1635, oil on canvas, 193.5 × 132.8 cm. The State Hermitage Museum, Saint Petersburg

over his possessions to creditors. Moes speculates, with good reason, that these difficulties may underlie Lievens' decision to move to Amsterdam in 1644.[77]

RETURN TO THE NETHERLANDS, 1644–1654

Although Lievens had chosen to move to Antwerp in 1635 rather than Leiden, The Hague, or Amsterdam, he presumably remained in touch with his family and with Dutch friends and colleagues, including his in-law Jan Steen as well as Rembrandt.[78] Otherwise, how would one explain the fascinating group of four tronies of exotic sitters from 1635 that Rembrandt based on prints Lievens had published in Antwerp (cats. 67–70)? How would Lievens have known Rembrandt's monumental *Sacrifice of Isaac* from 1635 (fig. 20), on which he based his own large rendering of the subject in the early 1640s (cat. 41)?[79] Moreover, Rembrandt owned a number of paintings — including landscapes, a head of a priest, and a depiction of Abraham and Isaac — that are characteristic of Lievens' work from his Antwerp years.[80]

When Lievens eventually moved to Amsterdam in 1644, it was the largest and most dynamic city in the Dutch Republic, brimming with energy, excitement, and wealth. For an ambitious artist who saw himself as a major figure on the world's stage, Amsterdam was a logical choice. It had an active artistic community, much like the one Lievens had enjoyed in Antwerp. In addition, his younger brother Dirck, by now a practicing artist, had moved to Amsterdam by the time of their father's death in 1640.[81] Finally, Rembrandt's dominance in the city's art scene had somewhat diminished, in part because of personal turmoil following the death of his wife Saskia in 1642, and in part because of strains that had begun to develop in his relationships with Amsterdam's highest political and social circles.[82]

Lievens must have believed that the international style of painting he had developed in Antwerp — combining the compositional grandeur of Rubens, the soft, blended modeling of Titian, and the sensitivity of Van Dyck — would appeal to Dutch sensibilities at the time. He was confident that his prior reputation in the Netherlands, his successes in London and Antwerp, and his ongoing contacts with Huygens would stand him in good stead. With the proper introductions, he clearly hoped to be able to procure important private, public, and courtly commissions.

Moving to Amsterdam with his wife and young son, Lievens rented a room from the artist Jan Miense Molenaer and his wife, artist Judith Leyster. Whether he lived there or rented studio space is not certain, but on March 1, 1644, he filed a lawsuit against Molenaer, demanding the return of an unfinished landscape

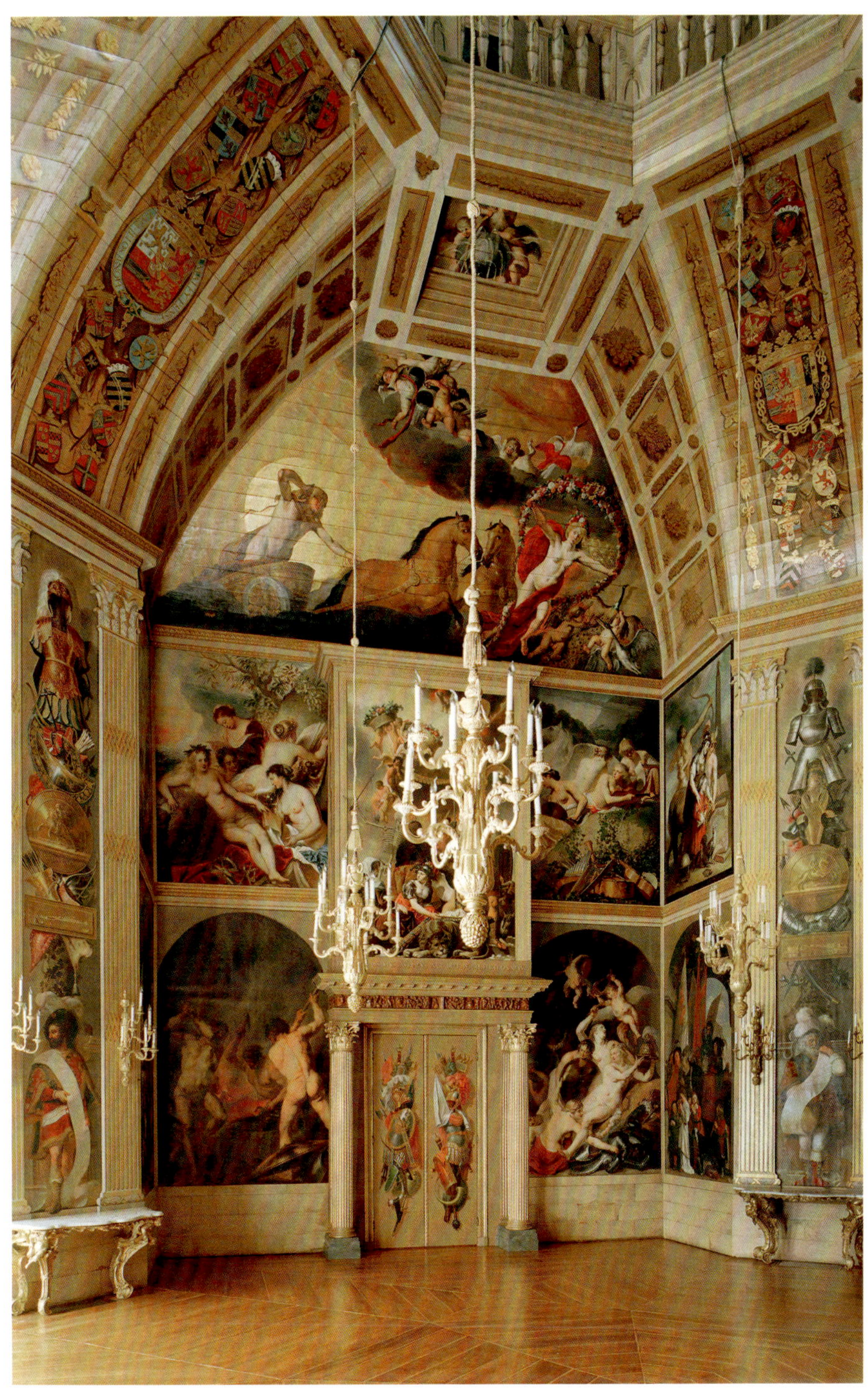

21 | View of the Oranjezaal, Huis ten Bosch, The Hague, showing Jan Lievens' *Five Muses* (fig. 22) to the upper left of the door

painting that Molenaer was holding in lieu of costs for artist materials he had provided.[83] This suit reveals not only that Lievens was still having financial difficulties but also that at the outset of his time in Amsterdam he was producing landscapes, perhaps as a means to earn income until he could establish a clientele for portraiture and large history paintings. Indeed, his wooded landscapes, which were more suggestively atmospheric than those of his Dutch contemporaries, seem to have resonated with the Amsterdam art dealer Johannes de Renialme, who had four such works in the inventory taken at his death in 1657.[84] Landscapes by Lievens appear often in Amsterdam inventories, including those of Rembrandt and Herman Becker.[85]

Unfortunately, Lievens' wife Susanna died shortly after the move to Amsterdam. Lievens remarried in 1648, this time wedding Cornelia de Bray, the daughter of the Amsterdam notary Jan de Bray, who was Catholic.[86] The couple initially lived on the Rosengracht and had six children who survived infancy. As Van der Veen argues (see his essay in this catalogue), the fact that the registers of the Reformed Church record Lievens' marriage but not the baptisms of his children suggests that Lievens returned to the Protestant faith but raised his children as Catholics.[87]

Lievens as History Painter The commissions Lievens anticipated in Amsterdam came quickly, and by the end of the 1640s his services were much in demand. The city's political, social, literary, and even artistic elite applauded his elegant, Flemish style of painting. More important, Lievens was correct in believing his associations with Huygens would lead to commissions from the House of Orange. Projects undertaken for the latter in the late 1640s and early 1650s cemented Lievens' reputation as one of the preeminent Dutch history painters.

The first of these commissions came following the death of Frederik Hendrik, Prince of Orange, in March 1647, when Lievens was invited to participate in the decoration of the Huis ten Bosch, a small summer palace near The Hague that the prince and princess had decided to build in 1645. Plans for the decoration of the interior changed radically when the prince died and his widow decided to transform the large cross-shaped central hall, the Oranjezaal, into a mausoleum. Paintings were to honor the life and accomplishments of Frederik Hendrik, particularly the peace and prosperity he brought to the Dutch Republic (fig. 21).

Huygens and Jacob van Campen, who supervised the decoration of the Oranjezaal, devised a complex program consisting of mythological, allegorical, and historical scenes that resembled, in concept, the decorative programs Rubens had created for the

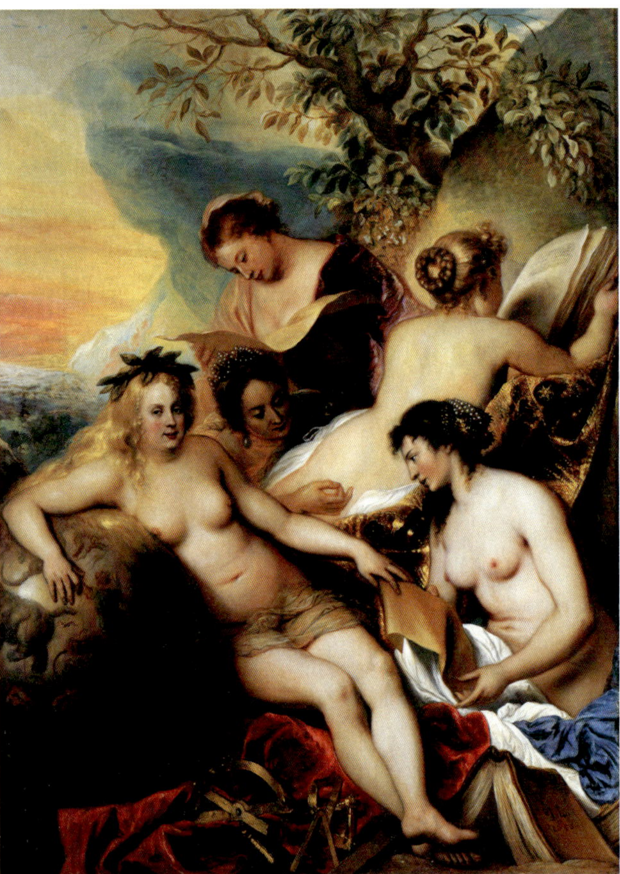

22 | Jan Lievens, *The Five Muses*, 1650, oil on canvas, 319 × 240 cm. Oranjezaal, Huis ten Bosch, The Hague

23 | Cesar van Everdingen, *Four Muses and Pegasus on Parnassus*, c. 1650, oil on canvas, 340 × 230 cm. Oranjezaal, Huis ten Bosch, The Hague

French and English courts. Huygens and Van Campen asked several outstanding Dutch and Flemish artists, including Lievens, to participate.[88] Van Campen then sent sketches and written instructions to the contributing artists, although none of these survive. The assignments were apparently given around 1648, and the works had been completed and installed by 1650.

Lievens' commission was to paint a large allegory, *The Five Muses,* to complement Cesar van Everdingen's *Four Muses and Pegasus on Parnassus* (figs. 22, 23). Huygens explained that Lievens' painting, placed adjacent to Everdingen's *Allegory of the Birth of Frederik Hendrik*, depicts muses "seeking his birth star," a concept that accords well with the way Lievens has represented them poring over books and papers using astronomical instruments and a celestial globe.[89]

The fulfillment of this commission almost certainly led to the request Lievens received in 1652 from Frederich Wilhelm von Hohenzollern, Elector of Brandenburg, and his wife Louise Henriette, the eldest daughter of Frederik Hendrik and Amalia van Solms, to come work for their court. Frederich Wilhelm, having married in 1646, invited various Dutch artists, among them Lievens, to participate in the decoration of the Schloss Oranienburg in Bützow near Berlin.[90] The elector probably also knew of Lievens' work from paintings offered to him in 1650 by the Amsterdam dealer Johannes de Renialme.[91] Lievens moved to Berlin in 1653 and completed a number of large *portraits historiés* and mythological paintings (cat. 50) for Louise Henriette's *lusthof* (country retreat) before returning to Amsterdam by the end of May 1654.

Lievens as Portraitist Lievens recognized that a market existed in Amsterdam for the type of refined portrait he had learned to make under Van Dyck. Yet he also knew enough about Dutch sensitivities to realize he would have to show a certain restraint in pose and technique. Thus, when invited to paint a likeness of Adriaen Trip, a member of one of Amsterdam's most prominent families, in 1644 — the very year Lievens arrived in the city — he showed the young aristocrat in a direct yet elegant manner (cat. 44). That Lievens, and not Rembrandt, received the commission is notable, for Rembrandt had portrayed Adriaen's mother and sister in 1639.[92] Whatever the reason, the choice of Lievens as portraitist indicates that his talents were immediately known to Amsterdam's upper class.

Lievens' associations with scholars and writers as well as with Amsterdam's political, military, and social establishment grew ever stronger in the following years. Some commissioned painted portraits, while others preferred a drawn or etched likeness reminiscent of images from Van Dyck's *Iconography*. Although the list of his sitters is extraordinary, only a fraction of the whole is known. Many documented portraits from this period are no longer extant. Among his illustrious patrons in the late 1640s were Anna Maria van Schurman and René Descartes (cats. 45, 112). Lievens also received a commission to paint life-size posthumous portraits of Admiral Maerten Harpertsz Tromp (whose likeness he had sketched before the admiral's death [cat. 116]) and his wife (Rijksmuseum, Amsterdam). Writer and playwright Joost van den Vondel, who sat for Lievens several times (cat. 85), wrote a panegyric to accompany the portrait etching that graces the title page of the 1650 publication of his *Poezy*: "so Livius of Leiden follows Titian and teaches you to understand Vondel's speech through his art, who has tried to establish Greek and Roman theater in the Netherlands."[93] A comparison to Titian was the highest compliment. Another notable poet and playwright, Jan Vos, also penned a tribute, no less admiring, on a portrait Lievens had made of him (cat. 118): "I am made immortal through Lievens' hand / the drawing pen serves Life as a weapon."[94]

The most revealing text related to a portrait by Lievens at this time comes from Sir Robert Kerr, First Earl of Ancram, who had returned to the Netherlands to live out his life following the death of Charles I. On May 30, 1654, Lord Ancram sent his son a letter, along with his painted likeness (cat. 51), and described Lievens as the "Duke of Brandenburg's painter," who "has so high a conceit of himself that he thinks there is none to be compared with him in all Germany, Holland, nor the rest of the seventeen provinces."[95]

ARTISTIC SUCCESSES IN THE HAGUE AND AMSTERDAM, 1654–1666

Lievens moved to The Hague in 1654, the same year he returned to Amsterdam after working at Schloss Oranienburg near Berlin.[96] His younger brother Titus was a teacher at the Latin School in The Hague, but it is not known if Lievens lived with him or received help interpreting Latin sources for civic commissions that required knowledge of antique sources. Lievens, in any event, quickly established relationships within the local artistic community, and in 1656 he became one of the founding members of the Confrerie Pictura, a newly formed artists' guild there.

The decision to move to The Hague in 1654 seems surprising given the radical changes that had occurred in the political climate since Lievens had been involved in the decoration of the Huis ten Bosch in 1648–1650. In 1650 Willem II, the Prince of Orange, had died suddenly from smallpox. The birth of Willem III after his father's death gave some hope for a continuation of the line, but in the meantime, the country had entered the so-called stadtholderless period under the *raadpensionaris* Johan de Witt. Thus, Lievens arrived in The Hague knowing that he could not expect to receive commissions from the House of Orange but believing that opportunities could be found in the new political environment unfolding under the leadership of the States of Holland.[97] And he was right. He soon received a major commission for an overmantel allegorical painting, *Arithmetica*, now lost, for the assembly room of the executive council (Gecommitteerde Raden) in a recently constructed building for the States of Holland in the Binnenhof.[98] The subject Lievens was asked to depict reflected the financial responsibilities given to the council.[99]

The architect Pieter Post, like Lievens, had once worked for the House of Orange in The Hague and was currently receiving commissions from the new political leadership. He had designed the Huis ten Bosch for the Prince of Orange and was now asked by the States of Holland to design their assembly room.[100] Although Post may have had input into the decision to invite Lievens to help decorate the room, the commission ultimately must have come from Amelis van den Bouchhorst, Lord of Wimmenum, the distinguished president of the executive council. Van den Bouckhorst, who served in this capacity from 1653 until his death in 1669, was a great admirer of Lievens, perhaps because of their mutual ties to Leiden.[101] He directed other commissions to the artist, including the large painting of Mars (fig. 1) for the meeting hall directly above the assembly room and two paintings for the Rijnlandshuis, Leiden headquarters of the Hoogheemraadschap van Rijnland, of which he was the head (cat. 55).

By the second half of the 1650s, while living in The Hague, Lievens continued to receive significant private and public commissions from patrons in Amsterdam. Indeed, he probably maintained some sort of residence or studio in Amsterdam to meet the demand for his services. Many portrait commissions came from members of prominent Amsterdam families allied with the republican ideals of the States of Holland and with Johan de Witt.[102] Many were connected to the powerful Andries de Graeff, whose political influence in Amsterdam was at its height in the early 1650s. The impressive list includes several burgomasters, not only De Graeff (cat. 117) but also Joan Huydecoper II and his wife (1656) and Lambert Reynst with his wife and children (c. 1664). Also in 1664 De Witt asked Lievens to paint posthumous portraits of his in-laws, burgomaster Jan Gerritsz Bicker and Agneta de Graeff.[103] Sadly, most of these portraits have disappeared, limiting appreciation for the scope of Lievens' artistic production in Amsterdam and The Hague during the 1650s and 1660s.

One enormously prestigious commission that came to Lievens in 1655, shortly after he moved to The Hague, was for an overmantel painting in the burgomaster's chamber of the Amsterdam town hall. For his large-scale *Quintus Fabius Maximus and*

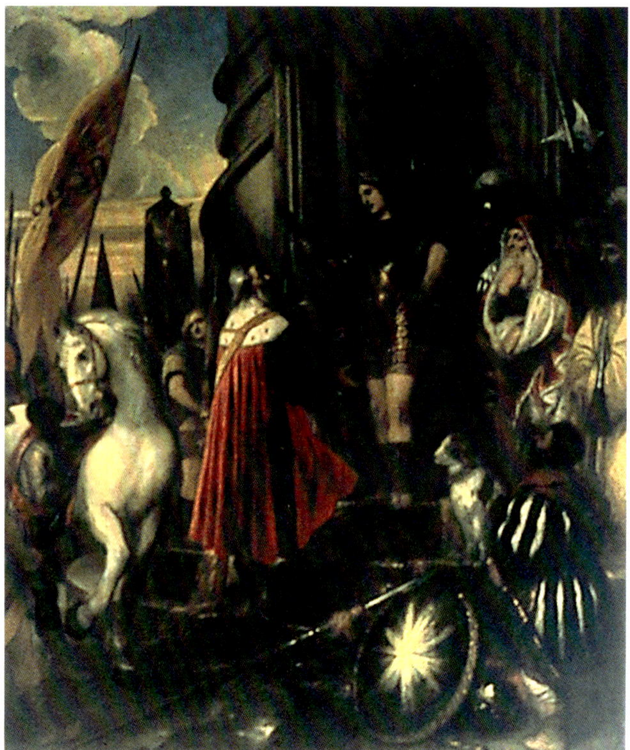

24 | Jan Lievens, *Quintus Fabius Maximus and His Son*, 1656, oil on canvas, 203 × 175 cm. Royal Palace, Amsterdam

His Son (fig. 24) he was paid no less than 1,500 guilders, identical to the amount paid to Govaert Flinck and Ferdinand Bol, who had also been invited to produce overmantel paintings for the same room.[104] All three paintings present exempla drawn from antiquity of proper behavior for civic leaders. In the episode Lievens represented, based on the writings of Valerius Maximus, Quintus Fabius approaches his son, the consul at Suesso. The son had ordered his father to dismount as a sign of respect for his office, and Lievens captured the moment when the father leaves his horse and climbs the steps toward his son, who stands at the entrance to a large classical structure. The son's pose, with one arm raised in the traditional gesture of the *adlocutio*, emphasizes the moral of the story — that public institutions take precedence over private duty. It also reinforces republican sentiments about the dangers of hereditary positions in government, such as that of the stadtholder.[106]

By March 1659, after five years in The Hague, Lievens had moved back to Amsterdam, where one of his children was buried in the Nieuwe Kerk. He was recorded as a citizen of Amsterdam in 1660 and lived there until 1669, although he maintained a nonresident membership in The Hague's Confrerie Pictura in 1660–1661. His reasons for returning to Amsterdam may have related to his desire to receive the commission for a series of eight large paintings for the lunettes at the ends of the galleries surrounding the central citizens' hall in the Amsterdam town hall.

The town hall had been officially open since 1655, but the lunette paintings had not been made, and the selection of an artist to receive the commission was imminent. Cornelis de Graeff (jointly serving as burgomaster with Joan Huydecoper) had devised an iconographic program to focus on the historic battle between the Batavians, under the leadership of Claudius Civilis, and the Romans — prefiguring the Dutch revolt against the Spanish.[107] Lievens, who had close connections within the De Graeff family, must have believed he would be a strong candidate for the task. But the lunettes had to be filled quickly because of an unexpected visit by the Prince of Anhalt and members of the House of Orange in August 1659, and Flinck, another De Graeff favorite, was asked to provide temporary decorations that would be ready in a matter of days.[108] His designs were so successful that he was given the full commission in November of that year.

Flinck, however, died soon thereafter, and in 1660 the burgomasters decided to divide the commission instead of awarding it to a single artist. Andries de Graeff, one of the magistrates that year, made sure that Lievens secured the commission to paint the *Brinio Raised on a Shield* lunette (fig. 25). Other artists who received commissions included Jacob Jordaens, who was to paint two lunettes, and Rembrandt, who was asked to paint *The Conspiracy of Claudius Civilis* (fig. 26) the following year. By January 13, 1661, Lievens and Jordaens had each completed one painting, for which they were each paid the large sum of 1,200 guilders.[109] Rembrandt's painting apparently did not satisfy the burgomasters, however, and it was removed shortly after it was installed.

One of Lievens' best-documented commissions in these years was for *Mars (The Allegory of War)* in Pieter Post's newly constructed assembly room in the Binnenhof (fig. 1). The enormous painting, finished in 1664, shows an armored Mars, the god of war, trampling both society's social compact (an open book with PRIVILEGIA written on its pages) and its religious foundations (a book titled BIBLIA) in a blood-stained landscape consumed by devastating fires. With bulging eyes and a drawn sword, he surveys the ruins with fierce satisfaction. The exaggerated characterization of the figure was highly praised in its day, although nineteenth- and twentieth-century critics reacted negatively to the work's excesses.[110] Lievens' violent image countered an equally large overmantel painting on the opposite wall, *The Allegory of Peace* by Adriaen Hanneman, another extremely successful artist in The Hague who worked in an elegant Flemish style.[111]

A letter from Lievens to Johan de Witt in April 1664 provides further information regarding *The Allegory of War*, not only indicating that the artist had sent an oil sketch of it to Van den Bouckhorst for approval but also offering a statement of his artis-

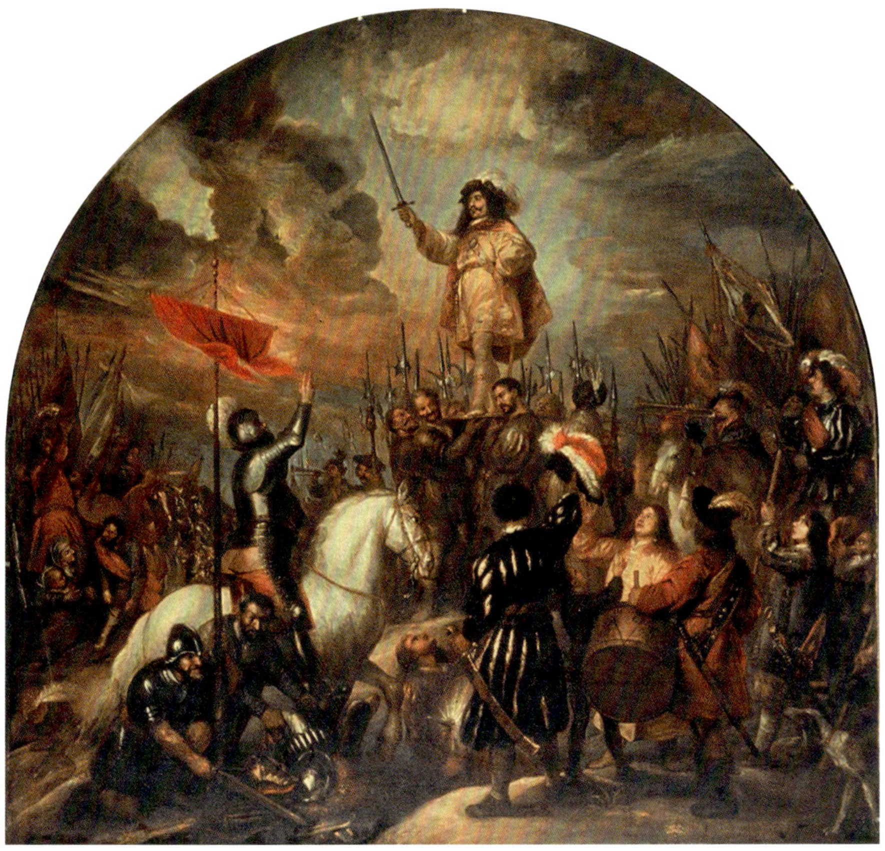

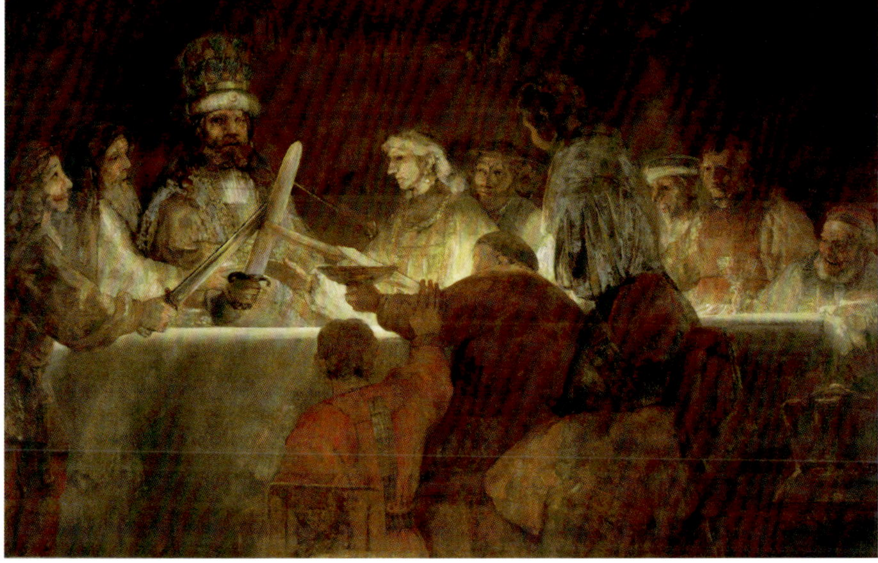

25 | Jan Lievens, *Brinio Raised on a Shield*, 1660, oil on canvas, 546 × 538 cm. Royal Palace, Amsterdam

26 | Rembrandt van Rijn, *The Conspiracy of Claudius Civilis*, 1661, oil on canvas, 196 x 309 cm. Nationalmuseum, Stockholm (cut down from original size)

tic intent: "I have a great desire to stir up something extraordinary in it, because War is a picturesque [*schilderachtich*] subject."[112] Lievens clearly welcomed the challenge of creating a work that resonated with power and emotional energy, and he wanted to stress the horrific rather than idealized character of Mars.

This same letter reveals that Lievens was continuing to experience financial problems. Given the generous payment he had received in 1661 for his work on the Amsterdam town hall, it seems surprising that he was having trouble paying his rent. He asks that his brother (presumably Titus, living in The Hague) be permitted to retrieve the oil sketch for *Mars* from Van den Bouckhorst so that Lievens could proceed with his work on the project.[113] This commission was profitable for the artist, bringing him 1,000 guilders when completed later that year.[114]

Trip to Cleves On June 27, 1664, Lievens wrote to Johan de Witt's brother-in-law Pieter de Graeff, saying that he was about to visit Cleves.[115] Little is known about this trip except that he made a number of atmospheric drawings of the village and its surroundings (cat. 129). It has always been assumed that Lievens was following the example of artists before him, such as Jan van Goyen and Aelbert Cuyp, traveling along the Rhine River to this picturesque and historically significant area of Germany in the early 1650s primarily for the landscape. A more probable motivation, however, was the hope that he would receive a commission to provide a painting for the castle of De Zwanenburcht, residence of Johan Maurits of Nassau, which was being renovated that year following the designs of Pieter Post.[116]

Maurits, who had been named stadtholder of the Lower Rhine in 1647 by Frederich Wilhelm, Elector of Brandenburg, had undertaken the modernization of this medieval structure because the elector and his wife often visited Cleves and wanted the castle to meet their expectations for comfort and refinement. It is uncertain whether Lievens ever painted anything for De Zwanenburcht. Nevertheless, the fact that the renovation was initiated at the behest of his former patrons from Berlin following plans by Pieter Post, with whom he had collaborated on projects for the States of Holland, argues strongly that the timing of the trip in 1664 was not entirely coincidental, particularly given his recent successes in Amsterdam and The Hague.

LIEVENS' LAST YEARS: AMSTERDAM AND LEIDEN

By the spring of 1666 Lievens was once again in Amsterdam living on the Hartestraat, but his return was not marked by domestic harmony. In April of that year he petitioned the city magistrates to arrest and discipline his son and student, Jan Andrea, who had run away from home and become engaged to an underage girl against his parents' wishes.[117] The resolution of this family crisis is not known, but it appears that the father and son were soon reconciled, for in May 1666 Jan Andrea named his father as "universal beneficiary" should he die.[118] In September of that year the two worked together on a chimneypiece for the office of Van den Bouckhorst in the Gemeenlandshuis of the Hoogheemraadschap van Rijnland in Leiden (cat. 55). When delivering this painting, *The Geographer*, Lievens described a figure "made by my son, composed and overpainted by me in many places."[119] He was paid only 300 guilders for this work, perhaps in view of his son's participation. The painting represents another instance of Lievens' having been asked to contribute to the decorative program for a building designed or renovated by Pieter Post, a frequent artistic advisor to Van den Bouckhorst.[120]

During this period Lievens continued to paint portraits and history paintings, but one has a sense that the supreme self-confidence that had supported him throughout his life was beginning to wane. Financial woes continued to mount, and many of his letters to patrons from the late 1660s focus on the timing and amount of payments. In 1667 and 1668, moreover, he entered into four separate arrangements with the collector Herman Becker to borrow money using paintings as collateral.[121] Another personal crisis befell him in March 1668, when his second wife, Cornelia, died. Finally, and perhaps most significantly for Lievens' financial well-being and artistic career, Van den Bouckhorst died on September 27, 1669, owing Lievens 1,900 guilders for paintings he had commissioned.[122] There is no evidence that the artist ever received these funds.

Lievens' humbled state is painfully evident, even before Van den Bouckhorst's death, in the invoice for his last major commission for the Hoogheemraadschap van Rijnland in Leiden. Sent in February 1669, the invoice estimates the painting's value to be 400 guilders but says that the artist will accept whatever sum his patron deems it to be worth.[123] One year later, on March 8, 1670, the new leaders of the organization decided to pay only 280 guilders, which Lievens accepted. The painting in question was a large allegorical image designed to be hung over the fireplace in the chamber of justice. Lievens described the theme as "Time bringing the Corpus Juris to Justice who is accompanied by the Goddess Athena."[124] This complex subject, largely drawn from emblematic concepts found in the 1644 Dutch edition of Cesare Ripa's *Iconologia*, was intended to emphasize the judicial responsibilities of the organization.

Prior to painting this work, Lievens submitted an oil sketch to Van den Bouckhorst for approval, as he had for *Mars* and *The Geographer*. His use of oil sketches suggests that he completed these three large-scale paintings with studio assistance, which might explain why he received a lower payment than anticipated.[125] Oil sketches exist for several other large compositions, including *The Lamentation* and *Brinio Raised on a Shield* (cats. 39, 54), and it seems probable that students assisted with these works as well. As indicated in a document dated 1653, Lievens also used student help to execute landscapes (perhaps from students like the orphan Erick van Weerelt).[126] Aside from assistance in executing painting commissions, students also provided Lievens with needed income, suggesting one reason why he accepted Jonas Witsen, son of the burgomaster Cornelis Joan Witsen, into his studio in 1669.[127] Even as late as 1670, when he was living once again in The Hague and seems to have had fewer large-scale commissions, Lievens took on a student named Denys Godyn.[128] Yet given the number of times he moved in the last twenty years of his life, it is unlikely that Lievens ever established a vigorous studio with students working under his close supervision.[129]

The description of the working process for *The Geographer* in 1666 is the only instance in which Lievens acknowledges painting with his son and student, Jan Andrea. Other collaborations between the two must have existed, for the few signed works known by the younger Lievens are remarkably close in style to those by his father. Attribution issues are particularly confounding when dealing with landscape drawings, for Jan Andrea seems to have emulated his father's atmospheric approach to depicting wooded vistas.[130]

Lievens remained in Leiden during the early 1670s, that difficult period in Dutch history when the country was besieged by France. As with many artists, including Johannes Vermeer, Lievens suffered financial losses when the art market dried up as his debts mounted. Even in this reduced state, however, his expertise in Italian art was recalled when a conflict erupted between his former patron Frederich Wilhelm, the Elector of Brandenburg, and Amsterdam art dealer Gerrit Uylenburgh. The authenticity of a group of Italian paintings the elector had acquired from Uylenburgh had been questioned, and Lievens and his son were among those asked to examine the paintings in Amsterdam in May 1672.[131]

Despite this fleeting recognition that his name still had value, Lievens' artistic career had come to a sad end. He returned to Amsterdam in April 1674, where he had rented a residence on the Rosengracht, but when he arrived on the doorstep with his furniture, he found the house locked and the landlord unwilling to let him enter before paying a security deposit.[132] Lievens, an artist whose work had always been highly esteemed by the powerful and the elite, died in poverty in June of that year and was buried in the Nieuwe Kerk.[133]

CLOUDED CRITICAL FORTUNES

Lievens' peripatetic existence during the last years of his life probably resulted from a number of factors. Undoubtedly, some moves reflected financial difficulties that plagued him most of his adult life; some stemmed from disagreements with landlords, as with Jan Miense Molenaer in 1644; some were driven by his belief that his artistic opportunities would be better in a different locale. It should not be forgotten that when Lievens returned to Amsterdam from Berlin in 1654 he brought impressive credentials. Yet he seems to have been burdened, as Lord Ancram's letter implies, by an exceedingly high opinion of his own talents. One can imagine that relationships with his contemporaries (and his family) would not have been easy, and indeed there is little evidence that he had close friendships later in his life.

There were also positive reasons for his many changes of residence. Lievens successfully combined his unassailable self-confidence with political savvy and a willingness to put himself in an advantageous position for receiving commissions. His services remained in demand throughout the 1660s in three major cultural centers: Amsterdam, The Hague, and Leiden. During these years he was often busy painting large works for a public building in one city while residing in another.

Considering the extraordinary success of his career after 1650, the broad neglect of this period in art historical literature remains puzzling. The cruel irony is that Lievens' artistic achievement, whether in assessments of individual works or his entire oeuvre, has come to be considered almost exclusively in relation to Rembrandt during his early Leiden years. To the detriment of Lievens, those comparisons are nearly always tinged by the cult of genius that surrounds Rembrandt, particularly since the romantic era in the nineteenth century. Adding to the lack of appreciation for Lievens' early innovations is the fact that so many of his youthful works have, until recently, been lost or attributed to other artists, primarily Rembrandt.

Quirks of history have also contributed to the obscurity of Lievens' later works, for most have either disappeared or are virtually inaccessible. Beyond issues of access, however, are changing tastes. Whereas Lievens' late paintings were greatly admired in the middle to late seventeenth century, the international style he devised — appreciated by the House of Orange, the States of Holland, and the burgomasters of Amsterdam — has fallen out of favor. His history paintings and even his portraits, infused with the spirit of Van Dyck and Titian, feel alien to the broader thrust of Dutch art, which privileges realism over idealization. Yet his painting style, with its blended brushstrokes and softly modulated forms, also differs from the typical clarity and crispness of Dutch classicizing traditions. Strikingly, Lievens was not included in a recent exhibition on Dutch classicism, though he certainly would have seen himself as belonging to that heritage.

At the same time, Lievens cannot be fully absolved from responsibility for the lack of recognition or low esteem accorded him by historians. He had artistic limitations that kept him from achieving some of his ambitious goals. His efforts to transform himself from a Dutch artist — who was exploring the new boldness of Caravaggio's pictorial vision, emphasizing the earthy reality of unidealized peasants in both tronies and history paintings — into a painter of refined and elegant figures suitable for courtly and aristocratic patrons created tensions in his art that he did not always successfully resolve. He never truly captured the luminosity of Van Dyck's and Titian's images because his paint application remained dense and relatively heavy throughout his career. While the Flemish and Venetian masters could soften forms with quickly applied strokes, Lievens' touch was more labored and his modeling sometimes appears muddy. Finally, one has the uncomfortable feeling that he tried too hard to satisfy too many conflicting desires by adapting his style of painting, thereby sacrificing his core artistic convictions for success in the marketplace. Interestingly, these issues are more problematic in his paintings than in his prints and drawings, which maintain a logical stylistic and thematic integrity throughout his career.

This exhibition offers an exciting opportunity to assess these issues and to come to a new understanding of the role and significance of Jan Lievens' pictorial innovations and stylistic approach within the wider framework of Dutch art. Lacunae are unavoidable, owing to losses, and the fact that some major commissions remain in situ, but Lievens should now, after so many years of existing in Rembrandt's shadow, reclaim his place in the light of history, with all of his great strengths and occasional flaws.

Notes

1 For the changing historical assessments of Lievens' relationship to Rembrandt, see Gutbrod 1996, 13–38.

2 The great majority of the Leiden-period paintings in this exhibition (except those recently on the art market) have at times been attributed to artists other than Lievens, usually Rembrandt, but also Nicolaes Maes, Gerrit van Honthorst, or Jacob Backer. In 1989 *The Feast of Esther* (cat. 6) was still widely attributed to Rembrandt.

3 No paintings survive from his time in London (1632–1635), and many major commissions from Amsterdam patrons in the 1650s and 1660s are lost.

4 Houbraken 1753, 1:296–301.

5 Weyerman 1729, 2:50–54; Descamps 1753–1763, 2:115–117, essentially followed Houbraken's text.

6 Weyerman 1729, 4:43.

7 Van Eijnden and Van der Willigen 1816, 1:395–396. Moes 1907, 150, records that the amount specified in the commission for this work in 1639 was 1,500 guilders. In 1640 the burgomasters paid 150 guilders, 14 stuivers, to Andries de Molyn when he brought the painting to Leiden from Lievens' workshop in Antwerp. The medal was struck in 1641 to express their pleasure with Lievens' work.

8 Smith 1829–1842. Hofstede de Groot 1907–1927 mentions Lievens only briefly in biography of Rembrandt and in a few catalogue entries of Rembrandt paintings.

9 Waagen 1857, 409, 150, and 41, respectively.

10 Bode 1883, 30.

11 Worp 1897. Huygens penned his autobiography in Latin in 1629–1631 while accompanying Frederik Hendrik, Prince of Orange, at the siege of 's-Hertogenbosch.

12 Moes 1907; Schneider 1932.

13 Bauch 1939; Bauch 1967; Gerson 1954; Gerson 1969; Schneider/Ekkart 1973.

14 See Braunschweig 1979.

15 For Rubens' painting, see Klessmann 1996, 182.

16 For Vogelaar and Van de Wetering, see Leiden 1991. See also Schwartz 1985; Gutbrood 1996; Van de Wetering in Kassel and Amsterdam 2001, 49–55; Schnackenburg 2004; and Van Straten 2005.

17 See Leiden 1991, 24–38, and 39–47. P. J. M. de Baar and Ingrid W. L. Moerman, "De symbiose van Lievens en Rembrandt," argue that there is no evidence the two artists shared a studio (and that each could have had a studio in his parents' home). Ernst van de Wetering believes that they did, in part because of the similarities in subject matter, style, and technique in the late 1620s.

18 Amsterdam 1991. See also Van Straten 2005, which contains almost as much information about Lievens as about Rembrandt during their Leiden years.

19 Schatborn in Amsterdam 1988; Dickey in Vlieghe 2001; DeWitt 2006.

20 Worp 1897. English translations of Orlers' and Huygens' comments are quoted in full in the Appendix.

21 Joris van Schooten (c. 1587–1653) was a portraitist and history painter. Lieven Hendrixsz (c. 1570–c. 1642) was a Protestant refugee who had come to Leiden from Ghent. He married Machtelt Jansdr van Noortsant (c. 1580–1622) on March 3, 1605, and they lived on the Pieterskerk-Choorsteeg. Jan was the second of four sons (he also had four sisters). His older brother Joost (b. 1606) registered at Leiden University on October 26, 1622, where he studied Latin. A younger brother Dirck (b. in 1613), enrolled in the Leiden Academy in 1635 to study mathematics but became a painter, moving to Amsterdam, where he lived until 1648, then traveling to the East Indies, where he died in 1650. The youngest brother, Titus (b. in 1616), studied literature at Leiden University before becoming a teacher in the Latin School in The Hague.

22 Orlers mistakenly dated the riots to October 4, 1618.

23 Although Orlers indicates that Lievens departed in 1631, the artist seems not to have left until 1632, for he signed a document in Leiden on February 2, 1632.

24 Orlers suggests that the king commissioned one large group portrait from Lievens, although the text could be interpreted to mean that Lievens painted a double portrait of the king and queen and separate portraits of the prince, princess, and "great lords." Orlers is likely recounting Lievens' own description of his activities in London, which cannot be independently confirmed.

25 Orlers mistakenly identified Susanna's father as Michiel Colijns. For the Colijns de Nole family, see Casteels 1961. Moes 1907, 146–147, notes that Lievens married Susanna in the Saint Jacobskerk in Antwerp in December 1638. She brought a handsome dowry: fl. 3,000 plus a share of various artworks and a promise of fl. 8,000 by year's end. The couple lived in the house "het Brandijzer" that they rented on the Saint Jacobsmarkt.

26 Simon van Leewen, *Korte Besgryving van het Lugdunum Batavoru. Nu Leyden*. (Leiden, 1672), 190–191, cited the location of this work as the room of the Board of Forty. For an English translation see Van Straten 2005, 351.

27 See DeWitt 2006, 42–43.

28 Bauch 1960, 112–119, sees close connections between Lievens and Haarlem, in part because Lievens' *Allegory of the Five Senses* appears related to Merry Company scenes painted by Haarlem artists, and in part because of stylistic connections between Lievens' early paintings and works by the Haarlem classicists, in particular Pieter de Grebber and Salomon de Bray. Gerson 1969, 139, echoes this opinion, doubting the attribution of some of Lievens' early paintings (cats. 2, 7, 9, 10). Stewart 1990 and Stewart 2004 argue that Lievens traveled to Antwerp in 1620–1621 to study with Rubens. See also Schnackenburg 2007.

29 See Slatkes 1965; San Francisco, Baltimore, and London 1997; and Judson and Ekkart 1999.

30 See Klessmann 1996.

31 Judson and Ekkart 1999, 14.

32 Virginia Treanor has suggested contacts between Lievens and this family date back to this period. Marten Jan Bok in Braunschweig 1987, 140, argues that Buchell referred to Andries, who had returned from Italy around the same time and shared a studio with his father Jan and his uncle Robrecht. Bok thinks Jan and Robrecht were in Utrecht at the time of Honthorst's return to settle the estate of a deceased brother. Lievens married Andries' daughter, Susanna, the year of her father's death.

33 They are described as such in the 1640 inventory of Orlers' collection. See Leiden 1976, 17.

34 See Braunschweig 1979, nos. 1–4.

35 Białostocki 1988, 144. Lievens probably learned his Latin from his older brother Joost.

36 Białostocki 1966, 591–593; Białostocki 1988, 144.

37 Hoogewerff and Van Regteren Altena 1928, 49; Braunschweig 2004, 121; DeWitt 2006, 37–38.

38 See Magurn 1955, 63–64.

39 See Leiden 1991, 49. Huygens accompanied Carleton on his trip to England in 1620–1621. See Colie 1956, 5–6. See also Worp 1897; Kan 1946; and Heesakkers 1994.

40 See Ekkart in Leiden 1991, 56.

41 In 1932 Schneider believed this painting was given to Sir Dudley Carleton when he returned in England in 1628. See Schneider/Ekkart 1973, 120, no. 116. But Christopher White, "Did Rembrandt Ever Visit England?" *Apollo* 76 (1962): 178–180, notes that the painting (attributed to Rembrandt) appears in Van der Doort's 1639 inventory of Charles I's collection as a gift from Robert Kerr. The canvas was very large (392.4 × 327.7 cm) and was unframed, thus probably not hanging on a wall. Van Straten 2005, 130–131, thinks Kerr returned to the Netherlands to visit his son, William Kerr (participating in the siege of 's-Hertogenbosch in late 1629), when the gift was presented. He posits that Kerr would have then visited the studios of Lievens and Rembrandt in Leiden, but there is no evidence to support that hypothesis.

42 Moes 1907, 142–143, quotes an article by Rammelman Elsevier from the *Nederlandsche Spectator*, April 17, 1875, quoting the *Journaal* of the Leiden civic guard, April 10, 1629.

43 Works attributed Lievens to in the 1632 inventory of the palace Noordeinde, The Hague, are: "Pluto Proserpina," "Sampson," "Een stuck schilderij de Melancolij...," "Symeon, sijnde in den temple... (by Rembrandt or Lievens)," and "Een stuck schilderie daer een waerseghster off een heyen in de handt goeder geluck seght." The first of three of these were by Rembrandt, not Lievens. See Corpus 1982–, 1:A39, A38, and A34, respectively. *Sultan Soliman* in is listed in the House of Orange inventory of 1707/1719. See also Drossaers and Lunsingh Scheurleer 1974–1976, 1:184–202, 530, listed as Rembrandt.

44 Van Straten 2005, 91, noted Lievens' dependency in these works on prints made after Rubens' paintings.

45 See the Appendix.

46 Drossaers and Lunsingh Scheurleer 1974–1976, 1:186.

47 Lievens' two still lifes (Heino, Hannema-De Stuers Foundation; and Rijksmuseum, Amsterdam [cat. 11]) are not universally accepted as being by the artist; see Haak 1969, 68–69; and Braunschweig 1979, 62–63, cat. 14.

48 For the argument that Rembrandt wrongly dated his *Samson Betrayed by Delilah* (Gemäldegalerie, Berlin), see Corpus 1982–, 1:249–257, no. A24. The painting is dated 1628, although Rembrandt probably executed it c. 1630.

49 The closest comparison is Rembrandt's etched *Self-Portrait, Open-Mouthed*, 1630. See London 1999, 128.

50 Jay Richard Judson (March 22, 2007) notes that Lievens' image, emphasizing the blood flowing from Christ's wound, differs markedly from Pontius' engraving after Rubens, where Christ has no wound and is still alive.

51 First proposed by Wheelock in Washington, Detroit, and Amsterdam 1980, 138.

52 See Walsh in *Van Dyck 350*, ed. Susan J. Barnes and Arthur K. Wheelock Jr. (Hanover and London, 1994), 223–244.

53 Millar 1960, 146, 161; Brown 1983, 670. In 1634 the children would have been two and four years old—ages at which they might pose "hand in hand."

54 See Amsterdam 1998, 58.

55 Worp 1892–, 2:246. Translation adapted from DeWitt 2006, 127. Schneider/Ekkart 1973, 161, no. 299, assumed this referred to a now-lost painting.

56 Schneider/Ekkart 1973, nos. Z166 and Z167.

57 Galleria Sabauda, Turin. See Washington 1990a, 284–287, no. 74.

58 See Keblusek in The Hague 1997, 54.

59 Van Dyck's collection of paintings by Titian was in Antwerp until after he returned to London in 1635, thus they were probably there when Lievens arrived. See Jeremy Wood, "Van Dyck's 'Cabinet de Titien': The Contents and Dispersal of His Collection," *Burlington Magazine* 132, no. 1051 (1990), 681. Lievens may also have been able to study Titian's paintings in London at the court of Charles I.

60 P. Rombouts and T. van Lerius, *De Liggern... der Antwerpsche Sint Lucasgulde* (Antwerp, The Hague, 1876), 2:61; and Van den Branden 1883, 863; Moes 1907, 146; Schneider/Ekkart 1973, 43–64.

61 Clippel 2003.

62 Sam Segal, *Jan Davidsz de Heem en zijn kring* (The Hague, 1991), 55–63, suggests that De Heem moved from Leiden to Antwerp in the early 1630s, perhaps because his father had come from there.

63 Lievens probably also knew sculptor Andries Colijns de Nole during these years. See note 32 above.

64 His *Diverse Tronikens* (cats. 63–66) resemble tronies after Pieter Bruegel the Elder.

65 This print was published by both Martinus van den Enden and Franciscus van den Wijngaerde.

66 This mood is entirely different from the panoramic, topographic quality of the drawings Lievens made in England under the influence of Van Dyck.

67 The tree in Titian's woodcut, *Saint Jerome in the Wilderness* (1525–1530), also inspired Lievens in his drawing *Mountain Landscape with Trees* in Berlin (Kupferstichkabinett der Staatlichen Museen, no. KdZ 376). See Braunschweig 1979, 194, no. 96.

68 Jegher created the woodcut from an oil sketch that Rubens had made in preparation for a ceiling painting for the banqueting hall at Whitehall.

69 Lievens' painting for the Jesuit church in Antwerp is lost. He painted his *Visitation* for the Jesuit church in Brussels. See Descamps 1753–1763, 5:65.

70 See DeWitt 2006, 163–164.

71 Van den Branden 1883, 865–866. Lievens and his wife had two children in the early 1640s. The first was baptized in Antwerp in July 1642; the other, Jan Andrea, was baptized in January 1644 and would go on to become an artist.

72 Lievens' presence in Leiden is confirmed by a document dated August 13, 1639. See Schneider/Ekkart 1973, 117–118, no. 106; and DeWitt 2006, 147, no. 39. See also Moes 1907, 150–152.

73 See above notes 7 and 26.

74 Rubens' original was painted c. 1617–1618 for the town hall in Brussels. See R. A. d'Hulst and M. Vandenveen, *Rubens: The Old Testament*, Corpus Rubenianum (London, 1989), 3:149, no. 46.

75 Huygens sent the request via his brother-in-law, David de Wilhem. See Schwartz 1985, 91; Inge Broekman, *De rol van de schilderkunst in het leven van Constantijn Huygens (1596–1687)* (Hilversum, 2005), 71.

76 Schneider/Ekkart 1973, 292–293. De Wilhem wrote two letters to Huygens concerning this matter. The first, dated June 6, 1640, presents Huygens with Lievens' proposal to complete the commission, which Lievens believed Rubens had not yet begun, let alone finished. The second, dated July 7, 1640, indicates that Lievens had been to Rubens' studio, where he had seen the backside of the canvas, which had an inscription "Hage" written in chalk. In the letter De Wilhem conveys Lievens' promise to spare no pains in bringing the painting to completion.

77 Moes 1907, 149.

78 Lievens' brother Joost (1606–1649) married Steen's father's sister, Marijtje Jansdr Steen, in 1632. Joost ran a bookstore on the Rapenburgh in Leiden, not far from Steen's parental home. See Marten Jan Bok in *Jan Steen: Painter and Storyteller*, ed. Guido M. C. Jansen [exh. cat., National Gallery of Art] (Washington, 1996), 28.

79 Broos 1972, 140–141, proposed that Lievens' painting inspired Rembrandt's, but Lievens must have executed his in Antwerp in the early 1640s after going to Leiden in 1639–1640 to paint for the town hall. See Marcus Dekiert, *Rembrandt. Die Opferung Isaaks* (Munich, 2004), 82–83.

80 Strauss and Van der Meulen 1979, 351, nos. 18, 19, 22; 355, no. 58; 361, no. 122. Other than the works in Rembrandt's inventory of 1656, no documents indicate interactions between the two artists after they left Leiden.

81 Bredius 1915–1922, 1:193.

82 For a discussion of the difficulties Rembrandt was experiencing, see Schwartz 1985, 226–234.

83 Schneider/Ekkart 1973, 7. As noted by Dennis Weller in *Jan Miense Molenaer: Painter of the Dutch Golden Age* [exh. cat., North Carolina Museum of Art] (Raleigh, 2002), 25 n. 35, "Molenaer stated he had purchased art supplies for Lievens and considered the painting his property."

84 Bredius 1915–1922, 1:231, 233, 238. See Schneider/Ekkart 1973, 168, no. 329. De Renialme owned no fewer than eleven paintings by Lievens at his death.

85 Strauss and Van der Meulen 1979, 349–388. Rembrandt owned three landscapes, which he hung in his entrance hall: no. 18, a landscape; no. 19, another by the same; no. 22, a "Moonlight Scene." He also owned other works by Lievens: no. 13, a candlelight scene; no. 42, a "Raising of Lazarus"; no. 46, a grisaille; no. 52, a small [picture of a] hermit; no. 58, a "Priest after Lievens"; no. 122, an "Abraham's Sacrifice"; no. 274, another engraved album with prints by Jan Lieven and Ferdinand Bol. For Herman Becker see Postma 1988, 1–21.

86 Jan de Bray was the son of Simon de Bray and the brother of Haarlem painter/architect Salomon de Bray. See A. van der Marel, "De kunstschilders De Bray en hun familie," *De Nederlandsche Leeuw* 81 (1964): 6–26.

87 DeWitt 2006, 199. As Moes 1907, 153, notes, the second child was named Frederik Willem, probably after the Duke of Brandenburg, for whom Lievens worked in 1653–1654.

88 As is noted in Rotterdam and Frankfurt 1999–2000, 176, a contemporary source indicates that the artists chosen were considered to be among "the seven or eight best painters in the land." Among the other Dutch artists who participated were Van Campen, Salomon de Bray, Pieter de Grebber, Cesar van Everdingen, and Honthorst. Also invited were Flemish artists, including Jacob Jordaens, Theodoor van Thulden, and Thomas Willeboirts-Bosschaert.

89 Rotterdam and Frankfurt 1999–2000, 178, 179, and pl. 3.

90 Also invited were Honthorst, Flinck, and Jan Mijtens.

91 Paul Seidel, "Die Beziehungen des Grossen kurfürsten und könig Friedrichs I. zur niederländischen kunst," *Jahrbuch der Königlich Preussischen Kunstsammlungen* 11 (1890): 122–123; and Moes 1907, 154.

92 Now in the Boijmans Van Beuningen Museum, Rotterdam, and the Rijksmuseum, Amsterdam.

93 English translation from Dickey 2004, 136–137.

94 Jan Vos, *Alle de Gedichten* (Amsterdam, 1662), 1:785. See also Houbraken 1753, 1:300. For a translation of the entire poem, see DeWitt 2006, 250.

95 The letter appears in John M. Gray, *Notes on the Art Treasures at New-Battle Abbey* (Middlothian, 1887), 12. For an excerpt, see Schneider/Ekkert 1973, 303.

96 Bredius 1915–1922, 1:198–199; Buijsen 1998, 190–193.

97 See Israel 1995, 700–730.

98 See Terwen and Ottenheym 1993, 163–172. Marion Bolten, writing a book on the Binnenhof, kindly shared her insights on this commission.

99 Schneider/Ekkart 1973, 119–120, no. 114; notes that the work was covered during the renovation of hall in 1913.

100 See Terwen and Ottenheym 1993, 163–172.

101 See Terwen and Ottenheym 1993, 30–32.

102 See Schwartz 1985, 267–271.

103 See following essay by Jaap van der Veen.

104 See Goossens 1996, 41, pl. XIV; 43, pls. XVI and XVII; 72–76. Bol's painting was *Fabritius and Pyrrhus*, while the one by Flinck was *The Incorruptible Consul Marcus Curius Dentatus*. See Fremantle 1959, 67.

105 Rubens often used this pose when depicting leaders receiving supplicants at the entrance of a building.

106 Both Vondel and Vos wrote poems celebrating this painting and the message it conveyed. Fremantle 1959, 67–68, notes that the subject was also found in a frieze by Artus Quellinus on the mantelpiece below it. For more on allegorical associations for Lievens' painting, see Brenninkmeyer-de Rooij in Washington, Detroit, and Amsterdam 1980, 68.

107 See Schwartz 1985, 318–320; Goossens 1996, 61–63.

108 See H. van de Waal, "The Iconographical Background to Rembrandt's *Civilis*," in *Steps Towards Rembrandt: Collected Articles 1937–1972* (Amsterdam and London, 1974), 31–33.

109 Bredius 1915–1922, 1:199–200.

110 See Buijsen 1998, 193.

111 See Vermeeren in Buijsen 1998, 60–64, pls. 7, 8.

112 Schneider/Ekkart 1973, 298–299. English translation from DeWitt 2006, 231.

113 Schneider/Ekkart 1973, 299.

114 Hanneman received 1,000 guilders, and it is probable that Lievens received the same amount for his work. See Vermeeren in Buijsen 1998, 64.

115 Schneider/Ekkart 1973, 299–300.

116 See Terwen and Ottenheym 1993, 82–87.

117 Bredius 1915–1922, 1:203–204; Schneider/Ekkart 1973, 279–283.

118 Bredius 1915–1922, 1:222.

119 Van Raay, Spies, Van Zoest 1987, 74–76.

120 See Terwen and Ottenheym 1993, 160–163.

121 Postma 1988, 2–7.

122 Bredius 1915–1922, 1:207–208.

123 Van Raay, Spies, Van Zoest 1987, 70.

124 See Van Raay, Spies, Van Zoest 1987, 69–74.

125 As suggested by DeWitt 2006, 230–231. For Van Weerelt, see Schneider/Ekkart 1973, 277.

126 Lievens' image has been badly compromised by numerous restorations and overpaintings, the most severe being that of Carl de Moor in 1699, so that no determination of its original appearance is possible. See Van Raay, Spies, Van Zoest 1987, 69–73.

127 An Amsterdam inventory of 1653 indicates that a "nephew of Godyn" participated in the painting of a Lievens landscape. See Bredius 1915–1922, 1:215.

128 Bredius 1915–1922, 1:206–207. Lievens received 100 guilders yearly for teaching Witsen.

129 Bredius 1915–1922, 1:208–210. Lievens apparently had already had a student related to the Godyn family (see note 127). By the fall of 1671 he was having financial difficulties with Godyn's father, Jeremias. Lievens subsequently moved to Leiden with his student, whom he housed temporarily, along with his three children, in the home of one of his clients. See Bredius 1915–1922, 1:210–211.

130 See Schneider/Ekkart 1973, 277–283.

131 Royalton-Kisch 1991b, 620–622.

132 Friso Lammertse and Jaap van der Veen, *Uylenburgh & Son: Art and Commerce from Rembrandt to De Lairesse 1625–1675* [exh cat., The Rembrandthuis] (Amsterdam, 2006), 85. Lievens and his son were among those who declared the paintings to be "rubbish and poor work."

133 Bredius 1915–1922, 1:186–189, 203–204, 213–214.

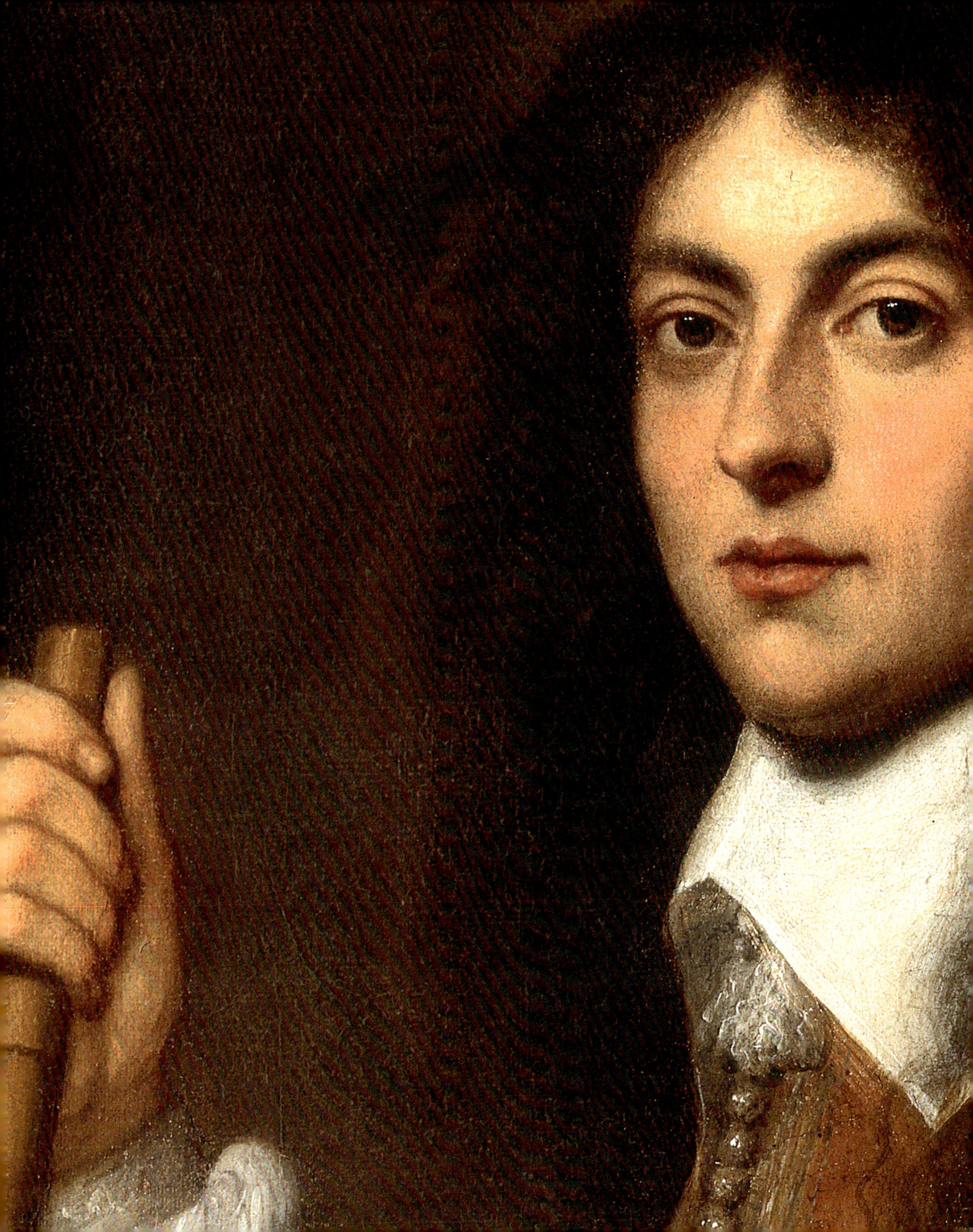

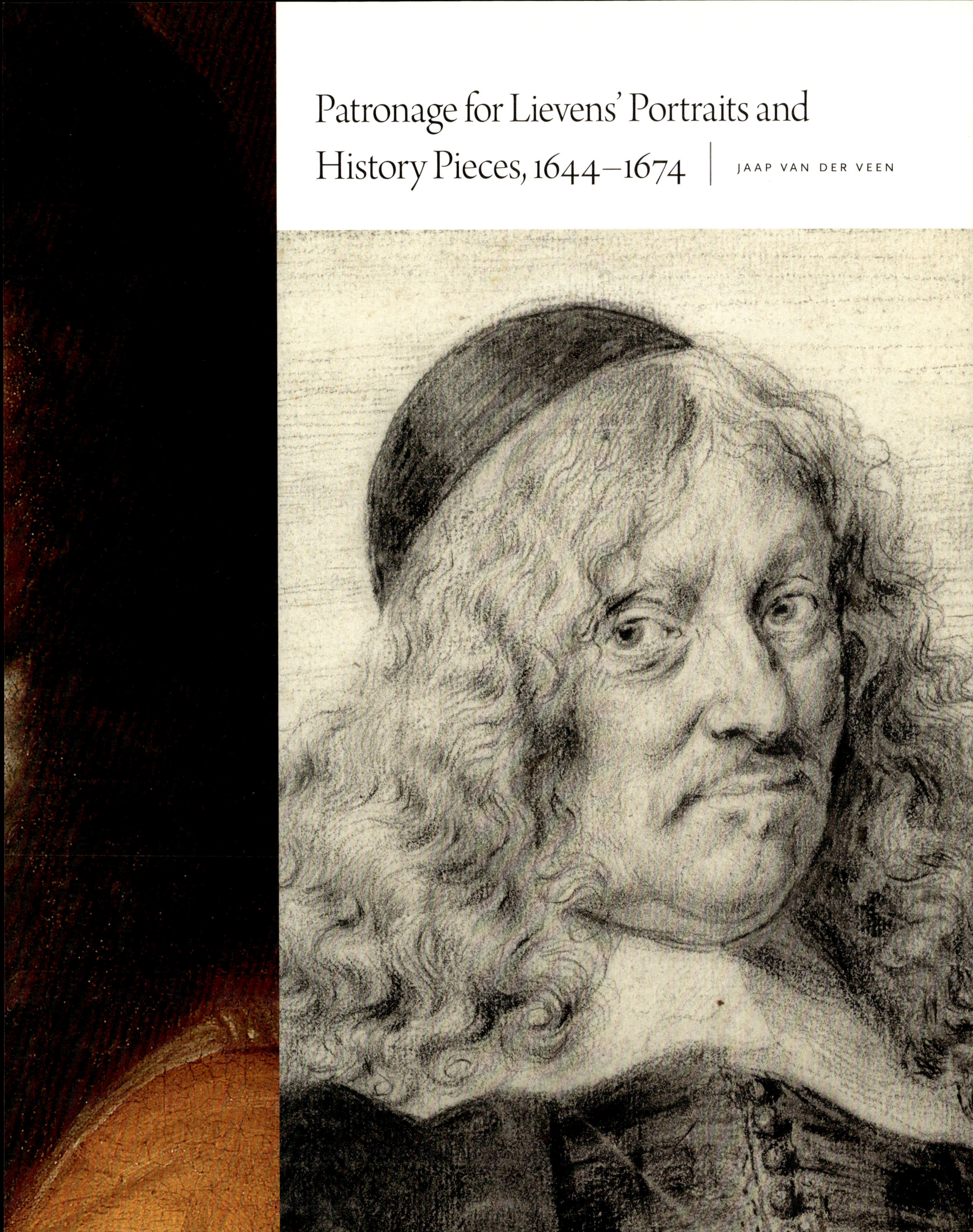
Patronage for Lievens' Portraits and History Pieces, 1644–1674

JAAP VAN DER VEEN

EARLY IN 1644 JAN LIEVENS moved from Antwerp to Amsterdam, where he remained active until his death, apart from brief sojourns in The Hague and Leiden. Yet relatively little critical attention has been paid to this long period of three decades. Art historians seem more interested in the youthful relationship and creative rivalry between Lievens and Rembrandt,[1] whereas Lievens attracted patrons in his later years from the highest political, economic, and cultural realms and was among the select few Dutch artists who contributed to the most important decorative programs of the 1650s and 1660s. Lievens seems to have returned to the Republic for several reasons. He had not fared especially well in Antwerp and was being pursued there by creditors — not for the last time in his career. Prospects in Amsterdam looked much brighter, with its prosperous middle class expressing an almost insatiable demand for art. Indeed, one of Lievens' first commissions in Amsterdam was a painted portrait of Adriaen Trip (see cat. 44), scion of a prominent family of local merchants.

Many seventeenth-century Dutch artists must have done work for the open market, producing paintings without a specific customer in line. Art was thus sold from stock, with the artist's studio serving as a salesroom. Other artists were able to work on commission, coming to an agreement with clients in advance regarding the subject, format, and price. Lievens may have created work for the open market, but he received many commissions between 1644 and 1674. He painted numerous portraits as well as history pieces in addition to making countless portrait drawings and etchings. Although he is often overlooked today in this respect,[2] Lievens' contemporaries considered him an important portrait painter, as reflected in the prices he could command and the circles from which his patrons came.

Rather little is known about the way commissions were secured at this time, and documentary material is scarce. Very few contracts survive, as agreements seem to have been reached verbally. Thus when artists' commissions are mentioned in written records, it is usually because a difference of opinion has arisen: over the price, quality, or missed deadlines. Remarkably, we do have essential documents regarding commissions that Lievens was awarded: an exchange of letters involving Lievens, Johan de Witt, and Pieter de Graeff, discussed later in this essay, is particularly illuminating. Moreover, there are many reports of portraits painted by Lievens that provide insight into his production and his circle of clients. His extant work does not give the impression that his output was especially significant, but wills, probate inventories, and other sources make clear that Lievens had an active business as a portraitist. The information to be gleaned from written sources is generally meager, but some cases present more detailed data. A commission Lievens obtained in 1659, for instance, from the Amsterdam patrician Joan Hydecoper (son of a well-known burgomaster of the same name and later burgomaster himself) offers a rich documentary record.

Diary entries written by Joan Huydecoper van Maarseveen, which have never before been published and which deal with an as-yet-unknown work commissioned from Jan Lievens, reveal just how close the contact could be between a painter and his patron.[3] These notes cover several interesting particulars. At the end of 1658, or early in 1659, Huydecoper conceived the idea of having Lievens paint a large group portrait. Apparently he had spoken with the artist about the project, for in a letter to a Haarlem art dealer he cites the high price demanded by "heer Lievens" for a painting in which his mother-in-law would be portrayed with her whole family.[4] The price was indeed very high: Lievens had asked a cool 2,500 guilders for the work, a colossal sum. Huydecoper was hoping that the dealer might be able to persuade Lievens to accept a considerably reduced price. The entire process of negotiating the contract can be followed in Huydecoper's journal for that year. On February 10 Lievens promised to paint the family portrait of Huydecoper's in-laws for 1,600 guilders. Nothing is mentioned in the journal concerning the format of the piece, the number of persons to be included, or other details, but these would have been fully discussed. Twelve days later Huydecoper noted in his diary: "Jan Livensen ate with us." Four days after this meal Huydecoper visited the artist's studio to sit for his portrait, which was to be "fitted into mama's painting."[5] The following day he brought his two children to the studio of Jacob van Loo to pose for a double portrait, while his wife, Sophia Coymans, went to Lievens' house for a sitting. The next day saw Huydecoper's "posture drawn with the *barlynskleet*." Although it is not clear what kind of costume this barlynskleet might be, Huydecoper was evidently wearing some kind of special attire for his portrait.

There were many visits to Lievens' house over the succeeding weeks. Huydecoper accompanied two sisters-in-law — sometimes together with another family member — to Lievens' studio to sit for the painter. Huydecoper himself had repeated sittings and checked regularly on the work's progress. On April 3 he went with a relative "to see the painting" and drank "a glass" with Lievens. There is an intriguing entry for April 22: "sat with Uncle Adrianus at heer Livensen's house." This uncle was none other than the earlier-mentioned Adriaen Trip, whose portrait Lievens had painted fifteen years before, and who was a brother of Huydecoper's mother-in-law, Sophia Trip, the central figure in the group portrait. The brief journal entry does not allow us to say with certainty whether Adriaen Trip also posed for Lievens at this time, but it is highly likely that he would have been given a place in the family group. Nor was the relationship between patron and painter limited purely to business. On one occasion Huydecoper went with Lievens "à la Montagne," to the famous lodging house "de Keizerskroon" in the Kalverstraat, where, shortly before this, the sale of Rembrandt's bankrupt estate had taken place; and on May 7 he writes that "Jan Livense and his wife ate with us." This all indicates a close personal relationship.[6] At the end of April Huydecoper went with the painter to an inn where they "discussed the painting," and on May 30, according to the journal, he sat for the last time. In October they again met at an inn.

Jan Lievens must have worked continuously on this group portrait for six months. Members of the Huydecoper, Coymans, and Trip families visited his studio on a weekly basis, if not daily. As far as the delivery and payment for the painting are concerned, Huydecoper's journal entries give us no information.[7] As mentioned above, Huydecoper noted that his own portrait would be fitted into the overall painting, suggesting that Lievens first made individual portraits of Huydecoper and his wife and subsequently incorporated their likenesses into the group portrait. Indeed, the Dutch eulogist Jan Vos sang the praises of these pendant portraits in a collection of his poetry that appeared in 1662. The portraits were hung in Huydecoper's new home.[8] Around this time Huydecoper was given "an image of Christ in the grave painted by Livense" as a gift for services rendered, but he quickly disposed of this *Entombment*, as he explained, so as not to "have any obligation."[9]

A curious feature of this commission is the high price Lievens thought he could command while at the same time maintaining personal relations with the patron. In this context, the fact that Lievens and his wife dined at the home of the Huydecopers is of considerable social significance. The individual portraits are no longer known, nor is the family group, which must have had a special place in Lievens' oeuvre. Lievens painted another group portrait, which has also not been preserved, this one of five children. Our knowledge of his production thus has notable gaps.

The steep price that Lievens originally asked, while rather audacious, reflects his status as a portrait painter in the 1650s. Yet Huydecoper obviously thought he could negotiate this price and brought in a third party to help do so. Lievens, for his part, certainly did not suffer from any lack of confidence. In a letter that Robert Kerr, an Englishman living in Amsterdam, wrote to his son in 1654, Kerr mentioned his portrait having been painted by Lievens that year (cat. 51), noting wryly that Lievens believed he had no peer as a painter in the Netherlands. Did the artist confide this opinion of his own worth during sittings?

Portraiture was not accorded the highest esteem in seventeenth-century Dutch art, but for many painters it was a necessary means to making a living.[10] And even established artists could rarely afford to reject portrait commissions, which brought high prices. Moreover, painting portraits brought the artist into close contact with clients, which could lead to other commissions. Sittings generally took place in the painter's studio, where potential patrons could see the artist's other works, both finished and unfinished. It is likely that a buyer would describe what he wanted in terms of format, support, pose, costume, and special features. One assumes that during dinners at Huydecoper's home — only a few days before the first sitting — the patron would have gone over such matters with Lievens. Perhaps a preliminary sketch was made. How much he was involved in the actual execution of the painting is difficult to say; but in Huydecoper's case, he came to Lievens' studio several times to gauge progress.

Certainly, painters were wary of overly demanding clients, especially those who claimed to be connoisseurs of art. A passage in Samuel van Hoogstraten's treatise on the art of painting (1678) put this very nicely, advising artists to arm themselves "with patient forbearance" whenever dealing with art lovers who possess more money than knowledge. Yet a patron's judgment is not always bad, the author admonishes, and he gives an example that clearly refers to Jan Lievens himself: "Our Livius had recently represented Truth, crowned by Justice in a piece," adding an old man who represented Time, as the allegorical subject seemed to demand; but when one of those who had commissioned the work (*een der aenbesteeders*) insisted that the old man "did not belong there," Lievens apparently removed him along with a few other figures and praised his adviser's wisdom.[11] So here, at least, Lievens accommodated the demands of a patron who wanted a change in a composition.

It is highly likely that Van Hoogstraten was recounting an actual situation, for Lievens did paint such a subject. In 1704 there was a painting in the collection of Pieter Six called "Time discovers the Truth by Jan Lievens," which is without doubt the work mentioned above.[12] The owner's parents, Pieter Six the Elder and Johanna Six, are known from various sources to have possessed a superb art collection, with many paintings and works on paper. Moreover, one can point to contact with Lievens: Jan Vos wrote a poem on a portrait of Johanna Six dedicated "to Ian Lievensen" as the portraitist.[13] Presumably Pieter Six acquired paintings from his parents' collection, including the one described here (as well as *A Councillor* and a portrait of Charles I, both also by Lievens,

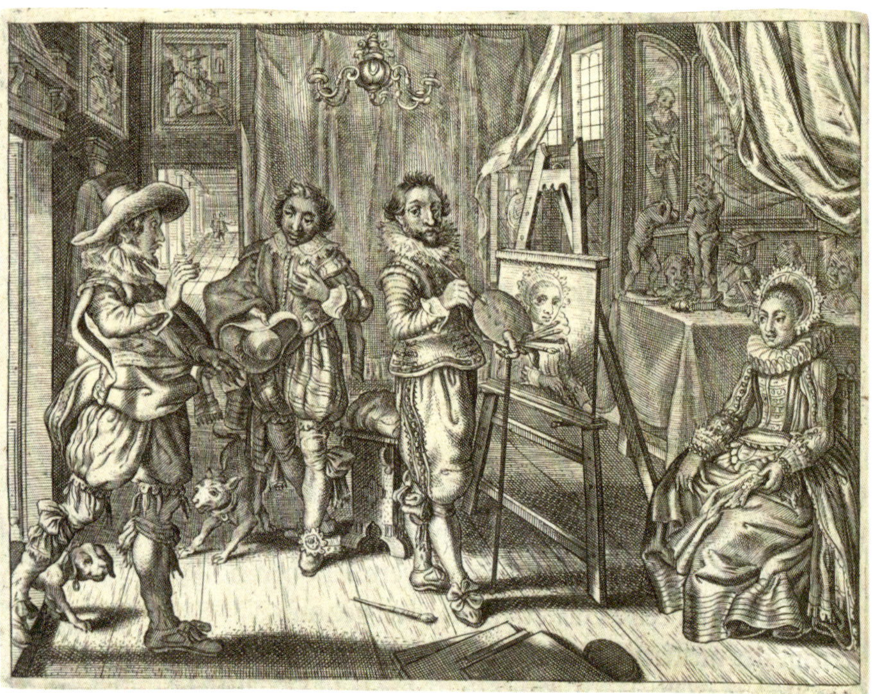

1 | After Adriaen van de Venne, *The Portrait Painter at Work*, engraving, in J. Cats, *Houwelyck. Dat is de gansche gelegentheyt des echten staets* (Middleburg, 1625). National Gallery of Art Library

probably dating from his time in London). In short, it looks as though Pieter Six the Elder had not only commissioned Lievens to paint a portrait but was also the *aenbesteeder*, in Van Hoogstraten's words, of a history piece whereby, during the execution of the work, he actually criticized Lievens' design.

LIEVENS' PORTRAIT PAINTINGS

Painting portraits was not an activity from which Dutch artists could earn great honors, but Lievens, like most painters, was not in a position to ignore this source of income (fig. 1). It is not easy to establish the extent of his production, however. If one judges solely by known works, he would seem to have painted no more than a handful of portraits between 1644 and 1674, but contemporary sources mention a significant number of others. One has to be careful, of course, with attributions of artworks to prominent artists in sales catalogues and other documents; it was very much in the interests of art dealers and sales organizers to offer paintings with famous names attached. In probate inventories too, one should accept the naming of painters with a degree of caution, for those who compiled these inventories were often unfamiliar with the material. With portraits, however, one assumes the putative heirs would have been present when the inventories were drawn up and would recognize the subjects of family portraits; whenever the artist is identified along with such subjects, the information may be fairly reliable.

A more important source are the wills in which explicit instruction is given concerning the inheritance of portraits. Several seventeenth-century wills have survived in which portraits by Lievens are specifically mentioned, which says a great deal about the significance that the subjects of the portraits, or their immediate descendants, assigned to the author of these works. In addition to Lievens' commissions from Trip in 1644 and from Huydecoper in 1659, a few other examples are known. Lievens' portrait of Aernout van de Cruijs is mentioned in 1698 in the will of a son of this Amsterdam merchant. He bequeathed to his eldest son "the portrait of the testator's father Aernout van de Cruijs painted by Jan Lievens."[14] No pendant is mentioned, and in all probability there was none, for Van de Cruijs was a widower beginning in 1646. He had determined in 1655 that his three children should divide his inheritance such that each should receive goods as he "had written in a certain book with his own hand."[15] In that book he would have specified to whom the portrait should go. The fact that Lievens is named as the portraitist at the beginning of the eighteenth century is a reflection of the reputation he still enjoyed at that time.

It is hard to know why Lievens would be chosen as a portraitist over the many others active in Amsterdam at the time. Perhaps it was because in London and Antwerp he had developed an elegant international style that was extremely fashionable in Amsterdam. In this regard, his portrait of Adriaen Trip set the tone. At the same time, the demand for expert portrait painters had grown enormously in these years. Some patrons had their portraits done by several artists. Thus in wills from 1664 and 1672 Jan Meures bequeathed to a nephew "two portraits of the testator, one painted by Bartholomeus van der Helst and the other by Jan Lievens."[16]

Jan Meures had close contacts with many painters. He and his wife he ran a smart hostelry, the Liesveldse Bijbel, in the Warmoesstraat, where Jacob Jordaens was resident in 1661 when he offered a painting to the city council of Amsterdam. Meures was a poet, a patron of the arts, and a regent of the Amsterdam theater. In 1653, together with the art dealer and connoisseur Marten Kretzer and two painters — one of them Van der Helst — he founded the Brotherhood of Painting (Broederschap der Schilderkunst). On that occasion, Lievens appears to have painted a portrait of writer and playwright Joost van den Vondel. Meures' art possessions can be assessed from the inventory drawn up by his widow on his death, in which a landscape by Lievens is listed.[17] The portrait by Lievens is not recorded, possibly because it had already been transferred to the beneficiary.

Based on source material as well as paintings that have survived, a conservative estimate of the number of portraits Lievens produced in this period amounts to at least forty. Some are mentioned in wills and personal documents that do not allow further systematic investigation. Others are known from accidental archival discoveries, such as that of Jan Meures and additional examples mentioned below. Extant portraits from the late 1640s and 1650s include those of Anna Maria van Schurman from 1649, Robert Kerr from 1654, and Jacob Junius from c. 1658 (see cats. 45, 51, 53). Portraits of Claes Calckoen and his wife Elisabeth Danckerts were also made about this time, listed in their probate inventory as "a portrait of the deceased and of his wife by Jan Lievens."[18] The wording might suggest a double portrait, but two portraits are known in the form of copies (figs. 2 and 3): a paper label on the reverse of the man's portrait gives his age as forty-two and the date as 165[4], while on the reverse side of the pendant is written the name of the subject and "geschildert door Lievense 1654" (painted by Lievens 1654).[19] Although not particularly well done, the copies would have reproduced the originals faithfully, including the decor, the unbroken balustrade, and the distant landscape. This commission appears to have been occasioned by Calckoen's purchase in the spring of 1654 of an imposing house on the Keizersgracht in Amsterdam, where the newly painted portraits would undoubtedly have been given a prominent place, alongside two additional "pieces" by Lievens — possibly landscapes, although they are not further described.

Another portrait painted by Lievens is documented in the probate inventory of one Gerard Schaep as a depiction of "the deceased Lord of Kortenhoef by Jan Lievens."[20] Gerard Schaep, Lord of Kortenhoef, was a prominent Amsterdam regent who was several times the city's burgomaster. A contemporary characterized him as a thrifty, miserly man of considerable means. He had a richly furnished house containing some seventy paintings, but whether he spent large sums on art is not clear, for the paintings with attributions were, with the single exception mentioned below, exclusively old masters, which one suspects he may have inherited. Schaep had certainly paid for the portraits. The inventory records three pairs of portraits of the man and his wife, Maria Spiegel, by Nicolaes van Helt Stockade, Jan van Ravesteyn, and an unknown portraitist. No pendant is recorded for the portrait by Lievens, which could have been ordered after the death of Schaep's wife in 1661.

The portrait was acquired for no less than 126 guilders, a hefty sum, though Lievens would originally have received considerably more than this.[21] A second indication for the execution of this work in the 1660s is the occurrence of the single "new" painting in Schaep's effects: "a Poma" by "the young Jan Lieves." In view of the birth of Lievens' son, Jan Andrea, in 1644, this *Vertumnus*

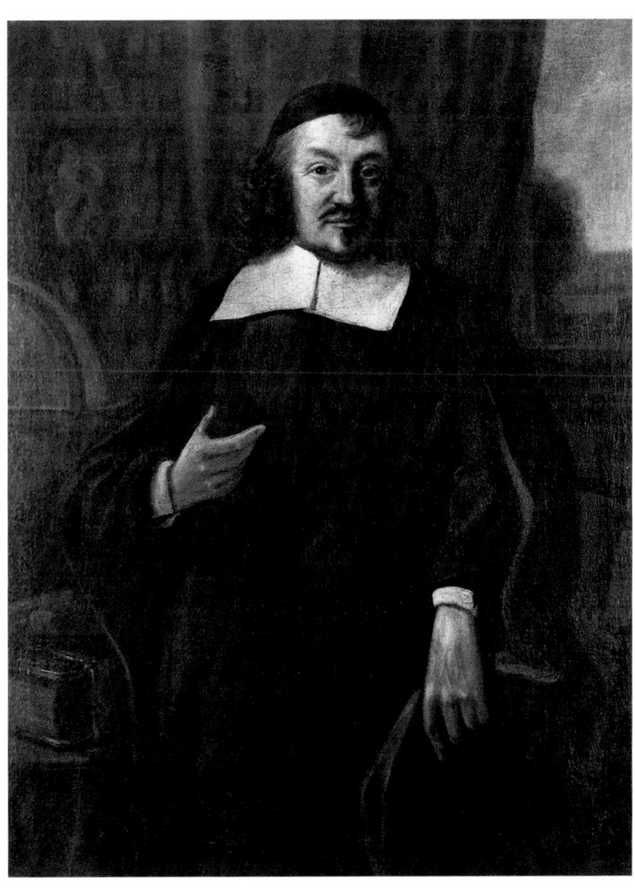

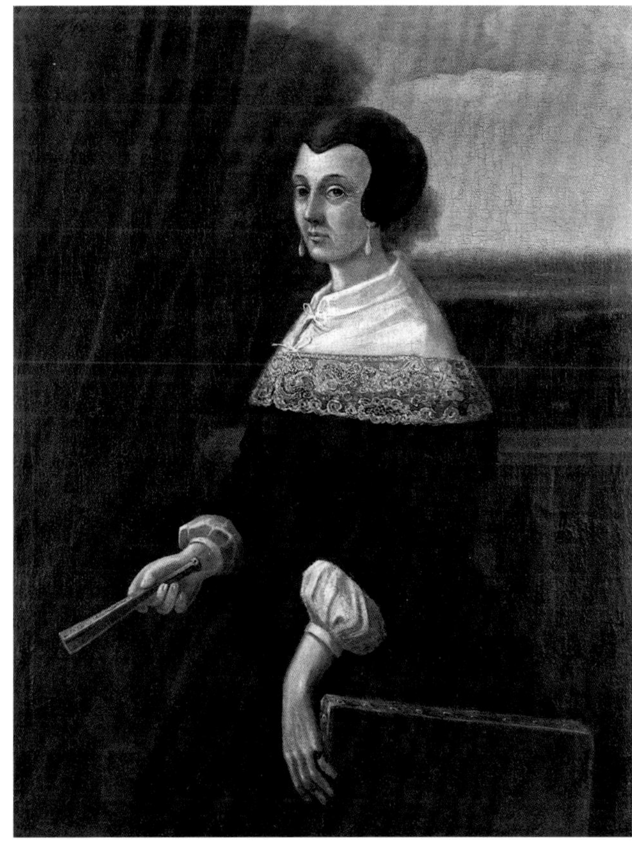

2, 3 | Copy after Jan Lievens, *Portrait of Claes Calckoen* and *Portrait of Elisabeth Danckerts*, oil on canvas. Instituut Collectie Nederland, Rijswijk

and Pomona could hardly have been painted before the early 1660s. Did Schaep acquire it during or soon after the time he sat for Jan Lievens? A third indication for the portrait's dating from the 1660s is its likeness to a marble bust listed among Schaep's possessions that now belongs to the Zeeuws Museum and that must have been made between 1663 and 1666.[22] Finally, the collection of poems by Vos that appeared in 1662 eulogizes several paintings in Schaep's possession but makes no mention of a portrait by Lievens.[23]

A previously unknown commission to Lievens is one from Timon Veneman and Helena Wijbrants, who had their portraits painted by him, possibly at the beginning of the 1660s. This extremely wealthy couple purchased a house on the Herengracht in 1661, into which they moved and must have furnished in an unusually luxurious manner. Possibly the portraits date from this time, although they were not mentioned in the will drawn up in 1663. Then in 1669 the wife stipulated that after her husband's death, his heirs must hand over to her mother "the portraits of the testators painted by Jan Lievens."[24] It is conspicuous that it was Helena Wijbrants who decided the fate of the paintings, which were evidently her possessions. Perhaps her mother had paid for them. In any case, the extent of the couple's household effects can be seen from the inventory of her estate in 1721, when the portraits were mentioned without naming the painter.[25] In fact, the artists' names are given for only two of the many paintings in the estate, so it is impossible to say whether the couple had bought works by Lievens, though at this time a brother-in-law owned at least two paintings by Lievens, a *Raising of Lazarus* and a *Deposition*.[26]

In view of Lievens' elite circle of clients, it is surprising that so few of his portraits are still traceable. Some vague references appeared in the eighteenth and nineteenth centuries, including mention of a portrait of Amsterdam regent Hans Bontemantel "by J.L."[27] Other documents are more tantalizing. In 1667 Lievens reminded Claude Blot of an agreement reached the year before for him to paint portraits of Blot and his wife, Maria van der Wel. The wife's portrait was ready, but Blot's was still only in the underpainting stage. Lievens had approached the client repeatedly, inviting him to his house, but he never managed to arrange the necessary sittings to complete the painting. Lievens stressed that he did not wish to be unreasonable and offered him the unfinished portrait if Blot would pay him 50 guilders for the work done.[28] This exchange makes it clear that sittings took place in Lievens' studio and that commissions were not without risk to the artist: the patron did not always fulfill his part of an agreement. After running into financial difficulties, Claude Blot was declared insolvent in 1667. Inventories drawn up both that year and following his death in 1670 include many paintings, but no portraits by Lievens.[29]

The individuals who offered commissions to Lievens were overwhelmingly but not exclusively Protestant. Lievens himself was of Protestant stock, but twice married into Catholic families. Did he convert to Catholicism while in London or in Antwerp? When he married Cornelia de Bray, a Catholic, the banns were announced in the Reformed Church; a note in the margin of the document records that the wedding took place on August 2, 1648, in Ouderkerk aan de Amstel, near Amsterdam, and that it was a Reformed preacher who officiated.[30] This suggests that Lievens remained a Protestant, although his children were probably baptized as Catholics. Whatever the circumstances, Lievens maintained good relations with his Catholic in-laws. He several times granted his brother-in-law Jan van der Hoeven power of attorney, while Van der Hoeven's widow appointed Lievens as guardian of her children during their minority.[31] One assumes that Lievens must have painted portraits of several of his wife's relatives. One concrete example is his portrait of Jan Denijsz Troncquois, a second cousin. They knew each other well, for several legal documents that Lievens had drawn up between 1660 and 1662 were signed by Troncquois. Troncquois, a merchant, lived in his mother's house from 1657 to 1666 and ordered the portrait in question during this period. A witness related how Troncquois' mother was present when Lievens delivered the portrait and had wondered why the painting was still wet, complaining: "Couldn't he keep it long enough for it to dry? Does he need the money so badly?" Troncquois had paid him about 100 guilders for the portrait.[32]

The question voiced by Troncquois' mother — that is, whether Lievens needed money so urgently — may have had substantial basis. Several times during his career the painter ran into financial problems, and it is conceivable that his increasing production of portraits beginning in the 1650s was related to financial needs. In the brief period he was active in The Hague and in Leiden, between roughly 1670 and 1672, this connection is clear. In matters of business, things were not going well for him at that time. On April 28, 1671, his goods were impounded in The Hague because of unpaid rent on his house, and he appears to have had other debts as well. In 1672 and 1673 creditors in Leiden forced the sale of his possessions, and a notary was appointed as the administrator. Occasionally Lievens paid off the balance of a debt by painting portraits — as in 1657, when he owed two persons some 700 guilders, from which 306 guilders were deducted for the delivery of three portraits.[33] Lievens thus received about 100 guilders per painting. But this means of settling debts could leave the

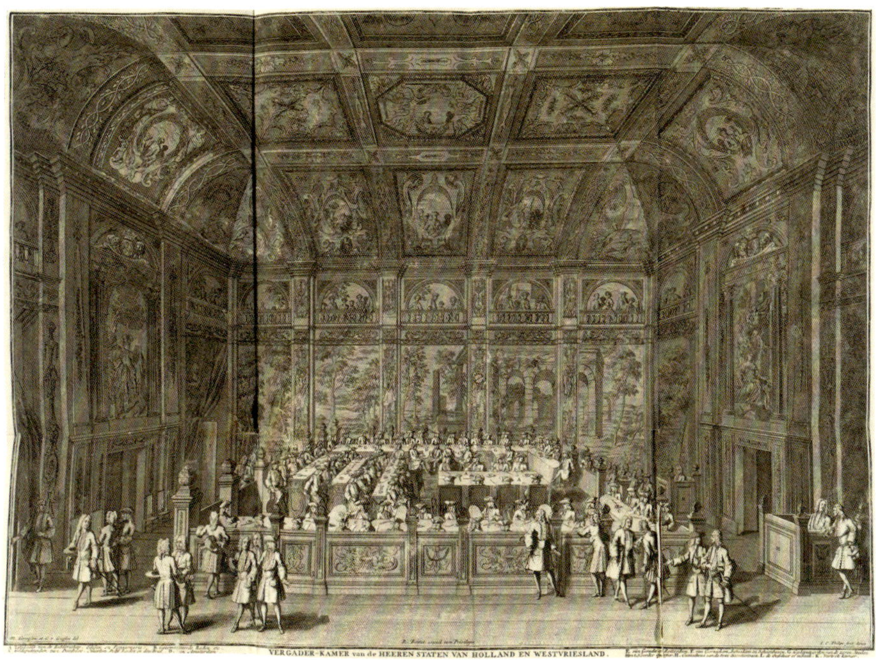

4 | Jan Caspar Philips after Mattheus Terwesten and Gerrit van Giessen, *The Assembly Room of the States of Holland and West-Friesland*, engraving, in J. de Riemer, *Beschryving van's-gravenhage*, 2 vols. (Delft 1730–1739). Universiteitsbibliotheek, Amsterdam

painter less well off than if he had sold his work in the open market. In 1671, for instance, Lievens agreed to paint the portraits of a Leiden citizen and his wife within a month in exchange for the 100 guilders he owed for room and board.[34]

Other portraits Lievens painted during this period appeared in a codicil to the will of Elisabeth van Peenen, who in 1683 bequeathed to the two sons from her first marriage "the two portraits of herself and her first husband, also done by Jan Lievens, painter."[35] She had married Adriaen le Pla in Leiden in October 1670, and the portraits would have been commissioned from Lievens, who was then living in Leiden, not long after the wedding. The document records that the portraits were "also" painted by Lievens, which suggests that the painting (just mentioned) for the chimneypiece in a room "lined with cloth" had been commissioned from Lievens. Adriaen le Pla had renovated and redecorated his house in 1671,[36] and moving into a new house, like contracting a marriage, was a preeminent occasion for commissioning painted portraits.[37]

IN THE GOOD GRACES OF GREAT MEN

It is clear that Jan Lievens, from the time of his arrival in Amsterdam, secured numerous portrait commissions from prominent individuals in the city. But he was not merely—or even primarily—a portrait artist, for in the same period he applied himself to creating major figural paintings with historical and mythological subjects, several of which he executed on a very large scale. He enjoyed considerable success with these and indeed was among the most sought-after painters of his time. During the last half of the seventeenth century he was one of very few artists asked to work on the most important decorative programs in the Dutch Republic.

In 1650 he produced a painting, *The Five Muses*, for the Oranjezaal of the Huis ten Bosch, dedicated to the memory of Frederik Hendrik, Prince of Orange (see Wheelock fig. 22).[38] Shortly thereafter he worked for the Elector of Brandenburg, who was married to a daughter of the prince and who from 1651 had the country seat of Oranienburg near Berlin rebuilt and decorated. Lievens must have painted at least two compositions for this residence, including *Mars and Venus* (cat. 50).[39] In 1656 he completed *Quintus Fabius Maximus and His Son* for the Amsterdam town hall (Wheelock fig. 24),[40] and in 1661 he painted *Brinio Raised on a Shield* for one of the lunettes in the upper gallery of the great citizens' hall (Burgerzaal) of this same town hall (Wheelock fig. 25).[41] Three years later he painted *Mars (The Allegory of War)* commissioned by the States of Holland for their meeting hall in the Binnenhof in The Hague (fig. 4 and Wheelock fig. 1).[42] The commission to paint an *Arithmetica* (now lost) probably comes from the same period. That work hung as a mantel painting in the new assembly room of the Gecommitteerde Raden, close to the hall of the States of Holland.[43] And finally, in 1666 and again in 1668–1669, Lievens worked partly in collaboration with his son on two commissions from the Hoogheemraden (water board) of Rijnland (cat. 55). It would seem that whenever there were commissions of importance, the choice for an artist fell on Lievens, a history painter who could handle large format works. In addition, it must have been significant that he worked quite quickly and delivered the painting within the time agreed. He probably completed *Brinio*, for example, within six months.

As in portraiture, few records survive to document large public commissions from the seventeenth century that would provide insights into the relationship between patron and artist. Most concrete information that does exist regarding such projects is given from the perspective of the commissioning patron. In the case of Lievens, however, there exists a unique group of letters that contain extremely interesting details—from the point of view not only of the patron but of the painter. The correspondence involved Jan Lievens, Johan de Witt, and Pieter de Graeff during the years 1663–1664 and concerned a commission given to Lievens; there are nine letters in total, two from Pieter de Graeff to his brother-in-law Johan de Witt—two from De Witt, and five from Lievens.[44]

Initially, Lievens was approached in 1663 by Johan de Witt—the famous councillor pensionary of the States of Holland and West-Friesland and the most powerful politician in the Dutch

Republic — and was asked to paint portraits of De Witt's deceased parents-in-law, Jan Bicker and Agneta de Graeff. In a comprehensive letter of April 13 Pieter de Graeff gave a progress report to De Witt, living in The Hague. Although it had been agreed with Lievens that he should first paint Agneta de Graeff and then her husband, he had begun with Jan Bicker's portrait. Lievens explained that he did not "have such a strong visual memory of her" as of Bicker, which implies that he must have known these eminent persons rather well.

Jan Bicker, a wealthy merchant, occupied various positions in Amsterdam and was appointed burgomaster shortly before his death in 1653. It is very possible that Lievens had worked for him. In any case, Lievens had to work mainly from memory, although he was given drawn portraits of the couple to use as models. This was more time-consuming than making a copy after an existing painting, the painter said, and when he had finished the first portrait, he asked 125 guilders for it. Meanwhile, Lievens felt little enthusiasm for painting the pendant, even though he had initially said that "he could picture her physiognomy no less vividly than his." De Witt wrote to De Graeff that he would try to be patient and hoped that Lievens would do the work, because he felt Lievens was the most appropriate painter for the assignment, "since he could call on his own imagination to help him." It would seem that De Graeff kept Bicker's portrait, because De Witt asked him to send another one and suggested that Lievens use his original painting as the model. Lievens painted a second portrait of Bicker and a portrait of Agneta de Graeff. In a letter of April 24, 1664, he wrote to De Witt that the portraits were ready but not yet dry enough to be sent. De Witt's wife noted in her household accounts that same year the payment of 200 guilders for portraits of her parents painted by Lievens.[45]

Lievens had outlined his prices in a letter to De Witt on May 8, 1664, saying that he normally charged 100 guilders for a painted portrait without hands and without a background landscape. About a month later he sent a similar letter to De Graeff but added that without having the subject before him "from life" the price was usually doubled. He was accepting 200 guilders for the two paintings in question "in order to maintain your good will and the favor of such a Highly Honored Gentleman," though he had previously been paid almost 160 guilders for a less challenging portrait. It is clear that Lievens, no doubt with an eye to future commissions, had gone to considerable lengths to cultivate the good graces of such highly placed gentlemen. De Witt promptly answered that the painter would have his money as quickly as could be expected.

In fact, De Witt was not pleased with Lievens' work and wrote that he was supported in that opinion by others who ought to know. In particular, the painting of his mother-in-law was not considered a good likeness. Lievens did not let this harsh judgment go unanswered, responding that De Witt might realize that the price was quite modest if he knew how much time and effort the artist had spent. Lievens also asserted that connoisseurs had been amazed that he had managed to convey such vitality in the posthumous portraits. He also expressed his desire to paint a subject "from life" for De Witt in order to demonstrate his abilities and regain the patron's favor. In his last letter to De Witt, Lievens said that as soon as he could travel to The Hague he would varnish the pendant paintings that had been delivered. He also wrote that he would paint a portrait of Wendela Bicker, De Witt's wife, that he hoped would please the great man more than the depictions of his in-laws, on which, wrote Lievens, "I have taken as much trouble as though it had been for the Prince of Orange."[46]

Lievens' likely dealings with Jan Bicker and Agneta de Graeff in the 1640s and early 1650s seem to have opened doors to his relationships with other members of the De Graeff family. In 1657 he drew a portrait of the powerful regent Andries de Graeff, who was burgomaster of Amsterdam that year (cat. 117).[47] Despite De Witt's dissatisfaction over the portraits of his in-laws, undoubtedly communicated to Pieter de Graeff, the latter reached an agreement with Lievens in 1673 to paint a portrait of his son Cornelis, two years old at the most and "naked as a cupid."[48] Lievens asked 50 guilders for this work, not a substantial sum for a painting that must have had a monumental format, being intended as a mantelpiece in De Graeff's house.[49] Other family connections included Willem Schrijver, the husband of Wendela de Graeff (sister to Andries and Agneta), who owned two landscapes by Lievens as well as a portrait that Lievens had painted of his father, Petrus Scriverius. An inventory of Scriverius' household estate described a "curious" landscape by Lievens, which was auctioned in 1663 along with a *Samaritan Woman by the Well*. These works may have been acquired on the open market, but the portrait commission raises the possibility that they were purchased directly from the artist.[50]

Lievens did paint such subjects to order, as indicated in a document from 1666 that records a *Samaritan Woman Speaking with Christ by the Well*, painted for a "sr. Daelder" for a price of 120 guilders.[51] A painting with this subject was listed in the inventory of the estate of Egbert Gerritsz Daelder in 1661,[52] and Lievens was trying to get payment from the man's heirs. In the books of one of Daelder's sons, Jan Lievens is listed with a balance of some 40 guilders,[53] thus commissions, it seems, were no guarantee that artists would actually be paid for their work.

Lievens' letter of April 24, 1664, to Johan de Witt sheds light on other commissions the artist had won as well as on relationships with his patrons. Asking whether the "Lord of Wimmenum" had shown De Witt an oil sketch of *Mars* that Lievens was painting for the States of Holland, the artist gives reason to believe that his private commission from De Witt had led to a public commission. The same appears to have occurred in his contact with the Lord of Wimmenum, Amelis van den Bouckhorst, who died in 1669 with what Lievens claimed was no less than 1,900 guilders in debts for various paintings Lievens had delivered.[54] Although the inventory of Van den Bouckhorst's estate mentions paintings by Gerrit van Honthorst, Adriaen Hanneman, Govaert Flinck, and Theodoor van Thulden, it lists only a single piece by Lievens, representing Hope.[55] Possessions from Van den Bouckhorst's country house, also described as part of his estate, included no works by Lievens, unless he had done in situ paintings such as mantelpieces or ceiling decorations, which would not have been specified in the inventory. Could Lievens have worked on the decorative paintings for this country house, built between 1662 and 1668? Van den Bouckhorst had been chairman of the Gecommitteerde Raden as well as *dike-reeve* (head) of Rijnland, and it is likely that Lievens obtained his commissions for both through the good offices of their leader. Certainly Lievens was in direct contact with Van den Bouckhorst, to whom he had given the modello of the *Mars* to show De Witt.

In the same letter from Lievens to De Witt in April 1664, the artist apologized that it had taken so long to finish the posthumous portraits of De Witt's in-laws, explaining that not only was it more difficult to work "from imagination" but he had been busy working for an important gentleman who wanted a subject depicted "outside, with beautiful skies and landscape."[56] Lievens does not identify his other patron, but apparently even a commission from the grand pensionary in The Hague had to wait! Most seventeenth-century artists produced their landscape paintings in the studio based on drawings and on visual memory. Much evidence shows that artists made drawings outdoors, "from life"; but painting outdoors must have been highly unusual.[57] The Dutch climate, often wet as well as cold, hardly invited the practice, and it is not by chance that the occasional reports of Dutch painters working outdoors did so in Italy; very little data testifies to this practice in the Republic. One of the few exceptions is a pen and ink drawing by Lievens of a woodland view in which a painter can be seen at work seated behind his easel (see Rubinstein fig. 7). On stylistic grounds, this sheet is dated to around 1655, and it is tempting to assume that Lievens has depicted himself.

The commissions Lievens received were therefore not restricted to history pieces and portraits. But important projects were entrusted to him in Amsterdam and The Hague. He worked for courts both at home and abroad and was much in demand as a painter of decorative pieces with historical or allegorical themes. As a portraitist, Lievens enjoyed a strong reputation among his contemporaries. He executed commissions for the most powerful political figures and members of the wealthiest and most socially prominent families in the land: Trip, Huydecoper, Coymans, Bicker, De Graeff, De Witt, Van den Bouckhorst, Schaep, Six, Bontemantel, Veneman, and Le Pla. How close the relations could be between patron and painter can be seen from the journal entries of Joan Huydecoper from 1659 and from the exchange of letters Lievens had with the brothers-in-law Johan de Witt and Pieter de Graeff in 1663–1664. Clearly, between 1644 and 1674 Jan Lievens stood in the good graces of great men in the Dutch Republic.

Notes

The following notes abbreviate Stadsarchief Amsterdam as "SA" and Notarial Archive as "NA" throughout.

1 Leiden 1991; Gutbrod 1996; Van Straten 2005; and Braunschweig 1979.

2 In the most recent exhibitions on seventeenth-century Dutch portraiture (Haarlem 1986; Amsterdam 2002–2003; and London/The Hague 2007–2008) not a single painted portrait by Lievens was included. Nor is there any mention of Lievens in two recent surveys of portrait painters active in the Republic (Ekkart in Amsterdam 2002–2003; and Ekkart in London and The Hague 2007–2008).

3 Joan Huydecoper van Maarseveen (1625–1704) was married to Sophia Coymans (1636–1714), whose mother, Sophia Trip (1615–1679), was the sister of an earlier patron of Lievens: Adriaen Trip (1620–1684/1687).

4 Joan Huydecoper to Sybrant Camay, Amsterdam, February 7, 1659, Utrecht, Het Utrechts Archief, Family Archive Huydecoper (access no. 67), inv. 55: "Den grooten eysch van monsr. Livissen voor een schilderij in 't welcke mijn schoonmoeder benevens hare gansche familie soude gerepresenteert werden."

5 The following paragraphs are based entirely on the journal for 1659. For this source and Huydecoper's circle, see Kooijmans 1997.

6 On May 16 Huydecoper recorded in his journal "met J. Livensen gekeven," but it is uncertain quite how one should interpret this verb. If they did indeed quarrel, it did not apparently lead to a break between them. At any rate, another sitting followed six days later.

7 The journals from after 1660 have not been preserved.

8 At the time of the commission given to Lievens, Huydecoper and his family were living with his mother-in-law while he was renovating a house he had inherited on the Lauriergracht, but there is no indication Lievens was involved in that project. See Vos 1662, 198–199. In wills made in 1693 and 1704 Huydecoper and his wife bequeathed their painted portraits to a son without mentioning the painter. Apart from Lievens this could also have been Jacob van Loo, for whom they sat in 1660. The portraits are not specified in the inventory made when Huydecoper's widow died in 1714.

9 Joan Huydecoper to "de heer Sandra," Amsterdam, September 16, 1660, Family Archive Huydecoper, inv. 56. He disposed of Lievens' *Entombment* to Gerrit Uylenburgh. This art dealer already had the piece in his stock in 1675, London and Amsterdam 2006, 298, no. 115. The "heer Sandra" was presumably the Sandra (1619–1707) who was married to Margaretha Tortarolis (1627–1681) and would subsequently marry Maria Leenderts (1641–1710), the widow of Jacob Junius, whose portrait Lievens must have painted around 1658 (see cat. 53). Members of the Leiden Tortarolis family of Leiden were among the earliest customers for Lievens' work.

10 Rembrandt posed no direct competition for Lievens, as he had not accepted portrait commissions for at least a decade since 1642. See Van der Veen in Melbourne and Canberra 1997.

11 Hoogstraten 1678, 315; Schneider/Ekkart 1973, 118, 300–301, no. 111.

12 SA, notary J. Lansman, NA 4720, 505–666 (July 17, 1704); it was sold the same year in Amsterdam. Pieter Six (1655–1703) was the son of a son of Pieter Six the Elder (c. 1609–1680) and Johanna Six (c. 1628–1689).

13 Vos 1662, 182–183. Whether Pieter Six the Elder was also portrayed by Lievens is not certain. In the inventory of his son of the same name there is mention of his portrait "by Coning" (Salomon or Philips Koninck); while in the estate of Jan Six (1618–1700) there are mentioned two portraits of his brother Pieter, although without mention of the name of the painter.

14 Aernout van de Cruijs (c. 1600–1655): SA, notary N. Brouwer, NA 3974, deed 54, 411–414 (July 23, 1698): "Het pourtraict van sijn testateurs vader zalr. Aernout van de Kruijs door Jan Lievens geschildert." The stipulation concerning the portrait is repeated in wills of 1704, 1706, and 1708 but does not recur in that of 1715. The portrait would have passed to the eldest son between 1708 and 1715.

15 SA, notary J. van Zwieten, NA 879, fols. 160v–162v (October 20, 1655).

16 Jan Meures (c. 1604–1672), SA, notary P. van Buijtene, NA 2770, 468–473 (August 10, 1664), and notary A. Lock, NA 2177, 30–33 (January 31, 1672): "Zijn testateurs twee contrefeytsels, het eene geschildert door Bartholomeus van der Helst ende het andere door Jan Lievens."

17 SA, notary J. van Loosdrecht, NA 2000, 149–167 (May 23, 1678); and Bredius 1915–1922, 1249–1250.

18 Claes Calckoen (1612–1687) and his wife Elisabeth Danckerts (1613–1670), SA, notary N. Brouwer, NA 3956, fols. 259v–276 (December 1, 1687–April 13, 1688): "Een conterfeytsel van de overleden en van sijn huysvrouwe door Jan Lievens."

19 Schneider/Ekkart 1973, 145–146, nos. 229, 236, and 333; the format of the two pieces is virtually identical to that of the portraits of their eldest son and his wife from 1666 by Herman Verelst (Haarlem 1986, no. 37), perhaps with an eye to possibly combining the portraits later?

20 Gerard Schaep, Lord of Kortenhoef (1598–1666), who had married Maria Spiegel (1604–1661), SA, notary N. Kruijs, NA 1857, 516–546 (July 26 and 27–August 5, 1666): "Nogh een [conterfeytsel] van de overleden heer van Cortenhoeff door Jan Lievess."

21 SA, notary N. Kruijs, NA 1857, 645–646 (September 7 and 8, 1666): "1 contrefeytzel van de heer van Cortenhoeff door Jan Livess. f 126."

22 Scholten 2006, 105–106 (fig. 15), 123, no. 16.

23 On the other hand a pair of portraits of the Schaep-Spiegel couple were listed without the name of the painter, see Vos 1662, 160–161.

24 Timon Veneman (1612–1673) and Helena Wijbrants (c. 1628–1721), SA, notary D. Doornick, NA 1938, 190–200 (November 8, 1669): "De conterfeytsels van hen testateurs geschildert door Jan Lievensz." The stipulation concerning the portraits is repeated in wills of 1671 and of 1672.

25 As "twee portraiten, het eene zijnde de heer Timon Veneman en het andere vrouwe Helena Wijbrands" (SA, Arch. no. 5073, inv. 988, doc. 1).

26 Vos 1662, 566 and 568 (Schneider/Ekkart 1973, 100–101, 103, nos. 31, 31a, 38, and 38a–b). See Van Gent 1998 for information on the portraits of Jan Jacobsz Hinlopen who was married to Lucia Wijbrants, a sister of Helena.

27 For Hans Bontemantel (1613–1688), see Kernkamp 1897, 1: xciii.

28 For Claude Blot (c. 1628–1670) and Maria van der Wel (c. 1629–after 1670), see Bredius 1915–1922, 1:205–206.

29 SA, Arch. no. 5072, inv. 594, fol. 165–171 (February 24, 1667) and inv. 598, fol. 104–108 (September 10, 1670). I suspect the portraits were never delivered.

30 SA, Baptism, Marriage, and Burial Registers (DTB), 465, 471 (April 23, 1648).

31 Jan van der Hoeven (1616–1657) was a notary in Amsterdam. Stadsarchief Naarden, notary J. Atten, NA 3677, deed 48 (December 21, 1663).

32 Jan Denijsz Troncquois (c. 1630/1640–after 1682), SA, notary N. Brouwer, NA 3944, fol. 404–405 (April 30, 1682); and Bredius 1915–1922, 1:201–202: "Noch verklaert sij getuyge dat sij daer bij en present is geweest als Jan Lievense schilder het contrafeytsel van Joan Dionijs Tronquoes ten huyse van juffr. Maria Deymans de Jonge zaliger heeft gebracht ende dat sij doleerde, seggende "waerom brenght hij mijn soon sijn contrafeytsel soo nat thuys? Kan hij dat niet houden soo langh als het droogh is? Heeft hij soo nodigh gelt van doen? Mijn soon sal hem wel betalen." Troncquois had the declaration drawn up because goods belonging to him — including the portrait in question — were in his brother-in-law's house. Troncquois could possibly have given these in keeping because of his bankruptcy. In the settlement of this bankruptcy, it turned out that the brother-in-law had a balance of around 15,000 guilders of which he was paid only 16 percent. An inventory of Troncquois' goods relates to the goods at his homestead at Sloten, not the goods that were stored with his brother-in-law (SA, Arch. no. 5072, inv. 1594, no. 361, and inv. 601, fol. 250–253 [October 10, 1676]).

33 Bredius 1915–1922, 1:198.

34 Bredius 1915–1922, 1:210; the landlord Daniel Dubordieu and his wife Geertruyt Vonck indicated that the work (possibly a double portrait?) should be as large "as sr. Heemskerck is painted." The form of this reference suggests that "sr. Heemskerk" had also had his portrait painted by Lievens.

35 Elisabeth van Peenen (1650–1700), who had married Adriaen le Pla (died 1675), Regionaal Archief Leiden, notary L. Overmeer, NA 978 (August 28, 1683): "De twee conterfeytels van haer vrouwe comparante ende haer eerste man za., mede gedaen door Jan Lievens constschilder."

36 Elen 1982, 88; in 1677 the widow still had a disagreement with a carpenter over the work carried out in her house, Leiden, notary J. van der Stoffe, NA 1193, deed 149 (February 12, 1677).

37 Ekkart in London and The Hague 2007–2008, 50; the commission for the group portrait from Huydecoper in 1659 could also have been related to his moving into a new residence.

38 Schneider/Ekkart 1973, 113, no. 89; Lievens received 600 guilders for this commission.

39 Braunschweig 1979, 110–113; and Sumowski 1983, 3: nos. 1208 and 1209.

40 Schneider/Ekkart 1973, 116–117, no. 102; for this painting Lievens received 1,250 guilders in 1656.

41 Schneider/Ekkart 1973, 115–116, no. 99; Lievens was paid 1,200 guilders.

42 Schneider/Ekkart 1973, 112, no. 86; nothing is known about the amount paid.

43 Schneider/Ekkart 1973, 119–120, no. 114. This painting is mentioned in an eighteenth-century source but has disappeared since the nineteenth century. I have looked for documents relating to this painting in the Nationaal Archief in The Hague without success.

44 Johan de Witt (1625–1672); Pieter de Graeff (1638–1707). The letters are in the Nationaal Archief in The Hague (inv.no. 3.01.17). Significant portions were published in Leupe 1874; Fruin/Kernkamp 1906–1913; and Fruin/Japikse 1919–1922. I have not been able to locate a letter from Johan de Witt to Pieter de Graeff, written in April 1663, in which Lievens must have been discussed.

45 She noted in 1664: "Portret van mijn vader en een van mijn moeder Bickers 200 [guilders], is geschildert van een meester Jan Lievisen, daeraen twee vergulden gesneeden lijsten"; SA, Family Archive De Graeff (Arch. no. 76), inv. 610. The portraits of the married couple, Jan Bicker (1591–1653) and Agneta de Graeff (1603–1656), in Amsterdams Historisch Museum (Amsterdam 1975–1979, 186–190, nos. 243 and 244) are thought to be copies (by Wallerand Vaillant?), possibly after the portraits by Lievens discussed here, Dudok van Heel 1983, 69 and n. 13.

46 Jan Lievens to Johan de Witt, July 24, 1664, offering to paint the portrait of De Witt's wife, Wendela Bicker (1636–1668), and defending his portraits of De Witt's parents-in-law: "Daer ick so veel arbeydts om gedaen heb alsof 't voor den prins van Oranien geweest waer."

47 For Andries de Graeff (1611–1678), see Weber 1985.

48 Dudok van Heel 1983, 66: "Heeft Jan Lievensz. schilder, in presentie van de Hr. Gerard ter Borgh, om mijn soon naeckt als een cupido uyt te schilderen geeijst f. 50."

49 Described in the inventory of Pieter de Graeff's household goods as "een jongetje verbeeldende den Hr. Cornelis de Graaff voornoemt [de Jonge] boven de schoorsteen door de oude Jan Lievensz," valued at 25 guilders. See SA, notary M. Servaes, NA 5001, 425–549 (March 8 and 9, 1709); and Dudok van Heel 1983, 66 n. 1.

50 Willem Schrijver (1608–1661), the husband of Wendela de Graeff (1607–1652), and son of Pieter Scriverius (1576–1660). The relations between members of the Schrijver family and Lievens extended over many years. In or shortly before 1673 Lievens painted the portrait of Willem Schrijver the Younger (1651–1673). Pieter de Graeff noted in one of his almanacs that he had sent Schrijver's widow "a large painting with the portrait of her deceased husband, our cousin Willem Schriver, painted by Jan Lievensz" (een groote schilderije offte conterfeytsel door Jan Lievensz. nae wijlen haer man, onse neef Willem Schrijver, geschildert), Dudok van Heel 1983, 66 n. 1. The widow was Margaretha Six (1653–1704), daughter of Pieter and Johanna Six; see above notes 12 and 13.

51 SA, notary J. Snel, NA 3581, 328 (September 5, 1667); and Bredius 1915–1922, 1:204–205.

52 SA, notary A. Loefs, NA 1603, envelope 6, fol. 41–48 (December 14, 1661).

53 SA, notary A. Loefs, NA 1605, envelope MM, fol. 9–13 (December 11, 1666).

54 Amelis van den Bouckhorst (1613–1669). Bredius 1915–1922, 1:207–208.

55 Bredius 1915–1922, 1:207 n. 3.

56 Jan Lievens to Johan de Witt, April 24, 1664: "Voor eerst dat ick meer bij uimaginatie als bij voorbeeldt heb moeten werken, en dat ick voor een groot heer doende was die gaern dinggen in een open dach in pleysant locht en lantschap uitgebeeldt sach." Very little is known about the customers for Lievens' landscapes, but he probably painted small landscapes for the open market rather than a specific purchaser. This intriguing passage from Lievens' letter indicates that he occasionally produced such works on commission.

57 Van de Wetering in Amsterdam 1998.

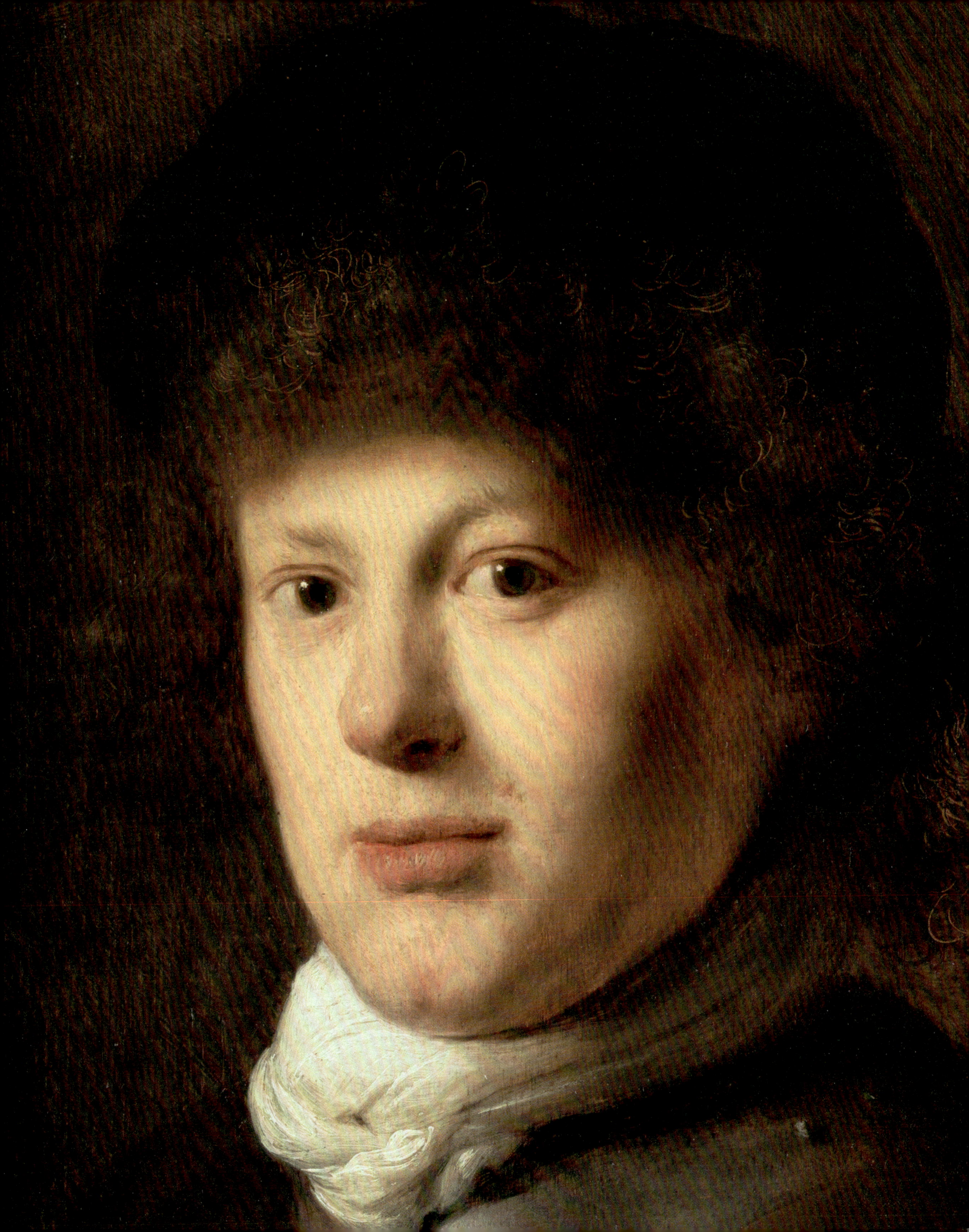

Lievens' Technique: "Wonders in smeared paint, varnishes, and oils"

E. MELANIE GIFFORD

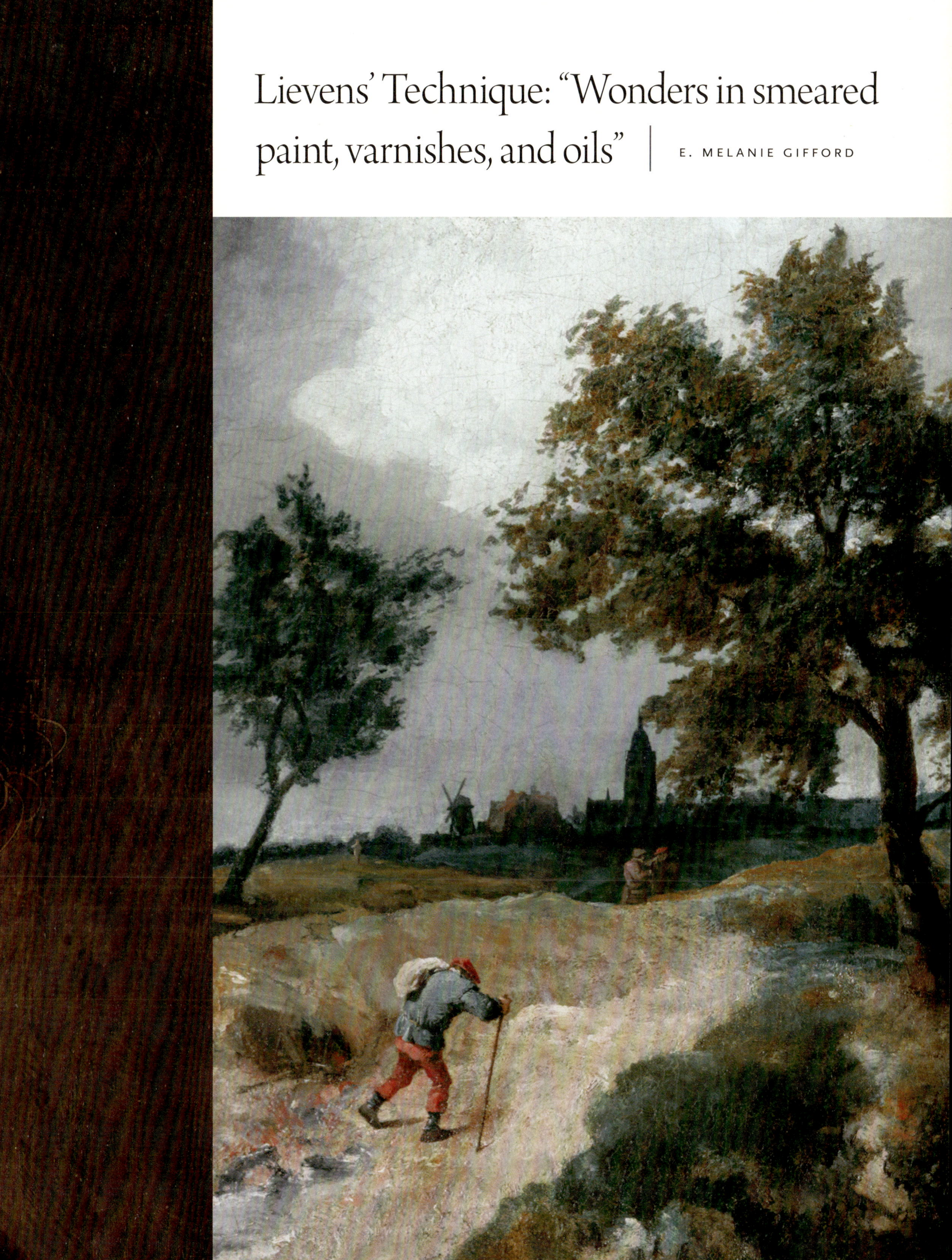

THE PAINTING TECHNIQUE OF Jan Lievens — artistic prodigy, court artist, and recipient of distinguished public commissions — offers a window on what a modern viewer might see as a bewildering variety of styles over the course of a long career. Technical examinations of forty paintings found that Lievens' diverse ways of painting do not resolve into a linear progression; instead, he worked in multiple styles virtually simultaneously.[1]

To understand how — and why — Lievens could have painted in several distinct styles at the same time, it is useful to consider three competing forces that shaped his oeuvre. The first was his extraordinary native talent; a bold and vivid handling of paint marks his earliest works in Leiden. This fundamental impetus was subsequently transformed to varying degrees by two other factors: his aspiration to paint for courtly audiences in The Hague or London in the 1630s, and the requirements of visual communication in large-scale paintings commissioned for public spaces: in Antwerp from 1635 to 1644 and in Amsterdam for the rest of his career. To meet the essential needs of these differing circumstances, Lievens adapted his native approach into distinct modes of painting that appeared concurrently throughout much of his life. The second half of this essay traces the three dominant modes in works from Lievens' maturity: large-scale public commissions, idealized portraiture, and landscapes in which his particular handling of paint served as a personal trademark.

THE STRUCTURE OF LIEVENS' PAINTINGS

Technical study has helped clarify Lievens' chronology, as it uncovered some variations in his materials. Like many of his contemporaries, Lievens chose his painting support — wood panel or canvas — based on size; smaller paintings were typically on panel, larger works on canvas. The ground layers that prepared the supports are typical for Dutch and Flemish artists. Panels were smoothed with a chalk-based lower ground followed by a toned upper ground; canvases usually had a tan or gray preparation: sometimes a single ground, sometimes a light-colored upper layer covering a reddish lower ground of earth pigments.

Lievens does not seem to have laid out his compositions with an underdrawing. Rather, he started with a brown painted sketch, as did his teacher Pieter Lastman and many contemporaries. From early in his career Lievens frequently made revisions to this sketch in black paint. After the sketch had dried, he blocked out the forms in a broadly handled underpaint, often following the standard practice of using subdued versions of the final colors.

The wide range of appearances that Lievens achieved in his paintings was primarily the result of his final paint application. He seems to have regarded the preparatory parts of a painting — the support, ground, painted sketch, and underpaint — as practical underpinnings that could be substantially changed in the subsequent paint layers, either by incorporating the first layers into the final presentation or almost entirely suppressing them.

LIEVENS' EARLIEST PAINTINGS IN LEIDEN

Lievens' innate talent was already apparent as a fourteen-year-old boy in 1621, when he painted a portrait of his mother that astonished Leiden connoisseurs.[2] This work may well be *Old Woman Reading* (cat. 1): dendrochronological dating suggests that the panel on which it is painted was available for use around 1618.[3] This early work illustrates Lievens' painting practices when he first worked in Leiden after completing his training with Lastman. Already his impatient, exuberant technique and the closely framed half-length composition, which depends on Utrecht prototypes, show a precocious independence from his master.

Like several of Lievens' earliest panels examined for this study, this portrait's wood support was crudely made; three roughly finished planks meet in fairly prominent joins.[4] At this period cabinetmakers usually sold panels for painters, and specialized "primers" prepared both panels and canvas supports with grounds.[5] In 1627 the Leiden guild of joiners and cabinetmakers requested that their charter be revised to make this prerogative explicit in order to stop a local woodturner, Jan Pietersz van den

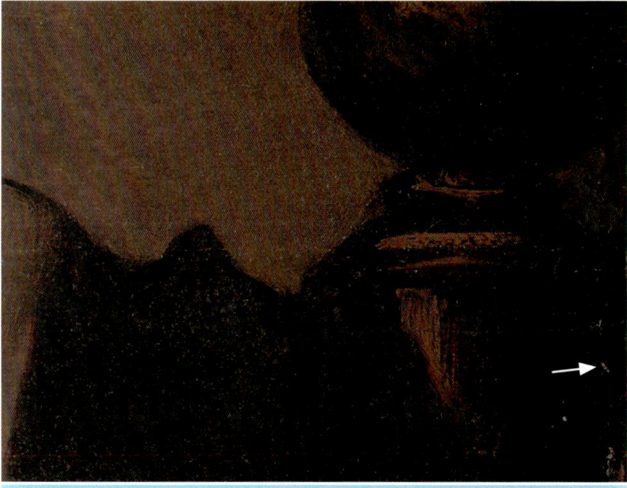

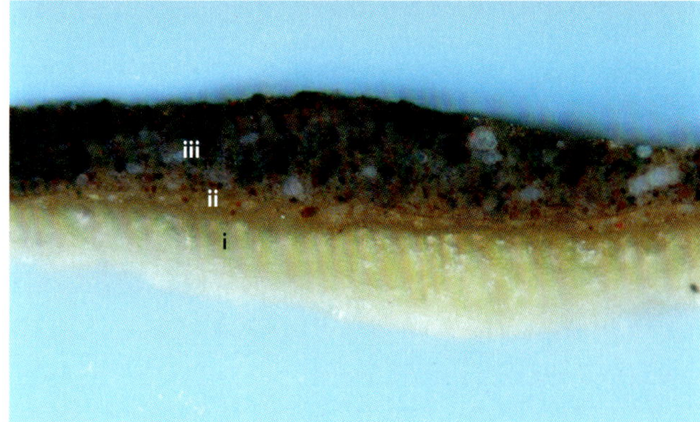

1 | Location of paint sample and cross section (JC487_S2) (25× objective) from chair finial in *Old Woman Reading* (cat. 1)

iii: brown paint of chair

ii: dark tan upper ground, with brush-marked surface

i: chalk lower ground (stained at upper surface)

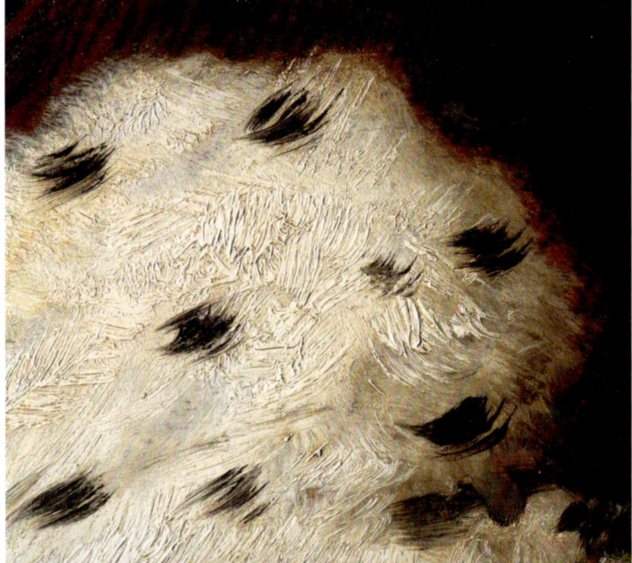

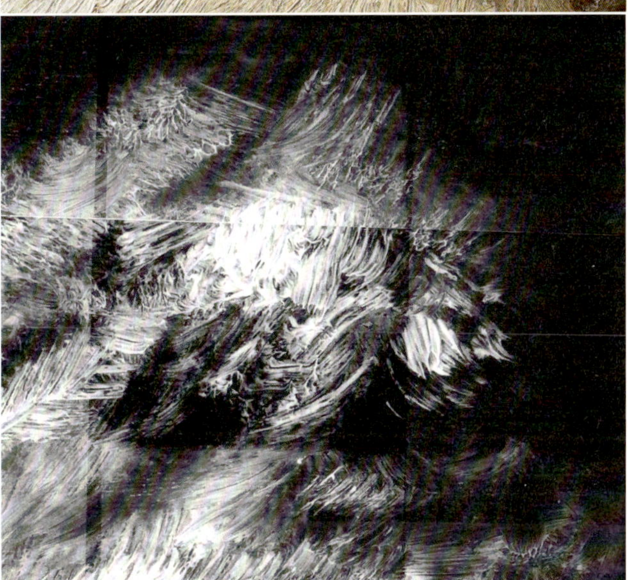

2 | Detail of ermine fur and x-radiograph of same area in *Old Woman Reading*

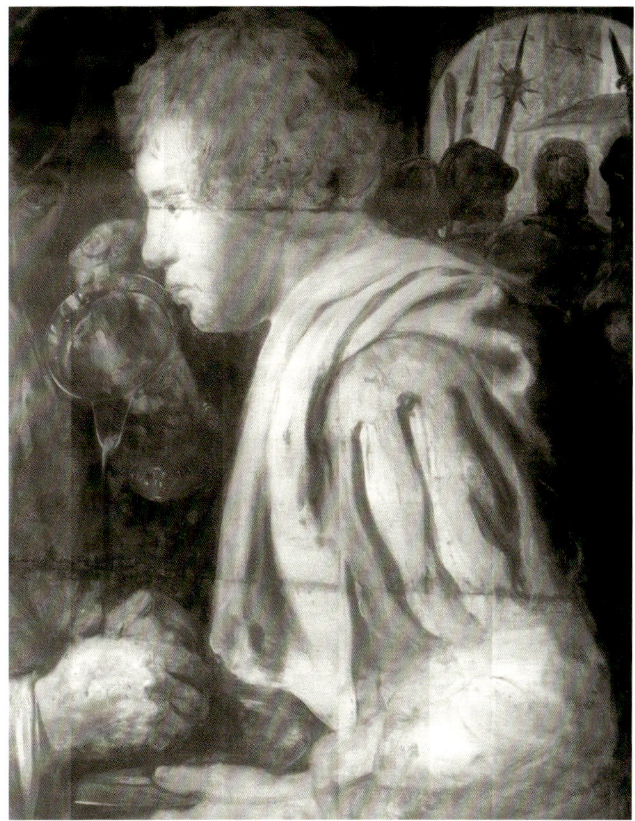

3 | Infrared reflectogram of detail from *Pilate Washing His Hands* (cat. 7)

Bosch, who had taken on this business.[6] The crude panels of Lievens' early paintings may have been Van den Bosch's presumably less expensive products.

This painting's preparation, a dark tan upper ground brushed vigorously over the chalk lower ground leaving a textured, brush-marked surface, resembles other grounds on Lievens' earliest paintings (fig. 1).[7] These grounds do not all share the same structure, but their similar colors and irregular surface suggest they could have been applied by the artist.[8] Lievens sketched out the composition with brown paint before indicating the colors with a thin underpaint. These preparatory stages are only occasionally visible: in the ermine they suggest the brown shadowed edge and the grayish undercoat of the fur. The completed painting is dominated by the dense final paint, which Lievens applied with an extraordinary freedom and confidence (fig. 2). He painted the wrinkled face with unblended strokes of yellow and pink and built up a sculptural impasto with brush, stick, and fingers to describe the heavy fur. Strikingly, no parallel for this brushwork exists in Lastman's work. It seems to be part of Lievens' native vocabulary, perhaps encouraged by the rough character of some of Dirck van Baburen's weathered faces, which he presumably saw during a visit to Utrecht (see Wheelock fig. 5).[9]

In the early Leiden years Lievens developed remarkably quickly, his creative process accommodating bold revisions as he transformed his Utrecht prototypes. In another painting on a crude panel, *Pilate Washing His Hands* (cat. 7), Lievens defined the composition with a sketch in brown paint, which he varied slightly in color. To indicate the pink-costumed servant, for example, he added red lake pigment. The infrared reflectogram (fig. 3) cannot reveal the reddish initial sketch, but it does show the black sketch paint with which he revised the forms.[10] With repeated strokes he lowered the elbow, thereby expanding the servant's form to counterbalance the massive figure of Pilate.

In *Pilate Washing His Hands* Lievens adjusted the paint handling to describe rich fabrics, stippling the surface of Pilate's coat and scratching into it while wet. The range of colors is restrained and the composition quiet by comparison with the somewhat

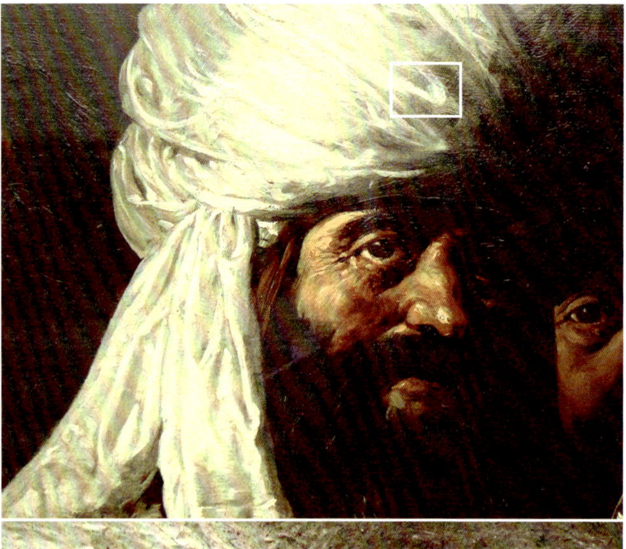

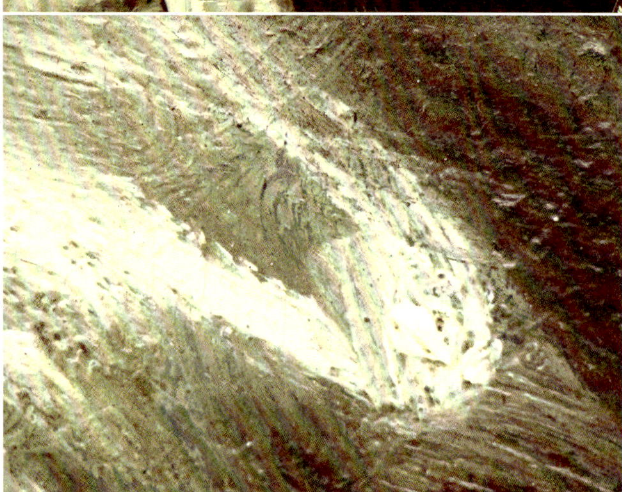

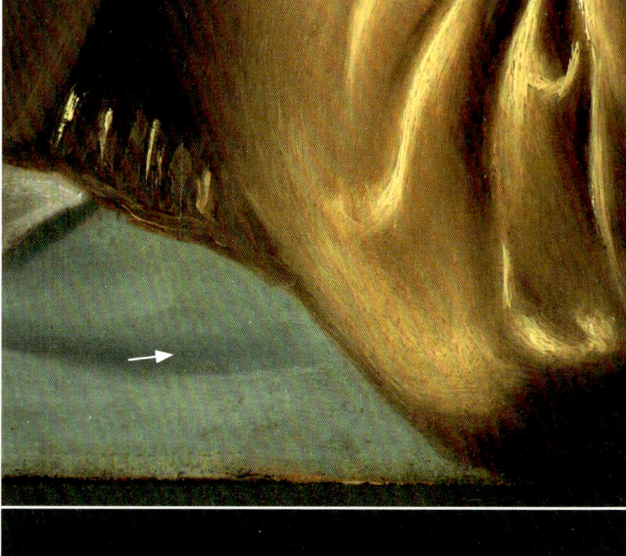

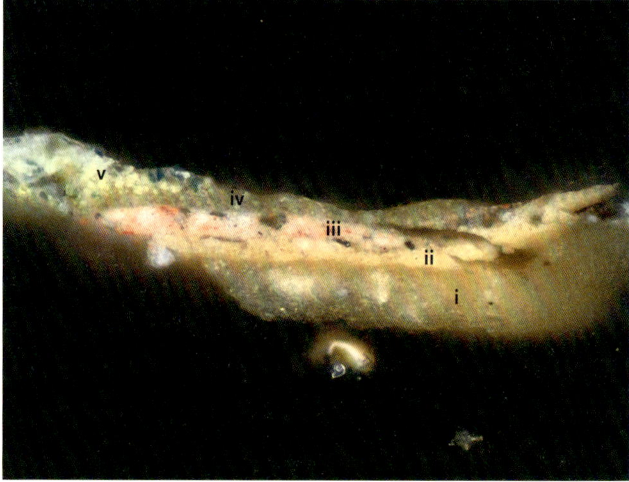

4 | Detail of turban with location of macro detail from *Pilate Washing His Hands*, blue stripe of the first version can be seen below white paint

5 | Location of paint sample and cross section (WAM 725) (20× objective) from revised green costume at lower edge of *Lute Player* (cat. 13)

v: green final paint of revised costume

iv: dull green underpaint of revised costume

iii: pink paint of original costume

ii: light tan upper ground

i: chalk lower ground

earlier *Feast of Esther* (cat. 6). Lievens consciously allowed the dark background and white turban and towel to set off the figures of Pilate and the servant, highlighting the psychological moment. He came to this solution after experimentation: microscopic examination demonstrates that Pilate's white turban was originally a patterned fabric with broad blue stripes crossed by fine stripes of blue and reddish brown (fig. 4).

LIEVENS AND REMBRANDT IN LEIDEN

Technical study illuminates the close artistic relationship between Lievens and Rembrandt after 1625, when Rembrandt returned to Leiden from his study with Lastman. The young artists not only bought materials from the same source, their paintings document an increasing exchange of artistic practices through the second half of the 1620s.

When Rembrandt first returned to Leiden, he may have patronized the same panel maker as Lievens. Panel makers tended to produce painting supports in standardized formats using consistent construction methods.[11] The maker of the crude panels in Lievens' early works used stock planks up to 29 cm wide rather than combining wider and narrower planks to place the joins away from the center of the composition. Rembrandt's two largest early paintings, *The Stoning of Saint Stephen* and *History Painting*, are on panels of the same format, and like Lievens' crude early panels, each is constructed of three irregular planks about 29 cm wide.[12] Evidence from a few years later suggests that the young artists may sometimes have bought supplies jointly. Dendrochronology has shown that Rembrandt's *Samson and Delilah* and Lievens' early *Self-Portrait* (cat. 18), both painted c. 1629–1630, are on panels made from planks of the same tree trunk; almost certainly the panels were bought in the same batch.[13]

Rembrandt and Lievens seem to have turned to more professionally produced panels around 1626 or 1627, either because the Leiden guild of joiners and cabinetmakers had put their former panel maker out of business or because they sought higher quality panels.[14] These panels were smoothly finished with almost imperceptible joins positioned off center. The later panels were also prepared with grounds that seem more consistent with one another and with Rembrandt's panels: a chalk-glue lower ground with an evenly brushed tan upper ground that is noticeably lighter than the early panels (fig. 5).[15] While these grounds are not identical, their relative uniformity suggests that they could have been commercially prepared.[16]

Lievens began painting *Lute Player* (cat. 13) around this time. Some time later he revised it, making a dramatic color change and transforming an explicit quotation of an Utrecht prototype.[17] In the energetic first composition the musician wore a bright pink costume, and the lute was painted in deep ruddy tones. The x-radiograph of the painting shows that the profile musician held his lute upright with the pegbox strongly foreshortened. The thumb pressed against the neck of the lute and a full sleeve swinging out to the left suggested movement (fig. 6). Lievens' emulation of Utrecht compositions seems to have a specific source: Hendrick ter Brugghen's *Lute Player in Lost Profile* of 1624 (fig. 7), which survives in three versions.[18] In revising his painting, Lievens shifted from Ter Brugghen's depiction of active music making to a more static, monumental figure reminiscent of the servant in *Pilate Washing His Hands*.

The color change from pink to dull green and yellow (seen in a paint cross section: fig. 5) also has implications for the date of the original painting and its revision.[19] Bright pink costumes appear in early works by both artists, including Rembrandt's *Music Lesson* of 1626 in which Lievens served as a model (see Wheelock fig. 12).[20] Both adopted a more muted palette after 1626, however, and Lievens' revisions to *Lute Player* must date from somewhat later. Rembrandt and Lievens were not alone among Leiden artists in this development. In the second half of the 1620s Jan Davidsz de Heem's monochromatic still lifes of books and Jan van Goyen's groundbreaking landscapes were at the forefront of a Dutch movement toward tonalism.[21]

In the later 1620s Lievens and Rembrandt developed new methods for their informal figure studies, known as tronies, incorporating evidence of the painting process into the finished work of art. Both began to leave their brown sketches uncovered in places, their paint surfaces were more varied, and both introduced expressive scratching into their painting technique that recalled their graphic works.

In Lievens' *Portrait of Rembrandt* (cat. 17) the warm brown sketch helps create shadows deep in the curly hair, while the light tan ground shines through the sketch paint as a russet halftone shadow at the edge of the face. This effect may correspond to the "glow" that Gerard de Lairesse attributed to the shadows of Rembrandt and Lievens among others. Paul Taylor suggests that the effect was used to create "a powerful sense of three dimensions" with vivid halftones counterbalancing bright highlights.[22] Lievens' varied surface does indeed create a lively three-dimensional effect. Blended handling makes the shadowed brown cloak recede, while vigorous descriptive brushstrokes in the kerchief and the studs on the gorget draw the eye to the center of the

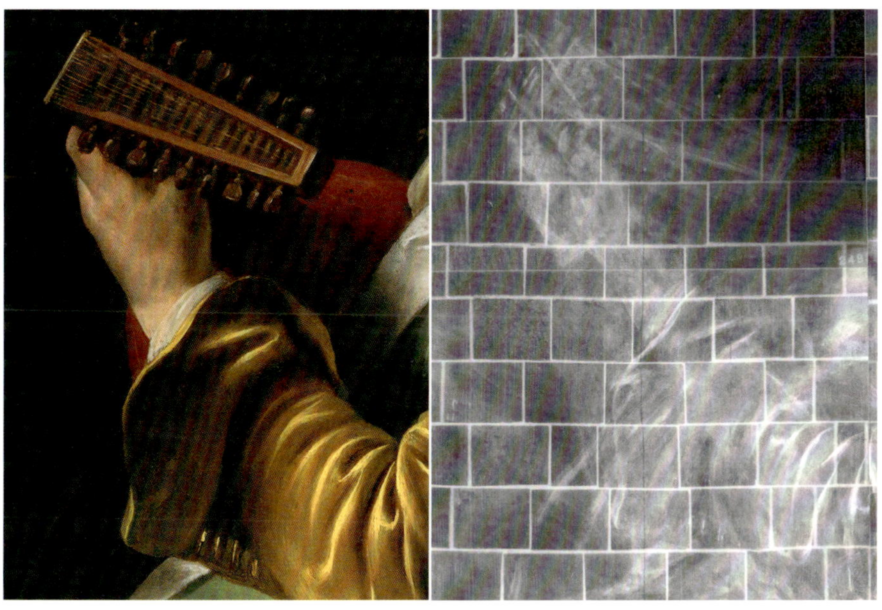

6 | Detail of lute and arm and x-radiograph of same area *Lute Player* (white rectangles show balsa blocks applied during prior conservation treatment)

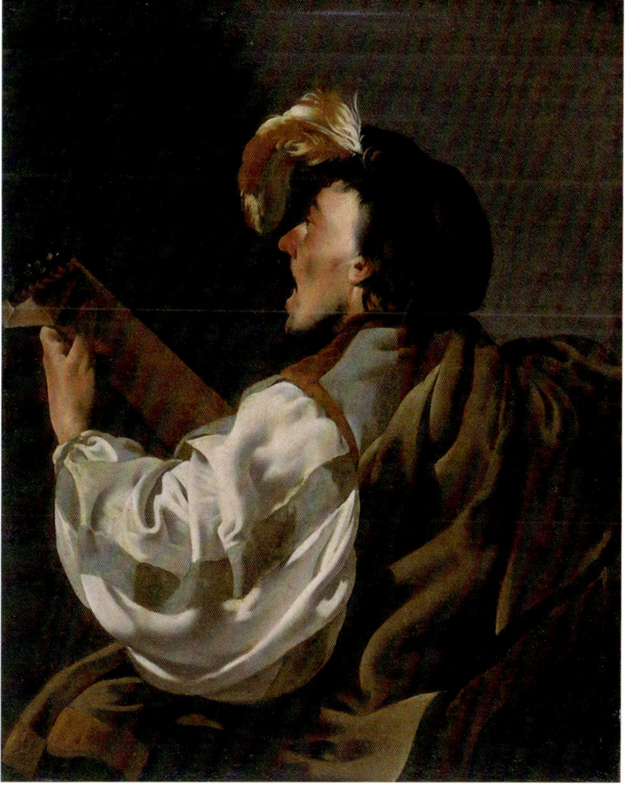

7 | Hendrick ter Brugghen, *Lute Player in Lost Profile*, 1624, oil on canvas, 104.5 × 84.7 cm. Musée des Beaux-Arts, Bordeaux

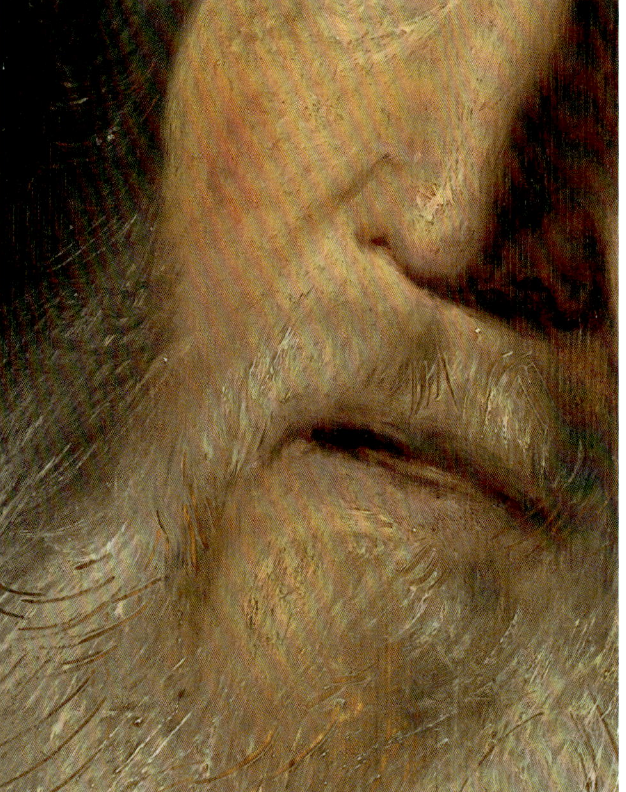

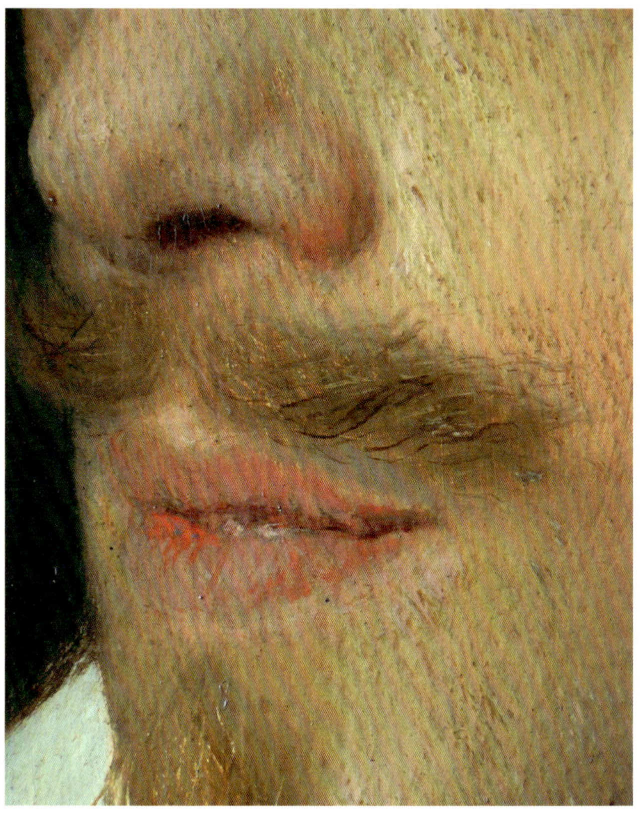

8 | Detail from *Bearded Man with a Beret* (cat. 20), showing the varied paint handling and free scratching typical of Lievens' tronies from late 1620s

9 | Detail from *Portrait of Constantijn Huygens* (cat. 16), showing smoothly brushed paint and minute final details typical of an idealized portrait

painting. In the face the treatment is far more convincing than his earlier method of placing sharply juxtaposed yellow and pink highlights with opaque shadows and rough blackish details over a grayish underpainting (compare, for example to the face of the servant in *Pilate Washing His Hands*). Instead, Lievens used moderate brushwork to build the forms and contrast the substantial face with the soft, shadowy hair.

Lievens' technique of scratching into wet paint became progressively more fluent in these years. In earlier paintings he had scratched a line or two to clarify contours or used random squiggles to break up a dense paint surface (see the heavy brocade in *Pilate Washing His Hands*). In revising *Lute Player,* Lievens' only changes to the face were to add highlights on the temple and the side of the nose; working almost intuitively, he reintroduced curls of hair and the lower eyelashes with quick notations scratched into the wet paint. In *Portrait of Rembrandt,* he extended this technique by suggesting curls with a combination of brushstrokes and varied scratches into the still-wet paint, sometimes making dark curls by exposing only the brown sketch, sometimes creating highlights by scraping down to the light tan ground. He united brushwork and scratching with a few final curls of blackish paint that crossed over both.

The expressive possibilities found in painting technique must have been central to the artistic interchange between Lievens and Rembrandt in the second half of the 1620s, but the two artists did not develop in lockstep. Rembrandt's "rough manner" must certainly be seen in the context of the heavily brushed paintings Lievens was already making in the early 1620s.[23] As Rembrandt increasingly developed the expressive qualities of dense paint, however, Lievens mastered his rough brushwork to evolve a progressively more refined manner. Lievens had depicted faces with thick paint and hard contrasts of light and dark in his early paintings. In later tronies such as *Bearded Man with a Beret,* from c. 1630 (cat. 20), his technique ranged from veils of color revealing the painted sketch in half-lights, to juxtaposed touches of ivory and pink impasto evoking the soft folds of a weathered face. His varied scratches into gently brushed wet paint suggest both the fall of the beard on the chest and wiry strands at the side of the face (fig. 8).

COURTLY ASPIRATIONS AND IDEALIZED PORTRAITURE IN LEIDEN

If these works show Lievens harnessing his innately audacious handling of paint, *Portrait of Constantijn Huygens* (cat. 16) offers the earliest case in which he undertook a different mode of painting to satisfy a patron's differing artistic expectations. In this portrait Lievens modulated his characteristic way of painting into an idealized mode that reflected his understanding of portraiture at the court in The Hague. The x-radiograph and infrared reflectogram document the concentration Lievens brought to this painting: changing the position of the sitter's head and gaze, and extending the hands to reveal the sitter's narrow wrists. Over the previous versions of the face he used a freely handled underpaint to block in the form of the face and hands, and then worked up the final paint in two sittings with a smooth, fluid touch and a level of detail entirely unlike his contemporary tronies. In the second and final sitting he worked wet-in-wet, dragging gray paint into flesh tone with a tiny brush to describe the beard and faintly stubbled jaw. He returned to add even finer details over dry paint: individual hairs in the moustache and eyebrows, infinitesimal dots of black beard on the shadowed jaw (fig. 9). The effect is more literally descriptive, and far less sculptural than his *Portrait of Rembrandt*.

Huygens reported that some people regretted that the "contemplative rendering... detracts from the vivacity of my mind," but he explained that Lievens had managed to capture the cares weighing on the sitter at the time. Two other paintings from the later Leiden years, *Boy in a Cape and Turban* and *Young Man in Yellow* (cats. 30 and 33), share the quality of self-contained detachment that characterizes the Huygens portrait as well its smoothly blended paint and minute final details. It seems that for these courtly patrons Lievens consciously sought to emulate the idealizing mode of portraiture practiced by court artist Michiel van Mierevelt. In doing so, he did not alter the freedom of his customary sketch and underpaint, but he did introduce a new manner of applying the final paint: fluidly blended, with smooth transitions that hide the artist's touch. For the rest of Lievens' career variants on this type of portraiture appeared concurrently with freely handled works.

Lievens' ability — and inclination — to work in more than one manner at once is not surprising, and his motivation here seems clear. As a very young artist he was already sensitive to the particularities of personal style. Orlers reported that he had painted copies after Cornelis Ketel so convincingly that they were later sold as originals. The ambition that Huygens recognized never waned throughout Lievens' career; he repeatedly modified the way he painted to suit his intended audience.

Another sign of his courtly aspirations appeared in his *Self-Portrait* of c. 1629–1630 (cat. 18). When Anthony van Dyck visited the court at The Hague in the winter of 1631/1632 and painted Lievens' portrait for his planned *Iconography,* he gave the young Leiden artist a graceful aristocratic demeanor more in keeping with styles at the English court than at The Hague (see Wheelock fig. 11). Lievens had intended to travel to England as early as 1629, and though he did not actually leave until 1632, he modified his own *Self-Portrait* to reflect his ambition to be a court artist. In the underlying sketch Lievens devoted considerable attention to capturing his characteristically square, narrow chin. In rapid revisions to the final painting he changed a cropped hairstyle to flowing shoulder-length hair worthy of a cavalier. The x-radiograph shows the background painted up to a point where the hair originally ended around the height of the cheekbones (fig. 10). Paint defects, including an area of "traction crackle" to the right of the face, suggest an impatience that may have pushed Lievens to make these changes before the paint of the first version was fully dry.

PUBLIC COMMISSIONS IN ANTWERP AND THE NORTHERN NETHERLANDS

Lievens left Leiden in 1632, and documentary evidence of royal commissions confirms Orlers' account that he worked for the court in England. Prints and drawings from those years testify to his close attention there to the work of Van Dyck. Although none of Lievens' paintings can be assigned to his stay in England, technical study of paintings made after he moved from London to Antwerp in 1635 shows his adoption of Van Dyck's elegant,

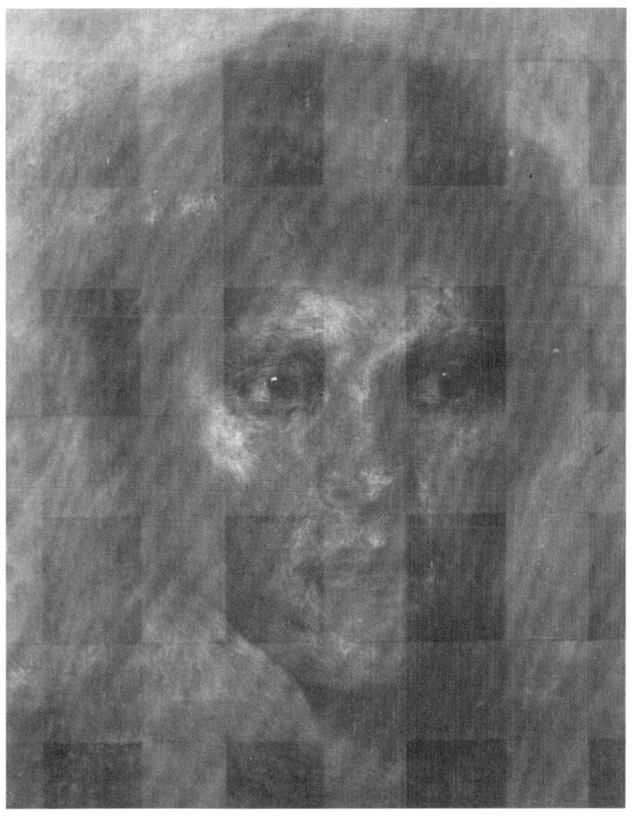

10 | X-radiograph of face in Lievens' *Self-Portrait* of c. 1629–1630 (cat. 18), showing original composition with short hair (grid pattern shows wooden cradle applied to panel in an old restoration)

expansive brushwork. In Antwerp, Lievens entered a new phase in his career, undertaking commissions for monumental religious works. He used the refined manner he had acquired in England to infuse his strong compositions with new grace.

Lievens does not seem to have adopted Van Dyck's disciplined painting practices, however: painted sketch, thinly washed underpaint, and final paint that rarely deviates from the planned design.[24] Instead, he created a similar effect by using his own robust preparatory stages and assimilating Van Dyck's elegant manner only into his final paint layers. In *Abraham and Isaac* from c. 1637 (see Wheelock fig. 17) Lievens laid out the large composition with a bold brownish black painted sketch, which reveals his sensitivity both to the narrative requirements of the subject and to its emotional force. Infrared reflectography shows that although he indicated Isaac's hand only schematically he also planned folds in Abraham's robe that would emphasize the boy's tight embrace. After blocking in the sketch, he freely indicated landscape, figures, and drapery with thick strokes of whitish underpaint that only loosely correspond to the finished painting. Lievens' final brushwork, however, forms a striking contrast to the free preparatory stages. He hid the sketch and underpaint with fluid, blended final paint. The refined tonal transitions show his debt to Van Dyck, suggesting the soft wool of Abraham's robe with translucent glazed shadows and scumbled highlights dragged over the surface (fig. 11).

For the major commissions that Lievens received in Antwerp, he seems to have adopted the practice of painting a preparatory *modello*. Judging from documents later in his career, Lievens must have shown such a study to the patron for approval before beginning an important work. He, and perhaps studio assistants, must also have referred to this preliminary work during the painting process (see Wheelock essay). Although there is no definitive evidence for studio assistants, at least one student appears in records from Lievens' years in Antwerp: Hans van den Wijngaerde began a six-year training in 1636.[25] Lievens contracted to provide room and board during his training but also to provide clothing during the final three years, which suggests that Wijngaerde would by then function as a productive member of the studio.[26]

Though only the modello for *The Lamentation of Christ* was examined in this study, comparison of the modello and the completed painting (cats. 39, 40) shows a remarkable consistency between the two compositions. In the modello Lievens used the black preliminary sketch to plan the layout and serve as a dominant design element. Where the black sketch can be glimpsed below the final paint, it serves as inky shadows and contrasts with the fiery sunset. Lievens frequently reinforced this effect by add-

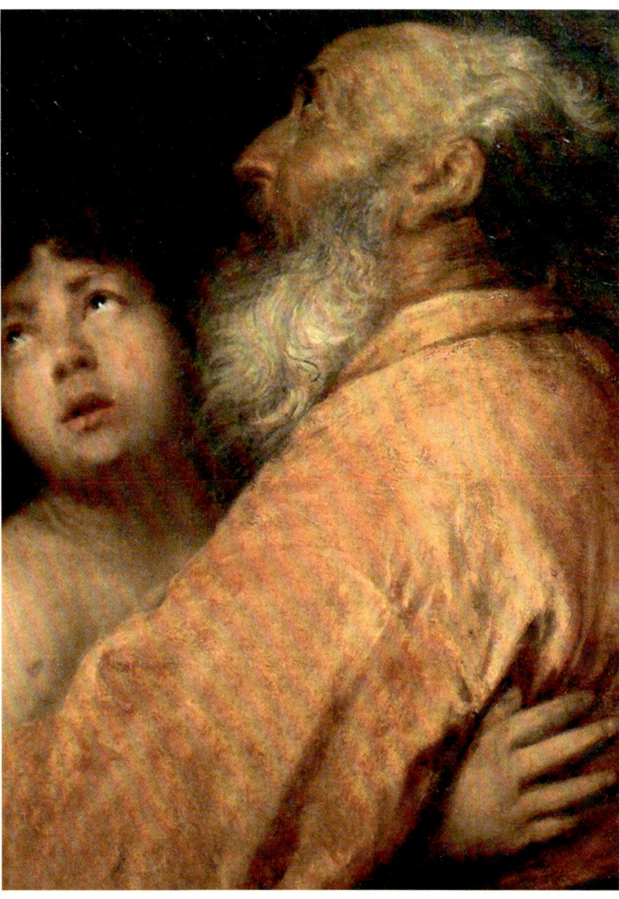

11 | Detail from *Abraham and Isaac* (Wheelock fig. 17)

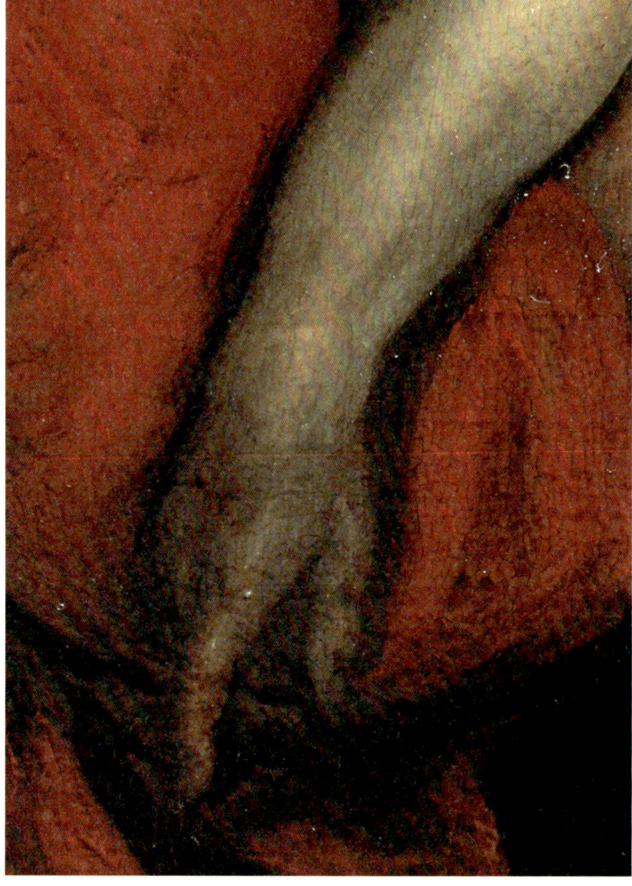

12 | Detail from the modello for *The Lamentation of Christ* (cat. 39)

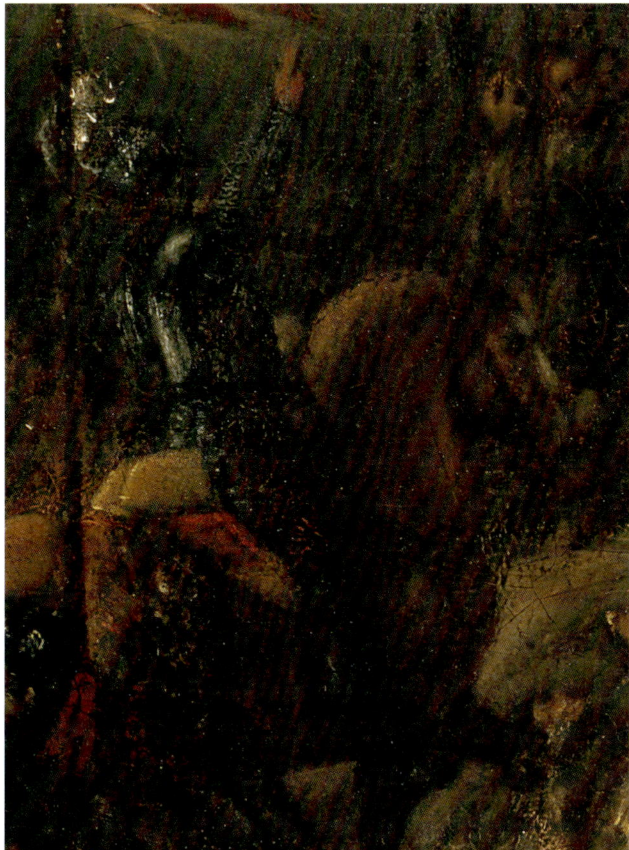

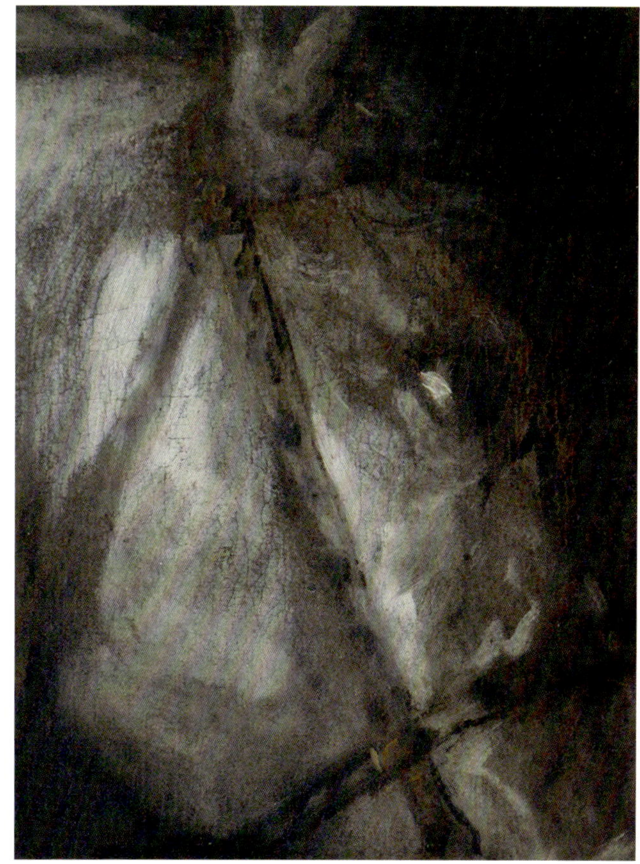

13 | Detail of foreground rider on dun-colored horse in the modello for *Brinio Raised on a Shield* (cat. 54)

14 | Detail of horse from the *Brinio Raised on a Shield* lunette (Wheelock fig. 25), which had been dun-colored, as in the modello, but was repainted white

ing final black contours (fig. 12), a technique that became standard in his later public commissions.

After his return to the Northern Netherlands in 1644 Lievens carried out numerous prestigious commissions for paintings in public spaces. These projects show a consistent method, a mode of painting that Lievens seems to have developed to achieve the greatest possible effect while working as economically as possible. During research for this technical study it was possible to examine both Lievens' lunette for the Amsterdam town hall, *Brinio Raised on a Shield*, and a preparatory modello (see Wheelock fig. 25 and cat. 54). Whereas the highly finished modello for *The Lamentation of Christ* seems characteristic of a study that a patron might consider, the modello for the Amsterdam town hall probably served as a working design. It was executed on paper in thick, wrinkled paint that Lievens must have built up during a process of experimentation.

In this modello Lievens placed the emphasis on the figure of Brinio, held aloft on a shield against a brilliantly lit sky. The artist first followed this emphasis on Brinio in the lunette, but he subsequently revised the composition's focus with his characteristically impatient technique to amplify its dramatic force. He hastily repainted the foreground knight's dun-colored horse bright white (figs. 13–14) and threw nearby figures into relief with heavy black shadows, thereby creating a stronger visual impact for a composition that was meant to be seen from below.

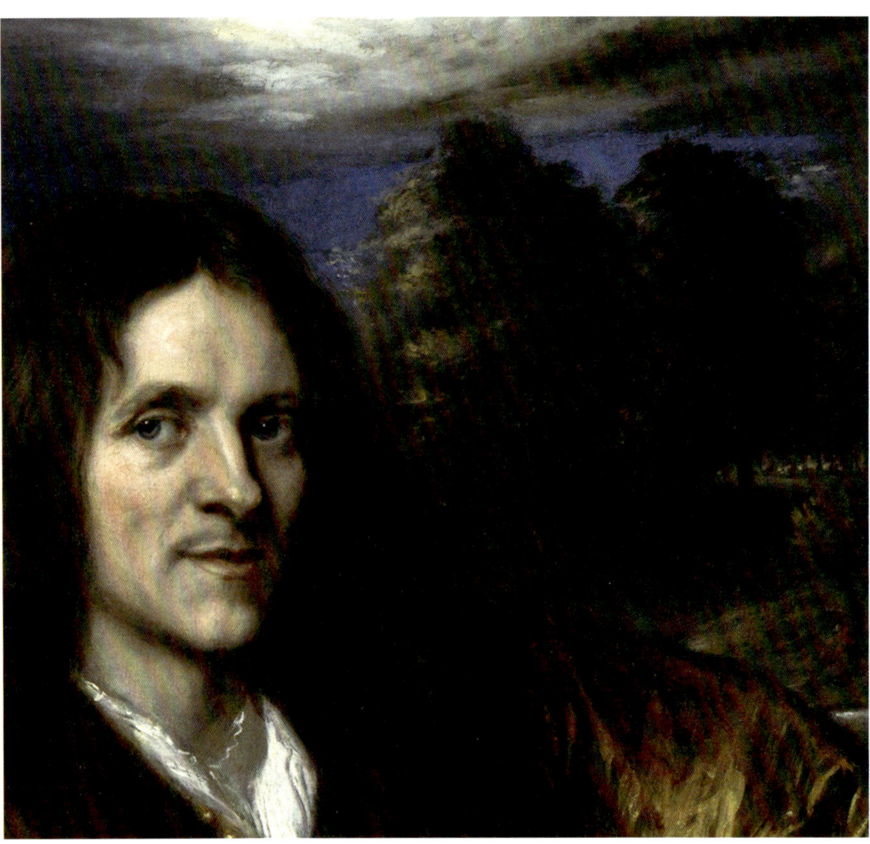

15 | Detail of face and landscape background in Lievens' *Self-Portrait* of the early 1650s (cat. 48)

To a remarkable degree Lievens used similar techniques and materials in both the modello and the finished painting. For example, he rendered the backlit clouds in the same way, with bright peach-colored underpaint suppressed by grayish paint and yellowish final details. In each, he first depicted the slashed coat of the foreground *repoussoir* figure with thick light-colored impasto covered by fluid black paint, exposing the underpaint in the slits of the fabric.

In both works the black paint seems to have a different composition than the other paints Lievens used here, and he may have mixed resin into his paint medium. The black costume in the modello was heavily damaged in old restorations, and tests on the lunette confirm that the black paint is unusually soluble.[27] This observation sheds light on one still-unanswered question. Some of Lievens' paintings from Antwerp, and all of the large public commissions in the Netherlands, show distinctive paint defects that suggest he had changed his materials some time after his early Leiden period. The darkest colors often are marred by "alligator" drying cracks, and in some freely brushed areas paint ran down the surface in long drips, eroding paints in the lower part of the composition. Medium analysis of two of Lievens' paintings has found evidence of pine resin added to the linseed oil in dark damaged paint, but not in lighter colors.[28] Possibly in an effort to speed the painting process, Lievens began adding pine resin to his darkest paints; he may also have continued work before these paints had dried completely.

Later writers, perhaps thinking not of Lievens' early works but of public compositions such as his *Brinio Raised on a Shield* lunette (see Wheelock fig. 25), were struck by Lievens' impulsive painting technique. Samuel van Hoogstraten reported in 1678 that "Jan Lievens was thoroughly at home seeking wonders in smeared paints, varnishes, and oils."[29] Gerard de Lairesse, who advocated a polished technique, was less complimentary. He warned artists against painting like Rembrandt and Lievens, "whose colors run down the piece like dung."[30] New research on the decorative program for the Oranjezaal suggests that Lievens' expressive manner of painting was purposely juxtaposed with Cesar van Everdingen's smooth and restrained classicism (see Wheelock figs. 22, 23).[31]

LIEVENS' TWO MODES IN THE MATURE PORTRAITS

Lievens' remarkable ability to vary his painting technique is highlighted in his mature portraits. In his *Self-Portrait* now in the National Gallery, London (cat. 48), Lievens presented himself as a supremely confident exponent of the Van Dyckian manner, portraying his distinctive chiseled features in a fine-boned aristocratic face. His relaxed posture, one arm draped over the back of a chair, and the dégagé air of his loose costume project the image of a painter fully at home in society.

Lievens also created this impression through the painting technique in his *Self-Portrait*, which is closer to Van Dyck's than any other of the paintings examined for this study.[32] He described the drapery with several stages of free wet-in-wet painting, using the orange pigment realgar, which is comparatively rare in Dutch painting.[33] In the face Lievens almost entirely covered the preliminary stages with finely finished paint in cool tones. His dark underlying sketch makes little contribution to the shadows. Instead, he modeled the forms wet-in-wet, creating shadows in the face by thinly dragging grayish tones with pinker flesh, and finished with bold touches of translucent brown (fig. 15).

After Lievens returned to the Northern Netherlands in 1644, he received portrait commissions from leading members of society. Some, such as Robert Kerr (see cat. 51), valued the fluent handling evident in Lievens' self-portrait. Not all Dutch patrons, however, seem to have sought portraiture in this expressive mode. For those who wanted to project a more restrained image, Lievens worked in a manner that is strikingly like the mode of idealized portraiture he had developed as a young man seeking commissions at the court in The Hague. *Portrait of Adriaen Trip* from 1644 shows a man dressed in the height of fashion, a hand on one hip in a confident stance (cat. 44). The paint handling, however, does not convey the flamboyant style of his London *Self-Portrait*. In the Adriaen Trip portrait Lievens depicts the sitter's oval face with smoothly blended tonal transitions and describes the almond-shaped eyes schematically with smooth outlines and just a single crease defining the hollow of the eye (fig. 16).

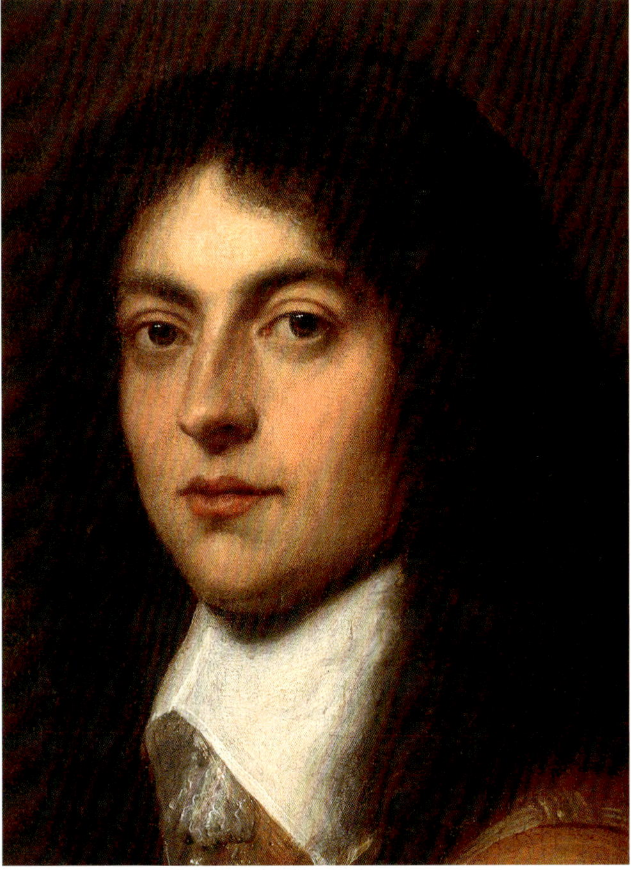

16 | Detail of face in *Portrait of Adriaen Trip* (cat. 44), before conservation treatment

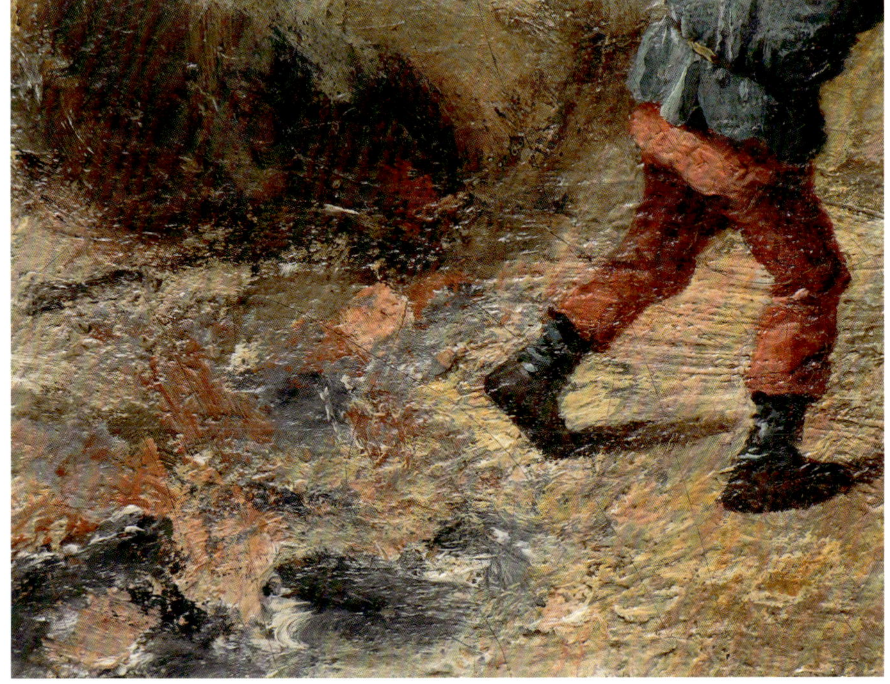

17 | Detail of foreground from the *Landscape with Peasants* (cat. 37), figures added by David Teniers II

RECOGNIZABLE TECHNIQUE AS A "TRADEMARK": LIEVENS' LANDSCAPE PAINTINGS

Lievens' varied production also includes landscape paintings that he probably produced for the open market. His distinctive landscapes, where the brushwork creates an idiosyncratic surface that completely dominates the image, were valued by his contemporaries.[34] No equivalent appears in landscapes by other artists, either in Antwerp or in the Northern Netherlands. In this type of painting Lievens capitalized on his native tendency toward an audacious handling of paint to create an instantly recognizable personal trademark.

A pendant pair of paintings, *Landscape with Peasants* and *Evening Landscape with Fisherman* (see cat. 37) exemplify the landscapes Lievens began producing in Antwerp. In several aspects these works show Lievens adopting typical Antwerp practices. The panels were locally made by an Antwerp panel maker.[35] The structure of the grounds also relates to Flemish practices: at least one has the streaky brown upper ground, or imprimatura, widely used in Antwerp.[36] In the pendants a pinkish upper ground can be seen between brushstrokes.

Lievens made the most of the characteristic tonality that warm grounds lent his paintings. He frequently depicted sunrise or sunset with glimpses of pink and orange sky seen between tree trunks, and he wove these colors throughout the composition. In *Landscape with Peasants* he painted brownish pink on the sandy path and combined it in one tree with translucent purplish lake glazes. Antwerp's art community valued collaboration, and David Teniers II was enlisted to paint the figures in these landscapes. Teniers responded to the pinkish accents when adding his figures, but he used different painting methods. He dressed his peasants in brilliant rose-colored trousers, then harmonized the color with Lievens' adjacent paint by dragging thin brown paint over the brightest red lake glazes (fig. 17).

The glimpses of warm light seen through the trees in almost all of Lievens' landscapes are a particular feature he could have seen in landscapes that Rubens made in the 1630s.[37] The way that detail was achieved — thick impasto accents dabbed in the spaces between tree trunks sketched in with brown paint—also corresponds to Rubens' practice. Yet Rubens used only an occasional accent of heavy paint in his otherwise free and fluid brushwork to create his landscapes. Lievens expanded the use of impasto in his landscapes and laid down densely overlapped and interwoven paint layers throughout the compositions.

Technical examination of *Dune Landscape with Trees* (cat. 43) confirms documentary evidence that Lievens continued to paint landscapes after his return to the Northern Netherlands in 1644: dendrochronology shows that panel was likely used after 1647.[38] Lievens nevertheless continued to apply a brush-marked brown upper ground, similar to the grounds he had used in Antwerp. Likewise, he laid out the composition with a brown sketch and underpaint, then worked and reworked the final paint so densely that it is almost impossible to follow the painting sequence.

Throughout Lievens' mature career three competing forces shaped his artistic production: native talent, courtly aspirations, and large-scale public commissions. Lievens could restrain his impetuous handling of paint when making court portraits. He channeled his facility for rapid production into large public commissions. But landscape allowed him free rein to express his artistic self-identity. Just as Lievens' figure in the elegant *Self-Portrait* (cat. 48) conjures up associations of nobility, so the setting, with a tree-lined allée glimpsed over his shoulder, implies an aristocratic park (see fig. 15). The light glimpsed through the row of tree trunks recalls Lievens' other landscape paintings, its free and suggestive brushwork as characteristic of the artist as his angular face.

Technical Examinations of Forty Paintings Undertaken in Preparation for This Essay

Old Woman Reading	c. 1621–1623	cat. 1
Allegory of the Five Senses	c. 1622	cat. 2
The Four Elements: Fire	c. 1624–1625	Wheelock fig. 7
The Four Elements: Air	c. 1624–1625	Staatliche Museen, Kassel
The Four Elements: Earth	c. 1624–1625	Wheelock fig. 6
The Four Elements: Water	c. 1624–1625	Staatliche Museen, Kassel
Pilate Washing His Hands	c. 1625–1626	cat. 7
Christ at the Column	c. 1625–1626	cat. 8
Still Life with Books	c. 1627–1628	cat. 11
Youth Embracing a Young Woman	c. 1627–1628	cat. 12
Lute Player	c. 1627–1628	cat. 13
Samson and Delilah (panel)	c. 1627–1628	Wheelock fig. 10
Samson and Delilah (canvas)	c. 1628	cat. 15
Portrait of Constantijn Huygens	c. 1628–1629	cat. 16
Portrait of Rembrandt	c. 1629	cat. 17
Self-Portrait	c. 1629–1630	cat. 18
Bearded Man with a Beret	c. 1630	cat. 20
Saint Jerome Meditating in a Grotto	c. 1630	cat. 23
Head of a Child	c. 1630	Museum Boijmans Van Beuningen, Rotterdam
Young Girl in Profile	c. 1631	cat. 28
Boy in a Cape and Turban	c. 1631	cat. 30
Young Man in Yellow (Self-Portrait?)	c. 1631–1632	cat. 33
Self-Portrait	c. 1635	cat. 34
Self-Portrait (replica)	c. 1635	Private collection, Oslo
Abraham and Isaac	c. 1637	Wheelock fig. 17
Landscape with Peasants (with David Teniers II)	c. 1638	cat. 37
River Landscape with Fisherman (with David Teniers II)	c. 1638	cat. 37, fig. 1
Tobias and the Angel in a Landscape	c. 1638–1640	National Gallery, London
The Lamentation of Christ (modello)	c. 1640	cat. 39
Landscape with Willows	early 1640s	cat. 42
Dune Landscape with Trees	middle to late 1640s	cat. 43
Portrait of Adriaen Trip	1644	cat. 44
Portrait of Anna Maria van Schurman	1649	cat. 45
Self-Portrait	early 1650s	cat. 48
Triumph of Peace	1652	cat. 49
Sir Robert Kerr, First Earl of Ancram	1654	cat. 51
Brinio Raised on a Shield (modello)	1660	cat. 54
Brinio Raised on a Shield (lunette)	1660	Wheelock fig. 25
Mars (The Allegory of War)	1664	Wheelock fig. 1
The Geographer (with Jan Andrea Lievens)	c. 1665	cat. 55

Notes

1 In order to include the most consistent information possible on Lievens' diverse production throughout his long career, the examination of a representative sample of forty paintings focused on Lievens' painting practices more than on specific materials. All of the paintings were examined under high magnification (8× minimum) to evaluate the paint handling and layering structure, including preparatory stages such as the painted sketch and underpaint. In many cases x-radiographs and/or infrared reflectograms were available for study of the preparatory stages and changes to the compositions. Cross sections from thirteen paintings were available for microscopic examination; some were made in the course of this study, and others were from earlier examinations. In most cases examination of the paint surface at magnifications up to 50× allowed visual estimations of pigment mixtures for comparison with observations made on paint samples.

I am grateful to the following colleagues for their help in examining these paintings and for sharing their own observations: Rachel Billinge, Mette Bjarnhof, Marion Bolten, Riccardo Buccarella, Edwin Buijssen, Steven Crossot, David DeWitt, Lloyd DeWitt, Taco Dibbits, Troels Filtenborg, Michiel Franken, Silke Gatenbröcker, Jeroen Giltij, Emilie Gordenker, Eric Gordon, Pia Maria Hilsenbeck, Hildegard Kaul, Larry Keith, Peter Klein, Nancy Krieg, Sabrina Meloni, Petria Noble, Eneida Parreira, Eva de la Fuente Pedersen, Viola Pemberton-Pigott, Jacqueline Ridge, Charles Roelofsz, Ashok Roy, Laurent Sozzani, Lidwien Speleers, Marika Spring, Lesley Stevenson, Dominique Suhr, Ken Sutherland, Gwen Tauber, O. Laman Trip, Mark Tucker, Michel van de Laar, Jaap van de Veen, Bob van den Boogert, Esther van Duijn, Anne van Grevenstein, Christiaan Vogelaar, Jørgen Wadum, Arie Wallert, Gregor Weber, and my colleagues at the National Gallery of Art.

2 See Appendix for texts by Huygens and Orlers.

3 Dendrochronology can establish the date at which a tree was felled by comparing the pattern of tree rings in a plank to a master chronology. In this case, the last datable ring of heartwood originated in 1601; all sapwood rings had been removed in processing. Peter Klein, report dated June 16, 2006, in the conservation department files, Philadelphia Museum of Art.

4 In another anomaly, the planks of the Philadelphia panel are oriented across the short dimension of the panel. The panel does not seem to have been cut down at a later time (there are traces of bevels on the four edges), but an unprofessional panel maker might have glued three planks for large panels, then made a smaller panel out of an off-cut. Other paintings with similar panels include cats. 2, 7, 8, 11, and *The Four Elements: Earth, Air, Water, Fire* (see Wheelock figs. 6–7). In some cases the reverse of the panel was not available for study and the evaluation and measurements were made from the front.

5 Van de Wetering 2000, 14–15; 21–22; Wadum 1998b, 165–168; Van Hout 1998, 213, 222 nn. 75, 76.

6 Van de Wetering 2000, 14.

7 These include Wheelock figs. 6, 7, and cats. 7, 11. Paint cross sections or magnified examination of the surfaces shows an upper ground based on a yellowish earth matrix toned with white and black.

8 In this case, the lower ground was irregularly applied and does not extend to the lower edge. In *Allegory of the Five Senses* (cat. 2) the ends of the panel show bare wood with a barbe, or build-up of ground, at the edge of the painted surface, suggesting that the ground was applied while the panel was secured with temporary battens across the end grain (for this structure see Rembrandt's *Artist in His Studio*, Corpus 1982–, 1:A18).

9 Painters in Utrecht in the early 1620s such as Ter Brugghen and Baburen usually worked with far more smoothly blended paint, limiting such emphatic handling to older faces. Lievens extended the handling throughout his paintings.

10 Infrared reflectography (IRR) shows black-containing materials in particular while other colors of paint are transparent to the infrared radiation. IRR of *Pilate Washing His Hands* was performed with a Hamamatsu C 2400-07 equipped with a N2606 IR vidicon, a Nikon Micro-Nikkor 1:2.8/55mm lens, a Heliopan RG 1000 filter, with a Lucius & Baer VM 1710 monitor (625 lines). Digitized documentation is done with a Meteor RCB framegrabber, 768 × 574 pixels, colorvision toolkit (Visualbasic). The IRR assembly reproduced here was made with Adobe Photoshop 9.

11 Van de Wetering 2000, 14–16; Bruyn 1979.

12 Corpus 1982–, 1:A1 (89.5 × 123.6 cm) and A6 (90.1 × 121.3 cm).

13 Peter Klein in Corpus 1982–, 4:655. The same is true for Rembrandt's *Andromeda* (Corpus 1982, 1:A31) and Lievens' *Profile Head of an Old Woman* (Sumowski 1983, no. 1272; Corpus 1982–, 4:656).

14 These paintings include cats. 16, 17, 18, and 30. *Lute Player* (cat. 13) probably should be included in this group, but some features on the reverse could not be evaluated because the panel is obscured by balsa blocks applied in an earlier conservation treatment.

15 Where analyzed, the upper ground has been shown to include white lead and chalk slightly toned with brown earth (ocher or umber) and sometimes black. Where samples were not available, microscopic examination of the surface showed brown and sometimes black particles lightly tinting a white matrix. For Rembrandt's early grounds see Karin Groen's analyses in Corpus 1982–, 4:660–661.

16 For professional preparation of grounds see Van de Wetering 2000, 21–22; Van Hout 1998, 213, 222 nn. 75, 76.

17 Gifford 1985.

18 Slatkes and Franits 2007, nos. A63, A64, A65.

19 The bright pink draperies that appear repeatedly in Lievens' early paintings were probably inspired by Lastman and seem to use his manner of painting. See *Orestes and Pylades Disputing at the Altar*, 1614, and *Christ and the Women of Canaan*, 1617, in Amsterdam 1991, nos. 7, 10.

20 Corpus 1982–, 1:A7. Rembrandt's earliest works included bright pinks even before he studied with Lastman, and this may reflect his contact with Lievens around 1624. See, for example, three paintings that survive from a probable series of the five senses: *The Three Singers (Hearing)*, *The Operation (Touch)*, and *The Spectacles Peddler (Sight)* (Corpus 1982–, 1:B1, B2, B3). Schnakenburg and Van den Boogert convincingly place these works under Lievens' influence before Rembrandt's study with Lastman in 1624–1625; see "The Mystery of the Young Rembrandt," in Kassel/Amsterdam 2001, 100–112 and 150–159.

21 In 1618 Van Goyen returned from his training with Esaias van de Velde in Haarlem. De Heem moved to Leiden from Utrecht in 1625. See Segal 1991, 60. Lievens could have met De Heem earlier in Utrecht; they certainly maintained a relationship in later life, as documents from Antwerp show (see Wheelock essay).

22 Taylor 1998, 171–173.

23 See Schnackenburg in Kassel/Amsterdam 2001, 92–121.

24 Thomas Marshall, "Observat d. Ant... Dykii" (Oxford, Bodleian Library MS Marshall 80) discussed in Kirby 1999, 13; Christensen et al. in Washington 1990a, 45–46.

25 Schneider/Ekkart 1973, 277.

26 De Jager 1990, 76.

27 Esther van Duijn, painting conservator, personal communication, July 20, 2007. Medium analysis has not been carried out, but solubility suggests that Lievens mixed resin into his black paint medium.

28 Raymond White used gas chromatography-mass spectrometry to analyze black paint with drying cracks in the London *Self-Portrait* (cat. 48), identifying heat pre-polymerized drying oil with some evidence of softwood pitch. Dark foliage paint with drying cracks in *Landscape with Tobias and the Angel* (NG 72) was identified as linseed oil that showed evidence of heat pre-polymerization and some pine resin components (analytical reports dated March 18, 1992, and April 4, 1992, on file at the scientific department, National Gallery, London).

29 "In d'aengesmeerde verwen, vernissen und olyen wonderen te zoeken was Jan Lievens dapper t'huis" (Hoogstraten 1678, 238).

30 "Op zijn Rembrands of Lievensz., dat het sap gelyk drek langs het Stuk neêr loope" (De Lairesse 1707, pt. 1, 324; translation in Van de Wetering 2000, 156).

31 I am grateful to Lidwien Speleers for discussions of her findings on the techniques of Lievens' *Five Muses* (Wheelock fig. 22). Full results will appear in a forthcoming book on the conservation and technical study of paintings in the Oranjezaal to be published by the Netherlands Institute for Art History (RKD).

32 The effect is strikingly similar to Van Dyck's portrait of *The Abbé Scaglia Adoring the Virgin and Child*, c. 1634/1635, National Gallery, London (NG 4889). See Roy 1999, 70–73.

33 Paint samples and analytical notes on file, scientific department, National Gallery, London. De Mayerne reported that Van Dyck used the related yellow pigment orpiment (Van de Graaf 1958, 175: no. 73).

34 Strauss and Van der Meulen 1979, 351, no. 18, 19.

35 *Landscape with Peasants* (cat. 37) was transferred from panel to canvas in the past, but the panels for both *Tobias and the Angel* (National Gallery, London) and *River Landscape with Fisherman* (cat. 37, fig. 1) are marked with an Antwerp brand and a six-pointed star, the personal mark of an unidentified panel maker. See Van Damme 1990, 234.

36 *Tobias and the Angel*, as in n. 28 above.

37 *Landscape with a Wagon at Sunset*, Museum Boijmans Van Beuningen, Rotterdam.

38 Dendrochronology findings by Peter Klein cited in Rotterdam 1988, 62.

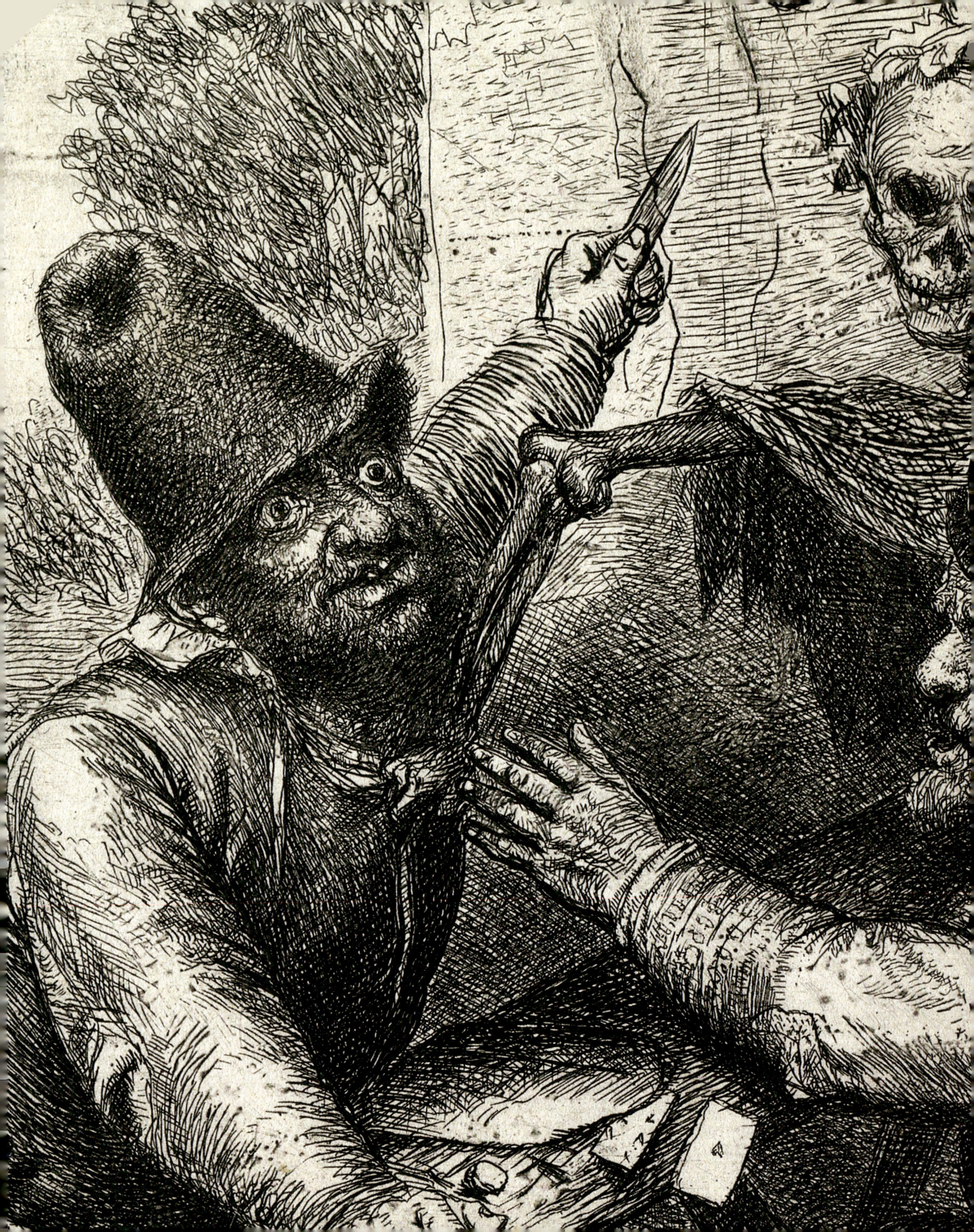

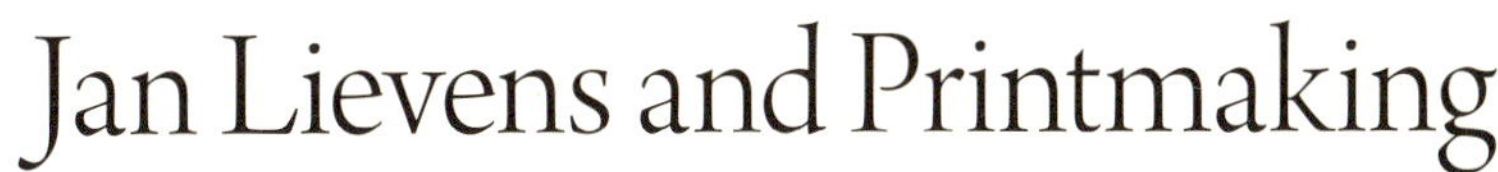

Jan Lievens and Printmaking

STEPHANIE S. DICKEY

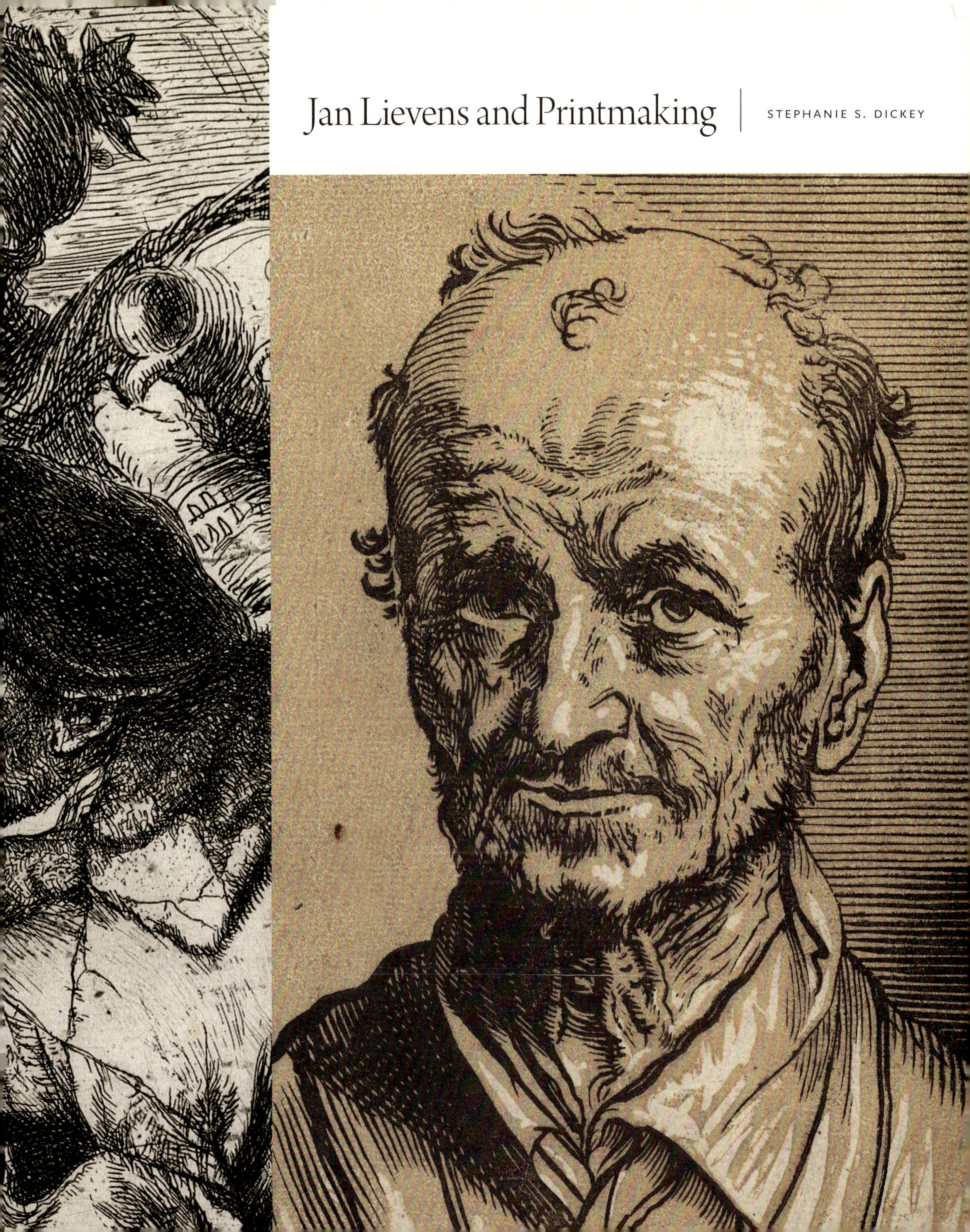

IN 1617 – 1618 THE TOWNS OF the United Provinces were embroiled in a religious and political controversy that threatened to divide neighborhoods, families, and even the fledgling Dutch Republic itself. Yet for one young artist, all of this turmoil paled next to his passionate pursuit of his craft. Jan Lievens, only ten years old in October 1617, ignored the riots in Leiden, according to his neighbor, Jan Orlers, to concentrate on "drawing prints by 'Witty Willem' [Willem Buytewech], for he regarded the love of art as more important than all the upheaval in the world."[1] Despite conventional elements (evidence of precocity and devotion were standard features of artistic biography),[2] this vivid story rings true. It illustrates the significance of prints as a model for artistic training, and for Lievens it marks the beginning of a fascination that would lead to a printmaking career of his own.

Lievens' prints have not been subjected to the same intense scrutiny as those of his Leiden colleague, Rembrandt van Rijn. No scientific study of watermarks or paper types has been undertaken, and the systematic cataloguing of his oeuvre, last attempted in a volume of the Hollstein series published in 1955, needs revision. Between the first catalogue by Gersaint (1751) and the Hollstein volume, the number of prints attributed to Lievens grew from 15 to 108, but several of Hollstein's attributions are problematic.[3] Chronology is difficult to establish, because Lievens did not date his prints. And it still remains to be discovered where, when, and from whom he learned the craft of etching.

Nevertheless, an outline of Lievens' career as a printmaker can be sketched by tracing the evolution of his style in relation to the sources and stimuli he encountered. It is important to consider not only his own production of etchings but also his interactions with other printmakers and publishers. His etched portraits, closely linked with his portrait drawings in black chalk, offer clues to the network of artists and patrons with whom he associated. Especially important after his departure from Leiden in 1632 are his relationships with printmakers in Anthony van Dyck's circle in Antwerp. His personal contacts with fellow artists and connoisseurs played a key role in his development. In printmaking, as in painting, his style evolved in response to the varying contexts in which he worked.

Taking a closer look at Orlers' account of the young Lievens absorbed in his study of prints by Buytewech, it is not surprising that the boy should learn by drawing from prints. For seventeenth-century artists in all media, drawing was an essential skill, acquired both by direct observation of nature and by emulation of the techniques of other masters. For many Dutch painters these lessons initiated a lifelong practice of consulting prints for formal and iconographic inspiration. Some, like Lievens, took up the medium of etching themselves as a creative alternative to painting that could supplement their income while helping to spread awareness of their achievements.

If Orlers, as a promoter of Leiden, had invented his story, we might expect him to put into Lievens' hands the work of that city's most famous printmaker, Lucas van Leyden. That Orlers linked him with Buytewech, active in Rotterdam and Haarlem, thus seems both credible and significant. It suggests that even at a young age Lievens took an interest in innovative, contemporary developments in art, and specifically in etching. Haarlem was known for the sophisticated engravings of Hendrick Goltzius and his followers, but Buytewech became one of the first printmakers to create etchings in a style that could sometimes evoke the graphic spontaneity of drawing (fig. 1).[4] It has been suggested that Lievens adopted from Buytewech the use of stippling (short, choppy flecks or dots) to create passages of delicate shading,[5] but this technique was not especially rare. Equally noteworthy is Lievens' tendency to define contour with long flowing lines, drawn and redrawn into the wax coating on the copperplate, a method comparable to the graphic style of Buytewech and his cohorts, such as Esaias and Jan van de Velde.[6]

Lievens took up printmaking at a time when etching was still a relatively new medium, open to innovation and discovery. His contacts in Leiden and Amsterdam, where he studied with Pieter Lastman, gave him access to many stimulating examples. In Lastman's studio he would have encountered printmaking as an artistic sideline and a commercial practice. Lastman's brother Claes was an accomplished engraver, and several artists in Lastman's circle had tried their hand at etching.[7] At home in Leiden, Lievens could have studied the work of local printmakers such as Bartholomeus Dolendo, with whom Gerrit Dou apprenticed before joining Rembrandt's studio,[8] or Willem van Swanenburg, brother of Rembrandt's first teacher, who had been a talented and prolific engraver.[9] Lievens may also have cooperated with Jan van Vliet, who reproduced several of his paintings.[10] Yet the most significant stimulus — for his early prints no less than his paintings — was his friendly rivalry with Rembrandt. The two artists developed their skills by trial and error, learning as much from each other as from more experienced printmakers, and ignoring the conventions of uniform finish and controlled hatching expected of trained engravers. Rembrandt's learning curve was marked by several failed plates. Lievens, although somewhat less audacious, seems to have progressed more smoothly. Both artists immediately began to treat the copperplate like a sketchpad, composing form and shading with scribbly, suggestive lines. A comparison of one of Lievens' earliest prints, *Mercury Lulls Argus*

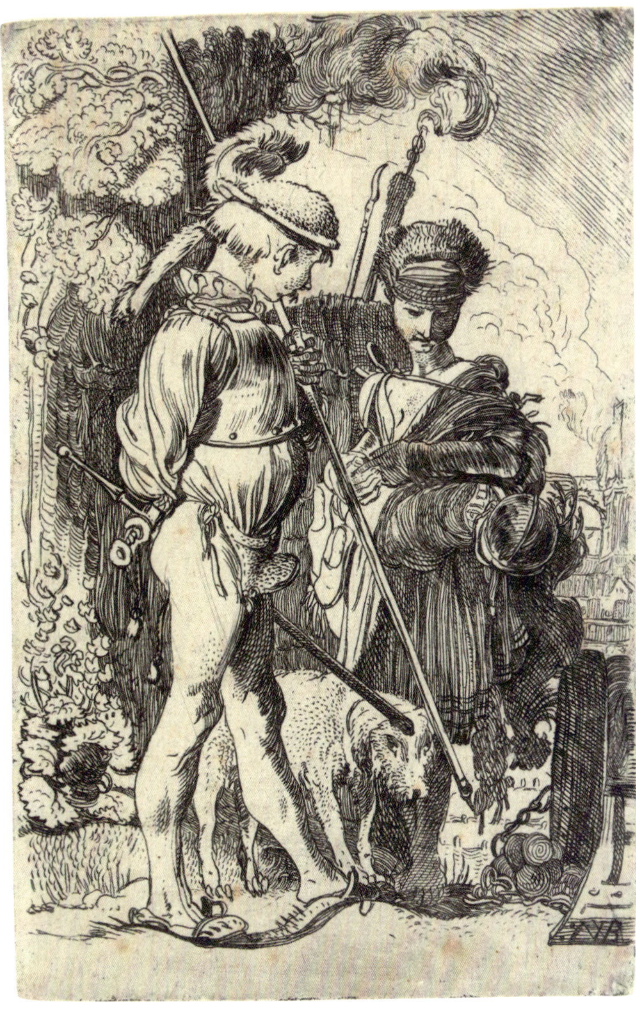

1 | Willem Buytewech, *The Gunner and the Sutler*, c. 1616, etching, published by Claes Jansz Visscher. Rijksmuseum, Amsterdam

to Sleep, with its preparatory study (cats. 58, 89) demonstrates that he sought to etch with the linear freedom of his drawings.

Mercury Lulls Argus to Sleep, *Saint John the Evangelist on Patmos*, and *Jacob Anointing the Stone* (cats. 56–58) form a group of three prints with historical subjects that Lievens probably etched c. 1625–1626. The compositions are simple but well conceived, the poses of the ample figures sedate but expressive. These qualities accord with Lievens' early paintings and are based on lessons he learned in Lastman's studio. *Mercury Lulls Argus to Sleep* and *Jacob Anointing the Stone* are signed "IL fec." in a neat calligraphic style, similar to the monogram that appears on prints and drawings throughout Lievens' career. *Saint John the Evangelist on Patmos* bears no monogram but was inscribed with Lievens' full name and the address of the Haarlem publisher Jan Pietersz Berendrecht. Berendrecht seems to have taken an interest in young artists working in a "modern" style, for he published several prints by Buytewech and one of Rembrandt's earliest etchings, *The Circumcision*. This may explain how Lievens came into contact with him.[11]

It has traditionally been thought that Lievens followed Rembrandt in learning to make prints, but in some respects Lievens took an early lead. When the young Rembrandt attempted to etch plates that are comparable in size and compositional type to Lievens' prints of the mid-1620s, such as *Saint John the Evangelist*, he often ran into trouble. In *Saint Jerome Kneeling: The Large Plate* (fig. 2), Rembrandt seems to have given up after barely sketching the cavernous setting.[12] *Peter Healing the Lame Man* and *Saint Paul at His Desk* fared no better.[13] The extreme rarity of these large plates confirms that Rembrandt did not consider them suitable for marketing. In addition, Lievens learned to create deep shadow with densely layered hatching in *Seated Hermit* and *Saint Jerome Meditating in a Grotto*, c. 1630 (cats. 71, 72), but Rembrandt did not master this effect until his *Annunciation to the Shepherds* of 1634.[14] While Lievens came to excel at depicting one or two figures on a relatively large scale, Rembrandt preferred to compose complex biblical scenes, such as *The Presentation in the Temple* (fig. 3), on plates half the size.[15] Lievens attempted this format at least once, with a nocturnal *Adoration of the Shepherds* (fig. 4), but for the most part, such tiny, intricate narratives were not his strength or interest.[16]

Lievens' dialogue with Rembrandt reached its peak in a sequence of paintings, drawings, and prints that depict the biblical story of Christ raising Lazarus from the dead. *The Raising of Lazarus* (cat. 73) is Lievens' largest and most ambitious etching, based on his own painting of 1631 (cat. 31). Even before the painting was completed (and thus presumably with Lievens' cooperation), it was copied in a print by Jacob Louys and published by

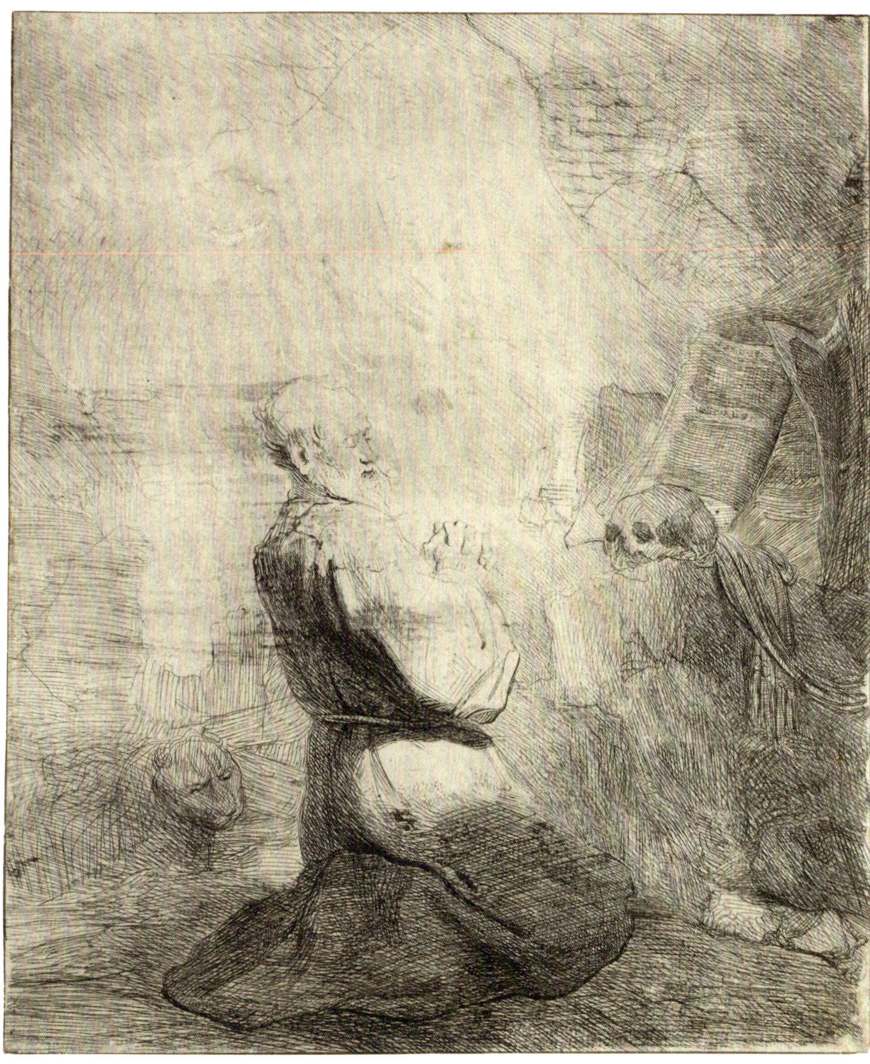

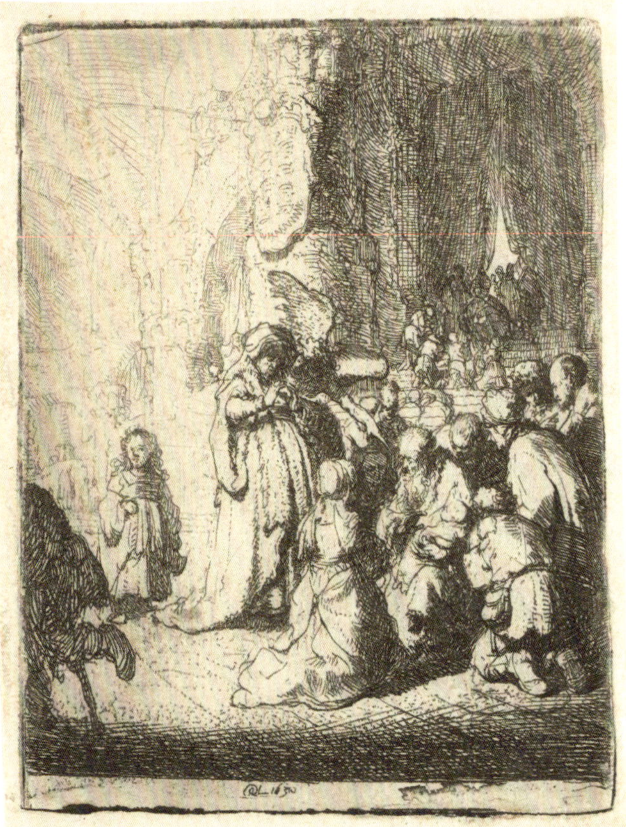

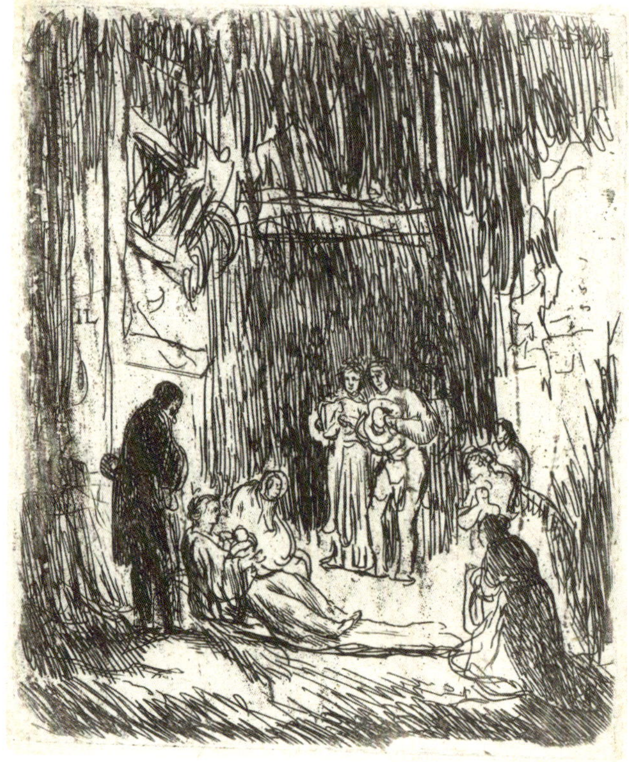

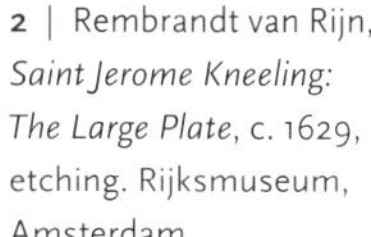

2 | Rembrandt van Rijn, *Saint Jerome Kneeling: The Large Plate*, c. 1629, etching. Rijksmuseum, Amsterdam

3 | Rembrandt van Rijn, *The Presentation in the Temple: The Small Plate*, 1630, etching. Rijksmuseum, Amsterdam

4 | Jan Lievens, *Adoration of the Shepherds*, c. 1630, etching. Rijksmuseum, Amsterdam

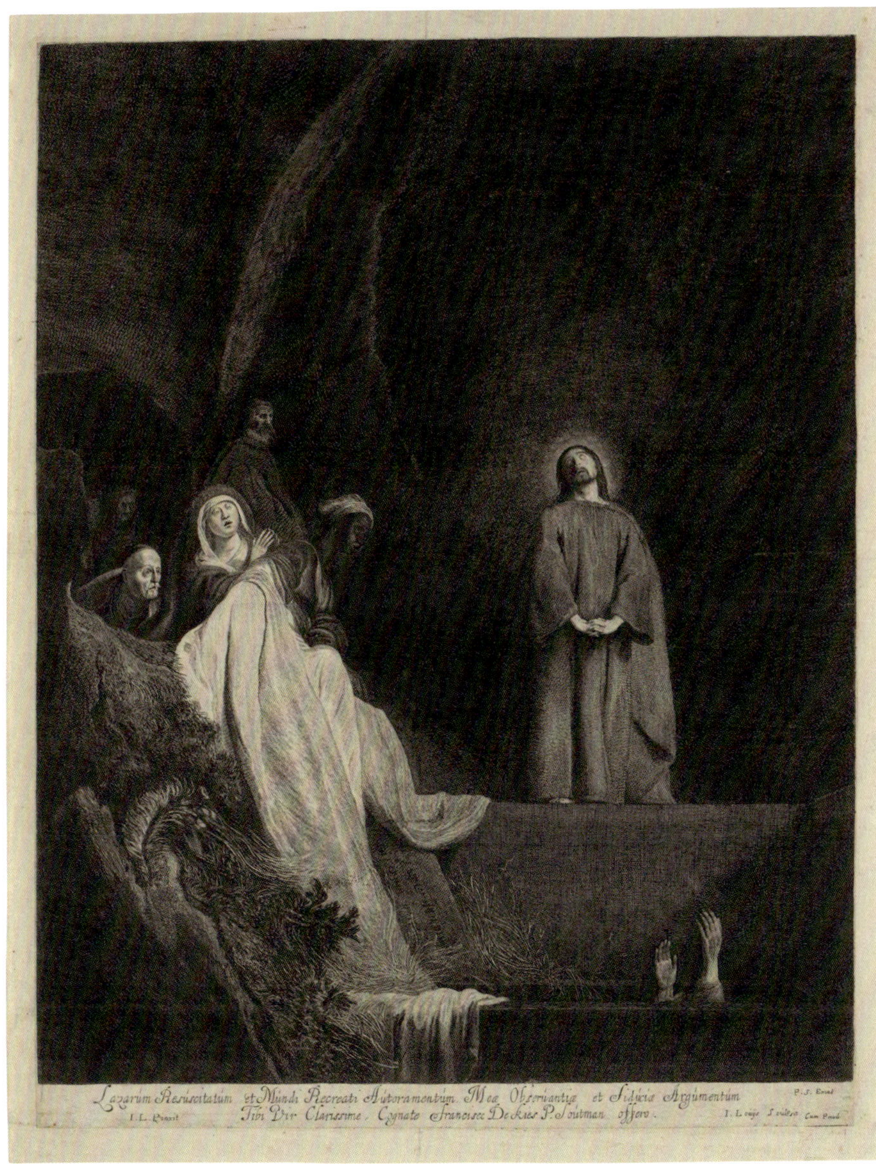

5 | Jacob Louys after Jan Lievens, *The Raising of Lazarus*, c. 1631, etching and engraving. The British Museum, London

Peter Soutman in Haarlem (fig. 5).[17] Soutman had studied with Peter Paul Rubens in Antwerp around 1615 and later traveled to Poland. Back in his native Haarlem by 1628, he was joined by printmakers who had worked with him in Antwerp, including Louys, and he continued to keep in touch with Flemish colleagues and print dealers.[18] Louys' reproductive print therefore helps to document Lievens' contacts with printmaking in Haarlem, while also setting the stage for his move to Antwerp. As an accomplished synthesis of etching and engraving, this print also exemplifies the graphic pictorialism that Lievens and Rembrandt strove to emulate in their nocturnal scenes. Yet in their *Raising of Lazarus* etchings the description of form and radiant light is achieved with greater spontaneity and expressiveness.

Although Lievens continued to paint historical subjects throughout his career, his focus as a printmaker turned increasingly to the single figure or bust, treated either as a formal portrait or as a study of human character and physiognomy. As a pictorial type, the character study, or tronie, began in the Renaissance as a preparatory exercise for history painting, but by the 1620s it had become an independent and highly marketable art form.[19] Rembrandt and Lievens developed a specialty in painting and etching colorful figure types, often in exotic dress. While the young Rembrandt focused his tiny etchings on elderly models and on himself, Lievens' models ranged from lovely young girls to proud cavaliers and wizened old men, captured on plates of different sizes (cats. 60–70).[20] In prints as in paintings, Lievens favored the profile view, often placing the figure in a corner against an expansive background. Some of his characters are vividly down-to-earth, while others are so extravagant in features and dress that they seem conjured from imagination rather than drawn from life. In the large *Bust of an Oriental with a Fur Cap* (fig. 6), the sagging eyelid, glowering brow, and wattled chin add vivacity to the corpulent head, but these details are exaggerated enough to verge on caricature.[21] Turbaned or richly clad, these imaginative character types suggest that Lievens took an interest in earlier physiognomic studies by artists such as Leonardo da Vinci. Lievens' etchings may, in turn, have inspired prints by other artists, such as Giovanni Benedetto Castiglione (fig. 7).[22]

The training in close observation required for such work proved useful not only for history painting but also for portraiture. In the early 1630s both Lievens and Rembrandt began to make portrait etchings.[23] As a means of replicating and distributing a likeness, usually with a laudatory caption, print portraiture was well suited to commemorating individuals of high status or achievement. Artists, along with aristocrats, theologians, and beautiful women, were among the celebrities frequently honored in prints, which could be collected in series or treasured as personal mementos. Most portrait prints were based on existing

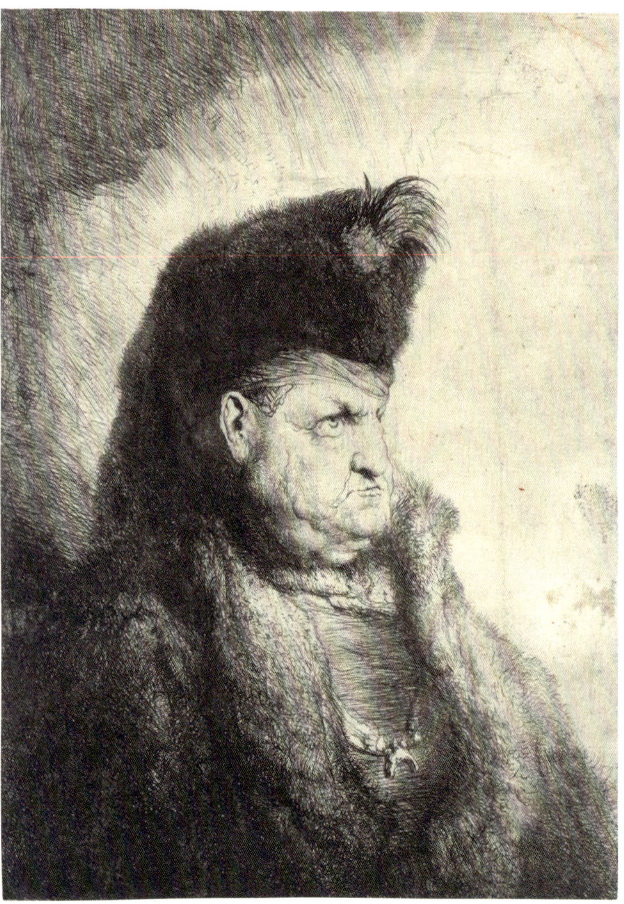

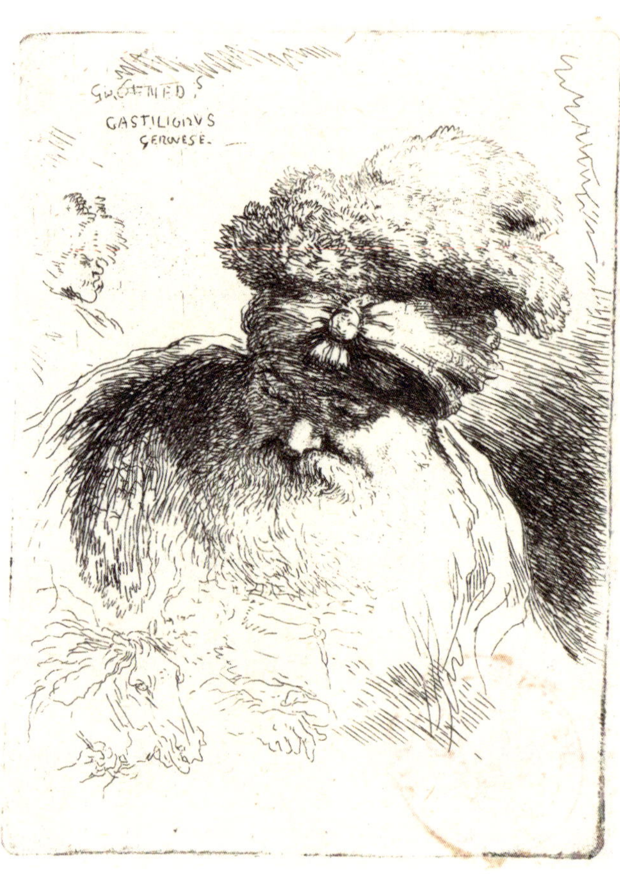

6 | Jan Lievens, *Bust of an Oriental with a Fur Cap*, c. 1630, etching. Rijksmuseum, Amsterdam

7 | Giovanni Benedetto Castiglione, *Man with a Beard and Moustache, Wearing a Tassled Headdress, Facing Left*, from the series Large Oriental Heads, c. 1645–1650, etching. Rijksmuseum, Amsterdam

paintings or on drawings from life, a medium at which Lievens also came to excel. It appears that his interest in graphic portraiture was sparked by an event that had profound consequences for his future career: Van Dyck's arrival in Holland in December 1631.

VAN DYCK, LONDON, AND ANTWERP

In the winter of 1631/1632 Van Dyck spent several months in The Hague, painting portraits and historical scenes at the court of stadtholder Frederik Hendrik. When he arrived, he had just begun work on a series of portrait prints that would be published as the *Iconography*. Compiled between 1630 and 1645, and eventually numbering a hundred plates, this series included likenesses of artists and art lovers, most of them known personally to Van Dyck and portrayed by him from life. Seventeen of the prints were developed from preliminary states etched by Van Dyck himself, but the rest were reproductive prints based on his paintings, oil sketches, or drawings. Several printmakers were involved in the project, primarily Lucas Vorsterman and Paulus Pontius, gifted engravers who had also worked for Rubens. While Van Dyck traveled between The Hague, Antwerp, and London, drawings and corrected proofs were sent back and forth for approval. On January 28, 1632, Constantijn Huygens posed for Van Dyck in The Hague, and on March 11, at the artist's request, he composed a caption for the resulting print, engraved by Pontius in Antwerp.[24]

Among the artists represented in Van Dyck's *Iconography* were a number of Dutchmen, among them Gerrit van Honthorst and Michiel van Mierevelt, who served the stadtholder's court and must have met Van Dyck through Huygens. Remarkably, this list included Jan Lievens, surely one of the youngest artists to earn a place in the series. In the first state of the print Lievens is still the "beardless boy" described by Huygens in his reminiscences of around 1630.[25]

Lievens' encounter with Van Dyck and his *Iconography* would have a lasting impact on his own portrait prints, but it had a more immediate effect as well. Perhaps encouraged by Van Dyck, Lievens departed for London sometime after February 2, 1632.[26] When Van Dyck moved there in the spring of 1632, he continued to work on the *Iconography* with the local assistance of the Dutch printmaker Robert van Voerst.[27] Lievens was soon introduced

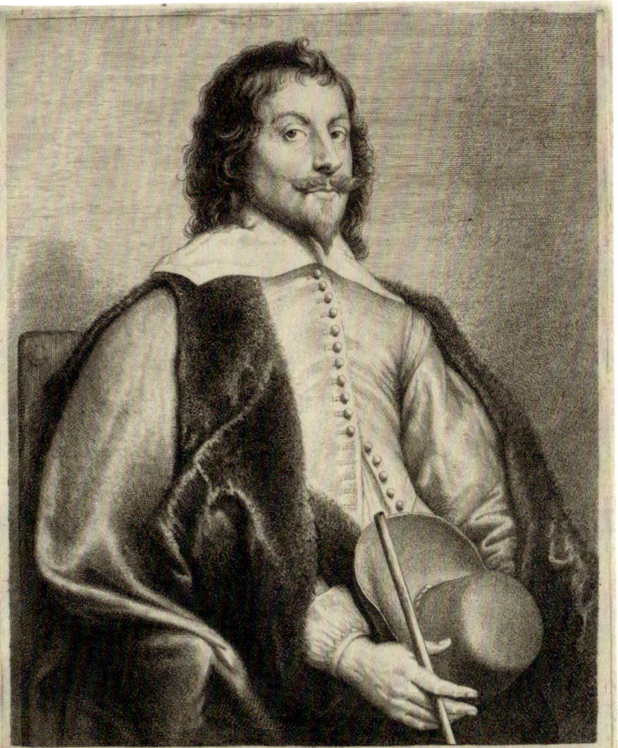

8 | Lucas Vorsterman after Jan Lievens, *Portrait of Nicholas Lanier*, late 1630s, etching and engraving. The British Museum, London

into this network, and the Van Dyckian idiom quickly began to affect his prints as well as his paintings.

When Lievens arrived in London, he was still a beginner compared with Van Dyck and his engravers, yet his expressive etching style would surely have attracted notice. The tronie had not yet taken hold as a collector's item in London, and Lievens may have aimed to create a sensation with his startlingly direct portrayal of an elderly bearded man, possibly the centegenarian Robert South. While the first state is expressively etched, the second state has been worked over with calligraphic engraved lines to add definition and shading (cat. 74). Did Lievens seek the assistance of a professional such as Van Voerst? Or might this be an early indication of his shift toward a more conventional linear style? In his portrait of the lutenist Jacques Gaultier (cat. 75) background details are described using standard methods, such as the moiré pattern produced by close, ruled strokes in the sky, which can only reflect a new attention to the practices of professional printmaking. Lievens most likely learned these techniques by observing Van Dyck and his team at work.

Gaultier was an internationally admired musician with an official appointment to Queen Henrietta Maria, and this was Lievens' first formal portrait print. He published it himself with a friendly dedication to the sitter, perhaps hoping to benefit from advertising his own success at court. Some time after he had painted the portrait of another court musician, Nicholas Lanier, he took the opportunity to publicize the commission by arranging for a reproductive engraving (fig. 8).[28] Appointed "Master of the King's Musick," Lanier was also a painter, engraver, art dealer, and collector.[29] The lost painting testifies to Lievens' participation in the community of artists and entertainers serving Charles I. But the engraving after it marks his place in the print economy of Antwerp, where he established relations with Van Dyck's engravers Vorsterman and Pontius and with the publisher Martinus van den Enden, who was publishing prints from the *Iconography* when Lievens arrived in 1635.[30] Franciscus van den Wijngaerde, a former student of Pontius, published the portrait of Lanier that was engraved by Vorsterman; Van den Wijngaerde's address appears on later states of many prints by Lievens himself.[31]

In this milieu collaborative entrepreneurship became as important to Lievens' printmaking as personal creativity. In 1639 he returned to Antwerp from a sojourn in The Hague with two portraits on paper. One was his black chalk drawing of Huygens, which he engaged Vorsterman to reproduce as an engraving (cat. 103), and the other was his own etching of the Leiden professor Daniel Heinsius (cat. 79).[32] Both prints were published by Van den Enden.[33] Comparison of the portraits of Heinsius and Huygens shows that Lievens profited from observing Vorsterman's coloristic techniques and adapted the dignified presentation of

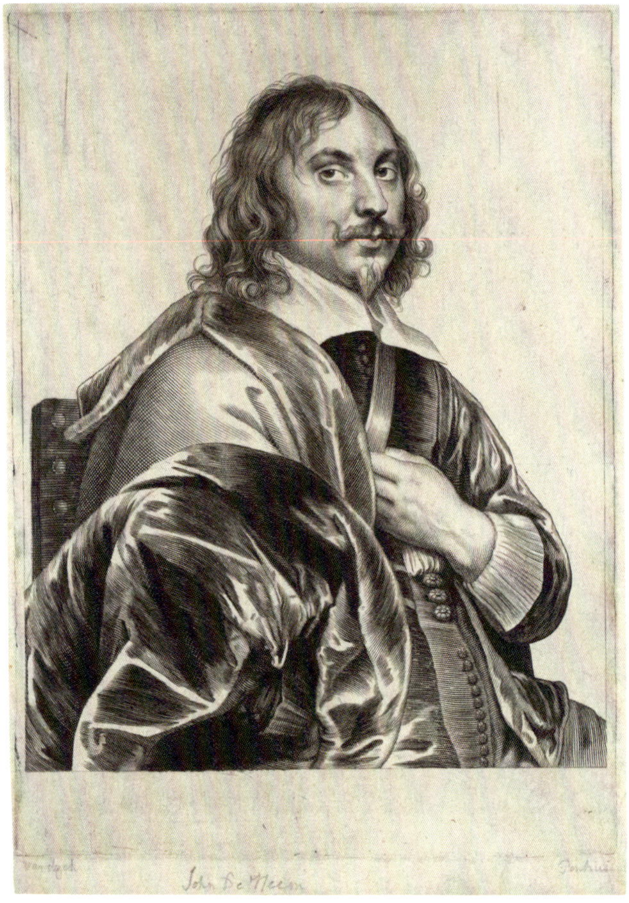

9 | Paulus Pontius after Jan Lievens, *Portrait of Jan Davidsz de Heem*, c. 1635–1640, engraving. The British Museum, London

his distinguished sitters from formats employed for prints in Van Dyck's *Iconography*.

Van den Enden also published several prints by or after Lievens that document the latter's relationships with two intersecting networks of artists: printmakers associated with Van Dyck, and friends of genre painter Adriaen Brouwer. A central figure linking these circles was Pontius, with whom Brouwer lodged in 1634.[34] Lievens painted a portrait of Pontius that was copied in engraving by Pieter de Jode II.[35] He also made portrait drawings of Brouwer (cat. 102) and still-life painter Jan Davidsz de Heem. Both were witnesses to Lievens' contract with a pupil in 1636, and De Heem, who had worked in Leiden in the 1620s, may have been an old acquaintance.[36] Pontius reproduced Lievens' black chalk drawing of De Heem in exactly the same size and format as the prints he was concurrently producing for Van Dyck (fig. 9).[37]

An important document of Lievens' collaborative working method is his portrait of the flower painter Daniel Seghers, which was engraved by Pontius and published by Van den Enden. Lievens' preparatory drawing is preserved (fig. 10), along with a proof of the print that has been corrected in black chalk with gray wash to clarify details of the background, probably by Pontius in consultation with Lievens (fig. 11).[38] The finished print by Pontius follows the revisions closely (fig. 12). Perhaps intended to compete with or even contribute to Van Dyck's *Iconography*, the portraits of De Heem and Seghers exemplify Lievens' engagement with reproductive printmaking.

Lievens' preference for the profile pose is well suited to conveying the sober demeanor of Seghers, who was also a Jesuit priest. Through the circulation of this portrait, Lievens could advance his own status by associating himself with a prominent, successful, and devoutly Catholic colleague.[39] While in Antwerp, Lievens produced one etching with a Catholic devotional theme, *Virgin and Child with a Pear* (cat. 76), and he continued to pursue his fascination with picturesque monastic figures (cat. 77). Lievens published *Virgin and Child with a Pear* himself, but it seems he soon decided that working with established publishers in Antwerp was more effective than competing against them. With *Fighting Cardplayers and Death* (cat. 78), published by Van den Enden, he must have hoped to profit from the trade in reproductive prints of Brouweresque themes.

Living in Antwerp, Lievens found himself in a community where painters like Van Dyck might make a few etchings but mostly supervised the reproduction of their designs by professional engravers. Lievens chose to play this role as well, yet he never completely lost interest in making prints himself. And with the venerable medium of woodcut, he found a new creative outlet.

By the 1630s the art of the woodcut had evolved from a functional, mainstream element of early print production, perfected by sixteenth-century artists such as Albrecht Dürer and Lucas van Leyden, to an aesthetic curiosity. Usually dependent on cooperation between designer and block carver, and limited in its capacity for fine detail, relief printing declined in proportion to the rise of the more expressive and personal medium of etching. Yet around 1600 woodcut experienced a revival in the hands of artists like Goltzius, Esaias van de Velde, and Werner van den Valckert.[40] Lievens may well have studied these antecedents, but he was also directly exposed to Christoffel Jegher's woodcuts reproducing paintings by Rubens, as reflected in his dramatic *Cain Slaying Abel* (cat. 81). His single landscape is more Venetian in its wild, woodsy motif, if not its jagged handling (cat. 80). His other woodcuts are male figures or character heads, crafted with a distinctive variability of line that encompasses broad areas of black, sweeping contours, and detailed physiognomies (cats. 82–84).

This unconventional approach suggests that woodcut, like etching a decade earlier, was a medium that Lievens taught himself. For his vivid tronies, he may have drawn from the Northern tradition of woodcut portraits after Dürer and Lucas Cranach the Elder, and from character heads by artists such as Christoffel van Sichem I and Werner van den Valckert. But his naturalistic profile heads, carved with stark linear economy (fig. 13), also recall wood-

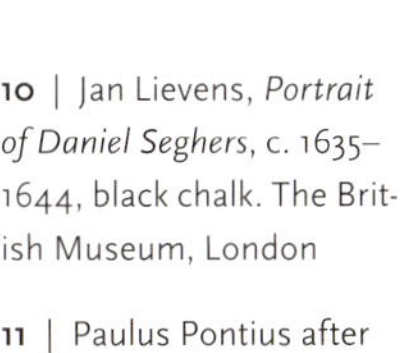

10 | Jan Lievens, *Portrait of Daniel Seghers*, c. 1635–1644, black chalk. The British Museum, London

11 | Paulus Pontius after Jan Lievens, *Portrait of Daniel Seghers*, c. 1635–1644, engraving, state 1 with corrections in black chalk and ink heightened with white. The British Museum, London

12 | Paulus Pontius after Jan Lievens, *Portrait of Daniel Seghers*, c. 1635–1644, engraving, state 2, National Gallery of Art, Washington, Rosenwald Collection

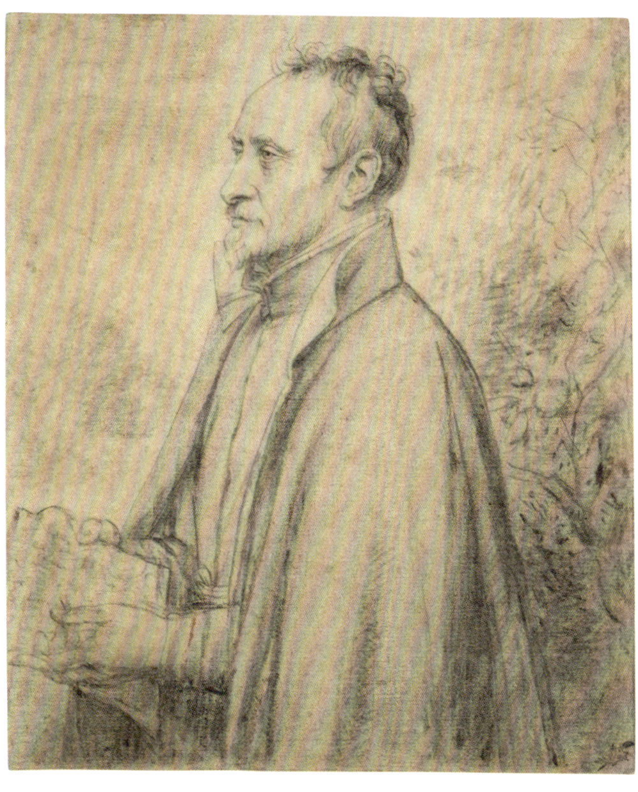

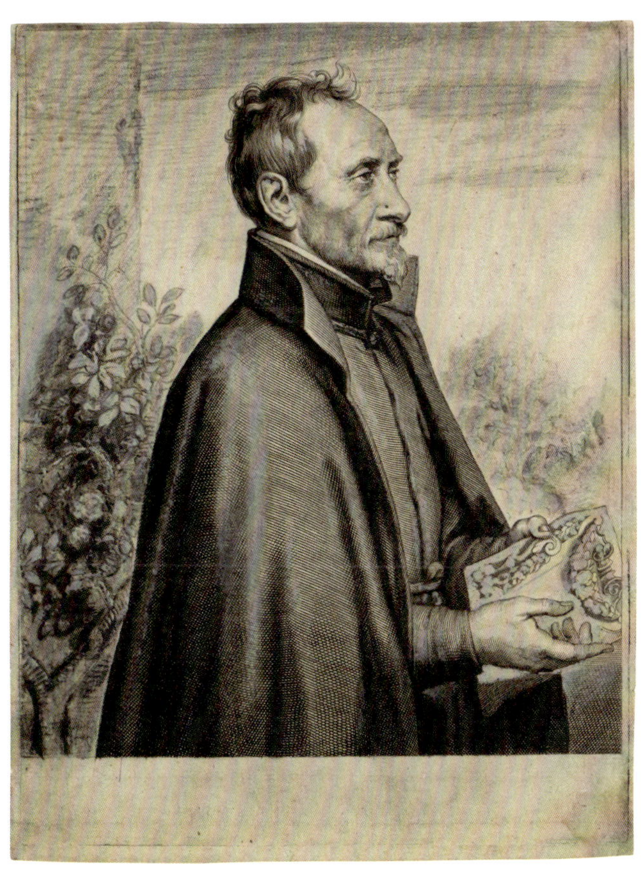

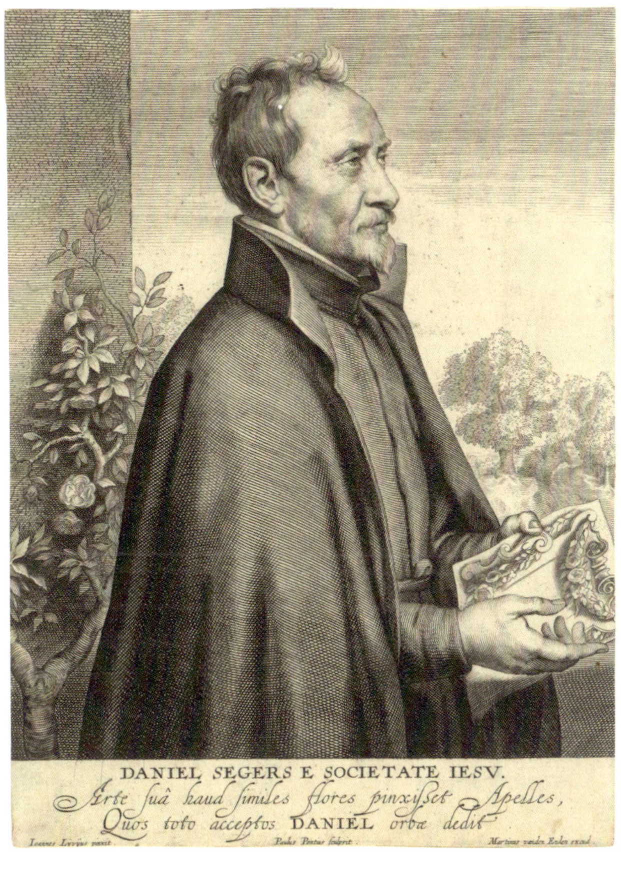

cut portraits by artists in Titian's circle, such as Giuseppe Porta Salviati (fig. 14).[41]

Most of Lievens' woodcuts are extremely rare, suggesting that he did not actively market them. The one commercial success may have been his single chiaroscuro woodcut (printed with one block for line and another for tone), still extant in many impressions (cat. 84). Recorded in Jan Steen's depiction of an artist's studio in the mid-1660s (fig. 15), this lively image must have been appreciated by Lievens' fellow artists. There are further clues that he treated this medium as an opportunity for personal creativity: unlike his etchings, Lievens' woodcuts show no evidence of a publisher's intervention, and his estate inventory of 1674 lists ten woodblocks but no copperplates.[42]

A final feature of importance for Lievens' printmaking activity in Antwerp is the fate of his copperplates. Lievens produced relatively few new plates in London or Antwerp, increasingly preferring to supply designs for prints by others. Yet he must have carried his Leiden copperplates with him, for many were issued at some point by Antwerp publishers. His small tronies were gathered into sets, possibly by Lievens himself and later by his Antwerp publishers (cats. 63–66). The mark of Pieter de Baillù, who also published prints after Rubens and Van Dyck, links a numbered set of seven larger tronies, including the so-called Oriental Heads copied in 1635 by Rembrandt (cats. 67–70). De Baillù was in Rome in the early 1630s and may not have set up as a publisher in Antwerp until 1642.[43]

Some twenty-five prints attributed to Lievens bear the address of the engraver and publisher Franciscus van den Wijngaerde.[44] These include the tronies already published by De Baillù as well as *Jacob Anointing the Stone* and *The Raising of Lazarus* from the artist's Leiden years. In most cases the address of Van den Wijngaerde appears on a third or fourth state of the plate, and often the plate has been reworked with engraving, usually to darken areas of shadow. In some cases, such as *The Raising of Lazarus* (cat. 73), the mechanical reworking may have been added by the publisher to strengthen a plate that was wearing out. Revisions in other prints show enough imagination and sensitivity to suggest that Lievens himself made efforts to freshen the plates before passing them along. For example, in *Bust of an Oriental in a Fur Cap* (see fig. 6), the lush fur cap is transformed into a silk-wrapped turban for the third state published by Van den Wijngaerde.

Van den Wijngaerde registered with the Guild of Saint Luke in 1636–1637 and was established as a printmaker and publisher by the time of his marriage in 1640. Apart from his own designs, many of the plates he published were acquired secondhand.[45] Thus it is not surprising that he took over copperplates from Lievens that were several years old. There is evidence that Lievens

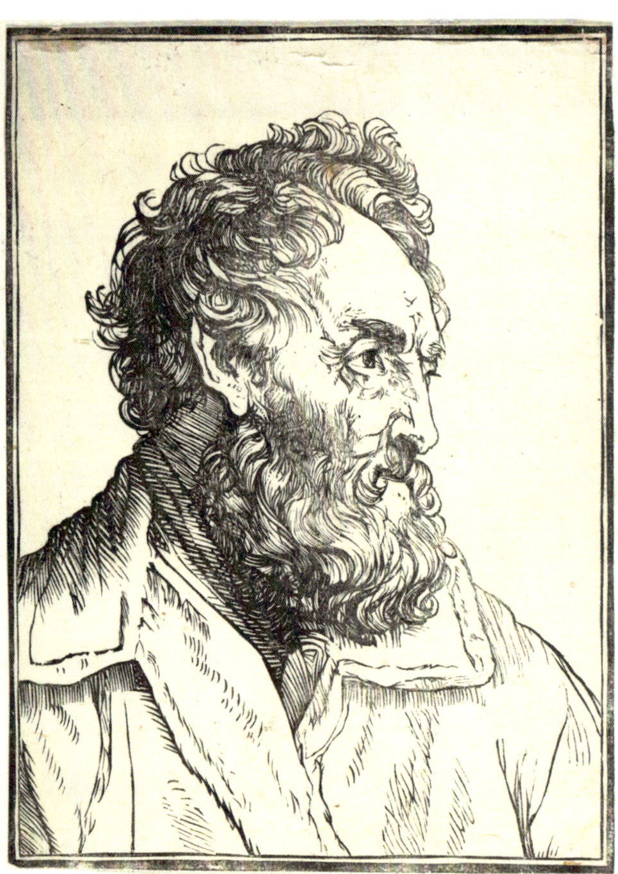

13 | Jan Lievens, *Bust of a Bearded Man, Facing Right*, c. 1640–1644, woodcut. Albertina, Vienna

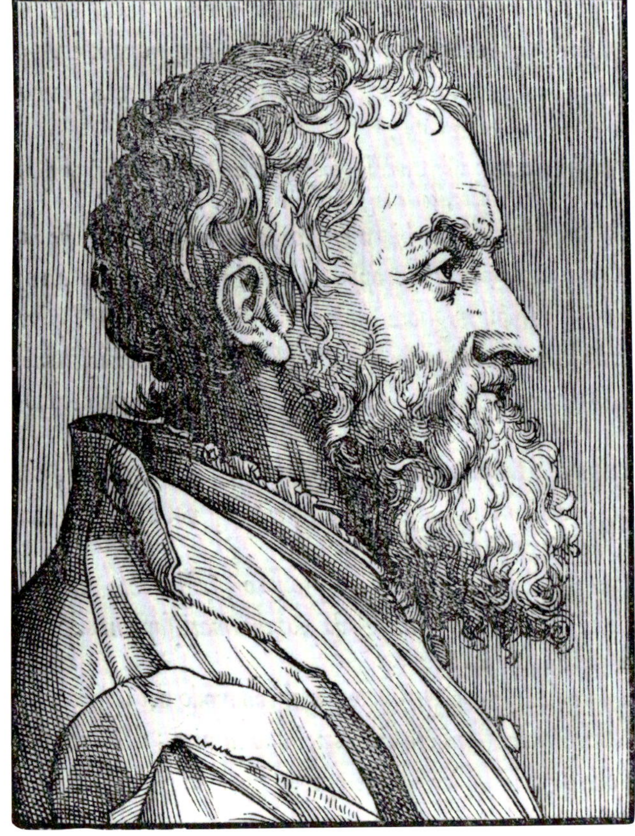

14 | Giuseppe Porta Salviati, *Portrait of Francesco Marcolini*, c. 1552, woodcut. Staatliche Museen zu Berlin, Kupferstichkabinett

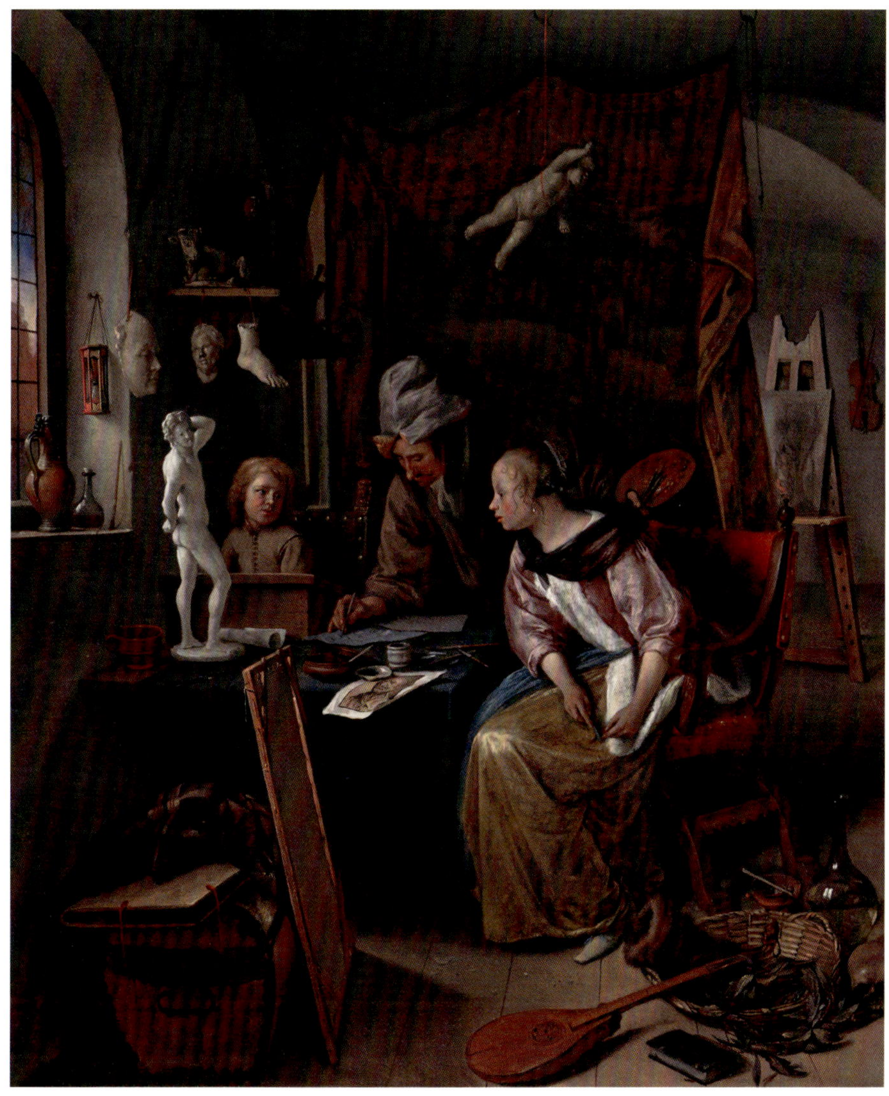

15 | Jan Steen, *The Drawing Lesson*, c. 1662–1664, oil on canvas. The J. Paul Getty Museum, Los Angeles

had begun to suffer from financial difficulties in the 1640s, and he may have transferred his copperplates to De Baillù and Van den Wijngaerde in an attempt to earn additional income. Around 1644, as a testament to an old colleague, he drew a portrait of Vorsterman that was etched by Van den Wijngaerde.[46] When Lievens moved to Amsterdam in 1644, he must have left many of his copperplates behind.

AMSTERDAM

In the last three decades of his life Lievens changed residences in Amsterdam several times and worked for patrons in The Hague, Berlin, and Leiden. He received commissions for several large public history paintings and painted many portraits. These circumstances must have left him little time or capacity for printmaking, and only four etchings can be placed after 1644.[47] He might have printed his woodcuts from blocks that were still in his possession; perhaps this is how an impression of the chiaroscuro *Balding Man* ended up in the painting by Jan Steen (fig. 15). According to Campo Weyerman, Lievens and Steen (who were related by marriage) saw each other almost daily in the 1660s.[48] And with or without Lievens' help, a few of his copperplates found their way to Amsterdam. Several small tronies were acquired and reprinted by the Amsterdam publisher Salomon Savery.[49] Danckert Danckertsz' inventory of 1667 lists a "Monk" by Jan Lievens; and Clement de Jonghe's inventory of 1679 (famous for its inclusion of many Rembrandt copperplates) lists a "Raising of Lazarus" by Lievens.[50] These publishers dealt primarily in secondhand plates. An intriguing potential conduit is Franciscus van den Enden, brother of the Antwerp publisher Martinus van den Enden. He had arrived in Amsterdam in 1648 and had taken lodgings with Leendert van Beyeren, a well-to-do follower of Rembrandt. By 1652 Franciscus was operating a shop, "De Konstwinckel," in the Nes, a street near the Dam Square. In 1670 he sent a maidservant to collect a debt of 90 guilders from Lievens.[51] This document hints at a long acquaintance that helped to maintain Lievens' ties with Flanders.

All of Lievens' etchings from this period are formal portraits, and like his drawings in black chalk, they served to support his ambitions as a painter. Both media were well suited as gifts of friendship, collegiality, or thanks, as Dürer and Goltzius had already recognized, but portrait prints had significant advantages: they could be replicated and distributed among friends or admirers of the sitter and embellished with inscriptions that clarified and reinforced their status as tributes.[52] Rembrandt seems to have understood this advantage, and he produced some of his most brilliant portrait etchings in the 1650s, whereas Lievens produced far more drawings than prints. Portraits in black chalk must have been a specialty for which he became known among the connoisseurs who gathered around Rembrandt's patron Jan Six. A number of men and women in this circle were painted or drawn by Lievens (cats. 45, 112), and his works were celebrated in verses by Joost van den Vondel and Jan Vos, both of whom he also portrayed (cats. 85, 118).

Prolific in composing occasional poetry, Vondel showed a decided preference for the work of Joachim von Sandrart (in Amsterdam from 1637 to 1645), Govaert Flinck, and Jan Lievens. It can be no coincidence that all three adopted a fluent pictorial style that tempered the vivid naturalism of Holland with a new elegance. Lievens' etched portrait of Vondel reflects his mastery of this idiom. Carefully developed with the help of a touched proof, and completed with a flattering inscription, it was issued initially by Lievens himself, some time before 1650, when Vondel published a poem about it (see cat. 85).

Lievens' most formal, imposing, and technically accomplished portrait print is his last. In portraying the prominent Jewish physician Ephraim Bueno, Lievens ended as he had begun, in competition with Rembrandt, who had etched a portrait of the same sitter in 1647. In the shimmering folds of Bueno's costume, we can almost feel Lievens striving to surpass Rembrandt's description of smooth black silk (cat. 87). With a larger format and more dignified presentation of the sitter, Lievens' portrait of Bueno is more conventional than Rembrandt's, but also better suited to the demands of honorific portraiture and more responsive to the Flemish-inspired grandeur that portrait patrons had come to prefer. The Latin inscription on Lievens' print, comparing the sitter with Avenzoar, a legendary Arabian physician from Bueno's native Andalusia, positions the portrait to appeal to an international market of collectors and admirers. More than any other, this remarkable etching offers a glimpse of the suave style that brought Lievens success at the highest levels of Amsterdam patronage.

At the beginning of his career as a printmaker, Jan Lievens embraced the medium of etching with an enthusiasm untempered by professional training or conventional expectations. Once he left Leiden, his goals and ambitions changed. After a few attempts at etching complex narrative scenes, he turned his attention almost exclusively to the human face and figure. While Rembrandt went on to experiment with printing techniques and retained control of his plates, Lievens took a more mainstream approach, embracing the standard methods of professional engraving and working with printmakers and publishers to reproduce his designs, especially portraits. The example of Van Dyck and printmakers working on the *Iconography*, especially Pontius and Vorsterman, played a decisive role in promoting this shift. When his relocation to Amsterdam removed him from the network he had established in Antwerp, he returned to etching only occasionally, retaining the focus on portraiture that had brought him success in the past.

How did Jan Lievens conceive of himself as a printmaker? Numerous accomplished painters were producing original etchings in Holland, and Lievens could have looked forward to a creative double life. Yet in England and Antwerp a distinct division of labor separated painters like Rubens and Van Dyck from the reproductive engravers who served them by translating their pictorial ideas into print. Key to this division was the balance between intellectual creativity and craft. In his quest for recognition as a painter, Lievens grew to value printmaking as a cooperative enterprise that could support his larger ambitions. In this context it is telling that only the blocks for his woodcuts stayed with him to the end. This was an art form that Rembrandt never touched and whose commercial market was limited. Perhaps it offered Lievens a creative outlet that could be uniquely his own.

Notes

I would especially like to thank Clifford Ackley, Anthony D'Elia, Franziska Gottwald, Martin Royalton-Kisch, Steven Nadler, Cecile Teinturier, and Pierre Tuynman for sharing their time and expertise.

1 See the Appendix to the present catalogue.

2 See also Haverkamp-Begemann 1959, 47; Schneider/Ekkart 1973, 14; Vasari 1987, 190–191.

3 Hollstein 1955, vol. 11. Descriptions of changes between states also need to be clarified. Lievens' oeuvre has been described in catalogues of Rembrandt and his pupils by Gersaint 1751; Daulby 1796; Dutuit 1881–1888; and Rovinski 1894. For Lievens as a printmaker, see also Linck 1859; Burchard 1917, 88–96; Köhne 1932, 44–69; Schneider/Ekkart 1973, 77–88; Boston 1981, 113–114; Braunschweig 1988–1989, 198–223; Amsterdam 1988; Schatborn in Leiden 1991, 60–79; Dickey 2001; Dickey 2004, 132–138; Van Straten 2005; De Witt 2006, 128–140, 186–192.

4 Willem Buytewech (1591/1592–1624), *The Gunner and the Sutler* (Holl. 16); Rotterdam and Paris 1974, 94, no. 121, pl. 41; Boston 1981, no. 57.

5 Burchard 1917, 55; Haverkamp-Begemann 1959, 47; Schneider/Ekkart 1973, 85; Ackley in Boston 1981, 113–115.

6 See also Boston 1981, nos. 58 and 59. Lievens must have shared his interest with Rembrandt, several of whose early works show the impact of prints by and after Buytewech. Compare *Tobit and Anna with the Kid Goat*, 1626 (Amsterdam, Corpus I, A 3), with Jan van de Velde print after Buytewech (New Holl., vol. 33, n. 6, Fr.-vd K. 49).

7 See Burchard 1917; Boston 1981, 37–38, 112–113, 126–127, nos. 20 (Jan Pynas), 69, 79 (Claes Moeyaert). For Claes Lastman (c. 1586–1625), see Hollstein, vol. 10.

8 For Dolendo see Ronnie Baer in Washington, London, The Hague 2000, 28; Van Straten 2005, 71, 268.

9 Schneider/Ekkart 1973, 14, suggests that Lievens could have learned directly from Willem van Swanenburg, but this seems impossible, as he was only five when Van Swanenburg died in 1612.

10 Watermark evidence dates Van Vliet's prints after Lievens to the mid-1630s, postdating Lievens' departure from Leiden; see Braunschweig 1979, nos. U2 and U3; Amsterdam 1996, 89–93, nos. 34, 35, but it is possible, as often supposed (see Hinterding in Amsterdam 1996, 24; and Van Straten 2005, 296), that Rembrandt, Lievens, and Van Vliet worked together in the late 1620s.

11 Burchard 1917, 90–92; Amsterdam 1988, 25; Leiden 1991, 60–63. Van Straten 2002 and Van Straten 2005, 36–38, 291–299, attribute *The Circumcision* to Lievens, but this has not supplanted the attribution to Rembrandt in Von Seidlitz 1895, no. 398. On Berendrecht and Haarlem printmaking, see Burchard 1917; Evanston 1993; Wyckoff 1998. For a new interpretation of Lievens' relations with art in Haarlem, see Schnackenburg 2007.

12 Bartsch 106; Van Straten 2005, 80–86.

13 Bartsch 95 and 149.

14 For Rembrandt see Bartsch 44; Amsterdam and London 2000, 129–131, no. 21. In Amsterdam 1988, 39, no. 15, the tonal approach in Lievens' *Seated Hermit* (cat. 71) is attributed to Rembrandt's influence.

15 Bartch 51. See also Rembrandt's *Circumcision* and *Christ Disputing with the Doctors* (Bartsch 48, 66), both c. 1630.

16 Hollstein's attribution of several small prints to Lievens (Holl. 1, 3, 6) is debatable; see Ackley in Boston 1981, 147.

17 Holl. 1; London 1992, 62–63, no. 11; Rotterdam 2006b, no. 39. The dedicatee of the print, "Francisc de Kies," must have been a member of the noble De Kies van Wissen family of Haarlem, possibly the A.F. de Kies van Wissen whose portrait by Soutman hangs in the Musée des Beaux-Arts, Brussels (with thanks to Christopher Atkins for this reference).

18 Antwerp and Amsterdam 1999, 384–385.

19 See Hirschfelder 2000; Gottwald 2007.

20 Later states often bear the signature of the Antwerp publisher Franciscus van den Wijngaerde (1614–1679), but the majority must have been etched in Leiden. Rembrandt's later tronies grew more varied but never achieved the range displayed by Lievens.

21 Holl. 30; Amsterdam 1988, no. 21; Luijten 1989.

22 *The Illustrated Bartsch* 21, no. 51 (33), 17.8 × 14.8 cm. See also Epinal 2003; Rutgers 2004.

23 For Rembrandt, see Amsterdam 1986; Dickey 2004.

24 Antwerp and Amsterdam 1999, 73–75, 84; Dickey 2001, 290–292.

25 Holl. 174 (Vorsterman) illustrates the first state in the Lugt Collection, Paris. The youthfulness of the likeness is evidence that Van Dyck met and drew the portrait of Lievens in Holland, not later, in London. The second state, where Lievens appears older, may have been completed after Lievens moved to Antwerp and met the engraver, Lucas Vorsterman (c. 1595–1675), face to face.

26 Moes 1907, 142–143; Schneider/Ekkart 1973, 3–4.

27 See Antwerp and Amsterdam 1999, 83–84, 386–387. For an overview of printmaking in Stuart Britain, see Corbett and Norton 1964; and Griffiths in London 1998.

28 DeWitt 2006, 133–135. Assuming the painting remained in London, Lievens must have brought a drawing to Antwerp. A study in pen and wash in the Fogg Art Museum, Cambridge, appears to be a careful copy after the painting, but not by Lievens (thanks to William Robinson for consultation on this drawing).

29 Wilson 1994; James 1999; Wood 2003. Van Dyck portrayed Lanier probably in 1628 (Kunsthistorisches Museum, Vienna) (Barnes et al. 2004, 320–321, no. III.92).

30 See Antwerp and Amsterdam 1999, 72–90.

31 See Antwerp and Amsterdam 1999, 370–371 (Van den Enden), 387–389 (Vorsterman), 381–383 (Pontius), 390 (Franciscus van den Wijngaerde).

32 Traced for transfer, the drawing of Huygens served as the direct model for the engraving (Holl. 163). The print faithfully follows the drawing, except that the devotional inscription on the paper held in Huygens' hand is replaced by illegible lines suggesting that he holds a letter addressed to him. The Latin encomium inscribed below the figure was composed by Daniel Heinsius' son, Nicolaes.

33 Both prints were later published by Jan Meyssens, who most likely acquired the plates from Van den Enden. Vorsterman also reproduced Lievens' portrait of Hieronymus de Bran (Holl. 136). Interestingly, this print bears a dedication to De Bran by Vorsterman, not Lievens.

34 Antwerp and Amsterdam 1999, 382.

35 Holl. 17; copied for the biography of Pontius in De Bie 1661, 497; DeWitt 2006, 191. Paul Pontius (1603–1658) also modeled for genre figures by Brouwer. See De Clippel 2003, 14–18.

36 Van den Branden 1883; Schneider/Ekkart 1973, 277. Nothing is known of the pupil, Hans van den Wijngaert, but it is tempting think that he was related to the publisher Franciscus van den Wijngaerde. See also Wheelock fig. 14; Dickey 2001, 298; De Clippel 2003, 4–6, 9, 15–18; DeWitt 2006, 186–193.

37 Drawing in the British Museum, London (inv. 1895.0915.119); print by Pontius (Holl. 85), subsequently published by Van den Wijngaerde. See also Schneider/Ekkart 1973, 44; Dickey 2001, 294–298, fig. 11–12.

38 Holl. 126; London 1977, no. 169. Van Dyck communicated with Pontius and other engravers in a similar manner. See Antwerp and Amsterdam 1999, esp. 19–25. For the impact of this method on Rembrandt and Lievens, see Dickey 2001.

39 Seghers (1590–1661), ordained a Jesuit priest in 1625, was active as a flower painter in Antwerp 1627–1661; see I. Haberland, "Daniel Seghers," *Grove Art Online* (accessed May 8, 2008). For Lievens' Jesuit patronage, see Wheelock essay.

40 For the evolution of the woodcut in the Netherlands, see Van de Waal 1940; Strauss 1973; Lehmann-Haupt 1977; Van Thiel 1978; Boston 1981; Washington 1983; Amsterdam and Cleveland 1992; Washington 2005.

41 Berlin 1970, 24, 58–59, no. 37; see also nos. 14, 38, 39, 40. For the Northern tradition compare Albrecht Dürer (Bartsch 163.154–155), Lucas Cranach (Holl. 132; Silver 2003, 11, 16, 17, and figs. 5, 12, 13), Christoffel van Sichem I, (Holl. 16; Boston 1981, 86, no. 51), and Hendrik Goltzius (Bartsch 239).

42 Bredius 1915–1922, 1:186–189, item 27.

43 Antwerp and Amsterdam 1999, 366, makes this supposition on the basis of financial records.

44 See also Schneider/Ekkart 1973, 5, 44, 81–82.

45 Antwerp and Amsterdam 1999, 390.

46 According to Schneider/Ekkart 1973, no. Z77, it was based on a lost chalk drawing. See also Dickey 2001, 297–299, fig. 14; and Dickey 2004, 140–141, fig. 153.

47 See cats. 85–87 and Holl. 25.

48 Lievens' older brother Joost was married to Jan Steen's aunt. Weyerman 1729, 353; Schneider/Ekkart 1973, 1–2, 60, 267, 278–279; DeWitt 2006, 251.

49 Savery, a Mennonite printmaker, etched prints after Lievens, Rembrandt, and Lievens' younger brother Dirck. His address appears on Holl. 40, 75, 76. Holl. 78 was probably etched by Savery after a painting by Lievens.

50 Rotterdam 2006a, 203, 207. The address of the Danckerts firm does not appear on any of Lievens' plates as described in Hollstein, and Clement de Jonghe's address is on only *Portrait of Ephraim Bueno*, produced in Amsterdam (cat. 87). Within Lievens' lifetime his prints were in collections in Amsterdam (e.g., Rembrandt's inventory of 1656) and as far away as Paris (Pierre Mariette owned prints by Lievens by at least 1666, when he inscribed impressions of both Holl. 42 and 44 [Teylers Museum, Haarlem; and British Museum, London]).

51 Bredius 1915–1922, 1:210; recording a visit by Altie Lucas, serving maid, on July 24, 1670. Franciscus van den Enden had trained as a medical doctor but joined his brother in the print trade; see Antwerp and Amsterdam 1999, 371.

52 Amsterdam 1986; Filedt Kok 1996; Zell 2002; Dickey 2004.

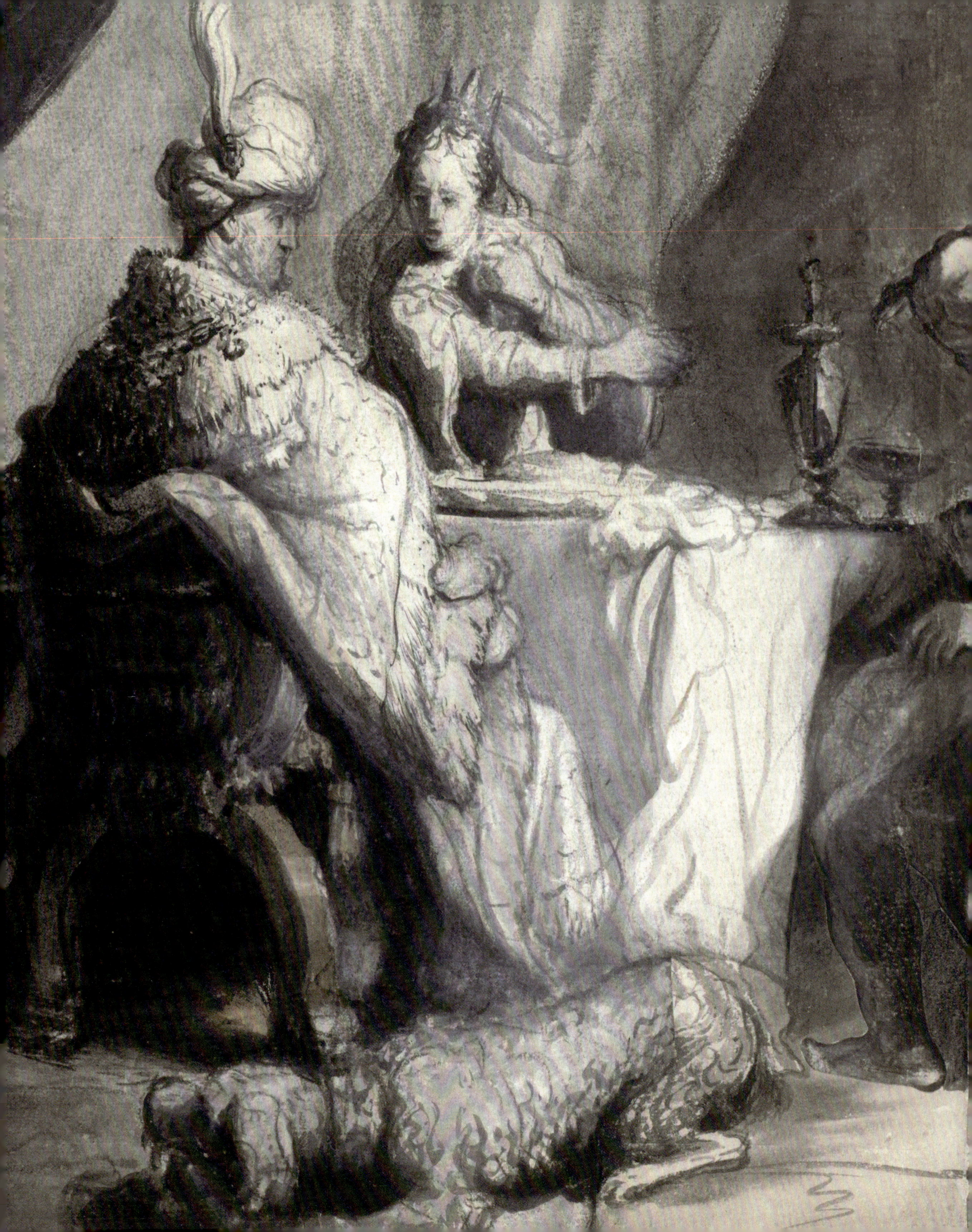

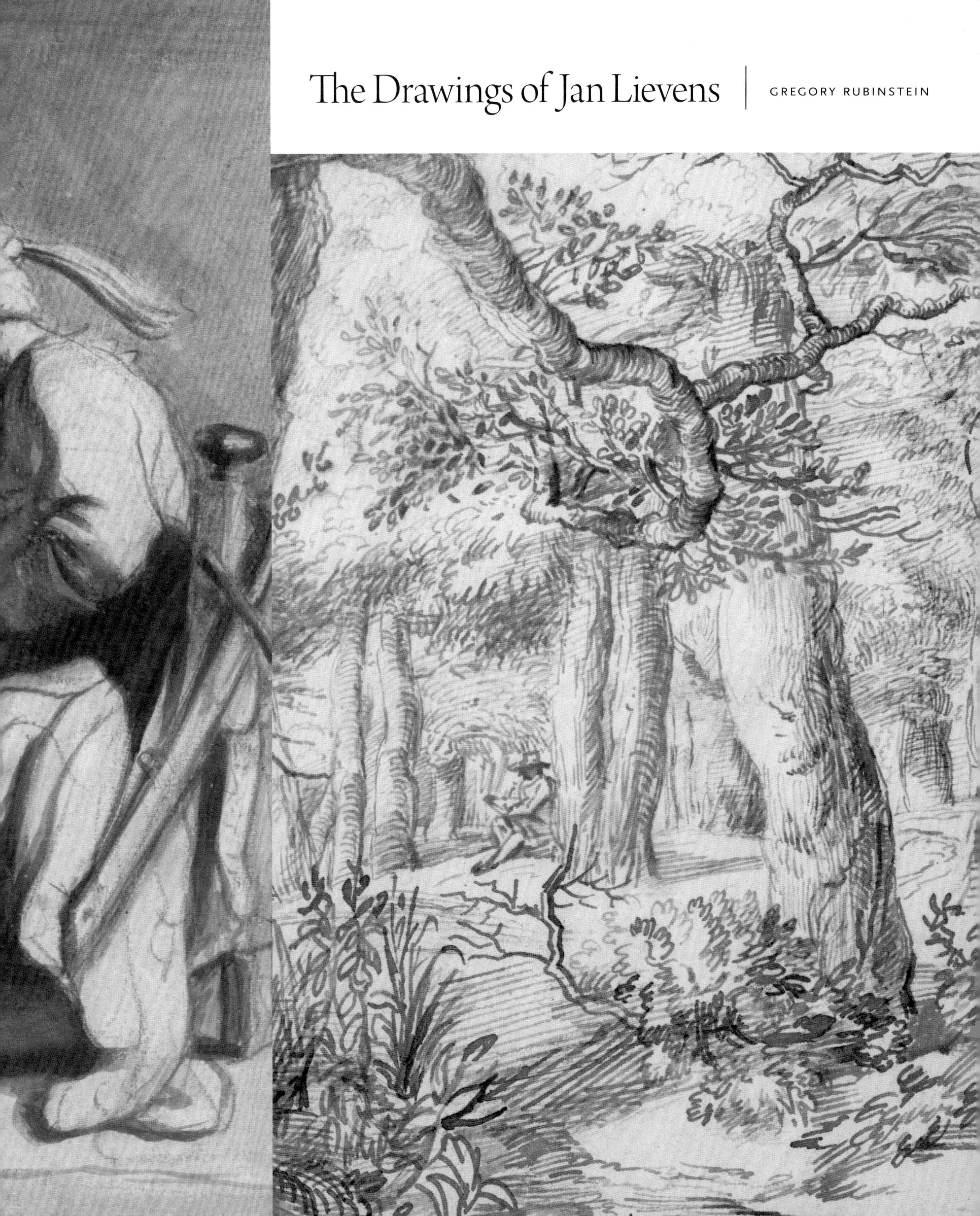
The Drawings of Jan Lievens
GREGORY RUBINSTEIN

JAN LIEVENS WAS A HIGHLY accomplished draftsman, who left a rich and distinctive body of drawings in various media. As in his paintings, Lievens' drawings demonstrate an unusually broad vision, a wide range of interests, and an awareness and keen understanding of several styles, both native and international. His restless travels exposed him to numerous artistic milieus and influences that had a profound effect on his drawing style. And while the works that resulted may not have profoundly changed the direction of seventeenth-century Dutch drawing, they constitute a remarkable record of achievement.

The ephemeral nature of unique works on paper means that we can never be sure how accurately the surviving drawings reflect the style and development of any artist. It is easy for the record to be distorted by the chance destruction of individual sheets, albums, or indeed the entire body of an artist's drawings.[1] In the case of Lievens, we probably have today only a fraction of the drawings that he made. Schneider's 1932 monograph listed 396 drawings, a total that Ekkart increased to 445 in his revised edition of 1973, but many of those entries simply repeated items from early sale catalogues, and barely half of these drawings can now be identified. In earlier times many more unrecorded drawings must also have been lost. Even so, certain categories and patterns can be detected in this partial account. Nearly half of the known drawings (at least eighty-five sheets) are landscapes, while portraits constitute the second largest group. Other works include compositional studies with religious and secular subjects, individual figure studies, and a few sheets with rapid, unconnected sketches in pen and ink.

A small number of Lievens' drawings relate directly to his work in other media — paintings or prints — but for the most part they represent either parallel explorations of similar themes or entirely independent creations. This is one of several factors that make it hard to establish a clear chronology within the artist's drawn oeuvre. Another is that so few of his works in any medium are dated. Only six known drawings are dated — five black chalk portraits (four from 1649–1650, one from 1657), and the 1665 pen drawing *Saint Jerome in a Landscape* (fig. 5) — but that is not so surprising for a seventeenth-century Dutch artist. The more unusual shortage of fixed points among Lievens' prints and paintings, however, poses an additional challenge. Schneider's monograph lists only eleven dated paintings, produced over thirty-five years (1629–1664); and just one of Lievens' more than one hundred prints is dated.[2] Nonetheless, many of the themes and interests that occupied Lievens in his paintings and prints are pursued in his drawings. And with the increasing understanding of the origins and development of his career,[3] it is possible to assign many drawings to at least a broad period, if not to establish the precise moment of their execution.

EARLY WORKS: INSPIRATIONS AND INFLUENCES

The intense scrutiny of Rembrandt's early career as a draftsman has inevitably thrown a spotlight on Lievens' Leiden-period works as well, but the frame of reference almost always centers on Rembrandt, leading to misunderstandings regarding inspiration and chronology that echo those in the paintings literature. The drawings that both artists produced at this time, especially in the second half of the 1620s, are indeed often extremely close in conception and style (see cats. 95, 97, 98), but there are also other crucial elements in the development of Lievens' early drawing style. As we now know, he began training as a draftsman much earlier than Rembrandt. Years before the latter embarked on his own artistic education, Lievens had studied with Joris van Schooten and Pieter Lastman. Moreover, there is also good stylistic evidence that he studied in Utrecht around 1620 within the vibrant artistic environment surrounding the middle-aged but still formidable Abraham Bloemaert. Several of Bloemaert's pupils had recently returned from Rome, full of enthusiasm for the exciting new style of Caravaggio. The powerful Caravaggist works of Gerrit van Honthorst, Hendrick ter Brugghen, and Dirck van Baburen clearly influenced Lievens' early paintings, though a direct link with the early drawings is less obvious. One problem is the lack of comparative material: Bloemaert drew ceaselessly, but hardly a drawing has been convincingly attributed to either Ter Brugghen or Baburen, and only a few to Honthorst. Yet there are definite parallels in compositional and facial type and in approach to lighting between an early Lievens drawing such as *The Stoning of Saint Paul at Lystra* (cat. 88) and the few known studies by Honthorst for his genre paintings and historical decorative schemes.[4]

The influence of Lievens' second teacher, Pieter Lastman, and other "pre-Rembrandtists" such as Claes Cornelisz Moeyaert and Jan Pynas likewise needs to be taken into account. Several characteristic early chalk drawings by Rembrandt and Lievens, such as the latter's *Head of an Old Woman* (cat. 95), reveal a swirling, flamboyant use of line similar to that in Lastman's drawing *Mercury*.[5] This influence is equally apparent in Lievens' unusual and impressive *Sermon of John the Baptist* in Dresden.[6] In his theatrical *Mucius Scaevola and Porsenna* (cat. 90) the rhythmic pen work, facial types, and approach to composition are reminiscent not only of Lastman but also of Moeyaert.

Only after this does the complex artistic dialogue with Rembrandt really begin. For a brief period around 1625, both artists produced works with similar themes and preoccupations, the attribution of which has exercised generations of art historians. One of the most coherent groups of Lievens drawings from this period consists of several relatively large-scale sheets, representing single full-length figures or compositions with a small number of figures. The drawings are boldly executed in pen and brown ink with gray and black ink wash, often over free preliminary sketches in black chalk, occasionally with touches of red chalk in the underdrawing. Despite their larger scale, the figures are sometimes defined with the engraving-like dots and hatching typical of the artist's earliest drawings — though by this time these touches were as likely to be applied with the point of the brush as with the pen. These drawings are characterized by bold compositions and handling and by dramatic lighting, which hint at the works of the Utrecht Caravaggisti. They also closely resemble many of Rembrandt's drawings and paintings of the early to mid-1620s.

The grandest of these drawings is the Dresden *Feast of Esther* (cat. 93), which shares a theme with one of Lievens' most important early paintings (cat. 6). The Dresden drawing and others like it differ from their painted counterparts in one notable way: namely, the scale of the figures within the compositions.[7] In the drawing the figures are depicted full-length, whereas the painting shows them half-length, from a much closer viewpoint, within a composition more reminiscent of the works of the Utrecht Caravaggisti. Other drawings in this group include *Trumpeter on Horseback* and *Christ Praying in the Garden of Gethsemane* (cats. 91, 92) as well as the dramatic *Foot Operation* (fig. 1). This last drawing is particularly Rembrandtesque in both subject and technique, and it shows that Lievens, like Rembrandt, was perfectly willing to make a monumental drawing of a mundane genre subject alongside more elevated religious or historical themes.

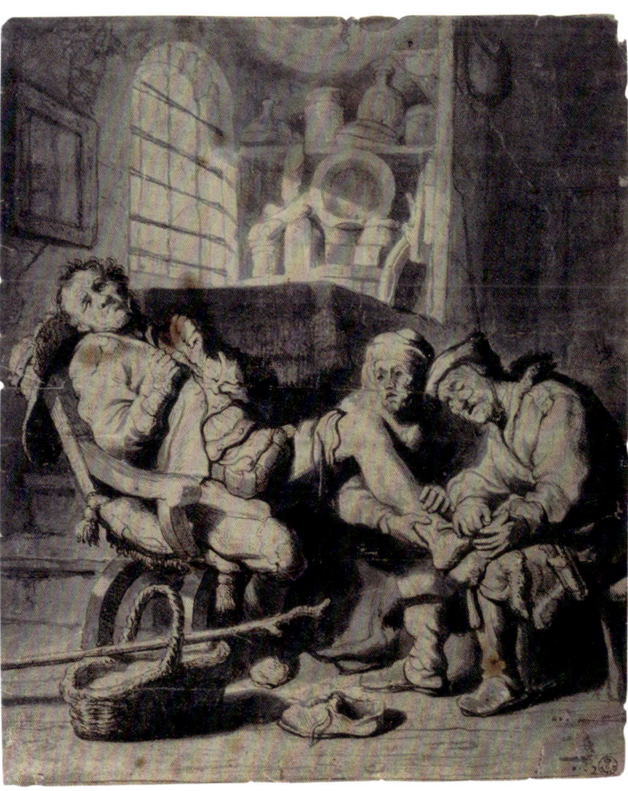

1 | Jan Lievens, *A Foot Operation*, c. 1628, pen and brown ink with gray wash. Galleria degli Uffizi, Florence

Lievens' chalk drawings from the 1620s, usually executed in a combination of red and black chalks but sometimes in just one or the other, relate closely to those Rembrandt was making at this time. These include various character studies of heads and figures, ranging from the immensely accomplished *Moorish Man with Turban in Half-Length* to the rapidly drawn, intimate *Bearded Old Man in Profile* (cats. 97, 98). Also close to Rembrandt in style, though in this case to the latter's drawings of c. 1630–1631, is Lievens' study (cat. 100) for his etching *The Hermit* (see cat. 71).

THE FIRST FOREIGN JOURNEY: LIEVENS IN ENGLAND

Lievens seems to have come into contact with Anthony van Dyck for the first time in the winter of 1631/1632, when the great Flemish master came to The Hague. During the course of this visit Van Dyck made the drawing or painting of the young Dutch prodigy, now lost, on which Lucas Vorsterman based his print for the *Iconography* (see Wheelock fig. 11) — a compendium of portraits, chiefly of illustrious artists of the day, engraved after original works by Van Dyck. Lievens was greatly impressed by what he saw: not only the artistic abilities and achievements of the Flemish master but also his courtly manner and high social position. In early 1632 Lievens realized his long-held ambition of traveling to London. It is not clear if he knew Van Dyck too was about to establish himself there, but whether by accident or design, Lievens' move to London gave him the opportunity to work closely with an artist who could almost be described as his idol.

Lievens remained in London for some three years, yet what he actually did there remains remarkably unclear. Abraham van der Doort's inventory of the collections of Charles I and Jan

Orlers' account of Lievens' life include tantalizing references to a group portrait by the artist representing the king's children,[8] and he is reported to have painted portraits of various members of the royal family, court, and nobility. But surviving works by Lievens from his English period are few. There is a pen-and-ink portrait of Charles I (fig. 2), possibly done from life, as well as record of another lost drawing of the king.[9] A few portrait prints depict personages at the royal court, such as the musician Jacques Gaultier (cat. 75), and the character and costumes of some sitters suggest that the artist may still have been in London when he made his first chalk portrait drawings. In particular, the portraits in Düsseldorf of an unidentified lady and gentleman (fig. 3) have a distinctly English air.[10]

In landscape, too, Lievens seems to have made his first experiments in England. Just as Van Dyck began in England to include topography and landscape in the backgrounds of his portraits, so also did Lievens: he placed the figure of the court lutenist Gaultier in front of a lush wooded landscape in his etched portrait. He drew an important view of Westminster from across the Thames (cat. 101) and another, less compositionally complete sketch now in Hamburg of the cathedral from the other side, the authorship of which is less certain.[11] The Westminster view is the earliest known landscape drawing by Lievens and is therefore the point of origin for the magnificent corpus of drawn landscapes from later in his career. Stylistically, the drawing resembles Van Dyck's pen views of Rye, in particular the example dated August 27, 1633, in the Pierpont Morgan Library, New York, with its precise topography, careful use of regular hatched lines to construct the buildings, and contrasting, more freely drawn hints of foliage in the foreground (see cat. 101, fig. 1). Lievens' later landscape style became more independent of Van Dyck's, but at this stage the parallels are striking.

A few intriguing inscriptions and references raise the possibility that additional topographical landscape drawings from Lievens' English period may once have existed.[12] One enigma is a sketchy, black chalk river landscape in Frankfurt (fig. 4), which, though unlike any other known landscape drawing by Lievens, is inscribed in an early hand, "Jan Lievense de oude… Buyten Londen na 't leven getekent."[13] Recently this old attribution has not been taken seriously, but similarities to the Düsseldorf drawings in the handling of the chalk suggest that this landscape should be restored to the list of possible attributions.

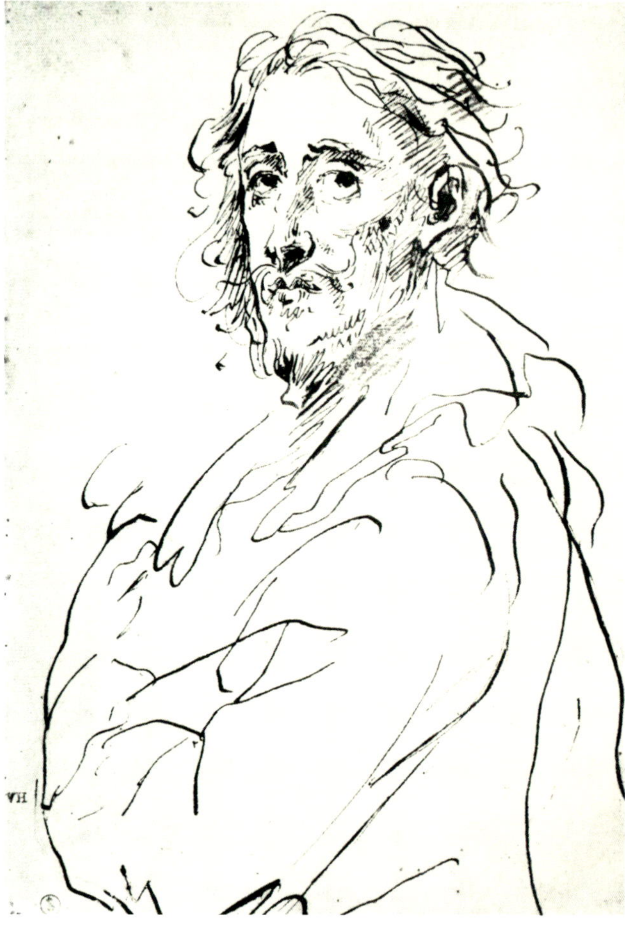

2 | Jan Lievens, *King Charles I of England*, c. 1632–1635, pen and brown ink, white gouache. Biblioteca Reale, Turin

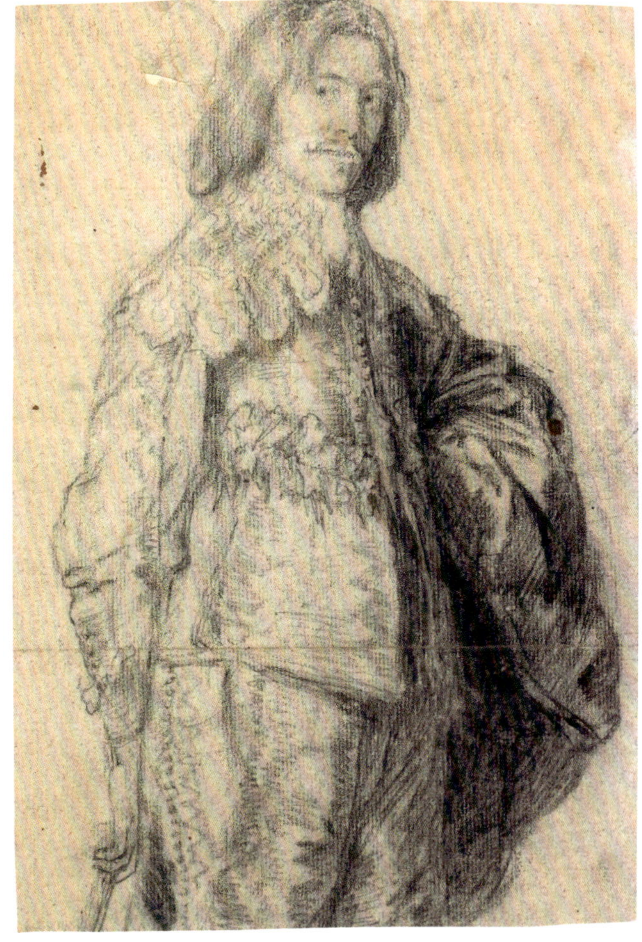

3 | Jan Lievens, *A Young Man Standing in Three-quarter Length, Facing Right*, c. 1632–1635 or 1635–1643, black chalk. Kunstmuseum, Düsseldorf

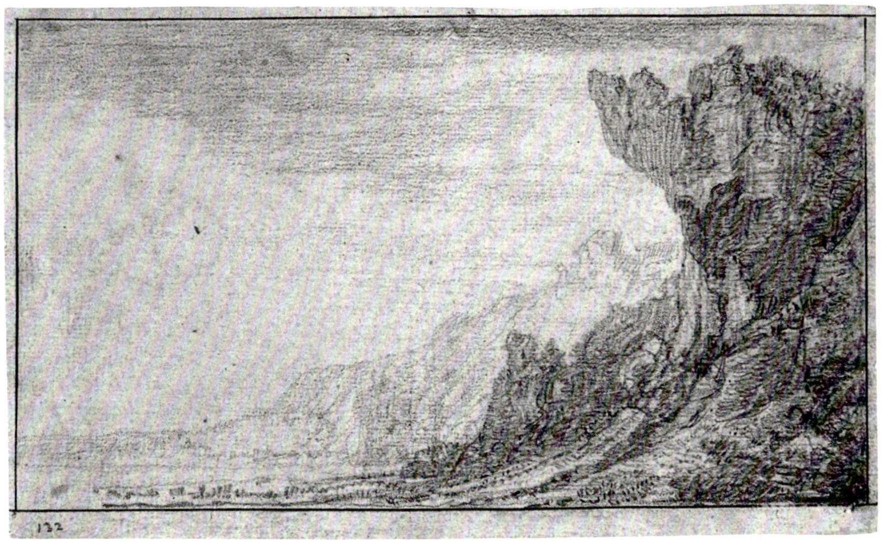

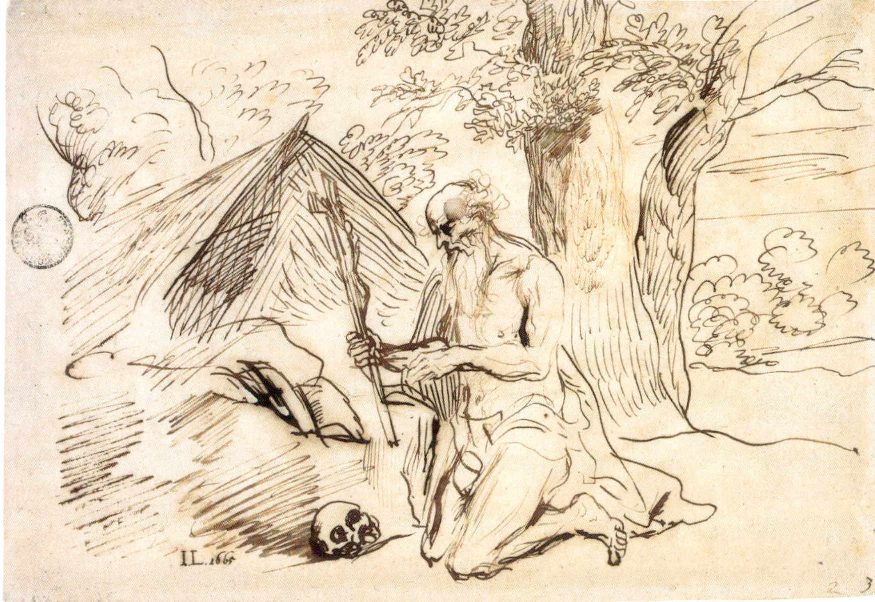

4 | Attributed to Jan Lievens, *River Landscape*, possibly c. 1632–1635, black chalk. Städel Museum, Frankfurt am Main

5 | Jan Lievens, *Saint Jerome in a Landscape*, 1665, pen and brown ink. Kunstmuseum, Düsseldorf

Lievens' artistic output during his time in England remains, however, remarkably thin. Maybe he slaved too hard in Van Dyck's studio to leave time for his own independent work, but even if this were the case, one would expect more than a handful of surviving works and references to show for three years in the life of this active and productive artist.

LANDSCAPE DRAWINGS: ORIGINS AND DEVELOPMENT

Rather than proceeding with a strictly chronological account of Lievens' career, it is instructive at this point to consider his landscape drawings further. Not only do they form a discrete aspect of his work, but once he began working in his mature landscape style, the dating of the drawings becomes more speculative. Only occasionally can meaningful dating parameters be established, as in the *View of Cleves* (cat. 129), which we know from architectural evidence to have been drawn before 1665. And only the Düsseldorf *Saint Jerome in a Landscape* (fig. 5) is dated (1665), but the peripheral nature of the landscape element and the lateness of the date limit its usefulness for comparison.

Following Lievens' move to Antwerp in 1635, his interest in painting landscapes developed for the first time,[14] but this does not seem to have been paralleled in his drawings. One or two drawings, such as the Abrams collection *Forest Landscape with a Pond* (cat. 110), show a continuing influence from Van Dyck and may have been made in Antwerp. Otherwise almost all of his eighty-five or so surviving landscape drawings appear to have been made after his return to Amsterdam in 1644. Given what we know of the renewed contact between Rembrandt and Lievens at this time, it is tempting to associate Lievens' growing interest in landscape drawing with contemporaneous developments in Rembrandt's work: in the mid-1640s, Rembrandt began his walks around Amsterdam, drawing and etching as he went.[15] But just as in the early years in Leiden, it is not possible to establish precisely the direction in which any influence may have flowed between these two strong artistic personalities. In any case, the similarities between Lievens' drawings such as *The Rollerbridge to the Sloterpolder* (cat. 111) and certain contemporary works by Rembrandt are more thematic than stylistic.

One of the most fundamental differences between Rembrandt's and Lievens' landscape drawings is that many of the latter's seem to have been made in the studio, as finished works for sale. Lievens did, of course, also make landscape sketches directly from nature, in accordance with contemporary art theory.[16] Indeed, he often included a self-referential figure of an artist at work in his landscape drawings. Generally, these artists

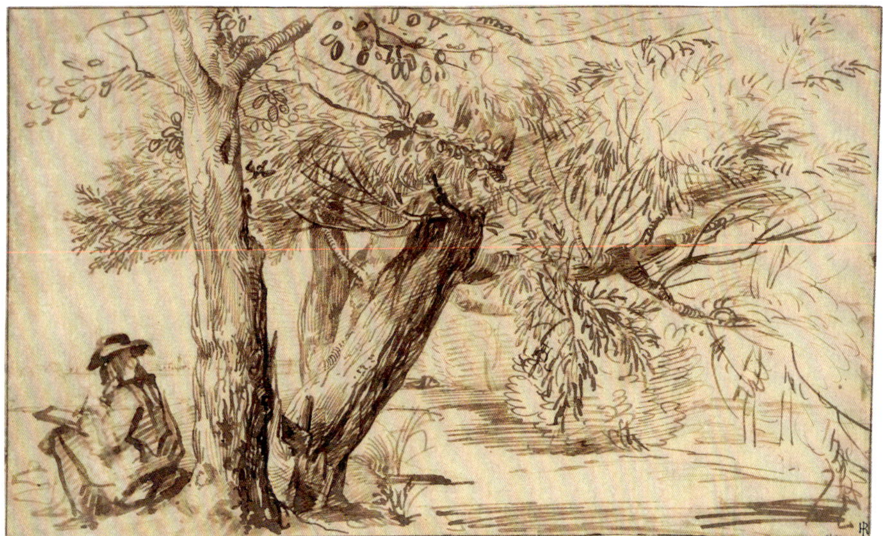

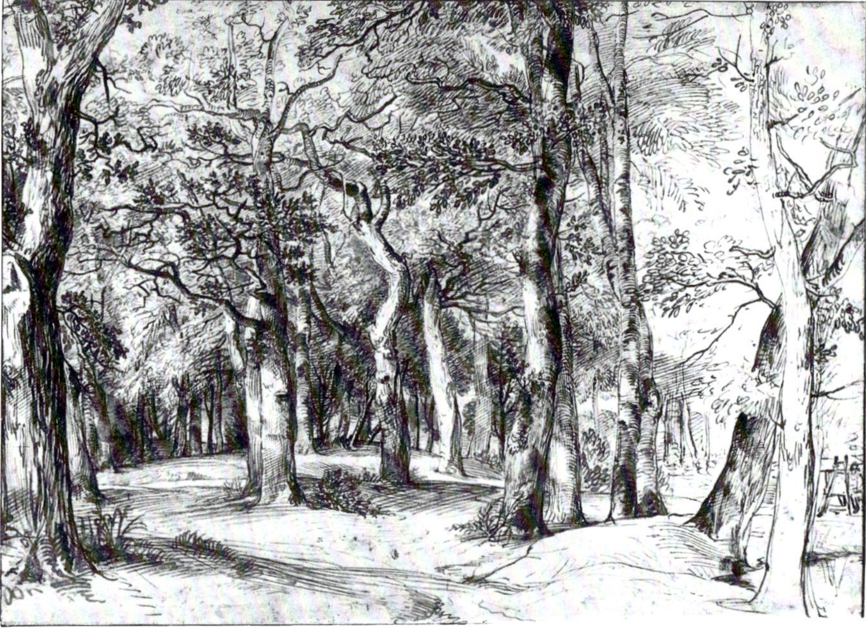

6 | Jan Lievens, *Woodland Scene with a Draftsman*, c. 1664–1665, pen and brown ink on oriental paper. Staatliche Museen zu Berlin, Kupferstichkabinett

7 | Jan Lievens, *Wooded Landscape with a Painter at His Easel*, c. 1655–1665, pen and brown ink with light brown wash on oriental paper. Städel Museum, Frankfurt am Main

are shown sitting on the ground to sketch (fig. 6), but in one exceptional drawing in Frankfurt (fig. 7) the painter has set up his easel in the woods. Our perception of Lievens' oeuvre may, however, be distorted due to selective survival: as Sumowski noted, an entire sketchbook by Lievens recorded in an inventory of 1686 is now unknown.[17]

Nonetheless, in one or two cases we have surviving examples of a small, sketchy drawing made from nature as well as a large, elaborate composition based on it, illustrating the artist's working method: *Farm under Trees* in Dresden (fig. 8) clearly served as the basis for the larger and more developed version of the same composition in New York (fig. 9). Technically, the sketch from nature is rather differently drawn, with strong, rapid pen strokes and deep areas of wash providing chiaroscuro structure. The final drawing is more measured in handling, and the compositional and lighting schemes are carefully constructed with the dense network of hatchings and looping pen strokes so characteristic of Lievens' finished landscapes.

Other drawings, such as the view on the outskirts of Haarlem (cat. 128), fall between the two previously mentioned sheets in terms of spontaneity and degree of finish but would still seem to have been made from life; whether their more developed nature signifies a difference in date, or a difference in time spent on the drawing, remains unclear. Finally, another group of small landscape sketches made from life, and often attributed to Lievens, do seem to originate from his immediate circle but not to be by him (fig. 10).[18] These drawings, characterized by flowing yet repetitive foliage and even pen work, are consistent in style and dimensions and may be sheets from dismembered sketchbooks.[19]

Given the distinctiveness of his landscape style, the long-running and complex debate that has surrounded the attribution of many of Lievens' landscape drawings may at first seem surprising. Only one of the artist's landscapes, *Houses among Trees* in the Abrams collection, is convincingly signed.[20] The same composition does, however, exist in two other versions, in London and New York (see cat. 126), and there are other examples where more than one version of a drawing exists (see cats. 136, 137). In some cases, the two versions are virtually identical, while in others there are minor differences in staffage or details of composition. Although almost all "pairs" of this type are on sheets of similar size, quite a few include one drawing on oriental ("Japan") paper and one on Western paper (see below). Sometimes one is slightly looser in execution and one more precise, but there are no clear and repeated patterns that would indicate which was made first, and whether or not both are by the same hand.

It has long been suggested that some of these drawings are in fact by Lievens' son, Jan Andrea, by whom we have two signed drawings incorporating significant landscape elements, *The Holy Family in a Landscape* (fig. 11) and *Sleeping Venus and Satyr in a Landscape*, both now in the British Museum.[21] Since the early eighteenth century, if not before, the works of the two artists have been confused in sales catalogues. Some drawings by the father have, remarkably, been listed as by the son,[22] while on the other hand the British Museum's *Sleeping Venus,* signed by Jan Andrea, was sold in 1761 and 1766 as the work of his father.[23] More recently, Van Gelder proposed that almost all of the landscapes are actually by Jan Andrea,[24] and similar claims have been made individually for a number of weaker sheets or second versions.[25] In the end, however, there appears to be a seamless continuum of both style and quality running through Lievens' landscape drawings, and there is no clear point at which the work can be separated into different hands. The two drawings by Jan Andrea Lievens in the British Museum are not particularly close in style to any Lievens landscape, which leaves two possible conclusions. One is that Jan Andrea at some point made a number of copies or imitations of his father's landscapes but left no works that bridge the stylistic gap between those drawings and his own. The other — and to me the more plausible — is that virtually all the landscapes under discussion are by Jan Lievens and that, like almost every artist, he made some works that are better than others.

8 | Jan Lievens, *Farm under Trees*, c. 1645–1655, pen and brown ink with brown and gray washes. Kupferstich-Kabinett, Staatliche Kunstsammlungen Dresden

9 | Jan Lievens, *Farm under Trees*, c. 1645–1655, pen and brown ink on oriental paper. The Metropolitan Museum of Art, Rogers Fund, 1961

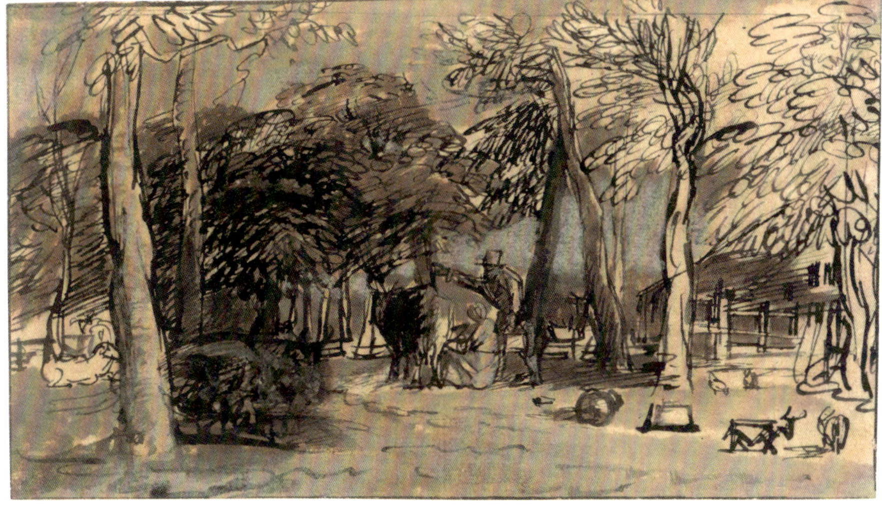

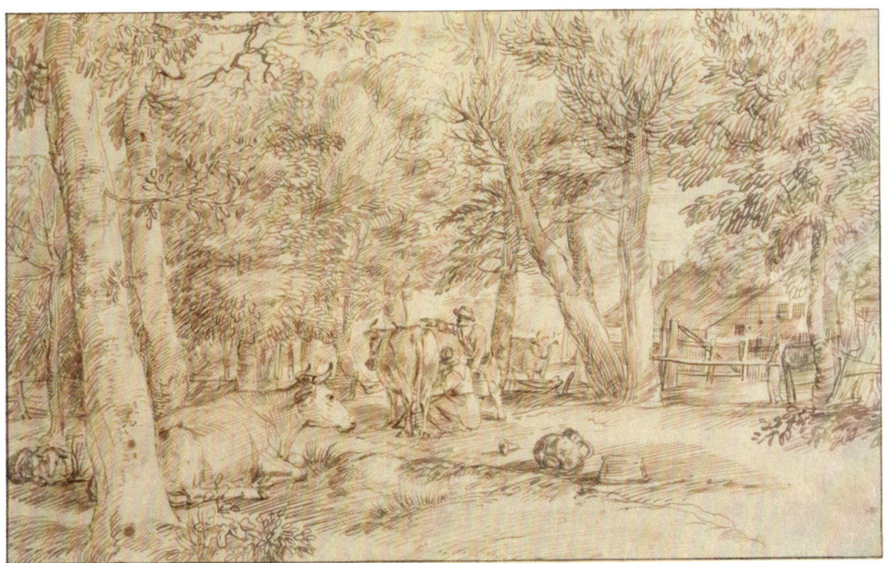

LANDSCAPE DRAWINGS: PAPERS AND DATING

For a significant number of his large, finished landscape drawings, Lievens used oriental rather than Western paper. The fine texture and slight surface sheen of these papers provided an attractive support for his brown ink drawings, similar to the vellum used by artists since medieval times, its absorbent and yet hard surface reacting with the artist's ink in a unique way. Rembrandt used such oriental papers repeatedly, though chiefly for etchings rather than drawings,[26] but he and Lievens were the only two artists of their time to explore the visual possibilities of these exotic papers in any depth.[27] The precise geographical origins of the oriental papers used by Lievens and Rembrandt remain unclear, though for Rembrandt's etchings they are traditionally described, very specifically, as either Chinese or Japanese, depending on their color and texture. There are two documented instances, in 1643 and 1644, when Dutch East India Company ships brought quantities of Japanese papers to Holland from the Dutch trading post near Nagasaki. This trading post was active from 1639, and Chinese papers are known to have been traded at least in the Far East before this date, so Japanese and Chinese papers may have reached the Netherlands before 1643, though probably in very small quantities.[28] In any event, Lievens' and Rembrandt's prints and drawings on oriental paper all seem to date from the mid-1640s or later. Their shared fascination with oriental papers hints, once again, at a renewed artistic contact between Rembrandt and Lievens in Amsterdam in the late 1640s and 1650s.

In principle, the structure of Western papers makes them more easily datable, and further study of those used by Lievens would be helpful in shedding light on the chronology of the drawings.[29] Nevertheless, several relatively coherent thematic and stylistic groupings of landscape drawings can be associated with different periods of his career. The grand, lyrical views of locations in the Haagse Bos (cats. 121, 122) were probably made c. 1654–1657, when Lievens spent significant time in and around The Hague. These drawings are characterized by an elegance and confidence of composition as well as by a refinement of execution that seem appropriate for this phase of the artist's career. In some ways similar are several drawings (see cat. 127) that depict slightly more open woodland scenes and views of farms seen through trees, populated with pastoral figures of milkmaids and piping shepherds. Though different in spirit from the artist's history paintings, the drawings in this group have a distinctly classicizing character, which suggests they should be dated to the later 1640s or early 1650s.

Utterly different in mood are another group of wooded landscapes, extremely densely worked, in which the artist's technique is more mannered and conspicuous (cats. 138, 139). The combinations of hatchings and looping strokes, always present to a varying degree in Lievens' landscapes, here take on a life of their own, to the point where in some drawings the technique itself almost seems to be the subject; in a few sheets the pen strokes reach such a fevered frenzy that the composition nearly falls apart entirely. Occasionally animals or shadowy figures of hunters emerge from the trees in these drawings, but their almost sinister presence could not be more different from the piping shepherds of the previous group. It seems reasonable to consider these late works.

Other evidence that should be considered with respect to Lievens' late landscape drawings includes a letter documenting his journey to Cleves in 1664,[30] which has been cited to support the dating of various drawings that represent locations around the Dutch/German border. Given how frequently and widely Lievens traveled, however, it is hard to imagine this was the only time he visited the lower Rhine towns that had attracted generations of Dutch landscape artists in search of picturesque views.[31] Unfortunately, only a limited amount of watermark analysis has been done on Lievens' drawings. The papers used for *Distant View of Haarlem* and *Forest Interior with a Draftsman* (cats. 130, 132), both in the Abrams collection, have almost exactly the same watermark, which has been dated by Churchill to 1664.[32] Two landscapes in the Lugt Collection (including cat. 136) both have versions of another watermark from the same period.[33] Yet despite all the recent advances in watermark research,[34] often all that can really be established is that a similar watermark is present in the paper of a firmly datable document, which by no means proves that the drawing in question was executed at the same time.

Ultimately, the chronology of Lievens' landscape drawings remains unresolved, but this does not diminish their quality, variety, and inventiveness. Indeed, these were arguably the works in which the artist most convincingly found his own voice and made his most personal contribution. Inspired by Van Dyck, Lievens created landscape drawings that are among the most distinctive and accomplished works of their kind, and they influenced a whole group of draftsmen of the next generation, including Johannes Leupenius, Abraham Rutgers, Jacob de Koninck, and Pieter de With.

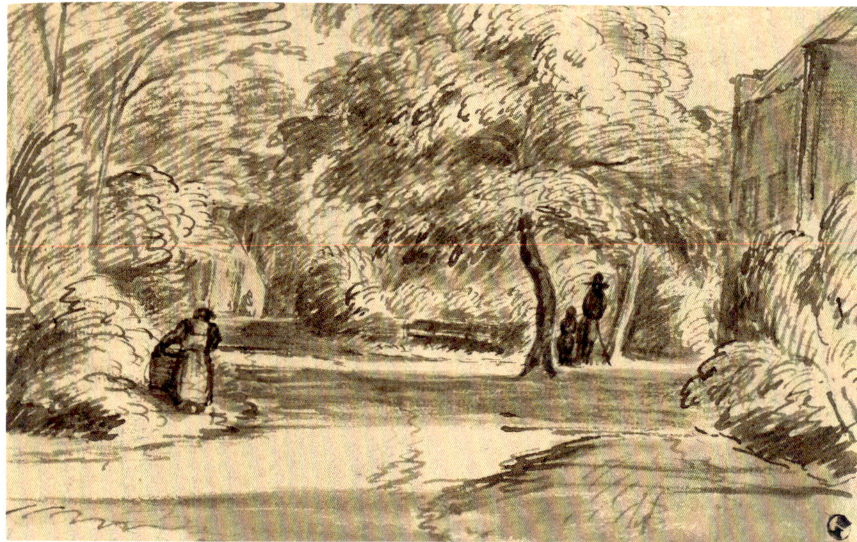

10 | Circle of Jan Lievens, *Road through a Wooded Village*, 1650s or 1660s, pen and brown ink with wash. Staatliche Museen zu Berlin, Kupferstichkabinett

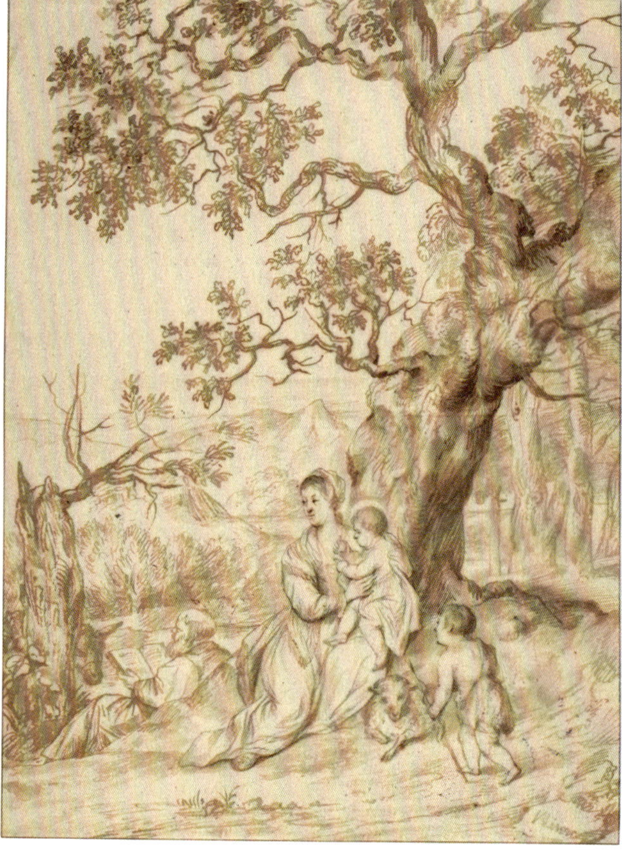

11 | Jan Andrea Lievens, *The Holy Family in a Landscape*, pen and brush in brown with black chalk. The British Museum, London

LIEVENS IN ANTWERP

When Lievens arrived in Antwerp in 1635, he had probably spent three years as a relatively anonymous member of Van Dyck's studio in London. Now he was stepping out into a new world of opportunity as an independent master in a city highly receptive to the styles he had learned and developed in England. Lievens rapidly established himself at the center of Antwerp's artistic life, forging strong relationships within a community of fellow artists that included Adriaen Brouwer, Daniel Seghers, and Jan Davidsz de Heem. Lievens' portrait drawings of his companions are the first clear evidence of his mastery of this type of subject and show him experimenting in a highly original way with media and techniques. The swashbuckling portrait of Brouwer (cat. 102), if a bit theatrical, is thoroughly Van Dyckian, in both pose and

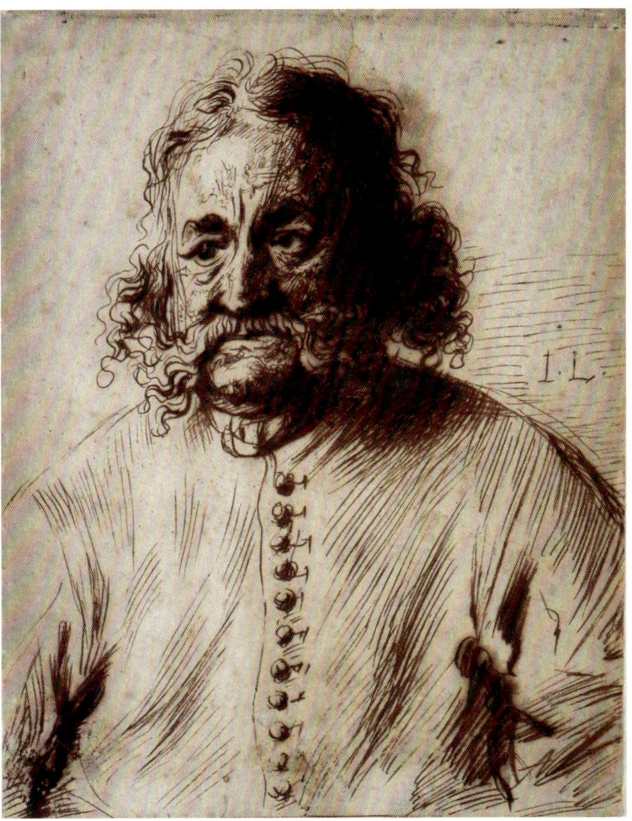

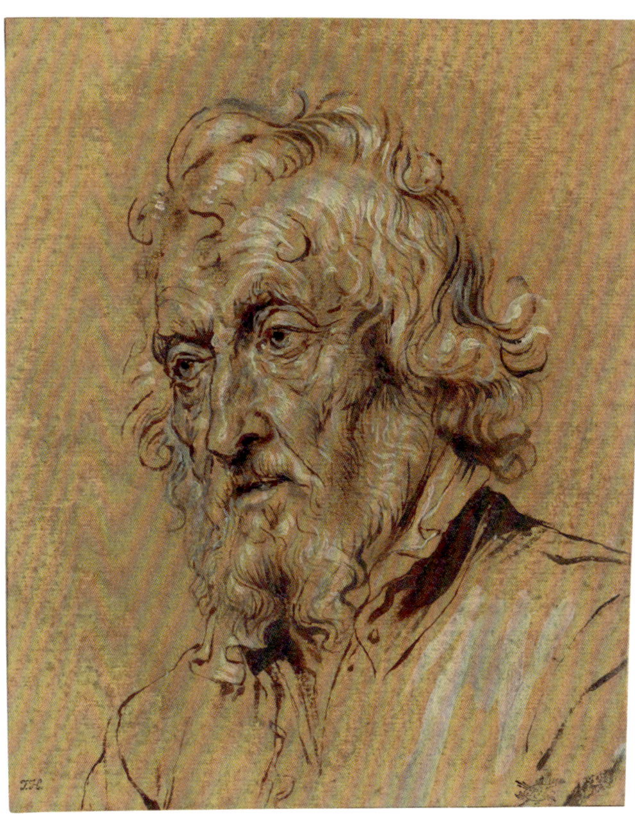

12 | Jan Lievens, *Portrait of a Man*, c. 1635–1643, pen and brown ink. Lugt Collection, Institut Néerlandais, Paris

13 | Jan Lievens, *Study of the Head of an Elderly Bearded Man*, c. 1635–1643, brush drawing with russet, black, and white oil and ink wash on yellow paper, Staatliche Museen zu Berlin, Kupferstichkabinett

technique. The figure is defined entirely with long, dashing chalk strokes of enormous freedom. The portrait of Seghers (see Dickey fig. 10) is drawn in a more varied manner, with chalk strokes of differing lengths and extensive stumping in the background to provide areas of continuous tone. The profile format was also something of a departure from previous portrait conventions and from the traditions of Van Dyck.

Occasionally Lievens drew portraits in pen and ink, as he had when portraying Charles I. The most notable example of this is the striking portrait in the Lugt Collection of a man sometimes identified as Jan Francken van Westerbaan (fig. 12), the servant of Johan van Oldenbarnevelt.[35] Somewhat similar in style is another intriguing drawing that depicts the head of a man in an unusual mixture of oil paint and ink wash on paper (fig. 13).[36] Though apparently unique in the artist's work, this fascinating sheet provides a clear stylistic link between Lievens' pen-and-ink portrait drawings, his more Van Dyckian oil sketches, and the Brouwer-inspired tronies that he painted after his arrival in Antwerp.

This was obviously a time of considerable technical experimentation for Lievens, both in drawings and in his printmaking. Preparatory drawings survive for various prints. *Saint Mark the Evangelist* in Vienna (fig. 14) is the study for one of a series of etchings of the Four Evangelists,[37] and the Rotterdam *Scholar Sitting in His Studio* (cat. 107) is a rare example of a study for a woodcut. Only in Antwerp did Lievens begin exploring this somewhat unfashionable medium, and though this drawing is indented with the stylus for transfer directly to the woodblock, the study is unusually freely executed, suggesting that Lievens himself cut the blocks and not a professional woodcutter.[38]

No drawings can be linked to any of the large historical compositions that Lievens painted in Antwerp or throughout the rest of his career,[39] but this absence is not unusual for a Dutch artist of his time. Rembrandt, for example, made very few direct preparatory drawings for his paintings. Lievens, on the other hand, did paint oil sketches as compositional studies, in the manner of Van Dyck and Rubens (cats. 39, 40), but did not follow their practice in also making detailed preparatory drawings of individual figures. A drawing such as the Washington *Seated River Gods* (cat. 105) demonstrates that he was perfectly capable of making masterful classicizing figure studies. Yet he seems to have done so very rarely and not in conjunction with paintings.

THE PORTRAIT DRAWINGS

It seems that Lievens' stay in Leiden in 1639 brought him into contact once again with Constantijn Huygens, the man who had been so encouraging at the outset of the artist's career. Having painted Huygens' portrait some eleven years earlier, Lievens now made a superb drawing of the great man (cats. 16, 103), in

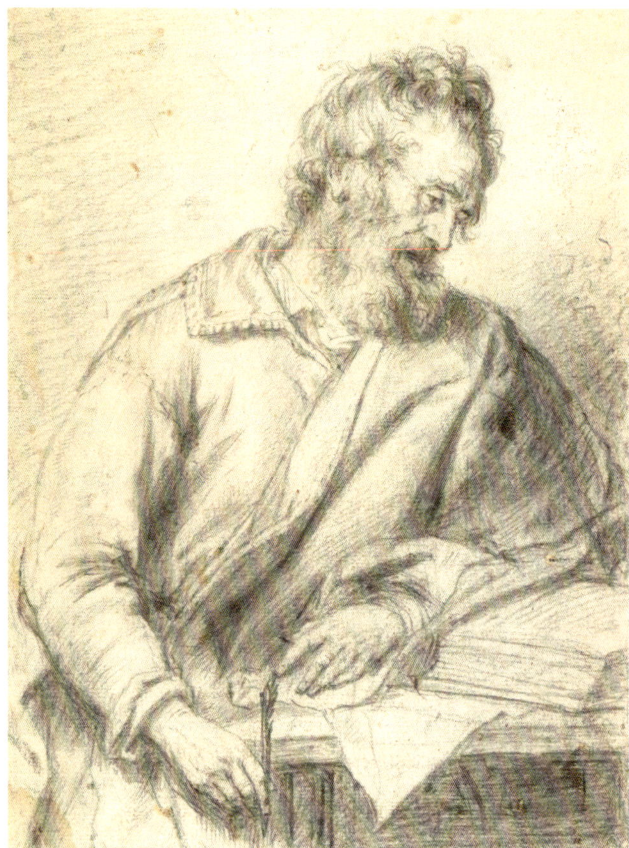

14 | Jan Lievens, *Saint Mark the Evangelist*, c. 1635–1643, black chalk. Albertina, Vienna

a bold and energetic style that falls somewhere between the Brouwer portrait and the Rotterdam *Scholar Sitting in His Studio* (cat. 107). This may be the earliest example of an elaborate portrait drawing by Lievens of an illustrious contemporary, a genre that later became one of the mainstays of his artistic production. The other important Antwerp-period example is the moving portrait of the exiled Earl of Arundel (cat. 109), which compellingly captures a sense of the sitter's troubles. Unusually, the Arundel portrait is drawn in a combination of red and black chalk, whereas almost all of Lievens' other mature portrait drawings are in black chalk alone.

Following his return to Amsterdam in 1644, Lievens drew a remarkable series of black chalk portraits of many of the leading cultural and political figures of his time (cats. 112–118). These were broadly inspired by Van Dyck's *Iconography* but have no other parallels in seventeenth-century Dutch or Flemish art.[40] His identified sitters included the philosopher René Descartes, patrician Johannes Wtenbogaert, theologian Caspar Streso, naval hero Admiral Tromp, and writers Jan Vos and Joost van den Vondel[41] — many of whom belonged to the cultural circle surrounding patrons such as Jan Six and Andries de Graeff (cat. 117). Interestingly, artists are absent from this group: Lievens' only known portraits of fellow artists are from his Antwerp period.[42] Dutch artists did not enjoy the social and political status of a Rubens or a Van Dyck, nor did they generally move in elevated intellectual circles. Perhaps by then Lievens was only willing to draw portraits of those of a certain standing, or those who would pay for his services.

In Lievens' portrait drawings the sitters are usually shown half-length or three-quarter-length, looking out at the viewer with a serious, knowing expression. These prominent personalities clearly appreciated the way that Lievens portrayed them, and the more literary among them, such as Vos and Vondel, composed poems in praise of the artist's powers of observation.[43]

ACHIEVEMENTS AND LEGACY AS A DRAFTSMAN

Though our understanding of the chronology of Lievens' career as a draftsman is limited, the overwhelming majority of his drawings after he moved to Amsterdam were portraits and landscapes — subjects that represent only a small percentage of his painted production in these years. In his maturity Lievens used the different media of painting and drawing for different and in some ways parallel purposes. A large proportion of the later drawings were made as finished works of art, almost certainly for sale. And those that were made for his own benefit were mostly sketches that recorded landscapes, buildings, and occasionally figures that might later be useful as the basis for more finished drawings.

Little in Lievens' drawn oeuvre would suggest that the artist was, in fact, an ambitious, classicizing history painter who contributed to all the major decorative schemes commissioned from Dutch artists of the day. Yet the corpus of drawings that Lievens has left us is at least as distinguished as his painted legacy. His drawing style was extremely varied but always original, powerful, and effective. In his drawings Lievens may have been less inhibited by his great ambitions as a history painter, and as a result he created a body of work that has an honesty of vision, freedom of expression, and quality of excellence that places him among the foremost draftsmen of his time.

Notes

1 A notable example is the marine artist Jan van de Cappelle, whose studio at his death had more than seven hundred drawings of his own, but by whom no securely attributable drawing is known today. The inventory of Van de Cappelle's studio was first published by Bredius in 1892; for an English translation, see Margareta Russell, *Jan van de Cappelle* (Leigh-on-Sea, 1975), 45–57.

2 The portrait *Johannes Chrysostomus van der Sterren* (Holl. 25) is dated 1649. The woodcut *Cain Slaying Abel* (cat. 81), though not actually dated, must have been made before 1654, when it was used as a book illustration.

3 See in particular Leiden 1991; Kassel and Amsterdam 2001–2002; and DeWitt 2006.

4 In chronological order, the most comparable drawings by Honthorst are *Death of Seneca* and *Backgammon Game*, both c. 1622; study for 1627 painting, *Diana on the Hunt*; study for 1628 Hampton Court painting, *Charles I of England and His Wife Henrietta Maria as Apollo and Diana* (Judson and Ekkart 1999, nos. D29, D49, D19, D44, respectively). Where and when Lievens might have seen the last two of these drawings remains unclear.

5 Lugt Collection, Paris; Amsterdam 1991, no. 33; and Kassel and Amsterdam 2001–2002, no. 4.

6 Sumowski 1979, 3632, no. 1632[x].

7 DeWitt 2006, 62–63.

8 See the Appendix and Millar 1960, 146, 161.

9 Sumowski 1979, 3914, no. 55.

10 Sumowski 1979, 3668, 3686, nos. 1645[x] and 1654[x]. DeWitt 2006, 140, refers to the costume research of Emilie Gordenker to support the dating of these portraits to Lievens' English period, but her view (e-mail communication) is that while the costumes in these portraits could well be English, dating from 1632–1635, this cannot be considered definite, as fashions of dress in England and Flanders during most of the 1630s were ultimately French-inspired and similar in many respects. The drawing of a youth and perhaps also the portrait of a young man, also in Düsseldorf (Sumowski 1979, 3670, 3672, nos. 1646[x] and 1647[x]), seem stylistically similar and may even depict members of the same family.

11 Royalton-Kisch 1998, 621, fig. 36, discusses the topographical evidence and proposes that neither drawing was made on the spot and that they were both based on rather later prototypes, drawn some time between the 1640s and the early 1660s. For further discussion, see cat. 101.

12 One of these references appears in Thomas Pennant's 1790 publication, *Of London*, where the text accompanying an engraved view of part of Old Whitehall Palace states that the image was based on a drawing by Lievens; but because that drawing remains unidentified, there is no way to verify the attribution. The print, entitled *The Cabinet of Charles I and Part of Old Whitehall*, faces page 100.

13 Städelsches Kunstinstitut (no. 7150); Schneider/Ekkart 1973, 225, no. Z238.

14 DeWitt 2006, 181, 251, cites thirteen landscape paintings, although many more were listed in seventeenth-century inventories. Of the thirteen, only three seem to have been made after Lievens' move back to Holland in 1644.

15 First described by Frits Lugt in his legendary publication, *Wandelingen met Rembrandt in en om Amsterdam* (Amsterdam, 1915), and memorably revisited in the beautiful exhibition, *Landscapes of Rembrandt, His Favourite Walks*, Gemeentearchief, Amsterdam, and Institut Néerlandais, Paris, 1998–1999.

16 Van Mander 1618, chap. 8, suggests that a landscape painter make drawings from nature, then use these studies as the basis for finished studio works. For an English translation, see Christopher Brown, *Dutch Landscape: The Early Years, Haarlem and Amsterdam 1590–1650* [exh. cat., The National Gallery] (London, 1986), 35–43.

17 Sumowski 1979, 3711.

18 The artist who made these drawings was apparently familiar with Lievens' landscape drawings on oriental papers. Among them: *Farm Buildings among Trees by Water*, Museum Boijmans Van Beuningen, Rotterdam (no. RP-R128); *Road through a Wooded Village* (fig. 10 here); *The Rhine West of Arnhem* and *Boathouse and Church*, both British Museum (nos. 1949.4.11.96 and 1910.2.12.155); and *View on the Rhine by Arnhem*, Lugt Collection, Paris (no. 1016; reproduced Paris and Haarlem 1997–1998, no. 92). The other proposed attributions — Esselens, Leupenius, and Van de Cappelle (as inscribed on both the Lugt Collection and British Museum drawings of Arnhem) — seem no more convincing, so these drawings must for now remain anonymous.

19 Because some but not all of these drawings are on oriental paper, they must come from more than one sketchbook. It would have been highly unusual to use oriental papers for sketching from nature or to bind them into a sketchbook.

20 See London, Paris, and Cambridge, MA, 2002–2003, no. 59. I am grateful to William W. Robinson and the conservation staff of the Fogg Art Museum for reexamining the drawing recently with infrared light of various wavelengths. This examination revealed no observable difference between the ink of the signature and that of the rest of the drawing.

21 Nos. 1836.8.11.343 and 1922.4.10.3; see Schneider/Ekkart 1973, 281–283, pl. 42; and Amsterdam 1988, no. 63.

22 *Wooded Landscape* (Courtauld Insitute, London), though clearly by Jan Lievens, even bears a seventeenth-century collector's attribution on the verso, "Jan Lievensz. de Jonghe"; Schneider/Ekkart 1973, no. Z281; Dennis Farr and William Bradford, *The Northern Landscape* [exh. cat., Courtauld Institute Galleries] (London, 1986), no. 50. I am grateful to Peter Schatborn for directing my attention to this drawing and for clarifying the dating of the inscription.

23 Schneider/Ekkart 1973, 281.

24 Van Gelder 1938, 60 n. 2.

25 For the British Museum version of the signed Abrams collection drawing *Houses among Trees*, identified as being by Jan Andrea, see Arthur M. Hind, *Catalogue of Dutch and Flemish Drawings preserved in the Department of Prints and Drawings in the British Museum*, vol. 1, *Rembrandt and His School* (London, 1915), 83.

26 The notable exceptions are his twenty-three drawn copies of Indian Mughal miniatures, which seem all to be on oriental paper: see Benesch 1954–1957, nos. 1187–1194, 1194A, 1195–1206; and Berlin, Amsterdam, and London 1991–1992, no. 37.

27 A few drawings on oriental paper are known by the Rembrandt pupils Philips Koninck, Anthonie van Borssom, and Pieter de With. Others by Adriaen van de Velde, Dirk Maas, and Cornelis Dusart also exist, but these artists seem to have used this type of paper only occasionally.

28 For Rembrandt's use of oriental papers, see "Rembrandt's Papers," in *A Collection of Etchings by Rembrandt Harmensz. van Rijn (1606–1669), formed by Joseph R. Ritman, presented for sale by Artemis and Sotheby's*, ed. Nancy Bialler et al. (1995), 269–274; and Jacobus van Breda, "Rembrandt Etchings on Oriental Papers: Papers in the Collection of the National Gallery of Victoria," *http://ngv.vic.gov.au/collection/conservation/rembrandt/mainpage.html* [accessed January 3, 2008]; the latter reference was very kindly provided by Bas van Velzen. I am also grateful to Frans Laurentius and Peter Bower for their helpful advice regarding papers.

29 Sumowski 1980, 372.

30 Amsterdam 1988, 82.

31 The view of Arnhem in Berlin (Sumowski 1979, 3852, no. 1731[x]) shows the Eusebiuskerk in 1650/1651, though the drawing may, of course, have been made at a later date, on the basis of an earlier travel sketch (perhaps even one by another artist).

32 Close to Churchill 1967, no. 423 (see London, Paris, and Cambridge, MA, 2002–2003, under nos. 60 and 61).

33 See Sumowski 1979, 3760, no. 1688[x]. Not absolutely identical, both watermarks are similar to Churchill 1967, no. 427, as is that in a signed and dated drawing of 1665 by Jacob Koninck (see Paris and Haarlem 1997–1998, nos. 75, 87, and 88).

34 Spearheaded in the field of Rembrandt studies by the work of Nancy Ash, Shelley Fletcher, Theo Laurentius, and Erik Hinterding; for a summary of the state of research, see Erik Hinterding, "Watermark Research as a Tool for the Study of Rembrandt's Etchings," in Amsterdam and London 2000, 23–35.

35 The other significant drawing of this type is *Bearded Old Man in Half-Length* in Bayonne. See Sumowski 1979, 3554, 3656, nos. 1593, 1640[x].

36 Though this study was previously considered to be by Lievens, Sumowski 1979, 6: 3414, no. 1532, reattributed it to Salomon Koninck, on the grounds of comparison with an etching that had been given to that artist. More recently, Holm Bevers has (in my view correctly) restored the drawing to Lievens. I am most grateful to him for bringing this important drawing to my attention.

37 Some believe the etchings to be by Lievens, others by Laurent de la Hyre after Lievens' designs. See Sumowski 1979, 3692, no. 1657[x]. The drawing does not seem to be indented for transfer. Though in reverse to the print, it does not correspond precisely in terms of composition.

38 Clifford S. Ackley has also noted that, while it would have been extremely unusual for an artist such as Lievens to cut the blocks after his designs himself, the freedom and originality of the woodcutting technique suggests that he may have done so (see Boston 1981, 142, 190).

39 In fact, the only drawing that can be directly linked to any of the artist's paintings is a Leiden period profile study of a man with a moustache in the Albertina (Sumowski 1979, 3550, no. 1591), which seems to have served as the basis for a painting once also in Vienna (in the Johann Hahn Collection in 1921; Schneider/Ekkart 1973, no. 184).

40 The nearest stylistic parallels are the works of Cornelis Visscher, who also made a specialty of portrait drawings. Visscher, however, does not seem to have had access to the elevated circles that provided Lievens with most of his subjects.

41 For the etched portrait of Vondel and Streso, see cats. 85, 86.

42 One drawing (Sumowski 1979, 3902, no. 1756[xx]) has sometimes been described as a portrait by Lievens of Rembrandt, but neither the attribution nor the identification of the sitter is totally convincing. The subject of the so-called Lievens self-portrait in Vienna (Sumowski 1979, 3598, no. 1615) also remains uncertain.

43 DeWitt 2006, 220, 245, 250; Amsterdam 1988, 70.

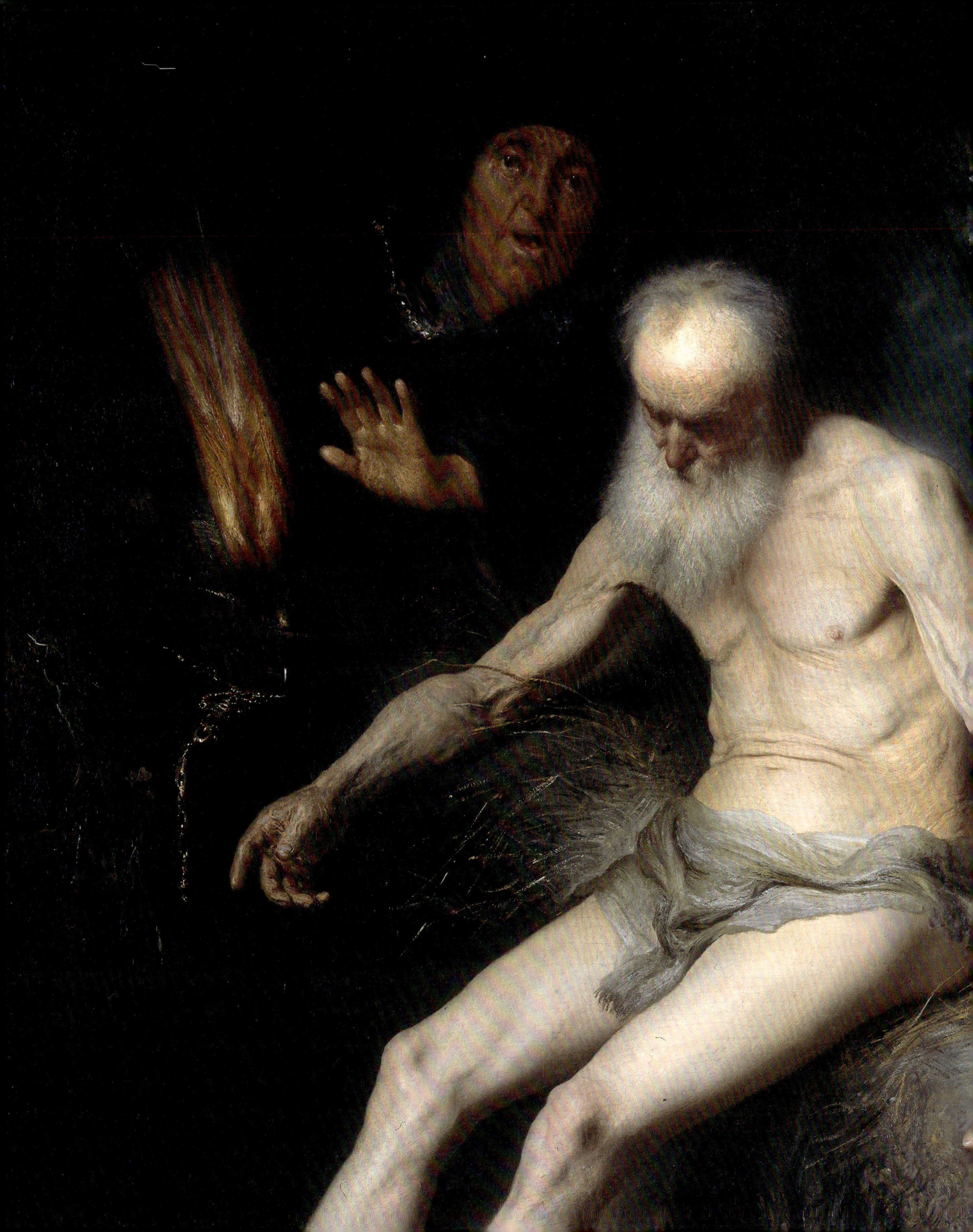

Catalogue

PAINTINGS, PRINTS, AND DRAWINGS

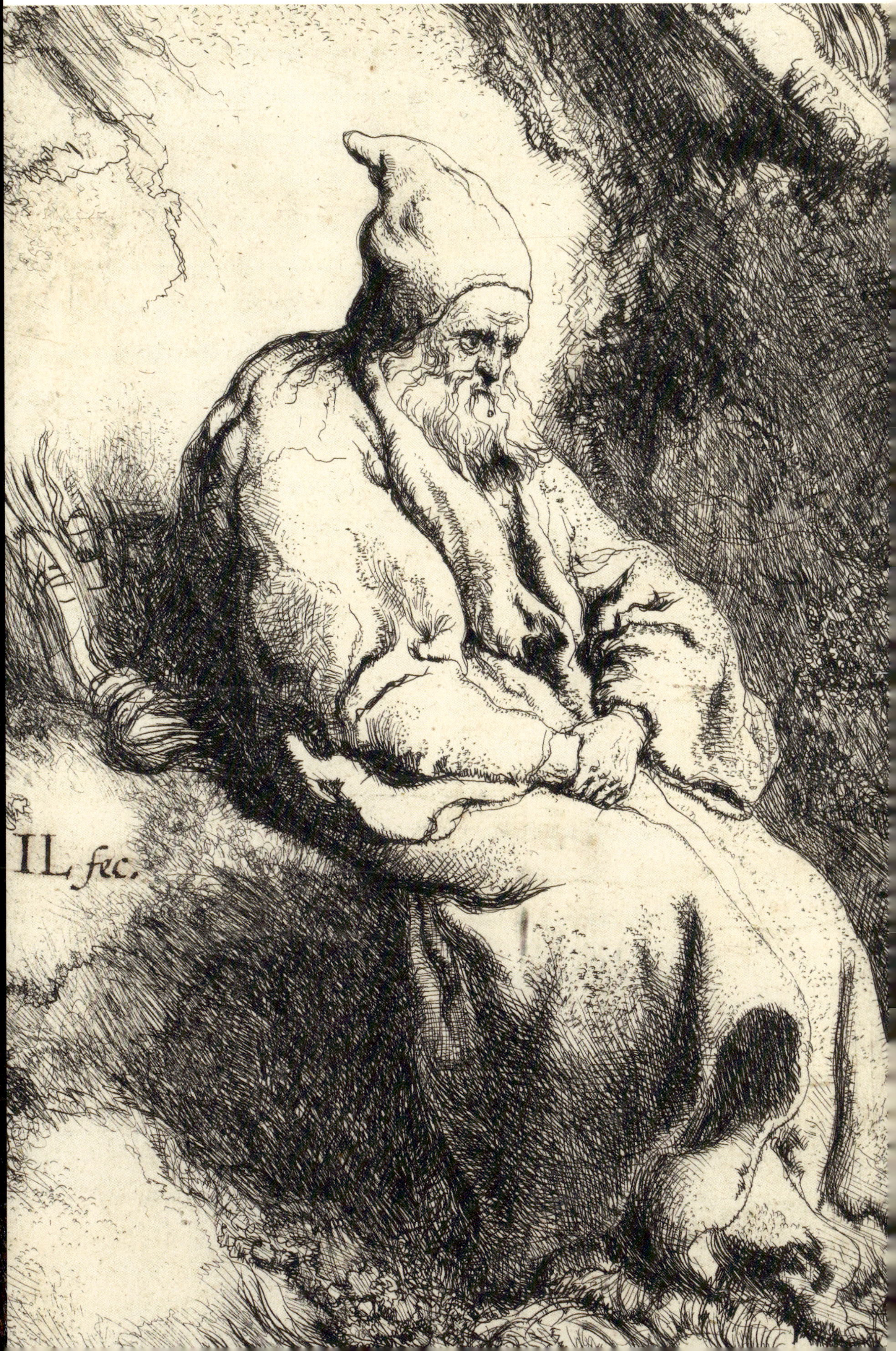

1 Old Woman Reading

c. 1621–1623, oil on panel, 68.7 × 64.6 (27 1/16 × 25 7/16). Philadelphia Museum of Art, John G. Johnson Collection, 1917

Inscription

Monogrammed on clasp of book: J·L

Provenance

J. D. Deuringer, Augsburg, 1813; (Durand-Ruel, Paris); acquired by John G. Johnson, Philadelphia, by 1909

Selected References

Schneider/Ekkart 1973, 342, no. xxxviii; Sumowski 1983, 3: 1789, no. 1214; Van Straten 2005, 22–24; DeWitt 2006, 42–44

A BESPECTACLED OLD WOMAN IS richly dressed in an ermine cloak over a bright red tunic with a heavy shawl over her head. Several leather-bound, metal-clasped books surround her, one of which she has opened and reads intently. This boldly painted, colorful image perfectly illustrates Constantijn Huygens' observation that Lievens preferred to make his figures larger than life-size. Its confident and forceful execution, especially the broad, visible brushstrokes, recalls the work of Dirck van Baburen more than Lievens' teachers, Joris van Schooten and Pieter Lastman.

One could imagine that Jan Jansz Orlers had paintings like this in mind when he noted in 1641 that Lievens' precocious talent astonished connoisseurs in Leiden. The deftness with which the young artist rendered the spectacles and other details belies the brashness he introduced elsewhere in the painting. His use of half-length figures indicates his adoption of Utrecht Caravaggism, whereas his light and color, still wedded to Lastman, suggest that this panel should be counted among Lievens' earliest works. The ermine and other rich textiles reappear in *The Feast of Esther* and *Pilate Washing His Hands* (cats. 6, 7), while a similar tablecloth and books appear in the artist's subsequent tronies.

Neither a history painting nor a formal portrait, *Old Woman Reading* is more appropriately described as a genre portrait. Its bold technique and shallow spatial construction have suggested to some that it was painted early enough to be the likeness of the artist's mother that Orlers credits Lievens with completing in 1621.[1] But although the work may date to that year, the apparent age of the sitter makes it is unlikely that she was Lievens' mother, Machtelt Jansdr van Noortsant, who died in childbirth in March 1622.[2] His mother's birth date is unknown, but if she married in her twenties, as was common, and gave birth to her first child, Joost, in 1605, she was probably less than forty years old at her death—considerably younger than this painting's model, whose age would more closely correspond to that of Lievens' grandmother, Margaretha Smuncx. If this is the portrait mentioned in Orlers' text, either Lievens exaggerated his mother's age for pictorial effect, or, as seems more plausible, Orlers mistakenly identified the sitter. LDW

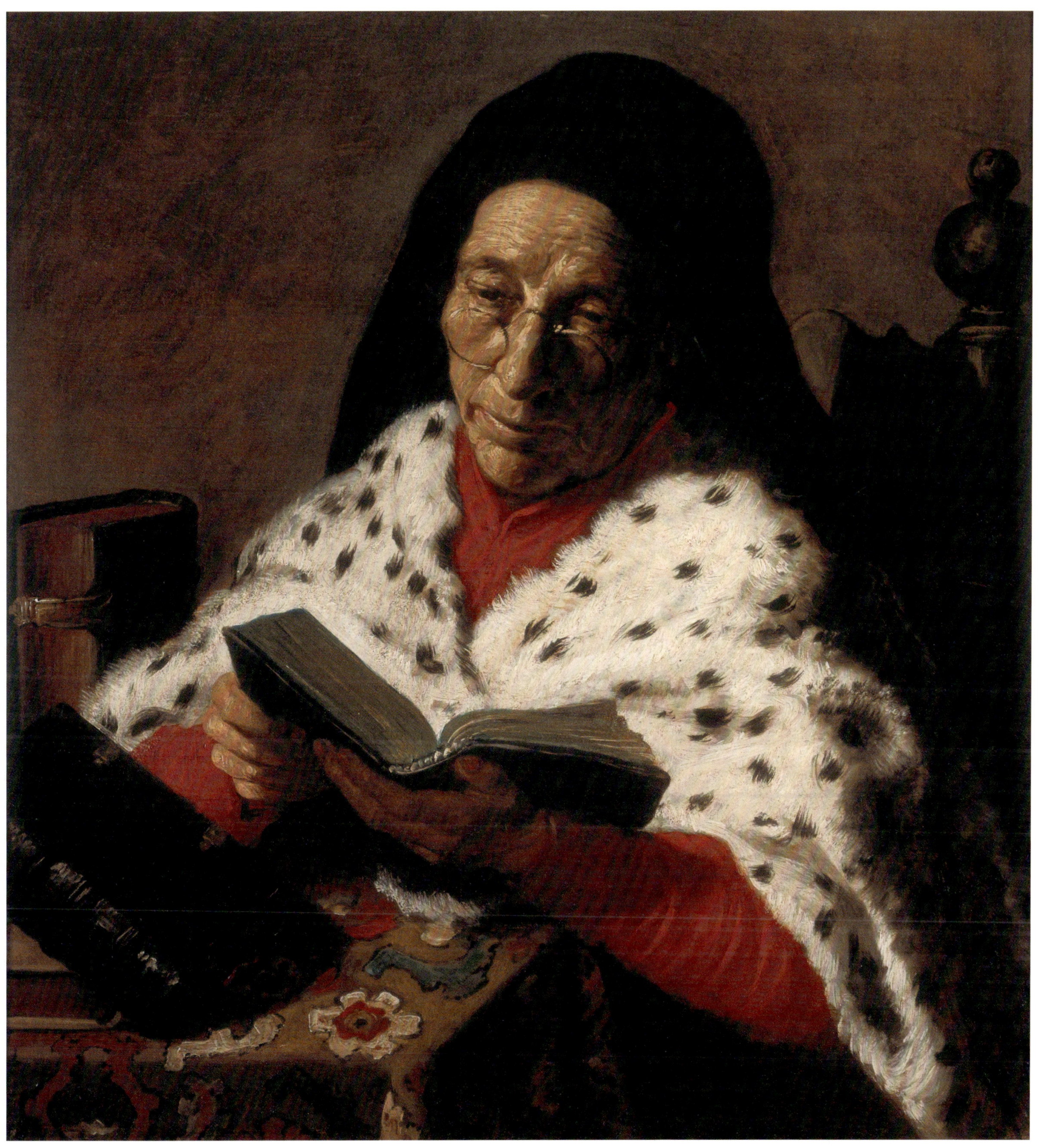

2 Allegory of the Five Senses

c. 1622, oil on panel, 78.2 × 124.4 ($30^{13}/_{16}$ × 49). Private collection

Provenance

Probably Adriaan van Leeuwen, Leiden, 1641; Prince W. Argoutinsky, Paris, 1934; Henry Taylor, Chicago; (Christie's, New York, May 31, 1990, no. 146)

Selected References

Schneider/Ekkart 1973, 118, no. 107; Sumowski 1983, 3: 1775, no. 1179; Kassel and Amsterdam 2001–2002, 102–103

IN THIS ODE TO THE JOYS OF sensual pleasure, the young Lievens produced one of his most intriguing works of the early 1620s. Luscious in paint and in the full-bodied figures, rich in costume and in the color of flushed cheeks, and evocative in the poses and gestures as well as in the surprising combination of five men and one woman, the painting welcomes viewers to gaze and enjoy the merry scene before us. Despite the focus on the Five Senses, the mood is remarkably innocent, as though one could ask no more in life than to touch a woman's breast and enjoy the taste of wine, the sound of a lute, the smell of tobacco, or the sight of a beautiful woman.

The celebrants, both male and female, exhibit no concern that sensual pleasures are but temporary, nor does the painting suggest that one's life should be led with greater purpose. The figures — which one must remember were painted by a teenage boy — fully enjoy the moment and seem to invite viewers to partake of their pleasure, not only through their direct gazes and expressive gestures but also through their close proximity to the picture plane.

Allegory of the Five Senses provides compelling visual evidence that Lievens had fully assimilated stylistic characteristics and thematic ideas of the Utrecht Caravaggisti by the early to middle 1620s.[1] As in paintings of musicians and lovers by Baburen and Honthorst from the early 1620s, Lievens composed his scene with a tightly compressed group of half-length figures that fill the field of the picture. He created a sense of immediacy through his bold brushwork, the figures' gestures, and their open expressions. Indeed, certain poses have direct prototypes in paintings by Utrecht masters: for example, the young man fondling the woman's exposed breast repeats a gesture seen in Honthorst's *Soldier and a Girl* (see Wheelock fig. 4). Eyeglasses as emblematic of sight are also found in Utrecht painting, as in Ter Brugghen's *Doubting Thomas* (fig. 1), where Thomas' companion peers through his glasses at Christ's wound.

Lievens' painting, however, would never be confused for a Merry Company or a Procuress scene by a Utrecht artist.[2] Instead of giving his protagonists Italianate costumes, Lievens clothed them as young Dutchmen wearing the latest in elegant fashion. Moreover, their features and physiques are not generalized or idealized, as in Utrecht painting, but are rather coarse and individualized. The lack of refinement stems partly from Lievens' intent to give this image a powerful feeling of reality, but it also relates to his lack of experience in modeling and sense of proportion. For instance, not only are the figures' heads generally too large for their bodies, but Lievens was clearly uncertain about female anatomy. Other awkward elements of the composition include the spatial relationships among the revelers, suggesting that this ambitious work is one of Lievens' earliest extant paintings.

In his biographical discussion of the artist, Jan Orlers described the enormity of Lievens' reputation among art connoisseurs in Leiden when the artist was only twelve years old. One of the art lovers who had acquired early works by this child prodigy was Adriaan van Leeuwen, whom Orlers notes owned a panel painting depicting the Five Senses, likely this very work. Christiaan Vogelaar has plausibly suggested that this patron may have been Adriaen Claesz van Leeuwen, a wealthy brewer at Het Lam.[3] AKW

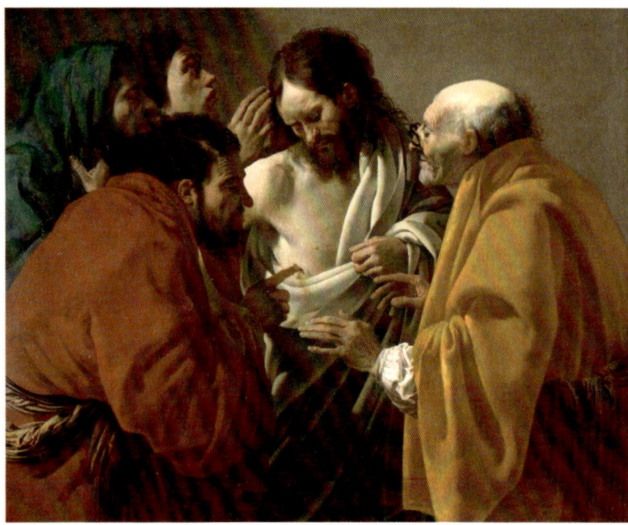

1 | Hendrick ter Brugghen, *Doubting Thomas*, c. 1621–1623, oil on canvas, 108.8 × 136.5 cm. Rijksmuseum, Amsterdam

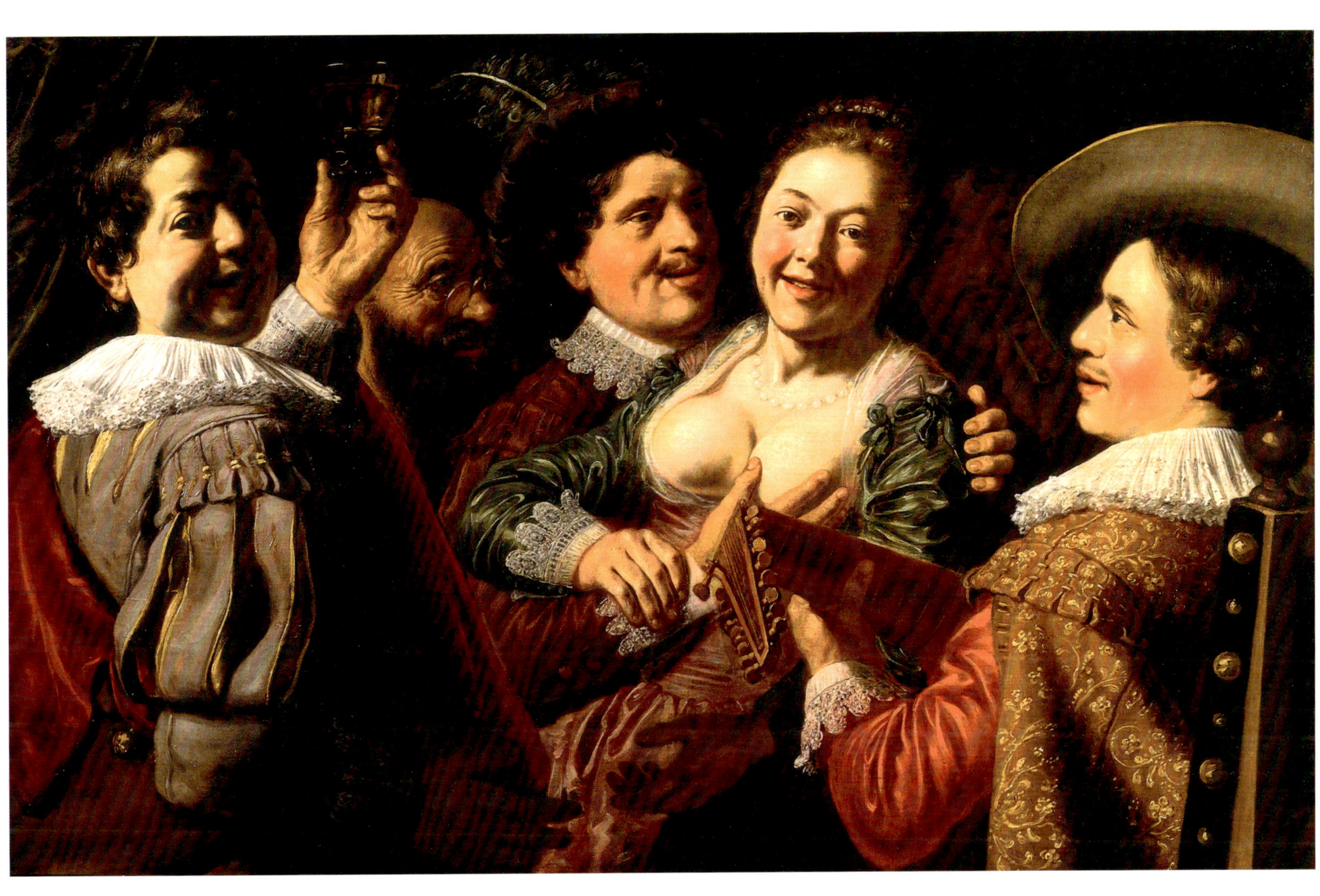

3 The Cardplayers

c. 1623–1624, oil on canvas, 97.6 × 105.6 (38 7/16 × 41 9/16). Private collection

Inscription

Monogrammed in upper left: IL

Provenance

Ovide Ghislain (d. 1944), Jemappes, acquired before October 1927; by descent to his grandchild; (Sotheby's, Amsterdam, May 8, 2007, no. 77)

1 | Workshop of Gerrit van Honthorst, *Card Cheats*, c. 1622–1624, oil on canvas, 97.6 × 105.6 cm. Gemäldegalerie, Wiesbaden

2 | Jan Lievens, *The Tric Trac Players*, c. 1624, oil on canvas, 98 × 106 cm. Spier Collection

TO JUDGE FROM THE CHALK MARKS on the back wall indicating drinks ordered from the innkeeper, it has been a long night of gambling. And to the intense pleasure of the kibitzers, the stakes have clearly risen with every card played. Lievens' painting, however, is not so much about the game itself as about the responses of the protagonists at that dramatic moment when one player realizes that he has lost. Holding his five of hearts loosely in his hand, the vanquished gambler stares in disbelief at the ace of hearts confidently presented by his helmeted opponent. Even without the obvious juxtaposition of the winning and losing cards or the eager gazes of the onlookers, the loser's body language and sober, downcast expression are enough to tell the story.

This striking painting, which has only recently come to light, demonstrates how thoroughly Lievens had internalized the compositional innovations of the Utrecht Caravaggisti. When Honthorst returned to Utrecht from Rome in 1620, he brought with him an artistic repertoire that featured depictions of cardplayers huddled around a table.[1] As with Lievens, Honthorst's compositions were tightly cropped, with the viewer situated close to the action. Gambling is a night sport, where passions and foolish behavior are allowed their full range, limited only by the size of the gamblers' purses. And in his *Card Cheats*, known today only from a workshop replica (fig. 1), Honthorst exploited the dark surroundings to unite the action, as light from a lantern on the table, hidden behind the arm of the silhouetted gambler, illuminates the faces of the players and their cohorts.

Not surprisingly, Lievens' painting was attributed to Honthorst before the discovery of the monogram "IL."[2] But the compositional similarities to Honthorst's gambling paintings are countered by significant differences in Lievens' figure types and poses, not to mention his brushwork. Lievens' gamblers are a coarse, lower-class group. They sit in an extremely close circle, their forms tensely compressed and restrained, while facial expressions rather than gestures become the painting's focus. Lievens' bold brushwork—rough, unmodulated, and totally in keeping with the character of the players seated at the table—also differs from Honthorst's smooth and elegant manner of painting. Finally, this work seems to offer no moral judgment on the actions of the figures (see also cat. 2). Whereas Honthorst followed a long iconographic tradition by emphasizing the deceitfulness and moral corruption of the game, Lievens' gamblers are involved in a game of chance, and his desire was to capture the emotions at the moment of truth.

Honthorst was not the only artist among the Utrecht Caravaggisti who closely cropped his compositions in the early 1620s. Baburen did so as well (see Wheelock fig. 5). Lievens must have known Baburen's *Mocking of Christ*, for he based his silhouetted cardplayer on the helmeted soldier in the latter's work. Lievens probably also responded to the aggressive chiaroscuro effects and the rugged physicality of Baburen's figures.

Lievens may have painted *The Cardplayers* as a pendant to another gambling scene, *The Tric Trac Players* (fig. 2), for the two works have virtually the same dimensions, a similar compositional focus, and both date from the early to middle 1620s.[3] Yet as Bernhard Schnackenburg has noted, *The Cardplayers* is compositionally more sophisticated than *The Tric Trac Players* and is painted in a far more assured technique.[4] These differences suggest that the two works were painted sequentially and thus demonstrate how rapidly Lievens matured as an artist in these years.

A fascinating aspect of this painting is that Rembrandt was almost certainly the model for the round-faced, smiling kibitzer holding a pipe. It would thus be the earliest known depiction of Lievens' friend and colleague. AKW

FIG. 1

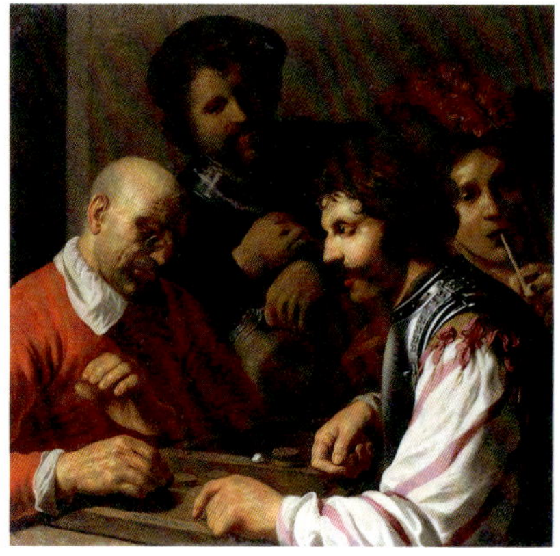

FIG. 2

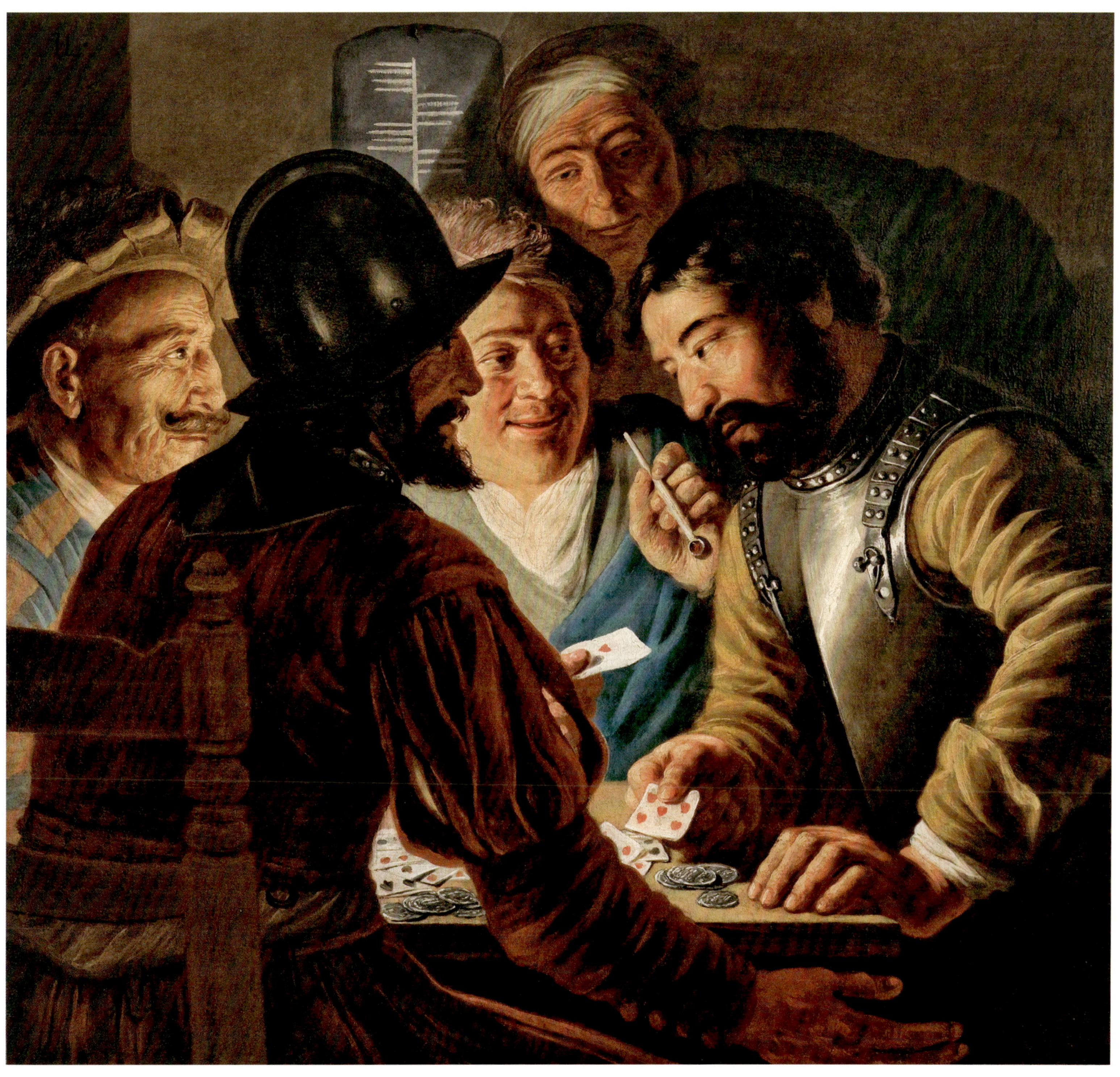

4 Saint Paul

c. 1624–1625, oil on panel, 94 × 78.7 (37 × 31). Agnes Etherington Art Centre, Kingston, Gift of Alfred and Isabel Bader, 2006

Provenance

(Jacques Goudstikker, Amsterdam, 1917, as Rembrandt); (Christie's, London, June 28, 1929, no. 39, as Rembrandt). (Newhouse Galleries, New York); Texas, private collection (Robert Doyle, New York, January 23, 1985, no. 43); Alfred and Isabel Bader, Milwaukee

Selected References

Schneider/Ekkart 1973, 172, no. xv, as not Lievens, 340; Sumowski 1983, 3: 1792, no. 1229, and 6: 3624; Milwaukee 1989, no. 14; Kingston 1996–1997, no. 23

1 | Jan Lievens, *A Man Singing*, c. 1624, oil on panel, 90.2 × 76.2 cm. Agnes Etherington Art Centre, Kingston, Gift of Alfred and Isabel Bader, 1991

2 | Anthony van Dyck, *Saint Thomas*, c. 1620–1621, oil on panel, 64 × 51 cm. The Art Museum, Princeton University

THE MAGISTERIAL FIGURE OF Saint Paul looms over the books piled on the table before him. His flowing white hair and beard frame a robust and full visage, setting it off against the bulging forms of his shoulders and arms. Even his fingers exude a herculean corpulence in their rounded forms. With his proper right hand Paul holds a short quill over the pages of an opened codex, a device of suspense. Lievens shows the apostle pausing in a moment of reflection and thereby evokes the divine inspiration moving him to write the epistles that assumed a place in Holy Scripture and shaped the theology of Christianity. His brooding visage, with his shaded eyes barely visible beneath furrowed brows, underscores the weight of his activity. The passing of the Old Testament is signaled by the extinguished candle behind his shoulder to the left.[1] Paul's attribute, the sword, emerges from under a volume to the lower right.

This large panel is linked to the series of the Four Evangelists (cats. 9, 10). Their dimensions are close, and they likewise include a conspicuously rich still life of books. Yet for the Evangelists Lievens created bolder arrangements of elements in the direct foreground and applied a wider range of handling, representing a more advanced stage of development. Stylistically, *Saint Paul* compares most closely to *A Man Singing* (fig. 1), which has a similar display of books and comparable thinness of paint.[2] Based on a comparison with Rembrandt's very early *Three Singers*, a date of 1624–1625 can be assigned to *A Man Singing*, and thus to *Saint Paul*.[3]

Here, the translucent layers and the diffuse spatial arrangement follow the precursors from which Lievens was drawing. The prominent still life is similar to that in the *Saint Luke* from Ter Brugghen's series of Evangelists produced in 1621.[4] The forward tilt of the head, the bearded visage, and the motif of the pen held prominently in a hand thrust forward appear to be taken from a 1623 *Saint Mark* by Ter Brugghen.[5] Lievens, however, must also have been aware of a painting that was Ter Brugghen's source, the *Saint Thomas* in a series of Apostles by Van Dyck that was in a Utrecht private collection around 1623 (fig. 2).[6] The flowing beard, thinning pate, and sharp lighting from the side are reminiscent of Van Dyck's image. At the same time, the robustness of this figure, which it shares with *A Man Singing* but not with the Van Dyck Apostles, points toward an awareness of the work of Peter Paul Rubens. The many sources synthesized in Lievens' *Saint Paul* attest to the young artist's great appetite and ambition.

Lievens likely produced his *Saint Paul* for a patron in Leiden. The university there attracted many scholars of theology who would have been drawn to images of the apostles and evangelists, whose texts they studied. The choice of the Apostle Paul may reflect the saint's significance in the religious-political context in which Lievens worked during the 1620s. The orthodox Calvinists, who had gained the upper hand in the Reformed Church at the Synod of Dordt in 1618, remained embroiled in a conflict against a liberal faction, the Remonstrants. Both sides cited the Epistles of Paul to support their theological positions, providing a ready interest and market for this image on either side of the conflict.[7] Paul's role as a writer of scripture also elevated his rank to that of the evangelists among the Calvinists, who regarded the text of the Bible as the sole source of revelation, and the focus of worship, following the dictum *Sola Scriptura* (scripture alone).

Lievens shows a remarkable approach to color, restricting the range to muted tones of gray and brown, even more than Ter Brugghen and Van Dyck, which further underscores the sober and serious atmosphere of his scene. Lievens' "tonal" palette places him at the forefront of a wider coloristic development in Dutch art lasting into the 1640s. DDW

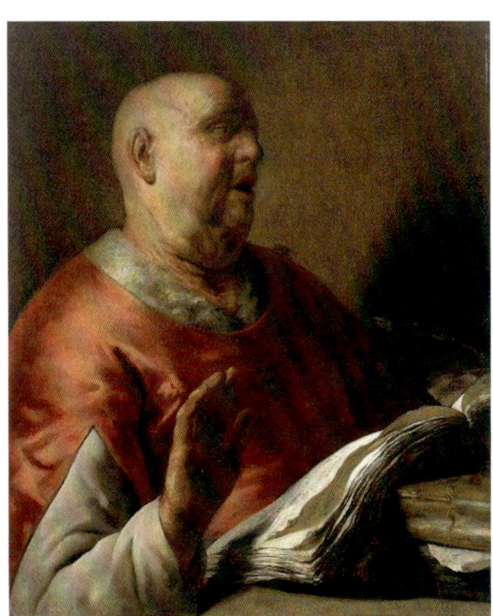

FIG. 1

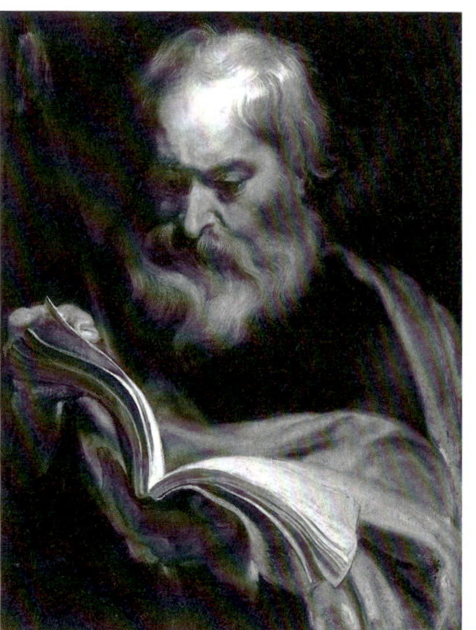

FIG. 2

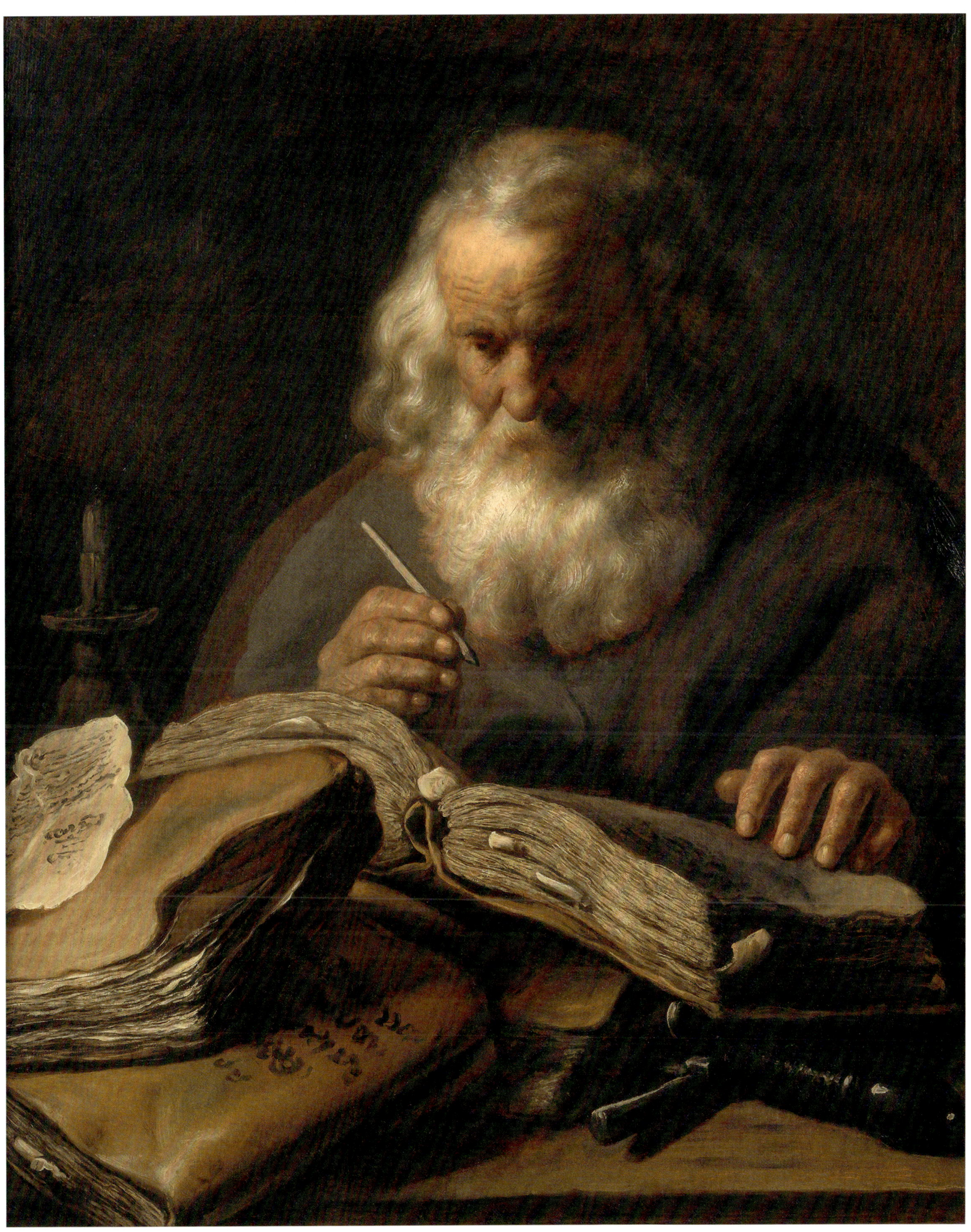

5 Saint Peter Released from Prison

c. 1624–1625, oil on canvas, 95 × 102 (37 3/8 × 40 3/16). Private collection, Israel

Provenance

(Sotheby's, London, July 6, 2000, no. 63)

THE STORY OF SAINT PETER'S escape from prison, as told in the Acts of the Apostles 12:6–10, stimulated the imagination of a number of Caravaggist artists working in Utrecht in the early 1620s, particularly Ter Brugghen and Honthorst. The story could not have been better suited to their sensitivities, for they specialized in using chiaroscuro effects to dramatize situations that involved sudden transformations in the state of a subject's heart or mind. The Bible relates that the night before he was to be condemned, Peter was sleeping soundly in his prison cell, chained between two soldiers, when he was roused by an angel of the Lord, who stood before him as "a light shone in the cell." The angel told him to "get up quickly," and the chains fell from Peter's wrists. The angel then instructed Peter to dress and follow him, which the apostle did, all the while wondering if what was happening to him was real or no more than a vision.

In their depictions of this subject Ter Brugghen and Honthorst either featured the moment when the angel burst into Peter's dark cell, turning it into a light-filled room, or when the angel, through his gesture, indicated that he, with God's help, would lead Peter to safety. Theirs are paintings of action and movement, reinforcing the sense that time was of the essence if this escape were to succeed.

Against this background, one can appreciate Lievens' radical reassessment of the story, as is evident in this fascinating painting. Lievens depicts neither Peter being freed from his chains nor his frightened gaze as the angel urges him to flee quickly. Rather, he focuses on the saint's quiet devotion and inner faith as, hands joined in prayer, he heeds the words of the angel. With his massive body covered by a voluminous red cloak, Peter seems slowly yet inexorably drawn forward, not so much by the urging of the angel as by an unseen source of light shining directly on his rugged, bearded face.

Nothing is known about the earlier history of this painting, or why Lievens chose to portray this subject, although it seems probable that a religious motivation underlay its execution. Xander van Eck has emphasized that the theme had a specific connotation that was significant for Utrecht artists: Catholics viewed Peter as a personification of the Catholic Church, and his freedom from oppression as a promise of salvation.[1] More generally, Protestant as well as Catholic theologians associated Peter's release from his chains with man's desire to be freed from sin, a reading that also seems appropriate to this moving image.

Given the large number of compositional borrowings from the Utrecht Caravaggisti in his paintings from the early and middle 1620s, Lievens' unusual interpretation of this subject is noteworthy. It suggests a certain freedom from the overriding influence of these artists and an eagerness to develop his own distinctive style. His strength as an artist lay in his ability to convey a figure's inner spiritual and intellectual life through the model's distinguishing features, particularly around the eyes, rather than through expressive gestures or dramatic chiaroscuro effects. Lievens' penchant for portraying individuals in profile helped serve this end, for this pose emphasized the distinctive physiognomy of his models. He enhanced the spiritual emphasis of this image by contrasting Peter's rough-hewn and careworn face, his eyes sparkling in the light, with the young and idealized angel who, with knowing gaze, gently instructs the aged apostle on his course of action.

The large and confidently rendered forms of Saint Peter and the angel are stylistically similar to the figures in Lievens' series of Four Evangelists (cats. 9, 10), which date from c. 1626–1627. Similarities exist with *The Evangelist Matthew*, not only in the apostle's furrowed brow and worried countenance but also in Lievens' use of the blunt end of a brush to articulate the apostle's beard. Also close in character are the faces of the angel here and in *The Evangelist John*, where Lievens seems to have used the same model (perhaps himself?). In this comparison, however, the model appears somewhat older in the latter work, suggesting that Lievens probably painted *Saint Peter Released from Prison* shortly before executing the series of evangelists.

This painting has suffered severe damages in the past, as the canvas support was once cut into twelve rectangular sections.[2] Although undocumented, this mutilation is said to have occurred when a former owner, a White Russian in the Ukraine, cut the painting into pieces to fit it into his saddlebags when he had to flee the Reds by horseback.[3] We are very grateful that the painting has recently undergone extensive restoration to allow it to be included in this exhibition. AKW

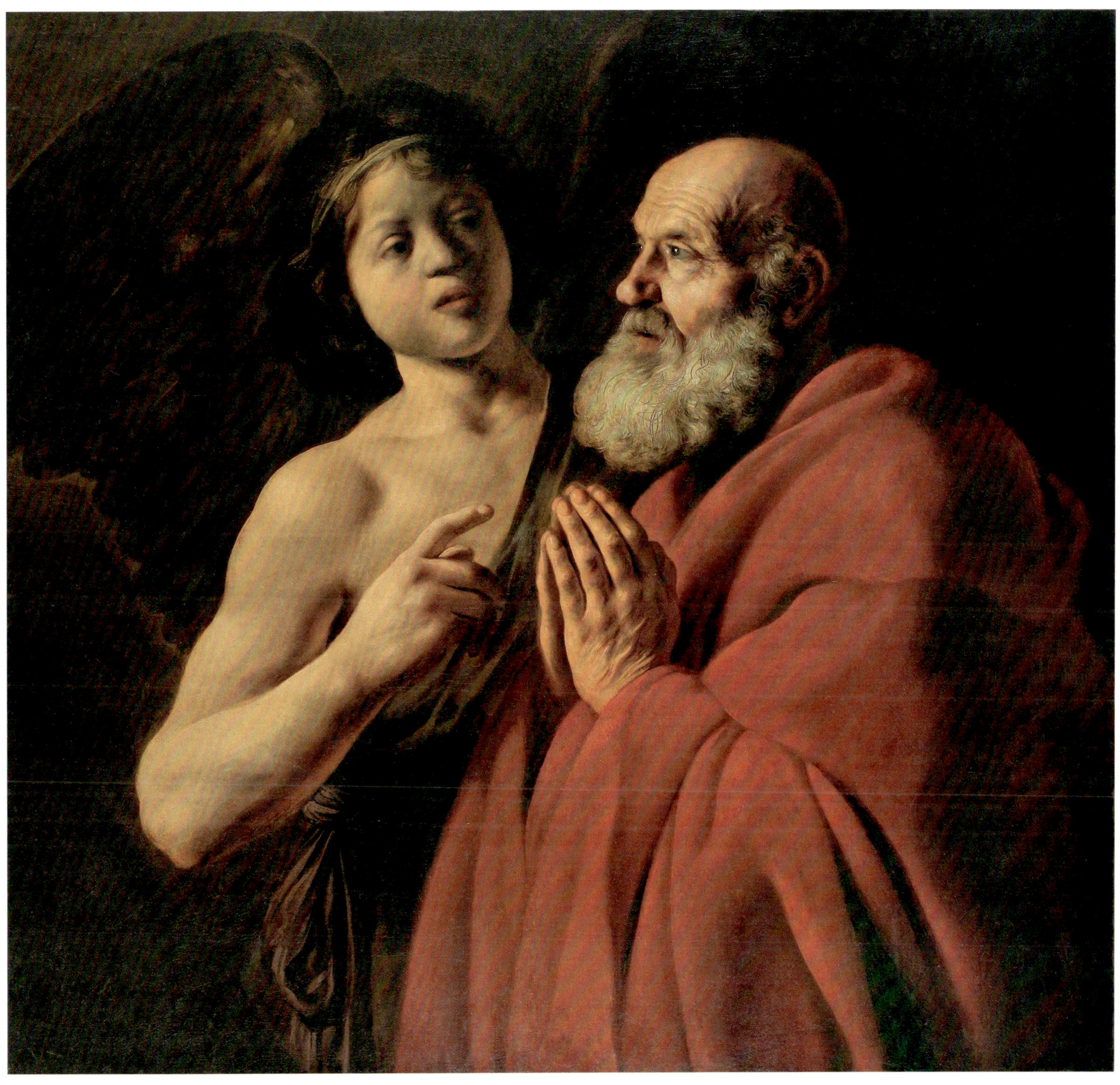

6 The Feast of Esther

c. 1625, oil on canvas, 134.6 × 165.1 (53 × 65). North Carolina Museum of Art, Raleigh, Purchased with Funds from the State of North Carolina

Provenance

Possibly Johannes de Renialme, Amsterdam, in 1657 inventory as Rembrandt; (possibly Compte C. A. de Calonne, Paris, London, March 25–28, 1775); (B. Sommelinck sale, Fievez, Brussels, December 16, 1936, no. 80, dated 1632, as by Aert de Gelder); (P. de Boer, Amsterdam, 1937, as Rembrandt); C. A. de Burlet, Basel, 1952; (Schaeffer Galleries, New York, 1952, as Rembrandt)

Selected References

Schneider/Ekkart 1973, 344, 349; Sumowski 1983, 3: 1776, no. 1181; Berlin, Amsterdam, London 1991–1992, no. 52L; Gutbrod 1996, 115–126, 134; Raleigh 1998–1999, no. 29

IN THIS EARLY MASTERPIECE OF biblical history painting, Lievens portrays the dramatic confrontation between the Babylonian king Ahasuerus and his court favorite Haman as told in the book of Esther 7:4–10. Queen Esther, in an eloquent speech at the feast she had arranged in order to expose Haman's perfidy, reveals to her husband Haman's plot to destroy her people, the Jews: "we have been sold, I and my people, to be destroyed, to be killed, and to be annihilated." The darkly silhouetted figure of Haman draws back and lifts his arm up defensively against Ahasuerus, whose fists express his swelling rage. The men's eyes meet across the table as Esther, leaning toward her husband, points an accusing finger at Haman, proclaiming him "a foe and enemy!" The darkness obscuring Haman seems to foretell his death, and when the eunuch Harbona, seen behind Esther, tells the king that the gallows which Haman prepared for Esther's uncle Mordecai stand ready, Ahasuerus promptly orders that Haman himself be hung on them.

The scene is a profusion of over-life-size figures and regal splendor compressed into a shallow, stagelike space. The painting, monumental in scale and composition, effectively communicates the sensational climax of the narrative. Not only the strong chiaroscuro, which Lievens turns into a tool for powerful psychological effects, but also the peculiar color combinations and striped fabrics relate to the style of the Utrecht Caravaggisti, as do many aspects of his work from this period.[1] Yet Lievens' drawing of the same scene (cat. 93), with its full-length figures, more muted chiaroscuro, and less dramatic action, recalls the style of Pieter Lastman.

Lievens' father, like many Flemish refugees who were members of the Reformed Church, was almost certainly Calvinist and would have sided with the Counter-Remonstrants in their struggle for authority in the latter part of the 1610s.[2] The patrician Jan Jansz Orlers — Lievens' neighbor until 1628 as well as a patron and promoter of the young artist — discussed the conflict in a lengthy section of the 1619 version of his panegyric to the House of Orange.[3] In it he celebrated the triumph of the Counter-Remonstrant cause through the agency of the stadtholder Prince Maurits. Lievens' relationship with Orlers strongly reinforces the notion that his family's religious sympathies also lay with the Counter-Remonstrants.

The association between Lievens and Orlers raises the further possibility that Lievens' *Feast of Esther* may be a political allegory, referring to the trial and execution of the States of Holland pensionary and Remonstrant Johan van Oldenbarnevelt for treason in 1619, at the instigation of stadtholder Prince Maurits. The Counter-Remonstrants viewed Maurits as a figure who, like Ahasuerus, had destroyed their enemy and liberated them from oppression.

Upon Maurits' death in April 1625 the rivalries were renewed during the stadtholdership of his brother and successor Frederik Hendrik, who adopted a policy of keeping the Counter-Remonstrant faction in check. While Leiden remained resolutely Counter-Remonstrant, in Amsterdam the poet Joost van den Vondel published his play *Palamedesz* in 1625, using the story of the ancient Greek tyrant Agamemnon who put to death the innocent Palamedesz as an allegory on the beheading of Oldenbarnevelt. The meaning was so thinly veiled that Vondel was fined for the work.[4]

Oldenbarnevelt's trial and beheading, like Haman's condemnation and hanging, brought about a swift reversal of fate.[5] Gary Schwartz suggests that Rembrandt's enigmatic *History Painting* of about 1625 (Stedelijk Museum De Lakenhal, Leiden) may in fact illustrate the climax of Vondel's censured play.[6] If, as Schwartz argues, the Leiden Remonstrant Petrus Scriverius commissioned Rembrandt's 1625 *Stoning of Saint Stephen* (Musée des Beaux-Arts, Lyon) as an allegory of Oldenbarnevelt's execution, a comparable underlying motivation, albeit with a contrary point of view, is possible for Lievens' picture.[7] The large size of the painting does suggest that it was a commissioned work.[8] LDW

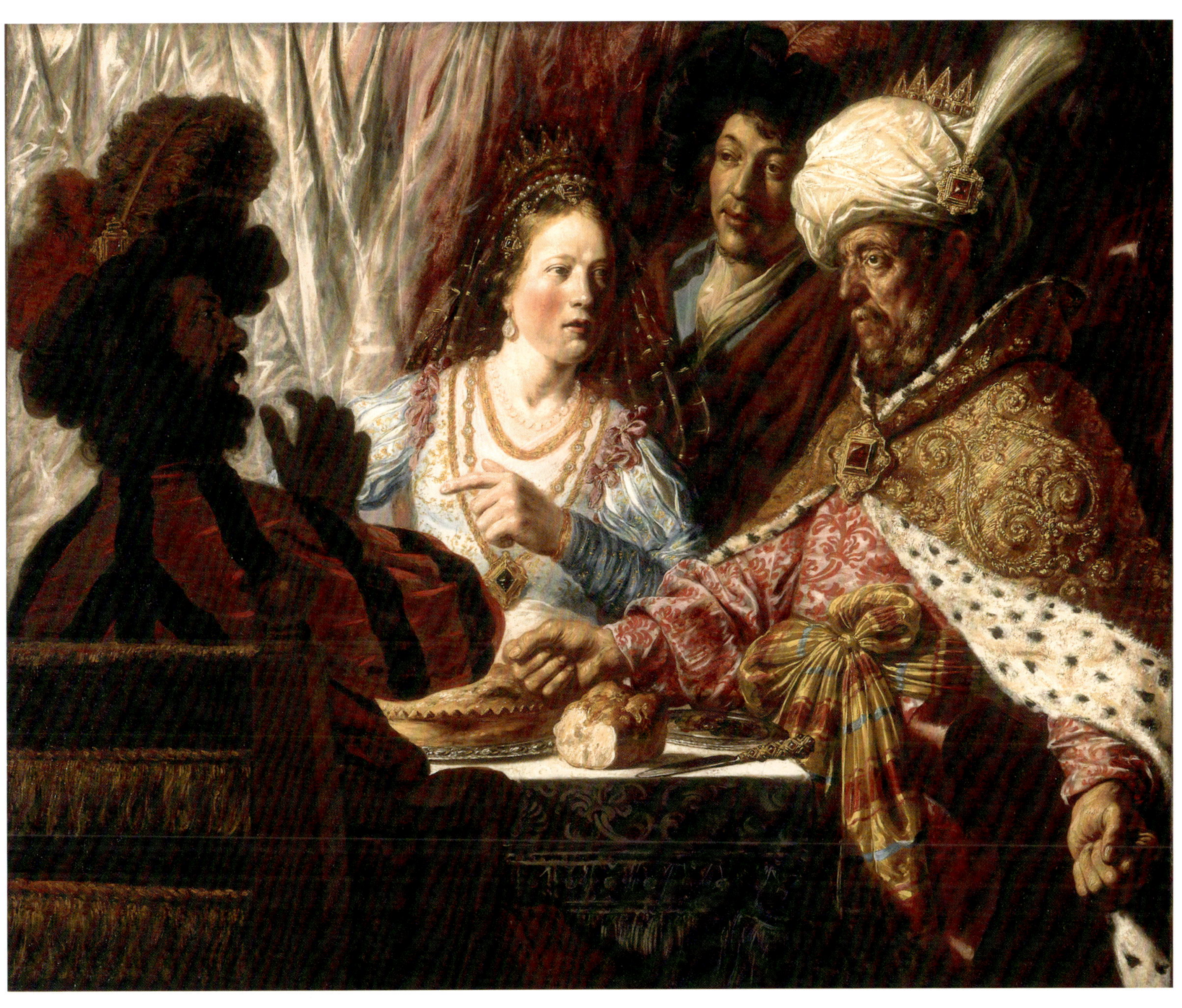

7 Pilate Washing His Hands

c. 1625–1626, oil on panel, 83.8 × 105 (33 × 41 5/16). Loan Stedelijk Museum De Lakenhal, Leiden, The Netherlands *(Washington, Amsterdam)*

Provenance

Probably Jan van der Graft, Leiden, c. 1640 (see Appendix); probably Jan Maire, Leiden, 1666; probably Hermen Becker, Amsterdam, 1678; (probably sale, D. Ietswaart, Amsterdam, April 22, 1749, no. 489); Sir Joseph B. Robinson, London; (Christie's, London, July 6, 1923, no. 57); Princess Labia, London/Cape Town, 1958; (E. Speelman, London, 1967); acquired by the museum 1977

Selected References

Schneider/Ekkart 1973, 102, no. 34, 346, no. S351; Braunschweig 1979, no. 8; Sumowski 1983, 3: 1775, no. 1180; Berlin, Amsterdam, London 1991–1992, no. 53; Kassel and Amsterdam 2001–2002, no. 24; Vogelaar 2003, 158

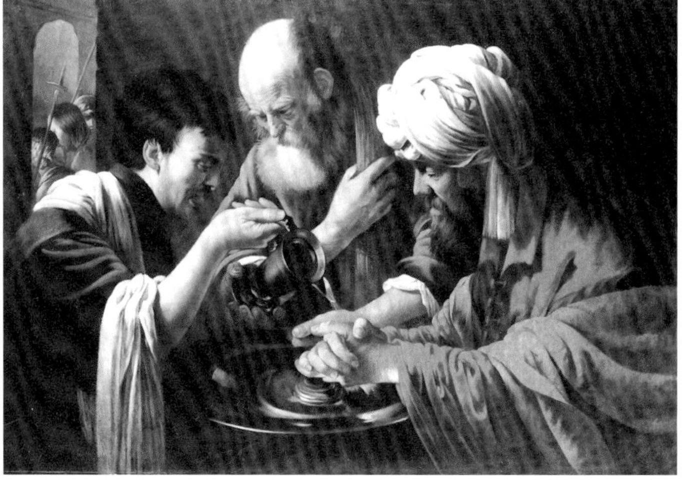

1 | Hendrick ter Brugghen, *Pilate Washes His Hands in Innocence* (old copy), c. 1620–1621, oil on canvas. Staatliche Museen Kassel, Gemäldegalerie Alte Meister

PILATE, GOVERNOR OF JUDEA IN AD 26–36, knew that Jesus was innocent of the accusations leveled against him by the priests and elders, but tradition decreed that the people, not he, could decide which prisoner to release at the annual festival of the governor. Offered the choice between Jesus and the notorious Barabbas, the crowd chose Barabbas and demanded that Jesus be crucified. Pilate responded in disbelief: "Why, what evil has he done?" But the people were adamant, and Pilate, fearing a riot, "took water and washed his hands before the crowd, saying, 'I am innocent of this man's blood; see to it yourselves.'"

This affecting story of a powerful political leader who was powerless to prevent the death of an innocent man is recounted in Matthew 27:15–26. In the visual arts Pilate's personal anguish is generally no more than a footnote to the far more significant consequences of this judgment: the condemnation and eventual crucifixion of Christ. Lievens, however, focuses squarely on Pilate's human tragedy and his attempt to absolve himself of guilt. With his swarthy, bearded face strikingly set off by his white turban, Pilate gazes directly out at the viewer, his eyes both appealing for understanding and disavowing the crowd's decision.[1] Simultaneously, he rubs his thick hands under a stream of water being poured from a pitcher by his young aide, symbolically washing away his guilt. Two soldiers, pressed closed to their leader, look to him for direction or a sense of what will transpire. In the background at the right three helmeted soldiers brandishing spears usher the condemned Jesus through an archway.

For this tightly cropped composition, Lievens drew fully on the inspiration of the Utrecht Caravaggisti.[2] He had an important prototype for his focus on this narrative moment: Ter Brugghen's *Pilate Washes His Hands in Innocence* (fig. 1). Ter Brugghen likewise shows Pilate reaching forward to have his hands symbolically cleansed, while soldiers in the background escorted Christ through an arched opening at the left. But Lievens radically transformed the emotional impact of the scene by having Pilate stare out of the painting, thereby emphasizing that the viewer must share the moral burden of the horrendous decision to crucify Christ. Also different is Lievens' brighter palette and the rugged physicality of his figures, which gives them an immediacy absent in Ter Brugghen's more monochromatic and thinly painted image.

A striking feature of this painting is the elaborate brocaded fabric of Pilate's fur-lined robe, which differs from any other fabric in Lievens' paintings, even the elaborate ermine-lined cloak worn by Ahasuerus in *The Feast of Esther* (cat. 6). The inspiration for Lievens' use of this fabric seems to have come from Abraham Bloemaert, who portrayed Melchior in a cope with a comparable red and gold brocade pattern in his *Adoration of the Kings* (Centraal Museum, Utrecht). As Van Thiel has noted, Bloemaert based his design on the cope of an important fifteenth-century bishop that is still preserved in Utrecht.[3] Lievens' adaptation of such an historic fabric was certainly intentional, and added to the symbolic content of his image.

Lievens probably painted this work in Leiden around 1626, shortly after executing his *Feast of Esther*. The surety of his modeling, not only in the figures but also in the gilt-silver pitcher and basin; the broad range of painting techniques, including the use of scratching to vary the texture of Pilate's robe, are characteristic of works he painted in the mid-1620s. The success with which he adapted his Utrecht models must have impressed his contemporaries, including Rembrandt, who may have posed as the young aide holding the water pitcher. In 1641 Orlers specifically mentions this painting in his discussion of Lievens, noting that it was in the collection of Jan van der Graft. AKW

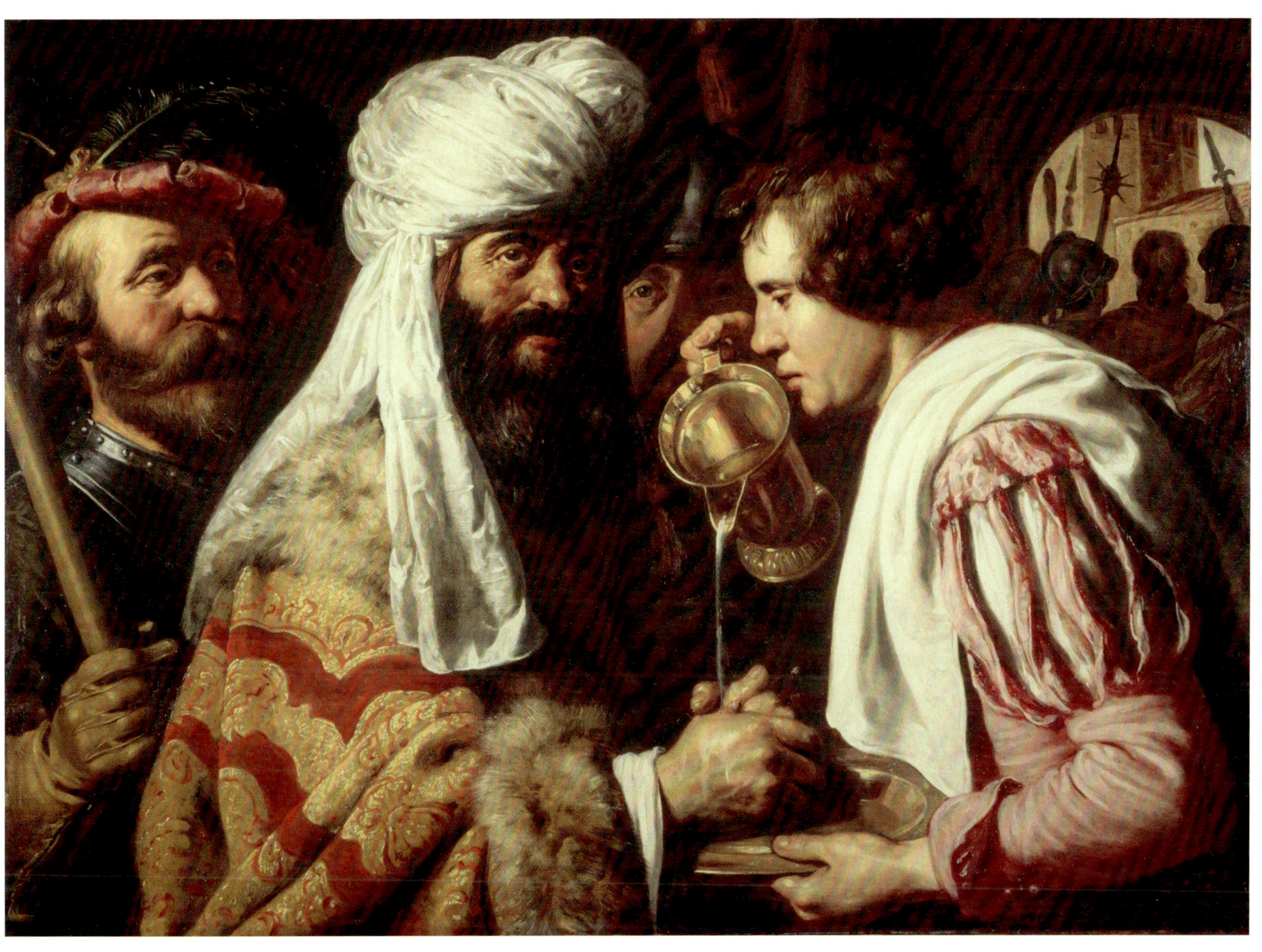

8 Christ at the Column

c. 1625–1626, oil on panel, 106.5 x 74.5 (41 15/16 x 29 5/16). Kremer Collection *(Washington)*

Inscription

Monogrammed in bottom left: IL

Provenance

Possibly Jean Franchois Tortarolis, Leiden, 1653; (Christie's, London, November 21, 1930, no. 102, as Hemling); (W. E. Duits, London, 1930–1931); (J. Leger & Sons, London, 1931); (P. de Boer, Amsterdam, 1932); J. Verheugen, Eindhoven; S.J.M. Slaats-Verheugen, Aarle-Rixtel, 1976; (Sotheby Mak van Waay, Amsterdam, April 24, 1978, no. 74); (S. Nystad, The Hague, 1979); (Charles Roelofsz, Amsterdam, 1989)

Selected References

Schneider/Ekkart 1973, 322–323; Braunschweig 1979, no. 9; Sumowski 1983, 3: 1790, no. 1220; Berlin, Amsterdam, London 1991–1992, no. 53; Van der Ploeg et al. 2002, 100–103, no. 21

BOUND TO A MASSIVE COLUMN, a crown of thorns pressed into his scalp, Christ is shown as he awaits scourging, mocking, and death under the watch of a soldier with a heavy pike. Tears run down his cheeks as he looks to heaven, clasping his hands over his head where they are bound by a chain. Christ's body is heroic and unblemished by torture, but the blood running down his head from the thorns foreshadows his crucifixion. The oddly inadequate chain binding his hands appears to reinforce the theme that Christ's real torment is his seeming abandonment by his heavenly father.

The thick impasto application, in visible strokes of pure color, is typical of Lievens' style in *The Feast of Esther* and *Pilate Washing His Hands* (cats. 6, 7), indicating that this work must also date to the mid-1620s. The dramatic lighting and half-length figure point to the dominant influence of the Utrecht Caravaggisti on Lievens' work at this period of his career. Honthorst's *Flagellation of Christ* (Rijksmuseum, Amsterdam) and Baburen's depiction of the same subject (see Wheelock fig. 5) both use strong illumination to emphasize Christ's suffering.[1] Yet in highlighting Christ's torso, stripped to the waist, Lievens also demonstrated his awareness of the art of Peter Paul Rubens, whose style would have a growing impact on the young artist in such paintings of the late 1620s as *Samson and Delilah* and *Man in Oriental Costume ("Sultan Soliman")* (cats. 15, 19). By confronting the viewer with a monumental and idealized figure in *Christ at the Column*, Lievens created a sense of the story's tragic dignity and pathos.

Artists traditionally depicted Christ in scenes of the Flagellation with his wrists bound near his waist rather than over his head. In conceiving this pose, Lievens may have been inspired by Rubens, specifically his *Prometheus* (fig. 1), which Sir Dudley Carleton, the English ambassador in The Hague, had acquired in 1618.[2] Rembrandt would later emulate the same model in his 1636 painting for Constantijn Huygens, the gory *Blinding of Samson* (Städelsches Kunstinstitut, Frankfurt).[3] LDW

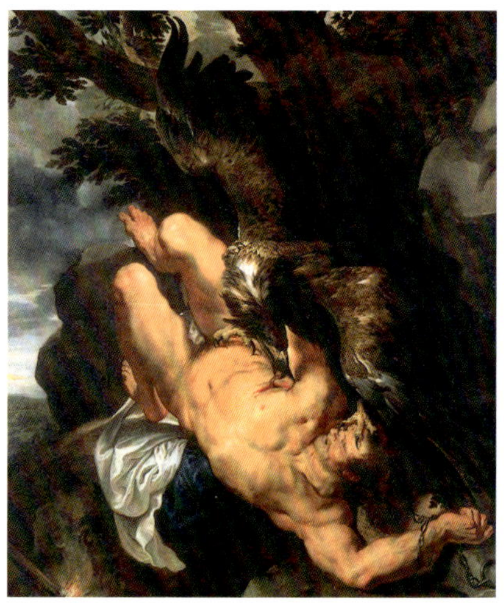

1 | Peter Paul Rubens and Frans Snyders, *Prometheus*, c. 1611–1612, oil on canvas, 242.6 x 209.5 cm. Philadelphia Museum of Art, W. P. Wilstach Collection, 1950

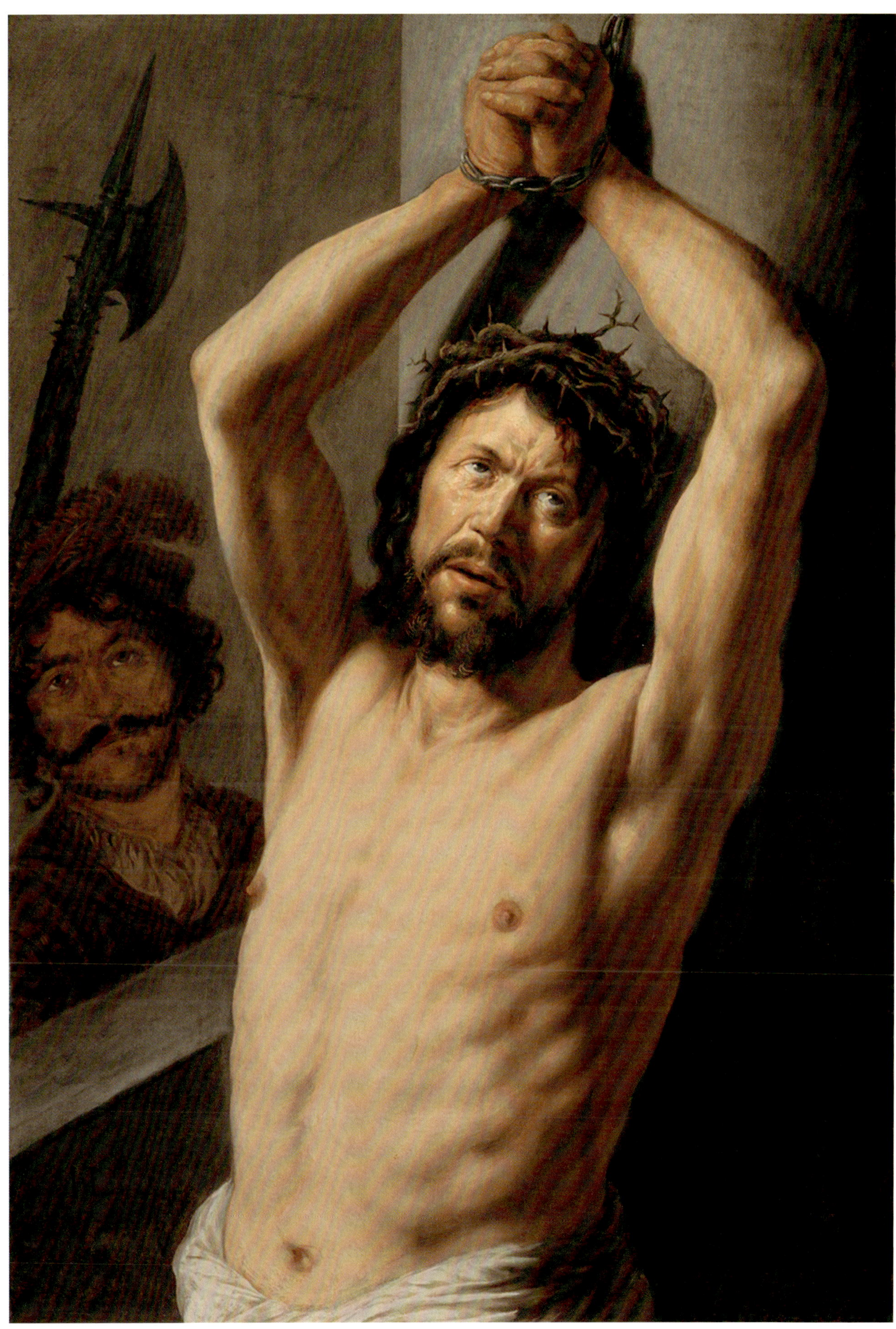

9, 10 The Evangelist Matthew *and* The Evangelist John, *from the series The Four Evangelists*

c. 1626–1627, oil on panel, 91 × 78 (35 13/16 × 30 11/16). Museen der Stadt Bamberg, Historisches Museum Bamberg

Provenance

Probably Jan Jansz Orlers (1570–1646); probably Jan Vogelesangh (1602–1659), Amsterdam; Josef Hemmerlein (1766–1838), Bamberg; Hemmerleinsche Stiftung an die Stadt Bamberg (1838); Städtische Kunstsammlungen Bamberg

Selected References

Schneider/Ekkart 1973, 346–347, nos. s352, s355; Braunschweig 1979, nos. 10, 13; Sumowski 1983, 3: 1793, 1794, nos. 1230, 1233

ONE OF JAN LIEVENS' GREAT strengths as an artist in the mid-1620s was his ability to capture the physical and emotional presence of individual sitters through the confidence of his touch and the forcefulness of his compositions. Although he would have trained with Pieter Lastman to be a history painter, the typical multifigured compositions of biblical, mythological, and allegorical subjects seem to have challenged Lievens' artistic skills.[1] He excelled, however, when focusing on a single figure brought close to the picture plane and portrayed slightly over life-size. He also had an exceptional talent for rendering abstract concepts in concrete terms. Early in his career he found an effective means of merging these two skills to ensure his status as a history painter: by starting to paint biblical or allegorical figures in series, as here or in the earlier Four Elements (see Wheelock figs. 6, 7).

The Four Evangelists have such a compelling physical and emotional presence that one could imagine each of these figures walking the very streets of Leiden that Lievens strode in the mid-1620s.[2] Neither their robes nor their physiognomies are those of early Christians living when the story of Christ's life was first being described and spread through the Gospels. Although the Evangelists' identities are confirmed by their attributes, these — particularly the lion, bull, and eagle in the backgrounds of Mark, Luke (figs. 1, 2), and John — are discreetly placed, dimly lit, and entirely subordinated to the overwhelming physicality of the saints themselves. Only in the painting of Matthew does the attribute take an active role in the composition, but the angel holding the tome in which Matthew writes — despite its prominent placement, bright lighting, and three-dimensional modeling — is shown from the back so that no sense of another personality intrudes on the scene.

Each of the Four Evangelists projects a great sense of moral authority, yet each differs from the others in its corporeal and psychological character. The full-bearded Matthew stares kindly yet imploringly at the young angel for guidance as he struggles to write his Gospel. Mark, dark in complexion, hair, and beard, intently sharpens his quill pen, his rugged hands seemingly unused to such delicate tasks.

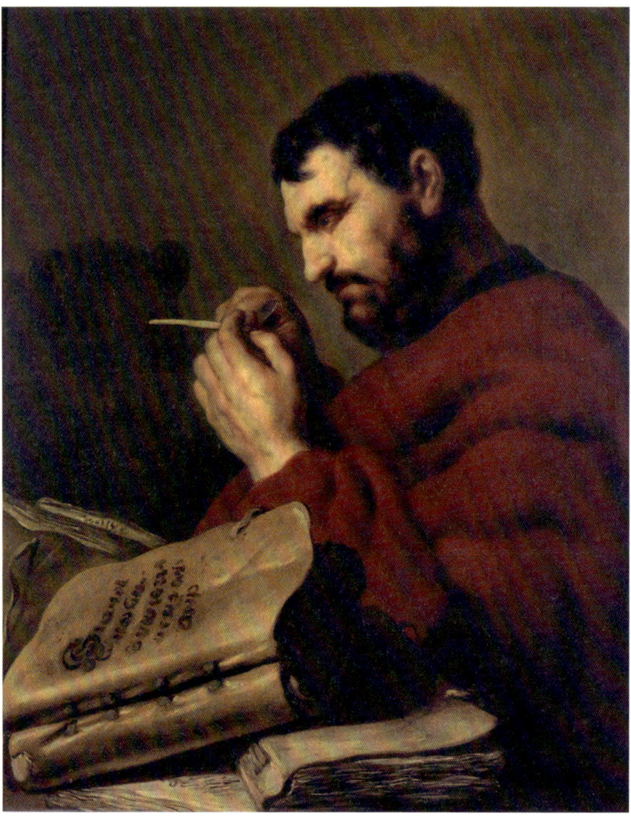

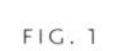

FIG. 1

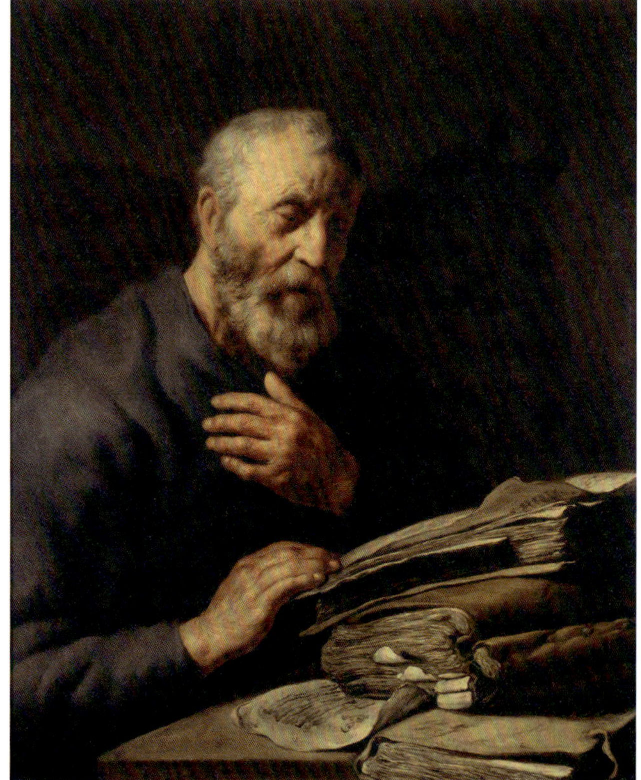

FIG. 2

1, 2 | Jan Lievens, *The Evangelist Mark* and *The Evangelist Luke*, c. 1626–1627, oil on panel, 91 × 78 cm. Museen der Stadt Bamberg, Historisches Museum Bamberg

3 | Workshop of Hendrick ter Brugghen and Dirck van Baburen, *Saint John*, c. 1623, oil on panel. Private collection, Westphalia

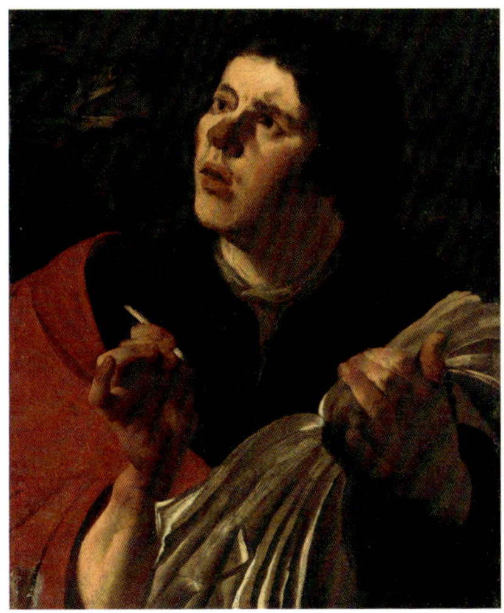

FIG. 3

Luke, a full-bearded, gray-haired scholar, reads quietly from one of the impressive books arrayed before him, his eyes almost shut as though trying to envision the language. He has brought his left hand to his chest in a gesture of his deep sincerity. Finally, the young John rests his head on his hand while leaning on a closed book. His quills lie on the table as he stares into the distance, seeming to reflect upon the ideals of the Christian faith he had so eloquently penned in his Gospel. The two images chosen for the exhibition, Matthew and John, establish its emotional parameters — from the evangelist who must search for guidance in the very formulation of his text to the one who is a visionary and able to conjure in his mind complex concepts that capture the full spiritual implications of the Christian story.

A long tradition for depicting the Four Evangelists existed in European art, but the search for a pictorial precedent for Lievens need not go beyond artists working in Utrecht within a tradition that inspired many aspects of Lievens' early work. Both Joachim Wtewael and Hendrick ter Brugghen painted series of the Four Evangelists,[3] but the closest prototype to Lievens' series is one created around 1623 in the joint workshop of Ter Brugghen and Baburen (fig. 3).[4] In this series the Evangelists were likewise shown close to the picture plane, actively involved in creating or contemplating their Gospels. Similarly, as in Lievens' series, attributes were discreetly placed in ways that do not distract from the essential presence of the saints.

Lievens painted his Evangelists in techniques that range from broad, smoothly modulated impastos, as in the face of John, to juxtaposed, thickly brushed strokes, such as those defining Matthew's features. In other instances Lievens vigorously scratched into the wet paint, as he did to articulate Saint Luke's beard and the creases around the saints' eyes. These techniques are consistent with those found in paintings that date from c. 1626–1627, which would seem an appropriate date for this series.[5]

Helga Gutbrod has made the intriguing suggestion that Lievens used himself as the model for John, an argument she buttresses with comparisons to Vorsterman's etching after a portrait by Van Dyck (see Wheelock fig. 11), which dates from the early 1630s.[6] Indeed, Lievens' somewhat idealized image of John does share many facial characteristics with his own youthful self-portrait from about 1629–1630 (cat. 18), including the broad cheekbones and full lips. One wonders whether any of Lievens' other models could be similarly identified, perhaps colleagues of Jan Orlers, the Leiden historian who was a friend and patron of Lievens and who likely first owned the series.[7] AKW

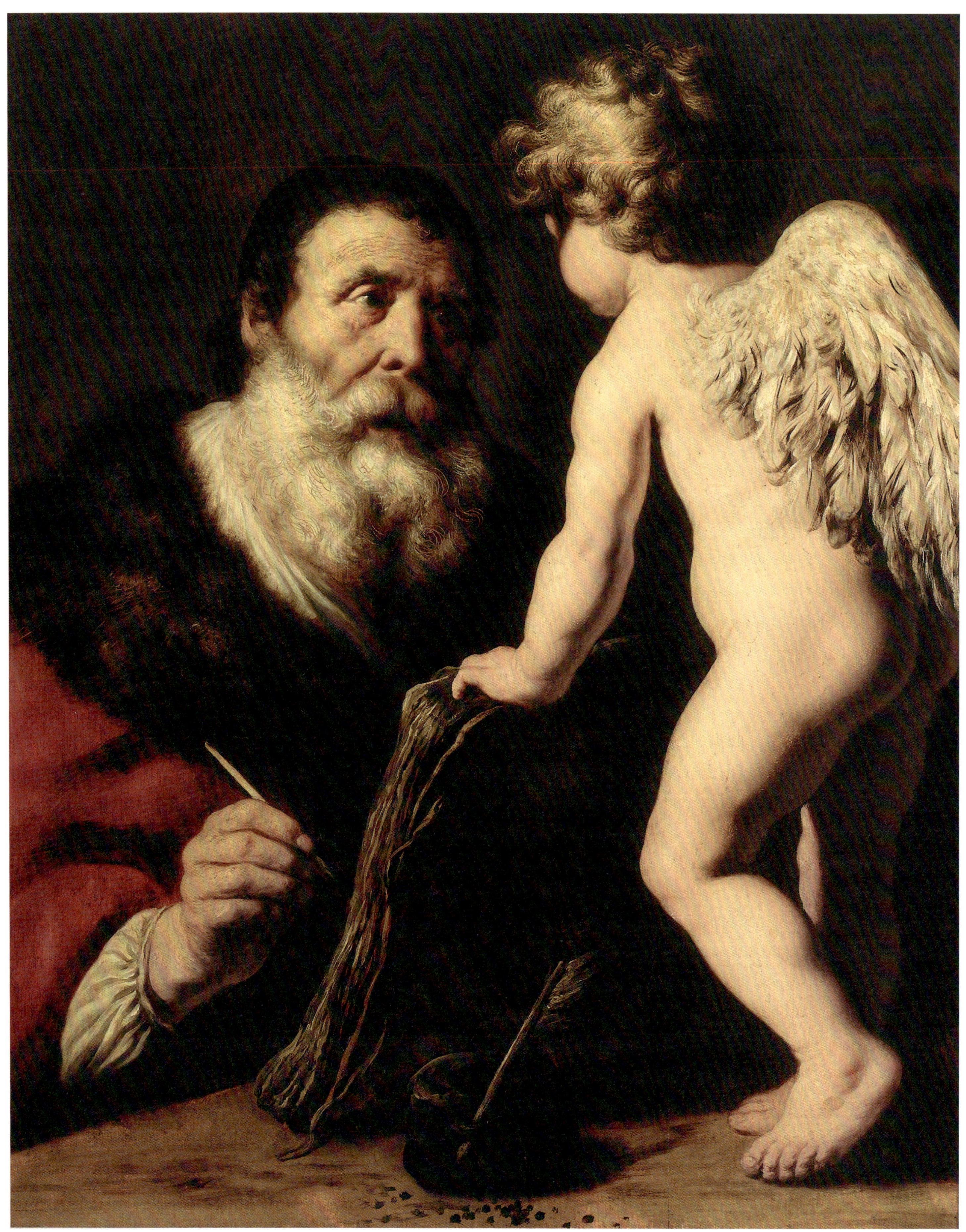

CAT. 9

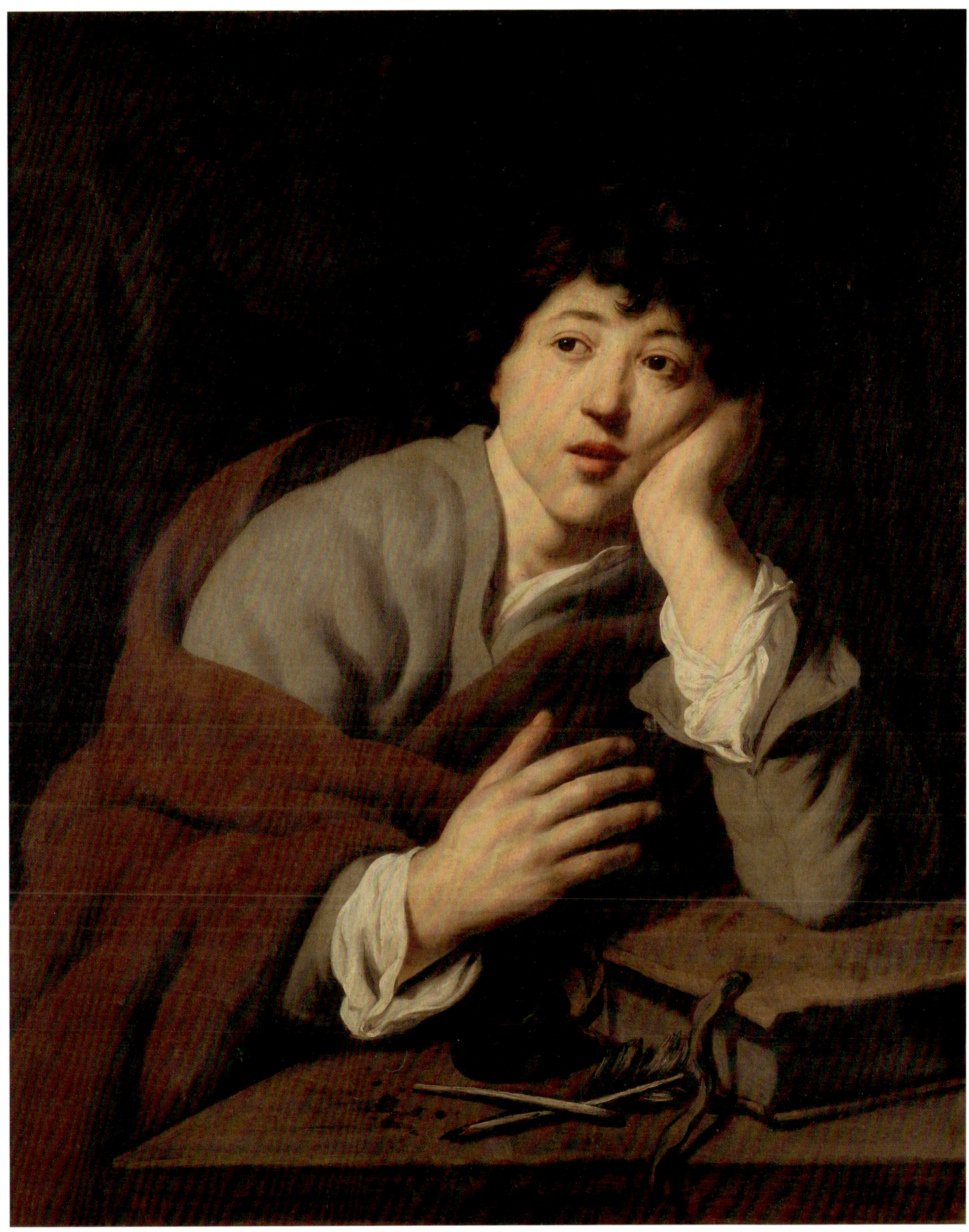

CAT. 10

11 Still Life with Books

c. 1627–1628, oil on panel, 90.3 × 119.3 (35⁹⁄₁₆ × 46¹⁵⁄₁₆). Rijksmuseum, Amsterdam

Provenance

Private collection, England; (Han Jüngeling, The Hague, 1963, as Rembrandt)

Selected References

Schneider/Ekkart 1973, no. S380, as Lievens and possibly Den Uyl; Sumowski 1983, 3: 1812, no. 1300; Amsterdam and Cleveland 1999, no. 18; Schnackenburg 2004, 33–34, 38–39; Wallert 2006a, as Lievens and Den Uyl; Vogelaar 2008, 277

THIS BOLDLY EXPRESSIVE STILL life was acquired by the Rijksmuseum in 1963 as a painting by Rembrandt, an attribution due in large part to the resemblance of the disorderly pile of books on the stone table to those in that master's small panel painting *The Goldweigher* (fig. 1). Yet it soon became evident that the differences in scale and paint handling outweighed the paintings' similarities, and a new attribution to Jan Lievens was proposed by Kurt Bauch in 1967.[1] One compelling stylistic argument supporting Bauch's attribution is the rugged appearance of the old books' pages and leather bindings. Similar books, painted with thick impastos, appear in a number of Lievens' compositions from the middle to late 1620s, as, for example, in *The Evangelist Matthew*, from Lievens' series of the Four Evangelists (cat. 9).[2] Nevertheless, Bauch's attribution did not immediately gain full acceptance, and the painting continued to be placed within Rembrandt's orbit, perhaps because Lievens was not generally regarded as a still-life artist.[3]

Attribution questions have also surrounded this work because x-radiographs indicate that the foreground pictorial elements — the glass, pewter pitcher, and plate with its roll — were added over an already-completed still life.[4] The theory was proposed that a different artist had executed these pictorial elements, probably the Amsterdam still-life painter Jan Jansz den Uyl, who was known for the smooth textural effects with which he rendered glass and metal.[5] Recent restoration of the painting, however, revealed that these pictorial elements were painted with the same energetic brushwork as the rest of the painting, quite unlike that of Den Uyl. As a consequence, Wouter Kloek and Alan Chong have attributed the entire painting to Lievens.[6] The attribution of this portion of the painting remains puzzling, however. Melanie Gifford has noted that the pitcher, glass, and plate with roll were executed in a single paint layer, as distinct from the complex layering of the books and other still-life elements.[7]

Beyond uncertainties of attribution, the subject of the painting has also been interpreted in different ways, with some seeing it as a *vanitas* still life and others as a grouping of scholarly and musical items related to the intellectual life of an artist or scholar.[8] The objects on the stone table — the books, globe, and wooden case for a lute — could support either reading. But with the absence of a skull or another specific reference to life's brevity, the *vanitas* interpretation becomes less compelling, particularly given the presence of a painter's palette and maulstick hanging on the wall. Additional tools related to the artist's profession, including brushes and a glass vessel containing oil or varnish on a shelf, are depicted in the shadowed area near the upper edge of the panel.

At the same time, the prominent pictorial elements in the foreground, belonging to a tradition of "breakfast" pieces, play a crucial role in the iconography of the painting, and their inclusion has never been explained. Bread and wine have Eucharistic connotations that offer religious overtones. By introducing them into a composition containing objects referring to art, music, and worldly knowledge, Lievens created an image that includes the spiritual and intellectual realms essential for nourishing both body and soul.

In addition, the importance of the bread and wine in the painting's composition and meaning raises the possibility that this was one of the two still lifes by Lievens listed in the 1640 inventory of his patron Jan Orlers, with one described as "a large breakfast piece painted by Mr. Jan Lievens."[9] Orlers, who had firm religious beliefs — and who owned the series of the Four Evangelists (cat. 9, 10) — was a book dealer as well as historian. One can imagine that he would have appreciated both the painting's iconography and the bold rendering of the books. AKW

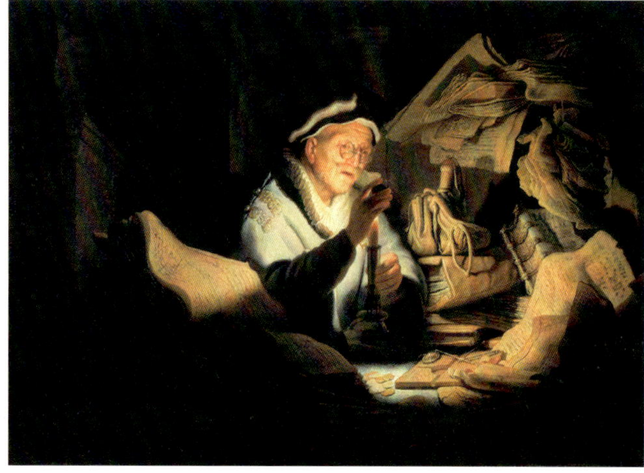

1 | Rembrandt van Rijn, *The Goldweigher*, 1627, oil on panel, 31.9 × 42.5 cm. Staatliche Museen zu Berlin, Gemäldegalerie

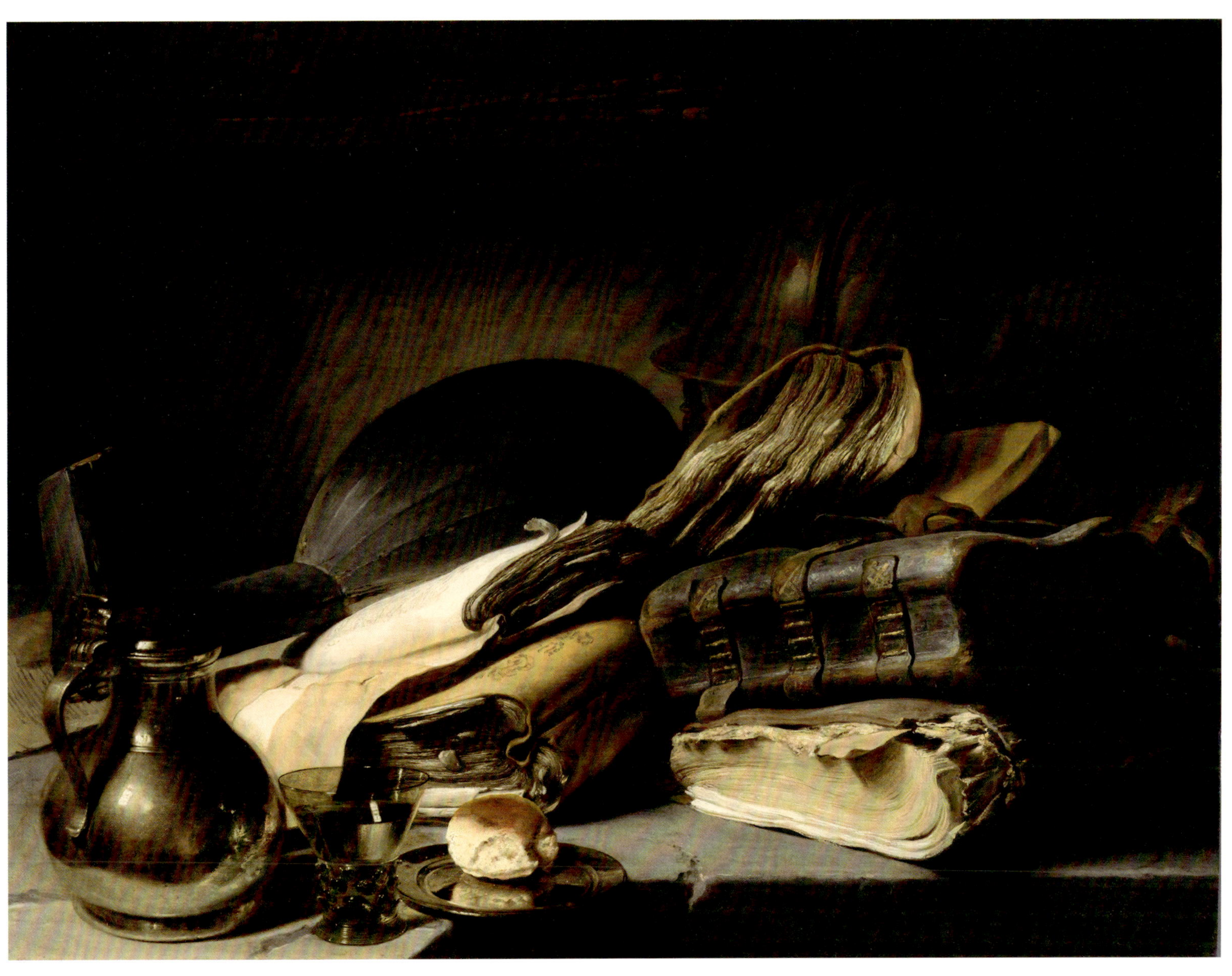

12 Youth Embracing a Young Woman

c. 1627–1628, oil on canvas, 97 × 84 (38 3/16 × 33 1/16). Private collection

Provenance

Duke of Arenberg, Brussels; (Galerie Georges Giroux, Brussels); (Christie's, Amsterdam, May 6, 1998, no. 120)

Selected References

Kassel and Amsterdam 2001–2002, 103

FEW PAINTINGS EXPRESS MORE vividly than does this evocative image the sheer pleasure of a physical embrace. The comely young woman gazes out at the viewer with sparkling eyes and an open smile as her male friend draws her close and grasps her hands. There is nothing delicate or fragile about these two lovers; rather they are full-blooded, sensual beings with plain features, color in their cheeks, and flesh on their bones. They seem a perfect match, and their warm embrace expresses both lustful desires and shared emotions.

Youth Embracing a Young Woman relates thematically to the central couple symbolizing Touch in *Allegory of the Five Senses* (cat. 2) but is executed with a freedom and surety not seen in that early work. The differences are many, not only in the proportions and gestures of the figures but also in the organic flow of their emotions. These differences in maturity suggest that some time must have elapsed between the execution of the two works. Given that the figures in this painting are somewhat larger than life-size, it seems probable that Lievens painted them around 1627, when many of his compositions have this characteristic.[1]

As with many of Lievens' earlier works, this embracing couple relates to bawdy genre scenes by the Utrecht Caravaggisti from the early to middle 1620s, when those artists often depicted the close physical and psychological interactions of two lustful figures (see Wheelock fig. 4). The connections with Utrecht are particularly close in relation to Lievens' buxom female model, whose blond hair, broad face, wide smile, and dimples are strikingly similar to features seen in one of Honthorst's favorite models from this period (fig. 1).[2] Unlike his Utrecht colleagues, however, Lievens painted with rich impastos rather than smoothly modulated surfaces, thereby adding to the physical sensuality of his image.

When this previously unknown painting was discovered in 1998, it looked quite different than it does now. Not only did it have extensions on the top and the right, but the young woman was somewhat more modestly clothed with a semi-translucent veil covering her breasts.[3] With these later additions removed during the painting's recent restoration, the bold physicality of the painting has been greatly enhanced. Whether the painting now fully represents Lievens' original intent, however, is uncertain. Technical examination suggests that the canvas support has been cut at the left and, to a lesser extent, at the right. One wonders if the gray shapes at the lower and upper left are remnants of a drapery, which served as a framing device for the two figures, or if it was part of a larger form, such as the robe of a third companion, as seen with the merry drinker in *Allegory of the Five Senses*. Another unresolved question is whether the painting was originally meant to be seen from below, as suggested by the position of the woman's outstretched right hand and the direction of her gaze. The Utrecht Caravaggisti often painted Merry Company scenes as overdoor paintings, and the same might have been intended for this work. AKW

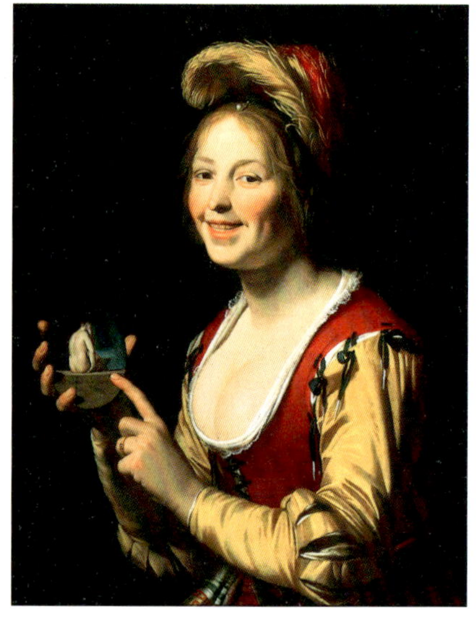

1 | Gerrit van Honthorst, *Young Woman Holding a Medallion*, 1625, oil on canvas, 81.2 × 64.3 cm. Saint Louis Art Museum, Friends Fund

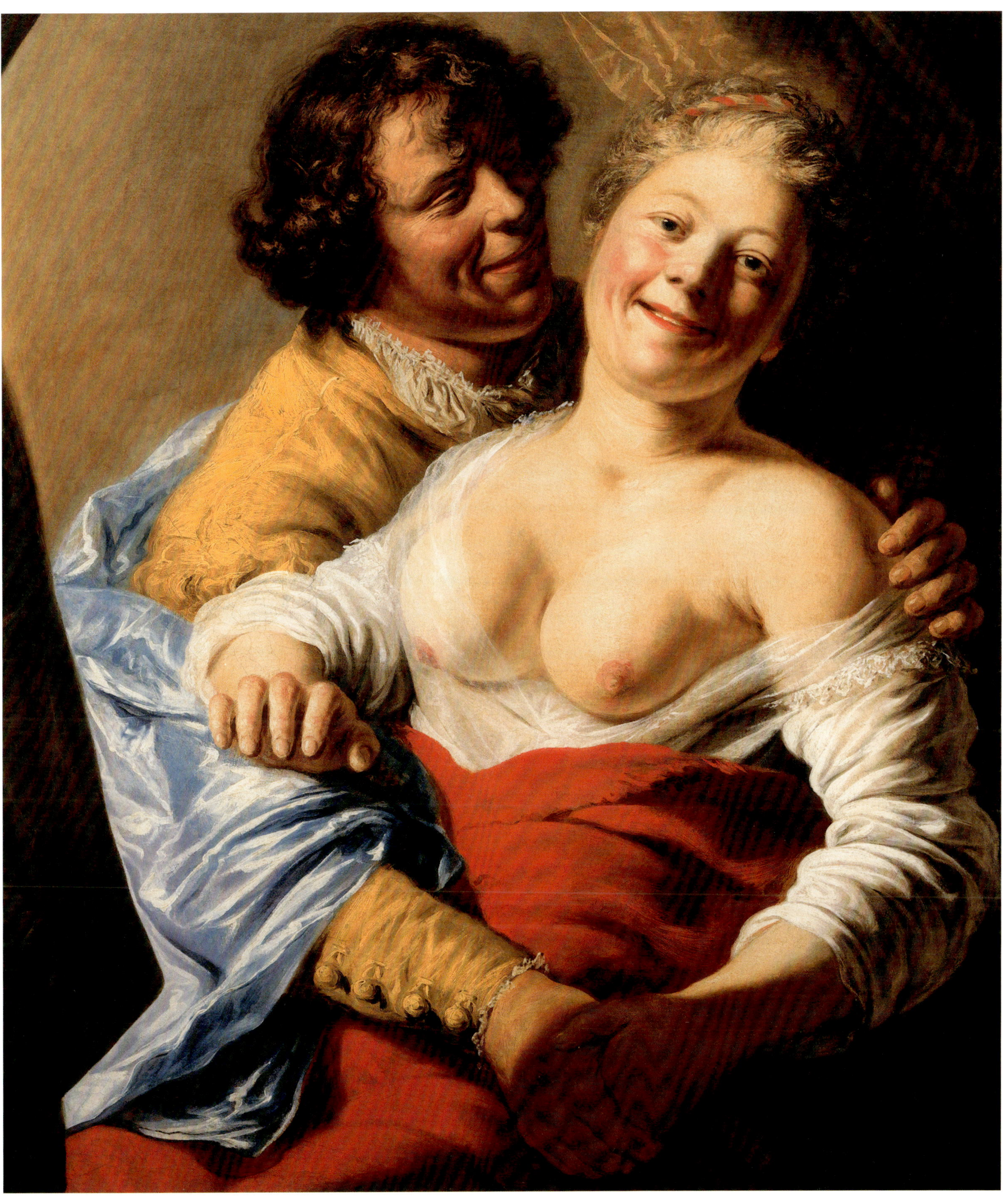

13 Lute Player

c. 1627, revised c. 1628, oil on panel, 92.7 × 78.3 (36½ × 30⅞). The Walters Art Museum, Baltimore, Maryland, Gift of the Dr. Francis D. Murnaghan Fund, 1973

Inscription

Monogrammed in lower left: I.L.

Provenance

Possibly Harmen Becker, Amsterdam, October 19, 1678; James A. Murnaghan, Dublin; Dr. Francis Murnaghan Fund, 1973

Selected References

Schneider/Ekkart 1973, 122, no. 122; Sumowski 1983, 5: 3109, no. 2125; Gifford 1985, 58–67; Postma 1988, 17; Van Straten 2005, 40–42

THIS HALF-LENGTH PROFILE image of a lute player is typical of the figures that Huygens had in mind when he wrote of Lievens: "Rather than depicting his subject in its true size, he chooses a larger scale."[1] The musician, with his striking green and yellow costume, dominates the picture plane, commanding the viewer's complete attention.

As with the majority of Lievens' works from these years, this painting reflects the influence of the Utrecht Caravaggisti. Yet Lievens imbues the figure with a timeless dignity quite different from the joyful spontaneity of the lutenists painted by Honthorst and Ter Brugghen (see Gifford fig. 7). Also characteristic of Lievens' paintings of the late 1620s is the broad and fluid application of paint that gives this figure its imposing physical presence. The strong profile and intense gaze of the lutenist can best be compared with *The Evangelist Mark* of c. 1626–1627 (see cat. 9–10, fig. 1). X-rays reveal that Lievens' *Lute Player* was executed in two phases, with an original pink robe replaced at a slightly later date by the present green and yellow one (see Gifford essay).

Technical analysis indicates that this work has much in common with paintings executed by Rembrandt at the same time. For example, the use of the end of the brush handle to scratch into the still-wet paint to create a sense of texture, as Lievens has done here to articulate the lute player's hair, was a device used by both artists. Aside from similar working methods, Lievens and Rembrandt also shared models (see cat. 20), sometimes even depicting each other.[2] Indeed, the slightly bulbous nose, double chin, and full lower lip of the lute player resemble Rembrandt's features in Lievens' contemporaneous portrait of him (cat. 17).[3] VCT

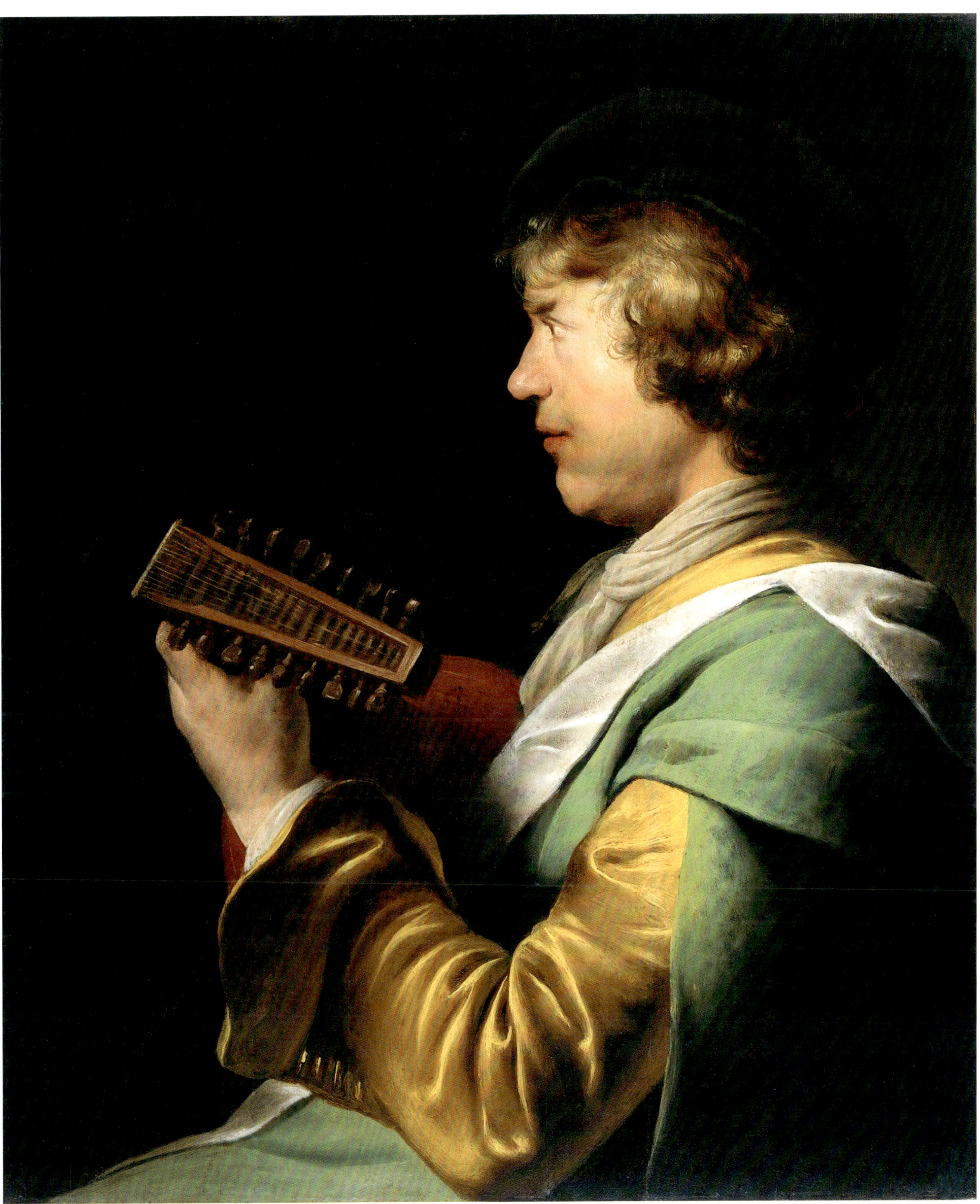

14 Young Man in a Beret

c. 1628, oil on panel, 83.5 × 49 (32⅞ × 19 5/16). Private collection, courtesy of Jean-Luc Baroni Ltd.

Inscription

Monogrammed at bottom left: L

Provenance

Austrian noble family since 1870 (sale, Dorotheum, Vienna, October 2, 2003, no. 85); (Jean-Luc Baroni, London)

EMPHASIZING one of the most important aspects of the tronie, *Young Man in a Beret* was clearly painted from life. There is no mistaking the individuality of this sitter, and Lievens' facility with portraiture, so lavishly praised by Constantijn Huygens, is evident in his characterization of this intense young man. While such tronies have a strong portraitlike quality, they were not intended to serve as painted memorials, but as character studies.

As is so often seen in Lievens' tronies, this young man is depicted in strict profile. His flat nose and pronounced underbite are reminiscent of the rough types that inhabit Lievens' tavern scenes, but his dress and the scale of the painting suggest a portrait perhaps of a fellow artist. The thickness of the paint, particularly in the flesh tones, and the use of the butt of the brush to indicate texture in the collar and hair are typical of Lievens' paintings from about 1628. MH

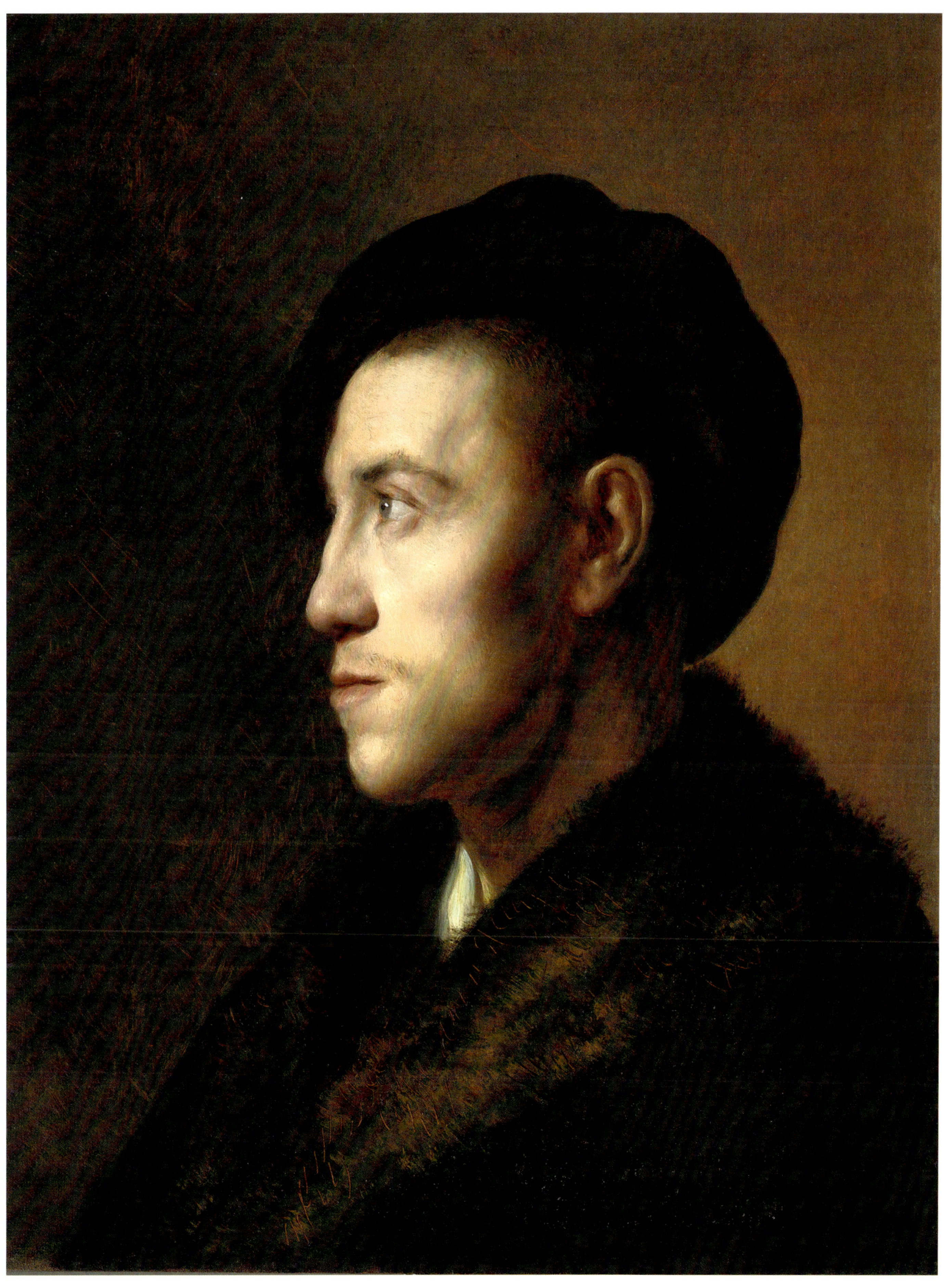

15 Samson and Delilah

c. 1628, oil on canvas, 128.5 × 109.5 (50 13/16 × 43 5/16). Rijksmuseum, Amsterdam

Inscription

Monogrammed at top left: IL

Provenance

J. S. Hensé, Bradford (1895)

Selected References

Schneider/Ekkart 1973, 319; Braunschweig 1979, no. 16; Sumowski 1983, 3: 1778, no. 1185; Gutbrod 1996, 144–149; Kassel and Amsterdam 2001, no. 27; Schnackenburg 2007, 207–208

1 | Gerrit van Honthorst, *Samson and Delilah*, c. 1621, oil on canvas, 129 × 94 cm. The Cleveland Museum of Art

2 | Jacob Matham after Peter Paul Rubens, *Samson and Delilah*, 1610, engraving. The British Museum, London

3 | Rembrandt van Rijn, *Samson and Delilah*, c. 1629–1630, oil on panel, 61.3 × 50.1 cm. Staatliche Museen zu Berlin, Gemäldegalerie

WITH A STERN LOOK, DELILAH thrusts a pair of shears toward her clearly apprehensive assistant, thus betraying the man who sleeps with his head in her lap. So begins the downfall of the mighty Samson, Delilah's lover, scourge of the Philistines, whose story is told in the Old Testament book of Judges (13:2 to 16:31). This treacherous episode comes after Delilah, allied with the Philistines, has convinced Samson to reveal the secret of his superhuman strength: his long hair. Then as Samson lies sleeping, she bids one of the Philistines to cut off the hero's hair. Once the deed is done, Samson is helpless, and his enemies are able to seize and blind him. But his hair soon grows again, and he takes revenge on the Philistines by bringing down the house in which they are celebrating, killing them all.

Lievens heightened the drama and the sense of urgency in this climactic moment of betrayal by bringing the viewer close to the action. The life-sized, half-length figures as well as the strong contrast of light and dark reflect the influence of Honthorst, who portrayed Samson similarly, with his head resting in the crook of his arm as he slumbered on Delilah's lap (fig. 1).[1] Substantial differences, however, exist between the two paintings: Lievens sets the scene in an ambiguous space rather than a specific interior, and he shows Delilah handing the shears to her accomplice instead of cutting Samson's hair herself. By emphasizing that Delilah is the instigator of this action, Lievens follows the biblical text: "she called a man, and had him shave off the seven locks of his [Samson's] head."

In depicting this specific narrative moment, Lievens may have found inspiration in Rubens' version of the subject (National Gallery, London), which he could have known through a print by Jacob Matham (fig. 2). Rubens' influence on Lievens was particularly strong at this time because of the Flemish master's presence in the Northern Netherlands and his visit to Honthorst's studio in Utrecht. Rubens also inspired Lievens' slightly later *Samson and Delilah* grisaille (see Wheelock fig. 10), which, it has been argued, influenced Rembrandt to paint his *Samson and Delilah* of c. 1629–1630 (fig. 3).[2]

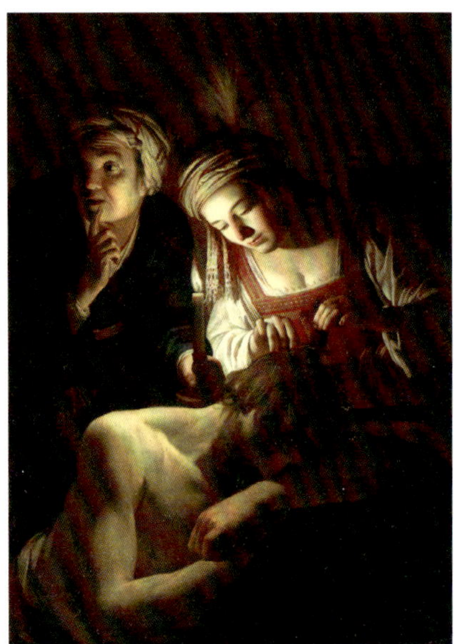

FIG. 1

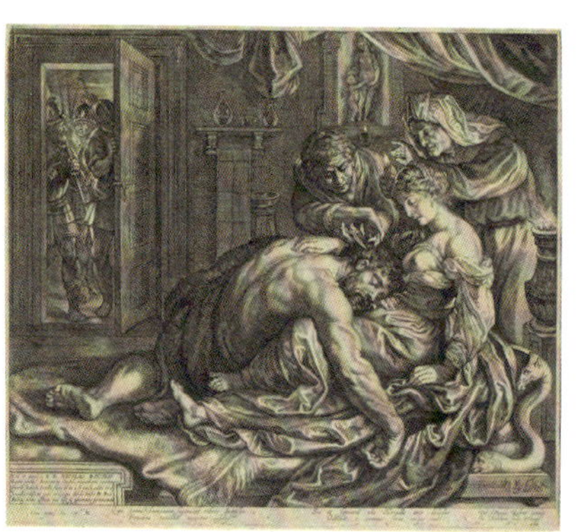

FIG. 2

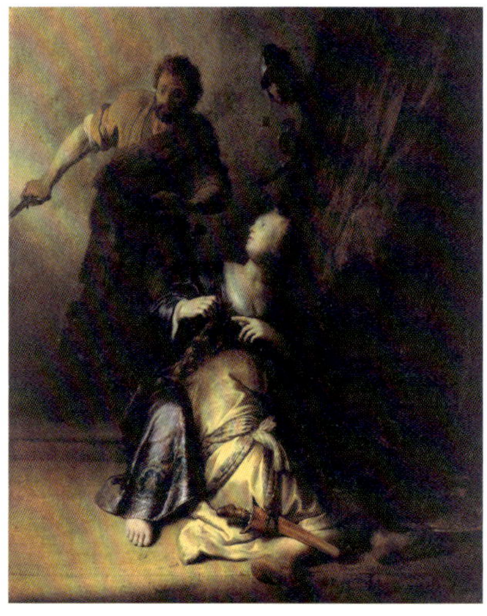

FIG. 3

Despite the impact of Honthorst and Rubens on Lievens' conception, the latter's painting differs from those of his artistic predecessors. His figures, while imposing, are markedly un-idealized. The glowering face of Lievens' Delilah bears no resemblance to the elegant women in either Honthorst's or Rubens' painting. Meanwhile, his Samson is the same bearded Dutchman who posed for his earlier *Christ at the Column* (cat. 8). VCT

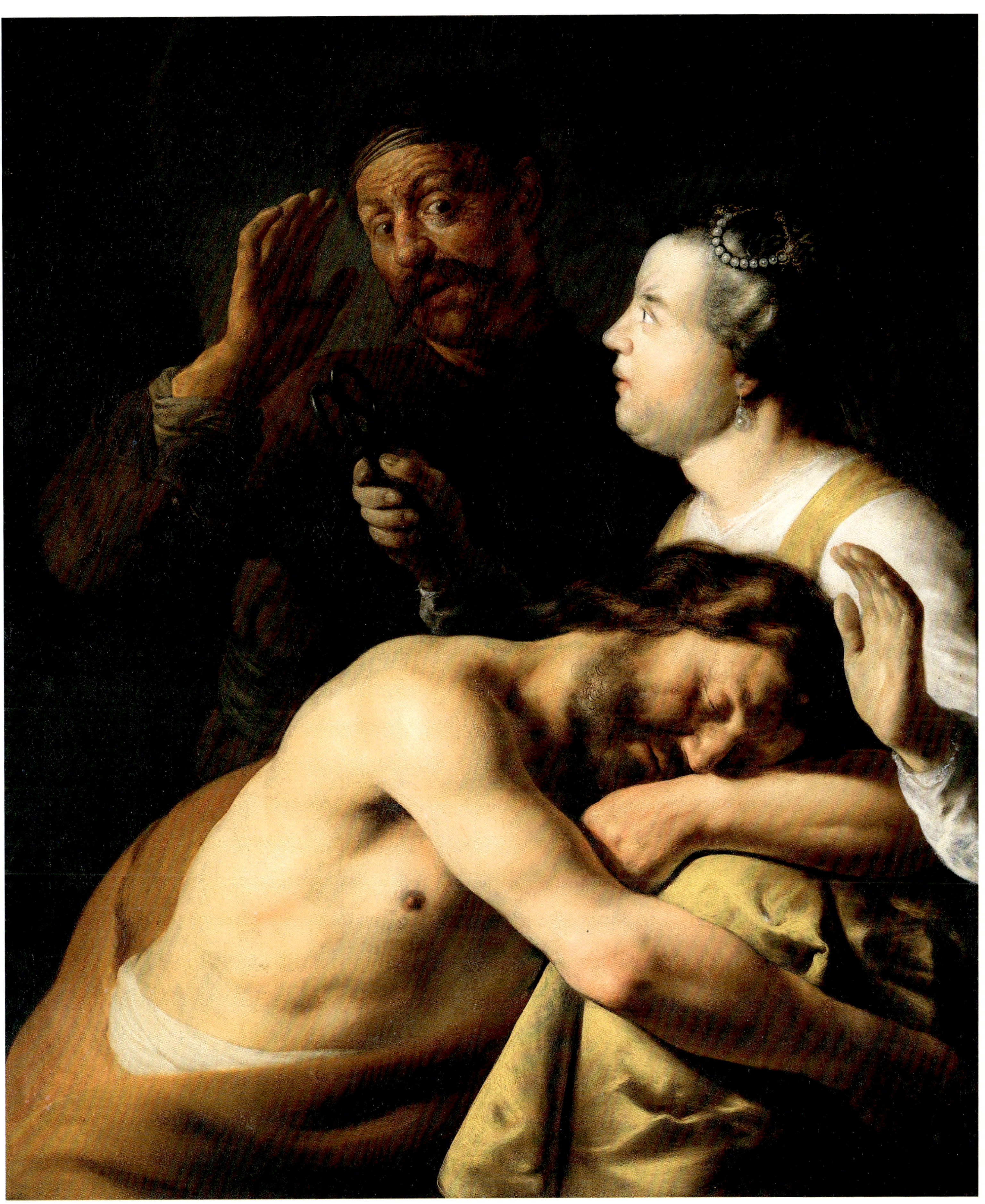

16 Portrait of Constantijn Huygens

1628–1629, oil on panel, 99 × 84 (39 × 33 1/16). Rijksmuseum, Amsterdam, on loan from the Musée de la Chartreuse, Douai

Provenance

(Favart, Douai); Dr. Enée Escallier 1836; acquired in 1857

Selected References

Schneider/Ekkart 1973, 309–311, 333; Braunschweig 1979, no. 17; Sumowski 1983, 3: 1807, no. 1286; Schwartz 1985, 76; Leerintveld 1989, 159–183; Van Straten 2005, 91, 107–108

CONSTANTIJN HUYGENS SITS, AT a three-quarter turn to the left, his hands clasped in his lap, gazing off with heavy-lidded insouciance. In this dark, nearly monochromatic painting, one tends to overlook the richness of Huygens' costume — with its fashionable loose ruff collar, cuffs, and a doublet hung with ribbons above and aiglets below, all black, as are the gloves and the expensive beaver hat. Careful observation rewards the viewer, however, for these elements of the sitter's dress — some English, some French, but all denoting Huygens' nobility — heighten the sense of his refined elegance.

Huygens was secretary to the stadtholder and an accomplished man of great intellectual breadth and complexity, not only a prolific writer, poet, playwright, and composer but also a high-level diplomat. On May 11, 1629, he began writing an autobiographical account in Latin for the benefit of his children while on a military campaign with Prince Frederik Hendrik. In it, he wrote extensively about artists, an interest that had taken him to Leiden the previous winter to meet Lievens and Rembrandt.[1] This record documents the genesis of the present portrait. After noting that he and Lievens "had no prior acquaintance," Huygens continued: "He was seized with the desire to paint my portrait. I assured him that I should be only too pleased to grant him the opportunity if he would come to The Hague and put up at my house for a while."

Thus, only shortly after their first meeting, Huygens agreed to have Lievens paint his portrait. Lievens appeared in The Hague before the agreed-upon time and completed the painting in two sittings: "he was content to paint my clothes and my bare hands, a task of which he acquitted himself most tastefully, and to postpone the portrayal of my face until the advent of spring." Huygens bought the finished painting, which he greatly esteemed: "not a day goes by but it is regarded by Mierevelt and countless others with the utmost admiration." This was high praise, as Huygens ranked Michiel van Mierevelt as Holland's leading portraitist.[2]

Huygens recognized the young painter's "acute and profound insight" and easy intelligence, and he particularly appreciated how Lievens managed to capture a sense of even the diplomat's guarded thoughts: "There are those who opine that the contemplative rendering of the face detracts from the vivacity of my mind, to which I can but respond that the fault is mine. During this period I was involved in a serious family affair of some importance and, as is only to be expected, the cares which I endeavored to keep to myself were clearly reflected in the expression of my face and eyes." Huygens also penned an admiring epigram about the painting on April 5, 1632: "The speech of this picture is not missing, nor does the voice trip you; / This is the face of Huygens, who was meditating, / If you look for the soul, you will each see the one who is full of breath, / If you will have brought to it Lievens' kind of insight."[3]

The portrait is not dated, which has led to speculation about the nature of the "serious family matter" (*tempestatum*) that provoked the anxiety Huygens sought to conceal. Two suggestions have been made — that Huygens was concerned either about his marriage proposal to Susannah van Baerle in 1627 or about the anticipated birth of his first son in March 1628.[4] But these dates are not consistent with the painting's refined style. The process of executing this portrait involved considerable struggle on Lievens' part: x-radiography demonstrates that he initially posed Huygens frontally, then changed to this three-quarter pose,[5] perhaps trying to achieve the reflective interiority the sitter valued.

The encounter in 1628–1629 established the beginning of Lievens' long relationship with Huygens. The artist remained in contact with Huygens during his sojourns in London and Antwerp, and he portrayed him again in 1639 (cat. 103). Later Huygens would serve as Lievens' agent for courtly commissions, such as the Oranjezaal in The Hague and likely also the Oranienburg near Berlin. He continued to be a supporter throughout Lievens' career. LDW

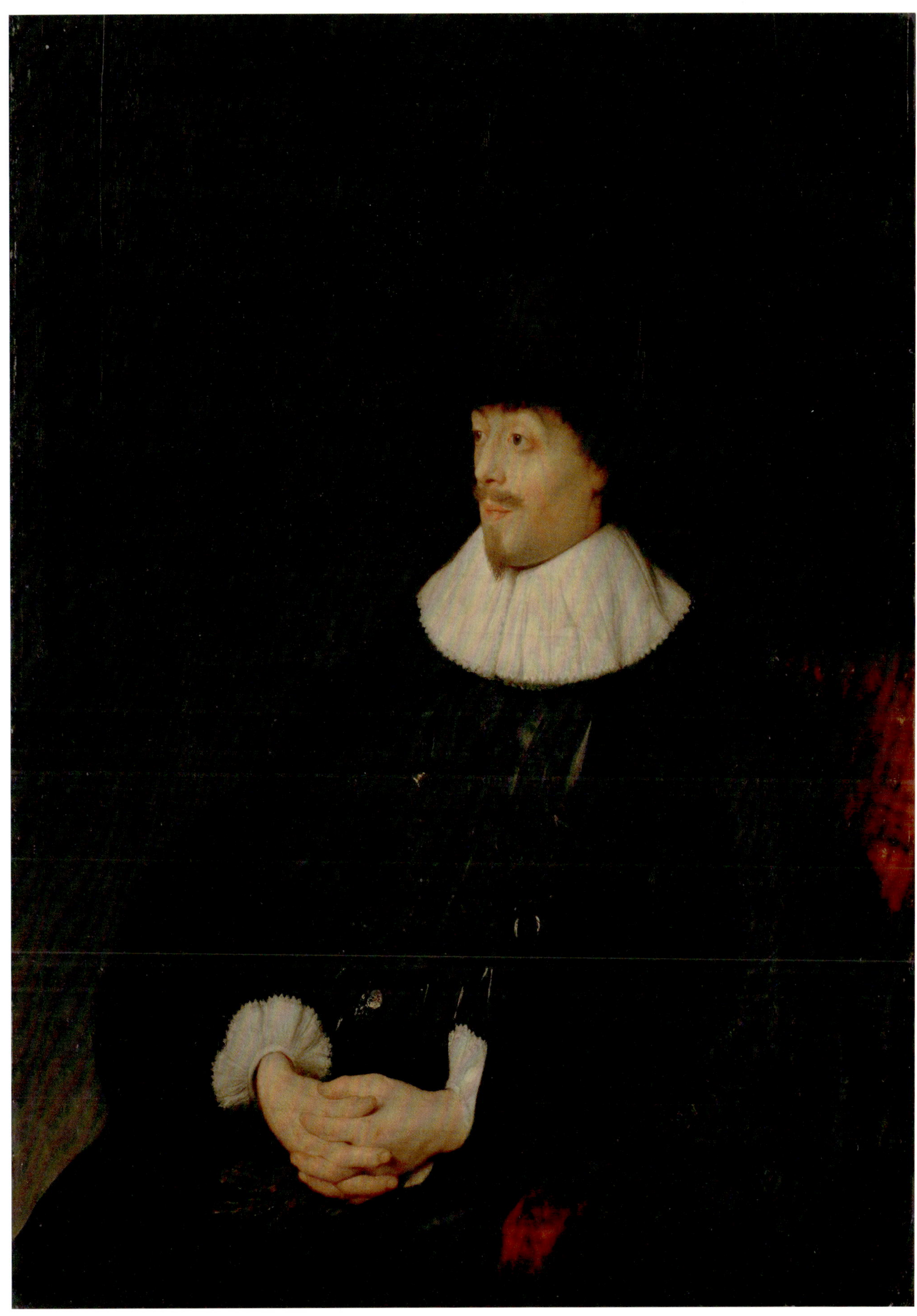

17 Portrait of Rembrandt

c. 1629, oil on panel, 57 × 44 (22 7/16 × 17 5/16). Rijksmuseum, Amsterdam, on loan from a private collection

Inscription

Monogrammed in lower left: I.L.

Provenance

Earls of Derby, Knowsley Hall, prior to 1736; (Christie's, London, July 17, 1964, no. 48); Daan Cevat Collection, Guernsey

Selected References

Schneider/Ekkart 1973, 335, 264b; Braunschweig 1979, no. 19; Leiden 1991; Sumowski 1983, 3: 1800, no. 1260; Gutbrod 1996, 197–205; Van Straten 2005, 204–205, no. 129

1 | Rembrandt van Rijn, *Self-Portrait with Gorget*, c. 1629–1630, oil on panel, 38 × 30.9 cm. Germanisches Nationalmuseum, Nuremberg

THIS YOUTHFUL SITTER, WITH rounded cheeks, a full lower lip, a bulbous nose, and wiry hair, bears a striking resemblance to images Rembrandt painted of himself in the late 1620s (see fig. 1). Although the fanciful dress with a gorget and felt cap is characteristic of tronies, Lievens captures Rembrandt's proud bearing and thoughtful countenance with a portrait-like precision. Smooth brushwork models the face, while Lievens defined tight curls in the hair by scratching into the wet paint with the blunt end of his brush — giving a hint of the unruly elements in Rembrandt's personality.

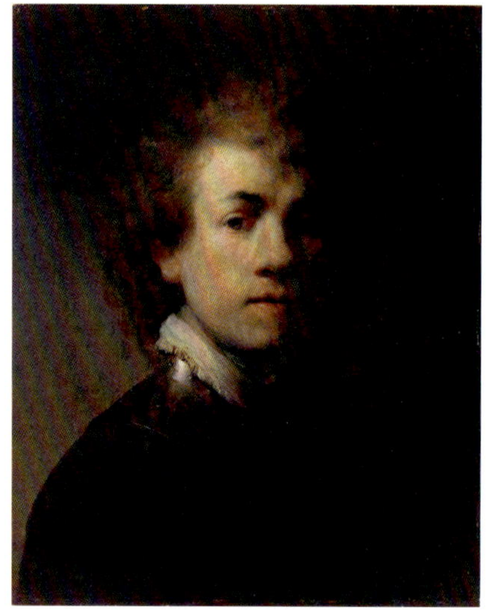

Lievens' chiaroscuro effects are softer than those Rembrandt used to describe his own features at this time. Light plays across all surfaces of the face and highlights the white scarf prominently bunched up below Rembrandt's chin and above his shiny metal gorget. Lievens created a ruddy glow by exposing the brown underpainting at the edges of the face (see Gifford essay).

Lievens executed this portrait around 1629 when the two artists were working closely together, possibly even sharing a studio (see Wheelock essay). Although Lievens and Rembrandt painted in comparable ways, the differences in their personalities and in their perceptions are revealed in their self-portraits and portraits of one another. Lievens' youthful self-portrait (cat. 18), with untamed wavy locks flowing down to his shoulders, exudes a far more romantic character than does his portrayal of Rembrandt as an earnest young man, gazing confidently out at the viewer. Rembrandt presented himself as a far more aggressive personality, his visage strongly accented with contrasts of light and dark. MEK

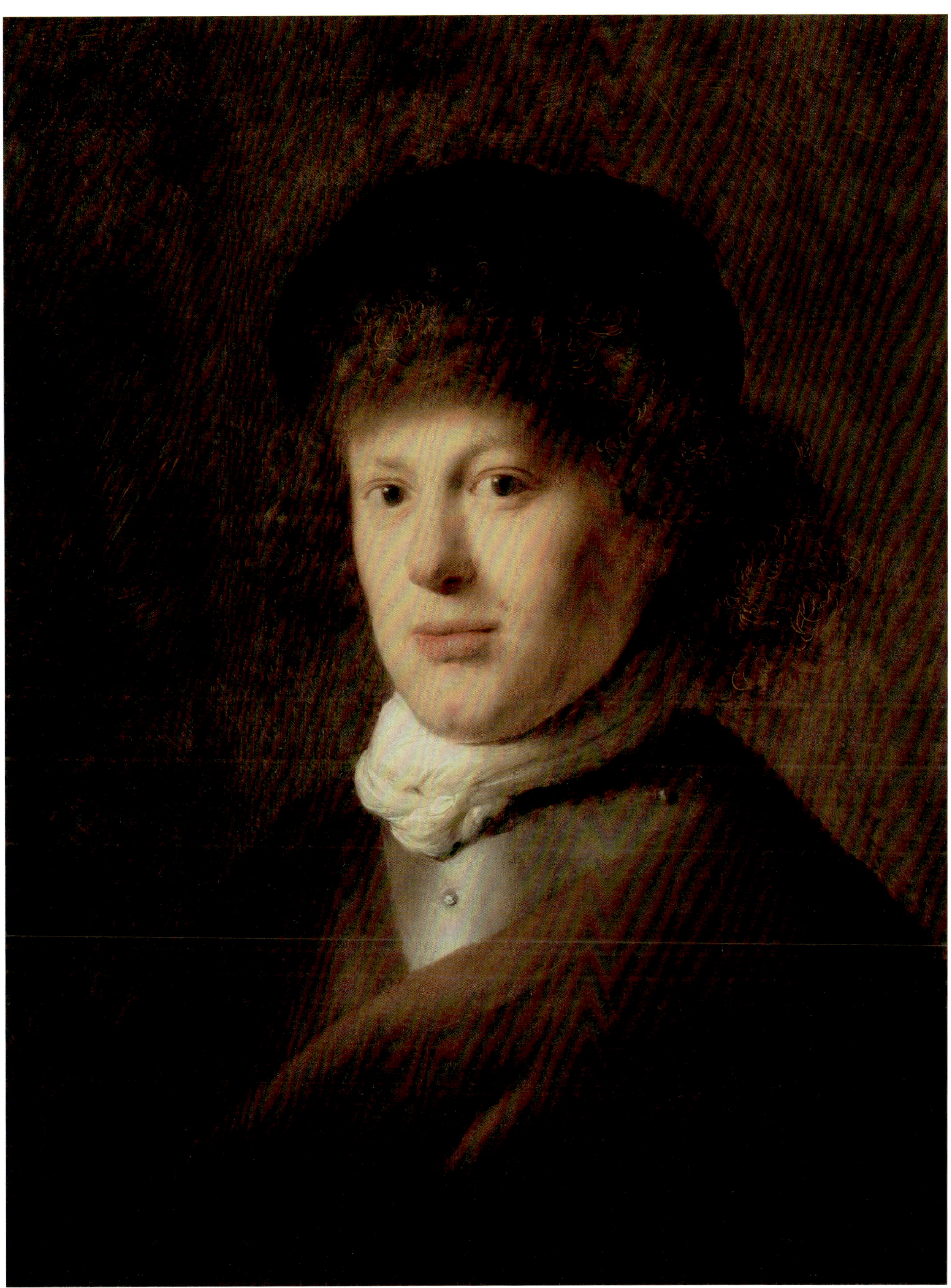

18 Self-Portrait

c. 1629–1630, oil on panel, 42 × 33 (16 9/16 × 13). Private collection

Inscription

Monogrammed in upper right: IL

Provenance

Private collection; (Sotheby's, London, July 22, 1953, no. 116); (A. Brod, London, 1957–1958); (Thomas Agnew and Sons, London, 2006); (Johnny Van Haeften, London, 2006)

Selected References

Schneider/Ekkart 1973, 352, 371, no. 56; Braunschweig, 1979, no. 32; Gutbrod 1996, 186 n. 8; Kassel and Amsterdam 2001–2002, 44 n. 76

WHEN HUYGENS TRAVELED TO Leiden in 1629 and met the young Jan Lievens and Rembrandt van Rijn for the first time, he discovered two dynamic artists whose striking personalities and artistic predilections he perceptively characterized in his autobiography. As for Lievens, Huygens celebrated him as a "prodigy" and admired his "vigorous, untamable spirit" and "acute and profound insight into all manner of things," even as he lamented his "stubbornness" and "excess of self-confidence." He praised Lievens' work ethic, talent, and immense production. If Huygens felt that Rembrandt was "superior to Lievens in his sure touch and liveliness of emotions," he thought that Lievens was "greater in inventiveness and audacious themes and forms." He was also convinced that Lievens should concentrate on "painting the human countenance," where "he wreaks miracles."

Standing before this handsome self-portrait, which Lievens probably began shortly after Huygens' visit, one can understand entirely the power of the young artist's forthright personality. Unlike Rembrandt, who in his early self-portraits of around 1629–1630 often obscured part of his face in shadow as he stared directly at the viewer, Lievens sought no such effect. A strong light from the upper left falls across Lievens' face to reveal his smooth skin, broad cheekbones, and distinctive features. His piercing eyes gaze to the right, suggestive of an active and searching mind. Light shimmering off his long, flowing brown hair, further enlivens the image. Lievens' pencil-thin moustache, similar to that seen in the portrait print for Van Dyck's *Iconography* (see Wheelock fig. 11), further confirms the sitter's identity.[1]

Although it was previously believed that Lievens painted this self-portrait around 1632–1634 when he was in England, a dating of 1629–1630 seems more likely for both technical and stylistic reasons.[2] Dendrochronological examinations have revealed that Lievens used an oak panel made from the identical tree that supplied the panel for Rembrandt's *Samson and Delilah* in Berlin, which dates to c. 1629–1630 (see cat. 15, fig. 3).[3] This suggests that Lievens and Rembrandt purchased their panels from the same panel maker and perhaps even purchased their panels jointly. X-radiographs indicate that Lievens revised his appearance during the course of painting in ways that were not simply neutral in character. He eliminated a hat, probably a painter's beret, which he had initially placed tilted slightly forward on his head, and he added freely rendered, cascading locks at the left, perhaps in emulation of English and/or Flemish courtly hairstyles. These changes transformed his presentation of himself into a dashing, almost aristocratic-looking young man, peering out past the viewer as though he had already left behind his Leiden persona in anticipation of the career he hoped would soon unfold at the court of King Charles I in London.[4] AKW

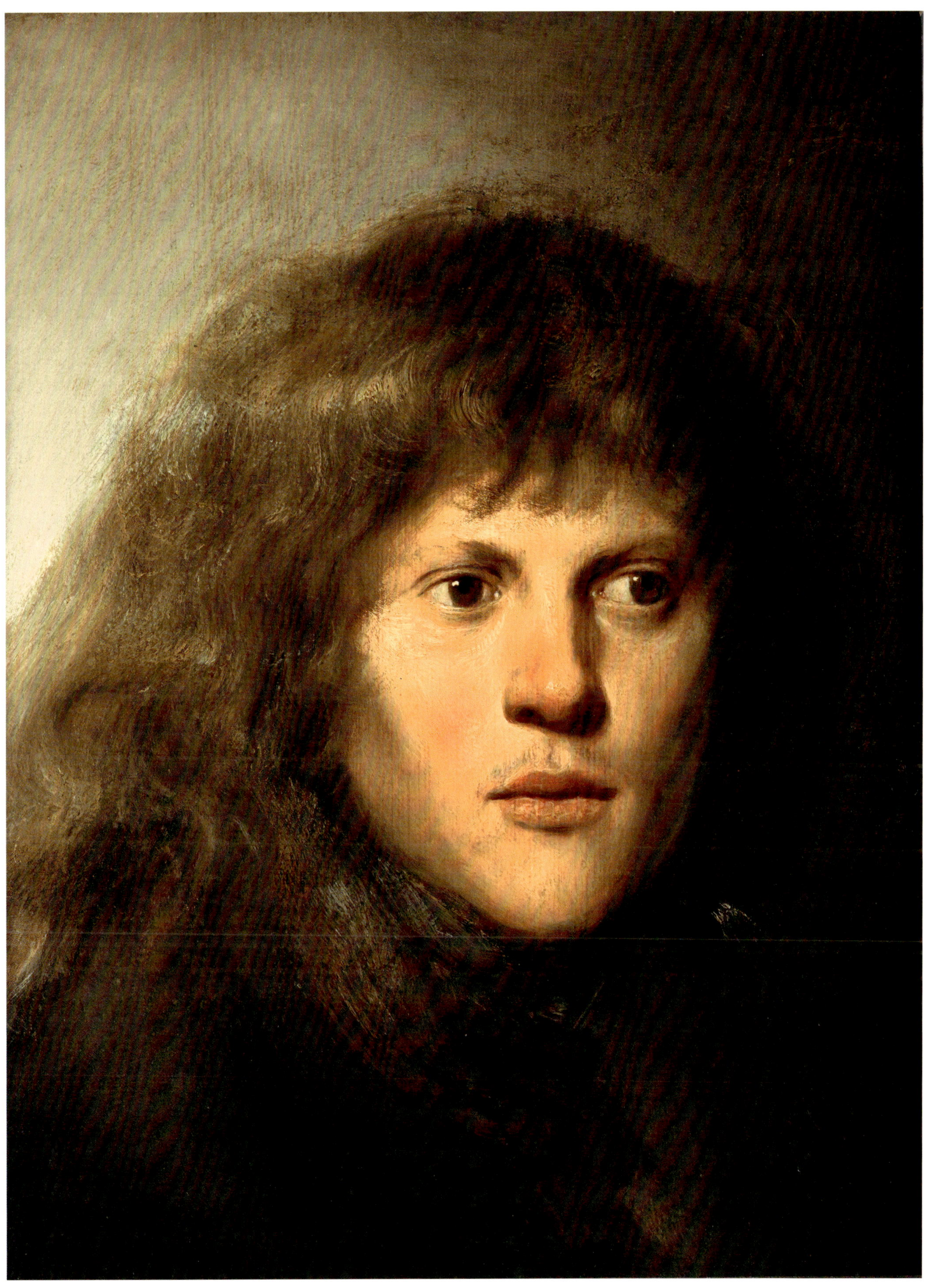

19 Man in Oriental Costume ("Sultan Soliman")

c. 1629–1631, oil on canvas, 135 × 100.5 (53 1/8 × 39 9/16). Stiftung Preussische Schlösser und Gärten Berlin-Brandenburg *(Washington, Milwaukee)*

Inscription

Monogrammed to the right of shoulder: L

Provenance

Frederik Hendrik, Prince of Orange, The Hague and Honselaarsdijk (inventory 1707, 1713, and 1719, no. 177, as mantelpiece in the audience chamber, "Sultan Soliman by Rembrandt"); by inheritance to the Electors of Brandenburg, Royal Palace, Berlin (inventory 1811, no. A 694)

Selected References

Schneider/Ekkart 1973, 29, no. 304; Drossaers and Scheurleer 1974–1976, 530, no. 177; Sumowski 1983, 3: 1795, no. 1236; Leiden 1991, no. 72; Gutbrod 1996, 283–286; Leiden 2005, no. 37; Van Straten 2005, 91–92

CONSTANTIJN HUYGENS REPORTS in his autobiography: "In the collection of our Prince is a painting of a man, purportedly a Turkish ruler, with the head of a Dutchman." Though the painting was listed in eighteenth-century inventories of the House of Orange as being by Rembrandt, Huygens' passage undoubtedly refers to the present work, which Lievens executed between 1629 and 1631.[1]

This majestic, half-length image of a man bedecked in Eastern-inspired garments was probably Lievens' first opportunity to impress the court in The Hague.[2] He positioned the subject against an unadorned background, while making use of strong lights and darks to emphasize the solidity of the figure. While still working in a large format, Lievens shifted from the broad, sweeping brushstrokes of his earlier technique to smaller, more refined touches that allowed him to create a more detailed image. This smooth style of painting was in vogue at court, which may have been the reason Lievens changed his working method. He took great pleasure in articulating the rich brocade of the cloak and the exquisite texture of the feathers of the aigrette.

So-called Orientals had been portrayed in Western art since the Middle Ages, often in representations of the Adoration of the Magi or other biblical stories (see cat. 7). Orientals did not appear as an independent artistic genre, however, until Lievens and Rembrandt began to paint them in the late 1620s.[3] Interest in such exotic costumes may have been stimulated by the visit of the Persian ambassador and his retinue to The Hague in 1626–1627, which may have prompted the commission for the present painting.[4] Lievens appears to have found artistic inspiration for his *Man in Oriental Costume* in one of the wise men Rubens depicted in his *Adoration of the Magi*, which Lievens could have known through a print by Vorsterman (fig. 1).[5] Rubens seems to have provided the source for the cloak fastened across the chest by a chain and the position of the man's hands grasping the sash around the waist.

The model for Lievens' *Man in Oriental Costume* is often identified as Rembrandt's father,[6] but he more closely resembles the model for *Old Man Holding a Skull* (see cat. 22), whom Jan Orlers describes in his 1640 inventory as "the keeper of the almshouse."[7] Although the man's features are somewhat more

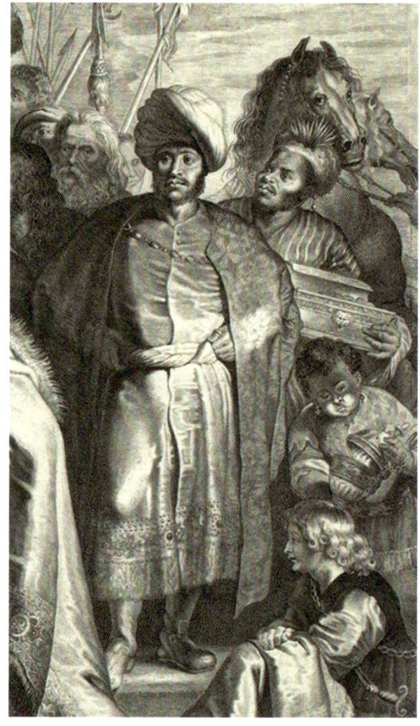

1 | Lucas Vorsterman after Peter Paul Rubens, *The Adoration of the Magi* (detail), 1621, engraving. Rijksmuseum, Amsterdam

idealized here, his thin lips, beaked nose, and deeply creased brow are recognizable. The present painting seems to have served as the impetus for Rembrandt's similar though slightly larger painting, *The Noble Slav* of 1632 (Metropolitan Museum of Art), evidence of the continuing closeness and competition between the two artists.[8] VCT

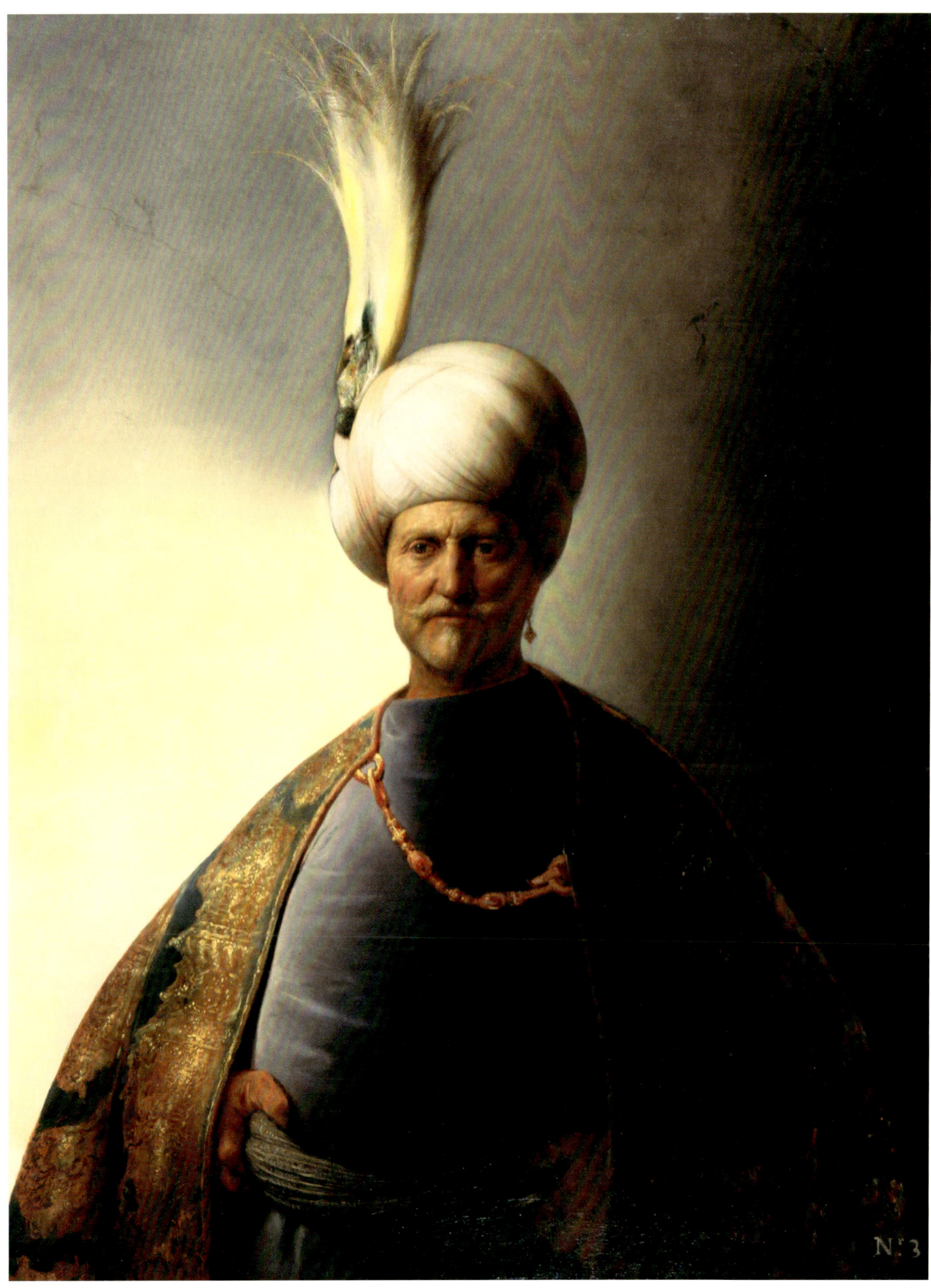
N: 3

20 Bearded Man with a Beret

c. 1630, oil on panel, 53.5 × 46.3 (21 1/16 × 18 1/4). National Gallery of Art, Washington, Gift (Partial and Promised) of the Kaufman Americana Foundation in honor of George M. and Linda H. Kaufman

Provenance

Marion Louise Nichols, Cambridge, MA; private collection, Boston (1975–1986); (Hoogsteder-Naumann Ltd., New York, 1986); George M. and Linda H. Kaufman Collection, Norfolk, VA, 1986

Selected References

Sumowski 1983, 3: 1799, no. 1253; The Hague and San Francisco 1991, no. 39

BEARDED MAN WITH A BERET is one of the best preserved and most expressive tronies, or head studies, of old men and women from the end of Lievens' Leiden period. In this nearly monochromatic image, an old man looks up to the left, with the incoming light glinting in his eyes. He is situated against a plain, dark background, his lips slightly parted as though he is about to speak. As is characteristic of Lievens' working method at this point in his career, the artist painted the wrinkled face and gray hair with thick impastos and short, meticulous brushstrokes, while modeling the beret and jacket with broad, fluid strokes. He also used the blunt end of his brush to scratch through the wet paint and create small furrows near the man's temples and flowing rhythms in his beard.[1]

As tronies were character studies rather than portraits of specific individuals, artists often incorporated fanciful costume elements, such as a beret, to enhance the expressive quality of the image. The beret, for instance, was an outmoded style of hat by the seventeenth century and was retained only in academic or scholarly dress.[2] Lievens may have intended such an association, for this sitter resembles the bearded scholar in Rembrandt's *Two Old Men Disputing* of 1628 (fig. 1).[3] Lievens and Rembrandt apparently used the same model for these paintings, as is often found in their works from c. 1630.[4]

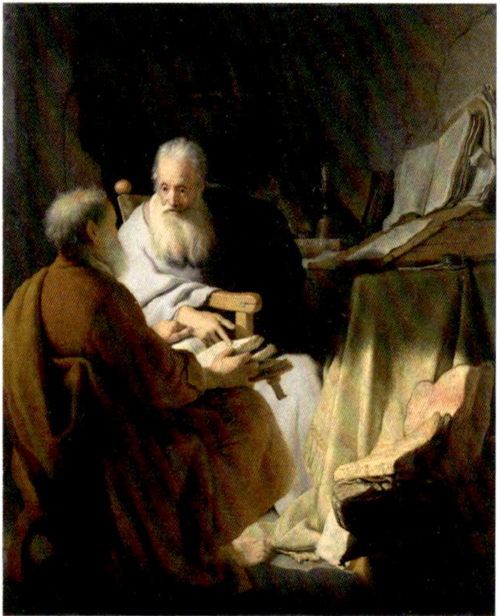

1 | Rembrandt van Rijn, *Two Old Men Disputing*, 1628, oil on panel, 72.3 × 59.5 cm. National Gallery of Victoria, Melbourne

Tronies were popular with seventeenth-century Dutch collectors. Generally painted from a live model, these evocative images were cherished both for their technical skill and for their picturesque subject matter.[5] Huygens records in his autobiographical account of 1629–1631 that a number of Lievens' tronies had already found their way into prominent collections, including those of stadtholder Prince Frederik Hendrik; his treasurer, Thomas Brouart; the artist Jacques de Gheyn III; and the Amsterdam tax collector Nicolaas Sohier. Huygens himself thought so highly of Lievens' ability to render human faces, calling it "miraculous," that he believed the artist would be well advised to make portraiture his specialty. Sympathetic images of elderly men in Lievens' graphic works from the end of his Leiden period (see cats. 71, 100) have a similar power to that of his paintings. VCT

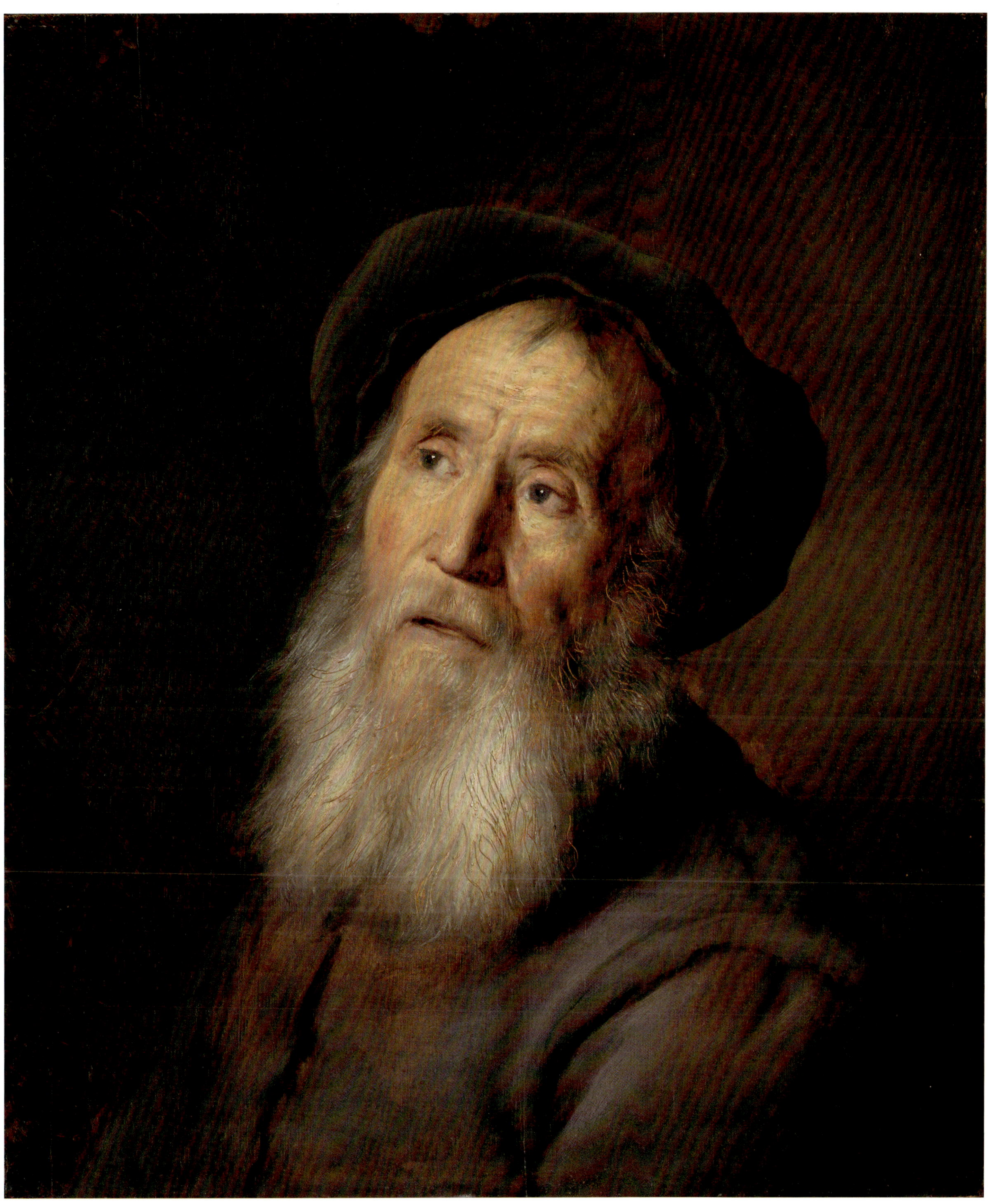

21 Profile Head of an Old Woman ("Rembrandt's Mother")

c. 1630, oil on panel, 43.2 × 33.7 (17 × 13¼). Agnes Etherington Art Centre, Kingston, Gift of Alfred and Isabel Bader, 2005

Inscription

Monogrammed upper right: RHL (in ligature), possibly originally IL transformed by a later hand

Provenance

Possibly Lucas Merens, Amsterdam; (sale, Amsterdam [Jan Yver], April 15, 1778, no. 92, as Rembrandt); Joseph Cardinal Fesch (1763–1839), Rome; (sale, Rome, March 17, 1845, no. 193); (J. F. Winterbottom sale, London [Foster], April 27, 1870, no. 290, as Rembrandt); (London, art trade, 1940); the Earl of Leven and Melville, London; (sale, London, December 12, 1945, no. 388); Loft & Warner, London; O. E. Johnson, London, 1950; (Leggatt Bros., London, 1956, as Rembrandt); Oscar and Peter Johnson, London; (K. and V. Waterman, Amsterdam); Linda and Gerald Guterman, New York, 1983; (sale, New York, Sotheby's, January 14, 1988, no. 22); Alfred and Isabel Bader, Milwaukee

Selected References

Braunschweig 1979, no. 18; Sumowski 1983, 3: 1801, 1900, 3062 n. 2, no. 1261; Bader 1995, 217; Melbourne and Canberra 1997, no. 35; Leiden 2005, no. 7; Edinburgh and London 2001, 70

A STRIKING OLD WOMAN WITH A prominent nose and toothless overbite appears in profile facing left. Her head is barely tilted back, her eyes are heavily lidded, and her lips are slightly parted in an expression of interest. She wears a richly embroidered translucent veil over a spectacularly patterned shawl. Lievens presents a tour de force of description, with passages of wrinkled skin set off against the fine embroidered cloth, and entrancing effects of reflection and transparency in the gauze of the veil. His penchant for monumental form is evident in the bold profile that fills the frame.

Lievens here draws on Turkish and Persian costume to cast his aged subject as perhaps a prophetess looking into the distance. Without an accompanying narrative or attribute, she cannot be specifically identified. This panel exhibits the new pictorial category of the tronie, which Lievens and Rembrandt forged out of the Flemish practice of creating head studies for history paintings.[1] These two artists clearly used local models whose features they followed closely, so that individuals are recognizable in various works, as is the case here. Lievens first rendered this particular woman in a painting of c. 1624, where she represents a prophetess.[2]

Despite longstanding tradition, it is highly unlikely that the sitter was Rembrandt's mother, Neeltgen Willemsdr van Zuytbrouck,[3] an assumption based on the belief that the two young artists looked no further than their immediate environment for subjects.[4] Nevertheless, the profound empathy that both artists demonstrate in their depictions of old men and women did probably arise out of their own familial bonds. The overall result in this instance is a compelling likeness far removed from the mundane sphere of family portraiture.[5] DDW

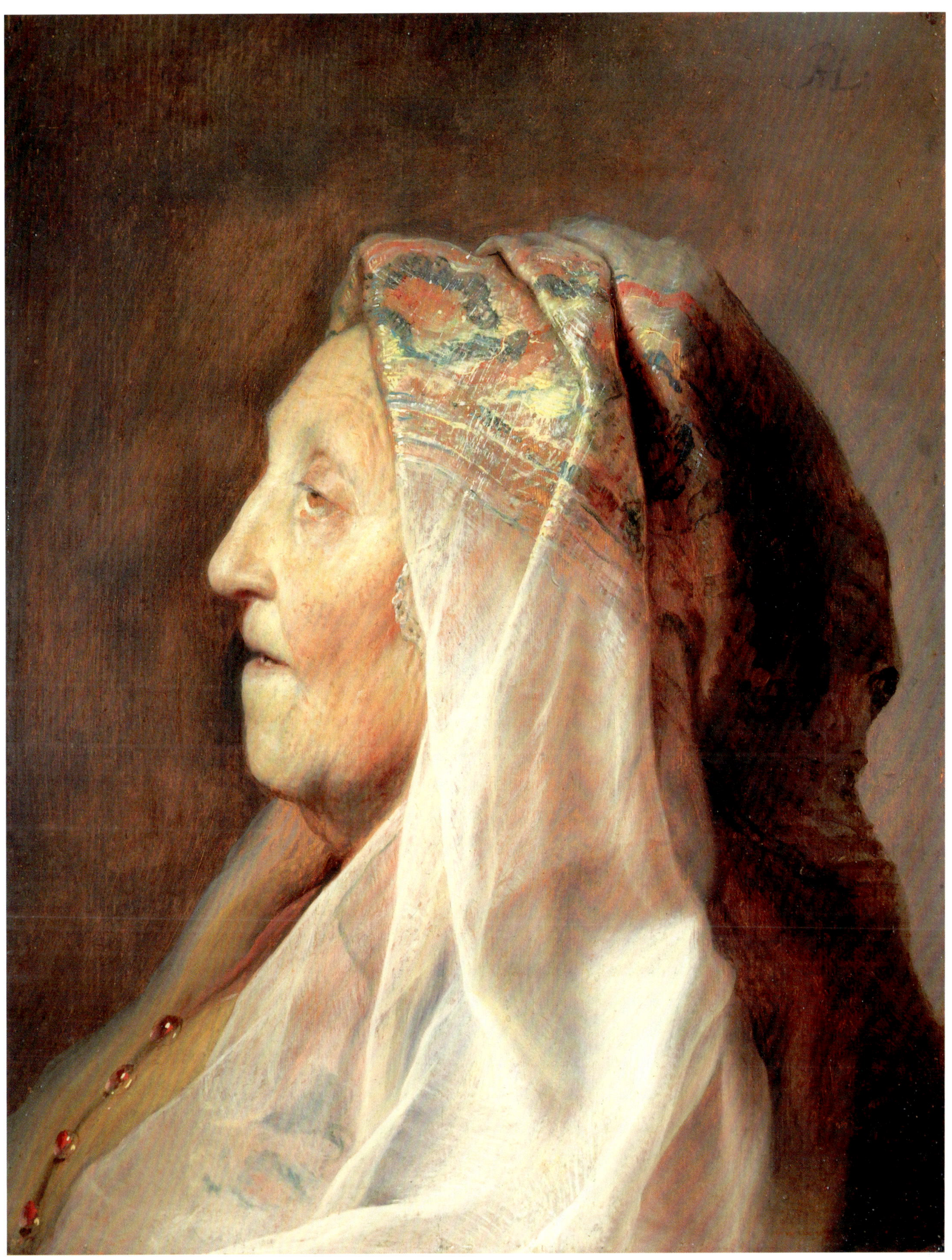

22 Old Man Holding a Skull

c. 1630, oil on panel, 61.6 × 48.3 (24¼ × 19). Johnny Van Haeften Ltd., London

Provenance

Jan Jansz Orlers, Leiden, inventory of 1640; Barton Booth (1681–1733), and by descent to his widow, Hester Booth (c. 1690–1773), and by descent to her grandson, Edward Eliot, later Craggs Eliot (1727–1804), 1st Baron Eliot of Saint Germans, and by descent at Port Eliot (Christie's, London, December 6, 2007, no. 56)

Selected References

Pelinck 1941, 198; Schneider/Ekkart 1973, 353

ONE OF THE MOST IMPORTANT recent additions to Jan Lievens' oeuvre is *Old Man Holding a Skull*. Painted in Leiden around 1630, it is both a remarkable *vanitas* image and an important example of the young artist's "astonishing talent" for depicting the human countenance.[1] It has remained in the same private collection for more than three hundred years.

Against a plain dark background, light falls from the upper left to emphasize the sitter's bald head, the wrinkles around his eyes, the prominent vein at his temple, and the skull he presents to the viewer. Lievens juxtaposed the sitter and the skull for maximum visual and iconographic impact. The man's prominent cheekbone and the shadow under his eye mirror the projections and hollows of the skull, even as his lively gaze contrasts with the skull's empty sockets.

Skulls and animated skeletons have appeared as symbols and harbingers of death in works of art since antiquity.[2] Though the predatory skeleton featured prominently in sixteenth-century works by artists such as Hans Holbein and Pieter Bruegel the Elder, it had largely been replaced in the seventeenth century by the detached inanimate skull, set within a still-life context or held in a sitter's hand. Frans Hals, for example, depicted sitters holding skulls in several paintings of the early 1610s, among them *Man Holding a Skull* in the Barber Institute of Fine Arts, University of Birmingham, and his lost portrait of the Catholic clergyman Jacobus Zaffius, known only through a print by Jan van de Velde.[3]

Hals returned to the theme in his *Young Man with a Skull*, c. 1627 (National Gallery, London). That painting, traditionally identified as a depiction of Hamlet, relates to a slightly different iconographic tradition of the transience of life, most vividly seen in Lucas van Leyden's engraved *Young Man with a Skull* (fig. 1).[4] In Lucas' print a young man wearing an elaborately feathered hat and fashionable outfit points to a skull half hidden beneath his cloak.[5] This overt juxtaposition of youth and death appeared almost unchanged a century later in a drawing of 1614 by Hendrick Goltzius, *Young Man Holding a Skull and a Tulip* (Pierpont Morgan Library, New York). The figure there stands before a ruined wall inscribed with a motto that reminds the viewer of death's inevitability: QVIS EVADET / NEMO (Who escapes? No man).[6]

Lievens' model, however, is neither young nor fashionable. As with Hals' portrait of Jacobus Zaffius, the artist was acquainted with his subject and clearly associated him with this dual iconography of life and death.[7] It is rare to know the sitter's identity in such images, but this painting is described as portraying "the keeper of the almshouse with a skull in his hand" in the 1640 inventory of Lievens' most important early patron, Jan Orlers.[8] The work was paired with another *vanitas* by Lievens, a boy blowing bubbles. Both works were described as having been painted from life.

Almshouses were charitable institutions that looked after the elderly and indigent. Thirty-five such facilities existed in Leiden at this time, nearly all funded by wealthy citizens who commissioned group portraits such as Hals' *Regentesses of the Old Men's Almshouse*, c. 1664 (Frans Halsmuseum, Haarlem), to depict themselves as purveyors of Christian charity. Lievens' sitter would have been responsible for the daily administration of the almshouse, making this pictorial warning more than a general reminder of life's brevity. To those who knew him, his appearance in Lievens' painting would have served not only as a reminder of death but also as an admonition to live well. MH

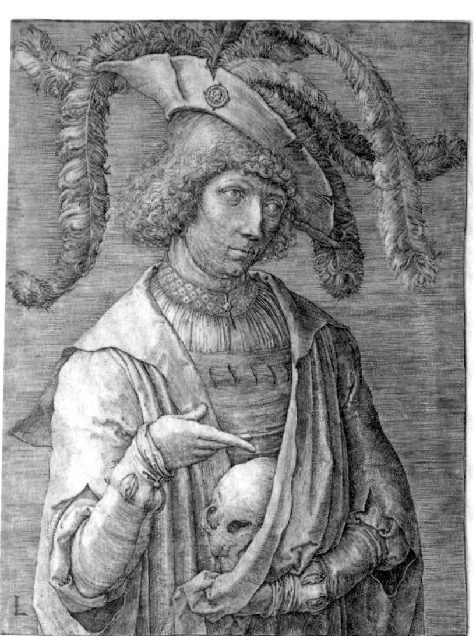

1 | Lucas van Leyden, *Young Man with a Skull*, c. 1519, engraving. National Gallery of Art, Washington, Andrew W. Mellon Fund

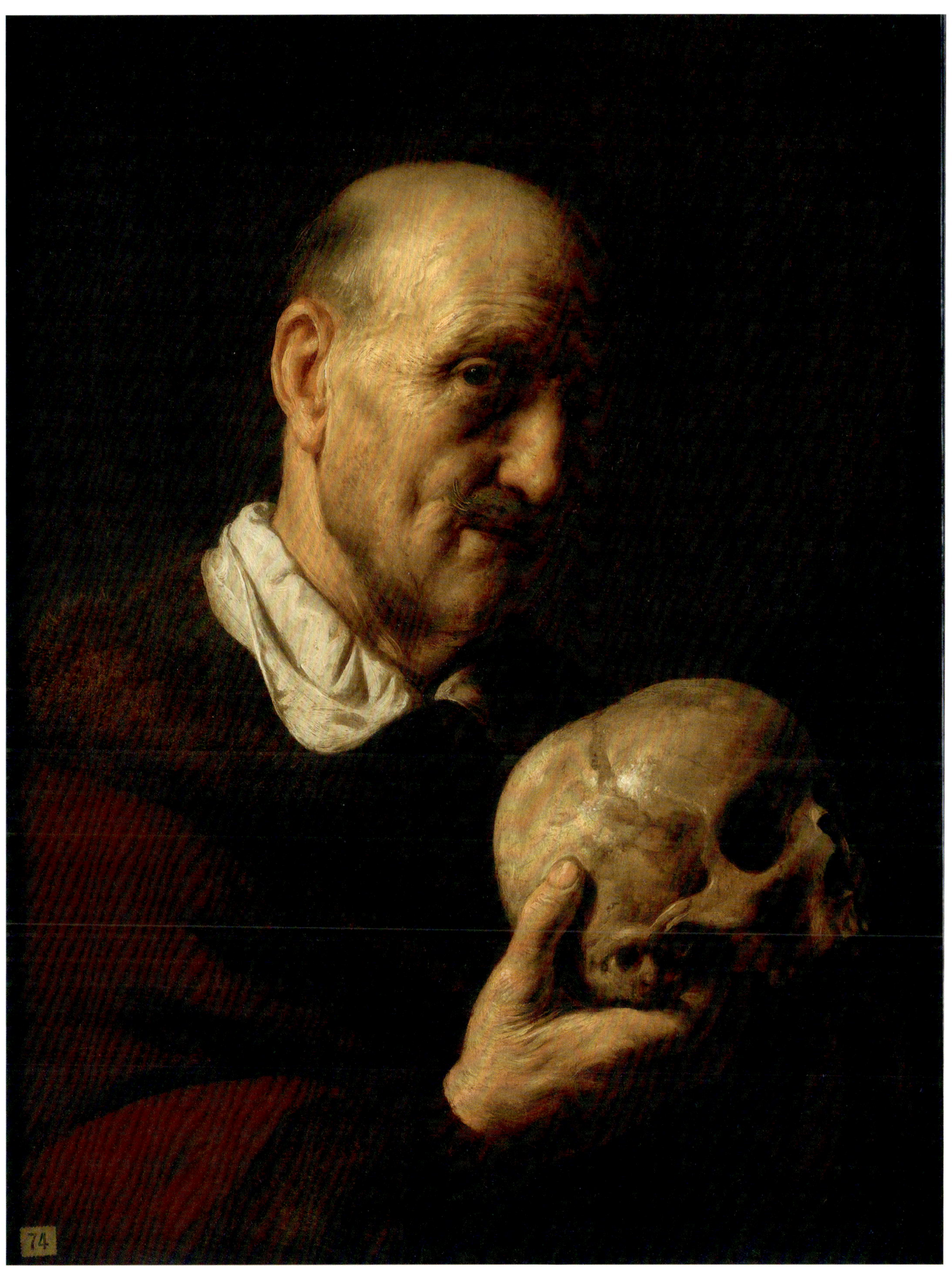
74

23 Saint Jerome Meditating in a Grotto

c. 1630, oil on paper on panel, 31.3 × 27.5 (12 5/16 × 10 13/16). Loan Stedelijk Museum De Lakenhal, Leiden, The Netherlands *(Washington, Amsterdam)*

Provenance

Dr. Torsten Stjernschantz, Helsingfors; Gösta Stenman (1926); Dr. Harry A. Johnson, Stockholm; (Bukowski, Stockholm, December 13, 1933, no. 13); Professor Dr. Einar Perman, Stockholm; (S. Nystad, The Hague, 1970)

Selected References

Schneider/Ekkart 1973, 36, 104, 328, no. 48; Braunschweig 1979, no. 24; Corpus 1982–, 1: 200, 444; Sumowski 1983, 3: 1797, no. 1242; Leiden 1991, 103–104

SEATED IN THE DEEP RECESSES OF a grotto, the aged Jerome stares intently at a skull resting in his lap as he holds a small, makeshift crucifix in his clasped hands. He is utterly alone, removed from the world and its temptations, his isolation reinforced by the darkness that surrounds him. Strong light shining down on his pale, emaciated body emphasizes his bald head, white beard, sunken chest, and sinewy arms and legs. Around him rest his slippers, staff, and an empty shallow bowl. One has a sense that they have not been used in some time and may not be picked up again in the near future.

This remarkable grisaille image, essentially a figure study in ochers and grays, is a powerful expression of this saint's intense spiritual devotion. It is also one of the first instances in which Lievens took the type of aged bearded figure he had favored in his drawn, etched, and painted tronies of the late 1620s and adapted it for a religious composition. He then used this small work on paper as a preparatory study for two evocative works, the etched *Saint Jerome* (cat. 72) and, the following year, the large-scale oil on canvas *Job in His Misery* (cat. 25). For the etching, which was Lievens' most ambitious print to date, the study helped him envision not only the composition but also the tonal range that he sought in the print. For the painting, this oil sketch established the body type and pose that Lievens used to depict Job sitting on a dung heap at the depth of his suffering.

One can imagine that Lievens made similar oil sketches as studies for other prints, but none are known to exist, making this work all the more exceptional and important for our understanding of Lievens' creative process, particularly during his Leiden period. It is not known where Lievens learned the advantage of making a grisaille study, although the technique seems to have been used by professional printmakers to a certain extent. Interestingly, Lievens anticipated Rembrandt's use of such sketches in preparation for etchings, a technique that Rembrandt seems to have developed only in the early to middle 1630s.[1] AKW

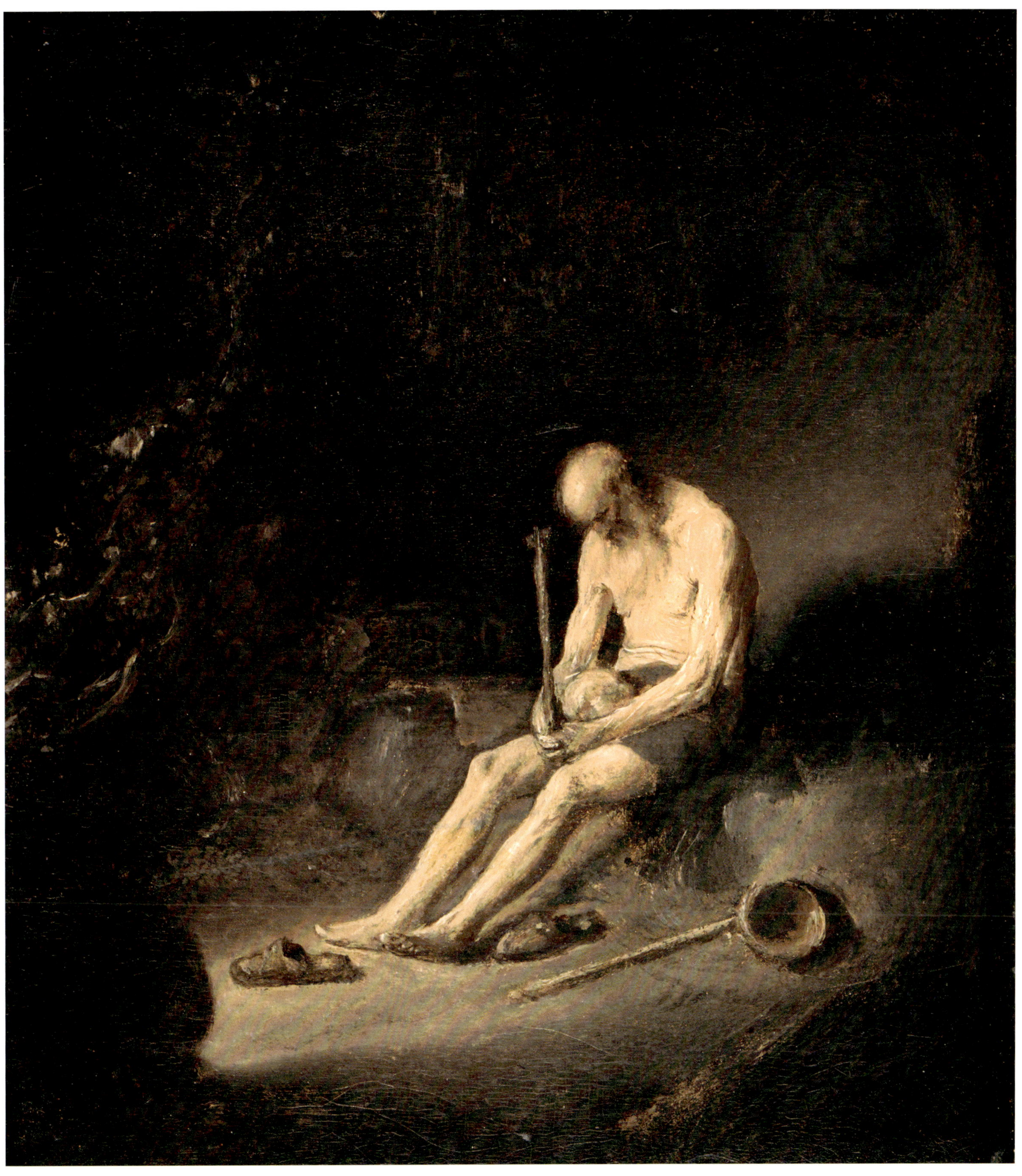

24 The Penitent Magdalene

c. 1631, oil on canvas, 63.5 × 49.5 (25 × 19½). Agnes Etherington Art Centre, Kingston, Gift of Dr. and Mrs. Alfred Bader, 1975

Provenance

Joseph Strecker, Vienna, 1965, as by Rembrandt; (Galerie Fischer, Lucerne); Dr. and Mrs. Alfred Bader, Milwaukee, in 1973

Selected References

Sumowski 1983, 3: 1795, 1876, no. 1237

AN OLD WOMAN TURNS TO THE left and looks up toward heaven while resting her hands atop a skull, contemplating the vanity of life and the promise of the hereafter. To judge from her plain, rough mantle, disheveled hair, and worn features, she has long adopted the life of a hermit. Jan Lievens had already specialized in sympathetic depictions of old age, but he exceeds all his previous efforts in this work's sober and unadorned presentation, one that audaciously turned on its head a widely popular pictorial tradition for representations of Mary Magdalene as a voluptuous, repentant sinner.

According to popular legend, Mary Magdalene followed Jesus after being healed of demons. Present at the Crucifixion, she was the first to whom Jesus appeared after the Resurrection. Later writers conflate her with other figures and trace her past to a life of pleasure, even prostitution, from which she repents.[1] She is also described as traveling to Provence and spending the last three decades of her life meditating in the desert, sustained only by heavenly music.[2] In Lievens' interpretation her most recognizable attribute, the oil jar, is missing, but the skull, her repentant attitude, and the long strands of loose hair confirm her identity.[3]

Lievens' haggard Magdalene differs markedly from sixteenth- and seventeenth-century renderings of the saint. Other artists invariably seized upon the Magdalene's sinful past as a license to incorporate an element of sensuality and emphasize her beauty, often by showing her as nude, covered only by her flowing tresses. Titian famously explained that he was depicting the Magdalene on the day after her repentance, still trailing the vestiges of her former life.[4] She was still portrayed in this manner by Hendrick Goltzius in 1614.[5]

Lievens' inversion of this tradition likely reflects the cautionary climate against sensual pleasure in Leiden as the Remonstrant conflict wore on in that city.[6] Indeed, Lievens appears to have perfectly captured the spirit of the searing criticism of sensual female figures in religious art expressed in the poem "Idolelenchus" that the defrocked Remonstrant preacher Jan Evertsz Geesteranus wrote in Latin in 1622.[7] Moral accusations and counter-accusations formed a staple of exchange between the Counter-Remonstrants and their various opponents during this period of open religious conflict. The assertive moralization of Lievens' *Penitent Magdalene,* like the *vanitas* imagery with which it is related, found a ready market in this climate.[8]

Lievens had already depicted the Magdalene at least once previously, in a roughly painted panel now in Douai that dates to around 1623–1624.[9] The thin, dry application and the extremely limited palette of muted blue and ocher of the present work link it directly to Lievens' astonishing *Job in His Misery* of 1631 (cat. 25). In both, the somber palette underscores the heavy moral theme of suffering and constancy. DDW

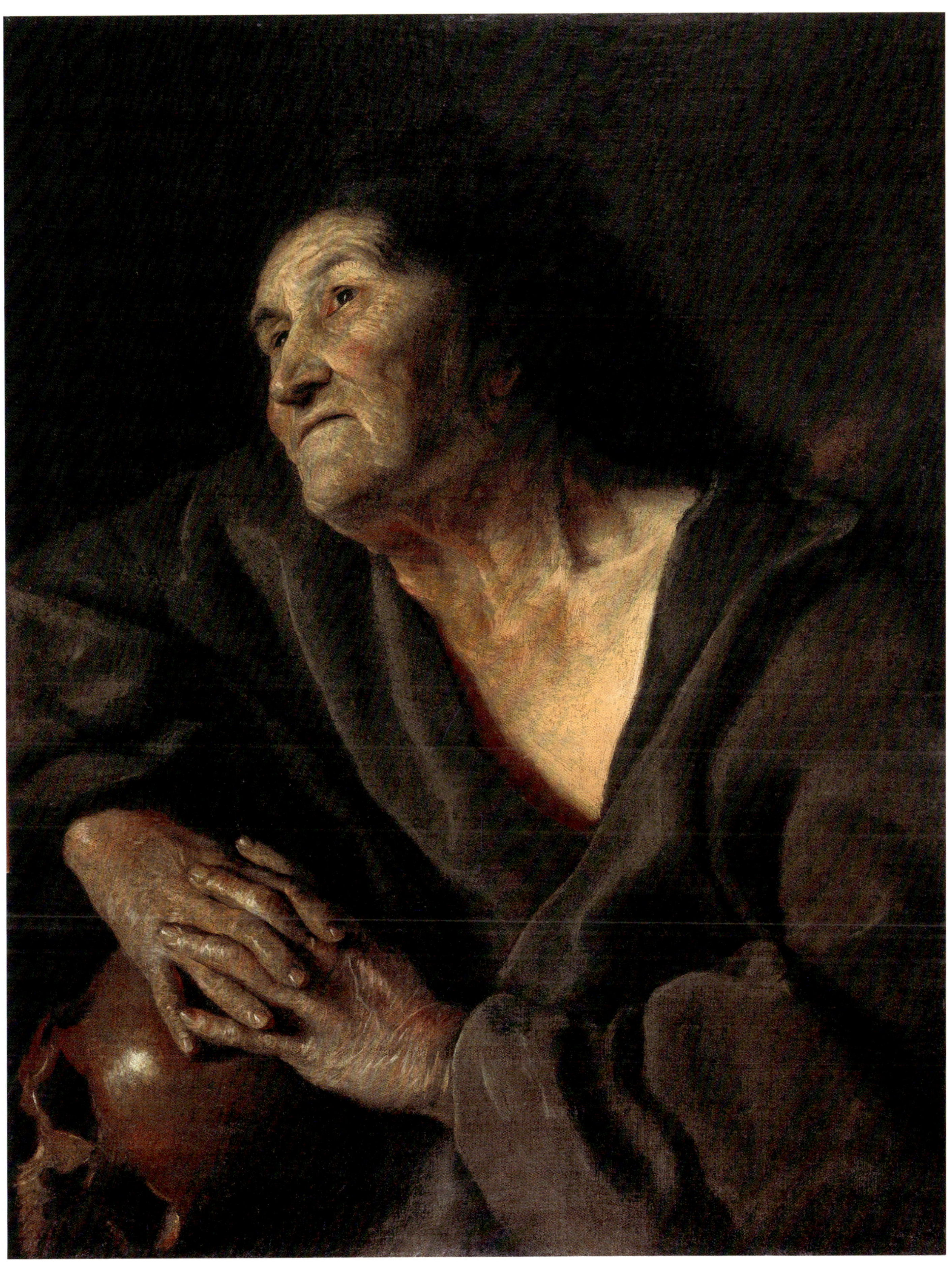

25 Job in His Misery

1631, oil on canvas, 171.5 × 148.6 (67½ × 58½). National Gallery of Canada, Ottawa, Gift of the National Art Collections Fund of Great Britain, 1933

Inscription

Monogrammed and dated in bottom right: IL/1631

Provenance

(Sale, Pieter van Copello, Amsterdam, May 6, 1767, no. 40); Johan van den Marck, Leiden; (Amsterdam, August 25, 1773, no. 160); (Amsterdam, July 26, 1775, no. 165); (J. Smith-Barry, London, 1857); Lord Barrymore, Marbury Hall, Norwich; (Sotheby's, London, June 21, 1933, no. 23)

Selected References

Stolow et al. 1969, 146–150; Schneider/Ekkart 1973, 35–36, 96, 320, no. 20; Braunschweig 1979, no. 25; Sumowski 1983, 3: 1780, no. 1191; Leiden 1991, no. 51; Gutbrod 1996, 15, 68 n. 7, 225

NUDE EXCEPT FOR A LOINCLOTH, the dejected Job sits on a low pile of straw-covered manure, the ground around him strewn with litter. His hair is disheveled, his body slumped, and his arms hang limply by his side, while his open hands express both helplessness and resignation. He is the victim of a bargain by which God has allowed Satan to torment Job as a test of his righteousness (Job 1:7–12). Black-horned and winged demon heads blow smoke and flames toward him, personifying the various plagues that Satan has inflicted in an effort to induce Job to curse God. Job's elderly wife is shown behind him holding a richly plumed turban and garments that she has encouraged Job to put on again if he will only reject God. She holds up her hand as she pleads with him: "Do you still persist in your integrity? Curse God and die!" (Job 2:9). But Job, even at the very depth of his suffering, refuses to do so.

In this painting Lievens gives full rein to his fascination with the physical effects of aging in his graphic rendering of Job's wrinkled skin, flaccid muscles, and protruding veins. He bases this depiction on earlier studies he had made. For example, Job resembles the figure in Lievens' drawing and corresponding print of a seated hermit (cats. 71, 100) and on his oil sketch and corresponding print of Saint Jerome (cats. 23, 72).[1] Lievens based Job's face on a tronie of an old man formerly in Schwerin and on drawings in The Hague and Washington (cat. 98).[2] Job's wife closely resembles the old woman in *Bathsheba Receiving King David's Letter* (cat. 27).

Job's slouched pose, aged body, and despairing gesture all express his physical and psychological affliction.[3] The consuming darkness is relieved only by a light from above that alludes to God as the focus of Job's persevering faith and anticipates his eventual restoration.[4] Lievens may have found inspiration for the demons in Rubens' more violent tormentors from the lost *Job on the Dung Heap*, possibly known to him through Vosterman's engraving (fig. 1).[5]

Lievens may have painted this work in response to Rembrandt's 1630 *Jeremiah Lamenting the Destruction of Jerusalem* (fig. 2) as part of the competitive dialogue he had with Rembrandt during the later years of his Leiden period. Rembrandt's Jeremiah sits farther from the picture plane and holds his head, overcome by melancholy. Lievens, who paints on a much larger scale, confronts the viewer inescapably with Job's suffering.[6] LDW

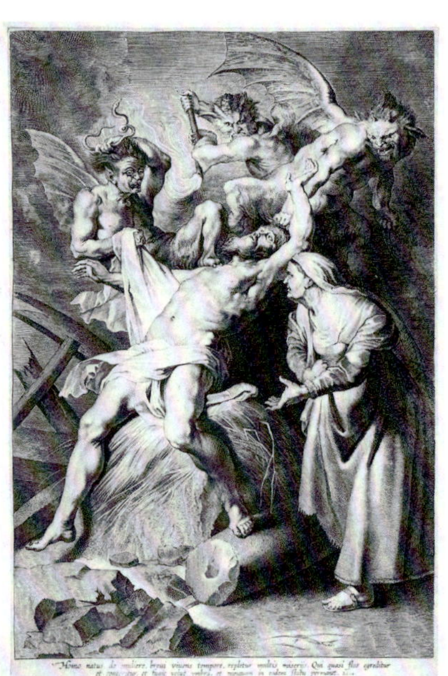

FIG. 1

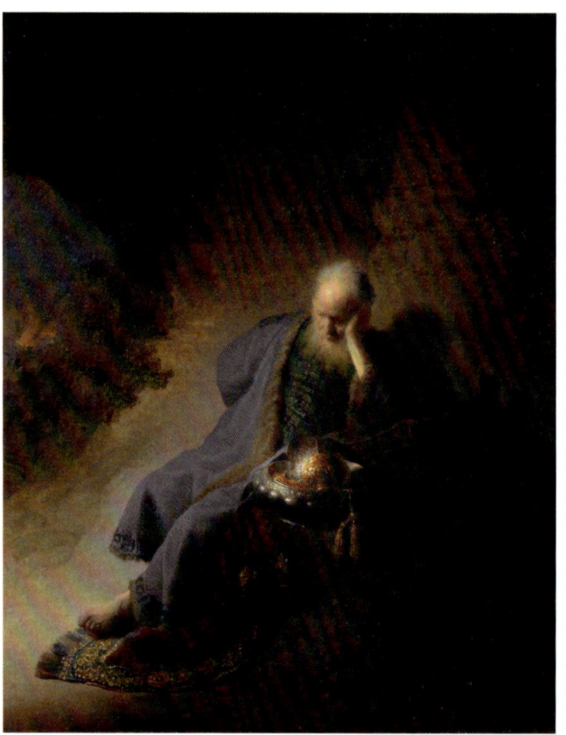

FIG. 2

1 | Lucas Vorsterman after Peter Paul Rubens, *Job on the Dung Heap*, c. 1620, engraving. Philadelphia Museum of Art, The Muriel and Philip Berman Gift

2 | Rembrandt van Rijn, *Jeremiah Lamenting the Destruction of Jerusalem*, 1630, oil on panel, 58 × 46 cm. Rijksmuseum, Amsterdam

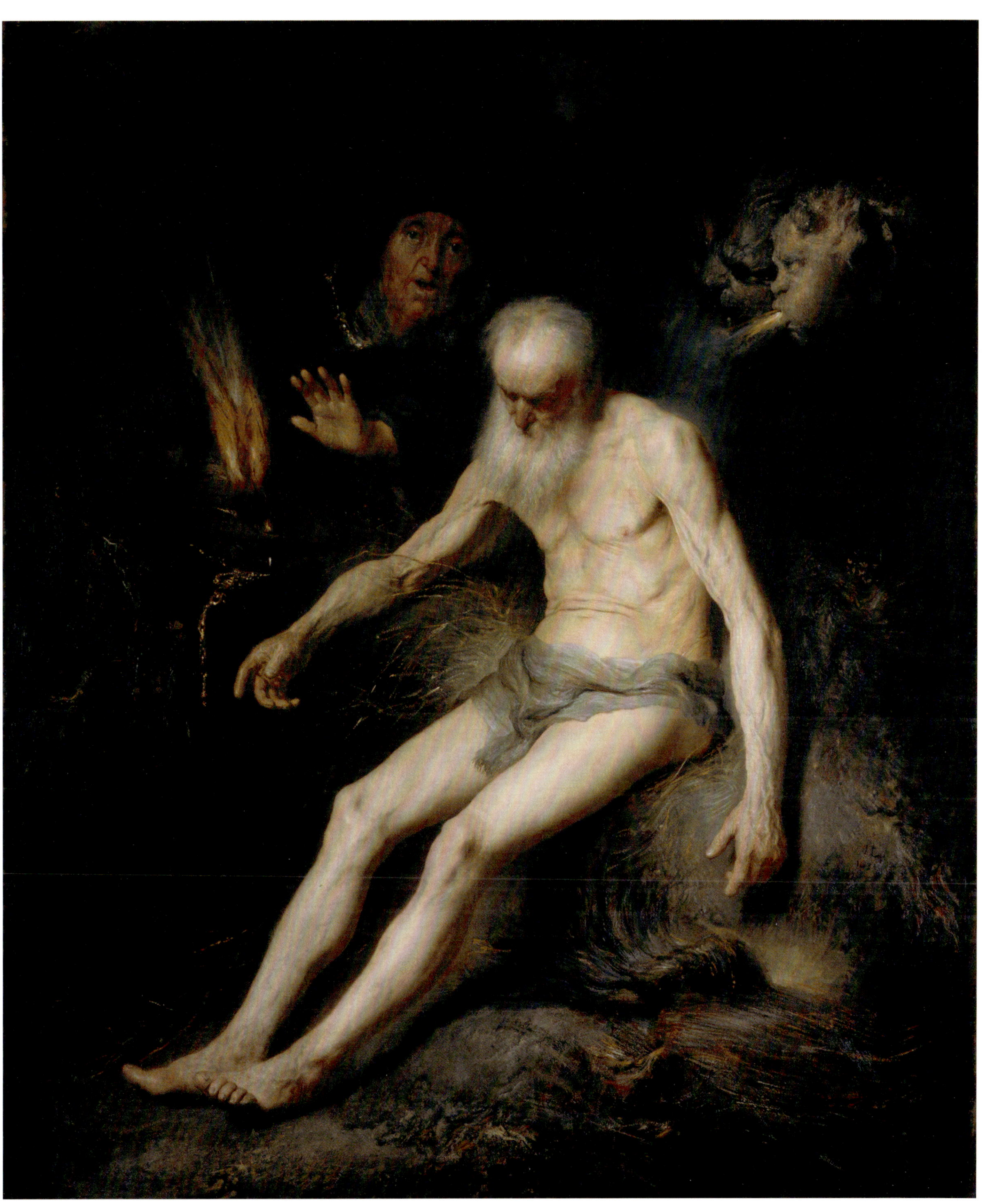

26 Preciosa and Doña Clara ("The Soothsayer")

c. 1631, oil on canvas, 161.2 × 142.3 (63 7/16 × 56). Staatliche Museen zu Berlin, Gemäldegalerie

Provenance

Palace Noordeinde, Prince Frederik Hendrik and Amalia van Solms, The Hague, 1632; Willem II, The Hague, 1647–1650; Willem III, Honselaarsdijk, 1650–1702, as Rembrandt; Friedrich Wilhelm I, Honselaarsdijk, 1702–1732; Friedrich II, Honselaarsdijk (until 1742) and Berlin, 1732–1786; Friedrich Wilhelm II, Berlin, 1786–1794; Friedrich Wilhelm III, Berlin, 1794–1829; Königlichen Museum, Berlin, 1830

Selected References

Schneider/Ekkart 1973, 31, 33, 35, 125–126, 328, no. 136; Drossaers and Lunsingh Scheurleer 1974–1976, 1, 202, 470, 528, nos. 496, 417, 141; Sumowski 1983, 3: 1779, 1826, no. 1187; Leiden 1991, 118, 119; The Hague 1997, no. 17

IN THE DARK INTERIOR OF A stone building a colorful group of characters gathers for a spell of palmistry. In the left foreground an old woman in tattered clothes stuffed with straw carries a bundled baby on her back suspended by a band around her forehead, a motif identifying her as a Gypsy. The piece of paper stuck to her forehead contains an illegible word, likely intended to be cryptic.[1] Addressing the viewer, she points to the outstretched palm of a wealthy woman seated across from her, who is dressed in fur accented by aglets of metallic thread. The proud black man standing in the background wears striking garb associating him with her household, as a Moorish slave in a Spanish context.[2] But the most remarkable figure in the scene is the radiant blonde girl with pale skin who stands at the peak of the compositional pyramid. She turns out to be the key to interpreting the picture, which has long eluded scholars: it depicts the fortune-telling scene from Miguel Cervantes' picaresque novella *La Gitanilla di Madril*.[3] The girl corresponds to Preciosa, who was kidnapped as an infant from her noble parents in Madrid and raised by the Gypsy Majombe. On one visit to the city Preciosa and Majombe are invited into the house of the noblewoman Doña Clara, who wants to have her fortune read but is impressed by Preciosa and remarks on her golden locks.[4] She is placated by a vague, double-ended fortune and the promise of more on a later visit. Lievens shows Majombe pointing to the lucky coin to be used in the palm reading by Preciosa, who in turn reaches toward Doña Clara.[5] At the same time, Preciosa looks out the window, an allusion to the nearby presence of Don Juan, who will fall in love with her and marry her.

The painting appeared in the 1632 inventory of the princely collections at Noordeinde, where it was identified only as a "Soothsayer," the specific literary source apparently not known to the scribe. Not previously illustrated, this scene counts among several obscure themes that highlight the patronage of the Prince of Orange, Frederik Hendrik, and probably reflect the intervention of his learned and cultivated secretary, Constantijn Huygens.[6] Cervantes had risen to great renown by the time he published his *Exemplary Novels* in 1613, and the next year they were already translated into French, the language favored by the court in The Hague.[7] A Dutch translation appeared in 1643, but by then *La Gitanilla di Madril* was already well known in the Northern Netherlands.[8] In 1637 the preeminent Dutch poet Jacob Cats had published a moralizing version (almost certainly based on the French translation), which was followed by two interpretations for the Dutch stage, both of which followed Cats in toning down the participation in Gypsy culture and practices by Preciosa and Don Juan.[9] Generally, depictions of the story by Dutch artists, most notably Paulus Bor, follow these Dutch transformations, and Lievens remains exceptional for his early conceptualization based on the French translation.[10]

Although the regal profile of Doña Clara bears some resemblance to that of Amalia van Solms, the consort of Prince Frederik Hendrik, the likeness is not exact, especially in the chin, mouth, and hair. Furthermore, the minor role speaks against such a representation.[11] In the story she serves only to highlight Preciosa's talents, in particular her soothsaying, depicted here, and in Lievens' composition she correspondingly occupies a secondary place. The celebration of a young woman of talent may point to the role in the commission played by Huygens, who maintained a correspondence with several female luminaries in the Dutch Republic, including Anna Maria Roemers Visscher and her sister, Maria Tesselschade. Not hitherto drawn to idealized female figures, Lievens was clearly sparked by the image of the young blonde woman he conjured for Preciosa, and he adapted it in quite a number of paintings of this period (see also cat. 27).[12]

The broad forms of the figures are consistent with Lievens' penchant for monumentality, although the overall smooth and even execution suggests that he adapted his style to reflect that of Gerrit van Honthorst, the Utrecht painter who dominated at court. Lievens' composition was recorded in a drawing by Leonard Bramer, which the Delft artist probably made after a painted copy of the present painting.[13] DDW

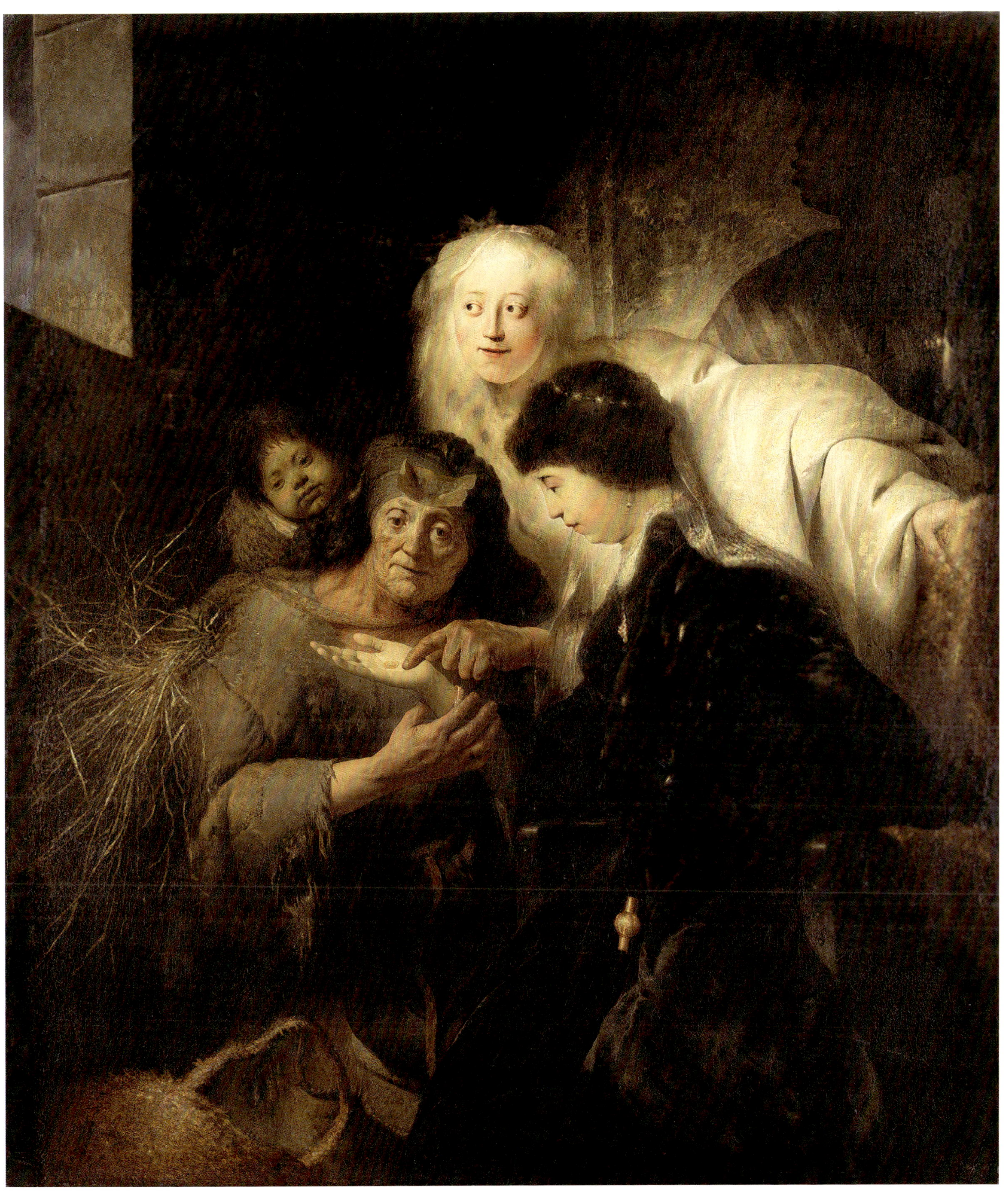

27 Bathsheba Receiving King David's Letter

c. 1631, oil on canvas, 135 × 107 (53 ⅛ × 42 ⅛). The Cooney Collection, Studio City, California

Provenance

(D. Katz, Dieren, by 1937, as Rembrandt); (P. Brandt, Amsterdam, March 17, 1964, no. 146); Frederic Stern, Los Angeles, 1965

Selected References

Schneider/Ekkart 1973, 344, no. 348, Sumowski 1983, 3: 1779, no. 1189; Los Angeles 1991–1992; Tel Aviv 1997, no. 3; Sluijter 1998, 56–59; Sluijter 2006, 340–341

A SEEMINGLY BASHFUL BUT COY young woman looks out at the viewer with a letter in her hand. She is Bathsheba, wife of Uriah the Hittite, and the letter is from King David. With her direct and steady gaze, she makes clear her compliance with this illicit appeal. Perhaps because of its moral implications, erotic overtones, and tragic consequences, the story of Bathsheba's affair with King David (2 Samuel 11) was one of the most popular Old Testament subjects for Dutch artists. Having spied on her from his roof while she was bathing, David secretly summoned Bathsheba to his palace and made love to her. When she conceived a child, David recalled her husband from his army camp and, to cover his own sin, encouraged Uriah to sleep with Bathsheba. When Uriah, out of solidarity with his fellow troops, refused to lie with his wife, David took the treacherous step of sending Uriah to certain death in battle with the Philistines. David then took Bathsheba as his wife. Although David repented of his sin when confronted by the prophet Nathan, his illegitimate child died. But Bathsheba went on to become the mother of Solomon, David's successor, making her an ancestor of Joseph, the husband of the Virgin Mary.

The golden light that glistens luxuriously over Bathsheba's long blond hair and silken cloak is comparable to that in *Young Man in Yellow (Self-Portrait?)* (cat. 33). Lievens contrasted the young woman's vain beauty and the messenger's old age with figures similar to those found in his tronies of around 1630 (cat. 61), a juxtaposition that also alluded to the theme of prostitution.[1] The Leiden artist and theorist Philips Angel interpreted a similar painting by Lievens (now lost) in his 1642 publication *In Praise of Painting* as though Bathsheba were a prostitute aided by an elderly, experienced procuress: "[Lievens] no doubt considered, after arranging the composition, that such a messenger would be an old woman well versed in the art of love, namely a procuress… who communicated the message not just in words but doubtless also brought a letter (as a token of a greater authority), which she handed to Bathsheba.… the reading of the letter arouse[d] a sweet blush of honorable shame in her (even if only slightly)."[2]

Bathsheba's knowing glance communicates more than the blush that Angel described in this other work. Yet by depicting Bathsheba as a young woman, Lievens places her between innocence and complicity: on the one hand, she accepts her obligation to obey her sovereign; but on the other, she willingly participates in the affair. LDW

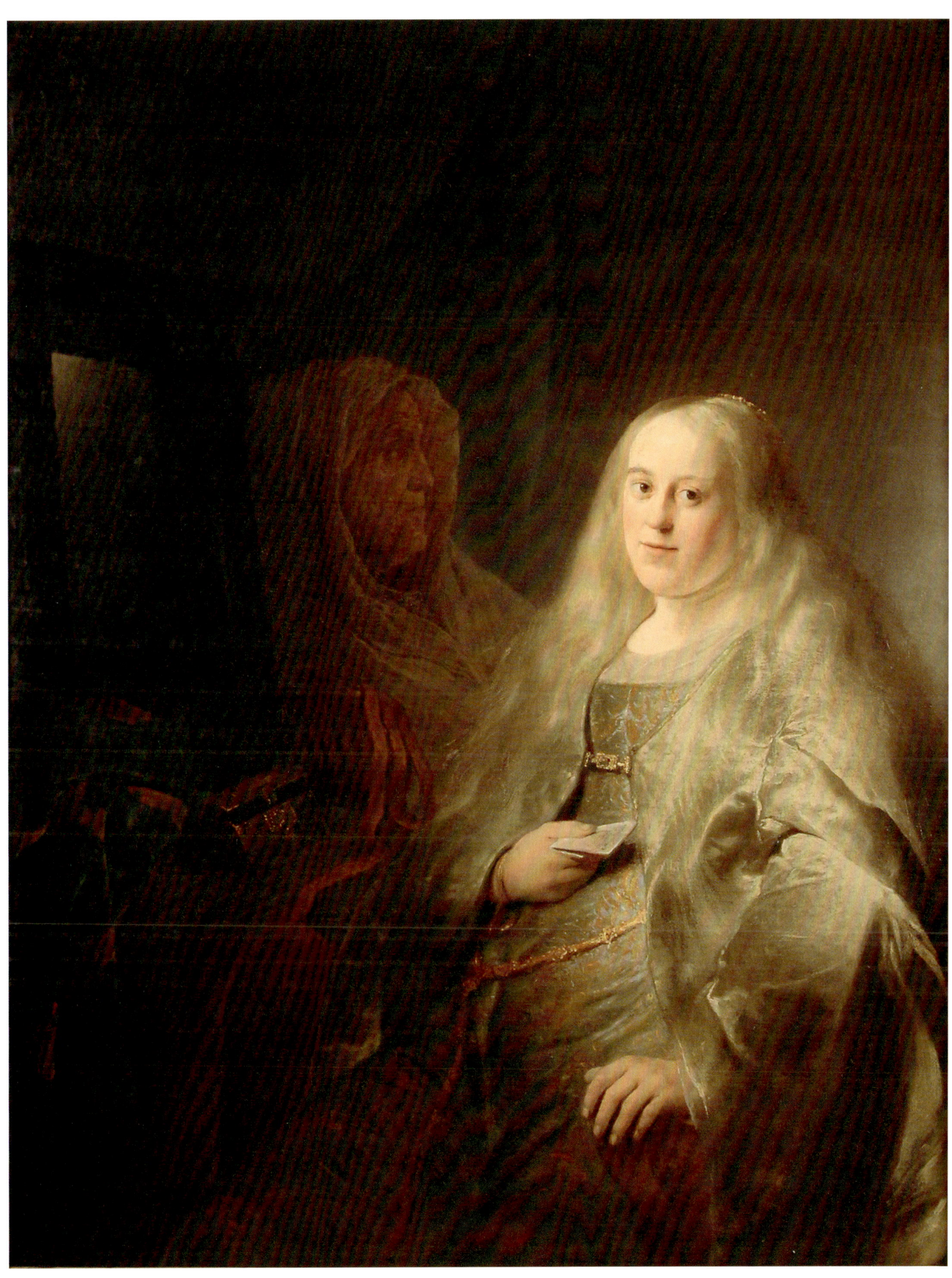

28 Young Girl in Profile

c. 1631, oil on panel, 45 × 38.3 (17 11/16 × 15 1/16). Eijk and Rose-Marie Van Otterloo Collection

Inscription

Monogrammed in lower left: L

Provenance

George V, King of Hanover (1797–1857); Baron von dem Bussche-Hünefeldt; Bernhard Hausmann (1784–1873), Hannover; (Fidi Commiss Galerie, Berlin, 1925, no. 38); (Simon Muller sale, Amsterdam, October 27, 1927, no. 27); Guttman Collection, Berlin, c. 1927; Bett family and by descent to the present owners; (Bonhams, London, December 6, 2006, no. 85); (David Koetser Gallery, Zurich, and Galerie Neuse, Bremen, 2007)

Selected References

Schneider/Ekkart 1973, 142, 332, no. 216; Sumowski 1983, 3: 1805

WITH SLIGHTLY DOWNCAST EYES and a partly opened mouth, a young girl with flowing blond hair pulled back by a pearl-studded red band stares quietly ahead, her pensive profile silhouetted against a plain dark background. In what is ostensibly a formal portrait mode — the strict bust-length profile image traditionally reserved for Roman emperors or humanist scholars — this painting is as much about the girl's inner life as about her soft, creamy complexion or her cascading locks. Although Lievens' young model may remain forever nameless, she creates an indelible impression. One is immediately touched by her expression and mood: that flickering of uncertainty of a child pondering what awaits her, even one who appears to enjoy a privileged upbringing.

Despite the extremely personal character of this image, it is not a formal portrait but a character study, or tronie, of the type that Lievens frequently created in paintings, prints, and drawings during his Leiden period. Such studies include an etching (cat. 59) and another painting of this very model (fig. 1), the latter of which was explicitly described as a tronie in an inventory of 1641.[1] These studies allowed Lievens to explore psychological aspects of his sitters, qualities that he also used to convey a sense of interiority in his formal portraits.[2] Constantijn Huygens rightly praised Lievens for this facility when writing in his autobiography that Lievens "miraculously combines the essence of the human spirit and body [in] painting the human countenance."

The present work exhibits all of the mastery of Lievens' painting techniques around 1631–1632. Light flooding onto the subject from the upper left illuminates the flawless complexion of the young girl's face, which Lievens modeled with carefully blended strokes, and it brings out the sheen of her golden hair, which he rendered with delicate parallel brushstrokes. He occasionally indicated wisps of hair by scratching into the wet paint with the end of his brush handle, and he softened the girl's skin tones by capturing areas of reflected light under her chin. Finally, his restrained color accents — the red of her hair band and lips as well as the pink of her cheeks — enliven the image despite her calm and reflective mood. AKW

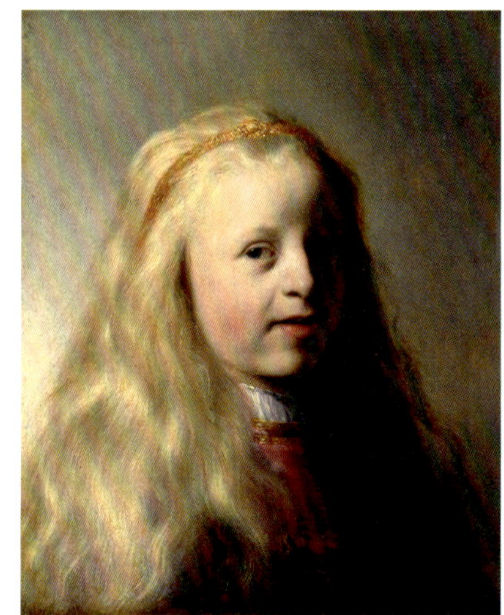

1 | Jan Lievens, *Smiling Girl with Long Blond Hair*, c. 1631–1632, oil on panel, 43 × 35 cm. Museum der Bildenden Künste, Leipzig

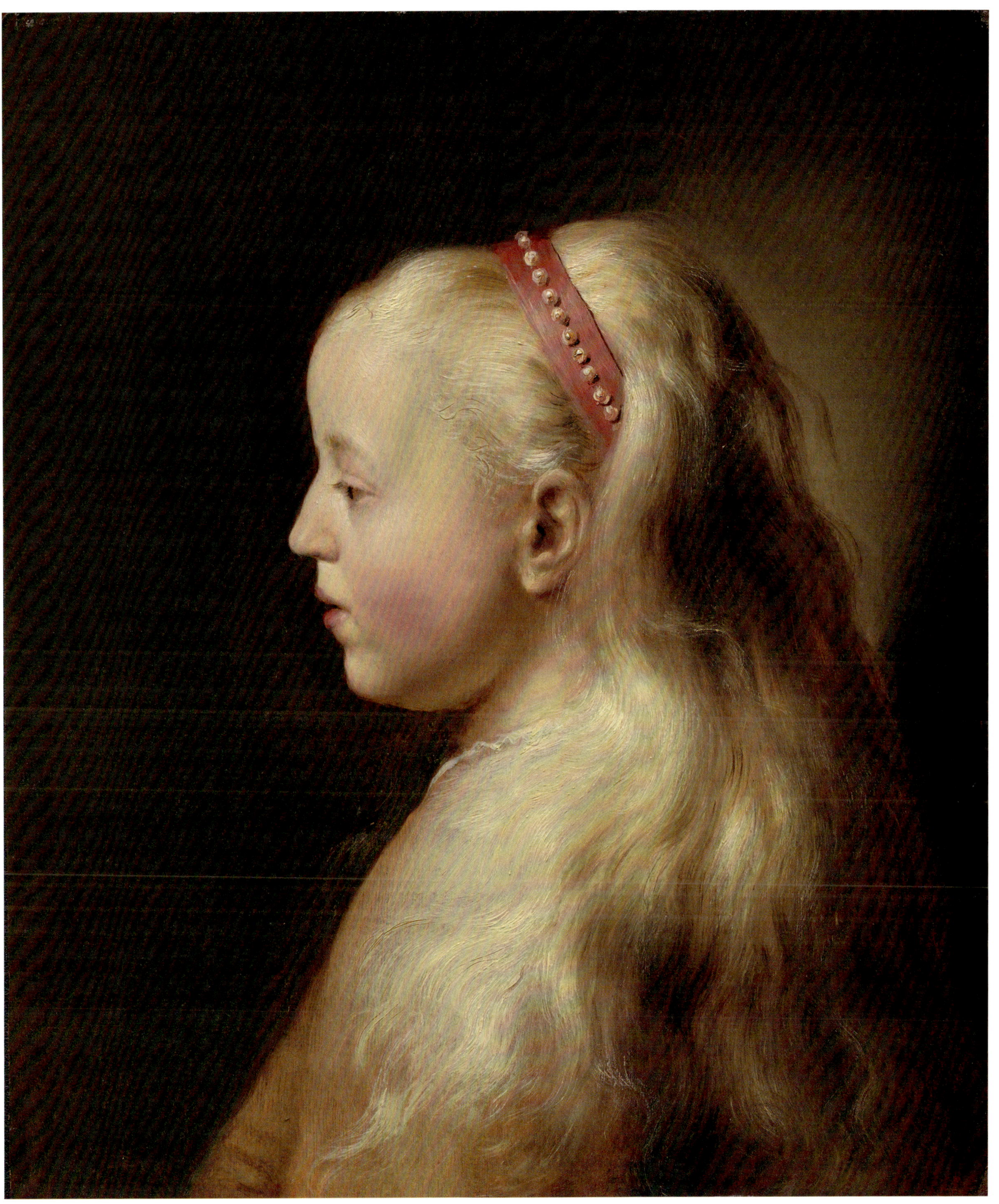

29 Prince Charles Louis with His Tutor, as the Young Alexander Instructed by Aristotle

1631, oil on canvas, 103.5 × 96.5 (40 1/4 × 38). The J. Paul Getty Museum, Los Angeles *(Washington, Milwaukee)*

Inscription

Monogrammed on armrest: IL/1631

Provenance

(A. Sydervelt, Amsterdam, April 23, 1766, no. 58); Earl of Craven, Combe Abbey, 1866, no. 20; Cornelia, Countess of Craven and J. Taylor, London; (Christie's, London, April 13, 1923, no. 11); Cornelia, Countess of Craven (Sotheby's, London, November 27, 1968, no. 88); (H. Shickman Gallery, New York)

Selected References

Schneider/Ekkart 1973, 328, no. 135; Braunschweig 1979, no. 28; Washington, Detroit, Amsterdam 1980, no. 32; Brown 1983, 663–671; Sumowski 1983, 3: 1778, no. 1186; Kassel and Amsterdam 2001–2002, 326–331; Vogelaar 2003, 161; Van Straten 2005, 205–209

1 | Rembrandt van Rijn and assistant, possibly Gerrit Dou, *Prince Rupert and His Tutor, probably as Samuel and Eli*, c. 1631, oil on canvas, 102.9 × 88.3 cm. The J. Paul Getty Museum, Los Angeles

A BOY IN A RICHLY EMBROIDERED lemon-yellow cloak, cinched by a tasseled sash, listens attentively to a stern yet sympathetic elderly gentleman, who wears a medallion on a gold chain and appears to be discussing the contents of an enormous volume lying open before them. The youth's sumptuous robes as well as the laurel crown on his head signify his royal status. He has been identified as Prince Charles Louis (1617–1680), eldest son of Frederick V and Elizabeth, the deposed king and queen of Bohemia, who had been living in exile at the Dutch court in The Hague since 1619. In 1628 Charles Louis enrolled at Leiden University, where he was taught by the distinguished tutor Wolrad von Plessen (1560–1632).[1]

The monochromatic golden aura of the painting suggests a richness, splendor, and sobriety in keeping with the regal yet restrained ethos of the courts in The Hague. Lievens portrayed Charles Louis and Wolrad von Plessen in historical guise as the young Alexander being instructed by Aristotle, a conceit undoubtedly suggested by Constantijn Huygens, who, as advisor to the king and queen of Bohemia,

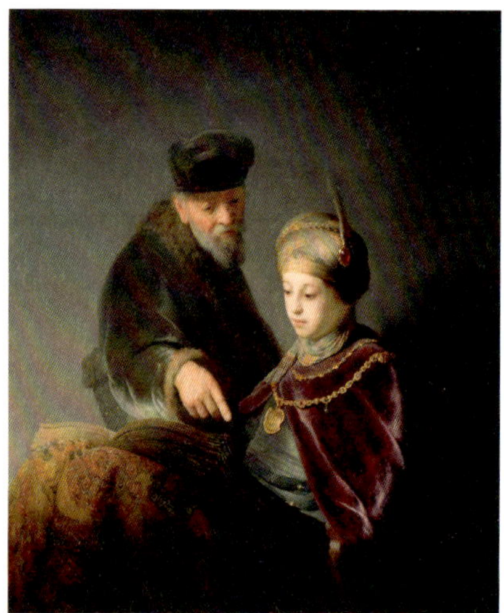

must have arranged for this important commission. This kind of *portrait historié* was in vogue both at the court of the exiled Bohemian monarchs and at that of the stadtholder.[2]

The classical allusions presumably engineered by Huygens do not end with the figures' historical guises. Pliny the Elder discussed a competition between the ancient Greek artists Xeuxis and Parhassius, and it seems Huygens may have arranged for a similar competition between Rembrandt and Lievens in relation to this commission.[3] Around 1631 Rembrandt began a *portrait historié* of Charles Louis' brother, Rupert, along with his tutor, probably in the roles of Samuel and Eli (fig. 1). The relationship between the proud and regal student, whose bearing seems well beyond his years, and his solicitous and patient tutor, is comparable in both works, although more effectively expressed in Lievens' painting.[4] As indicated by Von Plessen's "speaking" gesture, Lievens sought to convey the mesmerizing effect the teacher's words had on his student. It was just such an expression of reflectiveness that Huygens admired in the portrait Lievens made of him and that convinced him of Lievens' promise as a portraitist. LDW

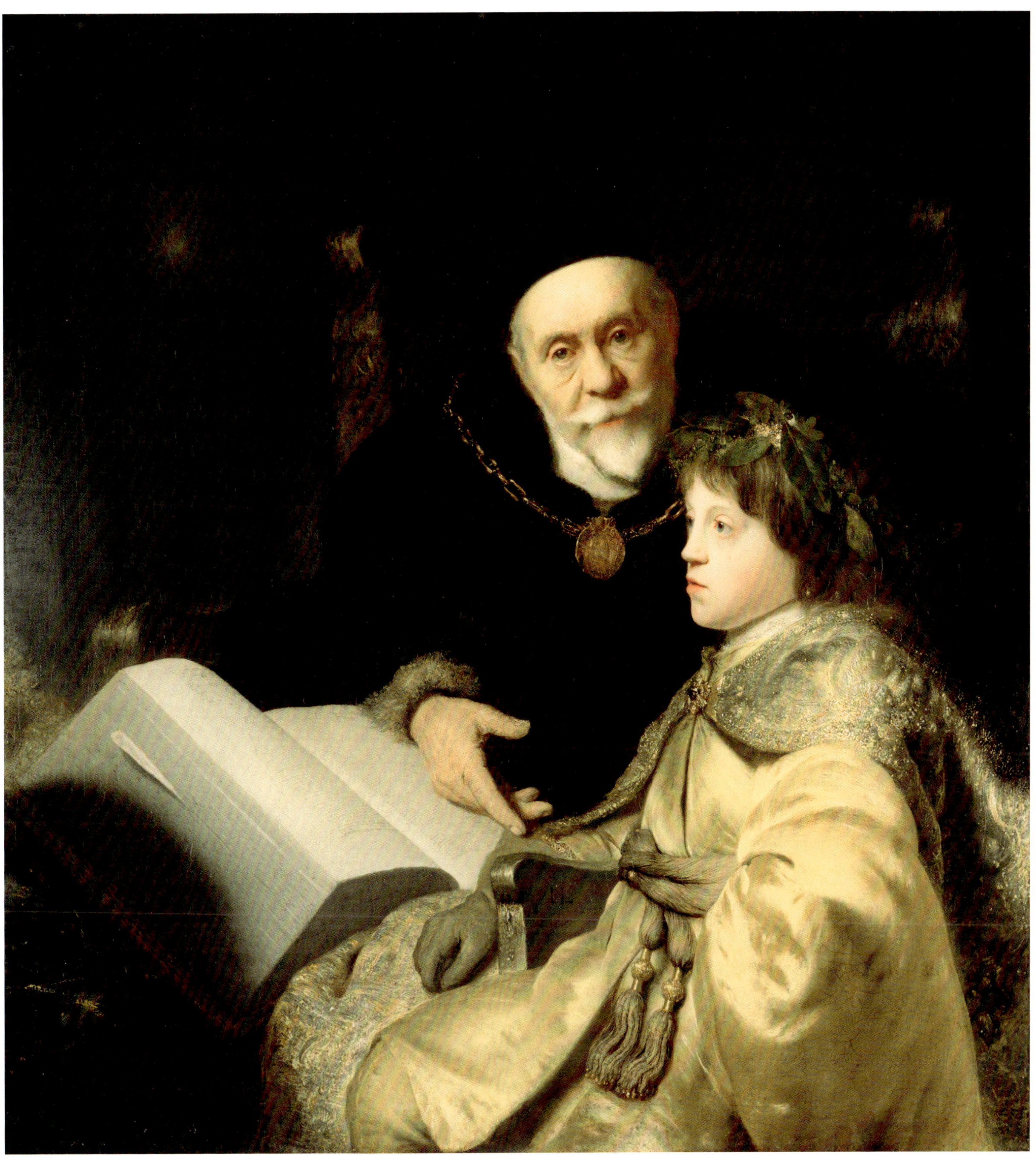

30 Boy in a Cape and Turban

c. 1631, oil on panel,
67 × 51.8 (26 3/8 × 20 3/8).
Private collection

Provenance

Jules Porgès, Paris; (Galerie van Diemen, Berlin, 1924); (Galerie Georges Petit, Paris, June 17–18, 1924); (S. Guttman, Berlin and London); (Bonhams, London, December 13, 1990, no. 102); (Emmanuel Moatti, Paris); (Christie's, New York, June 17, 2004, no. 72)

Selected References

Schneider/Ekkart 1973, 131, 329, no. 153; Sumowski 1983, 3: 1802, no. 1265

FIGURES IN ROMANTIC EASTERN dress appeared prominently in paintings by both Lievens and Rembrandt from the late 1620s and early 1630s, and *Boy in a Cape and Turban* is one of the most beautiful and compelling of these. Lievens renders the sheen of the fabrics with exquisite refinement and characterizes the boy's expression with great sensitivity. The combination of youth and dignity, tentativeness and grandiosity, distinguishes this sitter from the majority of such exotic subjects, most of which represent imposing older men described in contemporary documents as rulers, potentates, or sultans.

Lievens' first commission for the Prince of Orange was almost certainly *Man in Oriental Costume ("Sultan Soliman")* (cat. 19), on which the artist was probably working in April 1629 when he postponed a trip to England. Huygens later described that work as "a painting of a man purported to be a Turkish potentate with a Dutchman's head." This wording gives some sense of how such subjects were viewed by the artist's contemporaries. It suggests that the identification of a sitter as "Turkish" was a generalized concept at the time and that, while painted from a live model, it was not intended to be a portrait.

The model in *Boy in a Cape and Turban* adopts a pose similar to that in *Man in Oriental Costume*, with his hands on his hips beneath a stiff robe that fills the width of the picture. The closer viewpoint, however, emphasizes not his costume or his physical stature but his features and expression. His glance to the side and the softness and fullness of his cheeks betray his youth, and — unlike the formidable figure in *Man in Oriental Costume*, whose bravado almost repels the viewer's gaze — the boy's momentary vulnerability invites our empathy. The subtlety of Lievens' palette also holds the eye. No gold chains or medallions hang from the young man's neck, and no bottlebrush moustache announces his potency. Rather, the bird of paradise plume decorating his turban lights up like a flame that signals his vivacity and potential.

Lievens' *portrait historié* of Prince Charles Louis and his tutor Wolrad von Plessen (cat. 29), which he painted in 1631 for the king and queen of Bohemia, also focused on a young man wearing exotic Eastern dress. The belted robe and heavy cape worn by Charles Louis are identical to that worn by the subject seen here, with the only significant difference being that the laurel wreath has been replaced by a turban. The physiognomies of the two boys, from the broad flat face and protruding eyes to the heavy eyelids and long chin, are so similar that Charles Louis may also have posed for this work.

Nothing of the painting's early history is known. Yet the care with which Lievens painted every passage, from the sitter's face to the patterned fabric of his turban and sash, strongly suggests that this was a commissioned portrait and not a tronie. As Charles Louis became heir to the Palatinate in 1629, it would not be surprising for Lievens to have been asked to paint more than one likeness of him. The king and queen of Bohemia were keen to assert the legitimacy of their rule, as indicated by the flurry of commissions around 1631, including Rembrandt's and Gerrit Dou's *Prince Rupert and His Tutor* (see cat. 29) and Gerrit van Honthorst's group portrait of 1631 known as *The Palatinate Children* (Royal Collection, London). MH

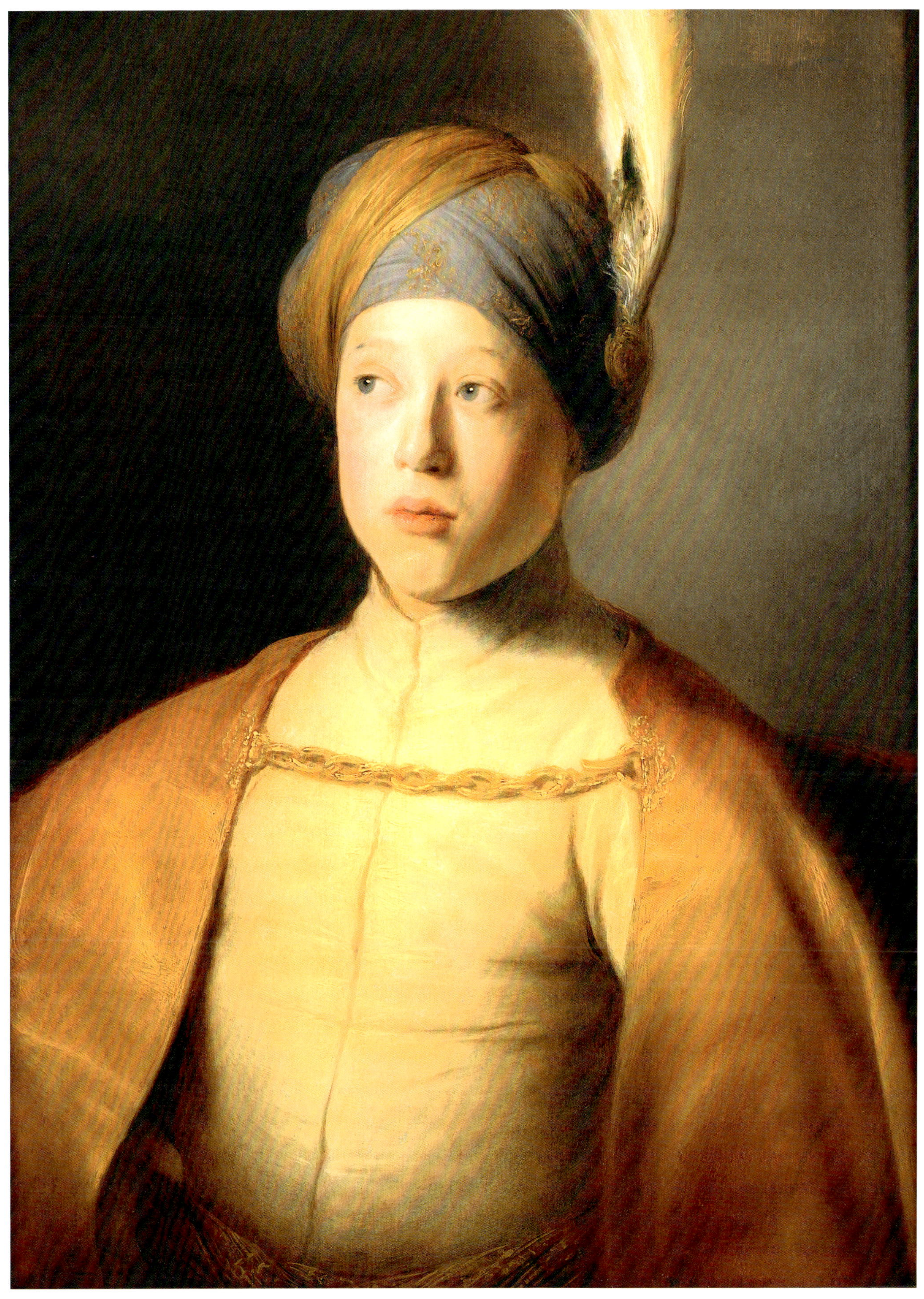

31 The Raising of Lazarus

1631, oil on canvas, 107 × 114 (42⅛ × 44⅞). Royal Pavilion and Museums, Brighton and Hove *(Washington, Milwaukee)*

Inscription

Signed on platform below Christ: IL 1631

Provenance

Possibly Rembrandt, July 25, 1656, inventory, no. 38; Jan Jacobs Hinlopen, 1662; (Van Kretschmar, Amsterdam, March 29, 1757, no. 32); (Amsterdam, June 21, 1774, no. 132); J. Knowles, London, 1838 (sale, Christie's, London, April 15, 1842, no. 113); J. Sidney North Collection, London; Baroness North Collection, 1871; (Sir George Buller et al., Christie's, London, June 7, 1884, no. 98)

Selected References

Schneider/Ekkart 1973, 38, 100, 322, no. 31; Braunschweig 1979, no. 26; Sumowski 1983, 3: 1781–1782, no. 1193; Leiden 1991, 110, 112; Gutbrod 1996, 68 n. 7, 146, 161, 225, 235–266; Leiden and Kassel 2006, no. 52

1 | Pieter Lastman, *Raising of Lazarus*, 1622, oil on canvas. Mauritshuis, The Hague

2 | Rembrandt van Rijn, *The Entombment*, over *The Raising of Lazarus*, 1631(?), red chalk. The British Museum, London

3 | Rembrandt van Rijn, *Raising of Lazarus*, 1632, oil on panel, 96.4 × 81.3 cm. Los Angeles County Museum of Art

THE MOST INNOVATIVE AND significant history painting from Lievens' Leiden period is *The Raising of Lazarus*. It illustrates that dramatic moment from the Gospel of John when Christ prays for his deceased friend Lazarus to be brought back to life (John 11:1–44). Christ stands on a ledge above the tomb, with a subtle aureole of light around his head, and calls, "Lazarus, come out!" An elegantly dressed black man lifts the long sweeping white shroud as two ghostly arms rise out of the tomb and bystanders react in fear and wonder.

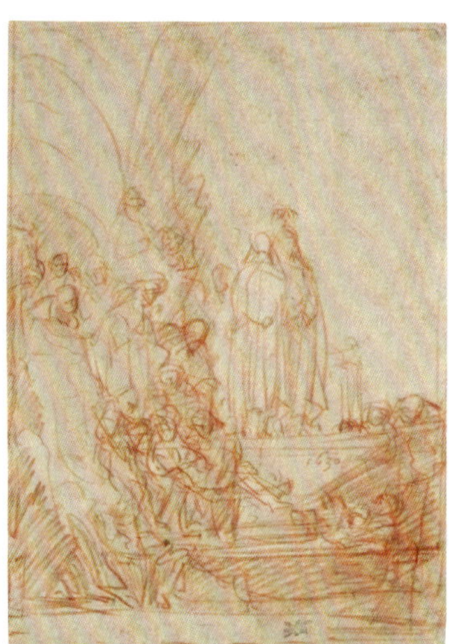

FIG. 2

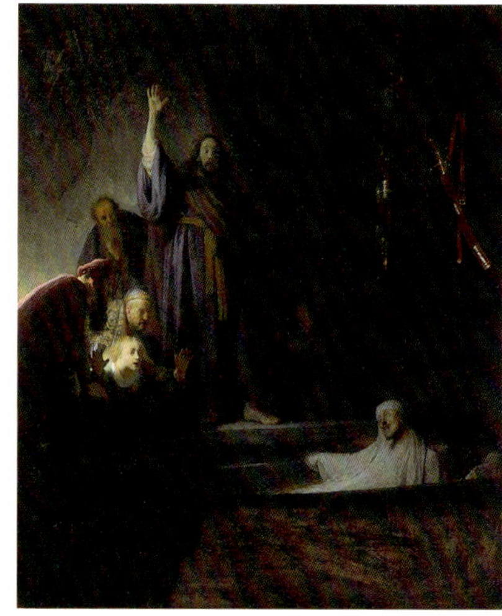

FIG. 3

The popularity of *The Raising of Lazarus* as an artistic theme in the early seventeenth century reflects the story's many compelling elements: profound human emotions, the drama of the miracle, and the theological implications, not only the foreshadowing of Christ's own death and resurrection but also the nature of salvation. Catholic artists, including Lievens' teacher Pieter Lastman (fig. 1), generally depicted Lazarus as physically fit and being helped from the tomb by Christ's disciples, emphasizing the importance of saintly intercessors.[1] Lievens approached the subject from a Protestant perspective, which taught that Christ was the sole agent through whom God granted new life; thus Lievens portrayed Lazarus as rising from the dead without the assistance of others.[2]

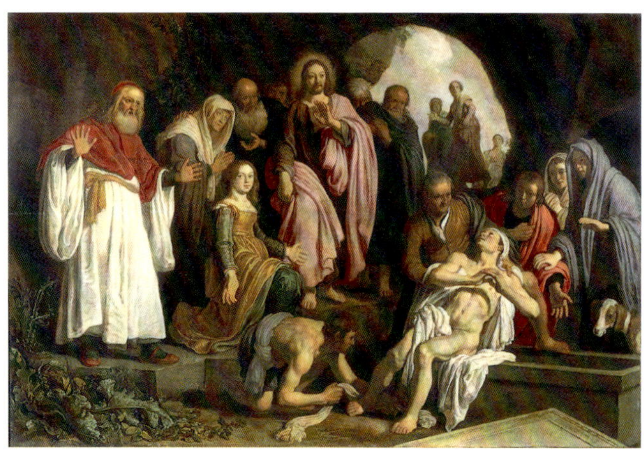

FIG. 1

Lievens published the image as a large etching in the very year that he painted it (cat. 73). The print shows Christ surrounded by a prominent aureole that fills the darkness with light. The space around the figures is also greater, suggesting that the painting was originally larger on all four sides, especially at the top.

Lievens' *Raising of Lazarus* is a quiet and austere image, though it emphasizes the emotional responses of the bystanders to the miracle they behold. Rembrandt, who made a red chalk copy of Lievens' painting (fig. 2), took a different approach when he painted his own version the following year (fig. 3),[3] showing Christ standing with one arm raised dramatically as he commanded Lazarus to "come out." Still, Rembrandt valued Lievens' achievement enough to acquire his friend's painting for his own collection. LDW

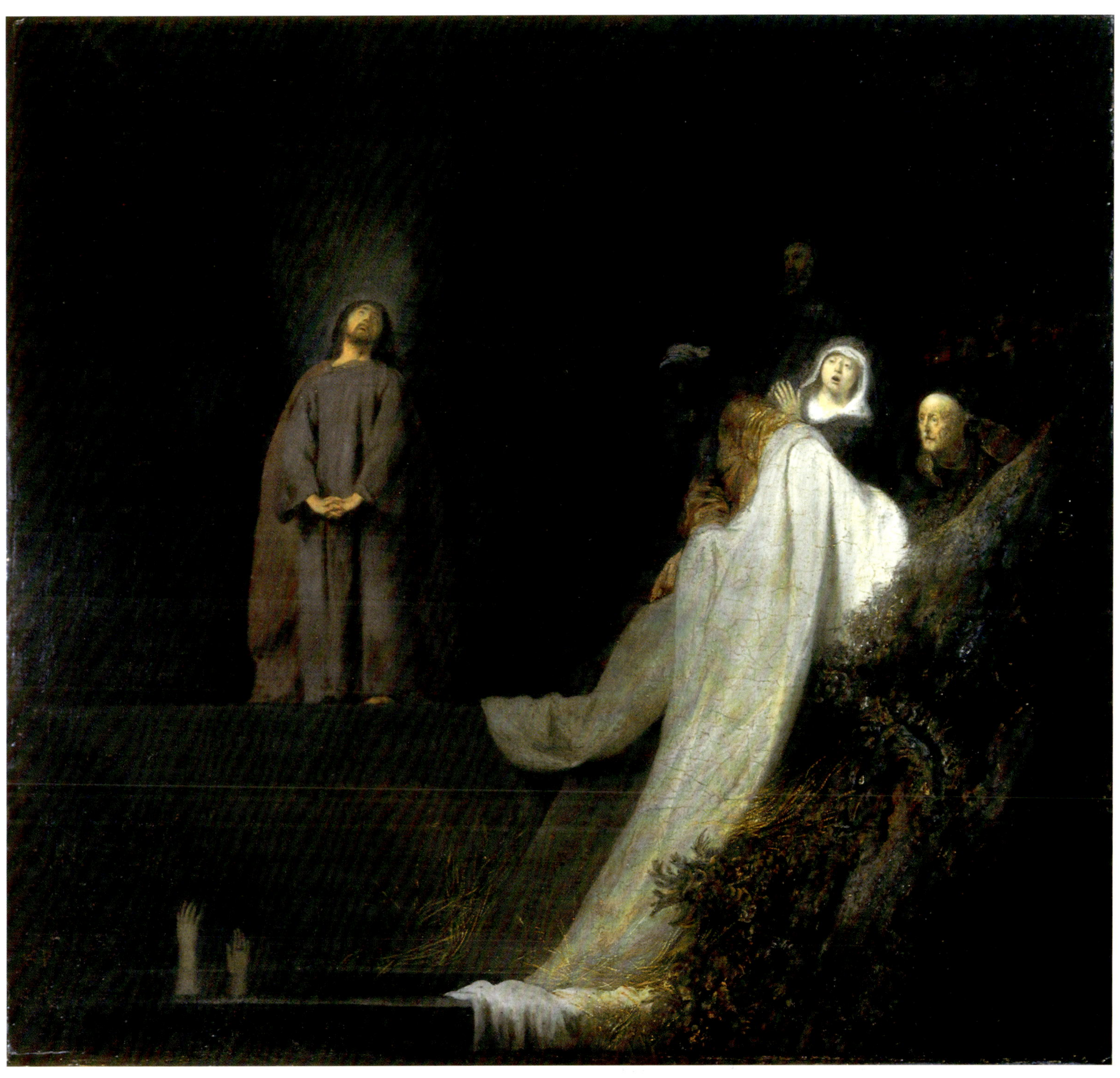

32 Christ on the Cross

1631, oil on canvas, 129 × 84 (50 13/16 × 33 1/16). Museé des Beaux-Arts, Nancy

Inscription

Monogrammed under cross: IL 1631

Provenance

Antwerp, Pieter Wouters (inventory, August 23, 1673); (auction, Amsterdam, October 8, 1700, no. 1); Camus Collection; purchased for the museum in 1793

Selected References

Schneider/Ekkart 1973, 102, no. 35; Braunschweig 1979, no. 27; Corpus 1982–, 1: 343–344; Sumowski 1983, 3: 1797–1798, no. 1245; Schwartz 1985, 86–89; Leiden 1991, no. 68; Gutbrod 1996, 272–276; Van Straten 2005, 203–205

THIS MOVING DEPICTION OF CHRIST on the cross is hauntingly powerful in its stark and unrelenting directness. Christ's body is illuminated by a strong light and seen against a stormy sky. Blood from the nail holes in his hands and feet and from the spear wound in his side stands out harshly against his pale skin. The *titulus* tacked horizontally above his head is written in Hebrew, Greek, and Latin: "This is the King of the Jews" (Luke 23:38). Thus the viewer, as though the sole witness to Christ's death, is encouraged to respond with devotional fervor, which Lievens reinforces with the altarlike shape of the arched picture.

Lievens painted this work in 1631, the very year that Rembrandt executed his own *Christ on the Cross,* now in the parish church in Le Mas d'Agenais, France (fig. 1). The shared date and similarities in concept have suggested to many that the two artists painted these works in response to a competition proposed by Constantijn Huygens as a means of determining who would secure a commission from the stadtholder for a series of paintings on the Passion of Christ.[1] Many differences do exist between the two works, notably their sizes: Rembrandt's painting measures only 99.9 × 72.6 cm. In addition, Rembrandt portrayed the moment just before Christ's death, whereas Lievens depicted the moment just after death. In Rembrandt's Crucifixion, Christ's body is taut, as he musters his dying strength to cry out to God (Luke 23:46), whereas Lievens' painting shows the body of Christ sagging under its own weight, the knees buckled and the mouth slack. If these paintings were products of an artistic competition, the parameters allowed a certain freedom of interpretation.

An engraving of the Crucifixion by Paulus Pontius after a painting by Rubens (fig. 2) is often cited as the model for both Lievens' and Rembrandt's paintings.[2] Yet this print could have served only as a prototype for Rembrandt's painting, whereas Lievens' portrayal of the dead Christ, with the wound on his right side and a small halo behind his head, is more akin to an engraving by Schelte à Bolswert after another *Crucifixion* by Rubens (fig. 3).[3] In following that model, Lievens chose to focus on Christ's body and blood as the sacrifice for humanity's sins.[4] VCT

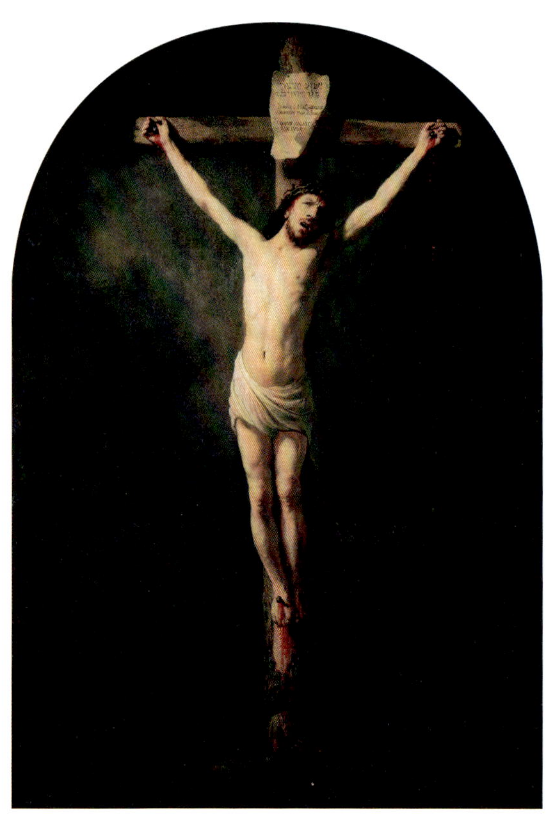

FIG. 1

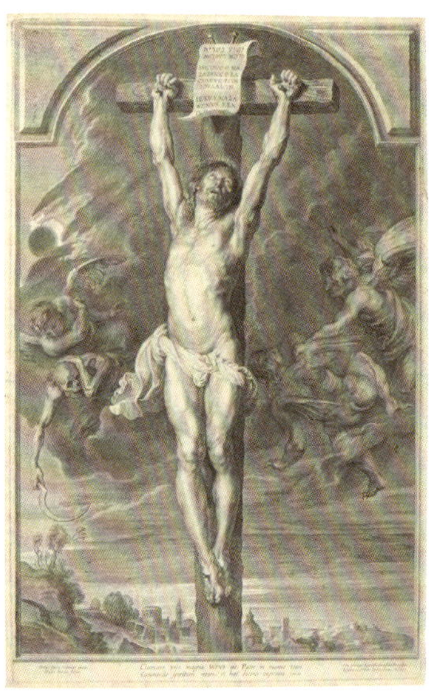

FIG. 2

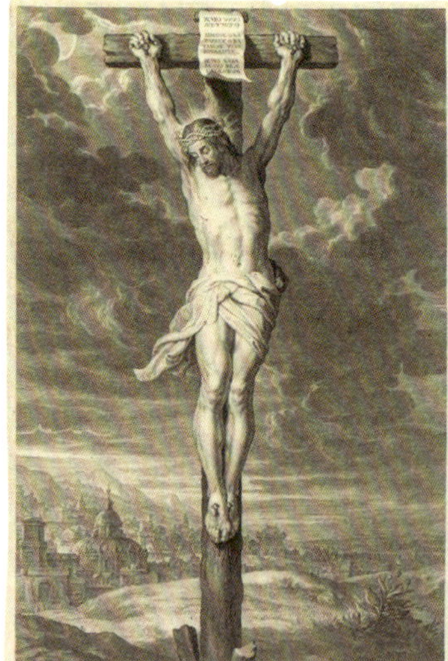

FIG. 3

1 | Rembrandt van Rijn, *Christ on the Cross*, 1631, oil on panel transferred to canvas, 99.9 × 72.6 cm. Parish Church of Le Mas d'Agenais, France

2 | Paulus Pontius after Peter Paul Rubens, *The Crucifixion*, 1631, engraving. Musée du Louvre, Paris

3 | Schelte à Bolswert after Peter Paul Rubens, *The Crucifixion*, engraving. The British Museum, London

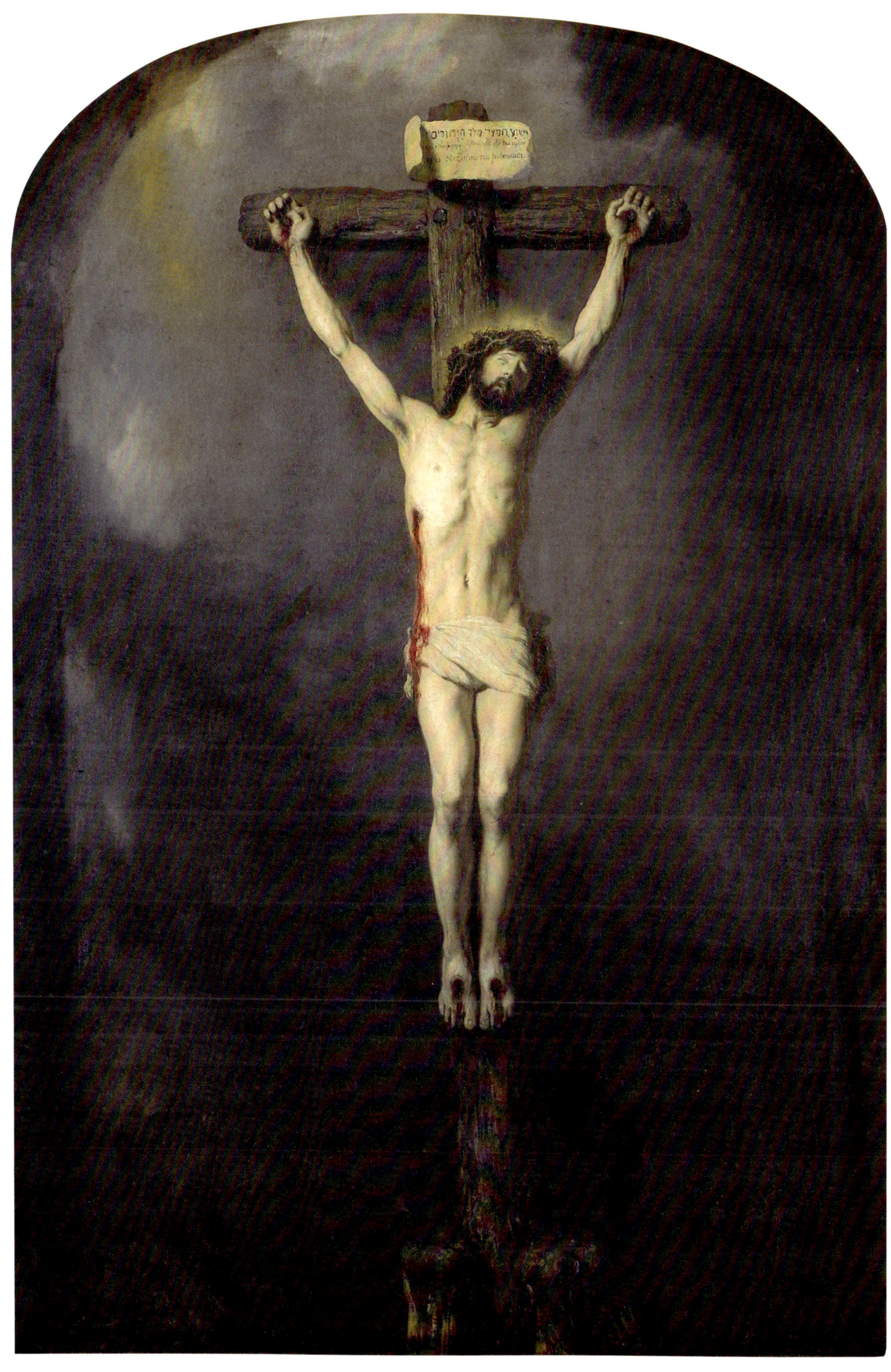

33 Young Man in Yellow (Self-Portrait?)

c. 1631–1632, oil on canvas, 112 × 99.4 (44⅛ × 38 3/16). National Gallery of Scotland, Edinburgh

Provenance

Mary, Lady Carbery, Castle Freke, County Cork, Ireland: (London, March 4, 1921, no. 9, as Gerard Dou); (H.M. Clark, London, 1921); (Thomas Agnew & Sons, London, 1922, as Ferdinand Bol)

Selected References

Schneider/Ekkart 1973, 29, 158, 336, no. 283; Braunschweig 1979, no. 31; Sumowski 1983, 3: 1802, no. 1264; Leiden 1991, 95, 97; Stockholm 1992, no. 95; DeWitt 2006, 4, 36, 71, 74–76, 239

IN THIS LUSTROUS PAINTING Lievens is thought to depict himself—with a supremely confident air, dressed not as a painter but as a prince, wearing a splendid golden robe and holding the baton of a commander. With his left elbow jutting forward and his right hand resting on the baton, the figure fills the composition. His sideways glance enhances the artificial formality of the pose, while simultaneously distancing the subject from the viewer. The lessons Lievens learned from the Utrecht Caravaggisti are vividly evident in the dramatic light that shimmers off his cloak and strikes his features from below, giving the work its strongly theatrical quality.

The identity of the sitter for this impressive work has actually been a matter of some discussion in the literature.[1] The broad, rounded face seems quite different from the relatively gaunt image, with slender chin and chiseled nose, seen in Lievens' profile *Self-Portrait* (cat. 34), a painting traditionally dated to the mid-1620s. It now appears, however, that the Copenhagen painting represents the artist as he saw himself around 1635. Lievens' appearance at the time of the present portrait can be more accurately judged from the dashing self-portrait he executed c. 1629–1630 (cat. 18). There one sees the same tousled hair, evenly rounded upper eyelids and eyebrows, broad cheeks with pronounced cheekbones, long chin, and peculiarly full upper lip. The one major difference seen here is the less prominent cheekbones, but that feature would probably be less obvious with the strong light from below.

The personality projected in this image is also consistent with the artist's traits as described by Huygens in his autobiography: self-assured, mature beyond his years, always striving for loftiness. Lievens seems to have taken his costume, in part, from the same figure on which he based his *Man in Oriental Costume ("Sultan Soliman")*: the Moorish king in Rubens' *Adoration of the Magi* (see cat. 19). Yet similar "Persian"-style yellow robes are found in a number of Lievens' paintings from 1630 and 1631, including *Prince Charles Louis with His Tutor* and *Boy in a Cape and Turban* (cats. 29, 30).

If indeed a self-portrait, Lievens assumes his commanding pose with grace and conviction, a manner one could imagine being reinforced by his close connections to both the Orange and Bohemian courts in The Hague around 1631.[2] Given that this painting was in England in 1772, when John Raphael Smith made a mezzotint after it, one wonders if Lievens may have taken it with him to London in 1632 as a demonstration of his artistic abilities.[3] Despite its large size, the painting's unusual light effects suggest that it was not a conventional commissioned portrait. LDW

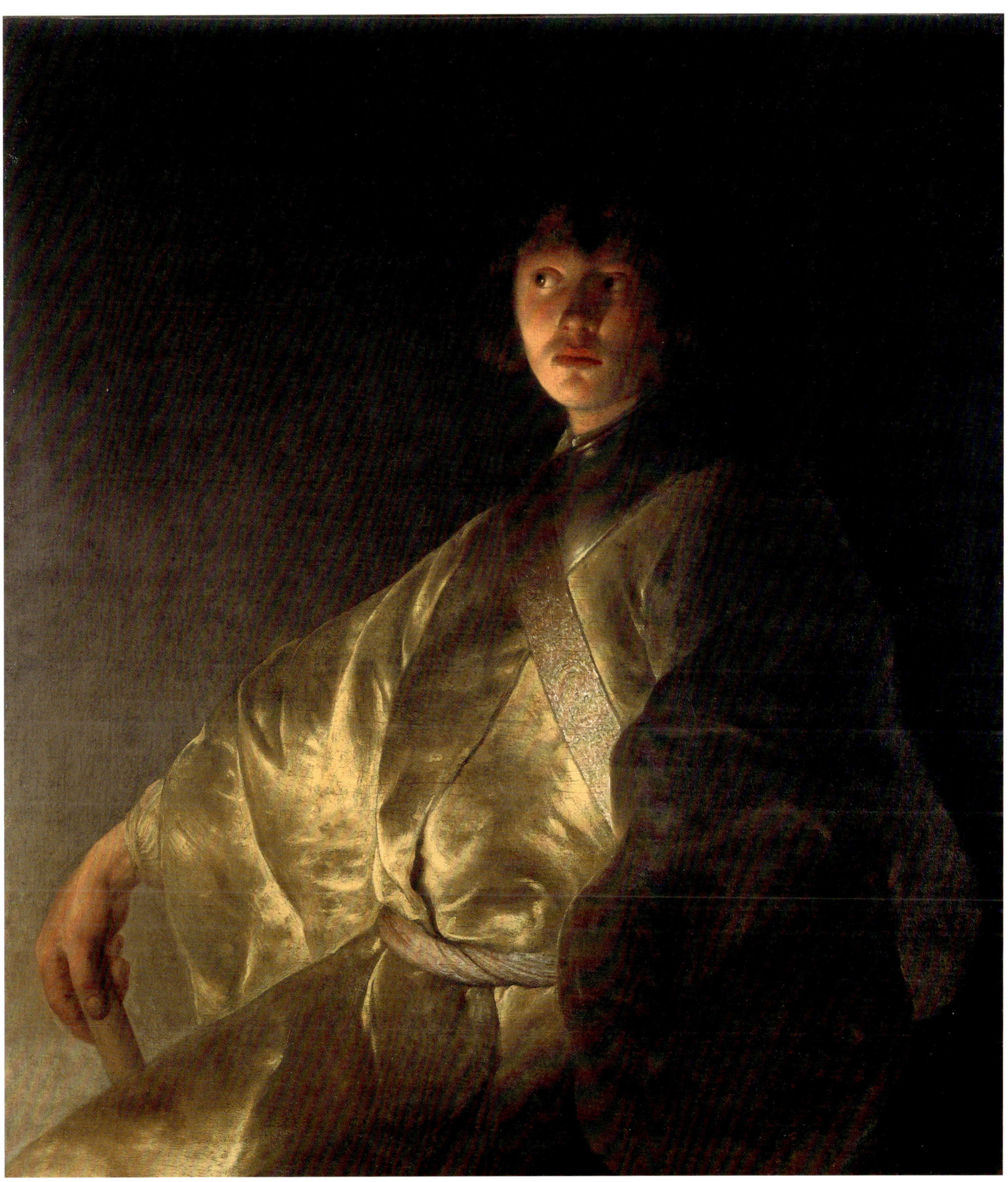

34 Self-Portrait

c. 1635, oil on panel, 50.5 × 41.4 (20½ × 15 15/16) (reduced on lower and left edges). Statens Museum for Kunst, Copenhagen

Inscription

Monogrammed under the sitter's chin: IL

Provenance

Acquired before 1773

Selected References

Schneider/Ekkart 1973, 69, 147–148, 334, no. 246; Sumowski 1983, 3: 1800, no. 1258; Gutbrod 1996, 190, 192, 193–197; Van Straten 2005, 105; Stockholm 2005, no. 34; Copenhagen 2006, no. 21

THIS REMARKABLE IMAGE, IN which Lievens presents himself in profile facing to the right and gazing into the darkness, is one of the artist's most ambitious portraits. The virtuoso performance of a self-portrait in profile, a difficult feat requiring exceptional concentration and the use of two mirrors, is nearly unique in Netherlandish art.[1] The many copies that were made of the painting suggest that Lievens' artistic achievement was widely recognized at the time.

Profile portraits, which have their roots in relief sculpture and coins from classical antiquity, are found in the oeuvres of Rubens, Honthorst, and the Haarlem "classicists" Salomon de Bray and Pieter de Grebber as well as Lievens (see cats. 21, 28). In this self-portrait light streams across Lievens' back, neck, and the side of his face, barely striking his nose while leaving part of his eye and his forehead in shadow. Instead of the theatricality of the Utrecht Caravaggisti, these light effects evoke a quiet, inner life. Although psychologically detached, Lievens' steady gaze projects a reserved tone tinged with melancholy.

This self-portrait has previously been dated to c. 1626 or 1627, but panel marks on the verso call those conclusions into question. In the center of the verso is the second of two marks used by panel maker Guillam Gabron, which appeared on panels in Antwerp between c. 1619 and 1638.[2] Dendrochological analysis, moreover, suggests that the panel was most likely available for use after 1633.[3] Thus Lievens likely acquired the panel after he arrived in Antwerp in 1635.

In addition, the painting's smooth brushwork and diffuse style correspond to Lievens' manner in Antwerp. The refined paint handling is closer to later works such as Lievens' self-portrait in London (cat. 48) than to paintings from the Leiden period. In the 1629–1630 self-portrait (cat. 18), for instance, Lievens had described the lighted planes of his face with distinctive impasto highlights that lie over the paint that defines the shadows. In the present painting, however, he described subtle tonal transitions by covering highlights with final veils of grayish flesh tone, much as he did later in the London painting.[4]

Lievens most likely painted this self-portrait to announce his abilities upon arriving in Antwerp in 1635. His youthful appearance and his use of light and shadow suggest that he drew on an earlier study from the Leiden years that he had brought with him to Antwerp (as he had brought copper plates of tronies he etched in Leiden). Replicas of this painting were made by several hands, probably students. Lievens took on his first pupil, Hans van den Wijngaerde, shortly after his arrival in the city. Issuing many copies of a self-portrait that depicted himself as a youthful prodigy would have been a bold self-promotional gesture in Antwerp, where his work was little known but where his portrait by Van Dyck had already been published as a print by Lucas Vorsterman (see Wheelock fig. 11). LDW, EMG

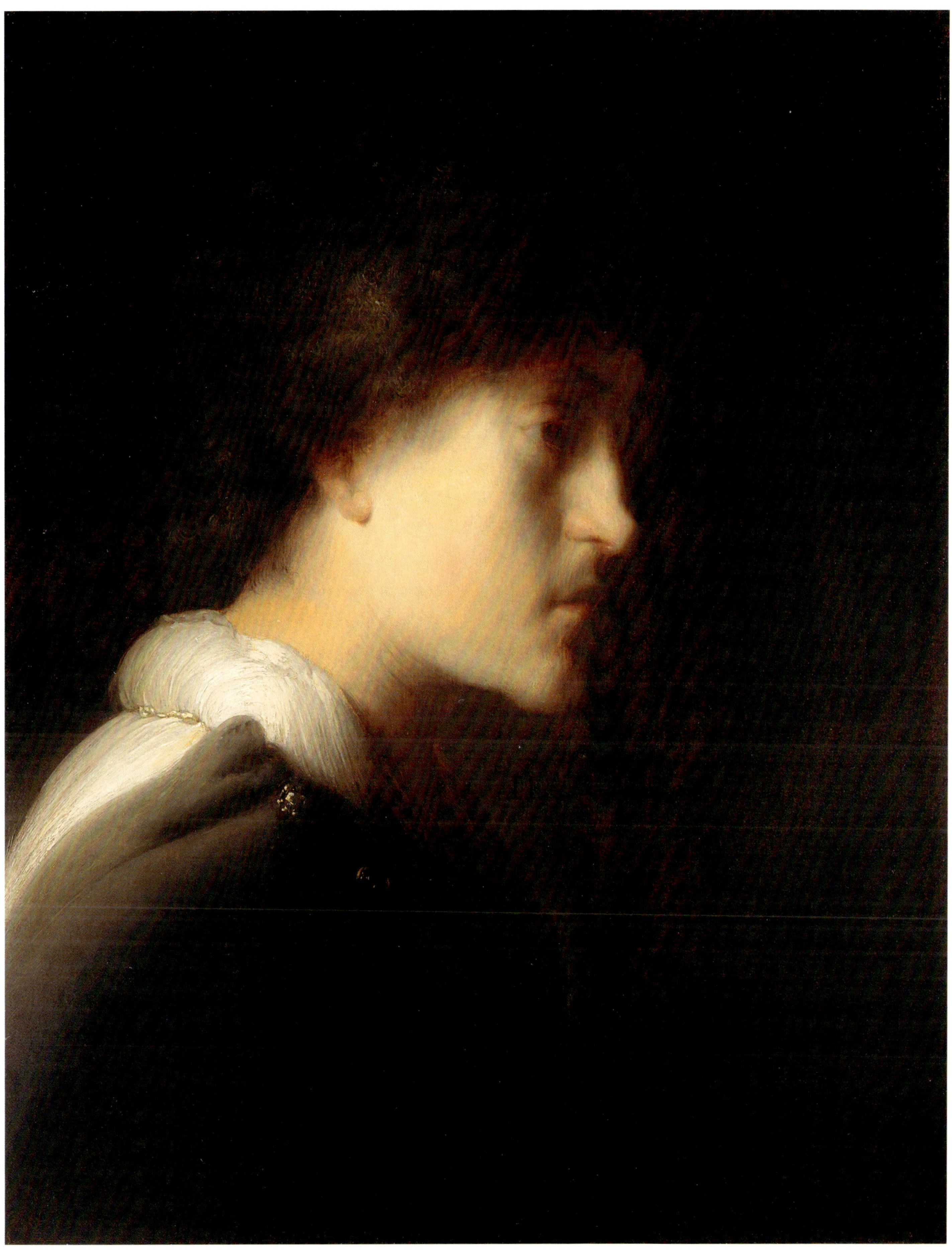

35 A Greedy Couple Surprised by Death

36 Fighting Cardplayers and Death

35
1638, oil on panel, 60 × 79 (23 5/8 × 31 1/8). Private collection

Inscription
On the chair at the right: I. LIVYVS FECIT 1638

Provenance
Maria Anna van der Goes, widow of Jacques Roelans, postmaster, Antwerp, inventory, November 3, 1663; Samuel van Huls, The Hague (The Hague, September 3, 1737, no. 161); Jacques de Roore, The Hague (The Hague, September 4, 1747, no. 129); Earl of Ilchester and by descent to the present owner

Selected References
Schneider/Ekkart 1973, 127; Braunschweig 1979, no. 34; Sumowski 1983, 3: 1783, no. 1197

36
c. 1638, oil on canvas on panel, 67 × 85 (26 3/8 × 33 7/16). Private collection

Inscription
Signed lower right: *J. Lievens*

Provenance
(A.D.S de Vahl et al., Christie's, London, February 20, 1920, no. 40 [as Arent de Gelder]); H.M. Clark, London 1921; (H. Kaven et al., Lepke, Berlin, October 27, 1925, no. 62); Dr. F. Schmidt-Benecke, Berlin, 1928; (H. Renner et al., Wertheim, Berlin, April 30, 1930, no. 56); Dr. A. Heppner, Berlin, 1931; private collection, Germany; (Johnny Van Haeften, London, 1999)

Selected References
Schneider/Ekkart 1973, 126, no. 137, 328; Braunschweig 1979, 104, 207; Sumowski 1983, 3: 1783, no. 1198

THESE TWO UNUSUAL WORKS WERE painted after Lievens moved from London to Antwerp, where he worked alongside low-life genre painters Adriaen Brouwer and David Teniers. Although they recall his earliest paintings — large Utrecht-inspired genre scenes with moralizing themes and compositions that revolve around the drama of arrested action — they also reflect Lievens' experiences in Antwerp. The figures in these works are similar to the rough and rural types that inhabit the tavern scenes of Brouwer, Teniers, and Joos van Craesbeeck, while the theme of Death intruding suddenly and unexpectedly recalls earlier Flemish artistic traditions.

A Greedy Couple Surprised by Death, signed and dated 1638, shows an elderly couple being interrupted in the midst of counting a hoard of money. Death appears in the guise of an animated skeleton that reaches toward the old woman, who dramatically pushes it away as the old man tightly clasps their bag of coins. The woman's wide-eyed expression registers shock at Death's unwelcome arrival, while the clock behind them warns that the moment of reckoning has come. With a leering smile and head cocked at an angle, Death almost seems to mock them and enjoy his ghoulish task.

In *Fighting Cardplayers and Death*, which must date from about the same time, Death revels in the battle for human survival that transpires between an enraged white-bearded cardplayer brandishing a beer tankard and his knife-wielding opponent. Death, wearing a vine wreath around his skull, gleefully grabs the latter's red tunic and prepares to club him with a thigh bone. As the card table falls into the man's lap, his bulging eyes and pale complexion suggest that he is all too aware of his bleak fate. Lievens also made an etching based on this painting (cat. 78).

Both of these paintings draw their subjects from a well-established iconographic tradition in Netherlandish art: death can come for anyone at any time. This theme appears in Pieter Bruegel the Elder's series of prints depicting the Seven Deadly Sins, where Avarice clutches his money in the face of Death.[1] Bruegel's *Triumph of Death*, from c. 1561 (Museo del Prado, Madrid), depicted the skeletal dead rising en masse from their graves to snatch the living from the bustle of daily activities. In addition, Rubens' earliest known drawings are copies after woodcuts from Hans Holbein the Younger's Dance of Death series, published in 1562. Rubens copied all forty-nine scenes, which show Death appearing to the unsuspecting in the midst of everyday life, including a scene of a skeleton snatching coins from a miser's table.[2]

Lievens was not the only artist of his generation to revisit the overtly moralizing Christian themes of the previous century. Themes related to life's brevity and the elusiveness of worldly possessions often occur in Dutch and Flemish art, primarily as *vanitas* still lifes that contain such motifs as an extinguished candle, an hourglass, or a skull. The jarring appearance of an animated and predatory Death, however, was far less common and may have been precipitated by the terrible plague that hit Antwerp as it spread across Europe in 1638. Indeed, the stumpy figures and blunt facial types of the old couple and the cardplayers — so unlike the elegant figures Lievens otherwise painted in the manner of Titian and Van Dyck during his Antwerp years — recall the art of Brouwer and suggest that Lievens may have painted them in homage to his friend fellow painter, who died of the plague in 1638. This plague may have inspired other works as well, including paintings by Van Craesbeeck, Rembrandt's print *Death Appearing to a Young Couple* of 1639, and Judith Leyster's *The Last Drop* (Philadelphia Museum of Art).[3] MH, AKW

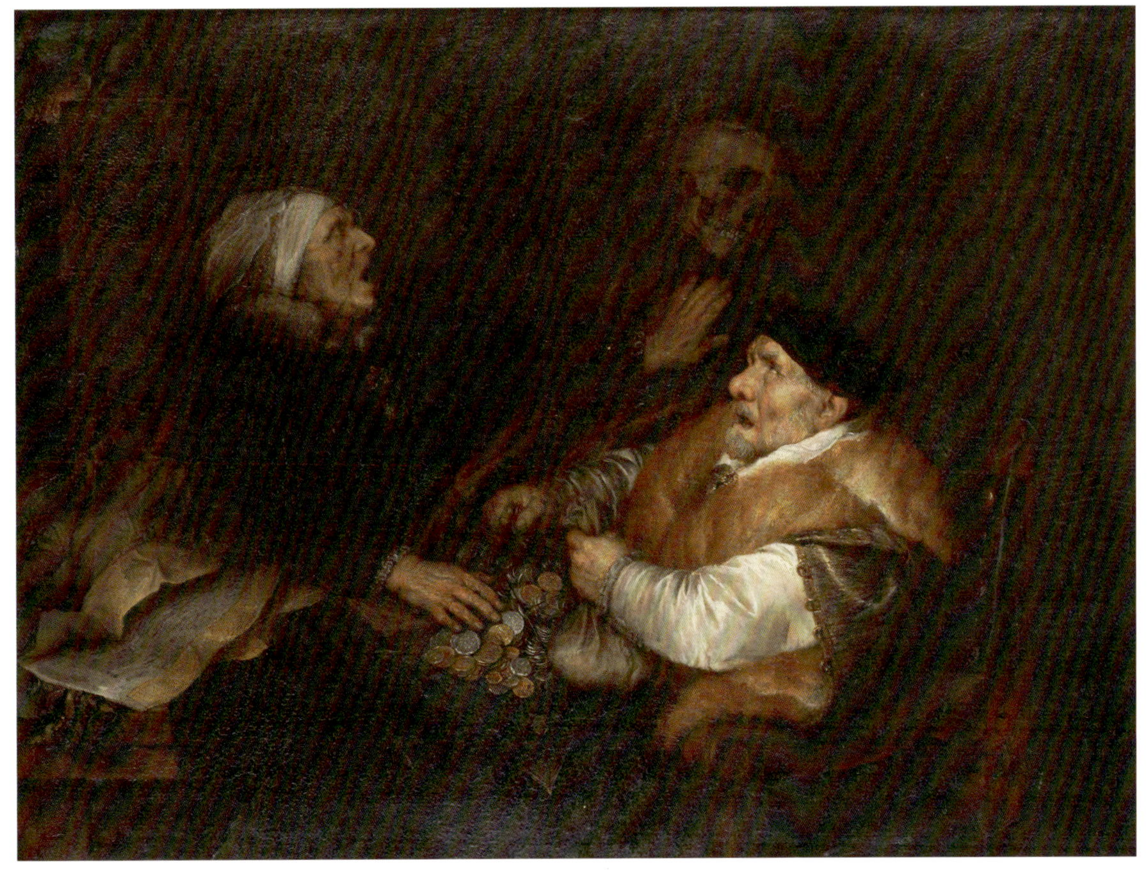

CAT. 35

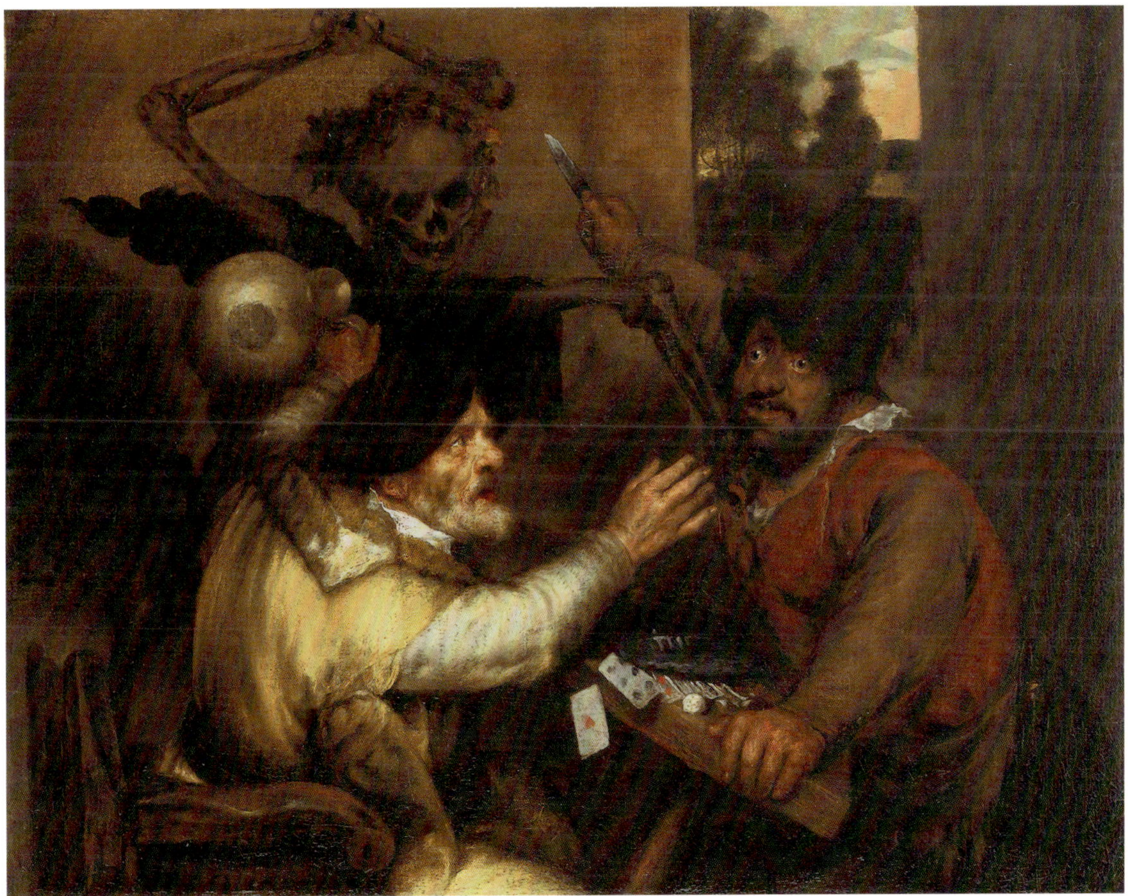

CAT. 36

37 Landscape with Peasants

Figures added by David Teniers II

c. 1638, oil on canvas, transferred from panel, 75 × 154 (29½ × 60⅝) (25 cm later addition at top removed in 2001). Kremer Collection *(Washington)*

Provenance

Admiral Lord Radstock, London, by 1821; (Christie's, London, May 13, 1926, no. 51, as Rembrandt and Teniers); Mrs. Tennant, London, as d'Arthois and Teniers; Dr. J. Seymour Maynard, London, 1927; (Christie's, London, January 29, 1945, no. 89); (L. Koetser, London); English private collection; (D. Koetser, Zurich); (Pictura, Maastricht, 1984); private collection, Düsseldorf; (Sotheby's, London, December 7, 1988, no. 115); (Robert Noortman, London and Maastricht, 1989)

Selected References

Schneider/Ekkart 1973, 58–60, 164, 337, no. 307; Sumowski 1983, 3: 1772 n. 32, as Brouwer school; Van der Ploeg et al. 2002, 104–107

ONE OF THE EARLIEST LANDSCAPES Lievens painted in Antwerp shows two paths leading into the distance — one to a village across the dunelike terrain at the left, the other passing through a dense forest at the right. Travelers depicted along these paths give a human dimension to the scene, which captures the windswept quality of the Flemish countryside. Although Lievens initially painted this landscape on panel, it has been transferred to canvas, probably in the eighteenth century. He originally paired it with another panel painting of comparable size, *River Landscape with Fisherman* (fig. 1), an evening scene, thereby creating pendants that represented two different times of day, a venerable tradition in Flemish art.[1]

This loosely painted vista emulates to a great extent the landscape style of Adriaen Brouwer (fig. 2), whom Lievens knew and even portrayed in a drawing of 1635–1637 (cat. 102). Indeed, until 1960 Lievens' painting was generally attributed to Brouwer, despite its large scale and relatively colorful palette. Lievens executed this work in a remarkably bold technique, dragging thick paint over loosely blocked-in forms. The mood and expressive character of the painting owe much to the large-scale landscapes that Rubens painted in the late 1630s.[2]

Lievens did not paint the staffage figures, which were incorporated into the scene after the landscape was completed.[3] These were probably added by David Teniers II, who also painted the staffage in its pendant.[4] Such a collaboration indicates that Lievens understood the marketing strategies of the Antwerp art world, where paintings were often valued more highly if more than one artist was involved. Lievens also collaborated with other artists, painting a landscape within a fruit and flower cartouche and a portrait within a flower garland by Jan van der Hecke.[5] LDW

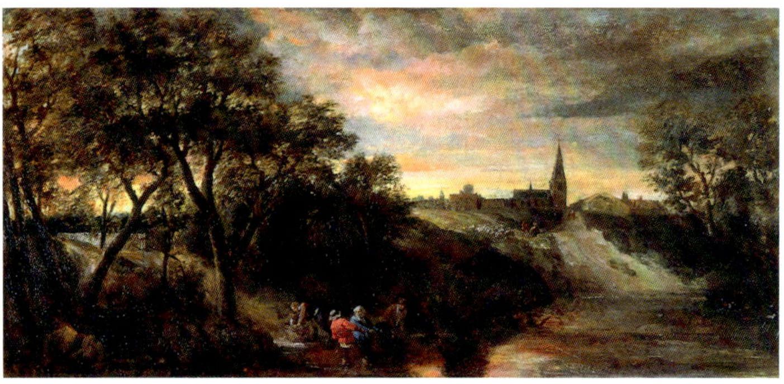

FIG. 1

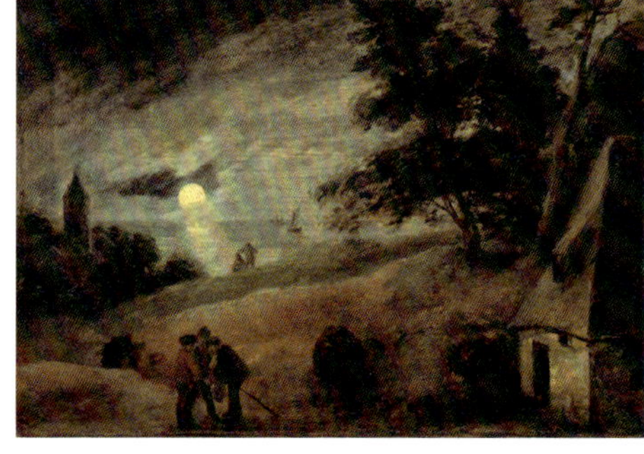

FIG. 2

1 | Jan Lievens, with figures by David Teniers II, *River Landscape with Fisherman*, c. 1638, oil on panel (seventeenth-century addition at top not illustrated). Private Collection

2 | Adriaen Brouwer, *Moonlight Landscape*, c. 1635–1637, oil on panel, 25 × 34 cm. Staatliche Museen zu Berlin, Gemäldegalerie

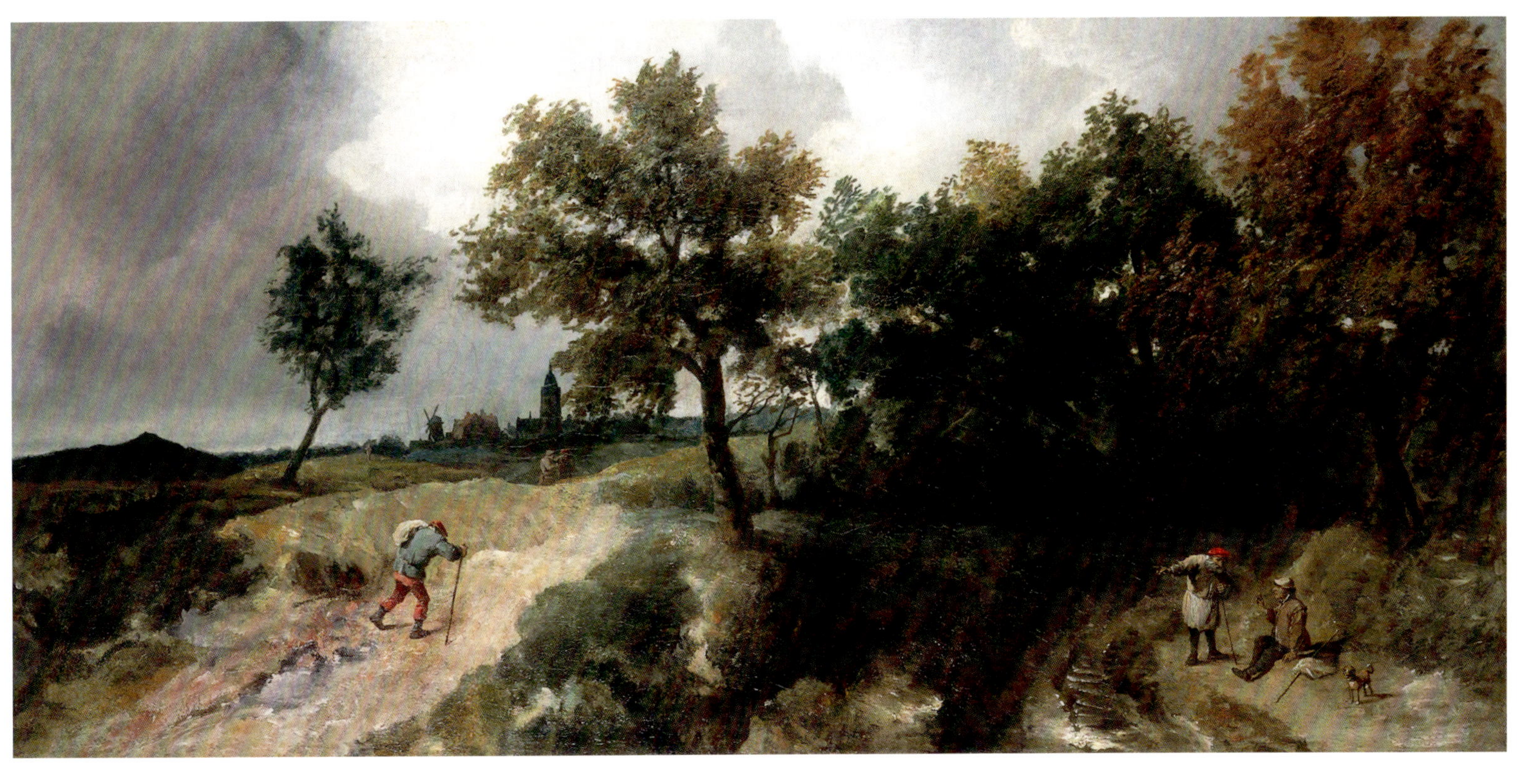

38 Head of an Old Man

1640, oil on canvas, 76.2 × 62.5 (29 1/4 × 24 1/8). New Orleans Museum of Art, Gift of Mr. and Mrs. Henry H. Weldon

Inscription

Monogrammed in lower left (reinforced): IL/1640

Provenance

Private collection, England; (A. Brod Gallery, London, 1957); Mr. and Mrs. Henry H. Weldon

Selected References

Schneider/Ekkart 1973, 351, no. S367; Braunschweig 1979, 108; Sumowski 1983, 3: 1922, no. 1284; New Orleans 1997, no. 26

ONE OF THE FINEST TRONIES Lievens made after he left Leiden, this evocative head of an old man demonstrates that his passion for studying the effects of aging did not abate during his Antwerp period. Stylistically, Lievens executed this full-bearded figure in a softer, more diffuse manner than he used to render *Bearded Man with a Beret* (cat. 20), but he imbued it with no less emotional intensity. Light, which catches a shock of hair on the old man's head and a soft wavy curl framing his face, fully models his worn features as he gazes soulfully into the distance. Lievens' portrayals of old men in the late 1630s and early 1640s, such as his black and red chalk portrait of the aged Thomas Howard, Earl of Arundel (cat. 109), are similarly tinged with emotion. Yet this tronie displays an unusual warmth and tenderness, which Lievens deepened by using reddish brown undertones in the shadows on the face.

Lievens seems to have had a personal rapport with this particular sitter, who may also appear in a number of the artist's religious paintings during his Antwerp years. The man resembles Joachim in *The Visitation*, for example (see Wheelock fig. 18), and Joseph of Arimathea in *The Lamentation of Christ* (cat. 40). Although Lievens rarely dated his tronies, this work is signed and dated 1640, making it quite distinctive. One wonders if it might represent the artist's father, who passed away around 1642 and whose will, registered on January 10, 1640, lists a painting of him "recently executed by his son" that was to be left to his youngest son.[1] Unfortunately, there is no way to confirm this connection. LDW

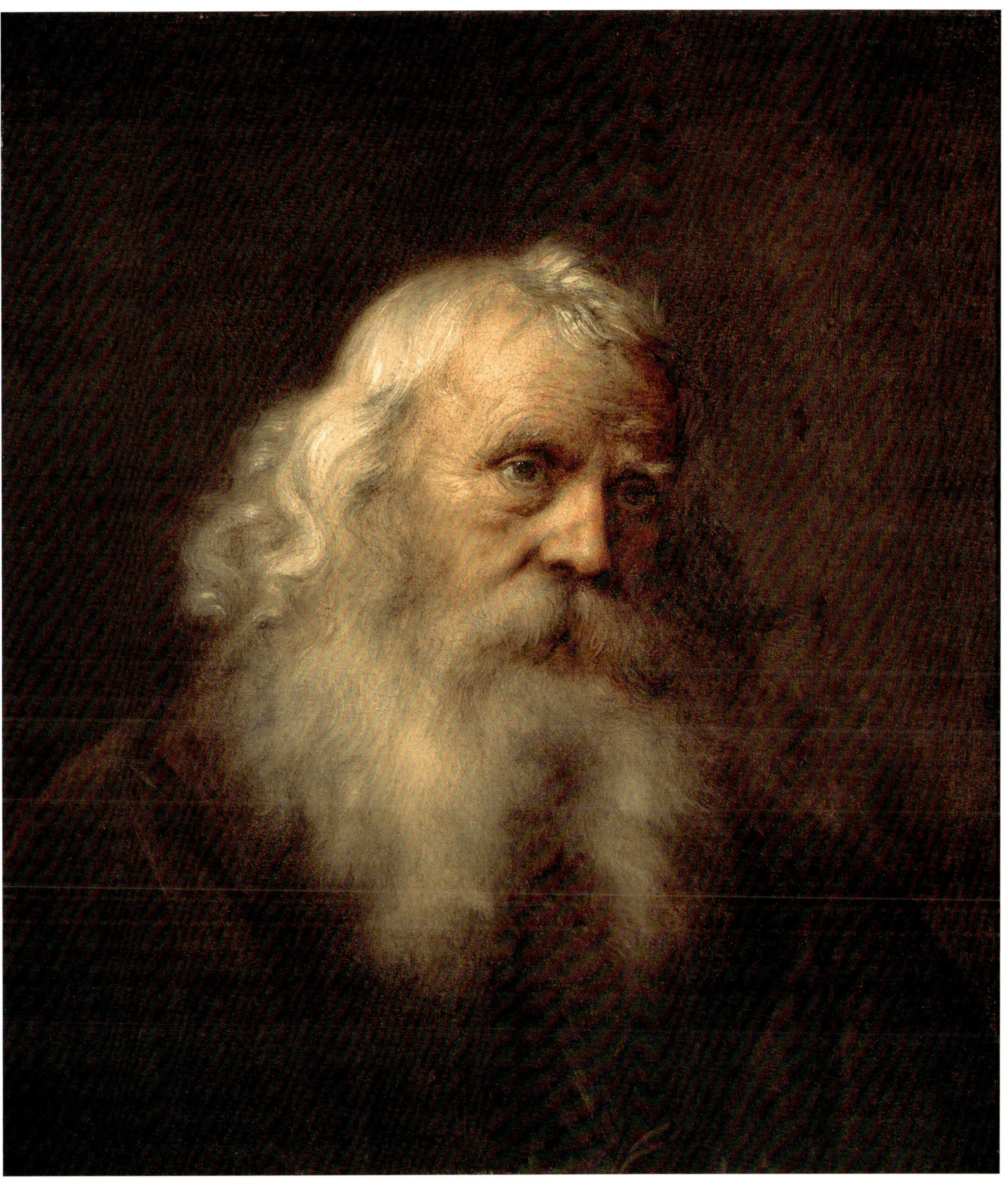

39 The Lamentation of Christ *(modello)*

40 The Lamentation of Christ

39
c. 1640, oil on panel,
39 × 54 (15 3/8 × 21 1/4).
Charles Roelofsz,
Amsterdam

Provenance
J. Jongekyk, Bundaberg Q.L., Australia (by 1979)

Selected References
Braunschweig 1979, 110 (as a copy or replica); Sumowski 1983, 3: 1784 (as a copy); Tokyo 2003, no. 53

40
c. 1640, oil on canvas,
141 × 216 (55 1/2 × 85 1/16).
Bayerisches Staatsgemäldesammlungen, Munich, Alte Pinakothek

Provenance
Fürstbischöfliche Galerie, Würzburg (as Anthony van Dyck, copy?)

Selected References
Schneider/Ekkart 1973, 51, 102, no. 37, 323; Braunschweig 1979b, no. 36; Brown 1979b, 745; Sumowski 1983, 3: 1784, no. 1200

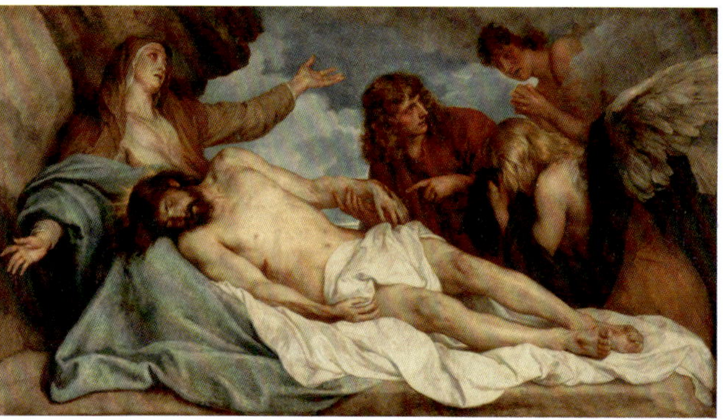

1 | Anthony van Dyck, *The Lamentation*, 1636, oil on canvas, 45.3 × 81.9 cm. Koninklijk Museum voor Schone Kunsten, Antwerp

IN A PAINTING RESONANT WITH grief, Mary, John, Mary Magdalene, and Joseph of Arimathea attend the dead Christ as he lies on a white shroud at the foot of the cross. Dark clouds and a deep reddish orange sunset give an eerie, otherworldly light to the scene. Lending spiritual support to the mourners are two angels, one looking heavenward, with wings partly obscuring the ladder used to retrieve Christ's body. In the foreground are the nails that had fixed him to the cross and the sheet of paper inscribed "INRI," or "Jesus the Nazarene, King of the Jews," which had been tacked above his head.

While Christ's body is the visual focus of the painting, the emotional core is the Virgin Mary's poignant expression as she gazes down at her son. Here, however, Mary does more than lament Christ's death: with her left hand she presents the crown of thorns to Joseph of Arimathea, who holds forth a gilded silver platter to receive it.

The provenance for the large painting does not extend back beyond the early twentieth century when it was in Würzburg and thought to be a copy after Van Dyck. But Lievens probably painted it on commission for a church or private chapel during his Antwerp years. The painting's subject, large scale, and horizontal shape suggest that it was conceived for a location over an altar. The unusual emphasis on the crown of thorns implies that this object had special significance for the patron, perhaps because the church possessed a relic.[1] One highly venerated "holy thorn" was at Sint Michielskerk in Ghent, although similar relics possibly existed in Antwerp and elsewhere in Flanders.[2]

No other painting demonstrates so vividly the extent to which Lievens entered into the spirit of Van Dyck's religious imagery while he was in Antwerp, not only with his broadly evocative brushwork but also with the tender emotions of the mourners.[3] As in Van Dyck's *Lamentation* for the Chapel of Our Lady of the Seven Sorrows at the Franciscan church of the Recolets in Antwerp, c. 1636 (fig. 1), Lievens illuminated the pale flesh tones of Christ's body—even though the scene unfolds as night falls, with only a thin orange band of light still radiant along the distant horizon. Also following Van Dyck's manner of painting, Lievens made use of two preparatory studies, one a study of an old man's head that served as the basis for the head of Joseph of Arimethea (cat. 38), and the other a compositional oil sketch on panel (cat. 39).

The compositional study is remarkably finished, which has given rise to the notion that it is a small-scale copy of the Munich *Lamentation*. But the study has a freedom of brushwork that belies that idea.[4] And Lievens seems to have seen the sketches as independent works of art that he could later sell. The sketch also demonstrates that the Munich painting has been trimmed on all sides.

Lievens frequently made oil sketches for major commissions later in his career, and we know that Hans van den Wijngaerde became his pupil in Antwerp in 1636. Given that *The Lamentation* was likely painted c. 1640, it is possible that Van den Wijngaerde used the sketch to assist Lievens in completing the altarpiece. There is a distinct difference between the modeling of the angels and that of the main figures, which may argue for such a division of labor. AKW

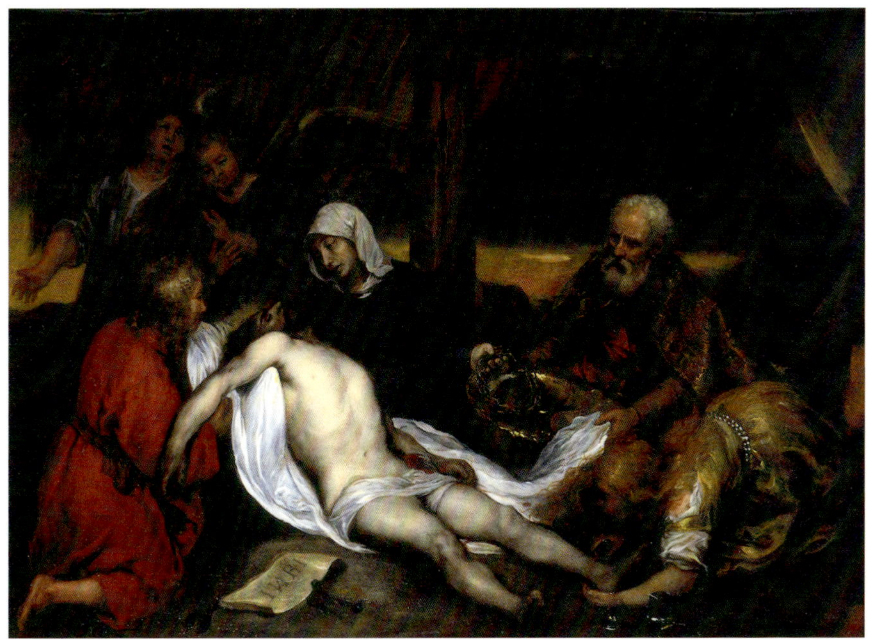

CAT. 39

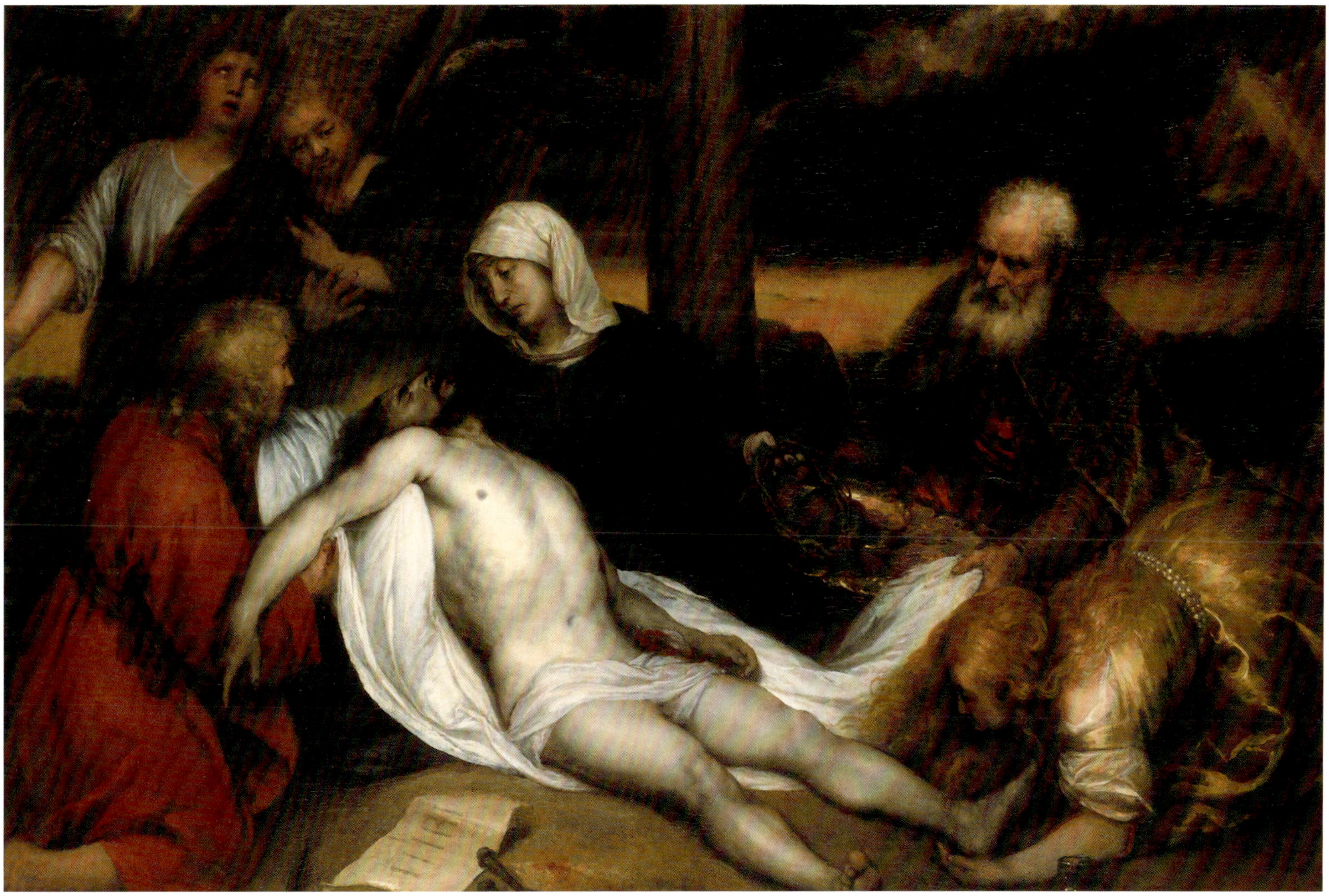

CAT. 40

41 The Sacrifice of Isaac

c. 1640–1643, oil on canvas, 234.4 × 174.3 (92 5/16 × 68 5/8). Collection Joseph and Lieve Guttmann, USA

Exhibition
Tel Aviv 1997, no. 1

IN ONE OF THE MOST DRAMATIC stories of the Old Testament (Genesis 22:1–13), the aged Abraham is instructed by God to take his only son, Isaac, to a mountain and sacrifice him as a burnt offering. Sorrowfully obeying God's command, Abraham brought a knife and fire to light the wood that the unsuspecting Isaac had been asked to carry. Abraham built an altar and was about to slay his son, when an angel of the Lord called to him: "Abraham, Abraham!... Do not lay your hand on the boy... for now I know that you fear God, since you have not withheld your son." Abraham then discovered that God had provided a ram, caught by its horns in the thicket, as a substitute for the burnt offering.

In this impressive painting Lievens has captured the emotional tensions of the moment when the angel suddenly appears from a cloudlike formation to stay Abraham's hand. Calmly addressing the patriarch, the angel gestures heavenward to indicate that he is an agent of God's will. Simultaneously, his left hand prevents Abraham from plunging his knife into Isaac's body and points to the ram in the underbrush. As the deep reddish orange fire burns on the altar, Abraham, his face drawn with anxiety, stares wide-eyed at the angel, still trying to comprehend the significance of the angel's words and actions. Isaac, his nude body lying defenseless on the stack of wood, reaches toward the angel with both arms, his eyes and mouth open in a mixture of horror and hope at this apparition.

This story of God's test of Abraham's faith excited the imaginations of artists for both its dramatic narrative and its theological meaning as an Old Testament prefiguration of the Crucifixion. In a large four-block woodcut and in a ceiling painting for Santo Spirito in Isola, Titian emphasized the angel's urgent intervention as he flies in and holds back Abraham's sword.[1] Around 1620 Rubens adapted Titian's compositional ideas in a ceiling painting for the Jesuit church in Antwerp.[2] Lievens, who painted a now-lost *Holy Family* for the Jesuit church, would certainly have studied this work.

But his primary source of inspiration for the present painting was Rembrandt's large-scale depiction of the subject, from 1635 (see Wheelock fig. 20). Rembrandt's and Lievens' works are similar in composition and narrative moment, yet different in mood and theological interpretation. Rembrandt stresses the story's physical reality, not only in the angel's firm grasp of Abraham's wrist but also in the forceful thrust of Abraham's hand on Isaac's face, both covering his eyes and exposing his throat. Lievens highlights the spiritual nature of the angel's communication with Abraham. The angel's hand passes over Abraham's extended arm, still holding the knife, but the two figures do not touch. And Isaac, his face obscured in Rembrandt's rendering, here reaches out toward the angel to embrace his salvation.

Lievens' interpretation, quieter and more focused on human emotions than Rembrandt's, derives not from the Bible but from Flavius Josephus' *Jewish Antiquities*.[3] In 1642 Philips Angel noted that Lievens had used this text to give an "uncommon naturalness" to his depiction of another episode in the story.[4] A distinguishing feature of Flavius Josephus' account is that Isaac, understanding the importance of obeying God and his father, consented to lie upon the altar without being bound, just as Lievens portrayed him.[5]

Lievens must have seen Rembrandt's *Sacrifice of Isaac* when he was in the Netherlands in 1639 and 1640 to paint *The Magnanimity of Scipio* for the Leiden town hall. Unquestionably, he painted the present work after returning to Antwerp, where a Catholic client would have welcomed the representaton of the angel as an intermediary between God and Abraham.[6] Lievens also adapted gestures from Van Dyck's *Saint Augustine in Ecstasy* altarpiece, in which an angel points toward the Holy Trinity and a penitent donor reaches prayerfully toward the saint with both arms.[7] Lievens' painting technique — much softer and more diffuse than Rembrandt's (compare the ways the two artists rendered Abraham's beard) — and the deep velvety colors of his palette reflect not only Van Dyck's but also Titian's manner of painting.

Lievens painted two versions of this composition, the second being in the Galleria Doria Pamphilj in Rome.[8] The primary differences are in the greater importance given here to flame burning on the altar and the radiance of the sky. Lievens probably availed himself of studio assistance in both works, for slight differences in handling are evident in the landscape and draperies.[9] AKW

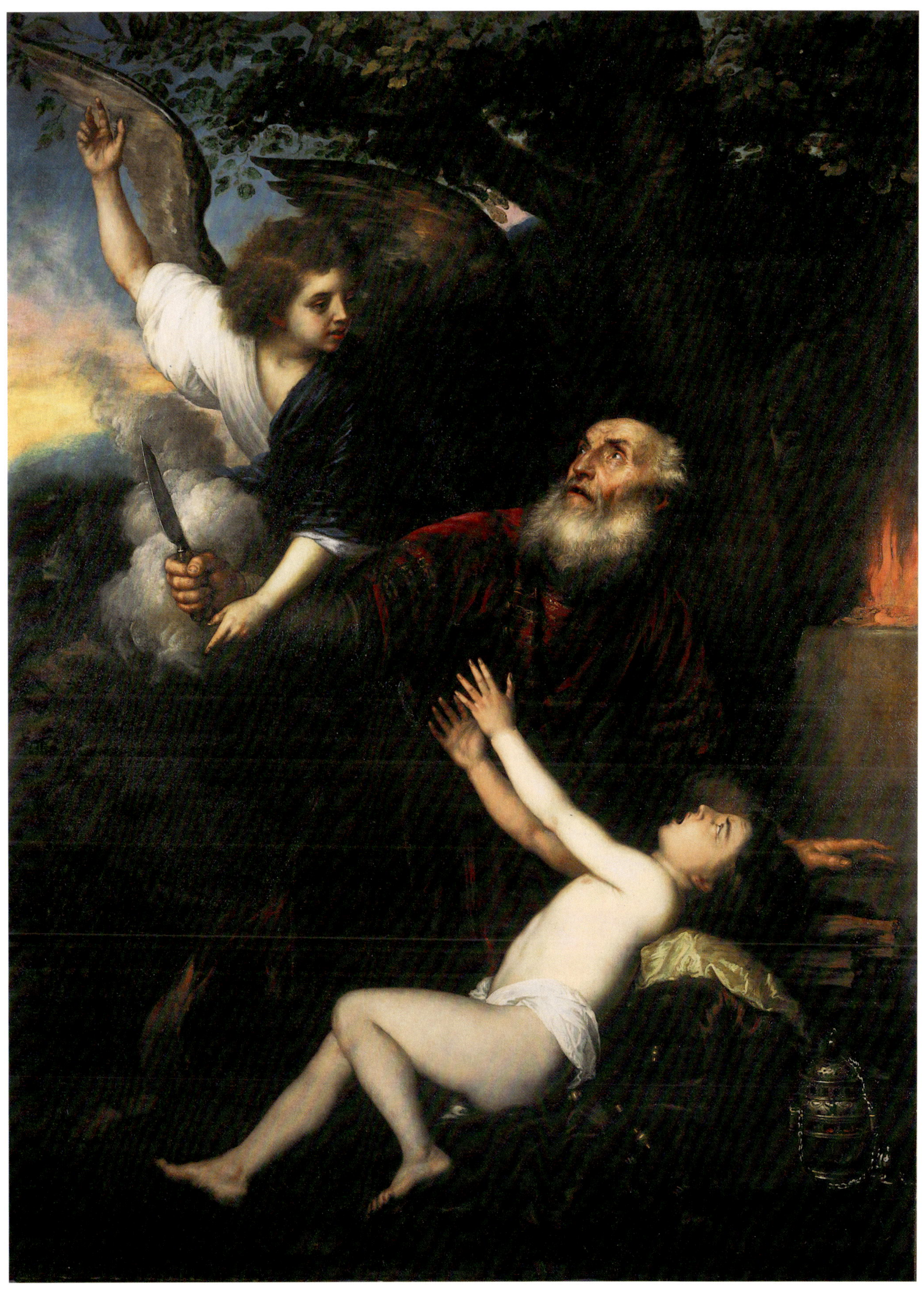

42 Landscape with Willows

early 1640s, oil on panel, original 26.1 × 39.9 cm, set into a collar 28 × 41 (11 x 16⅛). Frits Lugt Collection, Institut Néerlandais, Paris

Provenance

Probably Joan-Baptista Anthonie, Antwerp (1843–1929), by 1691; John Postle Heseltine, London (1843–1929); Frits Lugt, Maartensdijk, 1927

Selected References

Schneider/Ekkart 1973, 61, 164–165, 338, no. 308; Braunschweig 1979, no. 42; Brown 1979b, 745; Sumowski 1983, 3: 1813, no. 1305; Dickey 2001, 302 n. 51; The Hague 2002, no. 180

LIEVENS' PAINTED LANDSCAPES are all about mood. They are generally quiet woodland scenes, viewed at the end of the day, with a dense copse of trees silhouetted against the setting sun. In this small panel painting a man and a woman tending goats lie in the deep shade of three massive trees rising from the top of a small hillock, their forms almost lost amid the brushy undergrowth. In the middle distance a large manor house, partly obscured behind the foreground hill and situated near a small waterfall rushing off another hill nearby, further denotes the comfortable interaction of man and nature.

A precise chronology for Lievens' landscape paintings is difficult to determine because none of them is dated.[1] The brown tonalities of the present work, the powerful silhouettes of the pollard willows, and the way the bright yet cloudy sky appears between craggy branches and tree trunks closely resemble effects found in Lievens' Berlin landscape, which probably dates from the early 1640s (see Wheelock fig. 16). Spatially, however, this landscape is entirely different. Instead of a gentle recession into the middle ground, a compositional schema that owes much to Rubens' landscapes from the late 1630s, Lievens here established a dramatic foreground focus with massive trees densely filling the upper left quadrant of the painting.

In this landscape Lievens has embarked on a new, more personal style, emphasizing contrasts in scale to enhance the visual intensity of the scene. He has applied the paint more freely, particularly in the foreground, where organic forms are suggested with the juxtaposition of bold impastos and flat areas dominated by the golden brown ground and the brown and black underpainted sketches. To create the striking contrasts of sunlight glimpsed against the dark willows, Lievens laid in light-filled blocks of sky between the craggy tree trunks and branches. His final paint softened the contrast by adding twigs and fluidly handled foliage.[2] Much as Titianesque painting techniques and pictorial elements entered into Lievens' religious and mythological paintings from the latter years of his Antwerp period, so too did the glowing atmospheric effects of sixteenth-century Venetian landscapes influence his own work in this area.[3]

The probability is strong that Lievens executed this depiction of a rolling pastoral countryside in the early 1640s, soon after completing the Berlin landscape but before moving to Amsterdam in 1644.[4] As Sumowski has noted, this painting seems to have remained in Antwerp, where it was in the collection of postmaster Joan Baptista Anthoine (d. 1691). Anthoine's inventory lists a painting that, despite its cursory description, must be this work: "A little landscape with sleeping farmer[s?] by Lievens."[5] AKW

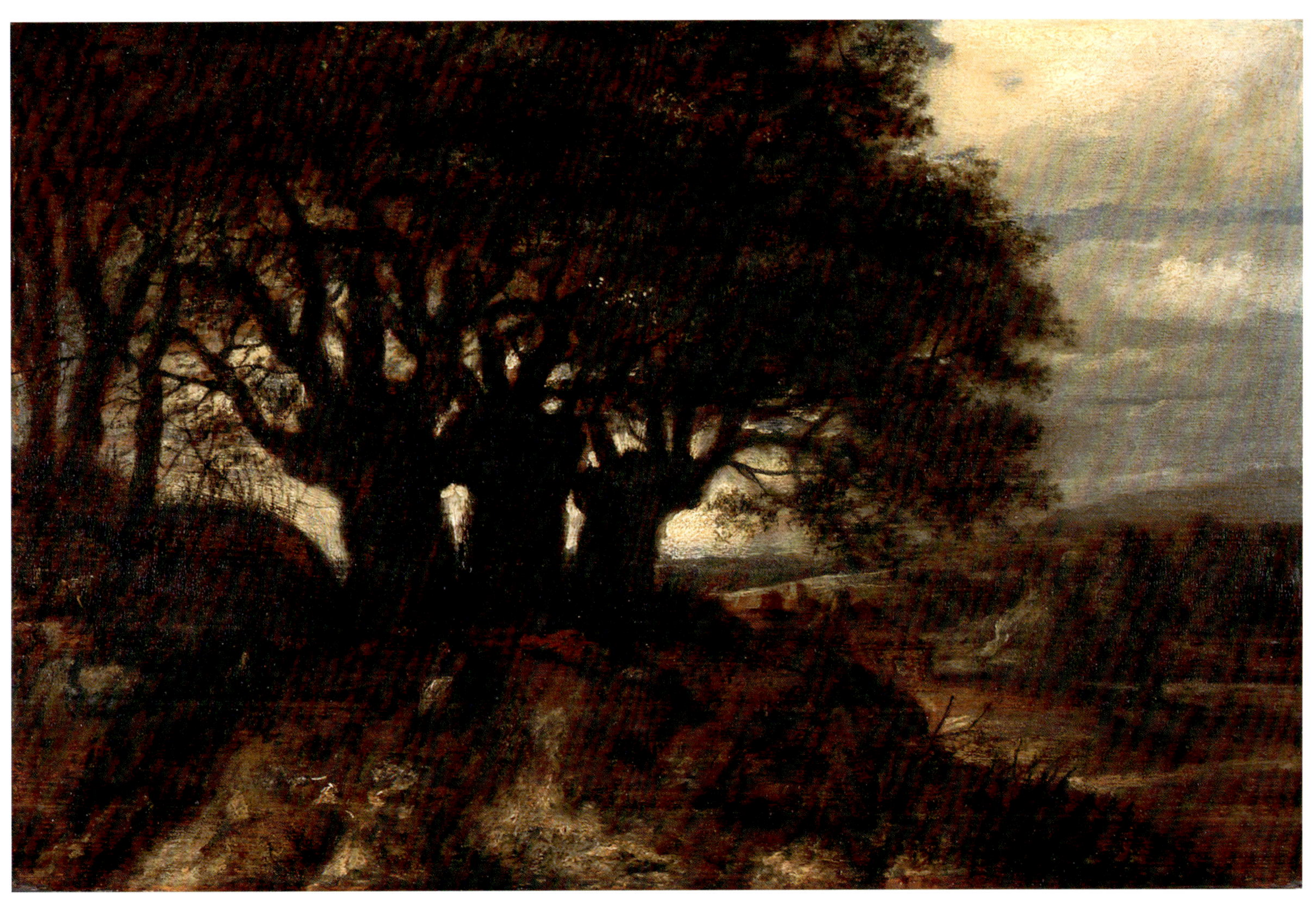

43 Dune Landscape with Trees

middle to late 1640s, oil on panel, 41.5 × 35.5 (16 5/16 × 14). Museum Boijmans Van Beuningen, Rotterdam

Provenance

(J. de Bary, Amsterdam, November 11, 1759, no. 32); (B. West, London, July 23, 1820); (S. Rogers, London, April 28, 1856); Lady Burdett-Couts; J. Pierpont Morgan, New York; Victor Koch, London; (N. Beets, Amsterdam, 1929)

Selected References

Schneider/Ekkart 1973, 61, 165, 338, no. 310; Braunschweig 1979, no. 46; Sumowski 1983, 3: 1812, no. 1302

THE LANDSCAPE INSPIRED LIEVENS in different ways, depending on whether he sought to capture its pictorial effects in woodcut, drawing, or painting. His masterful woodcut of a copse of trees from c. 1640 is boldly expressive, with twisting and knotted trunks and branches that Lievens articulated with firm lines and clarity of form (cat. 80). His landscape drawings are more measured and subtly rendered, with trees and buildings defined by long parallel hatchings and generally given equal weight. The Japan paper he often used for these nature studies imbues them with a soft atmospheric quality that enhances their contemplative character, even when he chose to situate the viewer deep within a woodland setting (cat. 123).

When Lievens approached landscape in painting, however, he sought to express its rugged irregularities. Trees stretch out and reach in unpredictable directions, rising out of uneven terrains that are more foreboding than welcoming. Clouds have a physical presence that suggests their movements within the sky and the impact of time or weather.

Landscape prompted Lievens to paint in his most evocative manner. Thick paints, dabbed onto the panel with little modulation, somehow capture the essence of the hard-packed dirt on a rocky hillside, the rough-textured bark of a tree, or the tips of leaves at the end of silhouetted branches. Reds, ochers, and greens — unmixed and seemingly randomly applied — somehow coalesce to form an image that is not only recognizable but also emotionally compelling. Small figures, here a rider and his companion, populate these landscapes, passing through them so inconspicuously that one is hardly aware of their presence. Where they are headed, or where they have been, is never divulged; even the paths they have followed are impossible to determine.

Lievens may well have derived his style of painting landscapes from Rubens and Brouwer, but if so, he quickly evolved his own approach. His manner of painting landscapes had little immediate influence on Dutch or Flemish artistic traditions, however, which continued to privilege descriptive realism above suggestive recreations of woodland scenes.[1]

The dating of Lievens landscapes is notoriously difficult, and *Dune Landscape with Trees* has been placed anywhere from the late 1630s to around 1650.[2] Similarities in spatial concept exist between this painting and the landscape from the early 1640s in the Lugt Collection (cat. 42), but the execution is somewhat freer and bolder here. Given that Lievens continued to paint landscapes in his "Flemish" style after he moved to Amsterdam in 1644,[3] it seems probable that he executed *Dune Landscape with Trees* soon after he returned to the Dutch Republic, probably in the middle to late 1640s. A relatively large number of Lievens' landscapes are listed in Amsterdam inventories, including those of Rembrandt and of Herman Becker. AKW

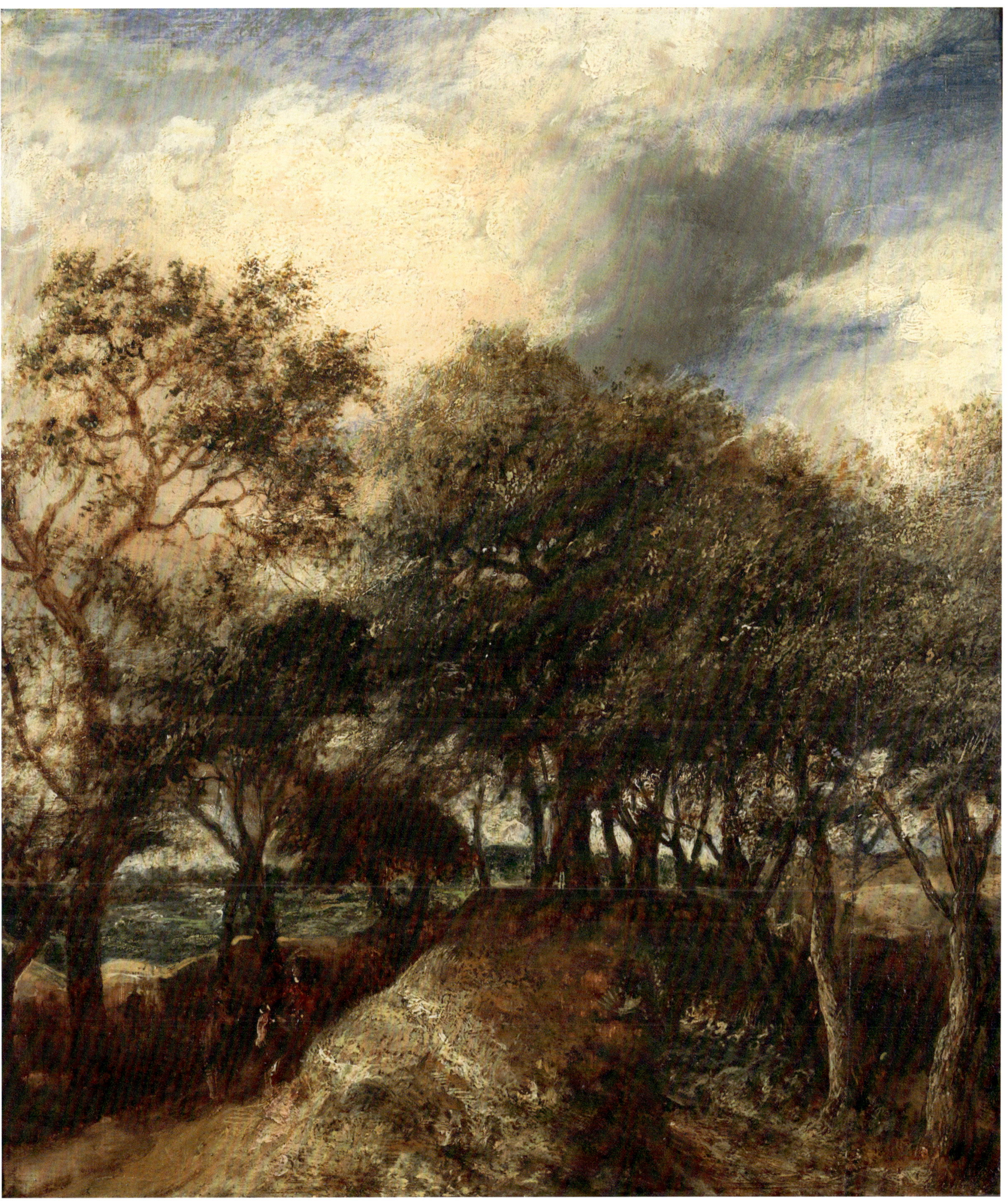

44 Portrait of Adriaen Trip

1644, oil on canvas (before conservation treatment), 107.5 × 83.5 (42 5/16 × 32 7/8). Museum Het Rembrandthuis, Amsterdam, on loan from a private collection

Inscription

Monogrammed and dated: I.L. 1644

Provenance

Through inheritance to the heirs of the sitter

Selected References

Schneider/Ekkart 1973, 151, no. 263; Sumowski 1983, 3: 1809, no. 1290; DeWitt 2006, 200, 240–241

THE PORTRAIT OF ADRIAEN TRIP, painted in 1644, must be one of the first works that Lievens painted in Amsterdam following his move from Amsterdam. The self-confident and elegantly dressed young man appears to be a nobleman, though in fact he was the scion of a prominent Amsterdam merchant family.[1] Adriaen Trip was born around 1620, the son of Elias Trip (1570–1636) and Aletta Adriaensdr (1589–1656). In 1645 he married Adriana de Geer (1627–1685), a daughter of the very wealthy ironware and arms dealer Louis de Geer (1587–1652),[2] and the couple moved to Sweden in 1646 to further the interests of the family business. They returned to the Netherlands in 1653 and settled in Beverwijk, a small town close to Haarlem where Trip owned property. Various well-to-do citizens of Amsterdam had country estates there, including Trip's mother as well as burgomaster Jan Bicker (see Van der Veen essay). In the mid-1660s Trip moved his family to Groningen, where he owned a large tract of land and was involved in extensive developments. He died there sometime between 1684 and 1687.

In this life-size, three-quarter-length portrait, Trip has been rendered with great élan. Wearing a highly fashionable yellowish brown outfit, he grasps a long staff in his right hand and sports a rapier at his hip. The small collar with hanging tassels is of the very latest style. The fluent manner of painting seen here — most striking in the face — is typical of Lievens and enhances the grace and dignity of the sitter. It is possible that the commission for the portrait came from the subject himself. At the time it was painted, the still-unmarried, twenty-two-year-old Trip was not yet living independently but was courting his future wife. The portrait could well have been intended for his mother's house, perhaps with an eye to advancing his appeal. In any case, the choice of Lievens as portraitist is significant, for it was Rembrandt who painted portraits of Trip's mother and probably his sister Maria in 1639, while Bartholomeus van der Helst painted likenesses of another sister Sophia and her husband in the same period.[3] Lievens' portrait of Adriaen Trip must have been appreciated, for around 1659 Joan Huydecoper commissioned him to paint a family group portrait around his mother-in-law, Sophia Trip. Huydecoper and Adriaen Trip visited Lievens' studio together and in all probability posed for the group portrait. If this surmise is correct, Trip's likeness was painted by Lievens on two occasions separated by fifteen years. JVDV

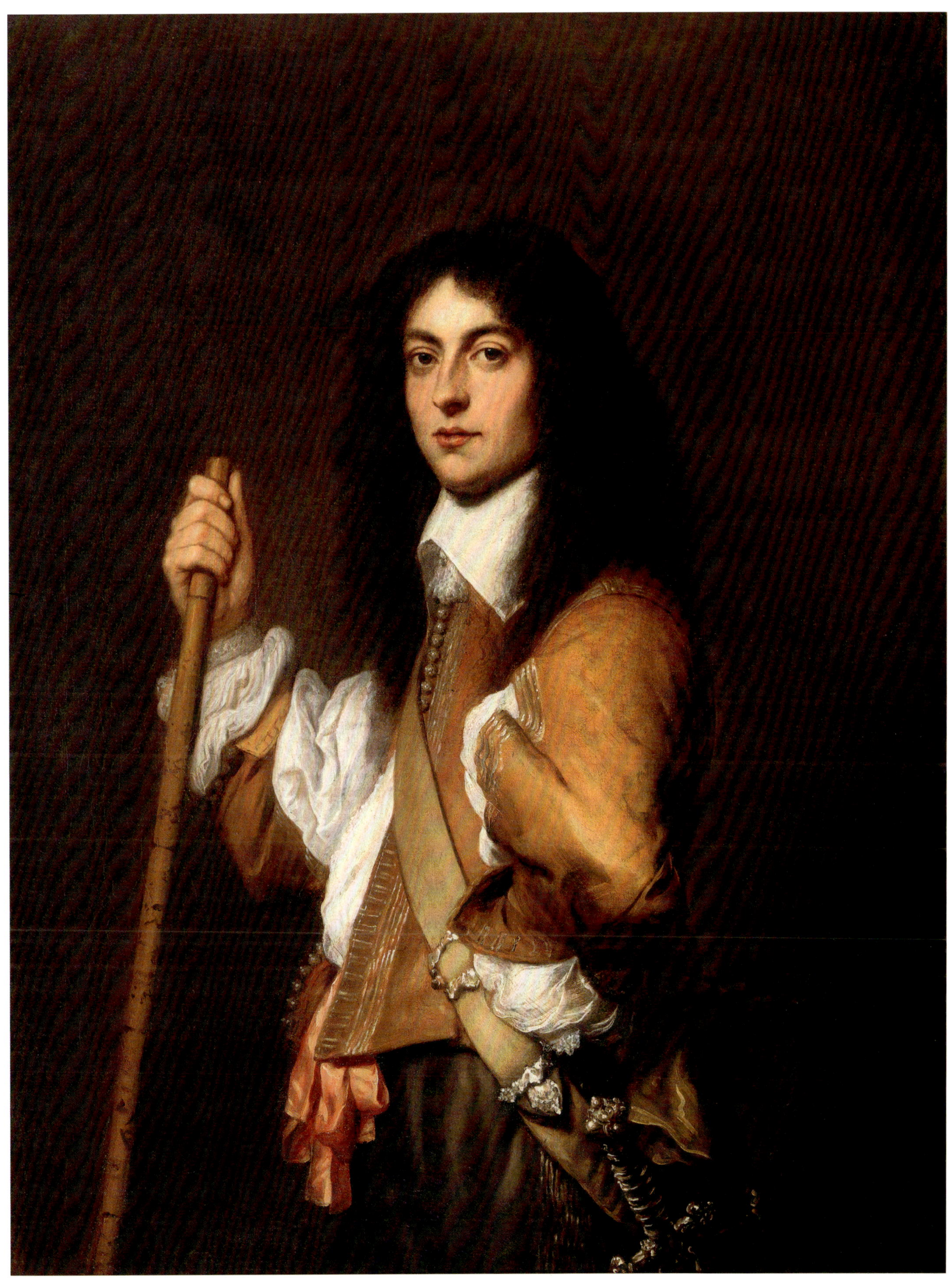

45 Portrait of Anna Maria van Schurman

1649, oil on canvas, 87 × 68.6 (34¼ × 27). The National Gallery, London, Presented by the Trustees of the British Museum, 1880

Inscription

Monogrammed and dated at left center: I.L./1649
Above sitter to the left, in a later hand: *Anna Maria Schurmam [sic]*

Provenance

Sir Hans Sloane bequest to the nation, 1753; presented by the Trustees of the British Museum, 1880

Selected References

Schneider/Ekkart 1973, 150, no. 258; Klessmann and Keiser 1983, 94; Sumowski 1983, 3: 1809, no. 1291; ; MacLaren/Brown 1991, 231, no. 1095; Franeker 2007

ANNA MARIA VAN SCHURMAN (1607–1678) gazes directly out at the viewer with a frank and open countenance. Seated behind a table covered with an oriental carpet, she holds an open book, the fingers of her left hand slipped lightly between its pages. An inkstand and ink pot sit before her on the table, perhaps to be used for writing in the book, whose pages are blank.[1]

Contemporary viewers would have known Van Schurman as having a vibrant and fertile mind. When Lievens painted her portrait in 1649, she had won renown throughout Europe as an unusually highly educated woman.[2] As the first female to attend university lectures in the Netherlands, she published her *Dissertatio* in 1641 on the education of women. Yet Van Schurman was not only an intellectual, she was also an accomplished artist. Although she maintained that she was self-taught, she probably studied engraving with Magdalena van de Passe, daughter of the Utrecht engraver and publisher Crispijn van de Passe. While a skilled engraver, Van Schurman also created works in oil, gouache, pencil, pastel, wax, boxwood, and ivory as well as paper cut into intricate patterns.[3] Lauded for her achievements in art, in 1643 she gained admission to the Utrecht Guild of Saint Luke as a "painter, sculptor, and engraver."

The identification of this subject as Anna Maria van Schurman is supported by comparison with her pastel self-portrait of 1640 (fig. 1).[4] Lievens had etched and drawn likenesses of *uomini illustri* throughout his career, including Joost van den Vondel, Adriaen Brouwer, Constantijn Huygens, René Descartes, and Jan Vos (cats. 85, 102, 103, 112, 118), possibly intending to create a series of images similar to Van Dyck's famous *Iconography*.[5] Lievens may have been commissioned to depict Van Schurman for such a series.[6] She was acquainted with both Descartes and Huygens, and it may have been through one of these connections that Lievens came to paint her portrait. VCT

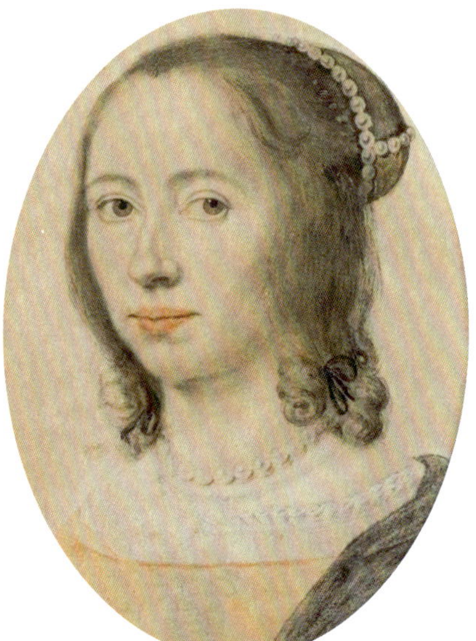

1 | Anna Maria van Schurman, *Self-Portrait*, 1640, pastel. Museum Martena, Franeker

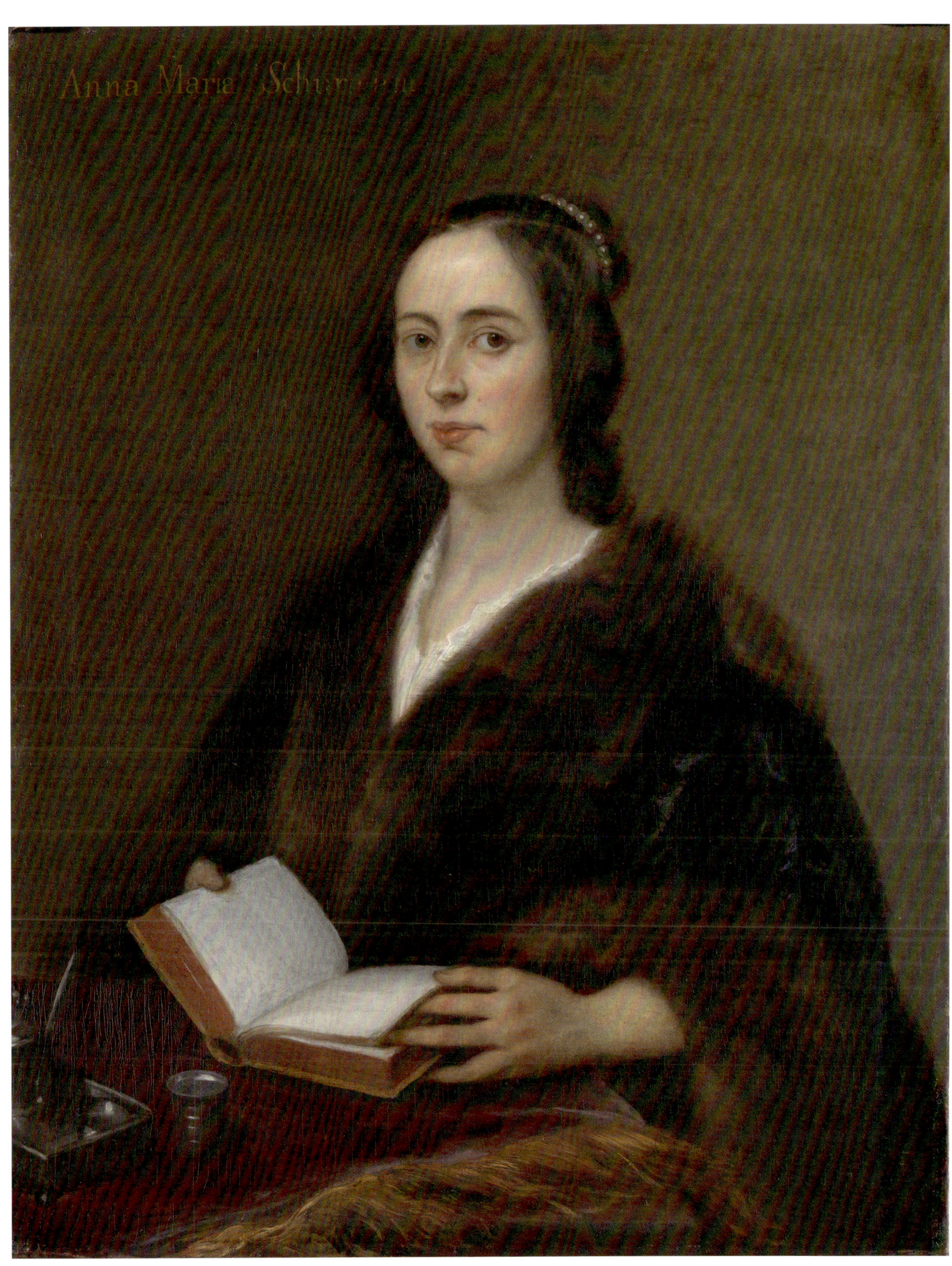
Anna Maria

46 Jacob Receiving Joseph's Bloody Coat

probably mid-1640s, oil on canvas, 55 × 73 (21 5/8 × 28 3/4). Collection Joseph and Lieve Guttmann, USA

Provenance

Perhaps Herman Becker, Amsterdam, 1678; perhaps Pieter Apostool, Amsterdam 1743

THE OLD TESTAMENT STORY OF Joseph excited the imagination of Dutch artists, not only for the marvelous exploits of the young leader but also for the jealousies, deceits, and betrayals that mark the complex narrative of his life.[1] The cause of intense boyhood jealousies was the "coat of many colors" that his father, Jacob, had presented to him, signifying that he was the favored son. The tragic consequences, with his older brothers turning against him, are described in Genesis 37. When Joseph, sent by his father to see if all was well with the brothers, who were herding sheep in the countryside, they conspired to kill him. Instead, they sold him into slavery in Egypt, then dipped his coat in the blood of a goat to feign his death and took it to the aged patriarch. In grief, Jacob tore his garments, donned sackcloth, and refused to be comforted.

The most influential of the many representations of Jacob's response to this horrific news was by Jan Pynas, a friend and colleague of Pieter Lastman in Amsterdam, who executed his large painting of *Jacob Receiving Joseph's Bloody Coat* in 1618 (fig. 1), the very year that Lievens was studying with Lastman. Pynas poignantly depicted the grief-stricken Jacob surrounded by his family. The power of this image was felt years later by the poet and playwright Joost van den Vondel, who credited Pynas' painting as the inspiration for his tragedy *Joseph in Dothan* in 1640: "where the bloody coat is shown to the father: such as we, in the closing (passages) of this work, have tried to emulate with words, the painter's colors, drawings, and passions."[2]

Lievens may well have seen Vondel's drama when he was in the Netherlands in 1640 to install *The Magnaminity of Scipio* for the Leiden town hall, and this perhaps prompted him to look back to Pynas' forceful composition when executing his own version of the story. Here, as in Pynas' image, Jacob has been shown the bloody cloak and falls back from a seated position inconsolable, his arms crossed, his family hovering around him. Lievens, however, intensifies the dramatic moment by bringing the action closer to the viewer and by eliminating extraneous compositional elements that Pynas had included to place the scene in a larger narrative framework.

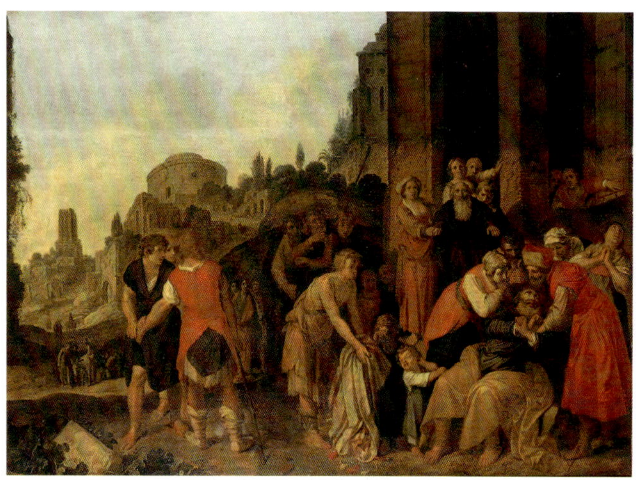

1 | Jan Pynas, *Jacob Shown Joseph's Bloody Coat*, 1618, oil on panel, 90 × 119 cm. The State Hermitage Museum, Saint Petersburg

He also changed Jacob's posture, making it more rigid and depicting him with his eyes closed, signaling that he has hardened his heart to the entreaties of those around him.

The parallels with Pynas' painting and Vondel's play argue that Lievens executed this work for the Dutch market, a hypothesis that is reinforced by early references to Lievens' paintings of this subject in Dutch collections. One version, now lost, was in Delft in the early 1650s, where it was copied by Leonard Bramer.[3] Another was listed in the 1678 inventory of Herman Becker, although it is not certain which painting he owned.[4] Stylistically, the smooth modeling of the drapery in this work differs from his brushwork during his Antwerp period, which also suggests its creation in Amsterdam probably in the latter half of the 1640s when his relationship with Vondel seems to have been particularly close (cat. 85).[5] Indeed, one wonders whether the gesture of the standing brother in this painting has its origins in a theatrical production of Vondel's play.

The work seen here is a modest-sized preliminary study for a large-scale painting (164 × 231 cm) in the Musée des Beaux-Arts in Aix-en-Provence.[6] Given the size of that work, and its awkward passages, it was probably a commissioned piece that Lievens executed with studio assistance. Compositionally, the two works differ primarily in the disposition of the background figures. AKW

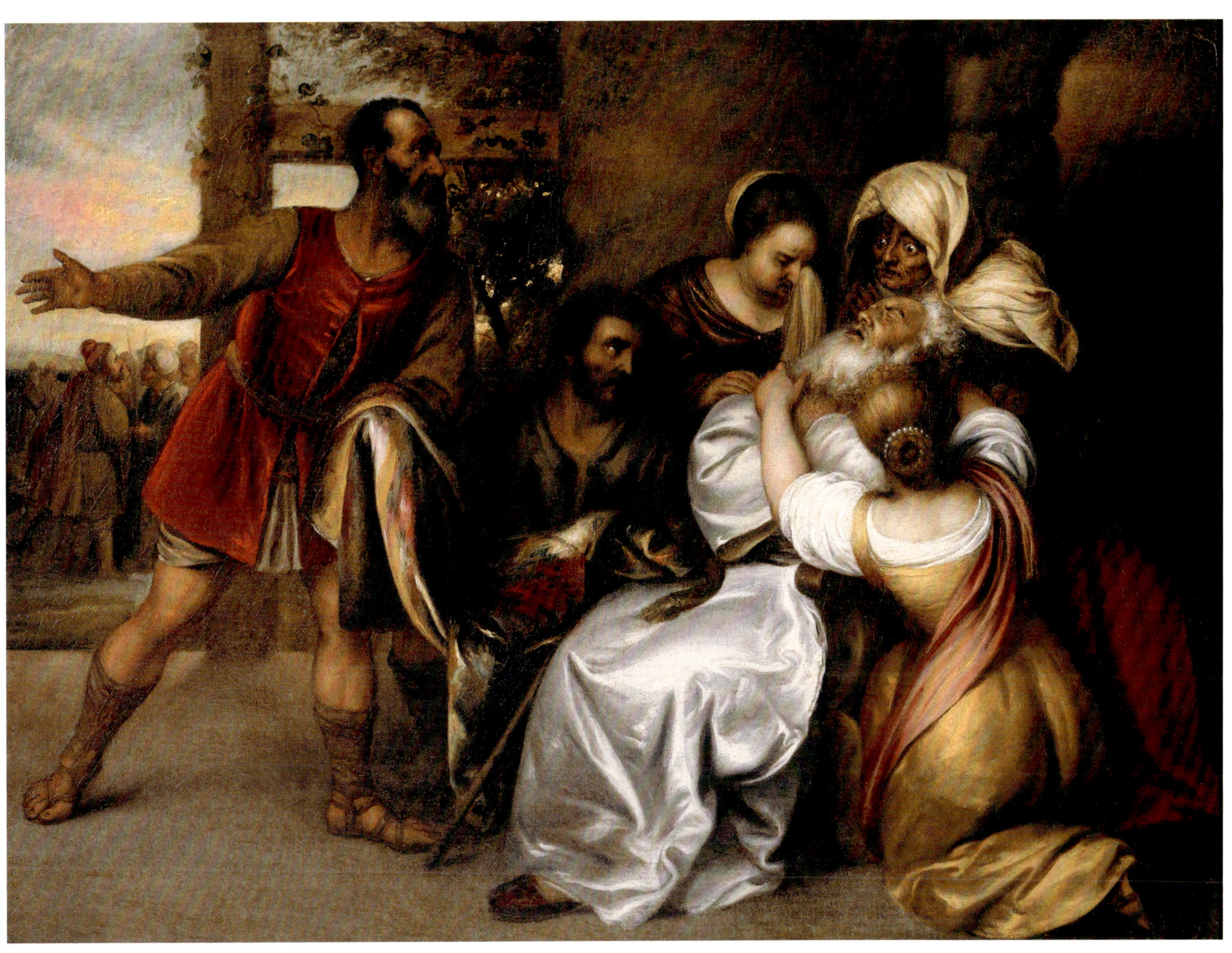

47 Gideon's Sacrifice

early 1650s, oil on canvas, 128 × 94 (50 3/8 × 37). Private collection

Inscription

False signature at the lower left: *Rembrandt. f. 1 (6?)*

Provenance

Art market, Rome 1995 (as Savoldo)

AS DESCRIBED IN THE BOOK OF Judges (6:11–21), an angel one day appeared to Gideon, the youngest son of an Israelite farmer, as he sat under an oak tree at Ophrah. Told that the Lord wanted him to rescue his people from their enemies, Gideon demurred and asked for a sign of God's favor. He prepared an offering of a young goat and unleavened cakes, then presented his gifts to the angel, who directed him to place them on a rock: "With the tip of his staff… the angel of the Lord touched the meat and the unleavened bread. Fire flared from the rock, consuming the meat and the bread."

This impressive canvas, unknown to scholars until recently, turned up on the art market in Rome in 1995 as a work by the Italian Renaissance painter Savoldo. A tentative attribution to Jan Lievens by the present owner was confirmed by Werner Sumowski, who dated the painting to the early 1650s.[1] Lievens combined elements in this painting from different periods of his career. The full-bearded Gideon is reminiscent of the kneeling Abraham in two depictions of the Sacrifice of Isaac from the 1630s (see cat. 41 and Wheelock fig. 17), as are the heavy folds in the drapery of Gideon's robe.[2] Yet the restrained gestures and muted emotions of the participants as well as the sophistication of the color scheme — with its contrast between the flaming red of the angel's drapery and the silvery shimmer of Gideon's garment — point to the 1650s. This dating is supported by the angel's elegant, almost classical facial type, comparable to figures in Lievens' mythological and allegorical paintings of the 1650s, including the companions in *Diana at the Hunt* of 1654 at Potsdam (Neues Palais). Trees with similar trunks and foliage can be found in other landscapes that Lievens painted in the 1650s, including *A Woodland Walk* in Edinburgh.[3]

Gideon's sacrifice is rarely seen in seventeenth-century Dutch art, and most known depictions of the subject are by artists associated with Rembrandt in the 1640s. Ferdinand Bol painted his version in 1641, followed by at least three paintings and a number of drawings by Gerbrand van den Eeckhout.[4] Despite his modest family background, Gideon appears in Lievens' painting clothed in elegant fabric decorated with a pattern of yellow golden flames that correspond to the flames engulfing the burnt offering before him.

This is the only known painting of Gideon by Lievens, thus it is likely the same one mentioned in a document related to financial transactions between Lievens and Herman Becker, an Amsterdam shipping merchant who was also a moneylender.[5] Becker counted a number of artists among his debtors, including Lievens and Rembrandt, and he was willing to accept paintings as pledges for the loans. Between May 1667 and October 1668 Lievens borrowed 400 guilders, using four paintings as security, one of them identified as a "Gideon."[6] When Becker died in 1678, an inventory of his possessions included 231 paintings,[7] but *Gideon* was not among the six paintings by Lievens in the list. Thus the artist was apparently able to redeem this painting by paying back that debt. VM

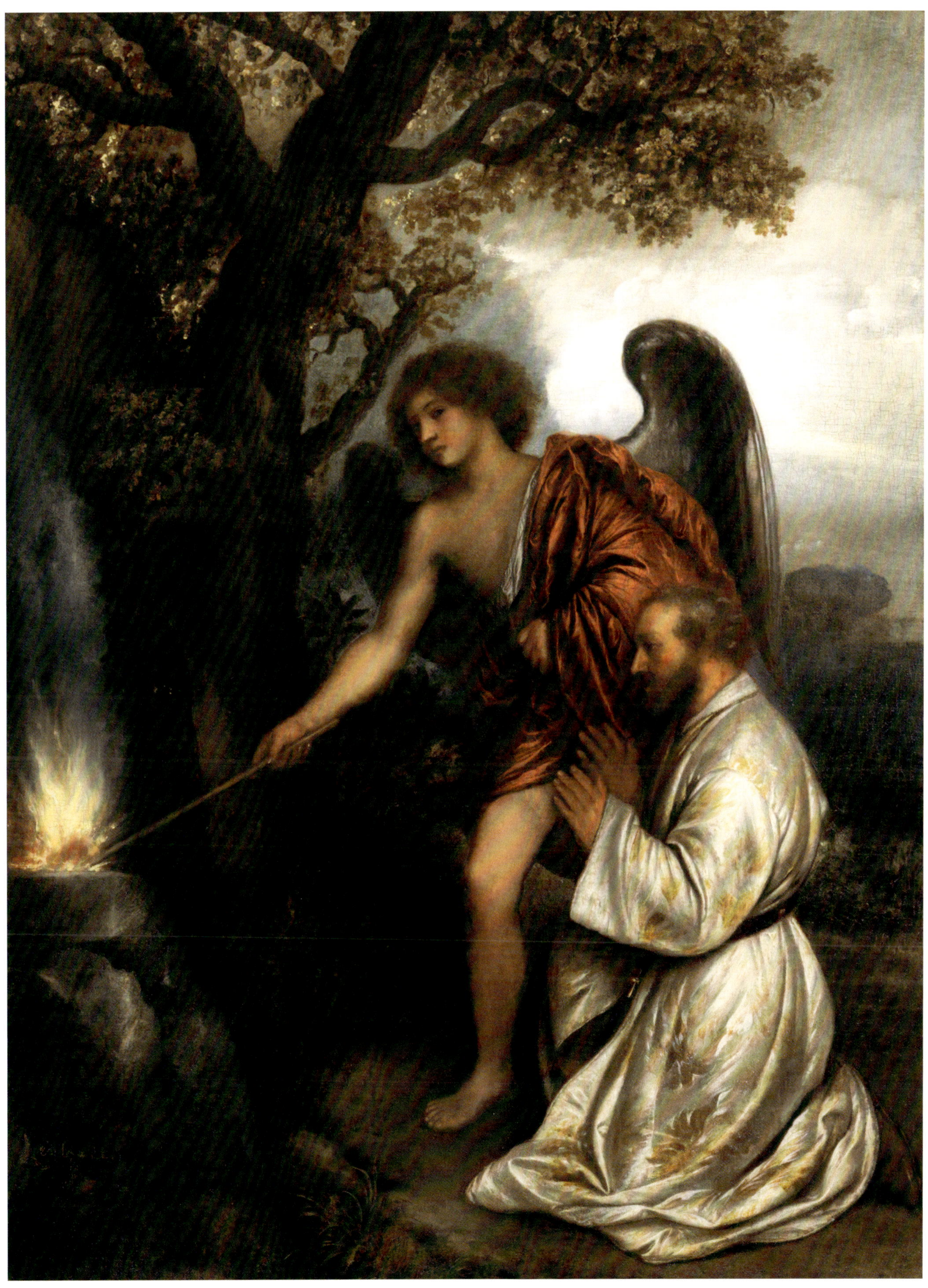

48 Self-Portrait

early 1650s, oil on canvas, 96.2 × 77 (37⅞ × 30⁵⁄₁₆). The National Gallery, London, Presented by Charles Fairfax Murray, 1912

Inscription

Monogrammed in center of the wall (barely visible): I.L.

Provenance

Possibly Susanna van Sonnervelt, widow of Simon Middelgeest, The Hague, 1696; (possibly Amsterdam, March 16, 1750, no. 102); Aert Schouman, The Hague, donated by him to the painter's association "Pictura" in 1792; (Gooden, London, 1896); C. Fairfax Murray, London

Selected References

Schneider/Ekkart 1973, 47–48, 68, 148, 334, no. 248; Braunschweig 1979, no. 33; Sumowski 1983, 3: 1809, no. 1289; Corpus 1982–, 1: 327–328; MacLaren and Brown 1991, 232–233, no. 2864; DeWitt 2006, 9, 237–240

IN THIS ELEGANT SELF-PORTRAIT Lievens presents himself as a successful gentleman, dressed in a shimmering golden robe and sitting before a large window that overlooks a twilight landscape with the setting sun illuminating the trees and the bottoms of the clouds. By posing with his right arm slung casually over the back of the chair, jauntily garbed in rolling masses of rich fabric, Lievens projects an air of luxury, gracefulness, and self-confidence. One senses that the "loftiness" Huygens observed when meeting Lievens in the late 1620s remained a firmly entrenched part of his public persona.

The identity of the sitter as Lievens has never been disputed because the distinctive features — particularly the nose, cleft chin, finely formed mouth, and dark flowing hair — relate so closely to Vorsterman's print after Van Dyck's portrayal of the artist c. 1632 (see Wheelock fig. 11). The date of this painting, however, has been a matter of discussion. While Lievens' features are clearly more mature here than in the engraving, his age might easily be anywhere from his mid-thirties to his mid-forties. Stylistically, the broad technique and elegant pose have long suggested to scholars that Lievens' painted this work after he had fallen under the sway of Van Dyck's style of portrait painting. But Schneider dated it to Lievens' Antwerp period, between 1635 and 1644, whereas MacLaren placed it in middle of the 1640s, raising the possibility that Lievens might even have executed it in Amsterdam. Sumowski placed it in the late 1630s, whereas Brown dated it variously to the early 1650s and to the late 1630s.

Costume considerations, however, make it clear that the painting can date no earlier than the 1650s, for the loose chamber gown, or *japonse rock*, that Lievens wears did not become fashionable in the Netherlands until that time.[1] Marieke de Winkel, who has noted that the billowing shirt sleeves and relatively wide ribbons Lievens wears around the forearm came into style in the early 1650s, would date the portrait to the early to middle 1650s on the basis of costume and the sitter's long, loose hair.[2] Such a date would also be consistent with the style of the background landscape, which is similar to that in *Portrait of a Young Woman* from 1650.[3]

The pronounced Flemish manner seen in this portrait, with its view through an opening onto a spacious landscape, differs substantially from the more restrained poses and carefully rendered likenesses commissioned from Lievens in Amsterdam in the late 1640s and 1650s (see cats. 51, 53). This is one reason it has often been dated to Lievens' Antwerp period. The general disposition of the figure and its relation to a distant landscape are indeed similar to that found in paintings by Van Dyck, including his portrait of Lucas van Uffel (1622), auctioned in Amsterdam on April 9, 1639.[4]

Although it is not known if Lievens arrived in the Netherlands in time to attend the Van Uffel auction, he was there in 1639 to discuss his commission for the Leiden town hall (see Wheelock fig. 19), and he may well have known Van Dyck's portrait.[5] Certainly when he came to execute this self-portrait in the early 1650s, he seems to have made a conscious effort to loosen his manner of painting to reflect his awareness of Flemish traditions, perhaps to ingratiate himself in European courtly circles, where this approach was very much in vogue. Indeed, it is interesting that the very year he was painting this self-portrait Lievens was in contact with Friedrich Wilhelm, the Elector of Brandenburg, and his wife, Louise Henriette, who had an enormous preference for this international style of painting and invited Lievens to help decorate their Schloss Oranienburg near Berlin. LDW, AKW

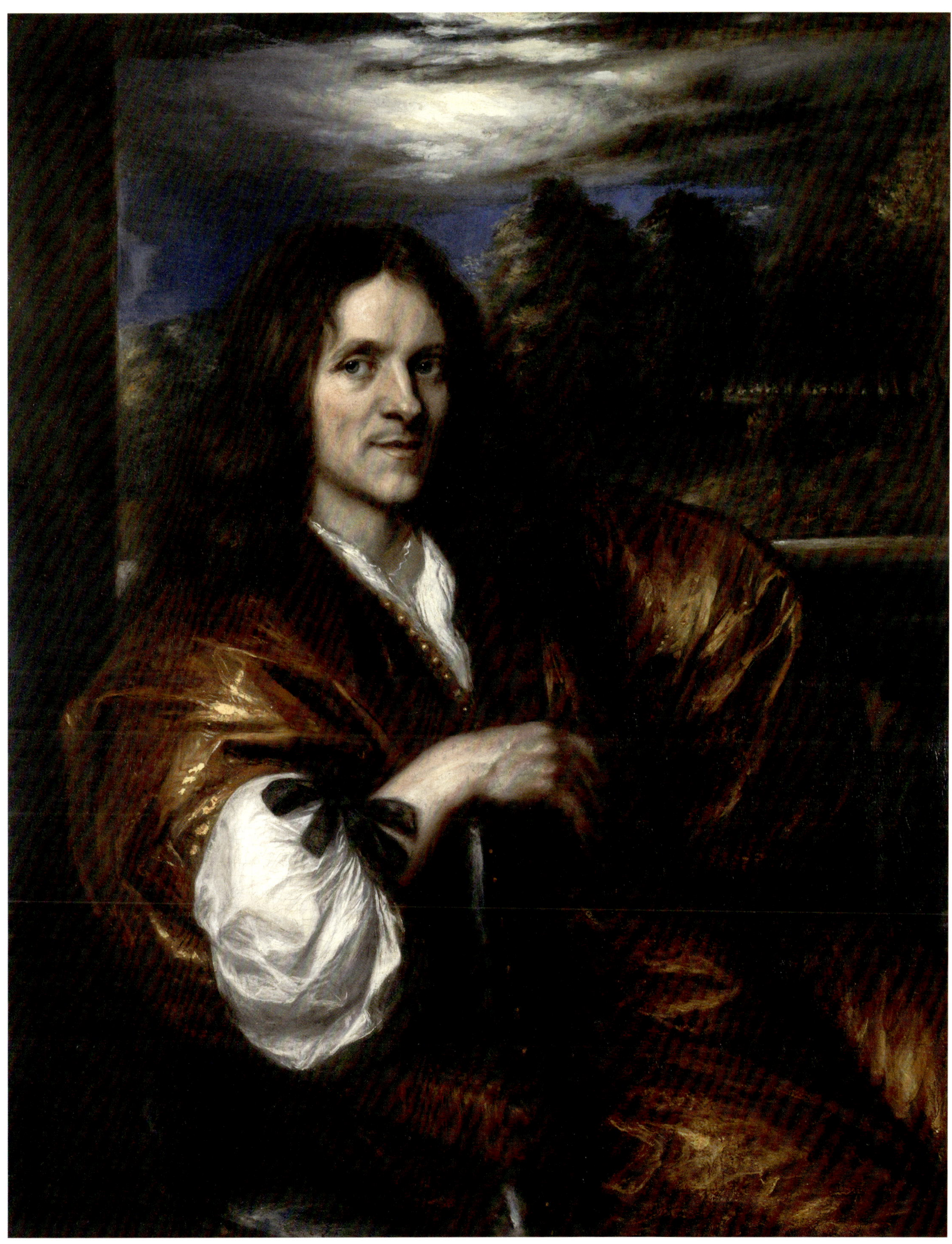

49 Triumph of Peace

1652, oil on canvas, 220 × 204 (86 5/8 × 80 5/16). Rijksmuseum, Amsterdam

Inscription

Monogrammed in bottom center: IL 1652

Provenance

Lievens' estate, Amsterdam, 1674; Offices of the Ministry of Finance, Spinhuissteg, Amsterdam until 1877

Selected References

Schneider/Ekkart 1973, 120, no. 115; Braunschweig 1979, no. 37; Brown 1979b, 745; Sumowski 1983, 3: 1786, no. 1207; Münster and Osnabrück 1998, no. 1162

ONE OF LIEVENS' MOST AMBITIOUS large-scale compositions, this painting is replete with symbols of the peace and prosperity that derive from overcoming the menace of war. At the center sits a jewel-clad woman representing Pax (peace), dressed in a white gown with a red cape and holding an olive branch. Minerva, recognizable by her plumed helmet, reaches forward to crown Pax with a laurel wreath, symbolic of her victory over Mars (war), the seething, hideous figure lying bound in chains under her feet. Mars' plight is mimicked by a putto at the left playfully binding another in chains, both of whom stare across to a smiling putto tapping on a war drum. Behind Pax are two elegantly dressed young women bearing cornucopia filled with a rich array of fruit, including exotic pineapples, representing the many benefits deriving from peace. Three putti hover nearby: one holds an olive branch, another presents floral crowns for Minerva and Pax, while the third, framed by the blue sky, places a bouquet of flowers into the hands of a grateful attendant wearing a splendid golden dress.

Lievens clearly intended *Triumph of Peace* to celebrate the signing of the Treaty of Münster in 1648.[1] Indeed, Pax even holds her olive branch as though it were a quill pen used to ratify such an agreement. In conceiving this work, Lievens drew on important allegorical precedents, among them Rubens' *Minerva Protects Pax from Mars* (fig. 1), painted as a gift for Charles I around 1629–1630 in honor of another peace treaty. In addition, Lievens' smooth, classicizing style is reminiscent of allegorical paintings made in The Hague by artists such as Gerrit van Honthorst.

No commission is known for *Triumph of Peace*, and curiously, Lievens owned it at the time of his death in 1674, when it was assessed at 100 guilders, nearly half the value of his meager estate. It is unlikely that such a large-scale allegorical work was painted on speculation, however. Rather, it seems probable that it was not accepted by its patron for some reason or was returned to the artist at a later date. *Triumph of Peace* is similar in concept and iconography to paintings Lievens made in 1653–1655 for the court of Friedrich Wilhelm, Elector of Brandenburg, and his wife, Louise Henriette, eldest daughter of the Prince of Orange and Amalia van Solms. These patrons had a preference for allegorical images, including Lievens' *Mars and Venus* (cat. 50) and his now-lost *Arts Triumphing over War*.[2]

One wonders whether Lievens painted this work in anticipation of a commission from the Elector and his wife, who were building their country palace, Schloss Oranienburg, near Berlin in the early 1650s.[3] Indeed, the model for Pax resembles Louise Henriette, with a sharp nose and small, rounded chin. The painting may have been a *portrait historié*, particularly as Pax is wearing a contemporary-styled dress, but the idealized nature of her features makes the identification far from certain.[4] LDW

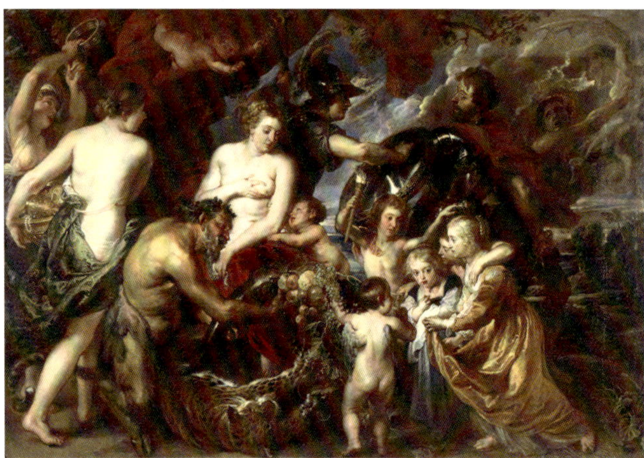

1 | Peter Paul Rubens, *Minerva Protects Pax from Mars*, 1629–1630, oil on canvas, 203.5 × 298 cm. The National Gallery, London

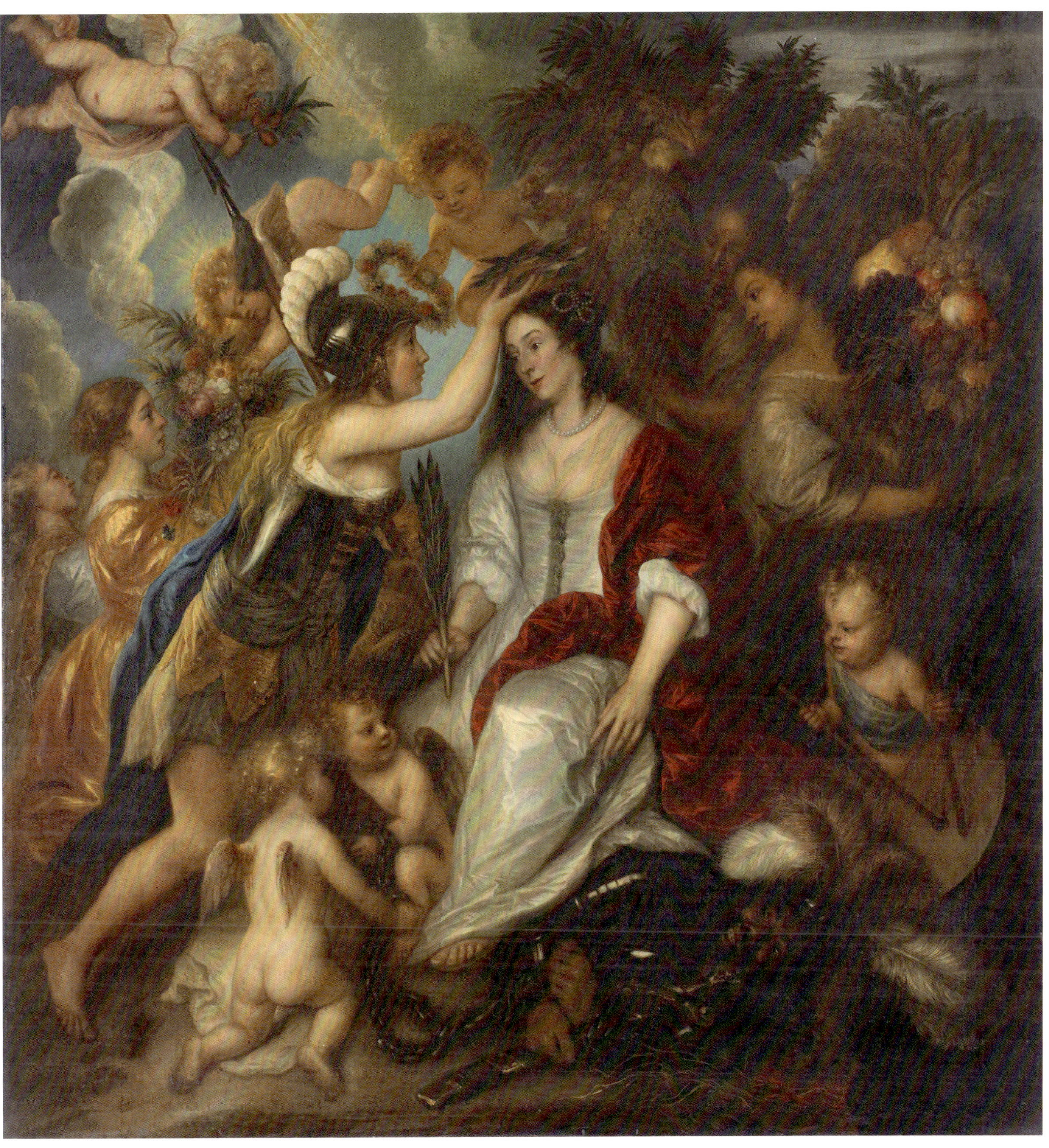

50 Mars and Venus

1653, oil on canvas, 146 × 136 (57½ × 53½). Stiftung Preussische Schlösser und Gärten, Berlin-Brandenburg *(Amsterdam)*

Inscription

Lower right: IL/1653

Provenance

Oranienburg Palace (inventory from 1699, no. 183; Berlin Palace (inventory, 1710, as Lievens; 1816; as Willeboirts); Niederschönhausen Palace (1909); Berliner Palace (1925); since 1932 in Jagdschloss Grunewald

Selected References

Schneider/Ekkart 1973, 325, no. 94; Sumowski 1983, 3: 1786, no. 1208; Haak 1984, 370; Potsdam 1988, v. 14; Krefeld, Oranienburg, and Apeldoorn 1999, 8/56

THIS LARGE PAINTING TAKES ITS theme from the classical tale of Venus, goddess of love, wooing Mars, the god of war. Painted in the smooth and refined international Flemish style that Lievens developed in Antwerp, it depicts the two figures gazing amorously into one another's eyes, while a bevy of putti remove Mars' helmet and sword, encouraging him to leave war behind and enjoy the fruits of love. The ambiguous setting suggests an intimate bedchamber that is open to the sky.

Scenes from mythology were popular in pictorial programs for European nobility, and during the 1650s Lievens developed a reputation as an artist who excelled at such works. His first major painting in this manner was *The Five Muses*, executed in 1650 for the Oranjezaal in the Huis ten Bosch as part of a cycle of allegorical paintings commissioned by Amalia van Solms to commemorate the life of her husband, Frederik Hendrik (see Wheelock fig. 22). Lievens' successful completion of this project led to his being invited by Friedrich Wilhelm, Elector of Brandenburg, and Louise Henriette, daughter of Frederik Hendrik and Amalia van Solms, to paint *Mars and Venus* for their Dutch-inspired pleasure palace, the Schloss Oranienburg.[1] The arched shape of the painting indicates that it was designed to be part of an architectural element, such as a mantelpiece.[2] Lievens also executed *Diana at the Hunt* (Neues Palace, Potsdam) and a painting depicting "the triumph of art over war," now lost, as part of the same decorative cycle.[3]

This allegorical depiction of the disarmament of war by love almost certainly refers to the end of the Thirty Years' War following the signing of the Treaty of Münster in 1648. The painting is also a *portrait historié* of Louise Henriette and Friedrich Wilhelm. When they were married in The Hague in 1646, Frederik Hendrik and Amalia van Solms commissioned a painting from Thomas Willeboirts Bosschaert that portrayed the young couple as Dido and Aeneas (fig. 1). These likenesses confirm the identities of the figures in Lievens' work.[4] Lievens clearly based his Venus on the same model

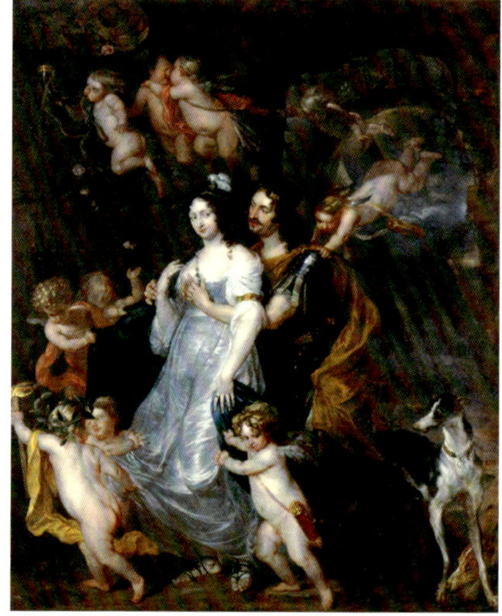

1 | Thomas Willeboirts Bosschaert, *Dido and Aeneas*, 1646, oil on canvas, 297 × 255 cm. Stiftung Preussische Schlösser und Gärten Berlin-Brandenberg, Bildergalerie Potsdam-Sanssouci

Bosschaert used for Dido, despite the differences in hair color, while Mars bears a strong resemblance to the Elector/Aeneas. The idealization inherent in *portraits historiés* allowed Lievens to depict Venus as a nude,[5] whereas such a state of undress would have been unthinkable in a formal portrait of Louise Henriette. Mars' gesture of grasping Venus' breast recalls the central couple in two of Lievens' early paintings, *Allegory of the Five Senses* and *Youth Embracing a Young Woman* (cats. 2, 12). VCT

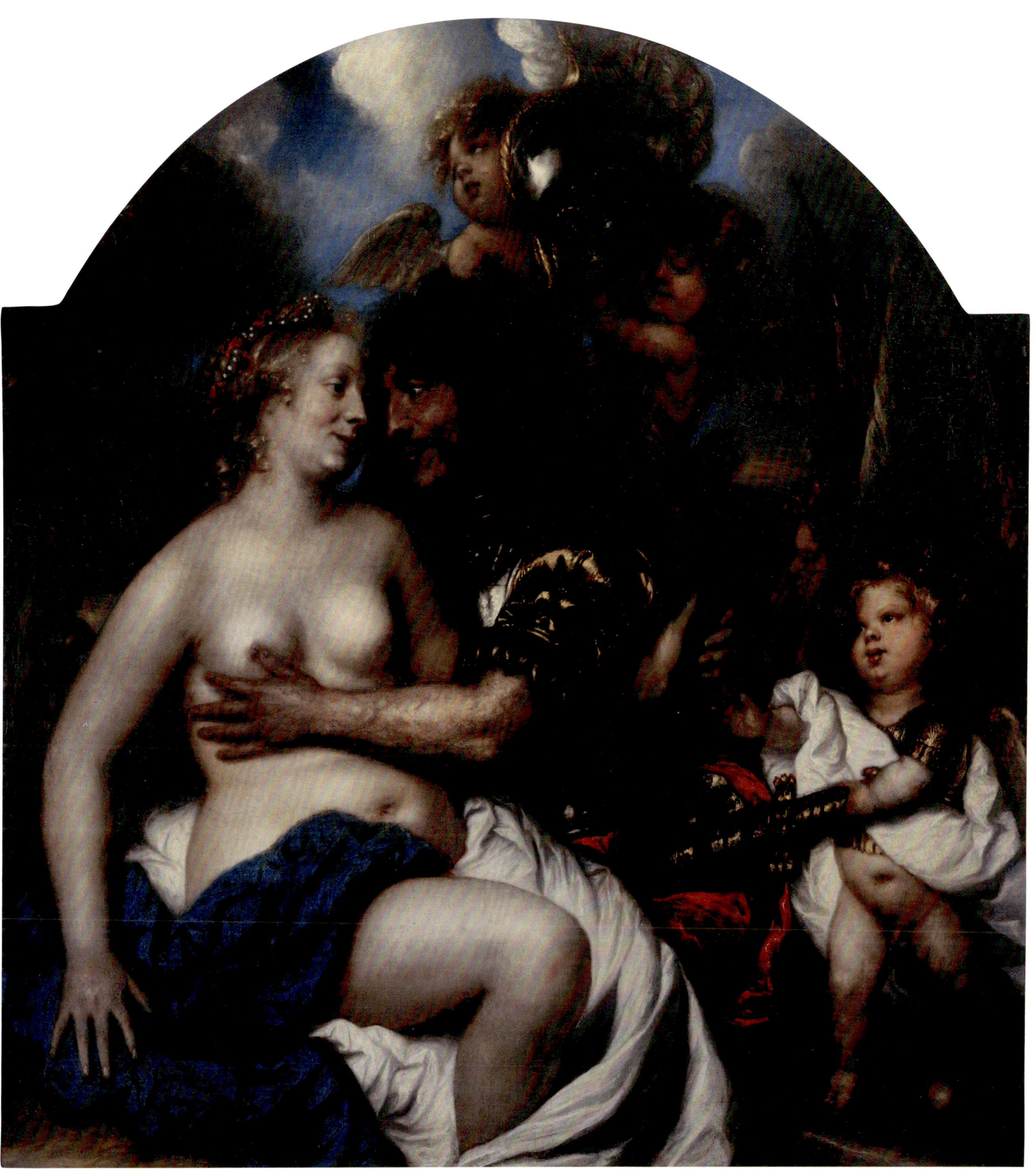

51 Portrait of Sir Robert Kerr, First Earl of Ancram

1654, oil on canvas, 62.2 × 51.4 (24½ × 20¼). Private collection, on long-term loan to the Scottish National Portrait Gallery

Inscription

Inscribed (twice) in upper left: *Earle of Earl of Ancram [sic]*

Provenance

By direct descent to the present owner

Selected References

Schneider/Ekkart 1973, no. 244, 147; Braunschweig 1979, no. 38; Sumowski 1983, 3: 1810, no. 1294; Haak 1984, 371; Edinburgh 1985, 16

PAINTED IN THE YEAR OF THE sitter's death, this portrait of the aged Earl of Ancram (1578–1654) is one of Lievens' most compelling portrayals of human dignity and frailty. Set against a dark background, the nobleman's angular face is imbued with a pathos that rivals that of Rembrandt's best portraits. Though his gaunt cheeks bespeak a man near his end, his piercing eyes convey the sharpness of his mind. Writing to his son shortly after Lievens had portrayed him, the earl lamented: "I grow very old, which showeth more in one year now than in the three before."[1]

In 1654 the Earl of Ancram was seventy-six, penniless, and living in exile in Amsterdam. A staunch royalist, he had left England for the Netherlands after the beheading of Charles I in 1649. This was not his first visit to the United Provinces, however, nor the first time he had met Lievens. He served as the English king's emissary to The Hague in 1629, when he first came to appreciate Lievens' artistic merits.[2] On his return to England later that year, he took with him two paintings by Lievens — *Capuchin Monk Praying* (see Wheelock fig. 9) and *Young Man Studying by a Peat Fire* (no longer extant) — as well as two by Rembrandt.[3] The earl presented the now-lost Lievens and the paintings by Rembrandt to Charles I as gifts from the Dutch stadtholder, Frederik Hendrik.[4]

We also gain insight into Lievens' prideful personality in the early 1650s through the Earl of Ancram, for in the same letter to his son, he wrote: "you may call for it [the portrait] at this town near the new market, out of the hands of Mr. Lievens, the Duke of Brandenburg's painter. He lives at the sign of the fleur-de-luce and you may be sure of a good one. He is the better because he has so high conceit of himself that he thinks there is none to be compared with him in all Germany, Holland, nor the rest of the seventeen provinces."

This evocative portrait shows that the artist had reason to be confident in his abilities. Having fully mastered the international Flemish portrait style (see cat. 44), Lievens adapted it for his Amsterdam clientele by using a darker palette and more restrained poses. His ability to penetrate and convey a sitter's psychological state is evident not only in this portrait but also in his *Portrait of Jacob Junius* (cat. 53).[5] VCT

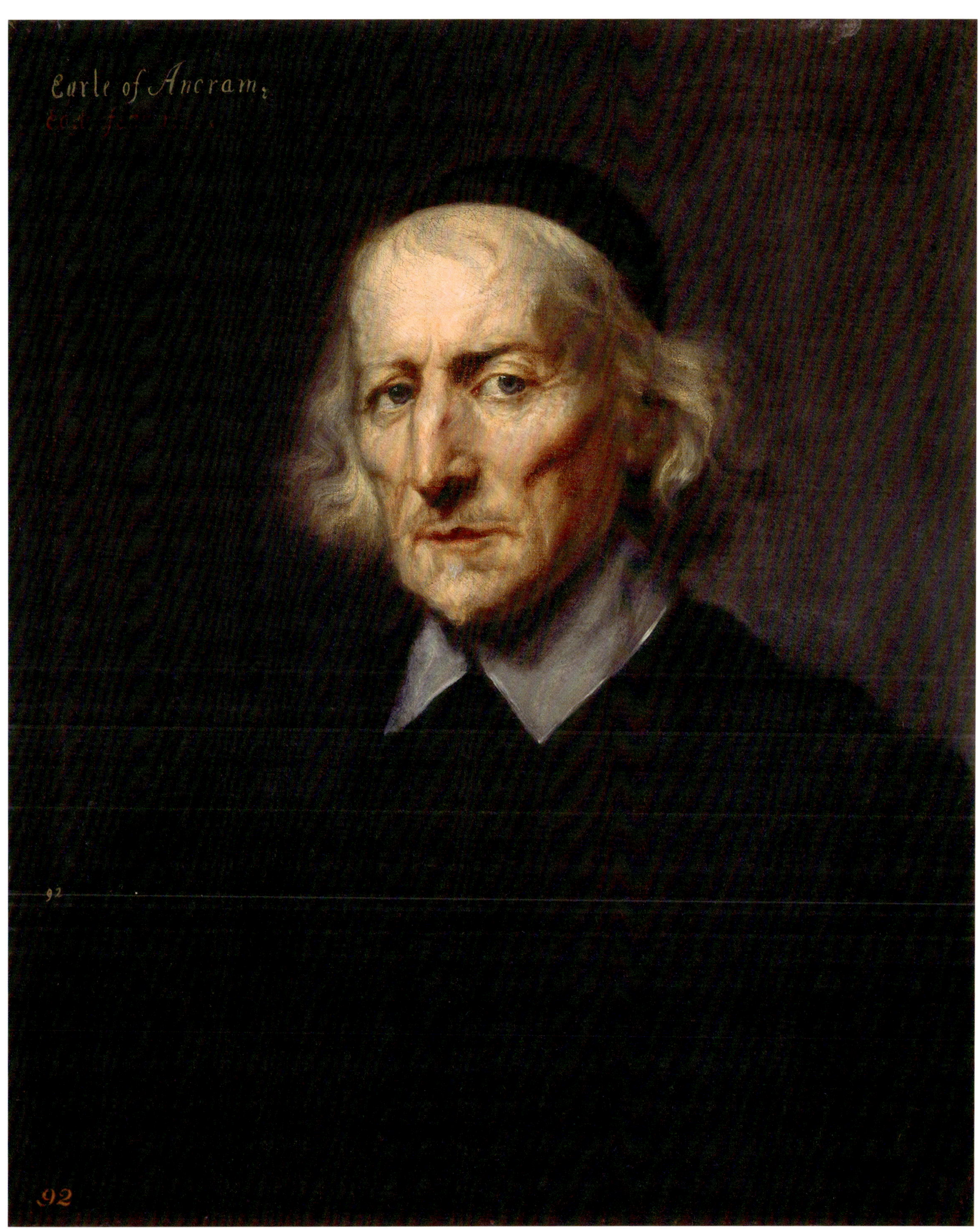
Earle of Ancram
92
92

52 Christ and the Centurion

1657, oil on canvas,
86 × 69 (33⅞ × 27³⁄₁₆).
Private collection, Europe, courtesy of Hoogsteder and Hoogsteder, The Hague, The Netherlands

Inscription

Monogrammed and dated in lower left: I.L. 1657

Provenance

Dr. Gaudinot, Paris; (Hôtel Drouot, Paris, February 15/16, 1869, no. 56); private collection, France; (Hôtel des Ventes, Saint-Germain-en-Laye, May 26, 1991, no. 96); (Hoogsteder and Hoogsteder, The Hague)

Selected References

Sumowski 1983, 6: 3964, no. 2356; The Hague 1992, no. 28; Gutbrod 1996, 299

STANDING IN AN OPEN GLADE WITH his followers, Christ welcomes the Roman centurion who has come to him to ask for help. As recounted in Matthew 8:5–13, the centurion tells Jesus that his servant is "paralyzed, in terrible distress," and Christ offers to come to the centurion's home and cure him. But the centurion replies: "Lord, I am not worthy to have you come under my roof; but only speak the word, and my servant will be healed." When Jesus heard this, he marveled at the man's faith, assured him that his request would be answered, and "the servant was healed at that very moment."

This encounter, which occurred as Jesus entered Capernaum, was one of a series of miracles that amazed Christ's disciples and spread news of his powers throughout the region. The story had a particular resonance at this point in Christ's life for it demonstrated that his influence had been recognized even by his Roman oppressors and that their faith could be more profound than that of the Israelites. Lievens captured the drama of this moment by depicting the Roman centurion on bended knee, looking up at the regal figure of Christ. The centurion's armor and the white feather atop his helmet shine in the sunlight, as Christ, his head surrounded by a golden nimbus, gestures toward him in a way that expresses both authority and compassion. In the background soldiers look on attentively, as do a group of exotic travelers from the East. A dog gazes toward the sky, an implicit reminder that Christ's powers come from God.

The quiet dignity of this scene is characteristic of Lievens' paintings of the late 1650s and undoubtedly reflects the experiences he had just had in executing the large *Quintus Fabius Maximus and His Son* for the Amsterdam town hall (see Wheelock fig. 24). Both of these works manifest the Flemish classicizing style that Lievens had developed during his years in Antwerp, where he had closely studied both Rubens and Van Dyck for figural types and compositional models. Yet *Christ and the Centurion* is somewhat more freely executed than is the painting for the town hall, notably in the rendering of the foliage. X-radiographs reveal that Lievens initially painted the figures at a much larger scale, then reduced them to integrate them better into the landscape.[1]

In 1657, the date of this painting, Lievens was living in The Hague, and it seems probable that he executed it for a patron there. The subject was not often represented in Dutch art, particularly after midcentury, and it is not clear why Lievens painted it at this time and whether it was for a Catholic or a Protestant client. DeWitt speculates that the painting's arched top indicates that it was conceived for an architectural setting.[2] AKW

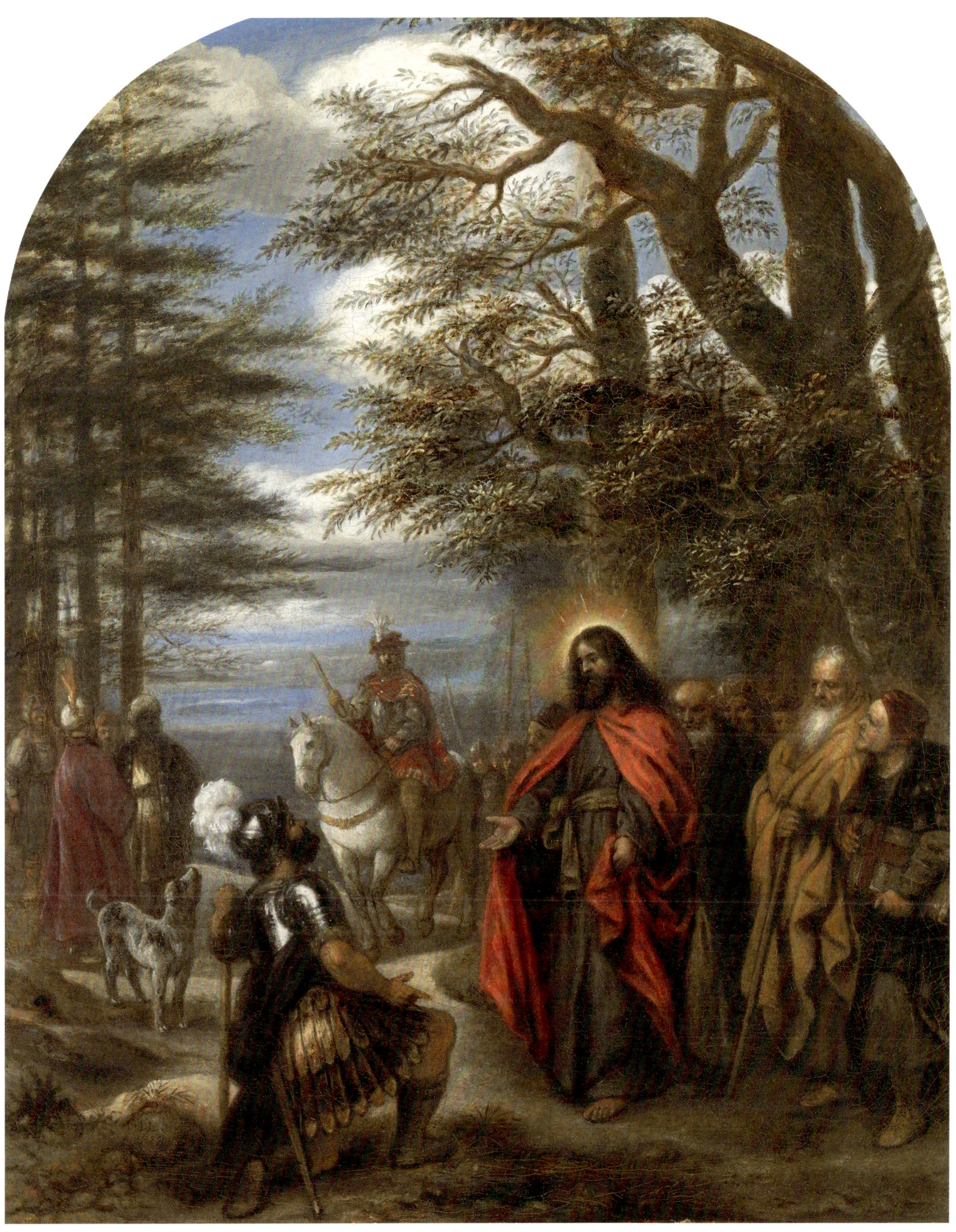

53 Portrait of Jacob Junius

c. 1658, oil on canvas, 79 × 53 (31⅛ × 20⅞). Alfred and Isabel Bader

Provenance

Delft, collection of the sitter, Jacob Junius; bequeathed to his second wife, Maria Leonards (1641–1710); by descent to their son Jacob Junius; by descent to his daughter Maria Jocoba Emmen; Slot Fraeylemaborg, Schlochteren, The Netherlands; by descent to Thomassen à Thuessink van der Hoop van Slochteren family; by descent to the De Sandra family; Boonstra Collection, 1971; (Han Jüngeling Gallery, The Hague, 1972); Alfred Bader, 1972; Bert van Deun, Beerse, Belgium, 1972; reacquired in trade by Alfred Bader, 1990

Selected References

Sumowski 1983, 3: 1769, 1810, no. 1295; Bader 1995; DeWitt 2006, 237, 241–242

THIS COMPELLING PORTRAIT depicts a man in a black doublet with a flat collar and tasseled ties who carries a black cloak over his right arm. The painting itself is undated and bears no information concerning the sitter except a later inscription on the reverse identifying "Junius." There is only one person to whom this could refer: the Delft regent Jacob Junius (1608–1671), son of the Reformed preacher Isaac Junius and his wife, Maria Duyckers. As a young man, Junius began studying law at the University of Leiden in 1626. After finishing his schooling, he sought adventure in service with the Dutch East India Company. He remained in the east until the mid-1650s, amassing a large fortune there. Once back in the Dutch Republic, Junius announced his betrothal in 1657 to the fifteen-year-old Maria Lenaerts (1641–1710) of Delft. They married in Amsterdam, where the bride was in residence, but established their home in Delft, where they were prominent and respected citizens. In 1667 Junius became regent of the Delft "Oude en Nieuwe Gasthuis."

Although this portrait is unsigned, it was unquestionably painted by Jan Lievens, and on stylistic grounds it can be dated to c. 1658.[1] The commission would thus have been secured around the time of Junius' marriage to Maria Lenaerts. It is difficult to say how Lievens was selected as the portraitist, but there are grounds for speculating that the contact was made through the bride's family. A portrait of Pieter Lenaerts, which was probably painted by Lievens, was included in the bequest of Elisabeth van Outen in 1680.[2] It is also noteworthy that after Jacob Junius died, his widow married Hendrick de Sandra (1619–1707), who was in turn the widower of Margaretha Tortarolis (1627–1681), a member of the Leiden family that was among Lievens' first clients.[3]

Without flattery or concealment, Lievens has created a penetrating likeness of Jacob Junius, his face visibly lined. The technique employed for this was not Lievens' smooth manner, but rather a bold, expressive paint application, which was very effective in capturing the man's aged and weather-beaten features. The work is one of the high points in Lievens' portraiture and shows compellingly why his services were so highly sought. JVDV

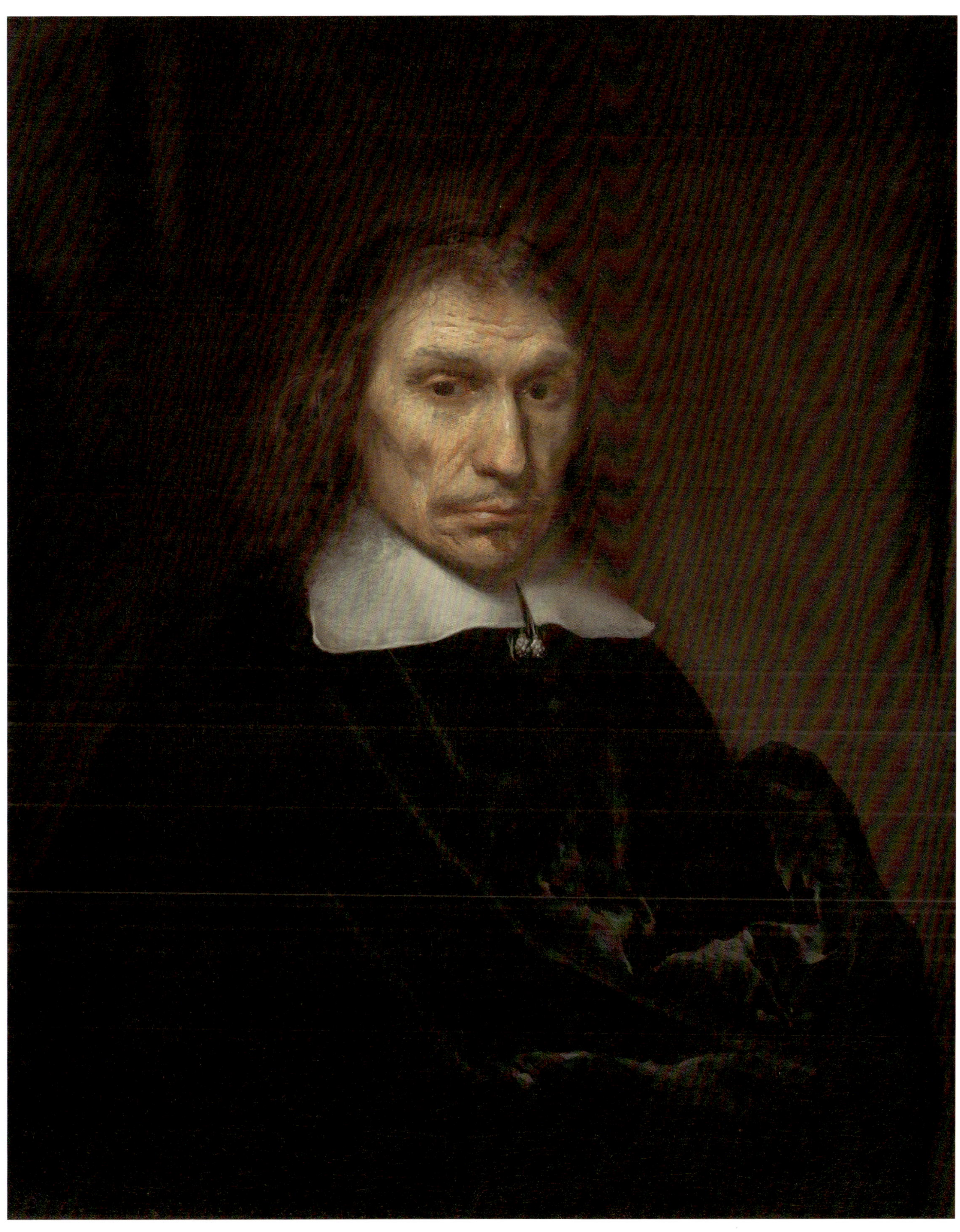

54 Brinio Raised on a Shield

1660, oil on paper on canvas, 60 × 59 (23 ⅝ × 23 ¼). Amsterdams Historisch Museum

Provenance

(Jeremiah Harman, London, May 17, 1844, no. 22, as Rembrandt, to Gardner); (E. F. Graf Von Hertzberg, Heberle, Cologne, March 10, 1902, no. 65); (Joseph Borsu, Brussels, May 13, 1929, no. 21); Hans Schneider, The Hague; donated to the museum 1940

Selected References

Schneider/Ekkart 1973, 326, no. 99a; Braunschweig 1979, no. 40; Sumowski 1983, 3: 1788, no. 1212; The Hague 1992, 222–223; Weber 1992 (giving provenance); Goossens 1996, 35, 63

LIEVENS' SMALL OIL SKETCH OF Brinio triumphantly standing on a shield held aloft by his comrades is a study for one of his grandest and most important commissions, a painting for one of the lunettes in the galleries of the Amsterdam town hall (see Wheelock fig. 25). This heroic scene, which Lievens executed in 1661 and which is still in situ, depicts an episode from the revolt of the Batavians, ancestors of the Dutch, against the Romans in AD 69. As described by the Roman historian Tacitus in *The Histories* 4:12–37, Brinio was a member of a tribe called the Cannenefates, who lived in the Rhine delta and who were allied with the Batavians in their struggle against the Romans. Prior to going into battle, the Cannenefates elected Brinio their leader. Tacitus writes that he was then "placed upon a shield in the tribal fashion and carried on the swaying shoulders of his bearers to symbolize his election as leader."[1]

The history of the commission for the paintings in the lunettes is complex, and many questions about the iconographic program and the choices of artists to paint the scenes remain unresolved. Nevertheless, the Batavians' epic struggle against the Romans had enormous symbolic significance for the Dutch, as it paralleled and gave historic precedent to their own revolt against the Spanish crown. The history of the Batavians had special resonance in Amsterdam, for the Batavians had settled in the province of Holland and citizens there believed them to be their direct ancestors. Claudius Civilis, the leader of the Batavians, was often linked allegorically with the leader of the Dutch revolt, William the Silent, Prince of Orange.[2] And although Brinio was not a major figure in the Batavian revolt, the episode in which he was raised up on a shield had important implications for the political structure of the Dutch Republic. It demonstrated that military leadership was an elected, not a hereditary position.[3] It thus served as a model for the Republican form of government that the burgomasters of Amsterdam, in particular, championed for their country.[4]

When the doors of the newly constructed Amsterdam town hall were opened in 1655, Dutch poets and historians proclaimed this architectural masterpiece to be the eighth wonder of the world.[5] The accolades had much to do with the classicizing design of its architect, Jacob van Campen, but also with the symbolic significance of this enormous civic structure to the city and to the Dutch Republic.[6] At that time, however, the lunettes at the ends of the galleries surrounding the "citizen's hall" and the two open courtyards remained unadorned. Jacob van Campen had planned to fill these spaces with classical allegories, but after he left the project in 1654, Cornelis de Graeff, Amsterdam's powerful burgomaster, changed the iconographic program. De Graeff, a Latin scholar, must have known the writings of Tacitus as well as Otto van Veen's *Batavorum cum Romanis bellum* (Antwerp, 1612), which featured Tacitus' account of the revolt of the Batavians. Van Veen's publication was illustrated with etchings by Antonio Tempesta, which would eventually serve as visual prototypes for the painted lunettes in the town hall.

The commission for filling the eight lunettes initially went to Govaert Flinck in 1659, but Flinck died unexpectedly shortly thereafter. In 1660 the burgomasters decided that the commission should be divided. Andries de Graeff, brother of Cornelis and Lievens' former patron (see cat. 117), secured for him the commission to paint the episode depicted in *Brinio Raised on a Shield*. Lievens completed the work by January 13, 1661, and received the large sum of 1,200 guilders.[7] Although Lievens may have had access to Flinck's preliminary study for the lunette that he had begun to paint before he died, his primary source of inspiration was Tempesta's etching for Van Veen's 1612 publication.[8] Lievens took over Tempesta's pictorial elements, including the Burgundian-styled clothing, but heightened the importance of Brinio. He centered the shield bearers and brought them closer to the foreground so that Brinio, posing proudly with sword drawn, would be dramatically silhouetted against a blue gap in a stormy sky. The viewer is thereby urged to join in with the cheering soldiers as they raise their hands and voices to salute their newly elected leader.

This roughly executed oil sketch, which Lievens must have used as a studio *modello*, differs very little from the final composition, the only major revision being the adjustment of the color of the horse to grayish white rather than reddish brown.[9] In this sketch Lievens was less interested in painting specific details than in establishing broad coloristic effects that would enhance the visual importance of Brinio in the composition. He applied his paint very freely, with dabs and stabs of the brush, although the wrinkling of the paper support has exaggerated the broken character of his brushwork.[10] Lievens also made a second, more finished oil sketch, which he probably presented to the burgomasters for their approval. AKW, MH

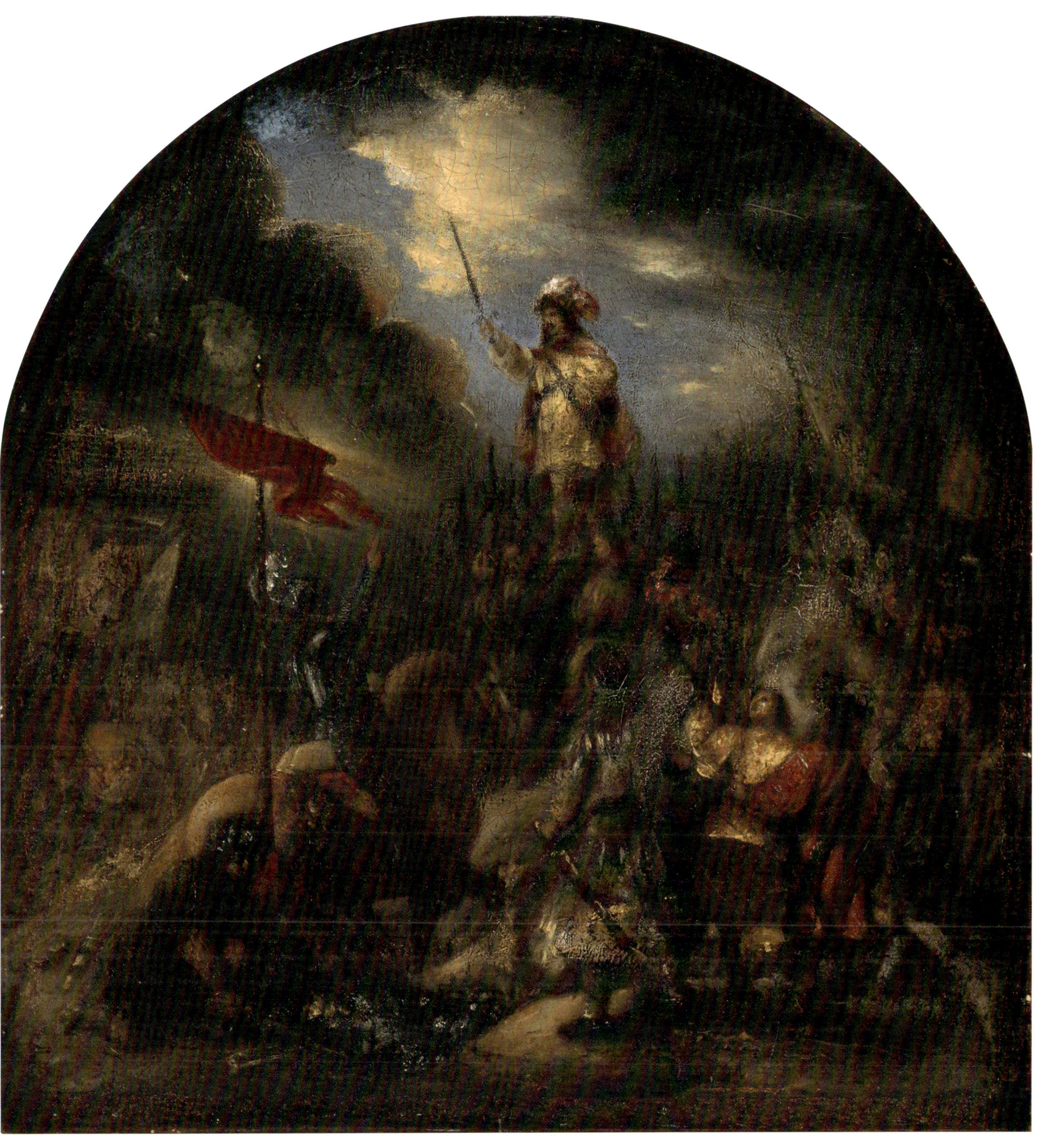

55 The Geographer

Jan Lievens and Jan Andrea Lievens

c. 1665, oil on canvas, 132 × 169 (51 15/16 × 66 9/16). Loan Hoogheemraadschap van Rijnland (water board), Leiden, The Netherlands

Inscription

Monogrammed: IAL

Provenance

Painted for the Rijnlandshuis in Leiden

Selected References

Schneider/Ekkart 1973, 121, no. 117; Sumowski 1983, 3: 1798, no. 1248; Van Raay, Spies, and Van Zoest 1987, 69–76

THIS INTRIGUING COMPOSITION shows a mathematician in his study, seated at a table covered with various measuring instruments as well as an inkpot and quill, a book, and a map. Behind him stands a celestial globe. The scholar wears a long dressing gown, with a beret on his head, and in his left hand he grasps a pair of compasses. Many of the objects depicted are related to geometry, while others, such as the protractor and the proportional compass, were also used by land surveyors. Given that the painting was intended for the chamber of the *dike-reeve* (or head) of the Rijnland in the Hoogheemraden (water board), an organization responsible for carrying out land surveys (among other duties), this image was a fitting subject.

It is clear from records that the painting was created around 1665 as a commission from the Hoogheemraden of Rijnland and served as a chimneypiece in the Gemeenlandshuis in Leiden. The work is extremely well documented. A written account by Jan Lievens dated September 18, 1666 — essentially an appendix that accompanied the settlement of the commission — states that the members of the water board received a painting to serve as a mantelpiece for the bedroom of the Lord of Wimmenum, Amelis van den Bouckhorst, who was then *dike-reeve*, and that the subject was "a geographer made by my son, composed and overpainted by me in many places." In this unique document, we thus have evidence of the collaboration between Jan and Jan Andrea Lievens. A year later Jan Lievens was paid the sum of 300 guilders for this commission.

The relatively low price received for this mantelpiece is probably related to the fact that the work was mostly executed by Lievens' son. It is difficult to be certain of the extent of Jan Lievens' retouching of the painting: possibly the white highlights applied to the book are by his hand, perhaps the strokes of red in the man's costume. The fact that Lievens so frankly declares the division of labor, however, leads one to assume that this had been discussed in the terms of the commission. Lievens would have had Van den Bouckhorst to thank for this commission as well as for earlier public projects and had personally overseen the work (see Van der Veen essay). Lievens had previously painted a composition for the assembly room of the Gecommitteerde Raden (executive council) in the Binnenhof in The Hague — the now-lost *Arithmetica*. Given the closely related subject and its function as a chimneypiece, that work could well have resembled the painting under discussion here. Two years after delivering *The Geographer*, Lievens did a second painting for the Hoogheemraden of Rijnland, this time an entirely autograph work. That allegorical work, which is still to be seen in the Rijnlandshuis, was drastically overpainted by Carel de Moor in 1699. JVDV

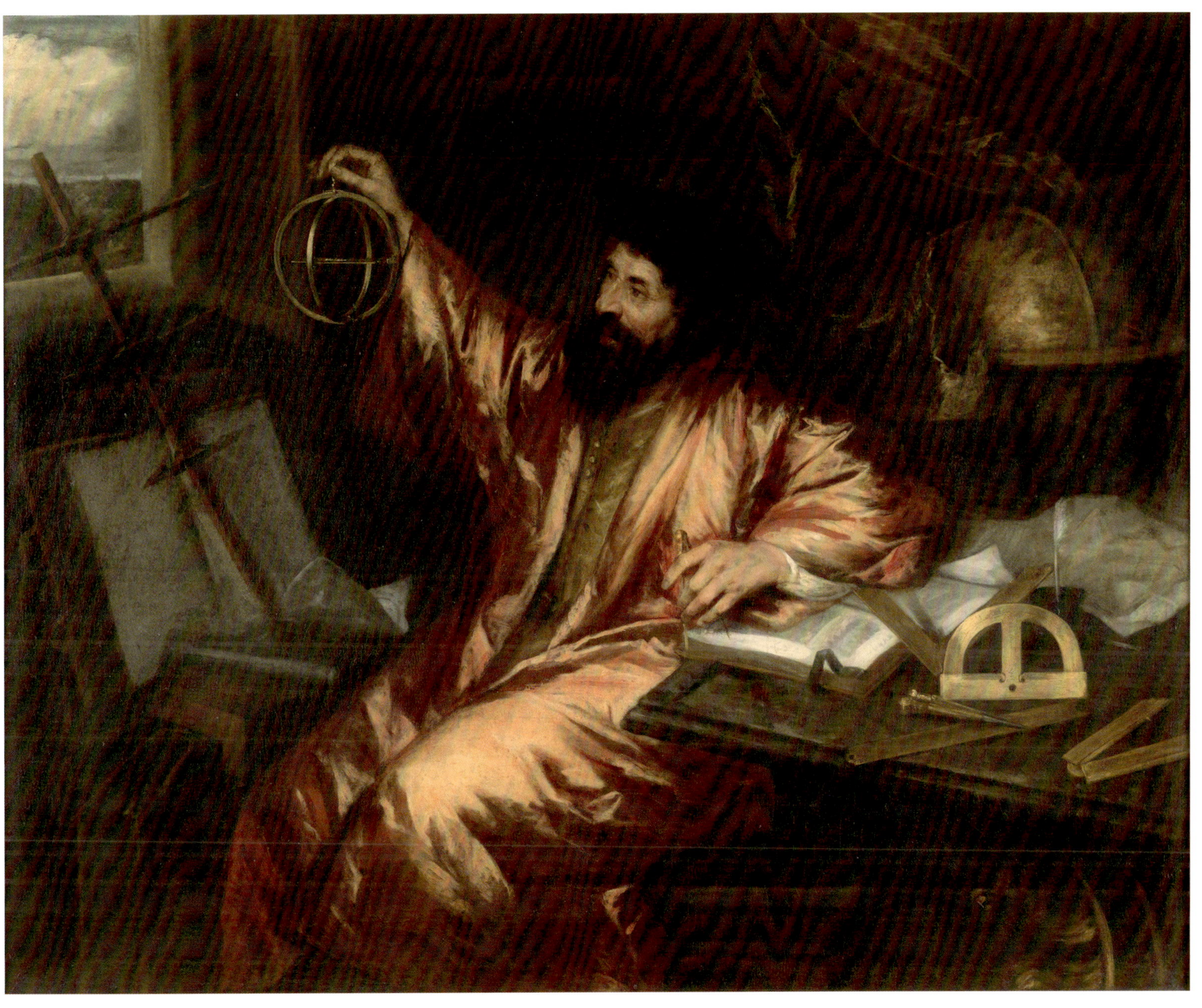

56 Saint John the Evangelist on Patmos

c. 1625–1626, etching, 15.6 × 14.1 (6⅛ × 5⁹⁄₁₆), state 2 (of 4). Museum Het Rembrandthuis, Amsterdam (342)

Selected References

Holl. 9. Schneider/Ekkart 1973, 19, 79, 83, 261; Leiden 1976, 63, no. P21; Braunschweig 1979, no. 99; Amsterdam 1988, no. 4; Berlin, Amsterdam, London 1991–1992, 161–162; Gutbrod 1996, 102–103, 106

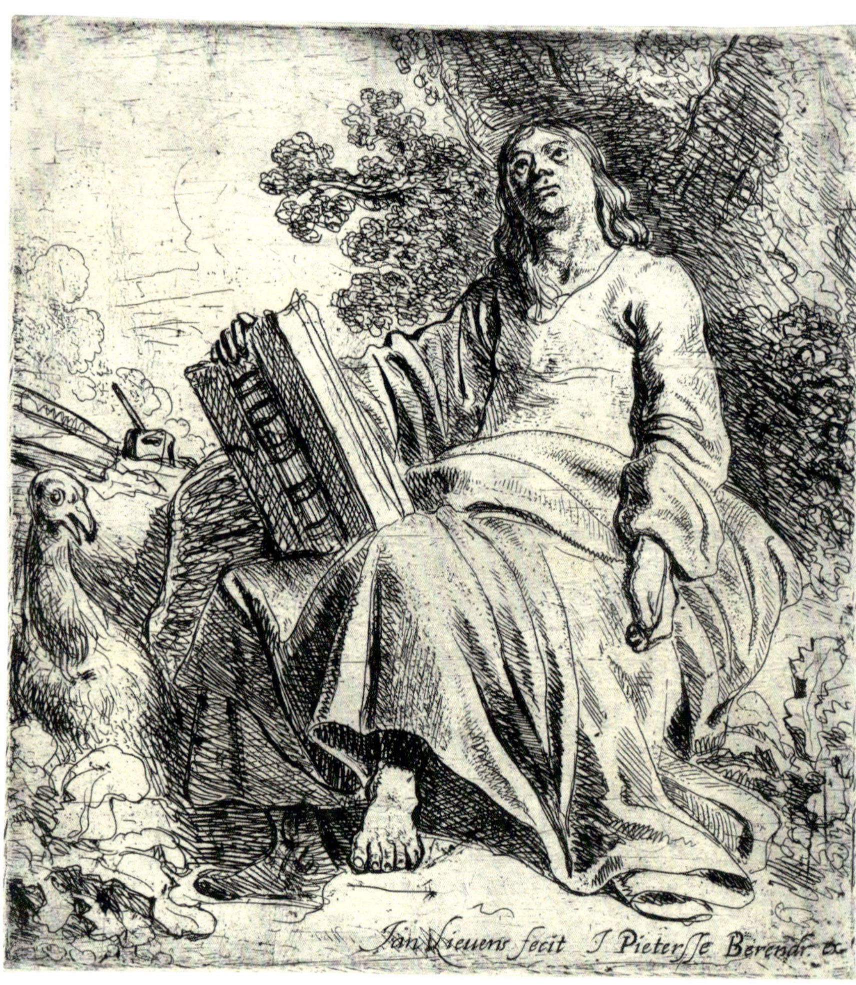

ACCORDING TO CHRISTIAN tradition, John the Evangelist was exiled to the Greek island of Patmos, where he wrote the Book of Revelation, the last book in the New Testament. The apocalyptic text was revealed to him in a series of visions, which a heavenly voice commanded him to record (Rev. 2:10–11).[1] By depicting John at work outdoors, Lievens follows a well-established pictorial convention. Every feature of the scene, from the youthful saint's companion eagle to his voluminous robe, upward gaze, book in hand, and even the inkwell by his side, can be found in manuscript illuminations and paintings by earlier Northern artists, including Lievens' teacher, Pieter Lastman. In prints Lievens could have consulted versions by Martin Schongauer, Master ES, and others. In pre-Reformation images and even in Lastman's version, however, John typically directs his attention toward a heavenly apparition of God or the Virgin Mary.[2] By eliminating this visual manifestation, Lievens may have been catering to Protestant distrust of visionary or iconic imagery. We are left to infer the object of John's gaze, so that his rapt expression in itself comes to symbolize his inspired communion with God.

Lievens minimizes the setting to focus attention on the ample figure, a formula he also favored in paintings of the 1620s (see cat. 4). The style and format of this etching relate closely to *Jacob Anointing the Stone* (cat. 57), but *Saint John on Patmos* was probably etched first: the draftsmanship here is looser and more tentative, and the modeling not quite as convincing. These qualities are similar to Rembrandt's earliest etchings, such as *The Circumcision* and *Rest on the Flight into Egypt*, but even at this early date, the use of stippling and strong contour lines separates Lievens' manner from that of his Leiden colleague.[3]

Both this etching and Rembrandt's *Circumcision* bear the address of the Haarlem publisher Jan Pietersz Berendrecht. *Saint John on Patmos* is not initialed with Lievens' characteristic monogram, but "Jan Lievens fecit" has been inscribed on the plate in the second state. The uniform calligraphy indicates that this inscription and Berendrecht's address were added at the same time. There is no other evidence of a relationship between Lievens and the Haarlem publisher, and it seems likely that Berendrecht acquired the plate some time after it was completed. He took an interest in the work of modern printmakers such as Willem Buytewech, whom Jan Orlers cited as an inspiration for the young Lievens.[4] SSD

57 Jacob Anointing the Stone

c. 1625–1626, etching, 20 × 16 (7⅞ × 6 5/16)

state 2 (of 2). Rijksmuseum, Amsterdam (RP-P-OB4227) *(Washington, Milwaukee)*

state 2 (of 2). Museum Boijmans Van Beuningen, Rotterdam (BdH 3783) *(Amsterdam)*

Selected References

Holl. 4. Schneider/Ekkart 1973, 19, 20, 79, 83, 262; Braunschweig 1979, no. 100; Boston 1981, 114; Amsterdam 1988, no. 3; Van Straten 2005, 44–45, 292–293

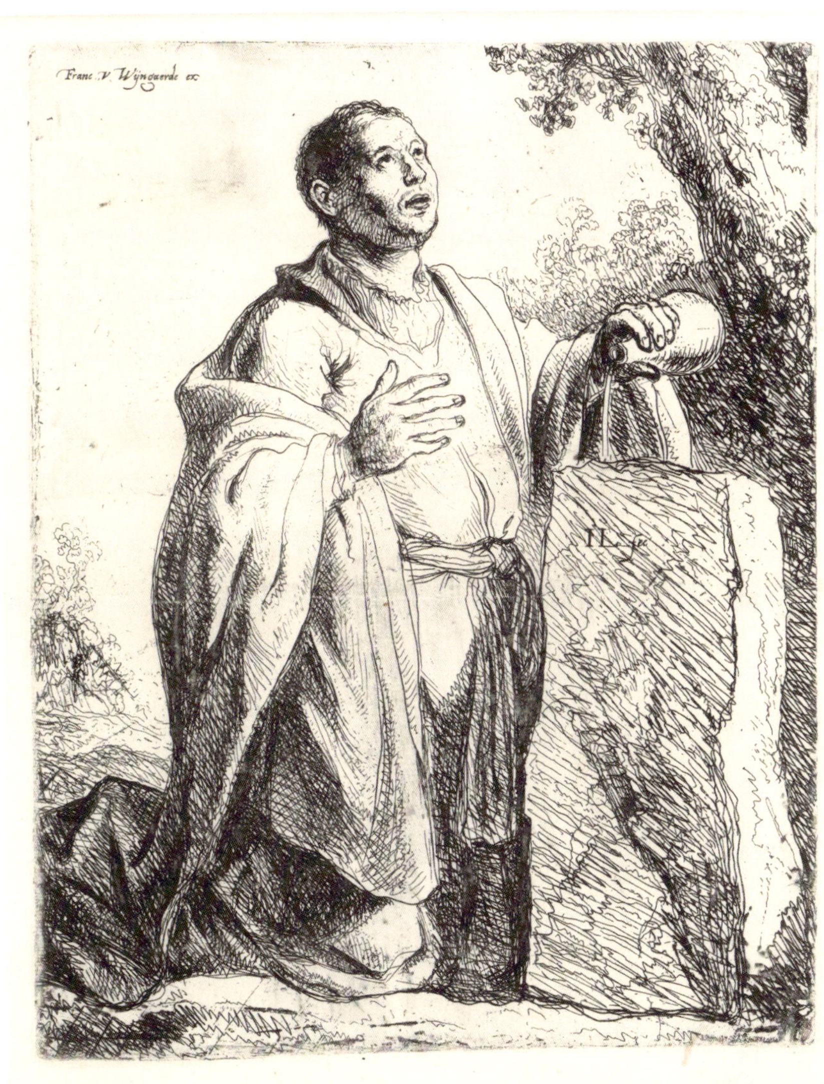

THIS ETCHING ILLUSTRATES AN event in the early life of the Old Testament patriarch Jacob. Traveling through the wilderness to escape the wrath of his brother Esau, Jacob fell asleep with a stone for a pillow. He dreamed of a ladder reaching from earth to heaven, with angels climbing up and down. From above, God spoke to Jacob, promising him a host of descendants and ownership of the land around him (Israel). When Jacob awoke, "he took the stone which he had put under his head and set it up for a pillar and poured oil on the top of it" (Gen. 28:18). Having thus sanctified the spot, he named it "Bethel," meaning "house of God," and vowed that in return for divine protection, he would worship God and return to him a tenth of all that he received.

The pictorial tradition for this scene stretches back through medieval times, but it was extremely rare in the seventeenth century.[1] Far more popular was the visionary imagery of "Jacob's Ladder," which became a favorite in the circles of Lastman and Rembrandt. Why Lievens chose this unusual motif is unknown. Luther and Calvin saw Jacob's action as a worthy expression of gratitude for divine favor.[2] Lievens captures Jacob's mood of awe and thankfulness: with his lips parted and eyes cast heavenward, Jacob kneels in reverence as he anoints the stone with oil from a simple flask.

With strong contour lines and scribbly hatching, Lievens sets his solid, volumetric figure in a summary but convincing outdoor space. The ample proportions of the robed figure and the narrative clarity of Jacob's active pose reflect lessons learned in the studio of Pieter Lastman.[3] The monogram "IL fec," written on the side of the stone pillar with the support of a carefully ruled guideline, reappears on prints throughout the first half of Lievens' career. The second state, exhibited here, was published by Franciscus van den Wijngaerde, indicating that Lievens took the plate with him to Antwerp. SSD

58 Mercury Lulls Argus to Sleep with His Pipe

c. 1625–1626, etching and engraving, 19.3 × 16.5 (7⅝ × 6½)

state 3 (of 3). Frits Lugt Collection, Institut Néerlandais, Paris (1972-P46) *(Washington, Milwaukee)*

state 3 (of 3). Teylers Museum, Haarlem (KG3951) *(Amsterdam)*

Selected References

Holl. 18. Burchard 1917, 89–94; Schneider/Ekkart 1973, 79, 83, 262; Boston 1981, no. 70; Amsterdam 1988, no. 2; Gutbrod 1996, 104–106; Van Straten 2005, 44–46

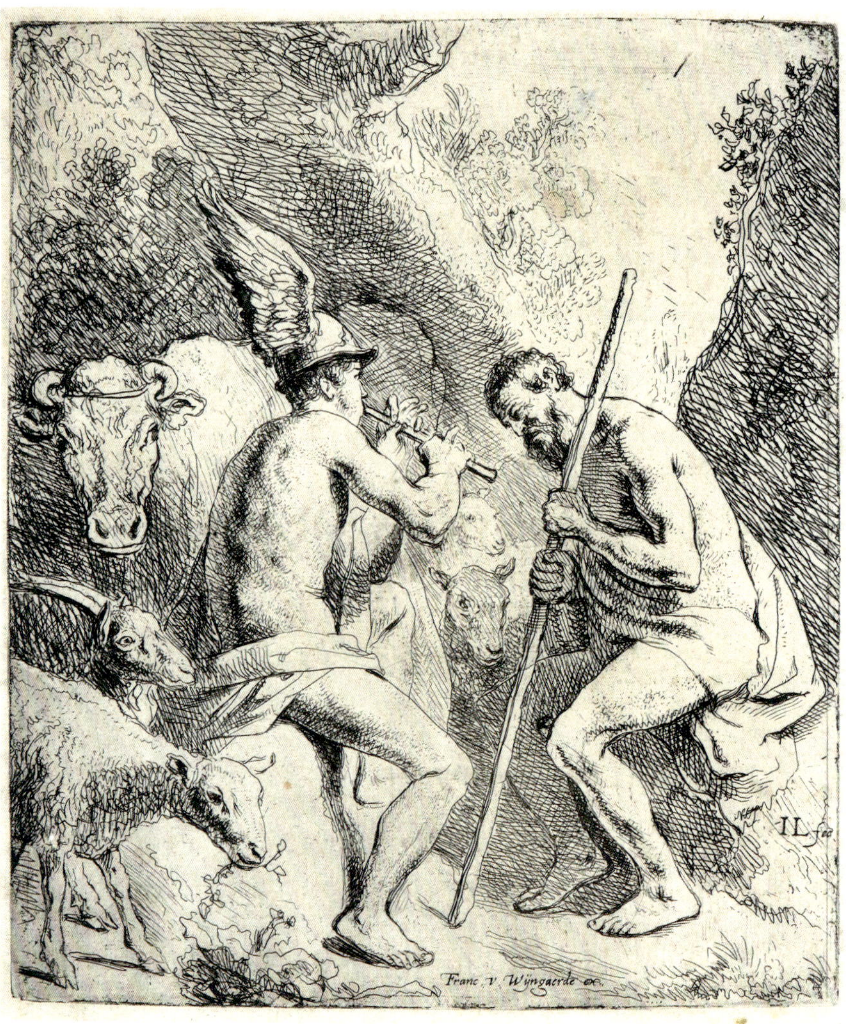

AS RECOUNTED IN OVID'S *Metamorphoses*, Jupiter became enamored of the priestess Io and transformed her into a cow to protect her from his jealous wife, Juno. Clever Juno claimed the heifer as a gift and set the many-eyed giant, Argus, to guard her, but Jupiter enlisted the help of Mercury, who lulled Argus to sleep and killed him. For his first Ovidian subject, Lievens may have turned to Karel van Mander (1604), who described Mercury leaning on a rock with the white heifer beside him, cheeks puffing as he plays his shepherd's flute and slyly glances over to observe the effect of his music on the drowsing Argus.[1]

In style and format this etching relates closely to two other prints from c. 1625–1626, *Saint John the Evangelist on Patmos* and *Jacob Anointing the Stone* (see cats. 56, 57), but here, the challenge for the young artist was more complex, requiring knowledge of ancient myth, mastery of the male nude, naturalistic depiction of animal life, and the orchestration of a narrative composition. It was not unusual for seventeenth-century artists to depict Argus as a human being rather than the fearsome giant described by Ovid, but Lievens' rendering of anatomy reveals a Northern penchant for realistic interpretation.[2] Argus is simply a grumpy old shepherd leaning on his staff, and Mercury, apart from his extravagant winged hat, looks more like a young Dutchman posed in the studio than a classical god. Stippling and free hatching define the lumps and bumps of their nude forms, caught in a play of flickering light and shadow. The young artist's mastery of movement and foreshortening are tested by the dynamic motif of Mercury's fingers plying the flute. This etching thus provides evidence of the ambition that earned Lievens a reputation for audacious confidence at an early age.

The composition follows Lievens' preparatory drawing (cat. 89) in all but a few details of the setting. Delicate foliage clings to the rock behind Argus and sprouts in the foreground, where a sheep chews placidly on a weedy branch. Lievens pulled a few trial proofs before adding the signature "IL fec" on Argus' rocky seat. Years later, in Antwerp, the publisher Franciscus van den Wijngaerde smoothed the rough edges of the plate and added his address. SSD

59 Young Girl with Long Hair

c. 1628–1631, etching, 16.2 × 14.3 (6 3/8 × 5 5/8)

state 2 (of 2). Städel Museum, Frankfurt am Main (6144) *(Washington, Milwaukee)*

state 2 (of 2). Museum Boijmans Van Beuningen, Rotterdam (BdH 15911) *(Amsterdam)*

Selected References

Holl. 43. Linck 1859, 275; Schneider/Ekkart 1973, 79–80, 83, 264; Amsterdam 1988, no. 32; Van Straten 2005, 156

THE MODEL DEPICTED HERE MAY be the same blonde girl who posed for several paintings by Lievens (see cat. 28). Her square-cut bodice, pleated blouse, and pearl necklace add a quasi-historical note, but the real subject of this etching is the girl's luxuriant hair — and the printmaker's ability to render its sinuous tendrils with wiry, undulating strokes that flow over her shoulders and curl in wisps around her face. Rembrandt may have drawn inspiration from this print for later etchings of his wife, Saskia.[1]

The first layer of etched lines failed to bite deeply enough and reads in most impressions as a grayish undertone. By the time the Antwerp publisher Franciscus van den Wijngaerde took over the plate, the delicate lines were wearing out,and the hair and other details were reworked for stronger definition.[2] The retouching preserves the expressiveness of the original concept and must have been done by Lievens himself before turning the plate over to his publisher, who added his address at the upper right. SSD

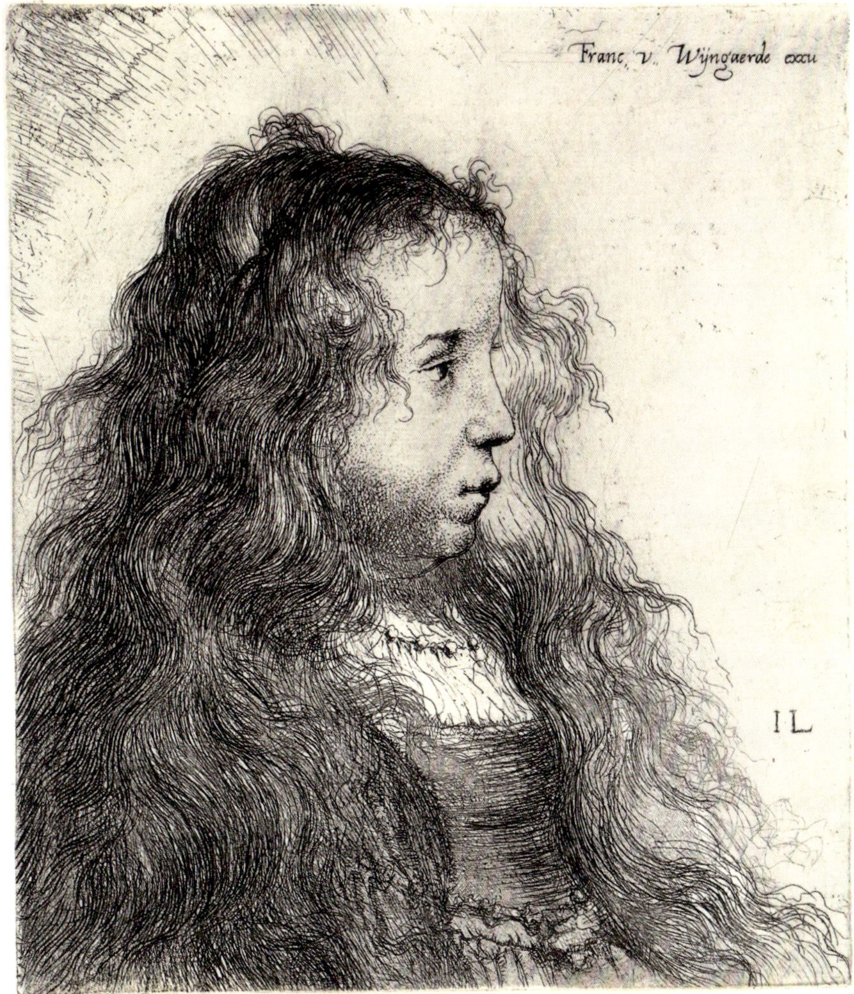

60 Young Woman in a Cap, in Profile

c. 1628–1631, etching, 14.6 × 12.4 ($5\frac{3}{4} \times 4\frac{7}{8}$), state 2 (of 3). Teylers Museum, Haarlem (KG3969) *(Amsterdam only)*

Selected References

Holl. 45. Schneider/Ekkart 1973, 79, 83, 264; Amsterdam 1988, no. 33; Van Straten 2005, 155–156

THE STRICT PROFILE VIEW LENDS gravity to this simple image of a country girl in plain muslin cap and dress. The sparse definition of form and open background give this sensitive likeness the quality of a sketch on paper. It is even possible that Lievens drew from life directly onto the copperplate. He varies his technique, defining the long nape of the girl's neck with a single deft stroke while giving more detailed attention to her plump chin and the soft fabric of her cap. The shadow crossing her face adds character and atmosphere.

It is likely that this print was etched in Leiden, c. 1628–1631, during the period when Lievens was most active in painting and etching character studies (tronies). Lievens printed a few proofs before signing the plate, then added his monogram at left.[1] Some collectors have trimmed away the expanse of white paper in front of the figure, little realizing that the airy background and asymmetrical placement of the bust are aesthetic features that distinguish several of Lievens' tronies from more conventionally finished figure studies. SSD

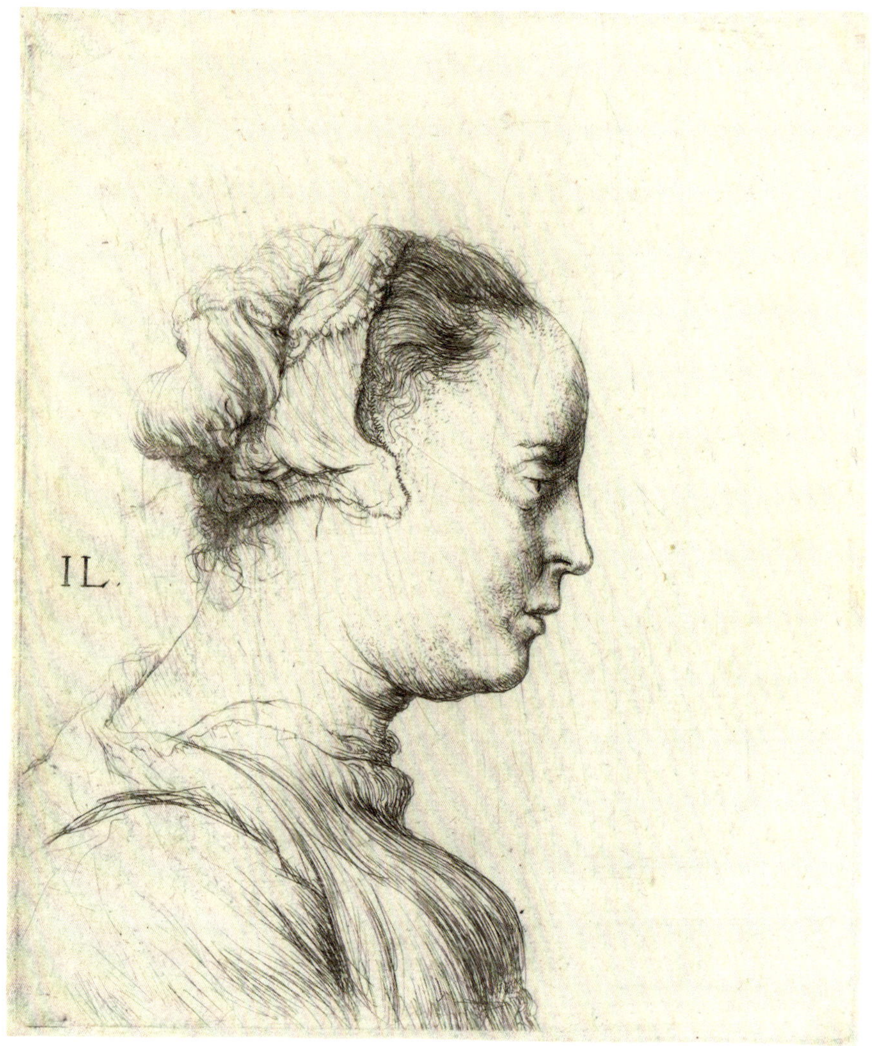

61 Profile Head of an Old Woman, Facing Left

c. 1628–1631, etching, 14.6 × 12.2 (5¾ × 4¾)

state 2 (of 2). Staatliche Museen zu Berlin, Kupferstichkabinett (905-13) *(Washington, Milwaukee)*

state 2 (of 2). Museum Boijmans Van Beuningen, Rotterdam (BdH 15913) *(Amsterdam)*

Selected References

Holl. 49. Linck 1859, 275; Köhne 1932, 47; Schneider/Ekkart 1973, 79–80, 83, 264; Van Straten 2005, 155–156

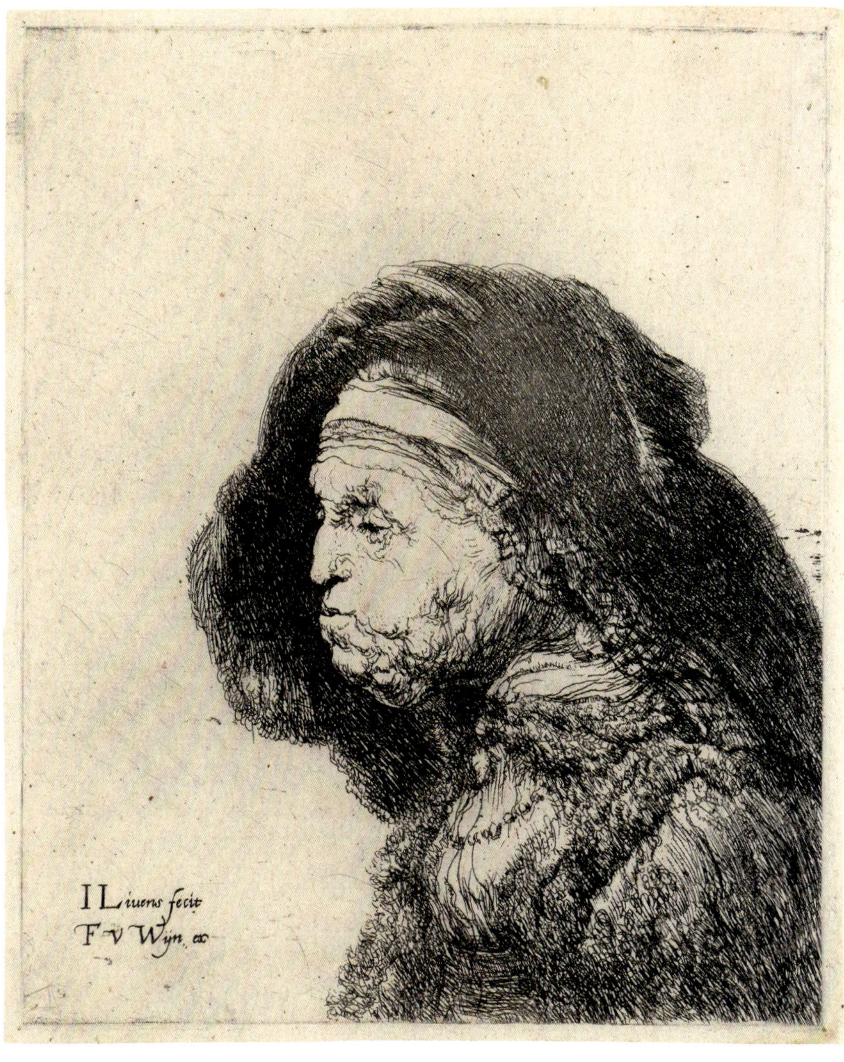

JAN LIEVENS' PAINTINGS AND prints depict a gallery of picturesque types, but especially striking is his treatment of elderly female figures. Whether sketching an aged model from life or imagining a historical character such as Saint Anne (see cat. 21 and Wheelock fig. 18), Lievens did not shy away from ugliness but relished capturing the ravages of time. Here, a pearl necklace and pleated linen blouse offer mocking adornment for a creature many years past her prime. The soft folds of her heavy, wattled chin are framed by her dark headdress. The costume may be meant to cast the model as a biblical prophetess, but the ultimate effect is a somber reminder of the brevity of life and beauty. This aspect of Lievens' work has always been admired: a painting copied from this print appears in a still life by his contemporary, Simon Luttichuys, and Gersaint described this etching as "executed in a very singular Manner."[1]

Lievens printed the first state of this etching as an unsigned proof. The intricate, scribbly hatching is characteristic of his Leiden period, but the plate was completed with his name and the address of his Antwerp publisher, Franciscus van den Wijngaerde. The motif reappears on a much smaller scale in a series of tiny tronies etched in Leiden and also published in Antwerp (see cats. 63–66).[2] SSD

62 Young Man in a Fur Cap

c. 1630, etching, 7.5 × 5.9 (3 × 2 5/16), states 1, 3, 4 (of 4); title page (unknown calligrapher): 7.6 × 6.1 (3 × 2 5/8). Rijksmuseum, Amsterdam (RP-P-OB12.595, RP-P-1952.634, RP-P-1962.281, RP-P-OB12.571) *(Washington, Milwaukee)*

Selected References

Holl. 72. Linck 1859, 278; Amsterdam 1988, 13

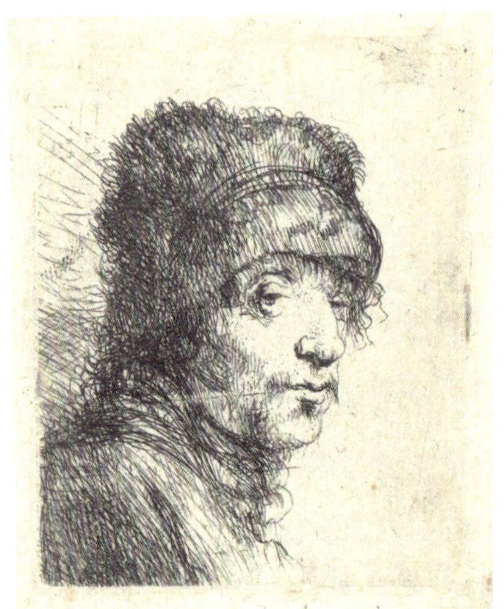

STATE 1

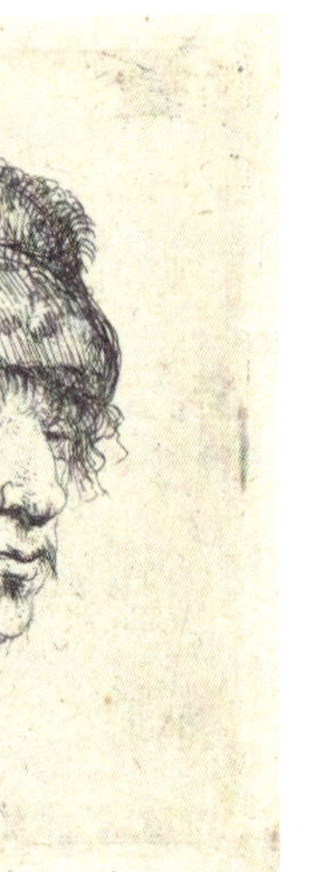

STATE 3

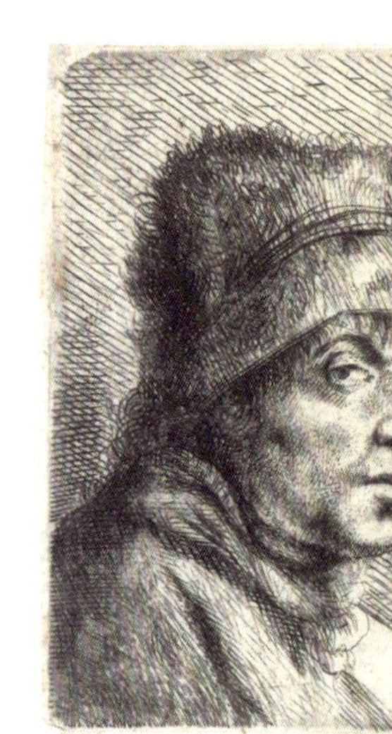

STATE 4

THIS LITTLE CHARACTER, WITH his fur cap, wispy moustache, and heavy-lidded gaze, is one of Lievens' most mysterious personalities. The three impressions exhibited illustrate the typical development of Lievens' small tronies, probably etched toward the end of his stay in Leiden.[1] The head is first sketched, possibly from life, against an open background. In the second and third states, further shading adds weight and definition. While this work has the spontaneity of Lievens' Leiden style, the pattern of hatching that covers the background in the fourth state is quite mechanical. It is possible that the end product reflects the intervention of a publisher, but it should also be noted that Lievens' own prints after 1632 show increasing awareness of conventional techniques (compare, for instance, his *Portrait of Jacques Gaultier*, cat. 75).

A title page of the same size, with a Latin inscription, identifies Lievens as a native of Leiden and creator of "Diverse Heads" — the term "effigies" is the equivalent of the Dutch "tronie," denoting a "face" or a character study without specific historial identity. It is difficult to know which of Lievens' many small character heads to place in this set. It was most likely a publisher who assembled the series, rather than the artist himself, and this could have taken place in Leiden or, more likely, after Lievens had moved to Antwerp, where other such series were published (cats. 63–66).[2] SSD

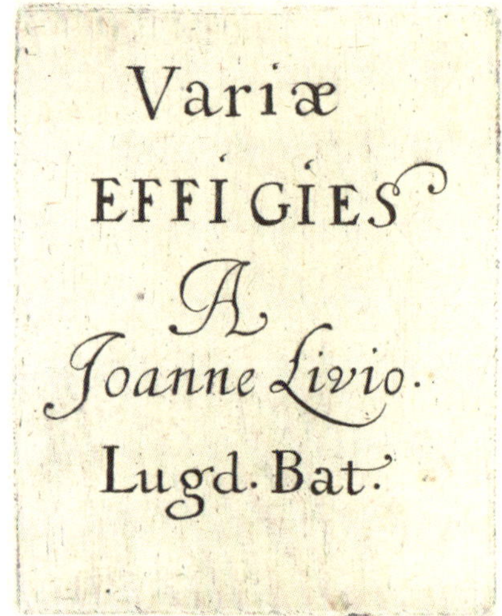
Variæ
EFFIGIES
A
Joanne Livio.
Lugd. Bat.

63–66 Tronikens: Character Heads in a Small Format

c. 1628–1635, etching and engraving. Staatliche Museen zu Berlin, Kupferstichkabinett (title page [likely by Jacobus Christianus]: 575-16; tronikens: 897-13, 899-13, 894-13, 890-13)

63
Young Gentleman, Facing Right

state 2 (of 3), 7.5 × 6.1 (2 15/16 × 2 3/8)

64
Man in a Cap ("The Cook")

state 2 (of 2), 7.7 × 6.1 (3 × 2 3/8)

65
Young Woman in a Headdress, in Profile to Left

state 2 (of 3), 7.7 × 6.1 (3 × 2 3/8)

66
Moorish Woman Facing Left

state 1 (of 3), 7.3 × 6.1 (2 7/8 × 2 3/8)

Selected References

Holl. 60, 62, 63, 66. Schneider/Ekkart 1973, 79, 83, 265; Boston 1981, 145 n. 2; Amsterdam 1988, 6, 9, 17, 20, n. 4; Hirschfelder 2000, 86–87; Van Straten 2005, 152–153

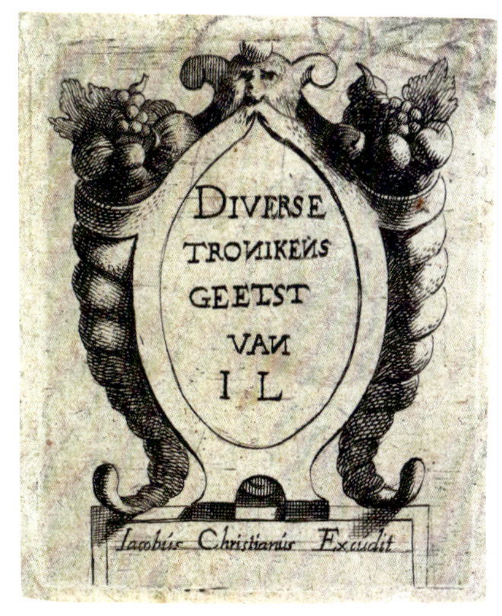

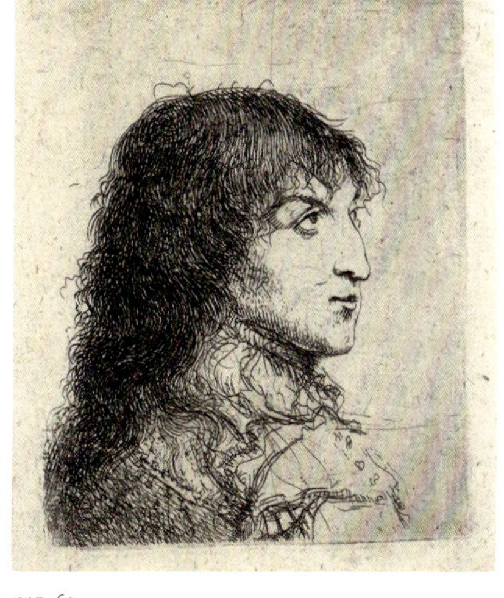

CAT. 63

THE TITLE PAGE SHOWN HERE identifies Jacobus Christianus as the publisher of a series of "Diverse Tronikens" etched by Jan Lievens. The term "troniken" is a diminutive form of "tronie." Hollstein lists eighteen prints as belonging to this series of plates, all measuring close to 7.5 × 6.1 cm (3 × 2 3/8 in.). Yet Lievens etched many more heads in a similar small format over the course of his early career. Another title page documents a different series, probably also published in Antwerp from plates begun in Leiden (cat. 62). Nothing is known of the publisher Christianus, but some of the tronikens ended up with Martinus van den Enden or Franciscus van den Wijngaerde, who published many of Lievens' prints in Antwerp. Twelve of the plates were reworked, usually in the third state, with shading behind the figure in a loose pattern of rectilinear cross-hatching, a common practice among Flemish engravers.

The men and women depicted in Lievens' small etchings range widely in age and social status. One sharp-eyed young fellow, with long locks and a falling collar, is clearly a gentleman (cat. 63), while a dark-bearded man in a cloth cap is traditionally identified as a cook (cat. 64). A plump young woman wears an elaborate

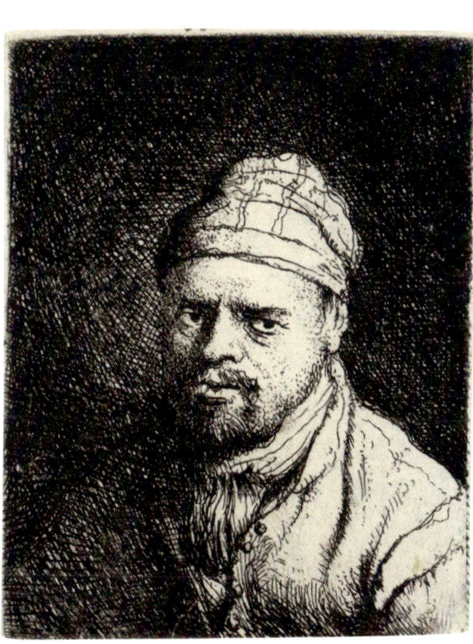

CAT. 64

headdress (cat. 65), but the most exotic model is a woman with Moorish or African features (cat. 66), recalling one of the bystanders in *The Raising of Lazarus* (cat. 73).[1] A wrinkled, elderly woman in a black hood (Holl. 61, not shown) reappears in several paintings and prints of the 1620s (cat. 61). These are clues dating the origin of at least the two female heads to Lievens' years in Leiden.

Lievens' tronikens are common in public collections, but no unified set exists to confirm how they were first sold or collected together.[2] It is likely that there was some variation and overlap between groups assembled by different publishers or dealers, as many of Lievens' plates changed hands during his lifetime. Collectors must have enjoyed arranging this assortment of striking faces in whatever order seemed most meaningful. As a theme for a print series, the array of diverse types goes back to prints after Pieter Bruegel the Elder and Leonardo da Vinci.[3] SSD

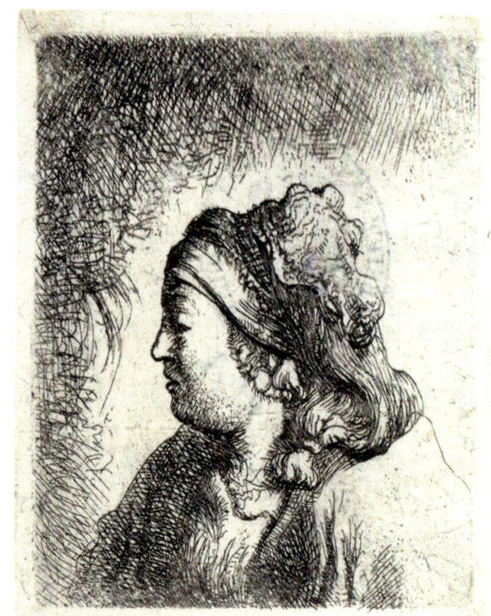

CAT. 65

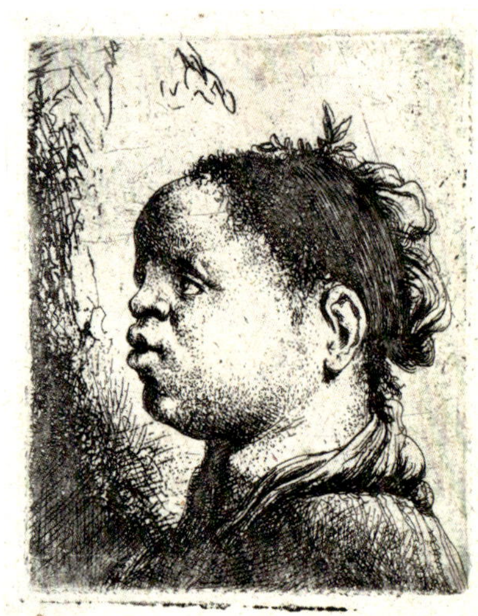

CAT. 66

67–70 A Series of Character Studies

c. 1630–1631

67
Young Man in Profile to Right

etching, 15.7 × 14.2 (6 3/16 × 5 9/16)

state 1 (of 5). Rijksmuseum, Amsterdam (RP-P-OB12.552) *(Washington, Milwaukee)*

state 4 (of 5). Museum Boijmans Van Beuningen, Rotterdam (4240) *(Amsterdam)*

68
Bearded Man in a Turban, in Profile to Left

etching, 16 × 14.3 (6 5/16 × 5 5/8)

state 4 (of 5), printed with plate tone. Rijksmuseum, Amsterdam (RP-P-OB12.554) *(Washington, Milwaukee)*

state 2 (of 5). Staatliche Museen zu Berlin, Kupferstichkabinett (919-13) *(Amsterdam)*

Rembrandt made a copy in reverse of this etching (see fig. 1 on p. 199).

69
Bearded Man Facing Left

etching, 16.2 × 14.4 (6 3/8 × 5 11/16)

state 1 (of 5). Collection of Tom Rassieur

70
Old Man Facing Forward

etching, 16.4 × 14.4 (6 1/2 × 5 11/16)

state 1 (of 3). Rijksmuseum, Amsterdam (RP-P-OB12.559) *(Washington, Milwaukee)*

Rembrandt made a copy in reverse of this etching (see fig. 2 on p. 199).

Selected References

Holl. 34, 35, 40, 36. Schneider/Ekkart 1973, 79–80, 83, 263; Braunschweig 1979, no. 104; Amsterdam 1988, nos. 23, 24, 26; Amsterdam and London 1991, 149–151; Leiden 1991, 76–79

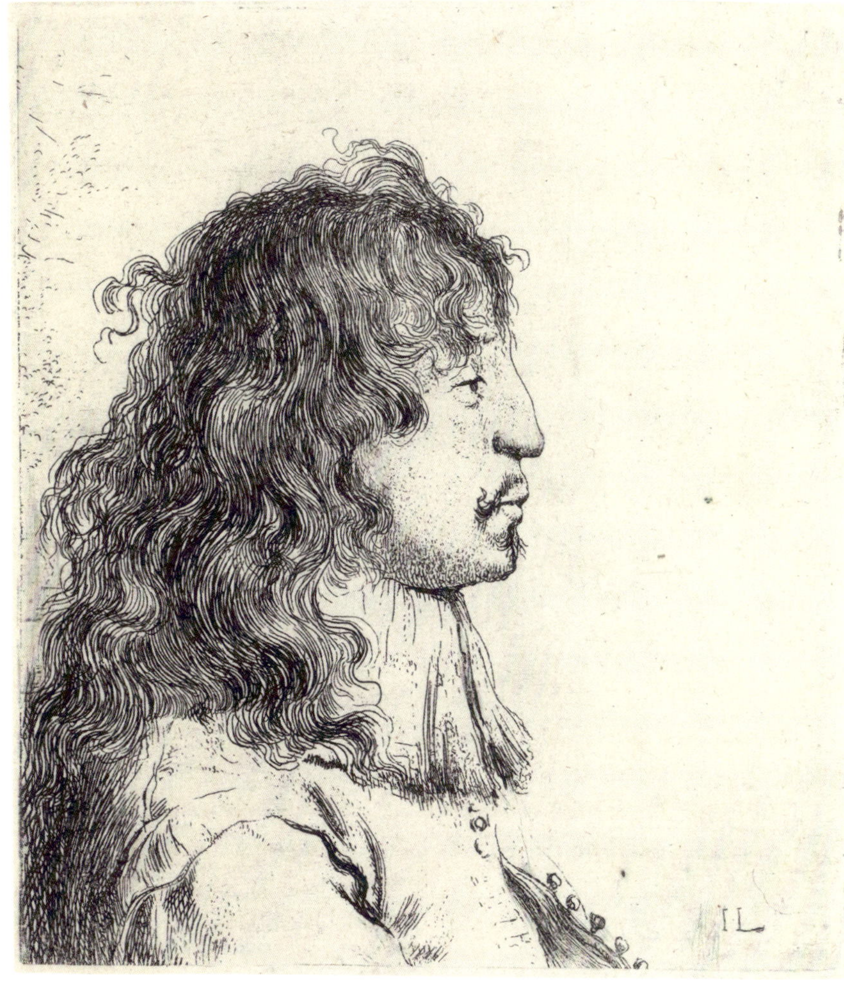

CAT. 67, STATE 1

SEVEN ETCHINGS OF BUST-LENGTH male figures, probably completed in Leiden around 1630–1631, are linked by a consistent size and format. They are numbered 1 through 7 in the upper right-hand corner. No title page has been preserved for this set, but the prints share a publishing history. The earliest states bear the artist's initials and the number, but no publisher's address. We can thus infer that Lievens himself gathered this group of tronies into a numbered series. Although none of the plates are dated, they are close in style and method to other etchings of Lievens' last years in Leiden and to tronies concurrently produced by Rembrandt and Jan van Vliet.[1] Close examination shows that Lievens worked up these plates in two stages, first etching the subject lightly and then enhancing details of hair, costume, and shading, a procedure also followed in many etchings by Rembrandt.

In Antwerp the publisher's address of Pieter de Baillù was added (in the second or third state) to six of the seven

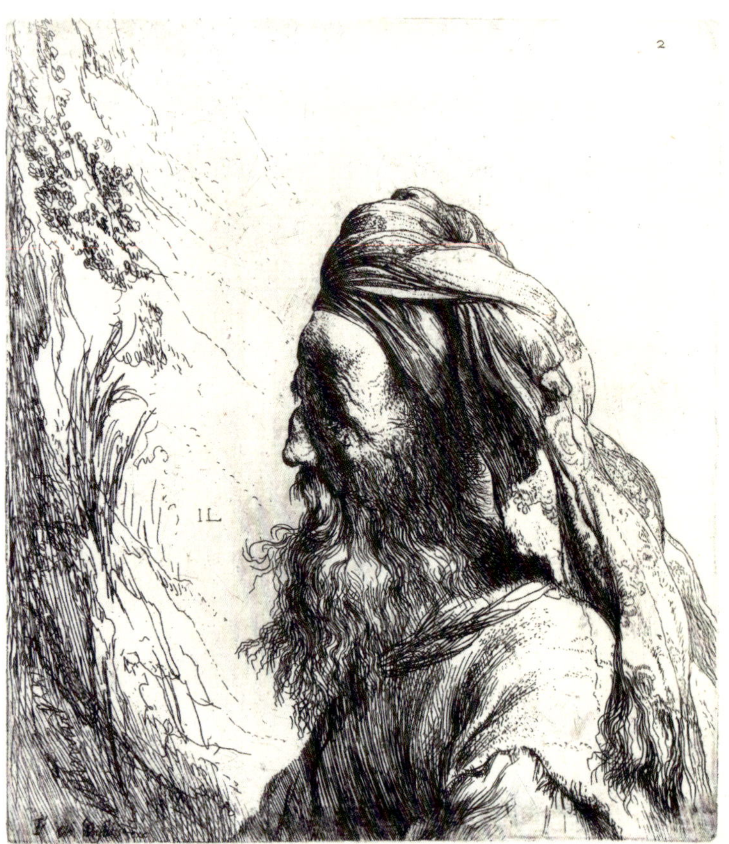

CAT. 68, STATE 4

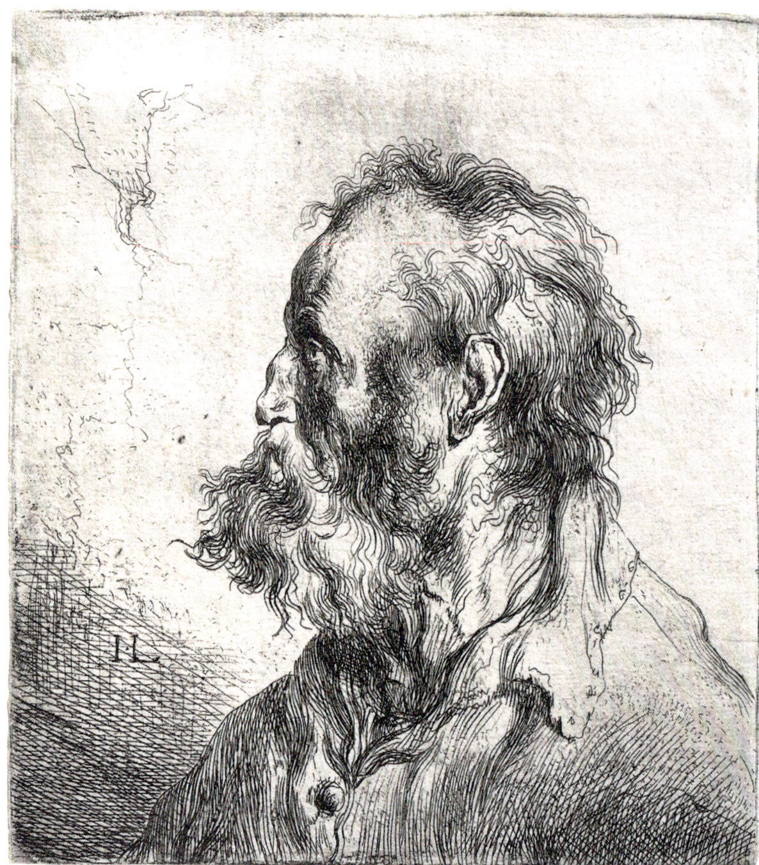

CAT. 69

plates, and later all seven were published again by Franciscus van den Wijngaerde. Both publishers maintained the images much as Lievens conceived them. Van den Wijngaerde was active from the mid-1630s onward, but De Baillù may not have established himself in Antwerp until after 1640.[2] Having carried the plates with him to Antwerp, Lievens must have turned them over to De Baillù sometime before he left for Amsterdam. Van den Wijngaerde probably acquired the plates from De Baillù; he also published many other prints by and after Lievens. In a final state the publishers' names are erased altogether.[3]

Despite the numbering, there is no clear logic to the sequence of heads in this group. Rather than suggesting a standard range of types, such as the four temperaments or the stages of life, Lievens may simply have meant to demonstrate his versatility in rendering details of costume and character or to increase sales by prompting collectors to acquire the whole series. Each plate presents a male head of sober demeanor and individualized physiognomy. Some figures are dressed in contemporary clothing, while others wear the exotic attire of a Turkish potentate or a character from the historical past.

The series begins and ends with profile studies of handsome young cavaliers wearing fashionable falling collars — the first sitter dark and moustachioed, the last clean-shaven and blond. Several of the heads of older men appear to be based on one model, recognizable by his strong nose and full beard. In plates 2 and 3, he wears a tall, silk-wrapped fur hat; in plate 4, a simple homespun coat; and in plate 6, a collared robe, possibly a cowl. Lievens' mastery of the profile pose is displayed in all but one of the plates.

Lievens' technique combines close hatching to articulate textures of fur, fabric, and hair with sharply drawn contours and delicate stippling to trace the planes and wrinkles of each rugged face. He clearly took delight in defining beards and costume details with wiry, curving strokes of the needle. Backgrounds are summarily indicated, focusing all attention on the figure, as if sketched from life.

The most vivid of Lievens' tronies were emulated by printmakers from Salomon Koninck in Amsterdam to Benedetto Castiglione in Italy.[4] Rembrandt took up three of these etchings as well as one that does not belong to the numbered sequence as models for a series of etchings usually called "the Oriental Heads." Rembrandt's etchings are dated 1635, thus providing a *terminus ante quem* for the prototypes by Lievens. In Rembrandt's versions (see figs. 1, 2), picturesque details of costume and setting are intensified. Gersaint, Daulby, and other early connoisseurs assumed that Lievens had copied Rembrandt. Three of Rembrandt's etchings bear the inscription *Rembrandt geretuckeert* ("retouched by Rembrandt"), and some twentieth-century scholars concluded that Rembrandt gave Lievens' etchings to a student to copy, then corrected the student's work. It is now more generally believed that Rembrandt etched these plates himself.[5] Significantly, he never came closer to directly emulating the work of another printmaker. Thus, although the inscriptions do not mention his source by name, these etchings show that Rembrandt maintained a competitive interest in his old friend's work long after the two artists parted company in 1632. It is likely that they became reacquainted when Lievens settled in Amsterdam in 1644. SSD

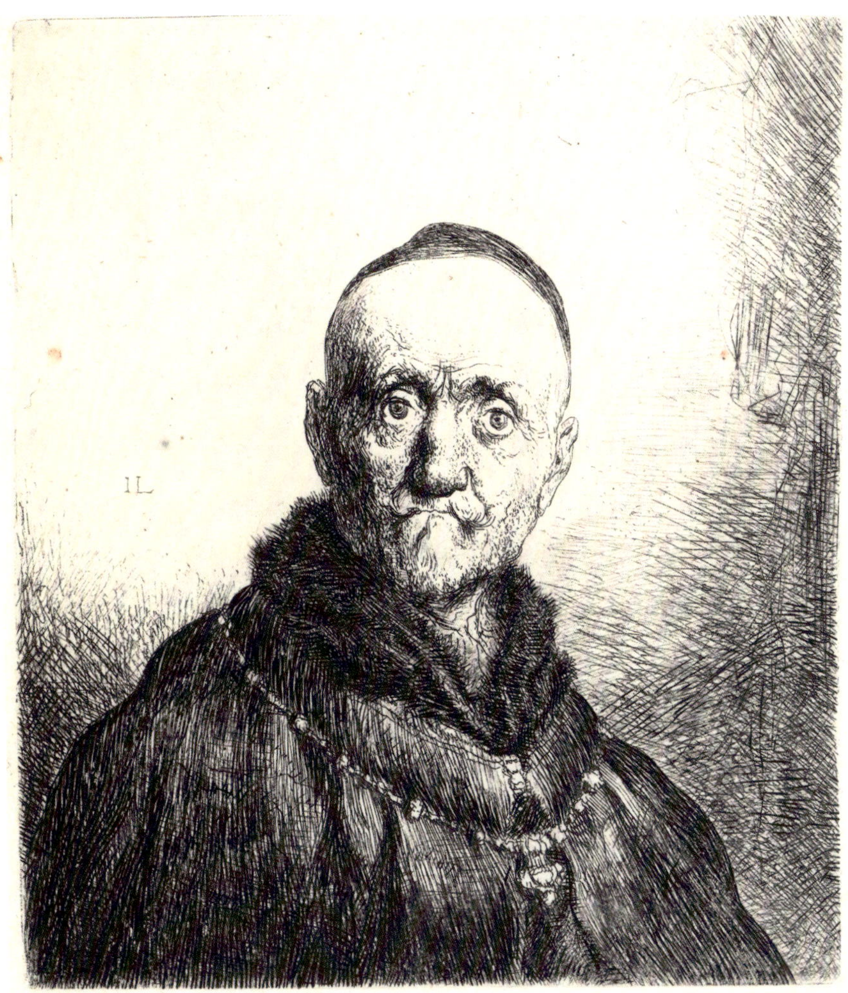

CAT. 70

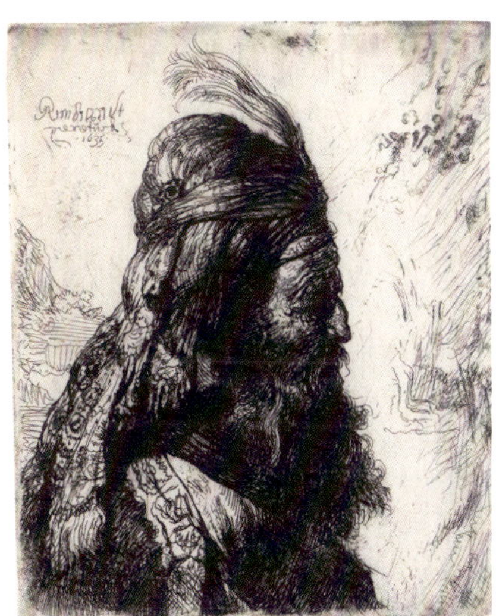

FIG. 1

1 | Rembrandt van Rijn, *Third Oriental Head*, 1635, etching. Rijksmuseum, Amsterdam

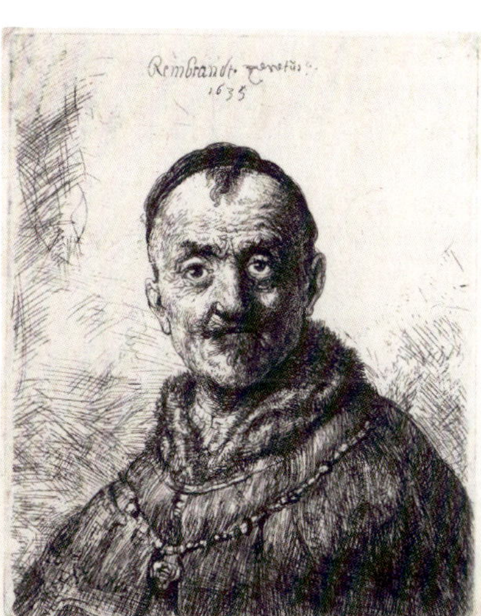

FIG. 2

2 | Rembrandt van Rijn, *First Oriental Head*, 1635, etching. Rijksmuseum, Amsterdam

71 Seated Hermit

c. 1630, etching and engraving, 23.9 × 18 (9 7/16 × 7 1/16)

state 1 (of 8), etching with *IL fec* added in pen and brown ink. The British Museum, London (S34) *(Washington, Amsterdam)*

state 5 (of 8). Rijksmuseum, Amsterdam (RP-P-OB12.538) *(Washington, Milwaukee)*

Selected References

Holl. 17. Linck 1859, 271; Köhne 1932, 50; Schneider/Ekkart 1973, 37, 79, 83, 187, 262; Amsterdam 1988, no. 15

THIS ETCHING IS BASED ON A red chalk drawing (cat. 100) that was traced onto the copperplate. Significant changes took place between the study and the finished print. Caught napping in a chair in the drawing, the old man is wide awake in the etching, staring from beneath heavy brows as he focuses on some unseen thought. He has been transported to a leafy grotto that is similar to the cave in which Lievens places Saint Jerome (cat. 72), but the setting here is less clearly described. Before constructing this densely worked image, Lievens etched the same figure on a much smaller plate, describing form with quick, suggestive strokes in the manner of a pen and ink sketch (fig. 1).[1] Although the figure wears the hooded robe of a monk, he is not meant to represent Saint Francis, as was once thought; no relevant attribute is present, and the white-bearded model is too elderly to resemble Francis of Assisi, who died at forty-four.[2]

In the first state Lievens begins to define the monk's rustic environment, with a combination of rocks and trailing foliage similar to that in the etched and engraved *Raising of Lazarus* (cat. 73). The network of scribbly lines is still relatively thin, allowing light to circulate throughout the scene. The monogram added in brown ink to the impression shown here suggests that Lievens may have considered stopping at this stage. Another impression of the first state in the British Museum, however, is heavily worked over with brown wash (fig. 2). Lievens continued to elaborate the setting, and by the fourth state the background is submerged in darkness so that the

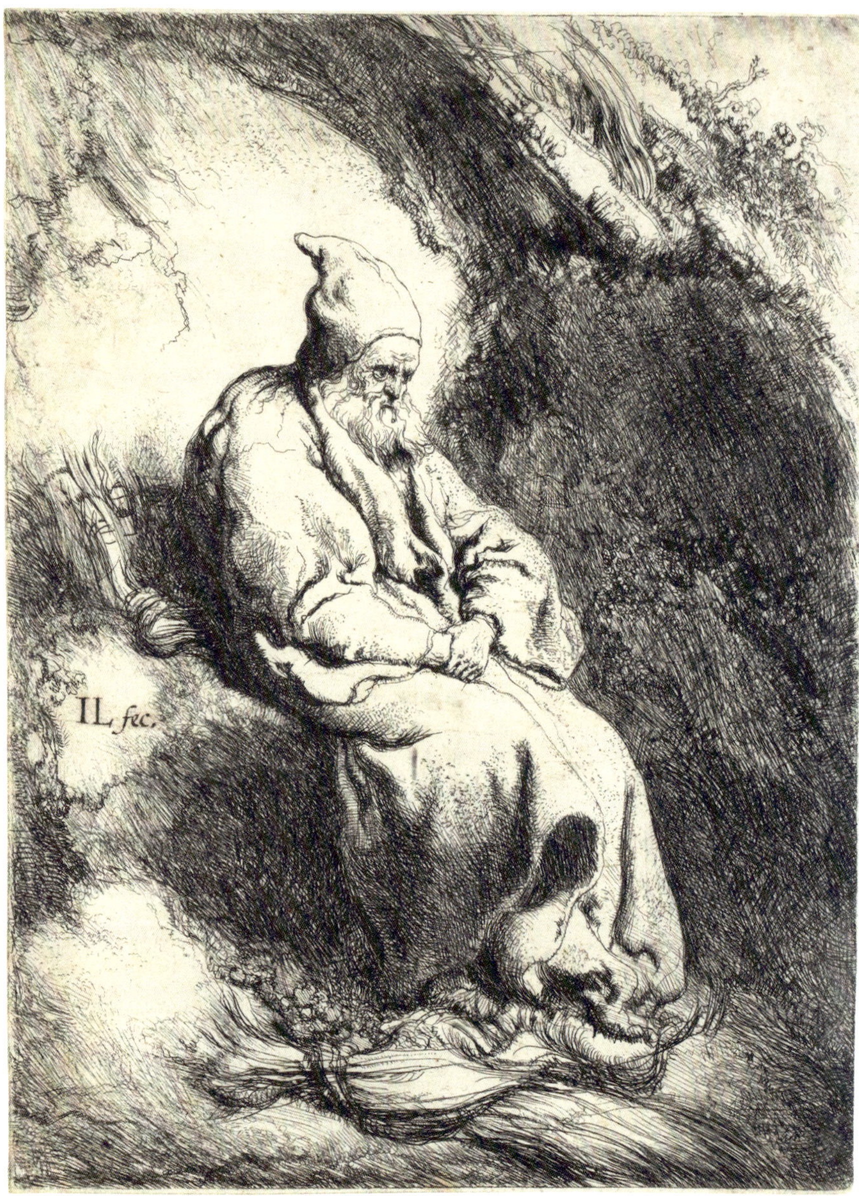

STATE 1

figure glows against it. In the seventh state he reintroduced highlights in the background by scraping, burnishing, and redrawing passages to the left and right of the figure, then added his signature at left. None of the states bears a publisher's address, and we can surmise that Lievens made the revisions in fairly quick succession.[3] The simple yet evocative motif seems designed to afford the opportunity for an experiment with nocturnal tone, most likely Lievens' first foray into this challenging aspect of printmaking. SSD

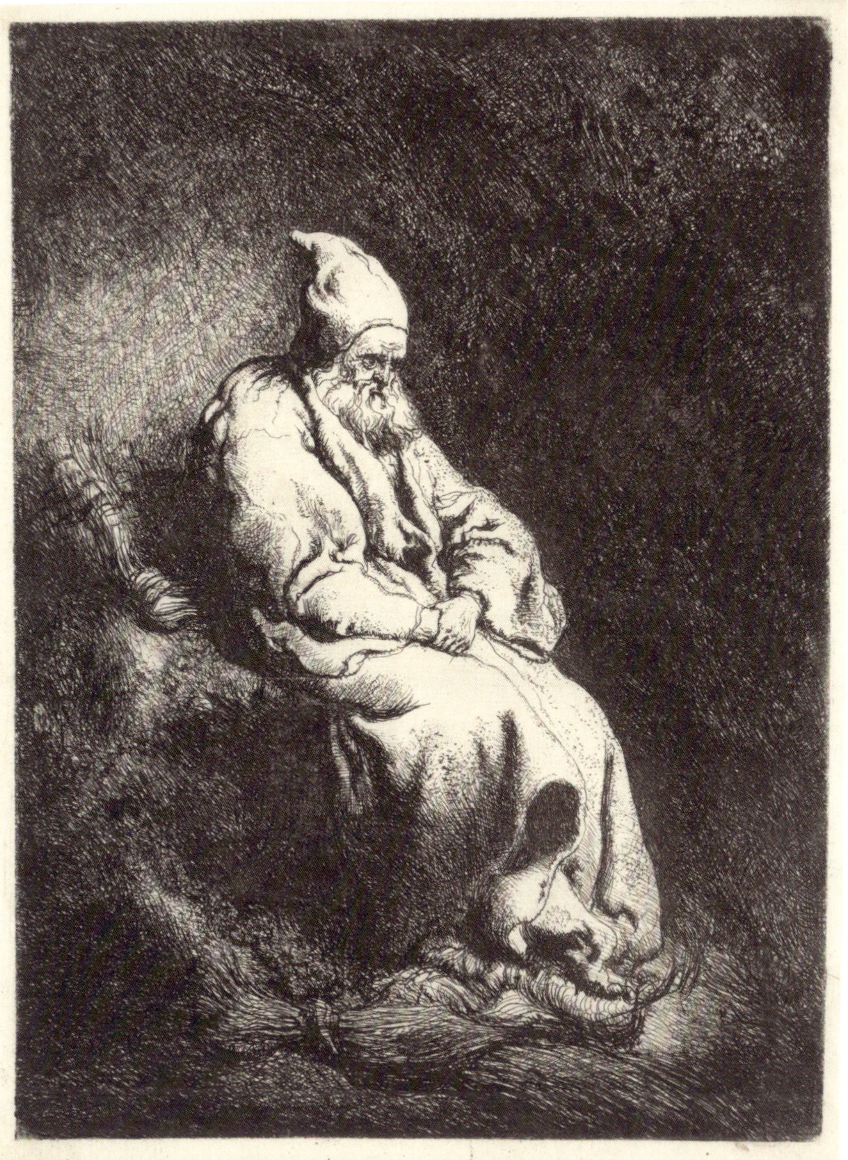

STATE 5

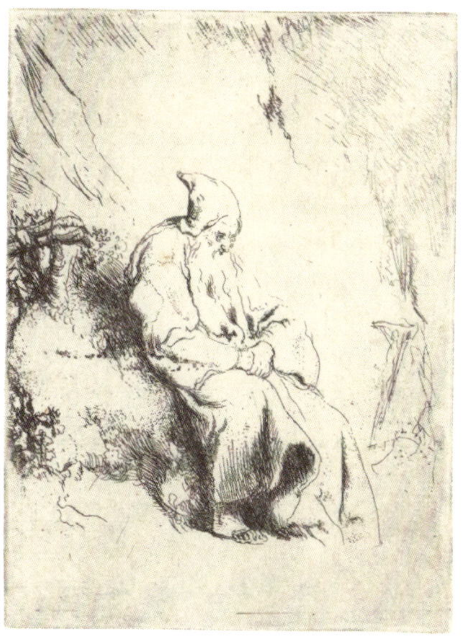

FIG. 1

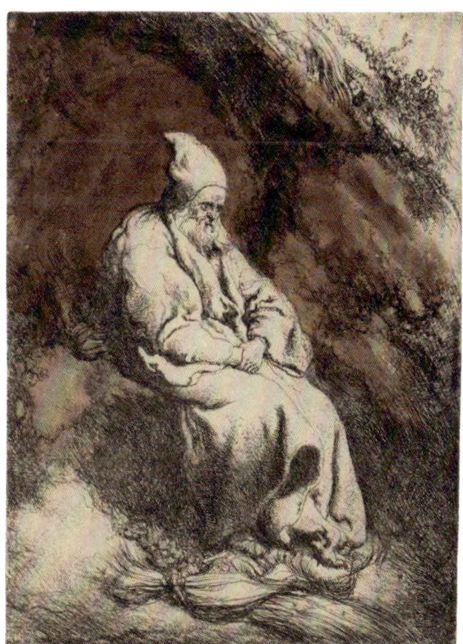

FIG. 2

1 | Jan Lievens, *The Hermit* (small plate), c. 1630–1631, etching. Rijksmuseum, Amsterdam

2 | Jan Lievens, *Seated Hermit*, c. 1630, etching and engraving, reworked with brown wash. The British Museum, London

72 Saint Jerome Meditating in a Grotto

c. 1630, etching, engraving, and drypoint, state 1: 32.3 × 27.1 (12 11/16 × 10 11/16); state 2: 24.5 × 21 (9 5/8 × 8 1/4); state 3: 24 × 21 (9 7/16 × 8 1/4)

state 1 (of 5). Museum of Fine Arts, Boston, Katherine E. Bullard Fund in memory of Frances Bullard (69.1060)

state 2 (of 5). Museum Boijmans Van Beuningen, Rotterdam (BDH 2084) *(Amsterdam)*

state 3 (of 5). Städel Museum, Frankfurt am Main (6126) *(Washington, Milwaukee)*

Selected References

Holl. 15. Linck 1859, 271; Köhne 1932, 50, 52–53, 62; Schneider/Ekkart 1973, 36, 79, 83, 100, 104, 262; Braunschweig 1979, no. 101; Boston 1981, no. 81; Amsterdam 1988, no. 20; Leiden 1991, 104

THROUGHOUT HIS YEARS IN Leiden, Lievens shared with Rembrandt an interest in depicting aged men, often in the guise of saints or scholars. Around 1630 both artists were engaged with the theme of Saint Jerome.[1] They sometimes sketched from the same models, and the balding, bearded man who posed for this etching appears in works by both artists, including Lievens' painting *Job in His Misery* (cat. 25).[2] Here, a radiant halo sanctifies the ascetic figure, who sits meditating over a hand-hewn crucifix in the mossy interior of a cave. Lievens takes pains to describe his sinewy, sagging flesh and the wispy curls of his hair and beard. In his lap is a skull, and behind him, a cardinal's hat and an hourglass. Sunlight spills through a gap in the rocks at right.

Lievens prepared for this print with an oil sketch, painted in grisaille on paper that has been affixed to a panel (cat. 23). This allowed him to work out the balance of tone in broad terms before approaching the complex process of creating shadow on the plate. He found precedents for the theme of the penitent saint, as well as technical models for depicting nocturnal darkness, in recent prints by artists such as Willem Buytewech, Willem van Swanenburg, and Jan van de Velde. Yet rather than emulating their conventional linear patterns, Lievens constructed tone with loose, unorthodox layers of hatching. Rembrandt employed a similar free technique but did not create such a deeply shadowed etching until his *Annunciation to the Shepherds* of 1634.[3] In content and tonality these prints had a continuing impact on artists in Rembrandt's circle.[4]

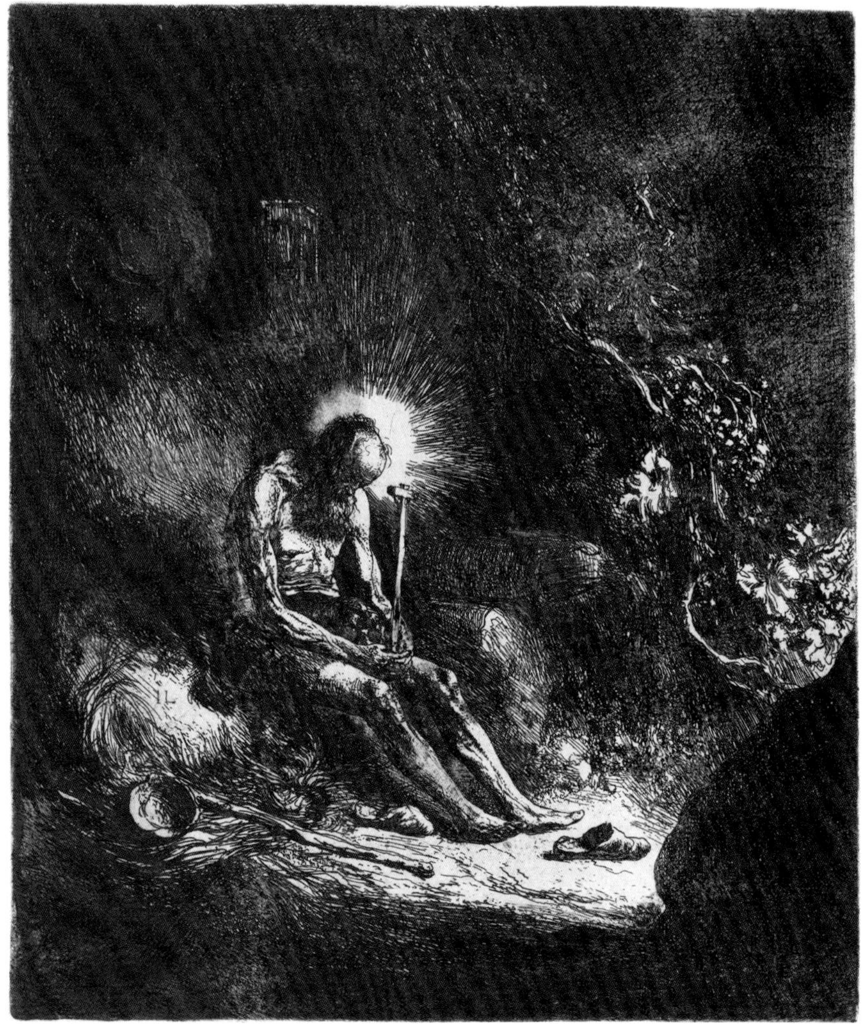

STATE 1

Clifford Ackley has observed that the somber intensity of *Saint Jerome* may have been achieved fortuitously. Because the plate stayed too long in the acid bath, some passages of hatching broke down into fuzzy tone.[5] This effect must have proved fugitive, for in the second and third states, the plate was cut down and extensively reworked with engraving. In the process, motifs in the background were clarified, the distracting repoussoir at right removed, and a large book and jug added beside the saint. The definition of these forms is relatively flat, and it is possible that Lievens enlisted the help of the publisher and engraver Franciscus van den Wijngaerde, whose address appears on the third state. The plate later passed through other hands. SSD

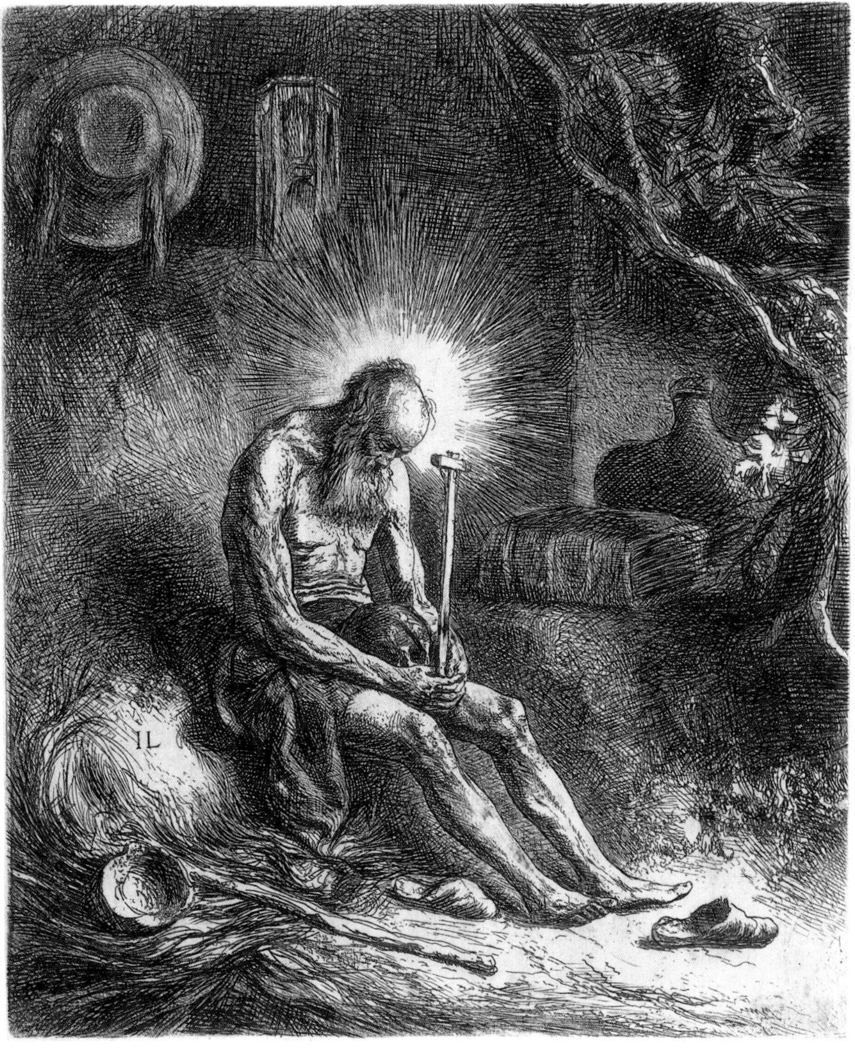

STATE 3

73 The Raising of Lazarus

1630–1631, etching and engraving, 36 × 31.2 (14 3/16 × 12 5/16)

state 1 (of 3). Rijksmuseum, Amsterdam (RP-P-OB12.859) *(Washington, Milwaukee)*

state 3 (of 3). Rijksmuseum, Amsterdam (RP-P-OB12.860) *(Washington, Milwaukee)*

state 1 (of 3). Staatliche Museen zu Berlin, Kupferstichkabinett (113-1881) *(Amsterdam)*

Selected References

Holl. 7. Schneider/Ekkart 1973, 38–40, 79, 83, 100, 261; Braunschweig 1979, no. 102; Boston 1981, no. 82; Schwartz 1985, 106–118; Amsterdam 1988, no. 17; Leiden 1991, 113; Gutbrod 1996, 224–225, 227; White 1999, 27–28; Amsterdam and London 2000, 118, 121, 122; Rotterdam 2006, 20–21

THE STORY OF CHRIST RAISING Lazarus from the dead is one of the most gripping narratives in the New Testament, with elements of faith tested, prophecy revealed, and sheer physical drama. Most baroque artists, including Rembrandt (fig. 1), depict the climactic moment when Jesus revives the dead man by crying "with a loud voice, 'Lazarus, come out'" (John 11:43), but in this etching and the related painting (cat. 31), Lievens emphasizes the moment just before, when Jesus lifts up his eyes in prayer (John 11:41–42). In the painting, darkness pervades the tomb, but in the etching Jesus stands in an aura of divine radiance. He is not the commanding figure depicted by Rembrandt, but a fragile conduit for the healing power flowing from God above.[1] Eyes wide and jaws dropping, the onlookers react with amazement as the ghostly arms of Lazarus reach up out of the tomb into the light.

Even as Lievens was at work on his painting and etching, the painting was copied in an engraving by Jacob Louys, published in Haarlem by Pieter Soutman (see Dickey fig. 5).[2] These concurrent projects set the stage for Lievens' activities in Antwerp, where he collaborated with reproductive printmakers while continuing to produce original etchings, including at least one other based on a painting of his own (cats. 36, 78). He brought with him to Antwerp a number of his Leiden copperplates, among them *The Raising of Lazarus*. The plate went through three states, and it is likely that only the first was completed in Leiden. In the second and third states various passages are reworked

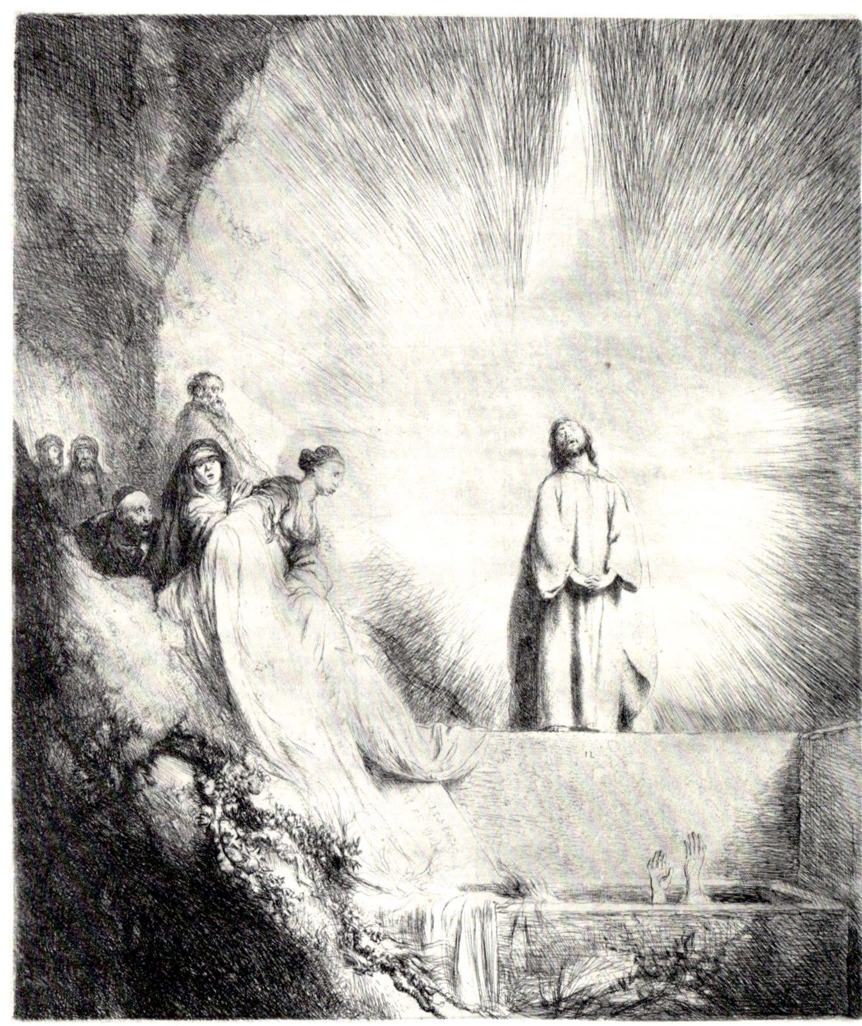

STATE 1

to strengthen shadows and add details such as the cascading foliage at upper left. The third state replaces the initials "IL," etched below Christ, with the signature "I Liuens fecit" and the address of Franciscus van den Wijngaerde, who published many of Lievens' etchings in Antwerp. While the treatment of foliage is evocative, there are more pedestrian engraved passages, such as the shading in the lower left corner, that suggest the intervention of the publisher (Wijngaerde was also a prolific engraver). The delicately etched plate wore out quickly, and fine impressions are scarce. SSD

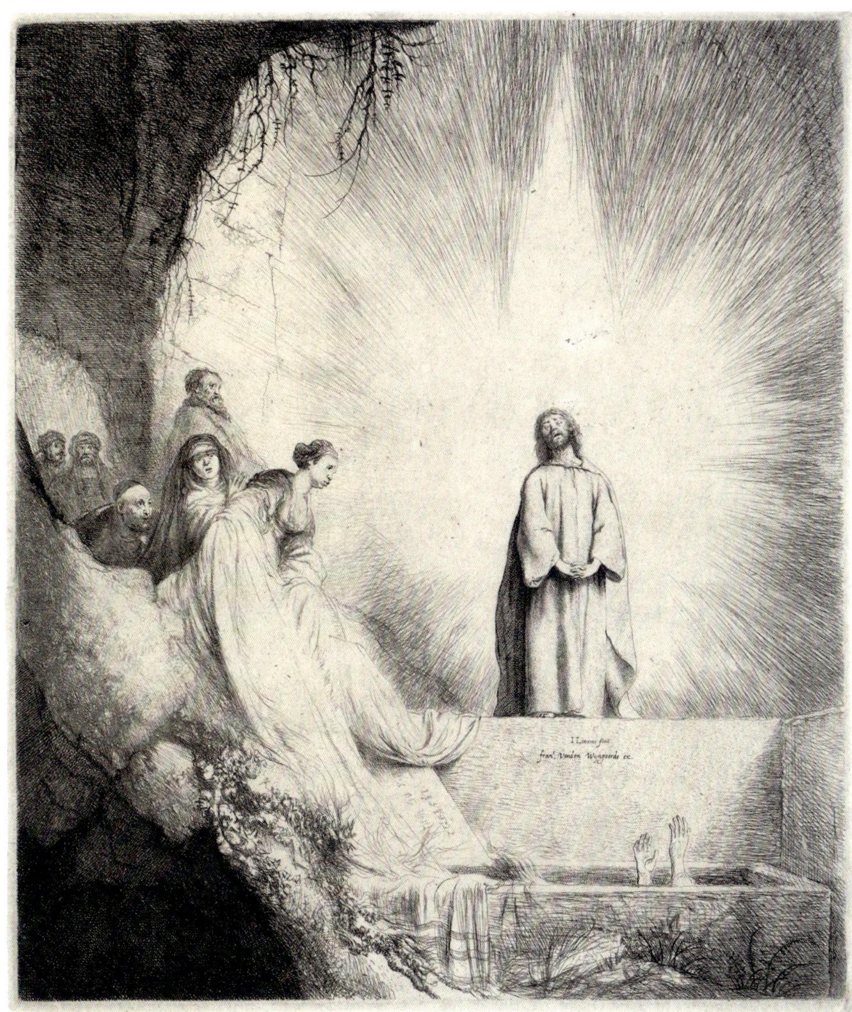

STATE 3

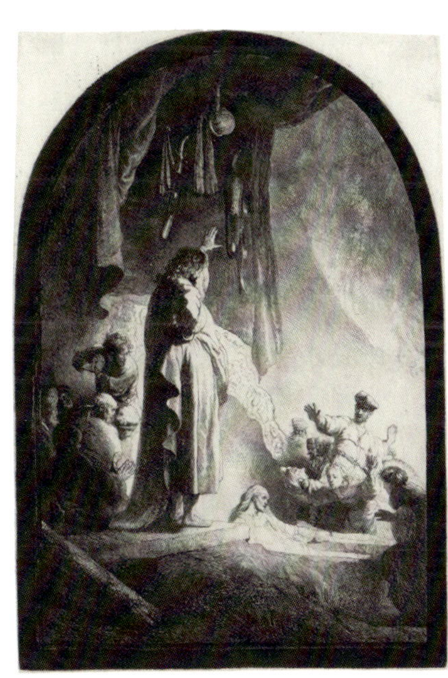

1 | Rembrandt van Rijn, *The Raising of Lazaus*, c. 1631–1632, etching. Rijksmuseum, Amsterdam

74 Portrait of an Elderly Man

c. 1632–1635, etching, engraving, and drypoint, 26.5 × 21.5 ($10\frac{7}{16} \times 8\frac{1}{2}$)

state 2 (of 2). Rijksmuseum, Amsterdam (RP-P-OB12.601) *(Washington, Milwaukee)*

state 2 (of 2), inscribed in pen and ink, by a later hand, *Joan. Livius fec. Robert South Anglois âgé de cent douze ans.* Museum Boijmans Van Beuningen, Rotterdam (BdH 20838) *(Amsterdam)*

Selected References

Holl. 28. Schneider/Ekkart 1973, 83, 270; Braunschweig 1979, no. 107; Boston 1981, no. 93; Amsterdam 1988, no. 36; DeWitt 2006, 128–131, 186–187

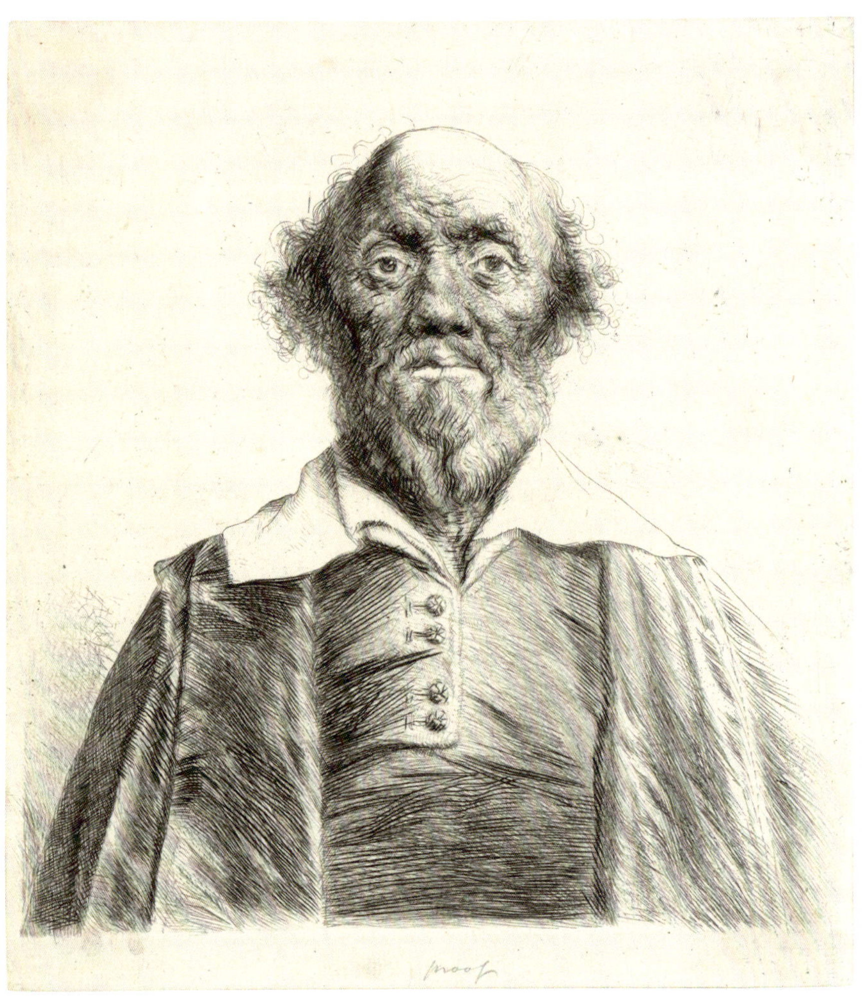

LIEVENS DEPICTS THIS BALDING old man with startling directness and unflattering realism. Such qualities are more characteristic of a figure study than a formal portrait, but handwritten notes on several impressions suggest that the identity of the model was once known, and that he was an Englishman. Two inscriptions link him with the prominent Digby family.[1] According to another notation, he was a musician at the Stuart court.[2] Most frequently cited is the French inscription on the impression from Rotterdam, naming him as "Robert South, one hundred and twelve years old." This reappears on an impression in Vienna, where a further note attributes the inscription to Theodor Matham, a printmaker whom Lievens may have known in Amsterdam.[3] While none of these identifications can be proven, the consistency of their association with England supports the dating of this print to Lievens' years in London (1632–1635). Despite the presence of an inscription field below the image, no signature or title was ever added to complete the plate, and the earliest connoisseurs did not recognize it as Lievens' work.[4] Yet the draftsmanship is unmistakably his.

Whether or not this study was intended as a true portrait, the frontal pose brings us face to face with an imposing personality. The costume is simple but genteel, and the serious demeanor and low vantage point add gravity. We are left with the impression that Lievens' model was a man of some consequence. Prints had long served the function of commemorating persons of great age, both for topical interest and as symbols of mortality, and late sixteenth-century portraits of elderly men by printmakers such as Jost Amman and Lucas Cranach anticipated Lievens' fascination with faces marked by time and character.[5]

The most significant stylistic feature of this plate is the change in technique clearly visible between the two states. In the first state, the intricate description of hair and skin is close to tronies of about 1630, such as *Bearded Man Facing Left* (cat. 69), but the shading of the coat is flatter and more angular. The second state, shown here, has been reworked throughout with sharp, parallel strokes of engraving, strengthening tone in the coat, beard, and other passages.[6] These harsh, rectilinear lines are quite different from the scribbly strokes that build up form in Lievens' Leiden etchings, and they reveal a new interest in the techniques of professional engraving. In London, Lievens must have interacted with Van Dyck and printmakers in his circle. From this point forward, their methods had an increasing impact on his graphic style. In subsequent prints he learned to blend etching and engraving with greater finesse. SSD

75 Portrait of Jacques Gaultier

1632–1635, etching, engraving, and drypoint, 26.5 × 20.2 (10 7/16 × 8), state 3 (of 5), trimmed just inside the platemark; touched with gray wash on the face. Museum of Fine Arts, Boston, Bequest of Washington Irving Jenkins (M26837)

Inscription

IACOBO GOVTERO INTER REGIOS MAGNAE BRITANNIAE ORPHEOS ET AMPHIONES / LYDIAE DORIAE PHRYGIAE TESTVDINIS FIDICINI ET MODVLATORVM PRINCIPI / HANC E PENICILLI SVI TABVLA IN AES TRANSSCRIPTAM EFFIGIEM IOANNES LAEVINI FIDAE AMICITIAE MONIMENTVM L.M. CONSECRAVIT.

Selected References

Holl. 23. Van Someren 1888–1891, 2: 290, no. 2078; Corbett and Norton 1964, 212, no. 1; Schneider/Ekkart 1973, 4, 43–45, 47, 84, 267; Braunschweig 1979, no. 108; Amsterdam 1988, no. 35; DeWitt 2006, 128, 131–133

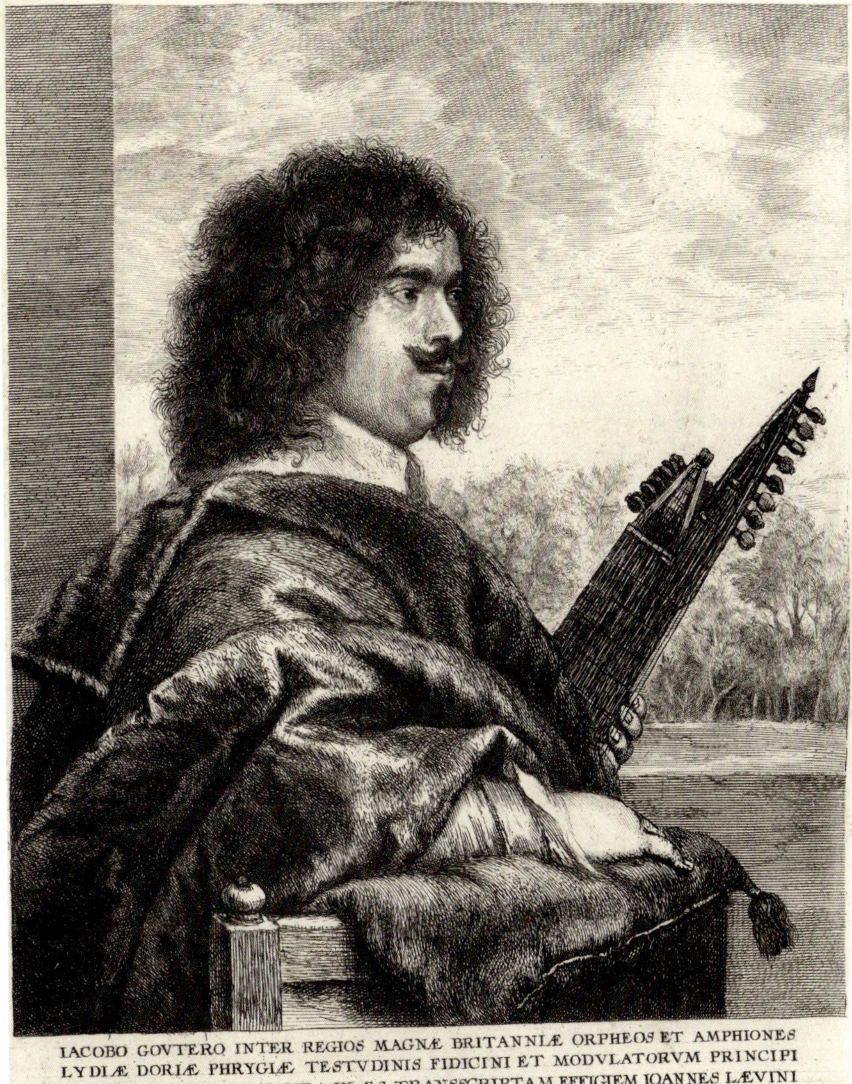

AT THE COURT OF CHARLES I IN London, where Lievens worked from 1632 to 1635, the king and his courtiers surrounded themselves with talented individuals who served their desires for art, music, and spectacle. This etching and a lost painted portrait of Nicolas Lanier, "Master of the King's Musick," provide evidence for Lievens' integration into this creative community.[1] Jacques Gaultier (fl. 1617–1652) moved to England from France in 1618 as a protégé of the Duke of Buckingham and became the foremost solo lutenist at the English court. The double-necked instrument he holds in the portrait may have been his own invention.[2]

In his youth Gaultier was a controversial figure, imprisoned for slandering the king and flirting with Queen Henrietta Maria, whom he tutored on the lute. By the mid-1630s, however, he had married and settled down to a successful career as royal entertainer, a post he retained throughout the reign of Charles I. Gaultier visited the Netherlands in 1630 and corresponded for many years with Constantijn Huygens, who may have encouraged Lievens to make his acquaintance.[3] Lievens published this print himself, perhaps hoping to gain status by advertising his courtly connections. The Latin inscription dedicates the portrait to Gaultier "as a sign of faithful friendship" and alludes in erudite terms to Gaultier's musical skill.[4]

This was Lievens' first formal portrait etching, and it taxed his printmaking abilities. He adopted his favorite profile view and synthesized formal conventions that were current in Dutch portraiture just before his departure, such as the supporting chairback and pillow. But the dense detailing of hair and costume seems somewhat stiff and overwrought, and the grove of trees in the background — an early indication of his interest in landscape — was resolved with some difficulty over the first three states. Apart from this, the treatment of the setting is surprisingly conventional, with ruled lines and dashes defining the flat stone wall and a curvilinear pattern creating a moiré effect in the sky. These passages suggest that Lievens must have studied commercial prints and consulted with Van Dyck and his engravers in London, such as Robert van Voerst. In Antwerp the portrait of Gaultier was republished by Jan Meyssens, who also acquired the plate of Lievens' *Portrait of Daniel Heinsius* of 1639–1640 (cat. 79). SSD

76 Virgin and Child with a Pear

c. 1635–1638, etching, engraving, and drypoint, 26.9 × 20.2 (10 5/8 × 7 15/16), state 4 (of 6). Museum Boijmans Van Beuningen, Rotterdam (BDH 16692) *(Washington, Amsterdam)*

Selected References

Holl. 8. Linck 1859, 273; Köhne 1932, 56; Schneider/Ekkart 1973, 263; Boston 1981, 145, no. 92

AS A CATHOLIC DEVOTIONAL image, the Virgin and Child was a popular theme in Antwerp, and this print must date from Lievens' Flemish period. The cherubic infant, with his chubby cheeks and curly hair, comes straight out of Van Dyck.[1] In accordance with tradition, Mary's pensive expression suggests her foreknowledge of Christ's future suffering, while the pear was a well-established motif symbolizing the virtuous sweetness of Mary and her child.[2] The inscribed caption, "Iesvs Maria," sets up the iconic function of the image as a focus for prayer and meditation, possibly invoking the familiar lines from the Ave Maria: "Blessed art thou among women, and blessed is the fruit of thy womb, Jesus."

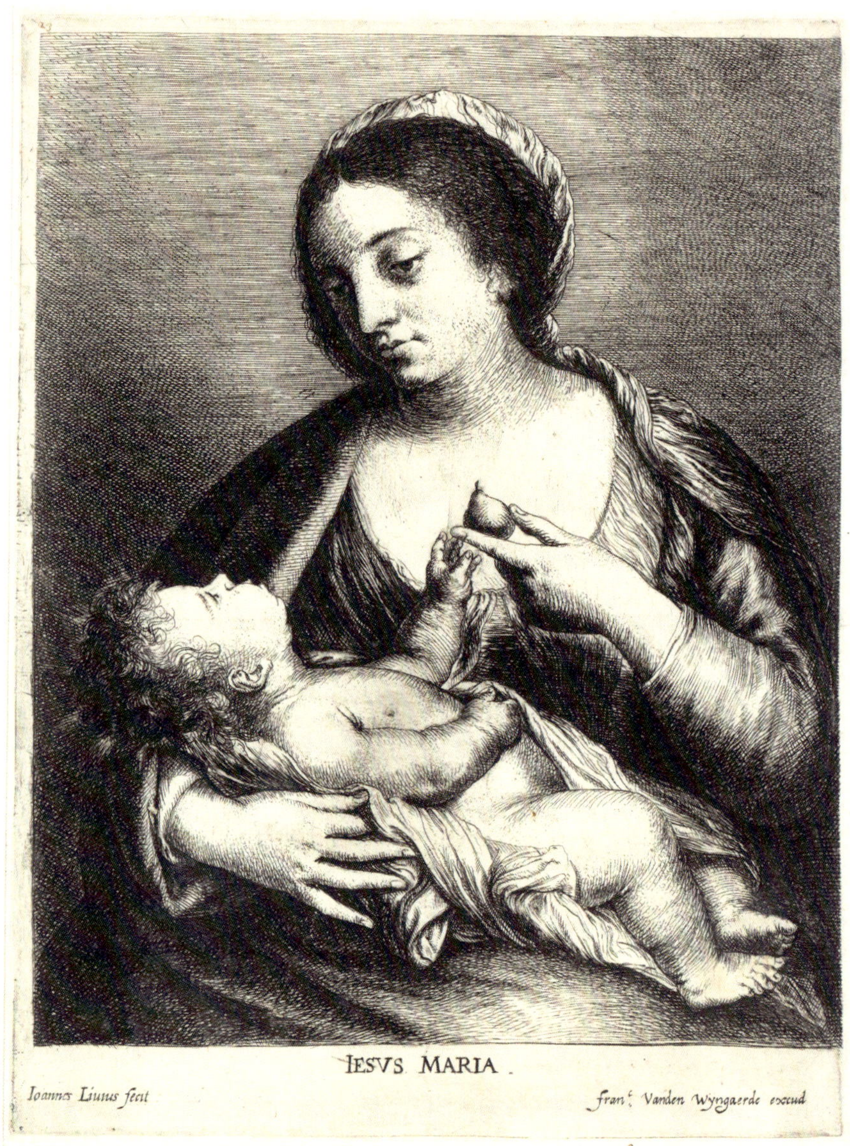

Lievens may have based this print on a painting that is now lost. Documents indicate that he painted the subject of the Virgin and Child several times; one version was still in his own estate in 1674.[3] The relatively tight, controlled technique of the etching may thus reflect his attempt to capture the tonal qualities of the painting. The moiré pattern created by closely spaced hatching in the background indicates that he studied the conventional methods employed by reproductive printmakers, including those in Van Dyck's circle (see also cat. 75).

Virgin and Child with a Pear is one of three etchings that Lievens officially published himself, as indicated by the inscription "fecit et excud." on the third state. It is likely that all three were published shortly after his arrival in Antwerp.[4] He must have had some success in marketing this print, for quite a few early impressions are still extant. Before leaving Antwerp in 1644, he turned the plate over to the publisher Franciscus van den Wijngaerde, who added his own address in the fourth state. SSD

77 Bust of a Capuchin Monk

c. 1635–1638, etching, 32 × 24.7 (12⅝ × 9¾)

only state. Staatliche Museen zu Berlin, Kupferstichkabinett (923-13) *(Washington, Milwaukee)*

only state. Museum Boijmans Van Beuningen, Rotterdam (BdH 16843) *(Amsterdam)*

Selected References

Holl. 27. Linck 1859, 273; Köhne 1932, 56; Schneider/Ekkart 1973, 263; Boston 1981, 145, no. 92

MONKS OF THE CAPUCHIN ORDER, founded in Italy, wore a hood (*capuccio*) and a long beard, and the traditional title of this print derives from these attributes. Although it seems likely that Lievens met his model in Catholic Antwerp rather than in Calvinist Leiden,[1] his interest in painting and etching monastic figures dates back to at least 1630 (see Wheelock fig. 9 and cat. 71). What distinguishes this print from works of his Leiden period is its broader conception, more fluent style, and imposing scale: the figure is more than half life-size. With an etching needle of such crystalline sharpness, this was a feat requiring virtuosic control (one, incidentally, never attempted by Rembrandt).

The stage was set for this audacious move by the almost equally large portrait of an old bearded man etched in London (cat. 74). Comparison of these two prints demonstrates Lievens' progression to a more polished style: in *Bust of a Capuchin Monk*, the hatching is more regular and controlled, combined with light stippling to model form with efficiency and precision. This departure from the more finicky, detailed rendering of earlier tronies seems to reflect the impact of Van Dyck and his circle: preliminary states of portraits for the *Iconography* display a similar technique.[2]

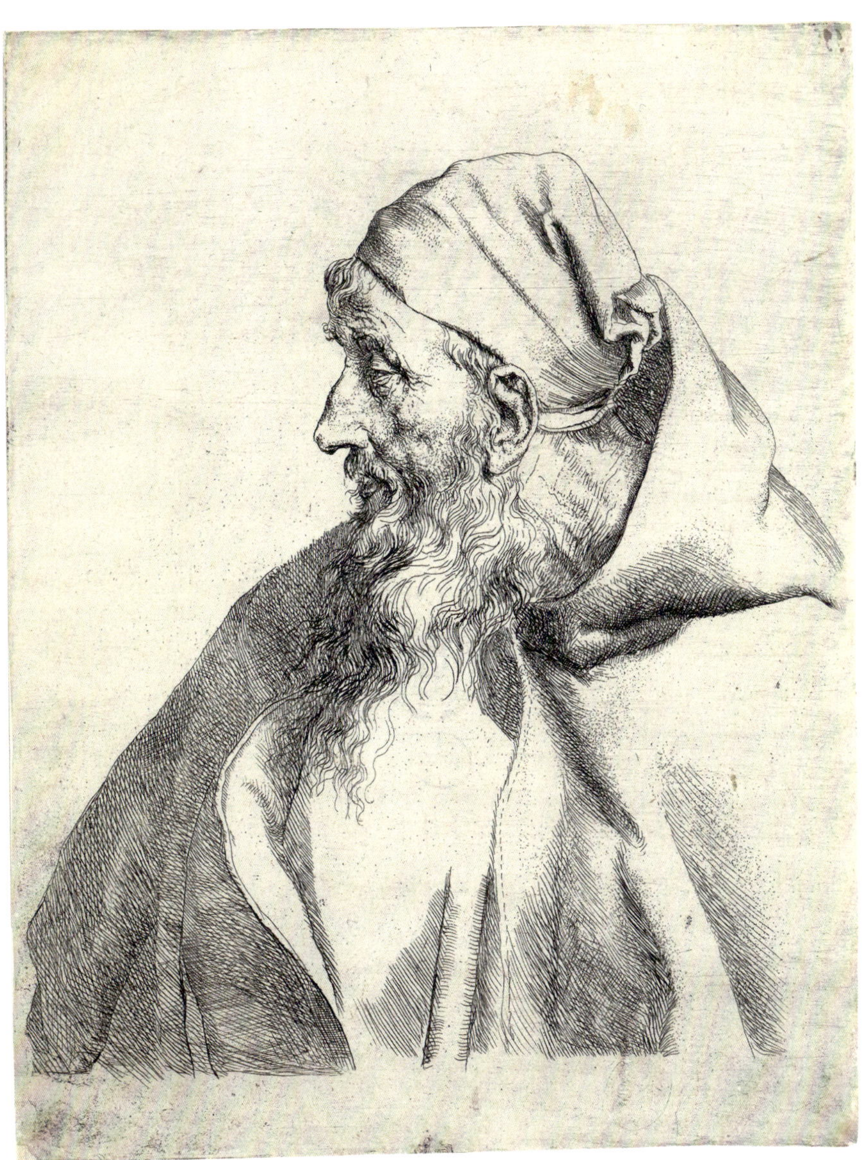

The same model, with his distinctive parted beard and long, beaked nose, appears with a caption casting him as Saint Anthony in an etching that Lievens published himself before turning the plate over to the Antwerp publisher Franciscus van den Wijngaerde.[3] The deeper tonality of that work, achieved with a combination of etching and engraving, illustrates what further work on *Bust of a Capuchin Monk* might have produced. But remarkably, this impressive plate is known only in a single state, unsigned and bearing no publisher's address. SSD

78 Fighting Cardplayers and Death

c. 1638, etching, 20.4 × 26.8 (8 × 10 9/16)

state 2 (of 3). Staatliche Museen zu Berlin, Kupferstichkabinett (926-13) *(Washington, Milwaukee)*

state 3 (of 3). Städel Museum, Frankfurt am Main (6133) *(Amsterdam)*

Inscription

Rixas atque odia salagit dispergere serpens / Antiquus, cuncta at iurgia morte cadunt.

Selected References

Holl. 19. Linck 1859, 272; Köhne 1932, 56; Schneider/Ekkart 1973, 79, 83, 262; Braunschweig 1979, no. 111; Munich 1982, no. 91; Van Straten 2005, 44–45, 292–293

LIEVENS BASED THIS ETCHING ON his own painting (cat. 36), depicting two gamblers quarreling over a game of cards. The intervention of Death, crowned with a vine wreath, indicates that alcohol has fueled their dispute and that it will end tragically. The moralizing message of this violent scene is reinforced in the print by the didactic Latin inscription, which can be translated: "The ancient serpent hastens to spread quarrels and hatred, but death cancels all brawls."[1] Both the print and painting must date from c. 1638, when Lievens painted *Greedy Couple Surprised by Death* (cat. 35) and was in contact with the genre painter Adriaen Brouwer (cat. 102), who specialized in raucous tavern interiors.

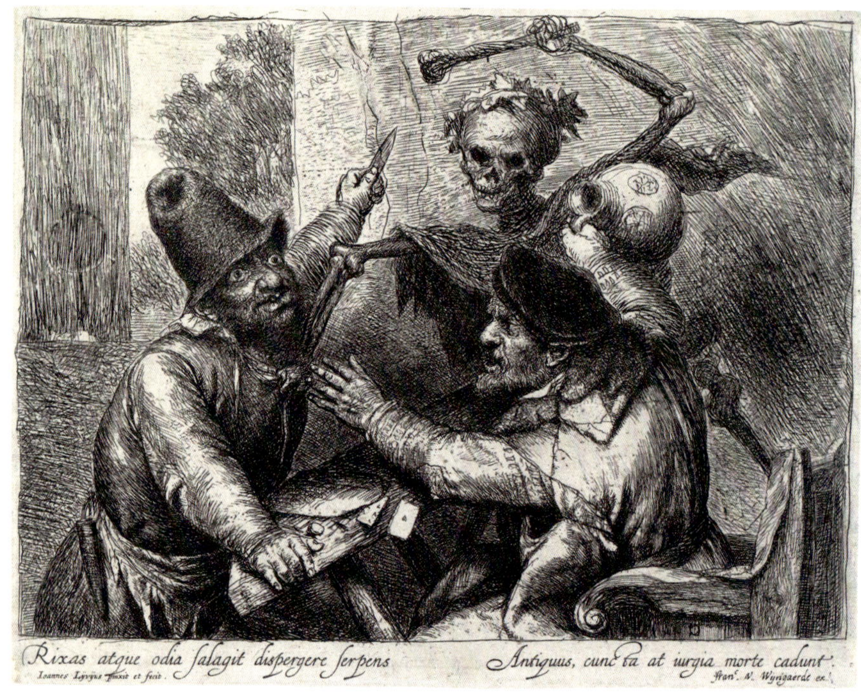

STATE 3

Lievens had not etched such a complex composition since leaving Leiden. His etching style, attuned to the rough subject, is looser here than in other prints of the period, such as his *Virgin and Child with a Pear* (cat. 76). The varied hatching captures texture and light, emulating the tonalities of his own colorful painting. The motif of the peasant about to bash his compatriot over the head with a jug occurs frequently in paintings by Joos van Craesbeeck, another Brouwer associate.[2] The skeletal figure of Death lends an allegorical tone absent from Brouwer's imagery, and the addition of the Latin inscription positions the print as a collectible for the educated buyer.

This etching demonstrates Lievens' interest in participating in the lively trade in prints after paintings, fostered in Antwerp by Rubens and Van Dyck. The engravers Lucas Vorsterman and Paulus Pontius made prints after these artists as well as after Brouwer and Lievens, with whom they were on friendly terms.[3] By making an etching after his own painting, Lievens played both sides of the coin, perhaps hoping to increase his profit while also advancing his reputation. He published three other prints himself in the mid-1630s, but he chose to distribute this etching through Martinus van den Enden, publisher of Van Dyck's *Iconography*. The plate was then acquired by Franciscus van den Wijngaerde. The existence of many worn impressions suggests that this was a popular and often reprinted image. SSD

79 Portrait of Daniel Heinsius

1639–1640, etching and engraving, 26.3 × 20.3 (10½ × 8)

state 3 (of 4). Rijksmuseum, Amsterdam (RP-P-OB12.602) *(Washington, Milwaukee)*

state 3 (of 4). Staatliche Museen zu Berlin, Kupferstichkabinett (498-52) *(Amsterdam)*

Inscription

DANIEL HEINSIUS EQVES SGRGN.MO SVECORUM REGI A CONSILIIS.

Bottom: *Hic ille Heinsiades, quem pingere solus Apelles, / Dicere quem digne solus Apollo potest: / Sola parens Diuûm meruit quem gignere Ganda, / Sola parens vatum Leida fouere sinu.*

Selected References

Holl. 22. Muller 1853, 2267–2268; Schneider/Ekkart 1973, 46, 79, 84, 196, 267; Ekkart 1974, III. 8; Braunschweig 1979, no. 112

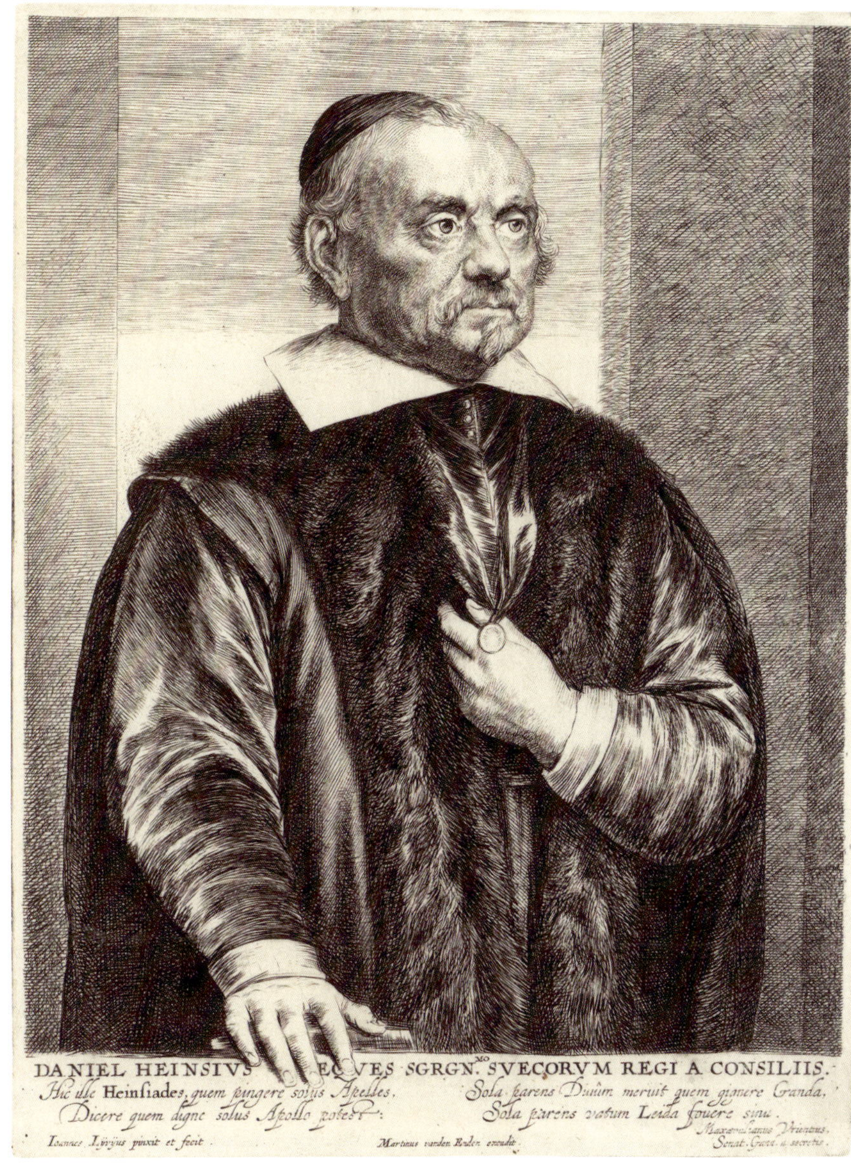

AS A DISTINGUISHED PROFESSOR at Leiden University, a poet, and a diplomat, Daniel Heinsius (1580–1655) was portrayed many times.[1] He must have posed for Lievens in 1639, when the artist returned from Antwerp to Holland to paint *The Magnanimity of Scipio* for the Leiden town hall. While in Leiden, Lievens made black chalk drawings of Heinsius (now lost) and of Constantijn Huygens (cat. 103).[2] By June 1640 he was back in Antwerp, where the drawing of Huygens was reproduced in an engraving by Vorsterman, issued by Martinus van den Enden, publisher of Van Dyck's *Iconography*.[3] Lievens chose to etch the portrait of Heinsius himself, perhaps completing the likeness in Leiden so that it could be approved by the sitter, but this print was also published in Antwerp by Van den Enden.

Heinsius had lived in Leiden since 1598 but had been born in Ghent, and the laudatory inscription is signed by the Ghent poet Maximilianus Vrientius.[4] With his own connections on both sides of the Dutch border, Lievens was well suited to produce this homage to a celebrated scholar whose appeal to fellow humanists and portrait collectors crossed political boundaries. Heinsius' international renown is emphasized by the caption, which refers to his appointment as councilor and historiographer to the king of Sweden. The medallion hanging conspicuously over his left hand must represent the Order of Saint Mark, awarded to him by the Republic of Venice in 1623.[5]

Lievens' print portraits were deeply affected by the suave style of Van Dyck's *Iconography*, beginning with his portrait of the court musician Jacques Gaultier (cat. 75). With the portrait of Heinsius, however, Lievens achieves a new confidence in both conception and execution. He worked out the sensitive modeling of Heinsius' broad face and velvety black costume with the help of a proof touched with gray wash, a practice commonly followed for the *Iconography*.[6] The simple format focuses attention on the dignified subject, who stands gazing out as if deep in thought. Heinsius' right hand rests on a book while projecting illusionistically into the inscription field below. This lively trick can be found in several portraits in the *Iconography*, including Vorsterman's engraving of the art collector Jacques de Cachiopin, completed while Lievens was in Antwerp.[7] SSD

80 Landscape with a Group of Trees

c. 1640, woodcut, 24 × 15 (9½ × 5⅞)

only state, touched with wash. Rijksmuseum, Amsterdam (RP-P-OB4634) *(Washington, Milwaukee)*

only state. Frits Lugt Collection, Institut Néerlandais, Paris (1860) *(Amsterdam)*

Selected References

Holl. 100. Hind 1913, 233, 235; Van de Waal 1940, 16; Schneider/Ekkart 1973, 86, 268; Braunschweig 1979, no. 116; Boston 1981, no. 127; Amsterdam 1988, no. 50

1 | Ugo da Carpi after Titian or Campagnola, *Tree with Two Goats*, c. 1518, woodcut in two blocks. Staatliche Museen zu Berlin, Kupferstichkabinett

THIS IS ONE OF LIEVENS' MOST rare and remarkable prints. The unorthodox carving of angular, jagged forms suggests that he learned to manipulate the medium of woodcut as he had learned etching years earlier: by trial and error. The result has an emotive force that anticipates German expressionism. This woodcut is known in a single state, preserved in only two impressions, but the impression in Amsterdam, seen here, has been worked up with brown wash, possibly in anticipation of creating a tone block. Chiaroscuro woodcut landscapes had been introduced to Dutch art around 1600 in the circle of Hendrick Goltzius.[1] Ultimately, Lievens produced only one print in color (cat. 84).

Beginning around 1635, Lievens painted and drew many landscapes. Yet apart from two portrait backgrounds (cats. 75, 85), this is his only treatment of an outdoor scene in print. In his drawings he took particular pleasure in sketching pollard willows and other hoary trees with long, gnarled branches (cats. 134, 135). The final results often seem to blend observation and imagination. This print probably developed from a sketch composed in the studio and traced onto the woodblock. The wild, woodsy motif was unusual in Dutch landscape prints, which more often depicted recognizable places or emphasized the traces of human habitation. But Lievens may have found inspiration for this bosky view in Venetian prints after Titian and Campagnola (fig. 1).[2] The fierce, choppy carving of the block seems purely his own, and its untutored energy suggests that it may be Lievens' first woodcut.

Most of Lievens' woodcuts are extremely rare, and they may not have been actively marketed. Ten woodblocks were still in his possession at his death in 1674.[3] It is possible that he took up this medium in the second half of his stay in Antwerp as a means of artistic expression apart from the more complex demands of painting and etching. SSD

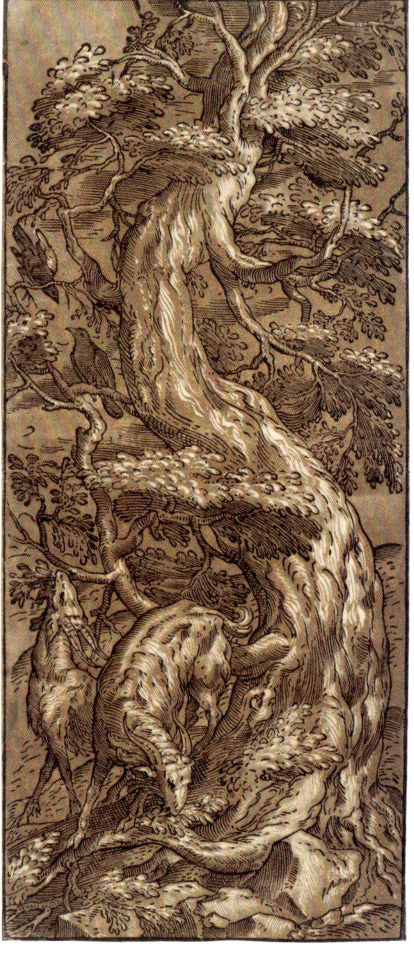

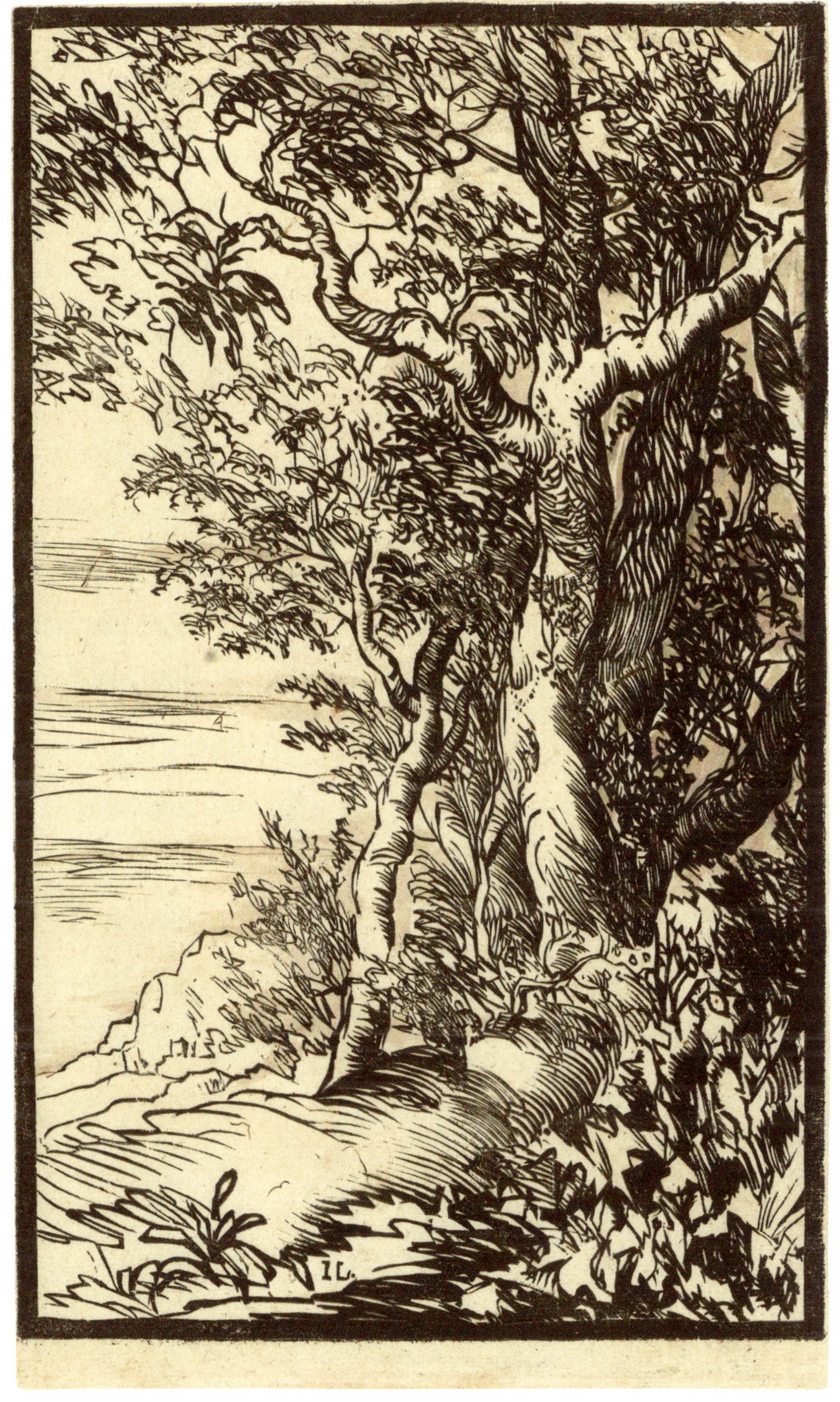

AMSTERDAM IMPRESSION

81 Cain Slaying Abel

c. 1640–1644, woodcut, 41.6 × 31.8 (16⅜ × 12½), only state. Rijksmuseum, Amsterdam (RP-P-OB12.862) *(Washington, Milwaukee)*

Selected References

Holl. 99. Linck 1859, 283; Van de Waal 1940, 10; Schneider/Ekkart 1973, 84–85, 268; Braunschweig 1979, no. 113; Münster 1994, no. 67; Amsterdam 1996, no. 3

SIBLING RIVALRY IS AS OLD AS time, and the image of Cain looming murderously over Abel, jawbone in hand, is as venerable in Netherlandish art as Jan van Eyck's Ghent Altarpiece (1432).[1] The story is recounted in Genesis 4:8: the firstborn son of Adam and Eve slew his brother Abel in a fit of jealousy after God preferred Abel's sacrificial offering to his own. Artists frequently chose the climactic moment just before Abel's death, but some, including Lievens' teacher Pieter Lastman, depicted the tragic aftermath when Adam and Eve mourn the loss of their son.[2]

The basic visual motif of menacing attacker and prostrate victim was central to scenes of conflict, from the Labors of Hercules to David slaying Goliath, and for this impressive woodcut, Lievens had recourse to a rich print tradition. Hendrick Goltzius' chiaroscuro woodcut, *Hercules Slaying Cacus* (1588), and Willem Buytewech's etching after Rubens, *Cain Slaying Abel* (c. 1608–1610), have often been mentioned as antecedents.[3] A more immediate source of inspiration was Christoffel Jegher, who worked closely with Rubens in the 1630s to produce a series of woodcuts after paintings by the master. It may have been Jegher who taught Lievens how to translate the form-hugging hatched lines of engraving to the less flexible medium of woodcut. The dramatic *Cain Slaying Abel* is Lievens' most Rubensian print, as well as one of his most ambitious compositions, recalling the combative, muscular figures of Jegher's *Hercules Fighting Fury and Discord* (fig. 1; another frequently cited source) and the simplified foliage, low horizon, and roiling clouds of his *Drunken Silenus*.[4] Yet Lievens may also have looked to an earlier woodcut where some of the same features are already present: Jan Gossaert's *Cain Slaying Abel* of c. 1525 (fig. 2).[5] Lievens treats the block more coloristically and adds his own interpretation of the emotional scene: Cain's rugged face is clouded with hatred, and the distraught Abel reaches up, not to fight back against his brother, but to plead for mercy against the fatal blow.

In 1654 Jegher's son made a reduced copy of Lievens' composition for a book illustration.[6] It seems that Lievens' woodcut was not widely sold, as it exists today only in this unique impression. SSD

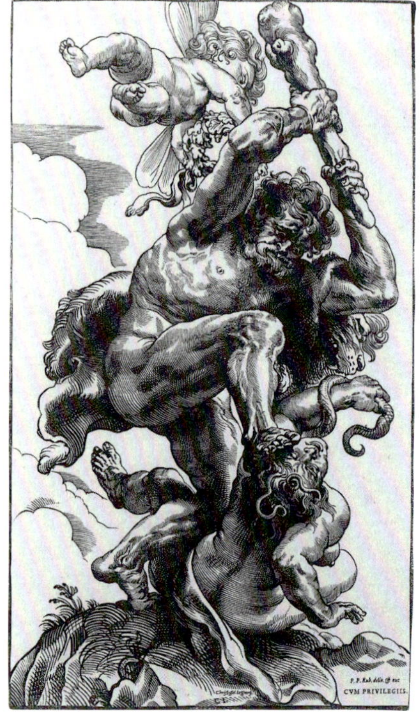

FIG. 1

1 | Christoffel Jegher after Peter Paul Rubens, *Hercules Fighting Fury and Discord*, woodcut. National Gallery of Art, Washington, Ailsa Mellon Bruce Fund

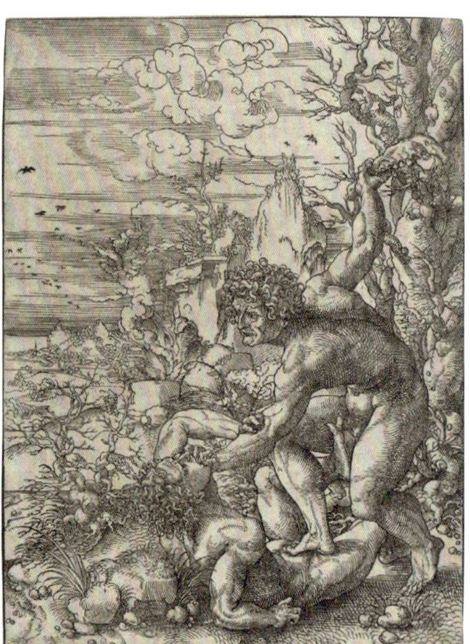

FIG. 2

2 | Jan Gossaert, *Cain Slaying Abel*, c. 1525, woodcut. The British Museum, London

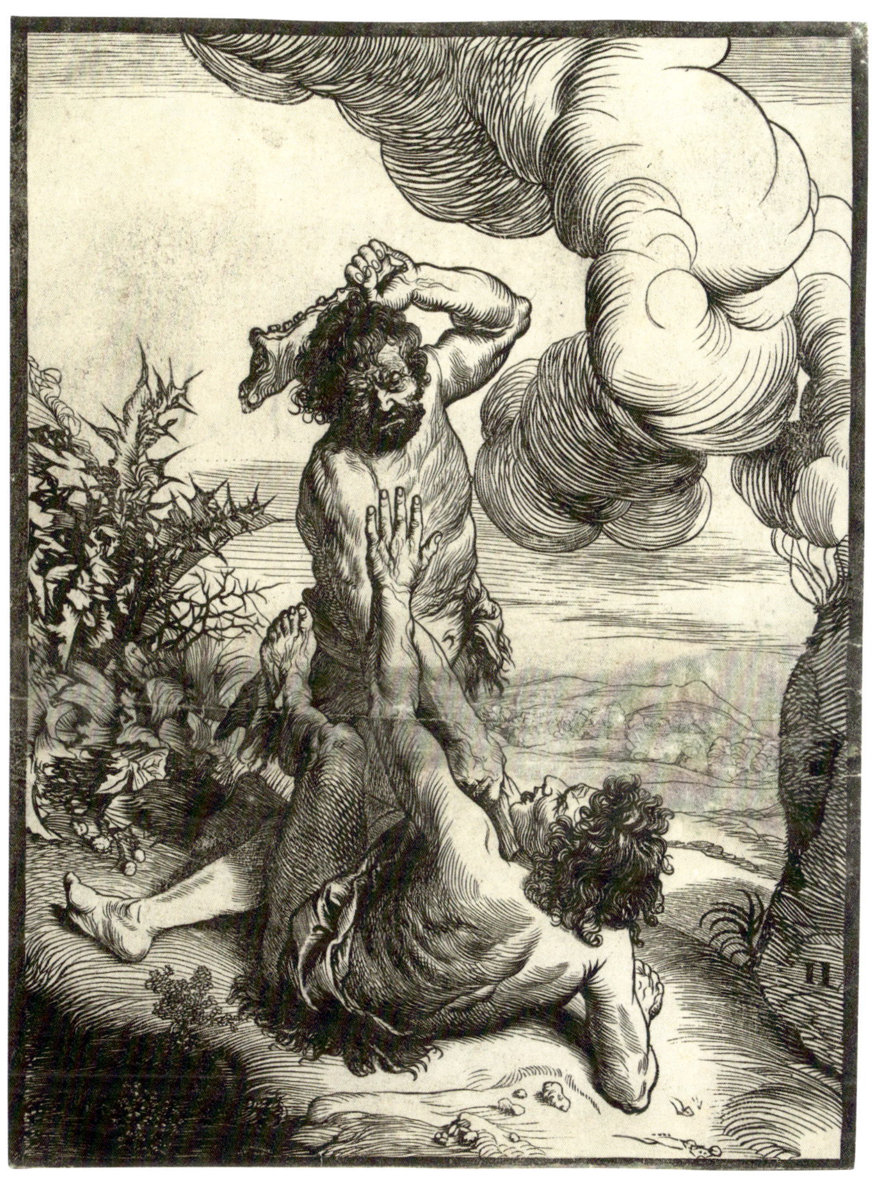

82 Man in a Cap Facing Left

c. 1640–1644, woodcut, 16.7 × 12.8 (6 9/16 × 4 1/16), only state, touched with brown ink. Museum of Fine Arts, Boston, Gift of W. G. Russell Allen (51.1332)

Selected References
Holl. 105. Hind 1913, 238; Chicago 1969, 197; Schneider/Ekkart 1973, 268–269

THE ONLY KNOWN IMPRESSION of this evocative figure study is exhibited here for the first time. The sheet of thin, possibly Japanese paper is closely trimmed, but the image might once have been framed with a border (cat. 83). The monogram has been strengthened with brown ink. This is one of Lievens' most sensitive wooduct tronies, carved with closely spaced diagonal hatching to model the torso and intricate, curving strokes for the hair and beard.

The pensive figure is related to an etching of Saint Mark, part of a series of the Four Evangelists for which *S. Marcus* and *S. Ioannes* were etched by Lievens while *S. Matthaeus* and *S. Lucas* have been attributed to Laurent de La Hyre. *S. Marcus* (fig. 1) is the only one of the four prints inscribed with Lievens' name and the address of his Antwerp publisher, Franciscus van den Wijngaerde. The etching is based on a sketch in black chalk, but the drawing is larger in scale; a painting may have been the original goal.[1] For the woodcut, Lievens removes the literary attributes and adds the dark cap, transforming the figure into a simple burgher. The old-fashioned costume and plain format suggest that he studied woodcut portraits by German artists of the sixteenth century such as Hans Baldung Grien and Lucas Cranach.[2] SSD

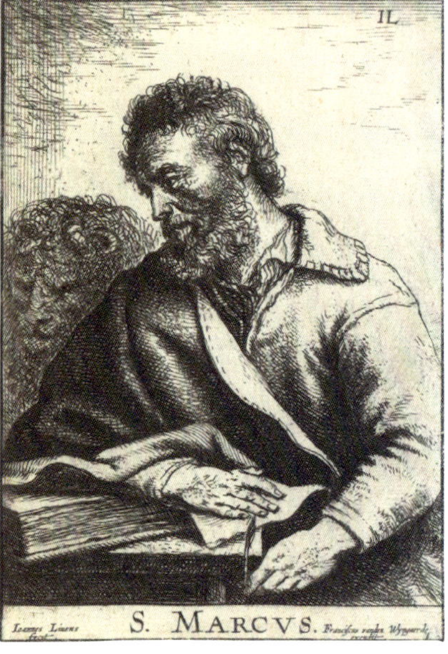

1 | Jan Lievens, *S. Marcus*, c. 1635–1644, etching. Rijksmuseum, Amsterdam

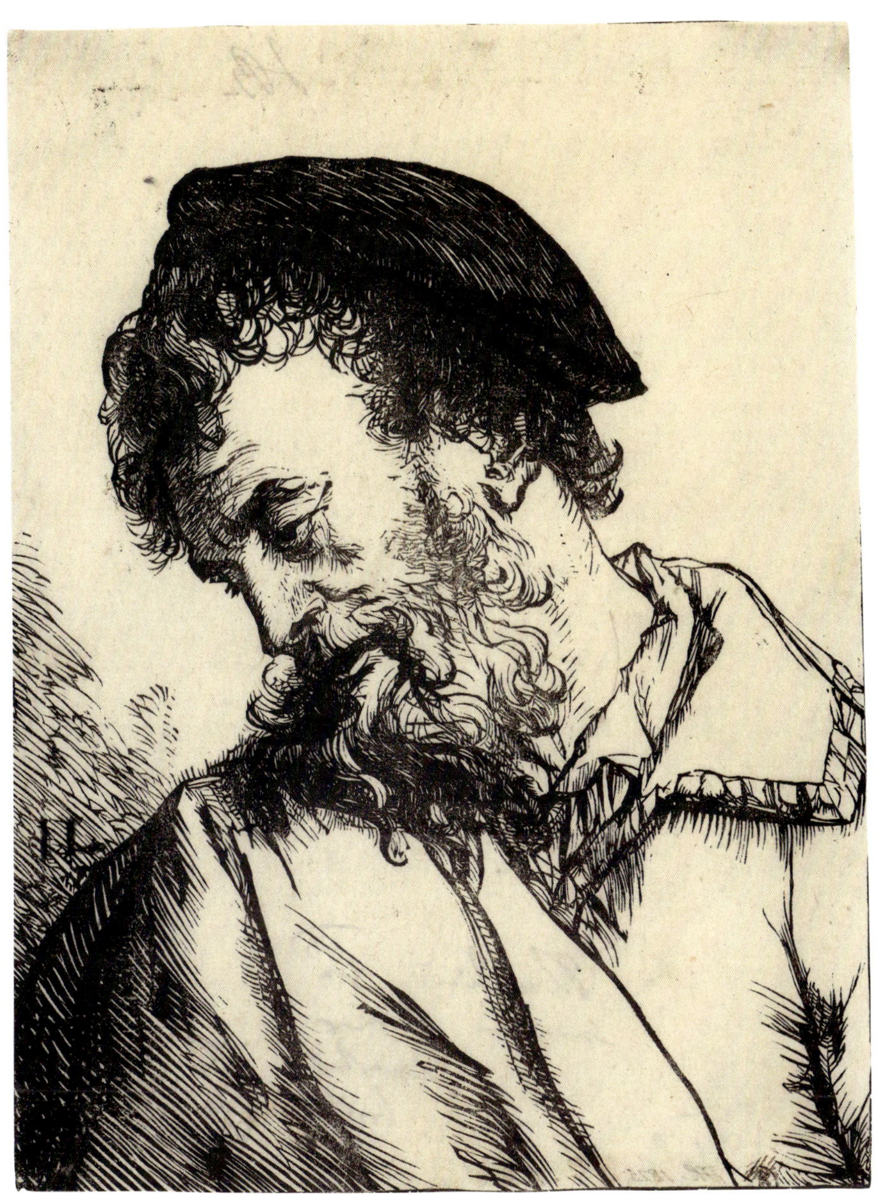

83 A Seated Cleric

c. 1640–1644, woodcut, 17 × 13.6 (6¾ × 5⅜), state 1 (of 2). Frits Lugt Collection, Institut Néerlandais, Paris (1716) *(Washington, Amsterdam)*

Selected References

Holl. 102. Linck 1859, 280; Van de Waal 1940, 14–15; Strauss 1973, 342; Schneider/Ekkart 1973, 85–86, 267–268; Braunschweig 1979, no. 115; Boston 1981, no. 90; Amsterdam 1988, no. 39

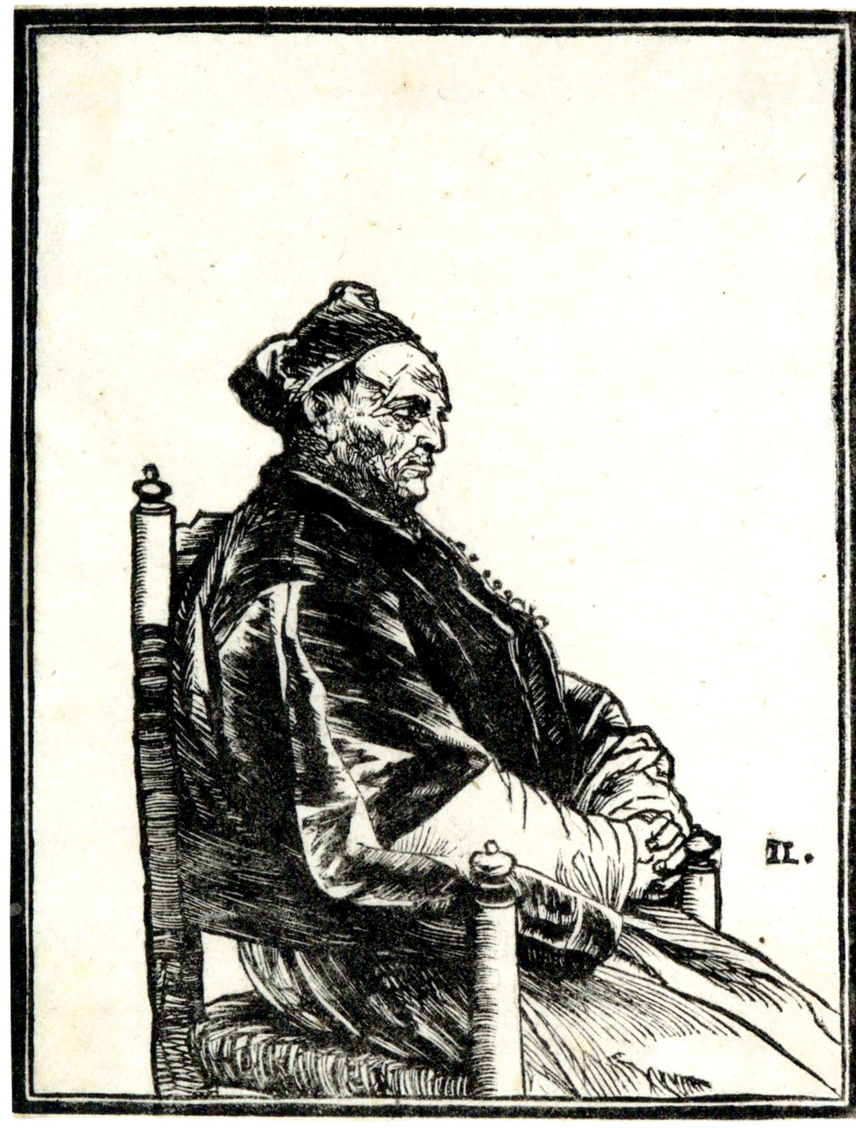

GERSAINT DESCRIBED THIS FIGURE in 1752 as "a Noble Venetian, seen in Profile, sitting in an easy Chair." The description was repeated in Hollstein, but Hind in 1913 had already recognized that the costume defines the subject as a clergyman. The figure wears a soft biretta on his head and a black mozzetta (short cape) over a white surplice, the informal dress of a Flemish prelate. Lievens must certainly have encountered such clerics in Antwerp, where he undertook several commissions for the Jesuit order and may have converted to Catholicism himself.[1]

The private nature of the image is clear in a preparatory drawing (cat. 107), where the same man is seen at home in a room littered with books, papers, and a globe. The drawing has the character of a sketch for a large, full-length, painted portrait, yet the central portion of the sheet was traced to the block to produce this stark, simple print. In the woodcut the man's facial features are defined with such care that the print may still have been meant to function as a portrait rather than a generic figure study.

Woodcut printing was usually a collaboration between designer and block carver, and Hind took the difference between the drawing and the print as evidence that Lievens did not cut his own blocks. Yet their unorthodox style suggests that he did. In this print and several other woodcuts, Lievens pushed the medium of relief printing to emulate the deep tonality of his intaglio portraits (see cat. 79), moving beyond the Rubensian manner of *Cain Slaying Abel* (cat. 81).[2] Passages of nearly pure black, relieved by angular, diagonal gouges to suggest the shimmer of fabric, are combined with long, clear strokes for contour and a web of delicate, irregular hatching to define facial features. Comparison of impressions shows that the most delicate lines (such as those in the face and chairback) broke down under printing and were sometimes touched up with brown ink.[3] This print is one of the least rare of Lievens' woodcuts. It is possible that the man portrayed chose to distribute impressions among his acquaintances, but his identity remains undiscovered. SSD

84 Bust of a Man Facing Forward

c. 1640–1644, chiaroscuro woodcut, 17.2 × 13 (6¾ × 5⅛), only state, printed from two blocks, border partly made up with ink. Museum of Fine Arts, Boston, Bequest of W. G. Russell Allen (1985.802)

Selected References

Holl. 106. Linck 1859, 283; Schneider/Ekkart 1973, 85, 87, 269; Braunschweig 1979, no. 117; Amsterdam 1988, no. 38

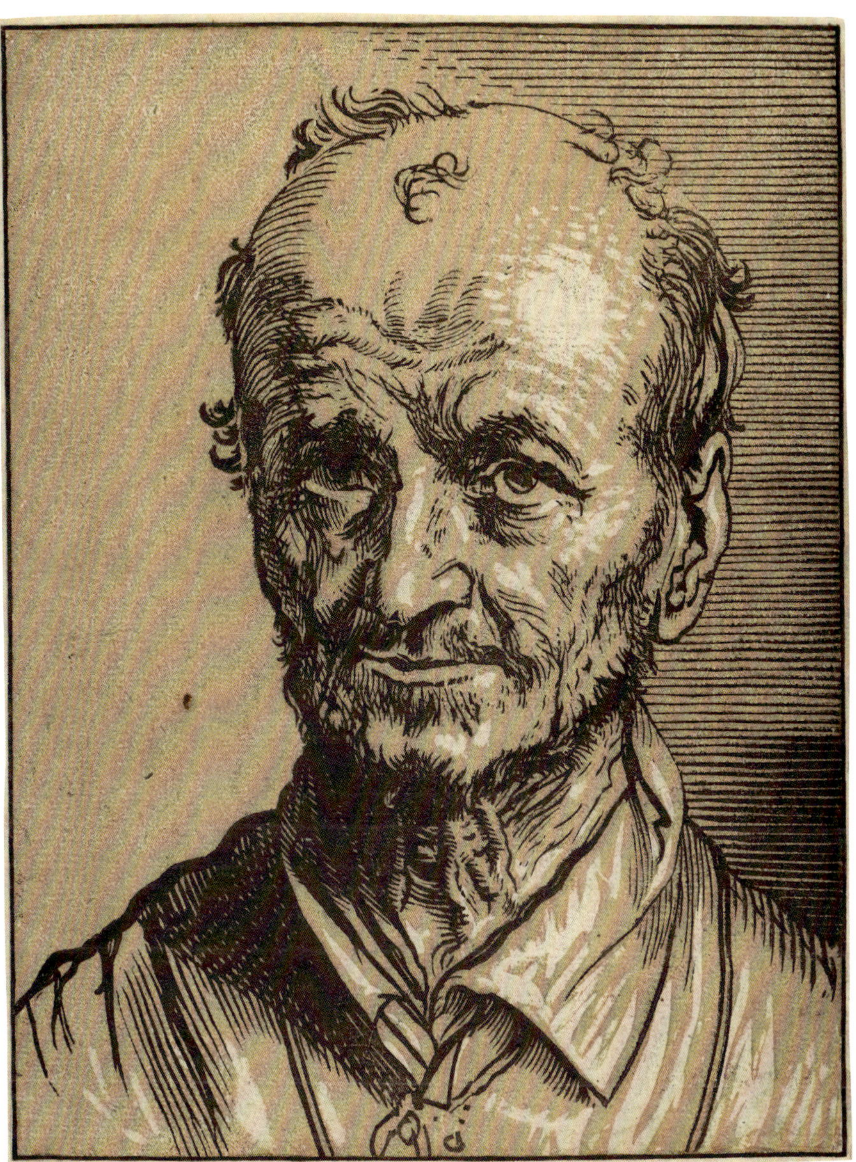

A REMARKABLE INFORMALITY characterizes this likeness of an aging man, his collar caught haphazardly in his simple coat. His sunken cheeks, scruffy beard, and penetrating gaze convey both the specificity of a sketch from life and the symbolic force of a meditation on the effects of privation and old age. This picturesque character study must have found a market among collectors, for many impressions survive.

This is Lievens' only foray into chiaroscuro woodcut, printed with one block for line and another for tone. Specialists in this technique sometimes used two or three color blocks to create tonal effects in imitation of painting, but Lievens' approach here is relatively simple, still relying primarily on the descriptive power of line.[1] The ocher color of the tone block varies slightly among impressions, as do the highlights where the white of the paper shows through. This suggests that Lievens continued to experiment with the effect of color as he pulled different proofs from the press. The handling of the line block displays Lievens' characteristic combination of angular hatching for the costume with more varied, evocative strokes to define the head and facial features. The horizontal patterning in the right background shows awareness of conventional methods for modulating shadow.

An impression in the British Museum bears an inscription in ink that has been read as "Ioannes Liuiyus pinxit" and "francisc. duSart sculp." This notation led Daniel Daulby to list the print in 1796 as a copy by one F. DuSart after Lievens, and later prompted Hind to suggest that the Flemish sculptor François Dieussart cut Lievens' woodblocks for him.[2] But Dieussart, an internationally successful sculptor in stone, is otherwise unknown as a woodcutter. Moreover, he traveled widely, and there is no possibility that he and Lievens could have met until after 1645.[3] By then, Lievens was in Amsterdam and had little time or opportunity for printmaking. Only a few etchings, all formal portraits, can securely be dated to the last phase of his career (see cats. 85–87). SSD

85 Portrait of Joost van den Vondel

1644–1650, etching and engraving, 32.2 × 24.6 (12⅝ × 9⅝)

state 2 (of 7), landscape background added with black chalk, inscribed in lower margin by a later hand. The British Museum, London (1853.3.12.225/PPA 127183) *(Washington, Amsterdam)*

state 5 (of 7). Frits Lugt Collection, Institut Néerlandais, Paris (1454) *(Washington, Amsterdam)*

Inscription

Bottom (state 5): *Agrippina parens ortum, pater Amstela sedem,* VONDELIO *famam Belgica Musa dedit, Priscaque Relligio, custos et nuncia veri, / Pandit iter,* JUSTUS *quo petit astra senex.* Signed *Prudenter*

Selected References

Holl. 21. Muller 1853, 5774; Van Someren 1888, 3, 662 (3938); Schneider/Ekkart 1973, 79, 84, 267; Braunschweig 1979, no. 119; Amsterdam 1988, no. 47; Dickey 2004, 61, 104, 135–136

JOOST VAN DEN VONDEL (1587–1679) was Holland's most renowned poet and playwright, author of dramas that drew crowds to the Amsterdam Schouwburgh as well as numerous verses honoring his many friends among the humanists and art collectors of the city. The Latin quatrain inscribed on Lievens' portrait was composed by Vondel himself, under the pseudonym Prudenter, and it encapsulates his life story.[1] He was born in Cologne, where his Mennonite parents had fled from Catholic Flanders. The family moved to Utrecht and then to Amsterdam, where Vondel spent his adult life. Around 1641 he converted to Roman Catholicism.

Vondel posed for several paintings and at least four portrait prints, including an engraving by Theodor Matham after Joachim von Sandrart and etchings by Jan Lutma the Younger and Cornelis Visscher as well as Lievens.[2] Some of these likenesses were in turn copied for use as book illustrations. A reduced copy of Lievens' portrait formed the frontispiece for an edition of Vondel's collected poetry published in 1650. This gives us a *terminus ante quem* for Lievens' etching. In another poem published with the frontispiece, Vondel compares Lievens to Titian and praises the artist's ability to suggest, through the gravity of Vondel's demeanor, the heroic content of the dramas he composed.[3]

Lievens portrayed Vondel several times and must have met the celebrated poet through mutual acquaintances in the circle of literati that included Rembrandt's patron Jan Six. His drawing of the rival dramatist Jan Vos (cat. 118) also resulted from his contacts in this milieu, but was never translated into print. The inscrip-

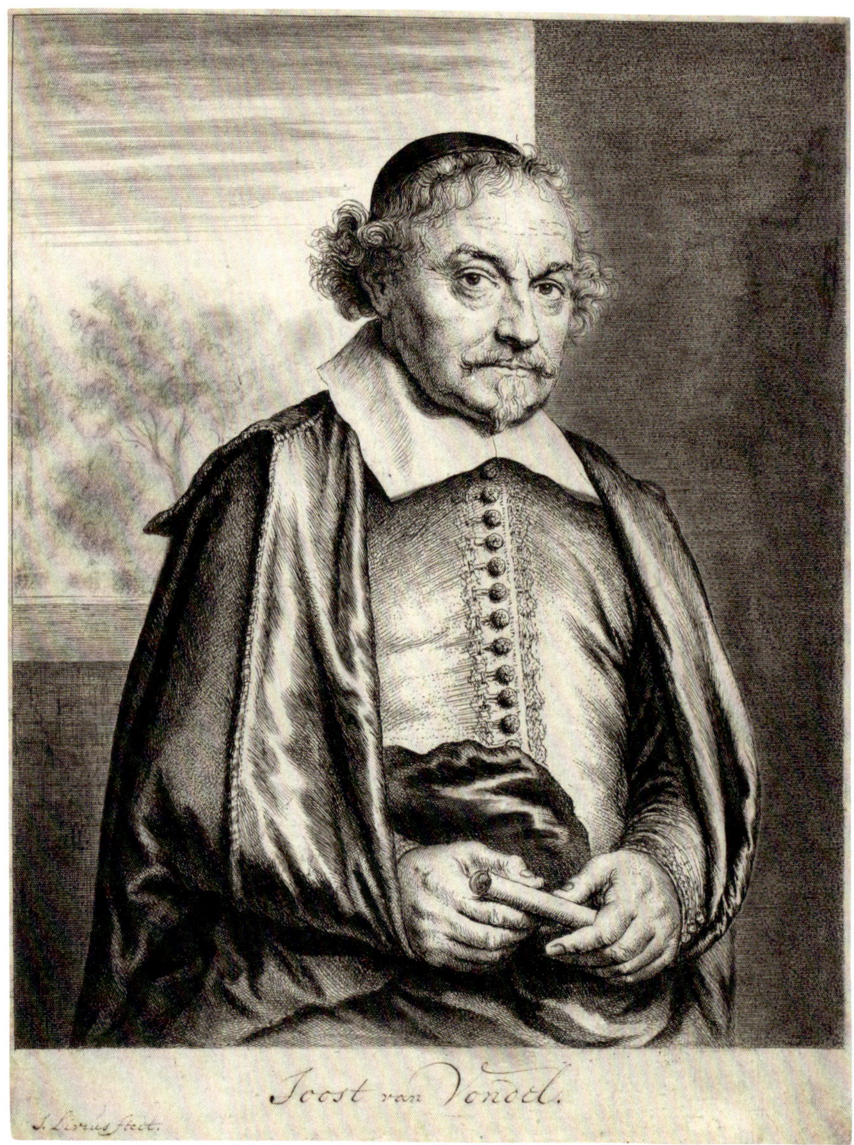

STATE 2

tion, "J. Livius delineavit," suggests that the etching of Vondel was also based on a drawing, but no trace of it survives.

Lievens' print eventually served a commercial purpose, passing through the hands of the publisher Adriaen de Wees and Theodor Matham before it was reprinted in the eighteenth century. The composition was complete in the fourth state, however, before the address of De Wees was added, and Lievens may have distributed preliminary impressions himself. The inscription targets an audience of Vondel's friends and fellow humanists: the viewer must infer the identity of the sitter by reading the Latin quatrain or by recognizing a familiar face.

In the first state Lievens begins with an airy sketch of the figure against a blank background, similar to his chalk drawings (see cat. 103).[4] He gives acute attention to the head, capturing the poet's alert expression and the unruly wisps of hair that emerge from beneath his cap. The scroll of paper in his hand alludes to his status as an author. In the next two states form and shading are refined, and an architectural frame anchors the figure in space. The sober, erect pose and the coloristic treatment of drapery recall Lievens' *Portrait of Daniel Heinsius* (cat. 79). But here Lievens adds a background feature more like that in his *Portrait of Jacques Gaultier* (cat. 75). Visible to the left is a stand of trees beneath a sky streaked with cloud. Although the format was already familiar, he took the trouble to work out details of the setting in black chalk on an impression of the second state, exhibited here for the

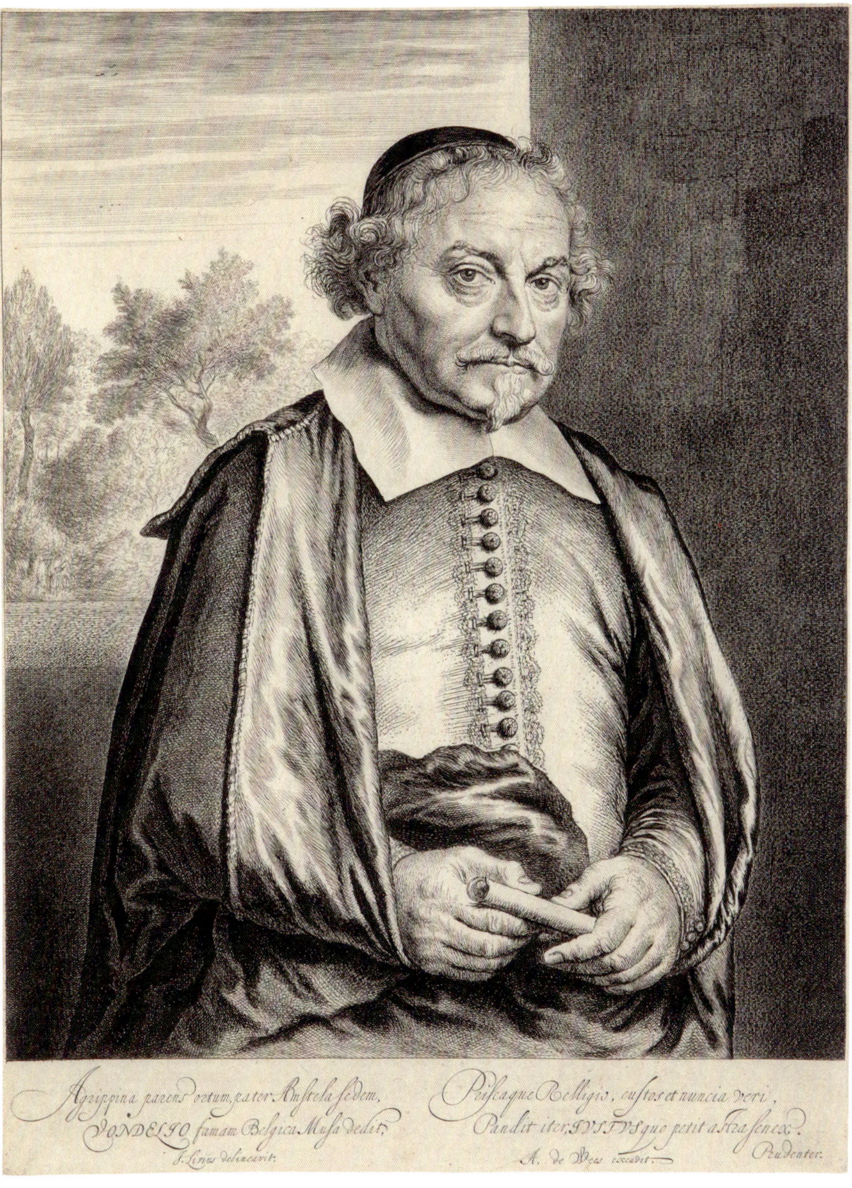

STATE 5

first time. This touched proof exemplifies Lievens' use of methods employed by printmakers working on Van Dyck's *Iconography*.[5] It also provides an important clue for the authentication of landscape drawings produced during his Amsterdam period. SSD

86 Portrait of Caspar Streso

1654–1655, etching and engraving, 29 × 24.5 (11 7/16 × 9 5/8)

state 1 (of 3), touched with black chalk. Rijksmuseum, Amsterdam (RP-P-OB12.598) *(Washington, Milwaukee)*

state 2 (of 3), with inscription in pencil by a later hand. Frits Lugt Collection, Institut Néerlandais, Paris (1965) *(Amsterdam)*

Selected References

Holl. 24. Van Someren 1888–1891, 5380; Schneider/Ekkart 1973, 79, 84, 270; Braunschweig 1979, no. 120; Amsterdam 1988, no. 48

IN 1654–1658 JAN LIEVENS WAS living in The Hague, and it must have been then that he etched this portrait of the distinguished Reformed pastor Caspar Streso (1603–1664). Originally from Anhalt, Streso had been a student at the seminary run by the Dutch Calvinist church at Austin Friars in London in the early 1630s; in 1638 he took up the post of preacher to the Reformed congregation in The Hague.[1] Lievens and Streso may have met as young expatriates in London, but it is more likely that Constantijn Huygens introduced them in The Hague.

Lievens prepared for this portrait with a drawing in black chalk, presumably sketched from life (cat. 113). The outlines of the drawing have been traced with a stylus to transfer the design to the copperplate. In the etching, however, we see more of Streso's figure and a table beside him. Lievens took care with these details, especially the long slender fingers of the hand resting on a book, where the fourth finger and pinky have clearly been redrawn. In the impression of the first state shown here, corrections in black chalk are visible in several areas, including the chair back, coat sleeve, Streso's mouth, and his curling hair.

In the second state the contour of the sleeve and the shading at left have been intensified so that the figure projects more forcefully in space. But the background remains blank, and the print retains the freshness of a sketch from life. (Compare, for instance, cat. 85, where the artist used a touched proof to develop an architectural backdrop for the figure.) Lievens' etching style is also freer and more economical here than in his other portraits, such as *Daniel Heinsius* (cat. 79). Long, parallel diagonal strokes define the folds of Streso's costume, allowing the white of the paper to shine through, while delicate stipples describe the play of light on the preacher's face. It took a certain audacity to present such an unconventional likeness, especially since Streso was well known for his conservative views.

The book on the table would be an appropriate attribute for any theologian, but it most likely alludes to Streso's status as the respected author of many religious tracts, several of which were published in the 1650s. In an address to the Great Assembly of the States General, held in The Hague in 1651, he expressed regret that the proliferation of alternative beliefs prevented the Reformed faith from gaining universal acceptance in the Netherlands.[2] In 1656 he published a treatise arguing against the rationalistic ideas of René Descartes.[3] It is therefore intriguing

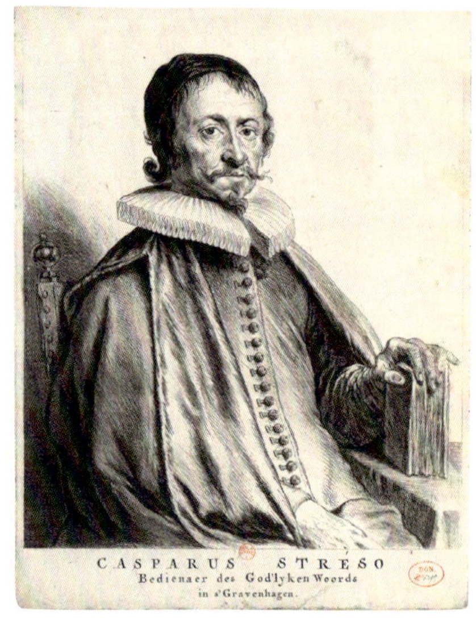

1 | Jan Lievens, *Portrait of Caspar Streso*, state 3, with caption in lower margin. Bibliothèque Nationale de France, Paris

that he should be portrayed by Lievens (probably a Catholic), who had served the Jesuits in Antwerp and drawn a portrait of Descartes before the philosopher left the Netherlands in 1649 (cat. 112). The commission is an indication that in the Dutch Republic, artistic excellence superseded political or religious affiliation.

Preachers were frequent subjects for portrait prints, which could be given or sold to colleagues, collectors, and faithful followers. Yet this etching is quite rare. It remained unsigned and uninscribed, and there is no trace of a publisher's intervention. This may be because the copperplate was handed over to the man portrayed, a frequent practice with private portrait commissions that allowed the sitter to control distribution of his own likeness. The informal quality of the image would have appealed to connoisseurs — or intimates who recognized Caspar Streso even without a label — more than to collectors of standard clerical portraits. But a newly discovered third state published here shows that someone eventually chose to complete the plate with an identifying inscription (fig. 1). Details of the background and costume have been strengthened with engraving to produce a more finished look. A touched proof of the second state in the British Museum, marked in many passages with black chalk to enhance shadows, may have been made in preparation for this.[4] The inscription on the third state identifies Streso and acknowledges his role as preacher in The Hague. Written in Dutch, this caption was not intended to appeal to the international collectors' market, but more likely to members of the Reformed faith who admired Streso as a spiritual leader. SSD

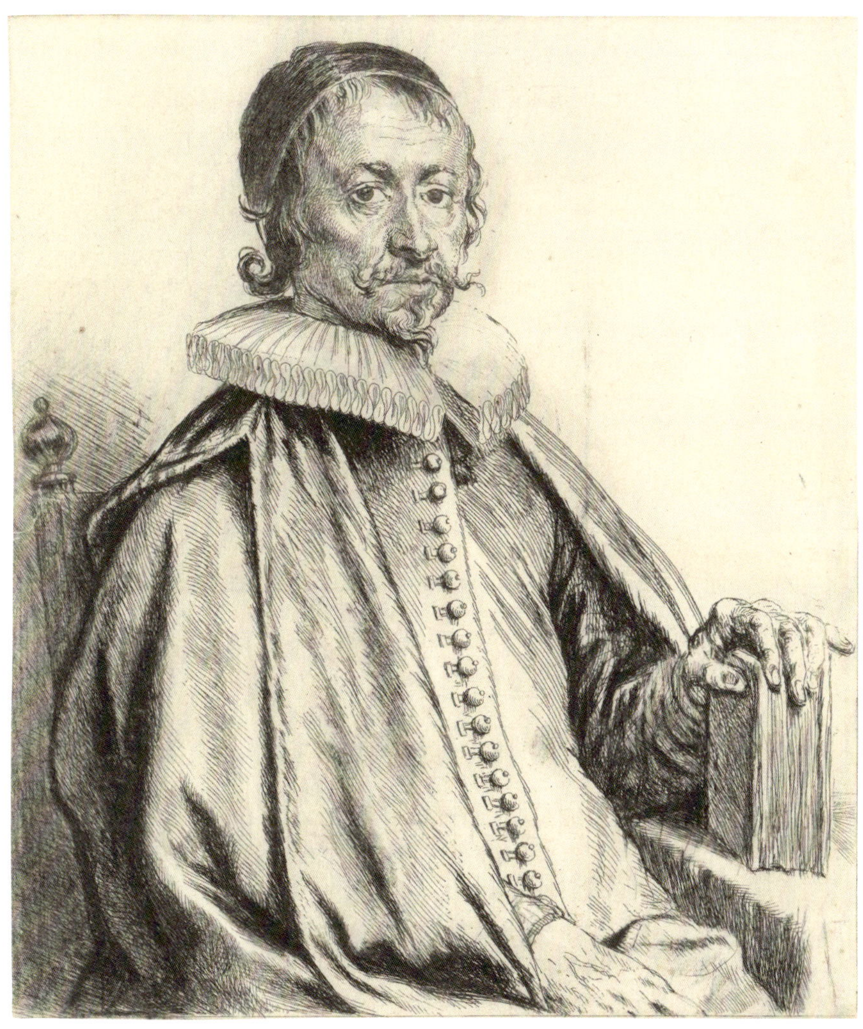

STATE 1

87 Portrait of Ephraim Bueno

c. 1656, etching and engraving, 34 × 26.2 (13 3/8 × 10 5/16)

state 5 (of 8). National Gallery of Art, Washington, Ailsa Mellon Bruce Fund (2005.18.1) *(Washington, Milwaukee)*

state 5 (of 8). Museum Boijmans Van Beuningen, Rotterdam (BDH 10391) *(Amsterdam)*

Inscription

D.OR EPHRAIM BONVS. MEDICVS HEBRAEUS

Bottom: *Alter Avenzooar grandi sub judice, magnus in medicis, magni discipulus que patris.*

Selected References

Holl. 20. Linck 1859, 279; Köhne 1932, 57, 69; Schneider/Ekkart 1973, 79, 84, 195 (Z52), 266; Amsterdam 1986, no. 36; White 1999, 144, 146; Paris 2007, no. 92

SINCE GERSAINT FIRST LISTED IT in 1752, this portrait has been recognized as a work of refined quality. It is almost certainly the last print Lievens made, and it represents the culmination of a stylistic development that led from early experiments in expressive sketchiness, pursued in competition with Rembrandt, to the mastery of accomplished techniques perfected by printmakers in the circle of Anthony van Dyck. Ironically, this project brought Lievens back into comparison with Rembrandt, who had etched a portrait of the same person in 1647 (fig. 1).

Ephraim Hezekiah Bueno (or Bonus) (1599–1665) was the son of a renowned Sephardic Jewish physician who had tended Prince Maurits on his deathbed. Bueno was born in northern Portugal, and the Latin inscription compares him with Avenzoar (Ibn Zuhr, 1091–1161), a legendary Arabian physician from Andalusia. Bueno followed his father's profession but also played an important role in the intellectual life of Amsterdam through his poetic writings, translations, and support of publications by fellow Hebraic scholars such as Menasseh ben Israel.[1]

With his silvery hair and heavy face, Bueno looks distinctly older here than in Rembrandt's etching. In the 1650s Bueno became a citizen of Amsterdam and published several books, including a Spanish

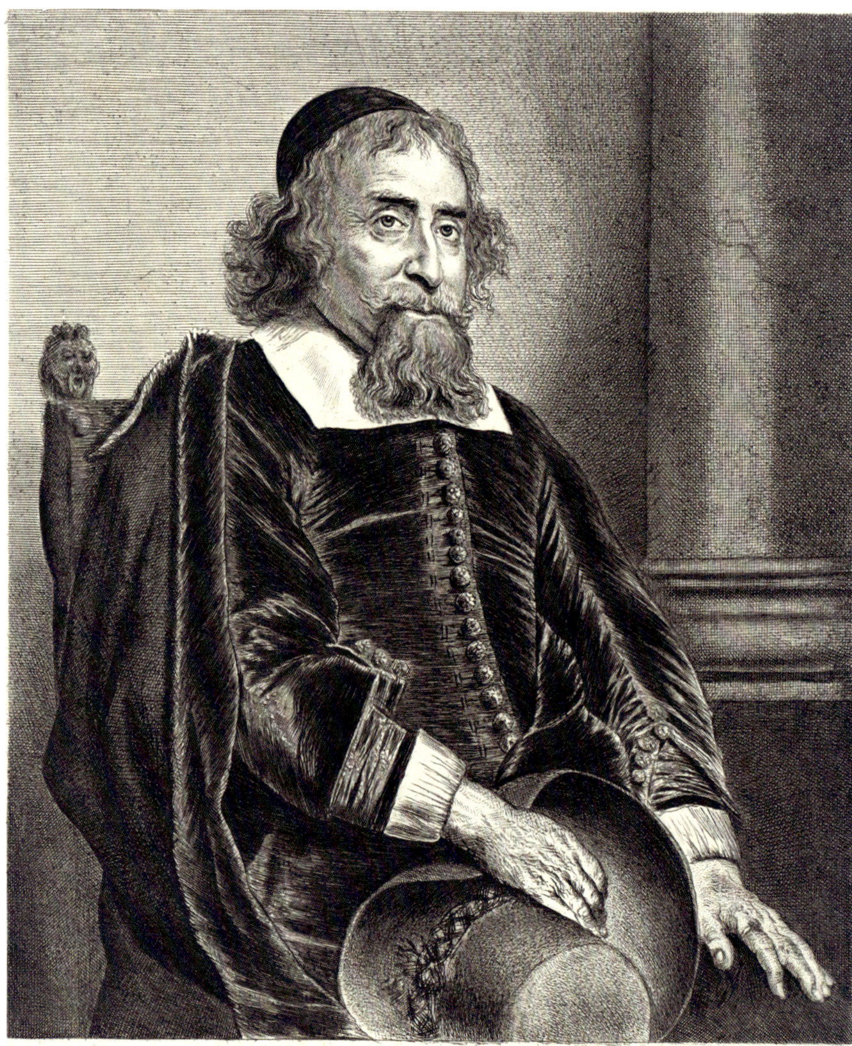

D.OR EPHRAIM BONVS, MEDICVS HEBRÆVS
Alter Avenzoar grandi sub judice, magnus in medicis, magni discipulus que patris.

Ioannes Livyus fecit

translation of the Psalms (1650), but it seems most likely that the portrait honors him as cofounder of the scholarly society Torah Or ("Law is Light"), established in 1656.[2] The formulaic staging of the portrait, with seated pose and grand architectural setting, could apply to any distinguished humanist. Bueno wears a cap similar to a scholar's *calotte*, but it is a *kippah*, the traditional head covering of devout Jewish men.[3]

Despite its sober, formal character, this was probably a private commission rather than a commercial undertaking. Not until the sixth state do we find the address of a publisher, Clement de Jonghe; the plate was later acquired by Johannes de Ram. Lievens might have cooperated with De Jonghe, as he had with Antwerp publishers, but there are numerous impressions of earlier states, indicating that the print was circulated before De Jonghe took over the plate.[4]

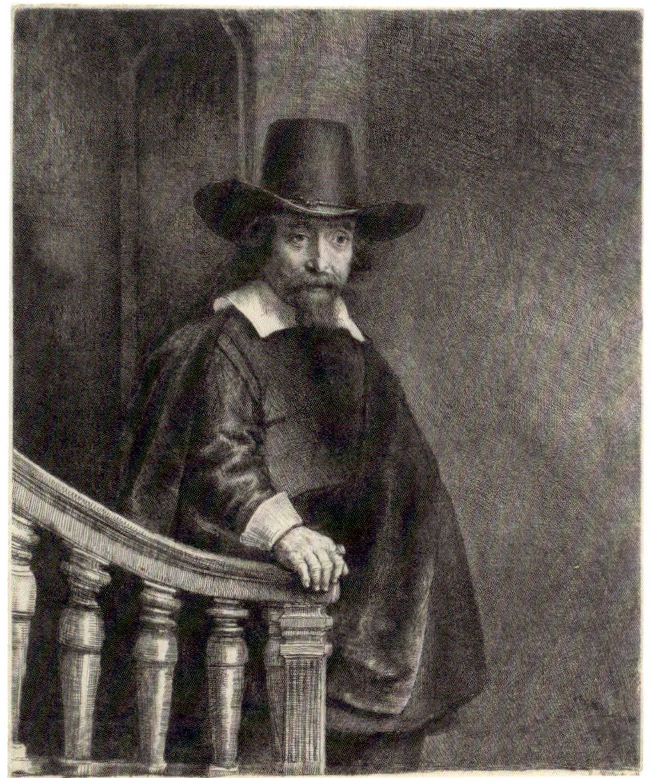

1 | Rembrandt van Rijn, *Portrait of Ephraim Bueno*, 1647, etching. Rijksmuseum, Amsterdam

Comparison with Rembrandt's etching shows how much their stylistic paths had diverged since 1630. Lievens' approach is more conventional in both style and content, but endows the figure with greater dignity and elegance. These were exactly the qualities, perfected in London and Antwerp, that brought him success with Amsterdam patrons in the classicizing climate of the 1650s. He renders the velvety black of Bueno's costume with greater assurance than in his earlier portraits of Jacques Gaultier and Daniel Heinsius (cats. 75, 79), using close parallel strokes in place of Rembrandt's modulated cross-hatching. He emphasizes Bueno's imposing presence with a low vantage point and captures his sitter in an attitude of cool attentiveness. The details of face and figure are sharply observed, while the geometric rendering of background elements is refined but somewhat mechanical, possibly completed with professional assistance. At this point in his career, Lievens was more occupied with major commissions for paintings. For prestigious acquaintances, he preferred to make portraits in chalk (cats. 117, 118). SSD

88 The Stoning of Saint Paul at Lystra

c. 1621–1623, pen and brown ink with brown wash, heightened with white gouache, over black chalk, 24 × 31 (9 7/16 × 12 3/16). The British Museum, London (SL 5236-124) *(Washington, Milwaukee)*

Provenance

Sir Hans Sloane (L.1363)

Selected References

Schneider/Ekkart 1973, 128, no. SZ410; Braunschweig 1979, no. 50; Sumowski 1979, 3612, no. 1622x

THIS DRAMATIC BIBLICAL SCENE must be one of Lievens' earliest drawings, clearly reflecting the handling and compositional approach of his teacher Pieter Lastman and the style of other so-called "pre-Rembrandtists," notably Claes Cornelisz Moeyaert. Indeed, Moeyaert was one of the two artists to whom the drawing was formerly attributed (the other being engraver Jan van Vliet).

The attribution to Lievens was first proposed by Kurt Bauch in 1939,[1] and although Gerson thought that the drawing might in fact be by Rembrandt, all other more recent scholars concur with Bauch.[2] The association with Rembrandt is understandable, for one of his early paintings, now in Lyons, depicts the same subject.[3] But Lievens and Rembrandt often shared common themes in their Leiden period works, and on stylistic grounds, the present drawing appears to predate Rembrandt's painting; the latter is dated 1625, but this drawing cannot have been made long after 1620, when Lievens returned to Leiden, following his training with Lastman.

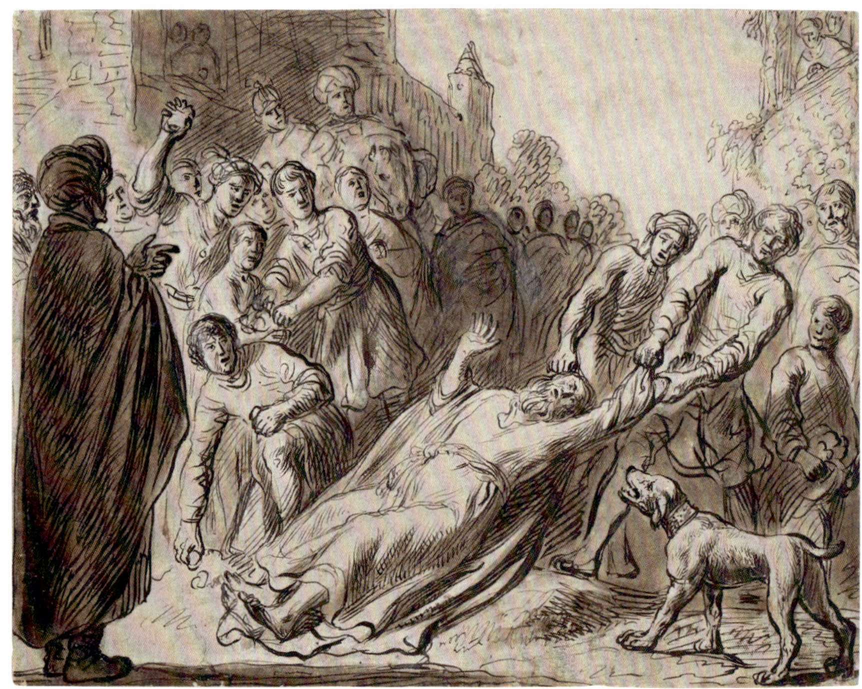

In conception, this powerful composition is entirely in keeping with the youthful Lievens' ambitions as a history painter, although it is not clear whether it was specifically made as a study for a painting. The intriguing possibility does exist that it was originally one of a series of drawings illustrating the story of the apostles: ten such drawings were listed in the catalogue of the 1732 sale of the collection of Lambert Hermansz ten Kate, a merchant, Baptist theological writer, and collector.[4] Because those drawings can no longer be identified, however, their attribution and possible connection with the drawing seen here cannot be verified. GMGR

89 Mercury Lulls Argus to Sleep with His Pipe

c. 1623–1625, pen and brown ink, heightened with white gouache, 20 × 16.7 (7⅞ × 6⁹⁄₁₆). Kupferstich-Kabinett, Staatliche Kunstsammlungen Dresden (C1980-465) *(Washington, Milwaukee)*

Inscriptions

Left center in ink: IL

Top left, in ink, by another hand: *Jan Lievert / principal*

Verso: *Jan Lieverz / principael*

Provenance

Probably acquired for the Royal Collection of Saxony from M.G. Wiedemann, Leipzig, in 1723

Selected References

Heuscher 1738, 83; Schneider/Ekkart 1973, 19, 190, 262, no. z26; Sumowski 1979, 3544, no. 1588; Amsterdam 1988, no. 1; Leiden 1991, no. 16

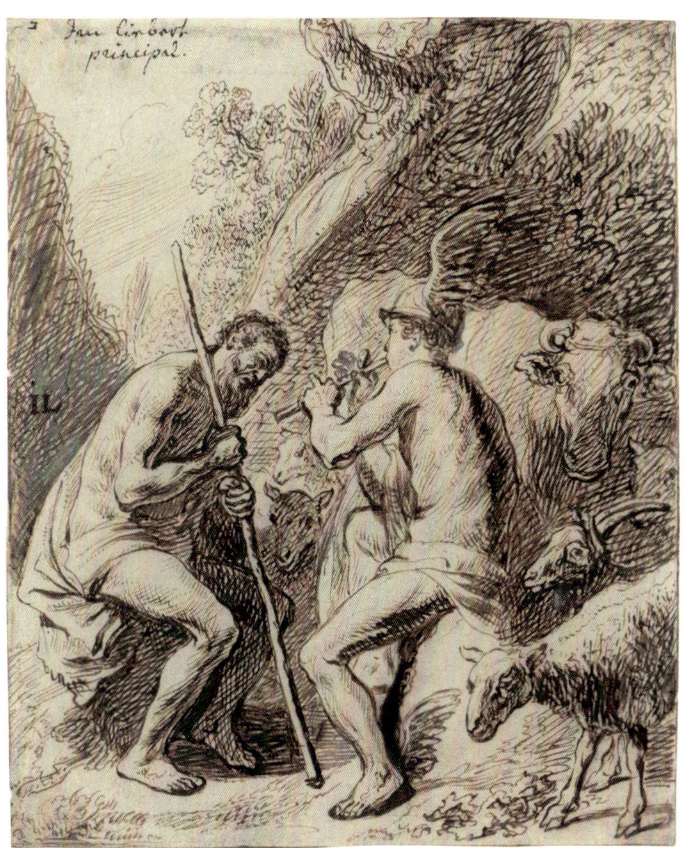

THOUGH NOT OBVIOUSLY INDENTED for transfer to a copperplate,[1] this is the preparatory drawing for one of a small group of stylistically similar prints that are Lievens' earliest etchings (cat. 58); the prints are traditionally dated c. 1625–1626. The pen work here is slightly more elegant than in the previous drawing, and the composition more sophisticated, but the stylistic debt to Lastman and Moeyaert remains pronounced. As Peter Schatborn has noted, there are close parallels with Lastman's pen style in particular, as seen in the small portrait of Nicolaes Lastman, drawn in 1613.[2] Thematically, there is also a clear link with the work of Abraham Bloemaert and his Utrecht contemporaries and pupils, who often painted similar mythological subjects, and this combination of influences suggests that the drawing could easily have been executed slightly earlier than the traditional dating given to the prints.

In the strong outlines and distinctive facial types, this drawing is rather similar to *The Stoning of Saint Paul* (cat. 88), but in other respects the technique is different: there Lievens used a combination of pen and wash, whereas here he has used pen alone to construct all of the tones and shadows. The drawing is densely worked with a combination of cross-hatchings and swirling, repeated strokes, which are closely followed in the etching; indeed, Lievens may well have used this distinctive and powerful pen technique precisely because the drawing was made as a design for the linear medium of etching. In some later designs for prints (see cats. 83, 107) the correspondence between print and drawing is less precise—as is the drawing technique itself—but here, at the very outset of his career as a printmaker, Lievens clearly felt it necessary to leave no room for doubt.

The use of pen alone, with only a small amount of white heightening, is unusual among Lievens' early drawings.[3] In the great majority of sheets from the 1620s, such as the following large-scale figural drawings (cats. 90–94), the pen was just one of the tools that the artist used to create works on paper, and it was combined with different colors and shades of wash and chalk. Yet later in his career Lievens often made drawings exclusively in pen and ink. Hardly any of his numerous landscapes incorporate wash, and several sheets of figure studies reveal only pen work (see cats. 104, 105, 119, 120), as do occasional compositional drawings such as *A Painter's Studio* (cat. 106).

The subject of this elegant drawing is an episode from Ovid's *Metamorphoses* (1:668–721) relating to one of the many loves of Jupiter. In a jealous rage, Jupiter's wife, Juno, transformed Io, the object of Jupiter's affections, into a white heifer. She placed Argus (described by Ovid as a hundred-eyed giant but usually, as here, depicted as a fairly ordinary shepherd) to guard over the animal. Mercury, sent by Jupiter to release Io, lulls Argus to sleep by playing his pipe, and then kills him. GMGR

90 Mucius Scaevola and Porsenna

c. 1625–1626, pen and brown ink with brown and gray washes, over black chalk, on two joined sheets of paper, 45.5 × 53 (17 15/16 × 20 7/8). Prentenkabinet der Rijksuniversiteit, Leiden (AW 903) *(Amsterdam)*

Provenance

(Probably sale D. Baron van Leyden, Amsterdam, May 13, 1811, portfolio BB, no. 10 ("Historical scene, a very large drawing with pen and washes, by a noble master, F. Bol"); H.W. Campe (L.1391); (sale, Leipzig, C.G. Boerner, May 9–10, 1930, no. 345, "school work in the style of early Rembrandt"); Dr. A. Welcker (L.2793c)

Selected References

Leiden 1948–1949, no. 41 (Lievens); Amsterdam 1956, no. 96 (Rembrandt); Amsterdam and Rotterdam 1956, no. 1 (Rembrandt); Schneider/Ekkart 1973, 384, no. SZ412; Leiden 1976, no. T.14 (attributed to Lievens); Braunschweig 1979, no. 49; Sumowski 1979, 3614, no. 1623ˣ; Amsterdam 1988, no. 6; Leiden 1991, no. 23; Kassel and Amsterdam 2001–2002, no. 15

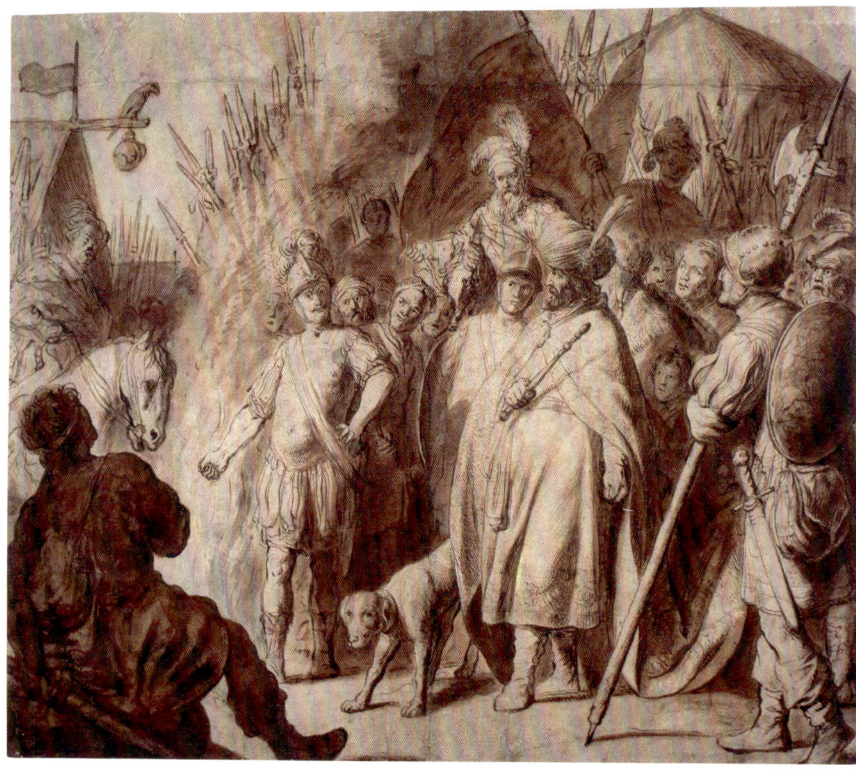

THE SUBJECT DEPICTED HERE, as recounted by Livy and other classical authors, is the episode from Roman history when the Etruscan king Lars Porsenna looks on in some consternation as the Roman noble Caius Mucius, having failed in his attempt to assassinate the king, holds his right hand in the flames of a fire to demonstrate his disregard for his own safety. Porsenna was so impressed that he forgave and freed Mucius, who was known thereafter as Scaevola, which means "left-handed."

This large, impressive drawing represents an important step away from the predominantly linear style of Lievens' very earliest drawings, such as *The Stoning of Saint Paul at Lystra* (cat. 88). Yet here too the basis of the composition is established with a dense network of pen lines, and even more than before, we see a structure of cross-hatching and stippling that is, as Bauch rightly noted, strongly reminiscent of the etchings of Willem Buytewech.[1] We have every reason to believe these prints were well known to the young Lievens, thanks to Jan Jansz Orlers' memorable description of how the ten-year-old artist chose to stay at home copying prints by Buytewech rather than go out into the streets during the Leiden riots of October 1617.[2]

In a departure from the previous two drawings, Lievens has here combined his elaborate structure of pen lines with two colors of wash, applied with the brush in a thoroughly painterly manner. This technique represents the starting point for a whole group of powerfully executed large drawings (including cats. 91–94 as well as other examples in Leipzig, Florence, Paris, and Vienna).[3] All of these drawings have at various times been identified as being by different artists — even *Christ Praying in the Garden of Gethsemane* (cat. 92), which bears an old attribution to Lievens — but are now universally accepted as important early works by Lievens. In the case of the present sheet, the previous attributions have included Jan van Vliet, Ferdinand Bol, and Rembrandt.

In compositional terms, an association with Rembrandt is more comprehensible than for other drawings in this group, which represent relatively large-scale figures, singly or in small groups. *Mucius Scaevola and Porsenna* is the only one with a complex, many-figured design, and there are clear parallels with some of Rembrandt's earliest paintings, notably the 1626 panel depicting an unidentified historical scene, now in Leiden, and the Basel *David with the Head of Goliath before Saul,* painted in the following year.[4] Because Lievens' compositions of this period generally show only a few figures, Sumowski concluded that he must have been influenced here by these Rembrandt paintings, therefore dating the drawing c. 1627.

Strong similarities with other works by Lievens suggest, however, that the drawing must date from slightly earlier — probably c. 1625–1626. The position of Porsenna's left hand, for example, is almost identical to that of Ahasuerus in the Raleigh *Feast of Esther* (cat. 6).[5] Moreover, as Christopher White noted, the face of Mucius Scaevola himself is stylistically similar to that of the saint in Lievens' print *Saint John the Evangelist on Patmos* (cat. 56),[6] providing further support not only for an early dating but also for the attribution. GMGR

91 Trumpeter on Horseback

92 Christ Praying in the Garden of Gethsemane

91

c. 1625–1628, pen and brown ink with gray wash, over black chalk, 28.1 × 22.5 (11 1/16 × 8 7/8). Rijksmuseum, Amsterdam (RP-T-1947-50) *(Washington, Milwaukee)*

Inscription

Upper left, in ink, by a later hand: *Rembrandt / f 1636*

Provenance

E. Calando (L.837)

Selected References

Rome 1951, no. 52 (Rembrandt); Benesch 1954–1957, 1: no. 21a (Rembrandt c. 1627/1628); Amsterdam and Rotterdam 1956, no. 5 (Rembrandt); Leiden 1966–1967, no. T.20 (attributed to Lievens); Schneider/Ekkart 1973, 385, no. SZ415; Sumowski 1979, 3620, no. 1626^{x}; Amsterdam 1988, no. 8; Leiden 1991, no. 22

IN THESE TWO DRAWINGS WE SEE Lievens taking the stylistic innovations of *Mucius Scaevola and Porsenna* (cat. 90) still further, exploring the myriad possibilities that adventurous combinations of media had to offer in the creation of large-scale figure studies. In both cases Lievens loosely sketched the figure in black chalk before working up the composition in pen and brown ink as well as wash in a very free manner, not always following his initial chalk underdrawing. As before, he used a distinctive, rather engraving-like combination of hatching and dots, although in these drawings he has applied these touches not only with the pen but also with the point of the brush. The greatest departure from the previous drawings, though, is in the lighting. Lievens has effectively thrown a powerful spotlight on the figures, and this, together with the free, broad draftsmanship, imbues the images with a new sense of energy and drama.

These compositional and technical developments seem to reflect Lievens' interest in the works of the Utrecht Caravaggisti and are echoed in many of Rembrandt's paintings of the middle to late 1620s. It is not surprising that these two drawings, and several others that are stylistically similar, continued to be attributed to Rembrandt until relatively recently; indeed, *Trumpeter on Horseback* was first attributed to Lievens only in 1956,[1] and it was still listed as a Rembrandt in the 1973 edition of Benesch's corpus of Rembrandt's drawings. The flamboyant draftsmanship seen here is, however, distinctive of Lievens' work, and there are few if any details in Rembrandt's drawings that parallel the elegantly sculpted rump and tail of the horse carrying the trumpeter or the obviously living foliage that seems almost to advance toward the figure of the praying Christ. Correspondences do exist between the poses of the rider in Lievens' drawing and the figure to the left in Rembrandt's 1627 painting *David with the Head of Goliath before Saul*.[2] But this may only signify that Lievens and Rembrandt were influenced by a common source: Lastman's painting of 1625, *Coriolanus Receives the Envoys*, which Rembrandt copied in a drawing in the British Museum.[3] As Schatborn has, however, pointed out, the horsemen in Lastman's and Rembrandt's compositions are not trumpeters, thus Lievens' primary source of inspiration may have been the famous series of prints after Jacques de Gheyn, *Exercises for the Cavalry*.[4]

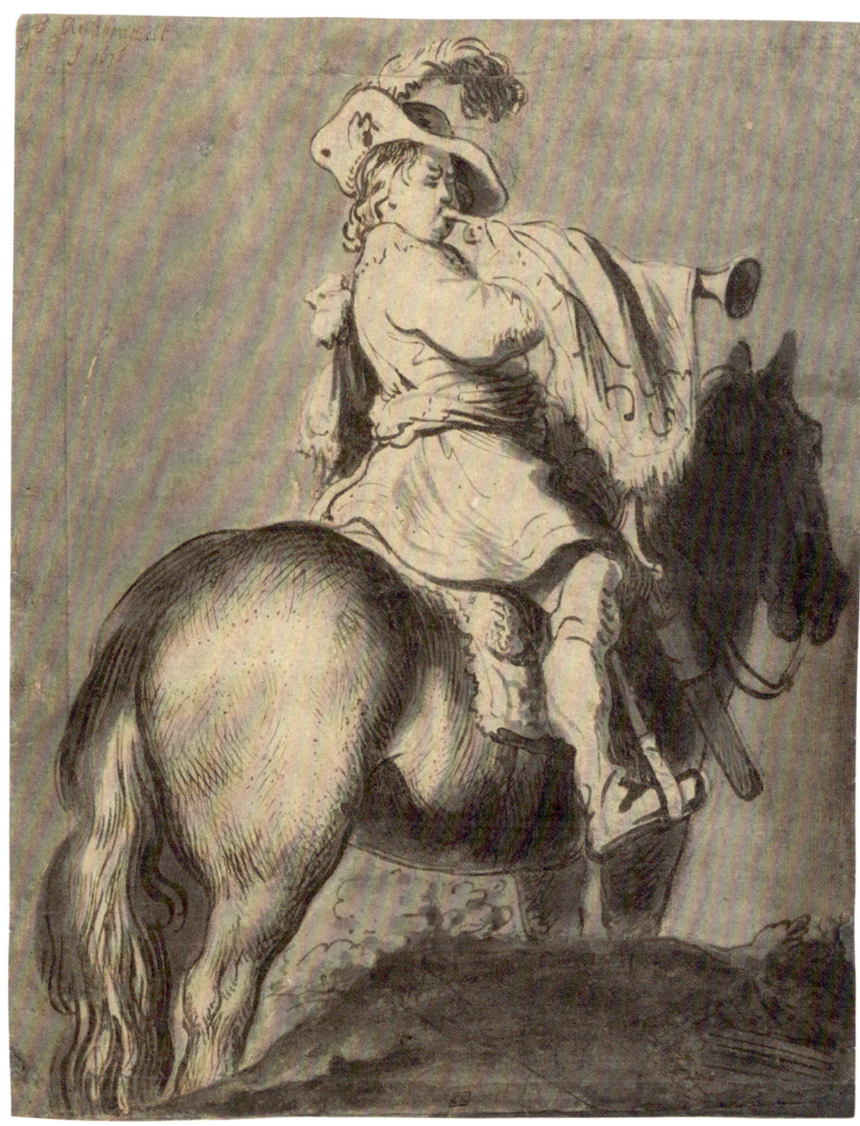

CAT. 91

92

c. 1625–1628, pen and brown ink with gray, black, with brown wash, the upper and lower right corners made up, 32.1 × 21.7 (12 5/8 × 8 9/16). Kupferstich-Kabinett, Staatliche Kunstsammlungen Dresden (C1437) *(Washington, Milwaukee)*

Inscription

Lower right, in ink, by an old hand: *Livens*

Provenance

Probably acquired for the Royal Collection of Saxony from M.G. Wiedemann, Leipzig, in 1723

Selected References

Schneider/Ekkart 1973, 18, 187, 359, no. z8; Sumowski 1979, 3618, no. 1625[x]; Amsterdam 1988, no. 7; Kassel and Amsterdam 2001–2002, no. 23

These two drawings form part of a distinctive series of about ten comparably handled sheets (see under cat. 90), but within this group they and *Old Man Reading* in the Louvre (cat. 94) are the only images of single figures. The others, such as the Dresden *Feast of Esther* (cat. 93), are compositional studies in which several figures interact. Although these highly accomplished and dramatic sketches depict religious or historical subjects, they nonetheless recall in some pictorial respects the Caravaggist single-figure genre scenes and tronies that Lievens, like Rembrandt, was painting at this time. They are also among the artist's most impressive early drawings.

Christ Praying in the Garden of Gethsemane is not listed in the early Dresden inventories, but it probably entered the collection in the early eighteenth century, at the same time as other early Lievens drawings (see cats. 89, 93).[5] Early sale catalogues and inventories suggest that albums of drawings from the studios of seventeenth-century Dutch artists often remained intact for several decades after their deaths — as was the case with the famous group of Rembrandt landscapes at Chatsworth, which had been kept together in the possession of Govaert and Nicolaes Flinck before entering the Devonshire collection *en bloc* in 1723. GMGR

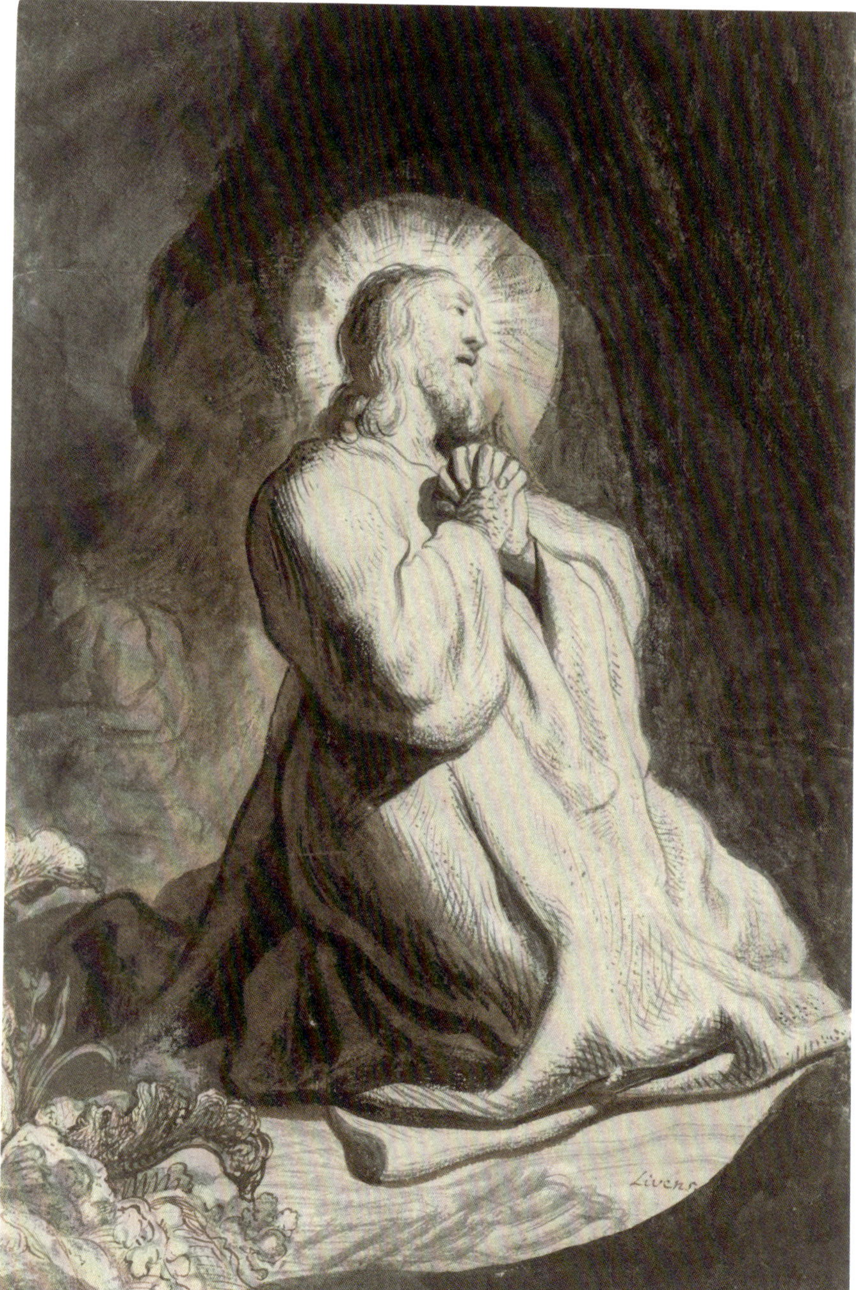

CAT. 92

93 The Feast of Esther

c. 1625–1628, pen and brush with brown and black ink, over black chalk and touches of red chalk, heightened with gray and white gouache, a section of paper replaced by the artist, bottom center, 45 × 56.5 (17 11/16 × 22 1/4). Kupferstich-Kabinett, Staatliche Kunstsammlungen Dresden (c1980-463) *(Washington, Amsterdam)*

Provenance

M.G. Wiedemann, Leipzig; acquired for the Royal Collection of Saxony in 1723

Selected References

Heuscher 1738, 81; Benesch 1954–1957, 1: 15, under no. 51; Schneider/Ekkart 1973, 381, no. sz399; Sumowski 1979, 3628, no. 1630x; Dresden and Paris 2004–2006, no. 47 (Dresden), no. 25 (Paris) (attributed to Lievens)

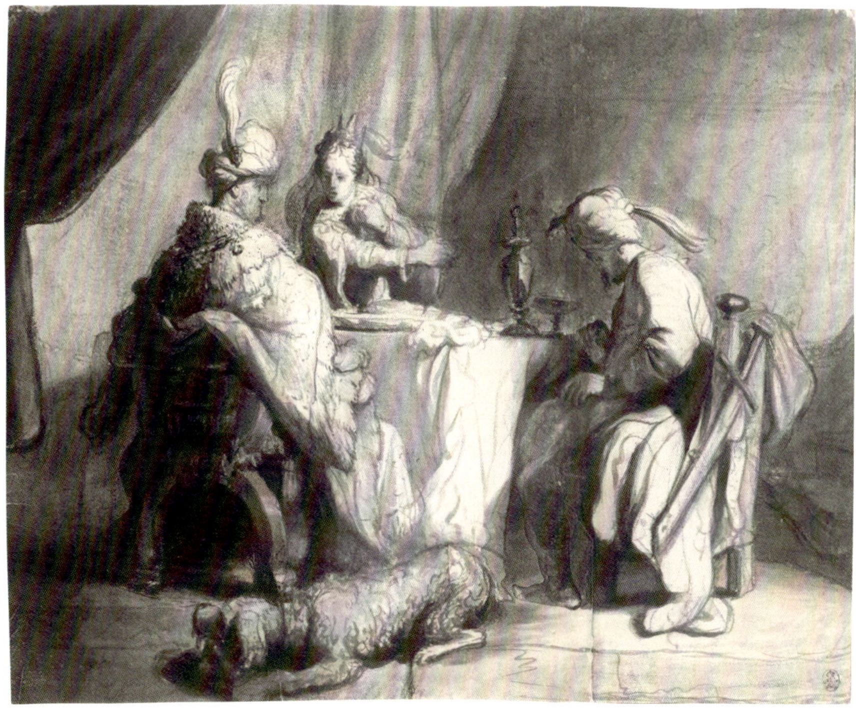

THIS COMPELLING DRAWING, the most monumental of a group of some ten sheets executed in a similar style c. 1625–1628, is particularly close in handling to *Christ Praying in the Garden of Gethsemane* (cat. 92). It is a full compositional study, thematically related to Lievens' important painting in Raleigh (cat. 6). In terms of overall configuration, however, the drawing and the painting differ in fundamental ways. The drawing depicts full-length figures in a clear architectural space, whereas the painting shows half-length figures closer to the picture plane. While the painting reflects the compositional ideas of the Utrecht Caravaggisti, the drawing recalls the tradition of Pieter Lastman (see Wheelock fig. 3).

Although no exact chronology can be established for Lievens' early drawings, it is possible that Lievens was reintroduced to Lastman's ideas when Rembrandt returned from Lastman's studio in 1625 and was painting compositions in which numerous full-length figures interact. It may well be that Lievens made the drawing subsequent to executing the painting of *The Feast of Esther* rather than as a preliminary study for it. Whether the drawing was a spontaneous reworking of the subject of the painting or a reaction to something he saw in the work of Rembrandt, Lievens produced a striking and dynamic image, exercising all his skill as a draftsman. A faint underlying chalk sketch reveals that he had previously placed the figure of Esther more or less equidistant between Ahasuerus and Haman before deciding to heighten the dramatic effect by moving her closer to King Ahasuerus. He also altered the design by cutting out a section of the paper — silhouetting Haman's leg in the process — and replacing it with another piece on which the rear of the poodle is redrawn. This very physical approach to revising a composition is found in a number of Rembrandt drawings, although the most notable examples date from some years later (see the British Museum's *Lamentation at the Foot of the Cross*).[1]

Taking all these factors into account, it is not surprising that this drawing and others like it have only recently come to be widely accepted as the work of Lievens rather than Rembrandt. Lievens' interpretation seems to have struck a chord with several of Rembrandt's pupils: a drawing tentatively attributed to Willem de Poorter repeats the composition with only minor changes, and Jan Victors painted versions of it at least three times.[2] GMGR

94 Old Man Reading

late 1620s, red chalk, pen and black and brown ink, brush and gray and black ink washes, 33.6 × 27.4 (13 ¼ × 10 ¹³⁄₁₆). Musée du Louvre, Paris, Département des Arts Graphiques (22.792) *(Washington)*

Inscription

Lower left corner, in ink: 175

Provenance

Acquired in the late eighteenth century

Selected References

Schneider/Ekkart 1973, 26, 192, no. z43; Braunschweig 1979, no. 52; Sumowski 1979, 3630, no. 1631ˣ

IN ITS INVENTIVE TECHNIQUE, free handling, and compositional power, this drawing resembles other large, early studies by Lievens of single figures, such as the Dresden *Christ Praying in the Garden of Gethsemane* (cat. 92), but the mood here is even more weighty and somber. The combination of extremely sketchy, almost wildly applied red chalk and dense, dark ink washes is comparable with Rembrandt drawings such as *The Apostle Paul,* c. 1629, also in the Louvre.[1] GMGR

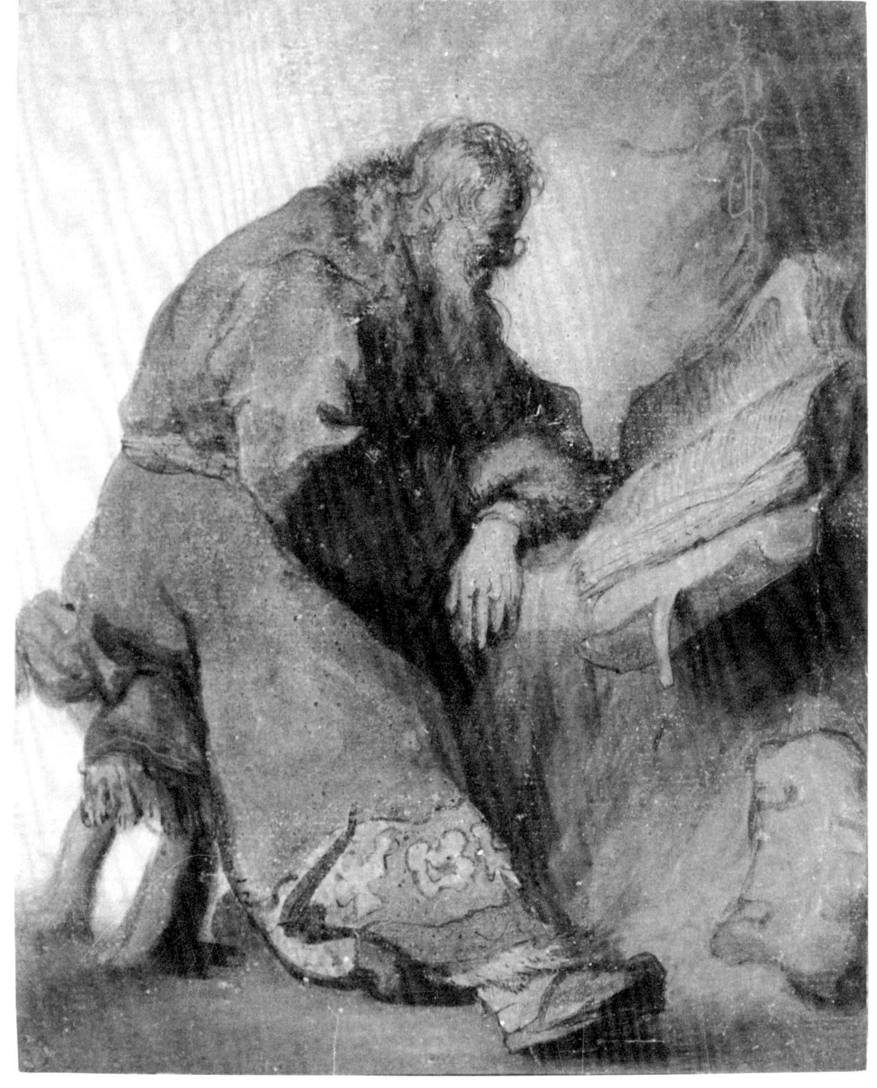

95 Head of an Old Woman ("Rembrandt's Mother")

c. 1627, red and black chalk on yellowish prepared paper, 10.8 × 8.3 (4¼ × 3¼). Private collection *(not in exhibition)*

Provenance

Collection P.H. (L.2086); Eugene Rodriguez; (his sale, F. Muller, Amsterdam, November 21, 1929, no. 17 [N. Maes]); Bernard Houthakker, Amsterdam (L.1272); F.W.A. Knight; (his sale, Sotheby Mak van Waay, Amsterdam, October 29, 1979, no. 25 [N. Maes]); Jacobus A. Klaver, Amsterdam (his mark, not in Lugt, on the mount); (sale, Sotheby's, London, July 9, 2008, no. 27)

Selected References

Amsterdam 1964, no. 57 (N. Maes); Sumowski 1979, 1168, no. 539xx (attributed to Gerard Dou); Amsterdam 1988, no. 11; Leiden 1991, no. 21; Amsterdam 1993, no. 34; Kassel and Amsterdam 2001–2002, no. 20; Leiden 2005, 103, fig. 85

PERHAPS INSPIRED BY THE DRAWINGS of their teacher Pieter Lastman, Rembrandt and Lievens both made a small number of energetic drawings in a combination of red and black chalk, on paper toned with a light yellowish ocher wash—a technique that Lastman used in several figure studies for paintings of the early 1620s.[1] Characterized by firm, rapidly drawn lines, dense shading, and considerable psychological intensity, these drawings by Rembrandt and Lievens form a small but distinctive group.

Even today their attribution remains a subject for debate, with the exception of *Seated Old Man with a Book* in Berlin (fig. 1),[2] on which Rembrandt based one of the figures in his 1627 painting *Saint Peter and Saint Paul*.[3] The present study of an old woman is strikingly close in handling to the Rembrandt drawing in Berlin, as is a comparable *Bust of an Old Man*.[4] But Benesch, Schatborn, and others have argued that the strong contours and the network of fine lines in the woman's hair and face are typical of drawings by Lievens.[5] While such arguments are compelling, this drawing remains among the most difficult to assign with certainty to one or the other of these two artists. They all must have been done c. 1627, about the same time as the painting by Rembrandt for which the Berlin drawing is a study.

The sitter for this drawing is the old woman traditionally known as "Rembrandt's mother."[6] Here, as in almost all representations of this woman, she is depicted in exotic costume, and the image can be considered as much a character head or tronie as a portrait.[7] GMGR

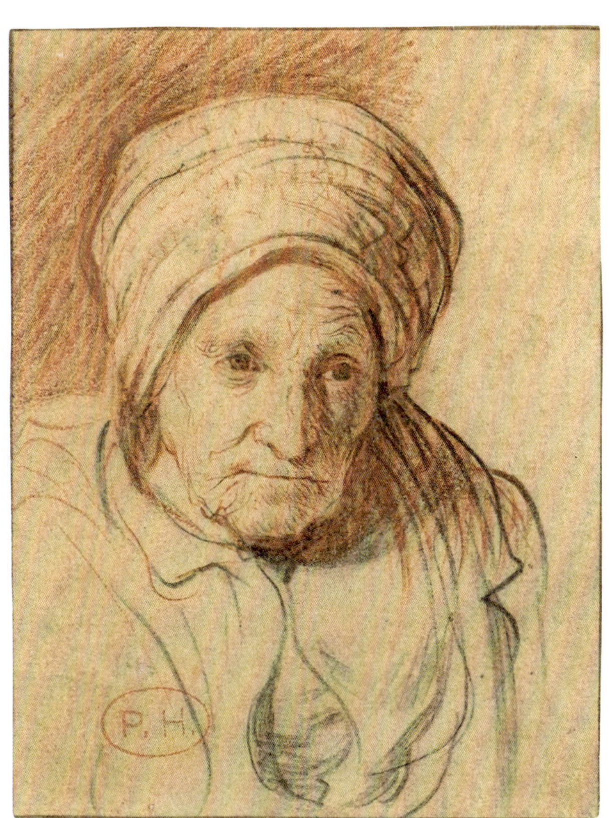

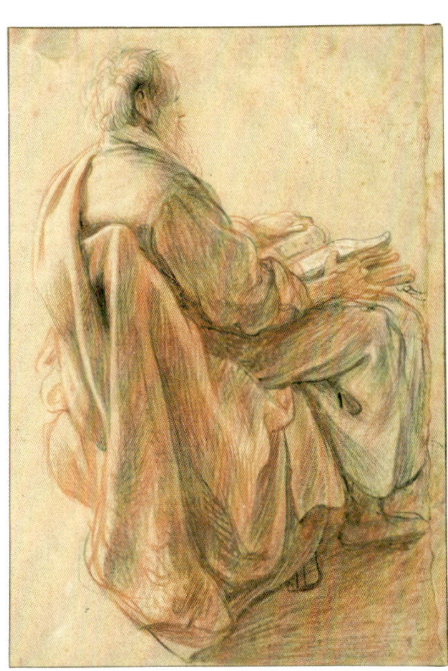

1 | Rembrandt van Rijn, *Seated Old Man with a Book*, c. 1627, red and black chalk. Staatliche Museen zu Berlin, Kupferstichkabinett

96 Old Woman in Half-Length Profile, Facing Left

c. 1628–1630, pen and brown ink with touches of gray wash, over traces of black chalk, 14.7 × 13.2 (5 13/16 × 5 3/16). Maida and George Abrams Collection, Boston, Massachusetts, on loan to Fogg Art Museum, Harvard University (25.1998.43) *(Washington, Milwaukee)*

Inscriptions

Lower right, in pen and brown ink: 9-

Upper right, in pencil, by a later hand: *Rem*

Verso, in pencil: *1256;* and *Rembrandt f.*

Provenance

Lord Nathan of Churt; (Faerber & Maison, Ltd., London); acquired in 1966

Selected References

Hanover, Wellesley, Providence, Storrs 1969, no. 2; Sumowski 1979, 3654, no. 1639x; Amsterdam 1988, no. 9; George R. Goldner, *European Drawings*, vol. 1, *Catalogue of the Collections: The J. Paul Getty Museum, Malibu, California* (Malibu, 1988), 254–255; Leiden 1991, no. 17; Amsterdam, Vienna, New York, Cambridge, MA, 1991–1992, no. 43; Kassel and Amsterdam 2001–2002, no. 21

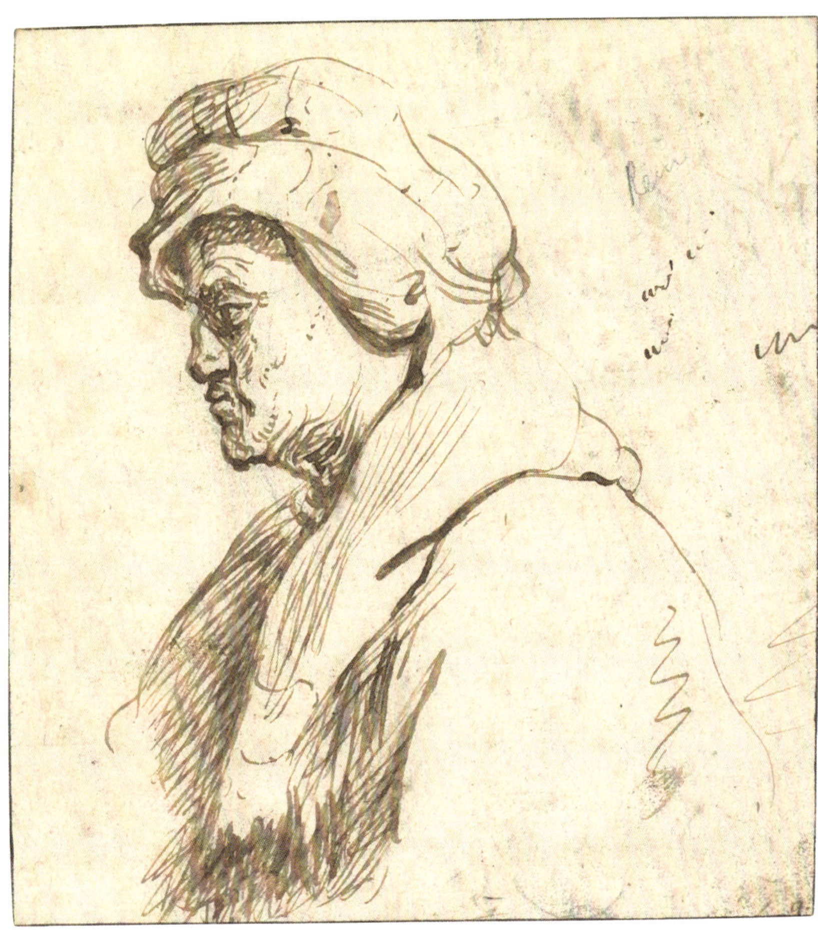

FRANKLIN ROBINSON, WHO FIRST published this drawing as Lievens in the 1969 Abrams Collection exhibition catalogue, dated it c. 1629–1630 on the basis of comparison with *Diverse Tronikens*, a set of expressive etchings of exotic figures, shown bust-length and in profile, which Lievens executed c. 1630 (see cats. 63–66).[1] This dating was revised by Peter Schatborn, who proposed that the drawing must have been made about the same time as one by Rembrandt, *Old Woman Seen from the Front*,[2] which is generally dated to 1628. The hatchings and overall use of the pen are indeed very similar in these two drawings, but the present work exhibits a greater fluidity of line. In that respect, it is closer to another drawing by Rembrandt of the same period, *Beggar Couple with a Dog*, formerly in the Koenigs Collection.[3]

Perhaps closest of all in style to the Abrams drawing is another fine half-length study of a woman in profile, which Sumowski associated with Lievens' Antwerp period, but which must in fact be an earlier work, also from about 1628.[4] Both drawings are strikingly similar in conception to certain Lievens prints, notably *Young Woman in a Cap* (cat. 60),[5] and there are definite links in draftsmanship with early pen drawings by the artist such as *Mercury Lulls Argus to Sleep* (cat. 89).

In this outstanding drawing of an old woman we see — more perhaps than in any other drawing by Lievens — his absolute mastery of the pen. With its highly expressive, fluid, yet powerful handling and bold composition, the drawing can be seen as carrying on the tradition of spectacular pen drawings of genre subjects established some years earlier by Hendrick Goltzius and continued by other Haarlem artists such as Jacob Matham. GMGR

97 Moorish Man with Turban in Half-Length

Attributed to Jan Lievens

c. 1627–1629, red and black chalk, 19.2 × 14.8 (7 9/16 × 5 13/16). Private collection, The Netherlands *(Washington, Amsterdam)*

Inscriptions

Verso: *Rembrandt*; and various collectors' numbers: *8 / 39* [Röver], and N2919 [Goll van Franckenstein]

Provenance

Valerius Röver (MS, Amsterdam University Library, portfolio 8, no. 39: Rembrandt, *Een Persiaan met een tulband, met rood en zwart krijt*); Jhr. Johann Goll van Franckenstein; (his sale, Amsterdam, July 1, 1833, no. F9); I. van Idsinga; (his sale, Amsterdam, November 2–6, 1840, no. H2); H. de Kat; (his sale, Amsterdam, March 4, 1867, no. 358 [Rembrandt School]); J. de Clerq; C.P. van Eeghen, Sr. (bears his mark, verso, not in Lugt)

Selected References

Benesch 1954–1957, 2: no. A4, fig. 593 (cannot convincingly be placed among Rembrandt's early chalk studies); Chicago 1969, no. 98 (Rembrandt); Sumowski 1979, 3666, no. 1644x

WRITING LITTLE MORE THAN A decade after this drawing had been included as an autograph work by Rembrandt in the major Chicago tercentenary exhibition, the words with which Sumowski began his description of the spectacular study are very revealing: "In spite of its superb quality, this drawing has no place in Rembrandt's oeuvre." If, as is now widely accepted, this sheet is actually by Lievens rather than Rembrandt, it is indeed one of his finest surviving drawings, in which line, tone, color, and mood work together to create a powerful and very moving image. Certain authors — including Sumowski himself at an earlier date — believed this to be a red chalk drawing by Lievens, reworked and strengthened in black chalk by Rembrandt, but Sumowski subsequently recognized that the drawing's various elements are totally complementary and must be by the same hand.

There are unquestionably aspects of the drawing that relate to works by Rembrandt, notably the similarity of the actual figure to one standing and holding a book in the center of Rembrandt's 1626 painting *The Baptism of the Eunuch*.[1] In terms of drawing style, however, the intense, highly coloristic way in which the artist has used the two colors of chalk has no close parallel in the work of Rembrandt, but is clearly evident in drawings by Lievens such as *Bearded Man in Half-Length, Facing Left*, and *Hermit in Contemplation, Sitting on a Chair* (cats. 99, 100). In the treatment of the background shading, the latter drawing is particularly similar to the present work.

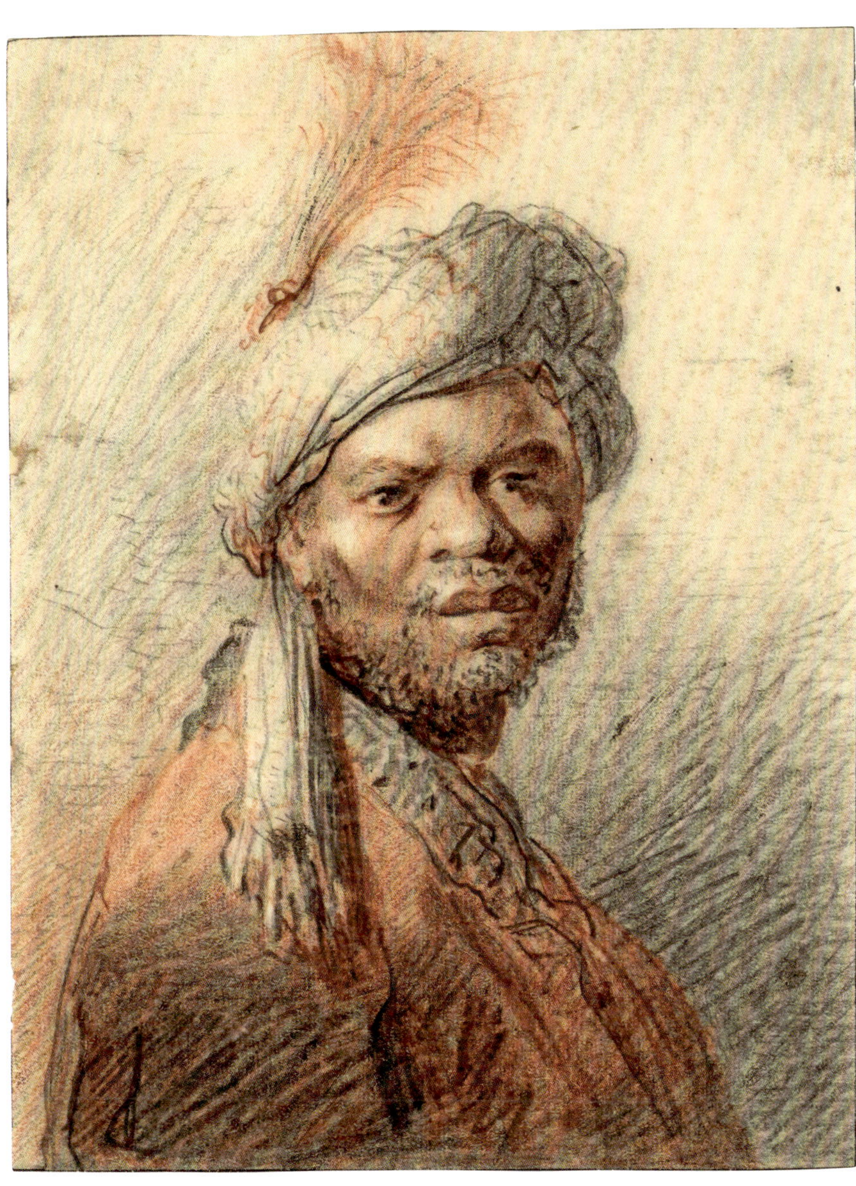

Although Lievens made numerous paintings and prints of exotic character heads, this is one of his very few drawings that could reasonably be described as a tronie. At the same time, the figure's pose, facing forward, and his pensive facial expression give the work the air of a portrait. GMGR

98 Bearded Old Man in Profile

c. 1628–1630, red chalk with touches of black chalk, 13.7 × 13.8 (5 3/8 × 5 7/16). National Gallery of Art, Washington, Gift of Mrs. Lessing J. Rosenwald (1987.20.11). *(Washington)*

Provenance

Charles Fairfax Murray; William Bateson (L.2604a); (sale Sotheby's, London, April 23–24, 1929, no. 228); Mrs. Lessing J. Rosenwald

Selected References

Benesch 1954–1957, no. 42 (as Rembrandt); Amsterdam 1988, 6, 12, 17, fig. IV; Martin Royalton-Kisch, "Recent Publications on Rembrandt Drawings," *Burlington Magazine* 132 (1990): 134 (as probably to be retained as Rembrandt); Leiden 1991, no. 25

THIS DRAWING WAS CONSIDERED to be by Rembrandt until 1988, when Peter Schatborn first attributed it to Lievens. Though indeed very close in style to various Rembrandt drawings of around 1631 (including the group of figure studies discussed under cat. 100), the bust here is essentially constructed with a dense network of lines, in a way that is characteristic of Lievens. Also typical is the profile pose, seen in many of Lievens' Leiden-period works, but much rarer in Rembrandt. The drawing is nonetheless a good example of how incredibly close in style some of Lievens' and Rembrandt's drawings of around 1630 can be.

A comparable drawing is the fine *Bearded Old Man with a Book* in Darmstadt,[1] where we see much the same cascade of swirling lines to define hair and beard, a technique that is also found in prints by Lievens, such as his *Bearded Man in a Turban* (cat. 68). Furthermore, in both the Darmstadt and Washington drawings, we also see the same specific treatment of the old men's undulating foreheads, with short, sharp touches of chalk used to indicate light reflecting off the surface. GMGR

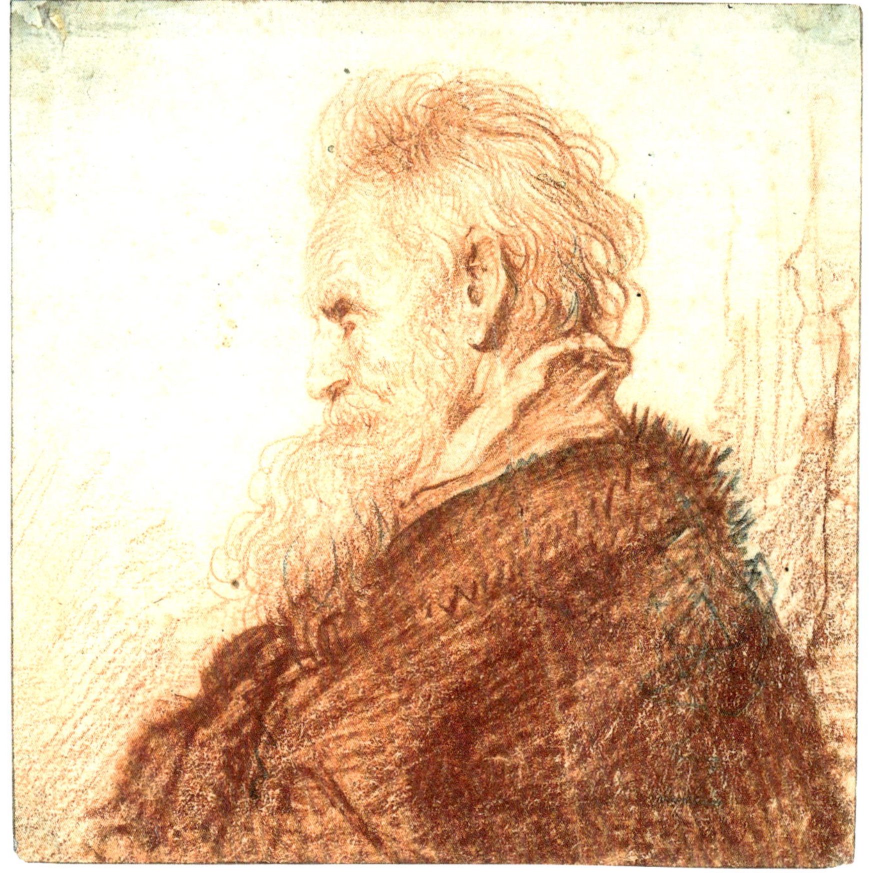

99 Bearded Man in Half-Length, Facing Left

c. 1630–1631, red and black chalk, 17 × 13.5 (6 11/16 × 5 5/16). The British Museum, London (1836.8.11.341) *(Washington, Amsterdam)*

Inscription

Left, at shoulder level: IL

Verso: in graphite, top left: *33 / 53* [Röver], and lower left: *£1.157;* red ink, lower left: N2920 [Goll van Franckenstein]

Provenance

Valerius Röver (L.2984; portfolio 33, no. 53: *Mans Pourtrait bij na in profil met root an swart krijt van Jan Lievense*); his widow, C. van Dussen, who sold his drawings to the dealer H. de Leth; Jhr. Johann Goll van Franckenstein (L.2987); (his sale, Amsterdam [de Vries...Roos], July 1, 1833, portfolio P, no. 14); John Sheepshanks (L.2333); acquired in 1836

Selected References

Schneider/Ekkart 1973, 203, 266, 363, no. z88; Sumowski 1979, 3546, no. 1589

THIS FINELY DRAWN STUDY OF A thoughtful young man shares a number of stylistic features with other drawings from Lievens' years in Leiden, but it also displays a sensitivity in capturing the character and mood of the sitter that hints at what was to come in his portrait drawings of the 1640s and 1650s. The sheet must date from not long before the artist's departure from Leiden in 1632. The way in which Lievens has combined and contrasted the red and black chalks is similar in the earlier *Head of an Old Woman* (cat. 95), as is the movement of the lines around the young man's shirt collar, though the overall effect of the drawing is much softer. Here the lines are set against a broader, more tonal backing, closer to that seen in *Moorish Man with Turban in Half-Length* or *Hermit in Contemplation, Sitting on a Chair* (cats. 97, 100).

The drawing was described by Schneider as the preparatory study in reverse for one of Lievens' prints (Hollstein 70), but as Sumowski has noted, the figure in that etching has long hair and is bare-chested. In any case, the drawing has more the feel of a study from life. Alone among Lievens' Leiden-period chalk drawings, it is signed with the artist's initials. GMGR

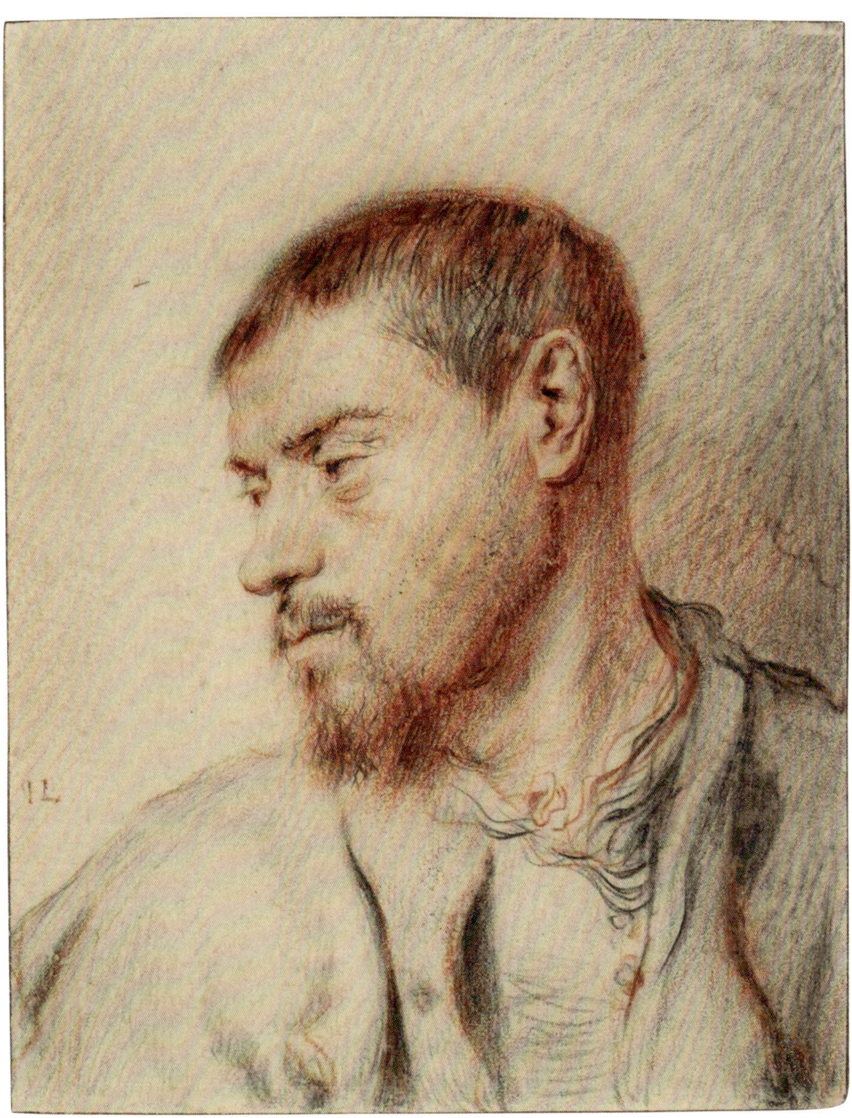

100 Hermit in Contemplation, Sitting on a Chair

c. 1630–1631, red chalk, indented for transfer, 19 × 14 (7½ × 5½). The British Museum, London (1836.8.11.347) *(Washington, Milwaukee)*

Inscription

Bottom right by a later hand: J.L.

Provenance

François Fagel; (his sale, London, T. Philipe, 2nd day, May 28, 1801, no. 96, to Thomson); John Sheepshanks (L. 2333); acquired in 1836

Selected References

Schneider/Ekkart 1973, 37, 87, 262, no. z11; Braunschweig 1979, no. 54; Sumowski 1979, 3548, no. 1590; Amsterdam 1988, no. 14

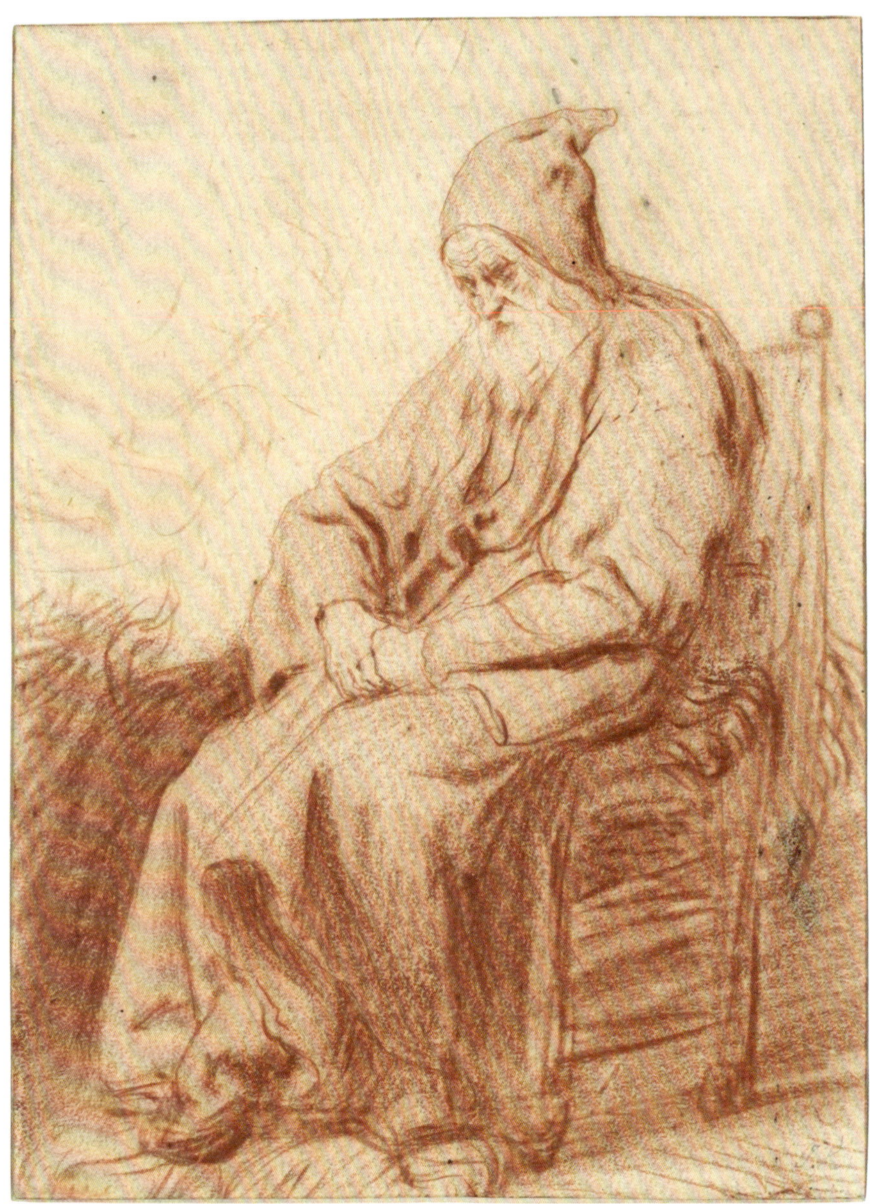

LIEVENS TWICE USED THIS STUDY as the basis for prints (cat. 71). In the larger of the two etchings Lievens continued to develop and change the composition, first placing the hermit on a rock in a cave, rather than seated on a chair, then progressively filling in the background, and twice cutting the plate down in size. In the drawing itself, there were also changes, in particular in the back of the chair, which was redrawn to make it higher.

It is possible that Lievens was envisaging the tonal effect of the print when he made this drawing, but whatever the reasons, the drawing style in this confident study is considerably less linear than in many of his other works from the Leiden period. In particular, the background tones here are defined in soft, broad chalk strokes, with sharper lines providing occasional accents. This handling is analogous to what we see in a group of red chalk figure studies by Rembrandt, some dated 1630 and 1631, most of which also show seated older men, seen from a similar viewpoint.[1] Among Lievens' chalk drawings, there are relatively few other examples in which the background tone is applied in this way, although there are some intriguing parallels with his stylistically unique and highly dramatic *Sermon of John the Baptist*, in Dresden, a drawing that may date from slightly earlier.[2]

In the context of Lievens' paintings, a dating of c. 1630–1631 for this drawing seems entirely appropriate: the composition and mood are comparable to those of his *Saint Jerome Meditating in a Grotto* (cats. 23, 72) and *Job in His Misery*, dated 1631 (cat. 25).[3] GMGR

101 View of London, with Westminster Seen from across the River Thames

c. 1633–1635, pen and brown ink with gray-brown wash, 21.8 × 37.3 (8 11/16 × 14 9/16). On loan from the House of Lords, London

Inscription

Bottom center by another hand: *Jan Livenze Fecit*

Provenance

Alfred Beurdeley, Paris (L.421); (Beurdeley sale, Georges Petit, Paris, June 8, 1920, no. 224); H.E. ten Cate, Oldenzaal (L.533b); (C.G. Boerner, Düsseldorf, 1964); (Gebr. Douwes, Amsterdam, 1965); Saam and Lily Nijstad, The Hague; (their sale "the Unicorno Collection," Sotheby's, Amsterdam, May 9, 2004, no. 71); (sale, Sotheby's, London, June 30, 2005, no. 228)

Selected References

Schneider/Ekkart 1973, 215, 366, no. z166; Sumowski 1979, 3834, under no. 1723x; Christopher White, "The Theory and Practice of Drawing in Early Stuart England," in *Drawing in England from Hilliard to Hogarth* [exh. cat., The British Museum] (London, 1987), 25; Royalton-Kisch 1998, 620–621 (as probably by Jan Andrea Lievens); Haags Historisch Museum, The Hague, *Grenzloos Goed, Tekeningen uit de Unicorno Collectie*, 2001, no. 59

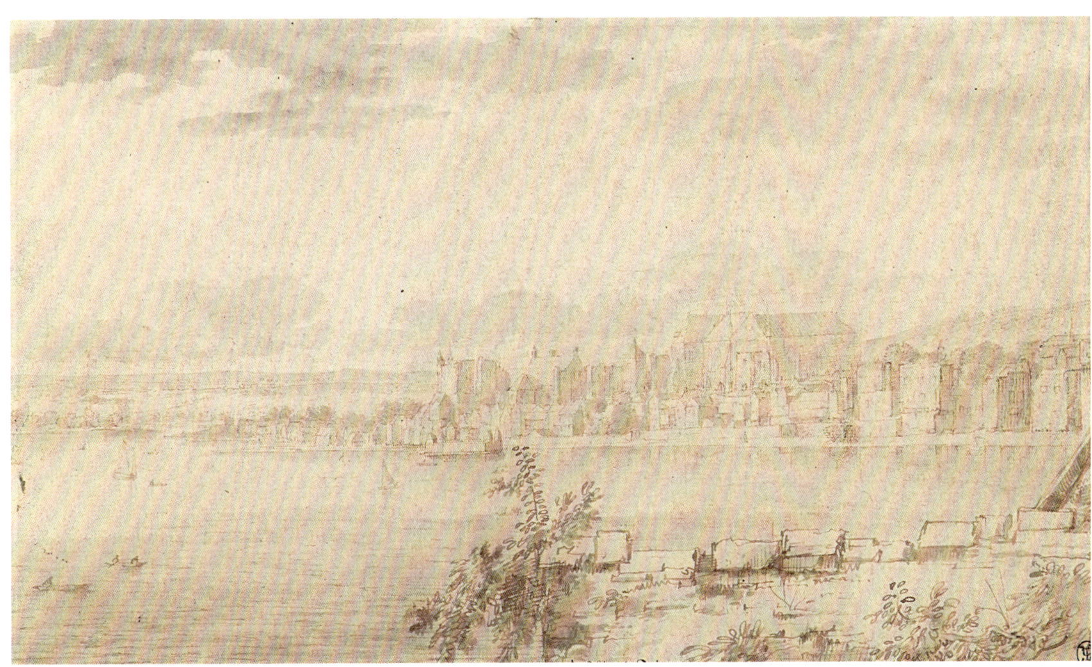

FIRST RECOGNIZED BY CHRISTOPHER White in 1987, the subject of this drawing is a view of Westminster. Seen from the south bank of the Thames, the great abbey church appears here to the right of center amid buildings of the old Palace of Westminster, where the English Parliament met until the great fire of 1834 (since replaced by Charles Barry's and Augustus Pugin's famous Houses of Parliament, still in use today). Despite the site's prominence, relatively few early views of Westminster survive. Two of the most notable are seen in the background of Anthony van Dyck's painting of King Charles I with Queen Henrietta Maria and their children, 1632 (Royal Collection, London),[1] and in Wenceslaus Hollar's etching from 1647.[2] The value of the present drawing resides in its being an early topographical portrayal of the English capital as well as the most significant visual record of Lievens' three years in London.

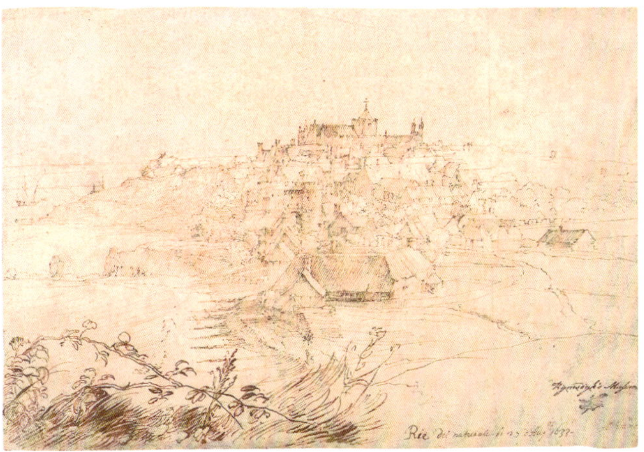

1 | Anthony van Dyck, *View of Rye from the Northeast*, August 27, 1633, pen and brown ink with touches of brown wash. The Pierpont Morgan Library, New York

Striking parallels exist with a small group of topographical drawings of the Channel port of Rye made by Van Dyck during his stay in England, particularly the treatment of the buildings and the details of the foliage in *View of Rye from the Northeast* (fig. 1). Dated August 27, 1633, that work is thought to have been made while Van Dyck was waiting to sail for the

Continent. This otherwise undocumented trip was probably a short one, as he was back in England before leaving again in March 1634 for a longer absence. Thus it is likely that Lievens had an opportunity to see Van Dyck's drawing in late 1633 or early 1634. The compositional parallels between Van Dyck's view of Rye and Lievens' drawing of Westminster are so close that it is impossible the latter was made without knowledge of the former. It can indeed be seen as something of an homage by Lievens to the work of the great Flemish master, in whose studio we believe he was working at the time.

Martin Royalton-Kisch has raised doubts about both the dating and the attribution of the present drawing, pointing out that both here and in the related *View of Westminster Abbey from the Northwest* in Hamburg, there is no sign of the crosses on the abbey's gable ends — included in most if not all other views up to 1647, and again after the dramatic fire of London in 1666, but which may have been removed for a time during the Commonwealth.[3] He also points out that this drawing seems to show hills in the distance at the right, which is inconsistent with the actual topography. On these grounds, he argues that these two London views were probably made in the studio, based on sketches from life executed during the late 1640s or 1650s, and he suggests that both may be by Jan Andrea Lievens rather than his father.

In the case of the Hamburg drawing, this theory seems plausible, but there is a striking stylistic and qualitative difference between that work and this one. Even if the present drawing had been completed in the studio, accounting for any minor topographical inaccuracies, its foreground details, clear debt to Van Dyck's Rye view of 1633, and superb quality argue strongly for its attribution to Jan Lievens, not his son, and its dating to the artist's English period. GMGR

102 Portrait of Adriaen Brouwer

1635–1637, black chalk, with touches of black ink, 22.1 × 18.5 (8 11/16 × 7 5/16). Frits Lugt Collection, Institut Néerlandais, Paris (1203) *(Washington)*

Inscriptions

Left, near shoulder: IL

Top left, in pencil: *A. Brouwer*

Verso (possibly eighteenth century): *Het Konterfeitsel van A. Brouwer* [possibly in the same hand as on the verso of cat. 113]

Provenance

James Kerr-Lawson, London (1864–1939); Frits Lugt, Maartensdijk and Paris (L.1028), acquired May 14, 1923

Selected References

Schneider/Ekkart 1973, 46, 71, 194, 361, no. z51; Sumowski 1979, 3556, no. 1594; Paris and Haarlem 1997–1998, no. 85

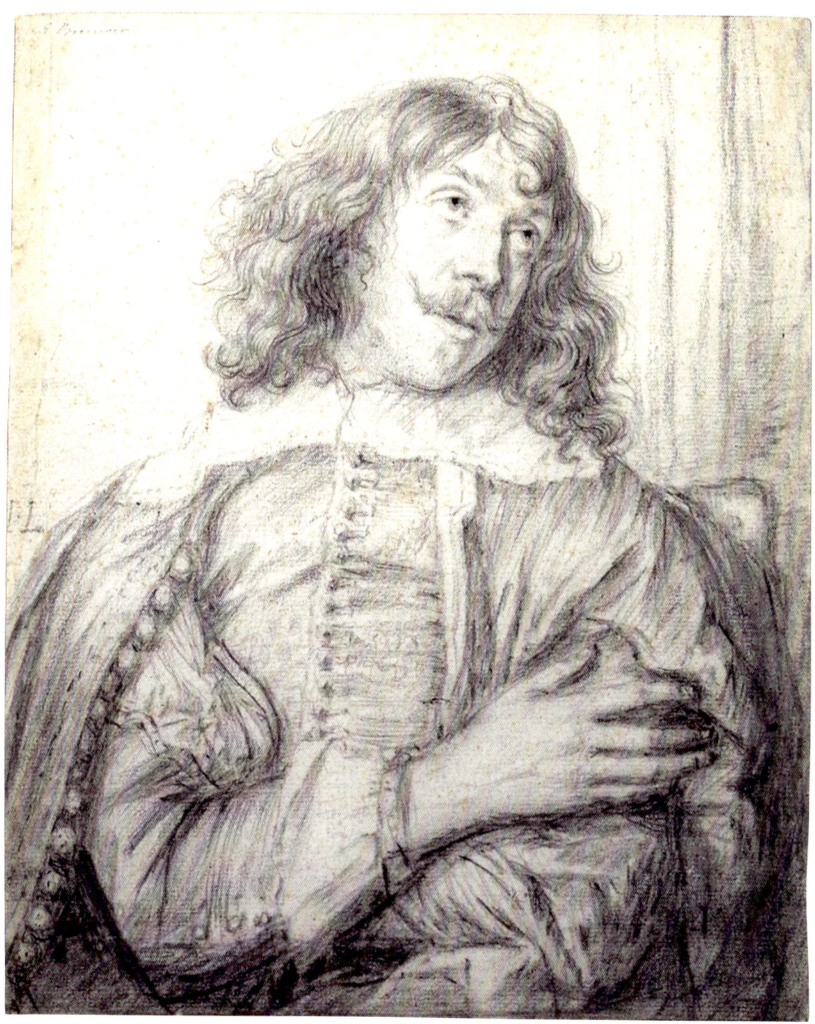

THIS IS ONE OF THE EARLIEST OF the great portraits that form such an original and important part of Lievens' drawn oeuvre. Lievens would have been aware of the portrait drawings by Van Dyck even before going to England in 1632, and he seems to have begun making such drawings himself shortly thereafter.

Lievens arrived in Antwerp in 1635 and soon fell in with a small group of fellow artists, who provided him with the subjects for several of his first portraits. In addition to this likeness of Adriaen Brouwer (c. 1605–1638) — whose painting style had such a great impact on Lievens' own — he also made excellent, and stylistically varied, drawings of Daniel Seghers (see Dickey fig. 10) and Jan Davidsz de Heem.[1] Later in his career most of his sitters would be statesmen, writers, theologians, and other cultural figures, but at this stage Lievens focused primarily on making drawings of his friends, with whom, to judge by Brouwer's depiction of the group (see Wheelock fig. 14), he led a very lively life.

His inspiration in making these elaborate portrait drawings was Van Dyck's famous portrait series, engraved and published in the *Iconography,* which depicted an array of celebrated artists (including Lievens himself). Prints were even made from Lievens' drawings of Seghers and De Heem, though not from this portrait, which is ironic, as it is the most Van Dyckian image of the group. Indeed, the extreme elegance of Brouwer's clothing and his highly theatrical pose make one wonder if the drawing may not even have had a deliberately tongue-in-cheek quality. Whether or not Lievens meant for this image of his friend to be serious or irreverent, it is a wonderfully lively and beautifully executed drawing, among the most spontaneous and accomplished of all Lievens' portraits.

Brouwer's early death in January 1638 means that the drawing must have been made within the first two years or so of Lievens' stay in Antwerp. Several other drawings that are stylistically related probably also date from the same years. These include the Vienna *Saint Mark the Evangelist* (see Rubinstein fig. 14) and *Bearded Man Seated, Holding a Skull,* in Amsterdam.[2] GMGR

103 Portrait of Constantijn Huygens

1639, black chalk, with touches of pen and brown ink, 23.8 × 17.4 (9 3/8 × 6 7/8). The British Museum, London (1836.8.11.342) *(Washington, Amsterdam)*

Inscriptions

Right, near shoulder: IL

On the letter: *vive Le/Roy de/Roys*

Provenance

John Sheepshanks (L.2333)

Selected References

Schneider/Ekkart 1973, 196, 361, no. z60; Sumowski 1979, 3564, no. 1598; Amsterdam 1988, no. 40

CONSTANTIJN HUYGENS WAS ONE of the most significant figures in Lievens' early career. As secretary to the stadtholder Frederik Hendrik — the Prince of Orange and the most influential man in the Dutch Republic — he was at the heart of the nation's political and cultural life. He was also a prominent man of letters and greatly interested in the visual arts. In October 1628 Huygens visited the Leiden studio of the young Lievens, after which, as Huygens recorded in his diary, the artist "was seized by the desire to paint my portrait." This resulted in an impressive painting (cat. 16),[1] which must have done much to cement Lievens' relationship with his appreciative sitter, who thereafter seems to have pulled strings on the artist's behalf on several occasions.

One such occasion may have been in 1639, when Lievens, then resident in Antwerp, was awarded the commission to paint a large history piece of *The Magnanimity of Scipio* (see Wheelock fig. 19) for the town hall in his native Leiden. While working on that canvas, he seems to have visited The Hague, where he made this fine portrait drawing. More severe in mood and direct in approach than the gentler painting of the same sitter from the previous decade, this drawing is among the most penetrating of Lievens' portraits. The emphasis is clearly on the great man's piety: he is shown wearing a quasi-ecclesiastical skull cap and holding in his hand a card or small book inscribed "Long live the king of kings" (i.e., God).

The drawing shows an exceptional combination of precision, energy, and freedom of execution. In its confidence and sense of vitality, it is stylistically comparable to the portrait of Adriaen Brouwer (cat. 102), but some aspects of the handling are more controlled. Underpinning the apparently broad, sweeping application of the chalk there is a fine tracery of key lines, drawn with a chalk point so hard and sharp that the effect is almost that of pen and black ink. Lievens used pen and ink in a few places, notably the face, to apply specific accents, though the ink there is brown rather than black. As discussed under *Man with a Moustache and Goatee* (cat. 108), this use of pen and ink for isolated accents is a very Rubensian technique.

The drawing was engraved by Lucas Vorsterman, apparently very soon after it was made, and its highly worked character would seem to indicate that it was intended from the start to be a study for a print.[2] GMGR

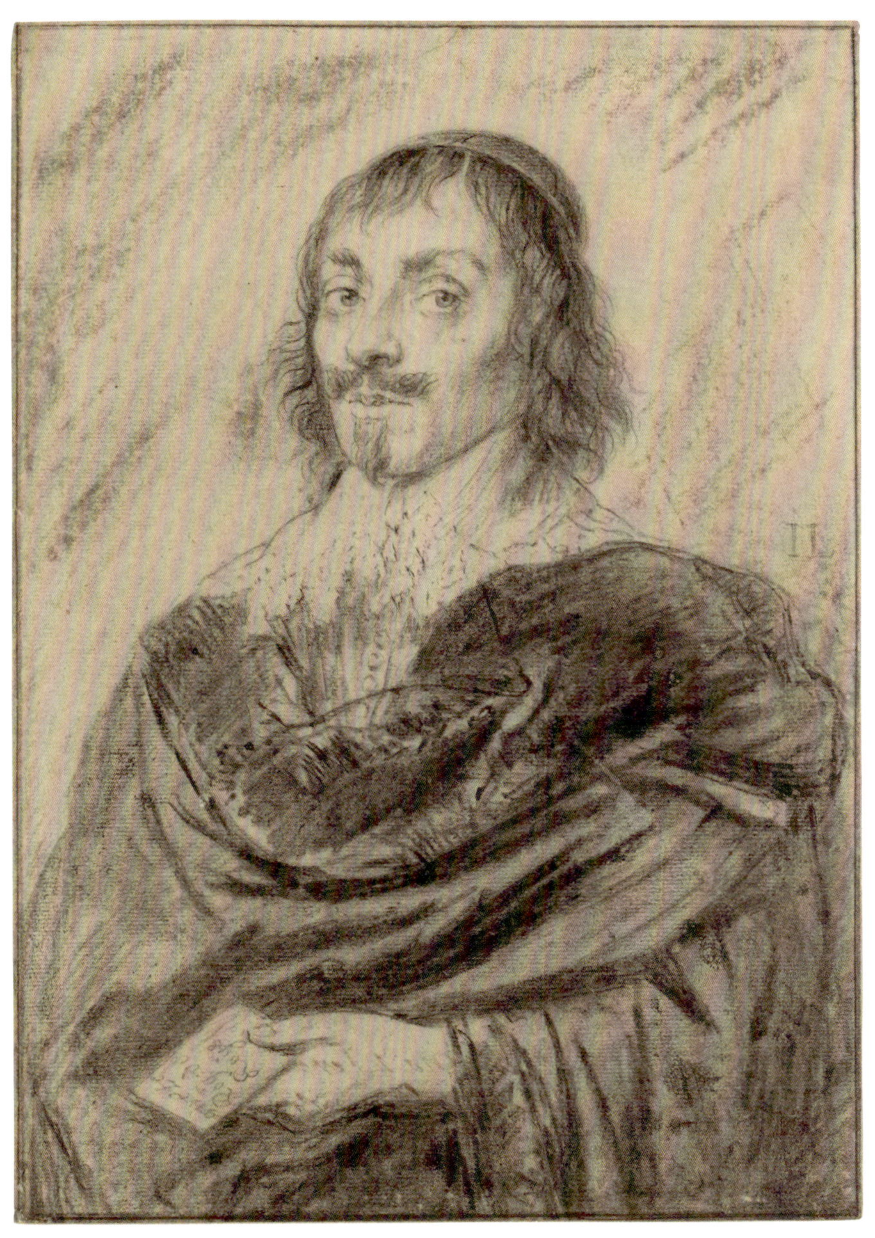

104 River God with an Eagle

105 Seated River Gods

104
c. 1638–1643, pen and brown ink over traces of black chalk, 14.6 × 20 (5¾ × 7⅞). National Gallery of Art, Washington, Ailsa Mellon Bruce Fund (1981.32.1) *(Washington, Milwaukee)*

Inscriptions
Verso, lower left: *J. Lievens*; lower center: *[f?]r.e.*; upper right: *61B*

Provenance
L.X. Lannoy; (sale, Amsterdam, May 19, 1925, in no. 401); J. Q. van Regteren Altena, Amsterdam; H. Schneider; Tobias Christ, Basel; (his sale, Sotheby's, London, April 9, 1981, no. 33)

Selected References
Schneider/Ekkart 1973, 191, 360, no. z32; Sumowski 1979, 3636, no. 1633[ax]

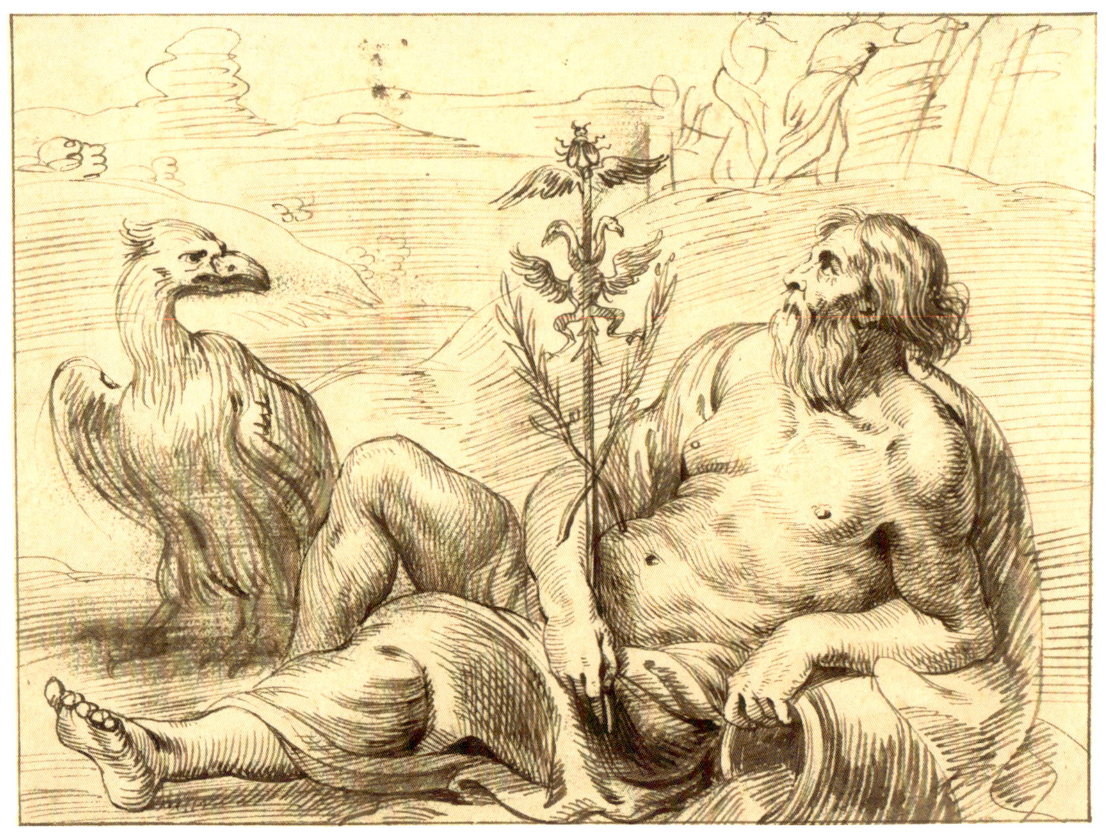

CAT. 104

THESE DRAWINGS ARE SOMEWHAT different in handling but related in their theme, which, as Elizabeth McGrath has noted, can be associated with a Rubens School drawing apparently representing the River Scheldt.[1] The overt classicism of the subject is perfectly in keeping with tendencies in Lievens' paintings from the late 1630s on, but it is unusual in his drawings.

Lievens' relationship with Flemish classicism is complicated. He and many of his contemporaries embraced the classicizing themes with enthusiasm,[2] but when it came to compositions and figural types, they did not always understand the lessons of Rubens and other Northern artists who cultivated the approaches and styles of Italian predecessors. Here, the Washington sheet is an accomplished figure drawing of a certain type, but it is executed in a passionless way that suggests Lievens was not totally engaged with the subject. The private collection drawing is more spontaneous and animated in character.

The dating of these two drawings is problematic. Given the clear reference to a Rubensian source, however, it seems likely that the two drawings both date from the latter part of Lievens' Antwerp period. GMGR

105
c. 1638–1643, pen and brown ink, 19.2 × 28.5 (7 9/16 × 11 1/4). Private collection *(not in exhibition)*

Provenance

L.X. Lannoy; (sale, Amsterdam, May 19, 1925, in no. 401)

Selected References

Schneider/Ekkart 1973, 191, no. Z3; Sumowski 1979, 3634, no. 1633[x]; Amsterdam 1988, no. 43

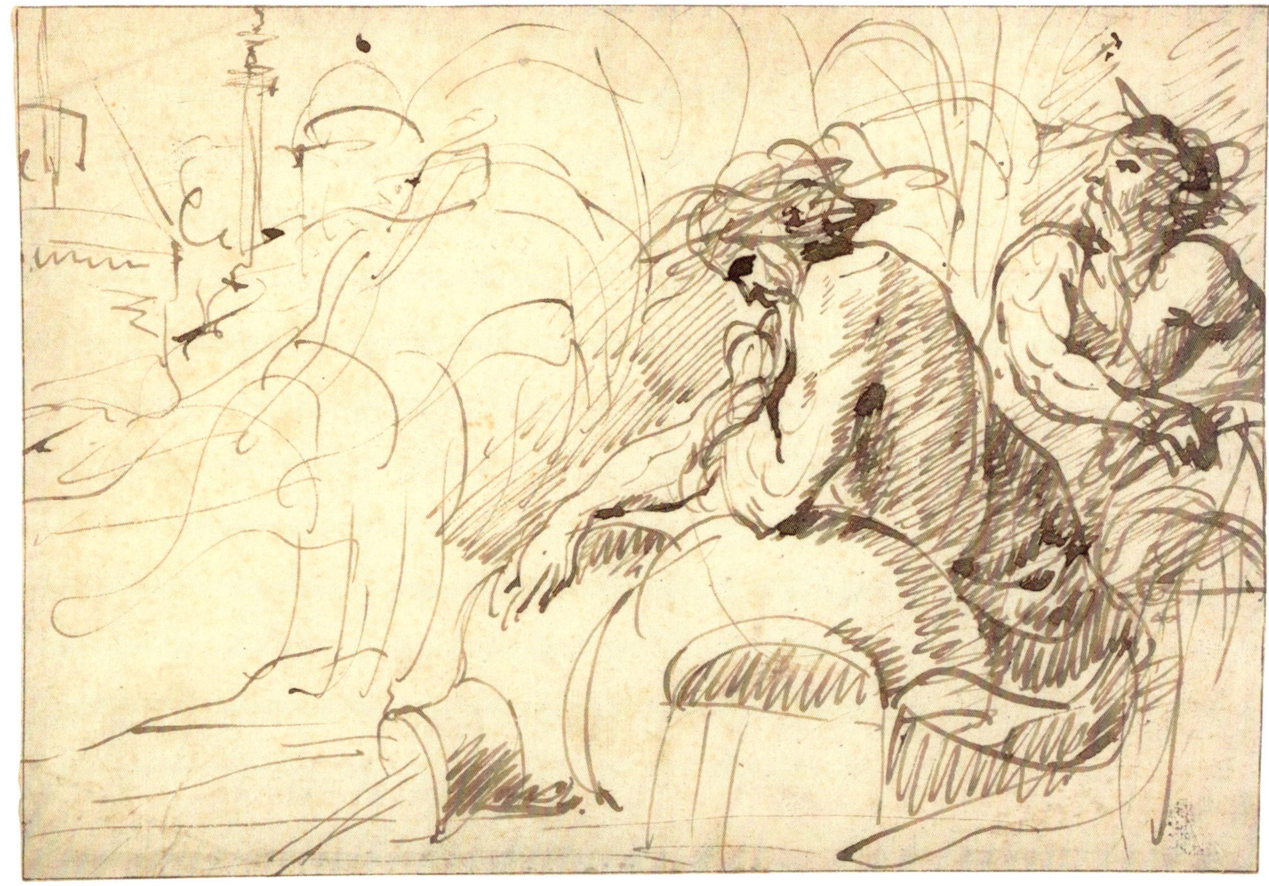

CAT. 105

106 A Painter's Studio

c. 1638–1643, pen and brown ink with brown wash, over black chalk, 38.5 × 29.5 (15 3/16 × 11 5/8). Private collection

Inscription

Verso, in brown ink: *Rembrandt*

Provenance

"Sensier, 1877"; (Sotheby's, London, February 19, 1936, no. 50, as Rembrandt School); Victor Koch, London; (Sotheby's, London, June 29, 1949, no. 88, as attributed to Lievens)

Selected References

Sumowski 1979, 3648, no. 1636b*; Amsterdam 1988, no. 44; J. Bolten and T. Folmer-von Oven, *Liberna Foundation. Catalogue of Drawings* (Hilversum, 1989), 154–155, no. 86 (with earliest provenance)

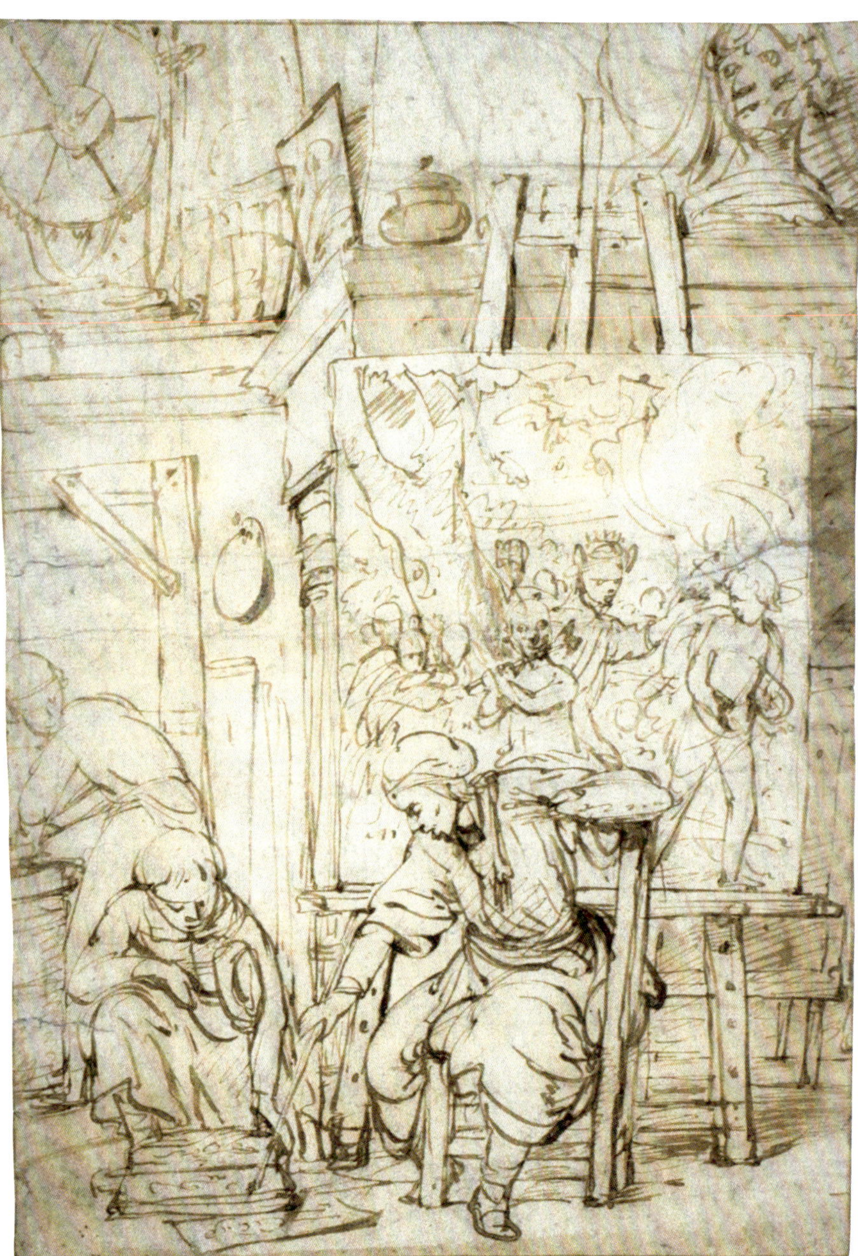

THIS SUBJECT, THE INTERIOR OF an artist's studio, is unique in Lievens' oeuvre; indeed only one other complete genre scene can be convincingly attributed to him.[1] The present drawing shows a seated painter pointing to an album of studies being shown to him by a kneeling student on the floor at his feet. On an easel behind the artist we see the painting on which he is working, while farther back another assistant grinds pigments, surrounded by other studio paraphernalia.

The key to interpreting this composition is the subject of the painting on the easel: *The Judgment of Midas*.[2] According to Ovid, Pan had the temerity to challenge the great Apollo — renowned for his lyre playing — to a musical contest. Apollo was judged the winner, but King Midas happened to be present and spoke out strongly against what he saw as an unjust verdict, whereupon Apollo awarded him the ass' ears, clearly visible on the central figure in our artist's creation. The subject is open to two cautionary readings. On the one hand, it served as a warning to any arrogant pupil who tried to surpass his master. On the other hand, it illustrated the perils of incompetent adjudication. Either way, the subject was of great relevance to the teacher-pupil relationship.

Sumowski compared the style of this drawing to the 1665 *Saint Jerome in a Landscape* (see Rubinstein fig. 5) and therefore dated it to the same decade. But its calligraphic style recalls earlier pen studies, such as those in London and Düsseldorf (see cat. 120), or even *Seated River Gods* (cat. 105) from 1638–1643. On grounds of quality as much as style, Schatborn considers this last dating appropriate for *A Painter's Studio*.[3] It is probable that this playful composition originated in the same period as Lievens' light-hearted portrait of Adriaen Brouwer (cat. 102). GMGR

107 Scholar Sitting in His Studio

c. 1640–1643, black chalk corrected with white, indented for transfer, 25.5 × 19.2 (10 1/16 × 7 9/16). Museum Boijmans Van Beuningen, Rotterdam (MB 197) *(Washington, Amsterdam)*

Provenance

F.J.O. Boymans

Selected References

Chicago 1969, no. 193; Schneider/Ekkart 1973, 85, 192, 360, no. Z42; Braunschweig 1979, no. 57; Sumowski 1979, 3650, no. 1596; Amsterdam 1988, 60–61, fig. 39a

INDENTED FOR TRANSFER, THIS drawing served as the study for Lievens' signed woodcut *A Seated Cleric* (cat. 83). In the print, however, the composition is reduced, with the figure appearing to be seated on a chair against a plain background, and with no indication of the surroundings suggested in the drawing. He is also shown in three-quarter length, rather than full length, and there are minor differences in details of the costume.

Opinions have varied as to whether or not Lievens took the unusual step of cutting his own woodblocks, but the evidence in this case suggests that he did. Not only has the composition been extensively rethought between the drawing and the final print, but the draftsmanship in the drawing is very loose, and the design would have been hard for anyone but the artist himself to follow. Lievens seems to have become interested in the then-unfashionable medium of woodcut following his move to Antwerp in 1635, probably as a result of exposure to Christoffel Jegher's spectacular woodcuts after Rubens. In Antwerp he must also have seen woodcuts by or after Titian, Domenico Campagnola, and other artists of the Venetian school, which were to have a significant influence on his subsequent landscape style. Even in the present composition, there are some echoes of the works of these Venetians.

The dominant influence on Lievens' drawing style here was Anthony van Dyck. As in several other drawings of this period, including the portrait of Adriaen Brouwer (cat. 102), the study in Vienna for the etching *Saint Mark the Evangelist* (see Rubinstein fig. 14), and the Amsterdam *Bearded Man Seated, Holding a Skull,*[1] Lievens' characteristic linear style is still in evidence, but is tempered by a softer, more tonal use of chalk and a generally lighter touch. GMGR

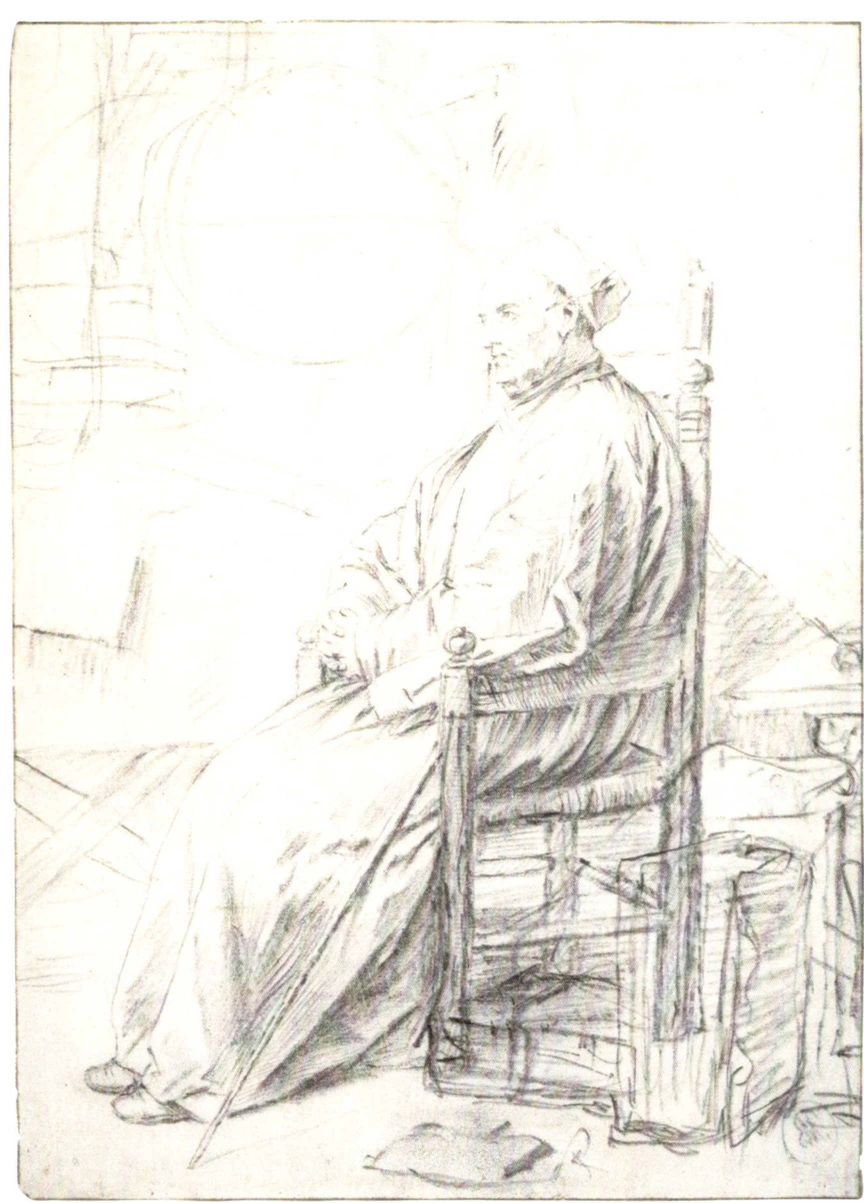

108 Man with Moustache and Goatee, Asleep

c. 1640–1643, black chalk, with touches of brown wash, 23.6 × 19.1 (9 5/16 × 7 1/2). Staatliche Museen zu Berlin, Kupferstichkabinett (KdZ 5729) *(Washington, Milwaukee)*

Inscription

Lower left: IL

Provenance

Jeronimus Tonneman, Amsterdam; (his sale, Amsterdam [de Leth], October 21, 1754, no. G34); Michiel Oudaan, Rotterdam; (his sale, Rotterdam [Bosch... Arrenberg], November 3, 1766, no. M6); Dirk Versteegh, Amsterdam; (his sale, Amsterdam [De Vries... Roos], November 3, 1823, no. 3 E31 [to Gruiter]); J.A.G. Weigel, Leipzig; (sale, Gutekunst, Stuttgart, May 15, 1883, no. 577); Adolf von Beckerath (L.2504); acquired with his collection, 1902

Selected References

Schneider/Ekkart 1973, 193, no. Z45 (as 1645/1650); Sumowski 1979, 3552, no. 1592 (as 1630/1631)

ALTHOUGH THE MISE-EN-PAGE and the form of the signature are comparable to those of portrait drawings by Lievens from the late 1640s and the 1650s, a firm *terminus ante quem* is provided by an intriguing painting by Simon Luttichuys dated 1644 (fig. 1). There the artist copied the figure from this drawing by Lievens and placed him in an interior alongside a scholarly still life.[1] Other paintings by Luttichuys from the period also incorporate motifs copied from Lievens, and it seems likely that the two artists knew each other quite well around the time of Lievens' return to the Netherlands from Antwerp in 1644. Indeed, their contact may have begun much earlier, as Luttichuys, who was born in London, was still there when Lievens lived in the English capital between 1632 and 1635.[2]

While almost the entire drawing is in black chalk, Lievens added a number of small touches of grayish-brown wash — for example, under the little finger, the right cuff, and on the left side of the shirt collar — that provide subtle accents and add to the three-dimensionality of the work. This technique was used regularly by Rubens and occasionally by Van Dyck, which suggests that Lievens had studied the works of these artists very closely in London and Antwerp. The draftsmanship is less flamboyant and Van Dyckian than that in the early Antwerp-period portrait of Adriaen Brouwer (cat. 102), but there are similarities with the slightly more sober handling in the portrait of Constantijn Huygens (cat. 103), which Lievens executed c. 1639. It is likely that the present drawing was also made at or soon after that date. GMGR

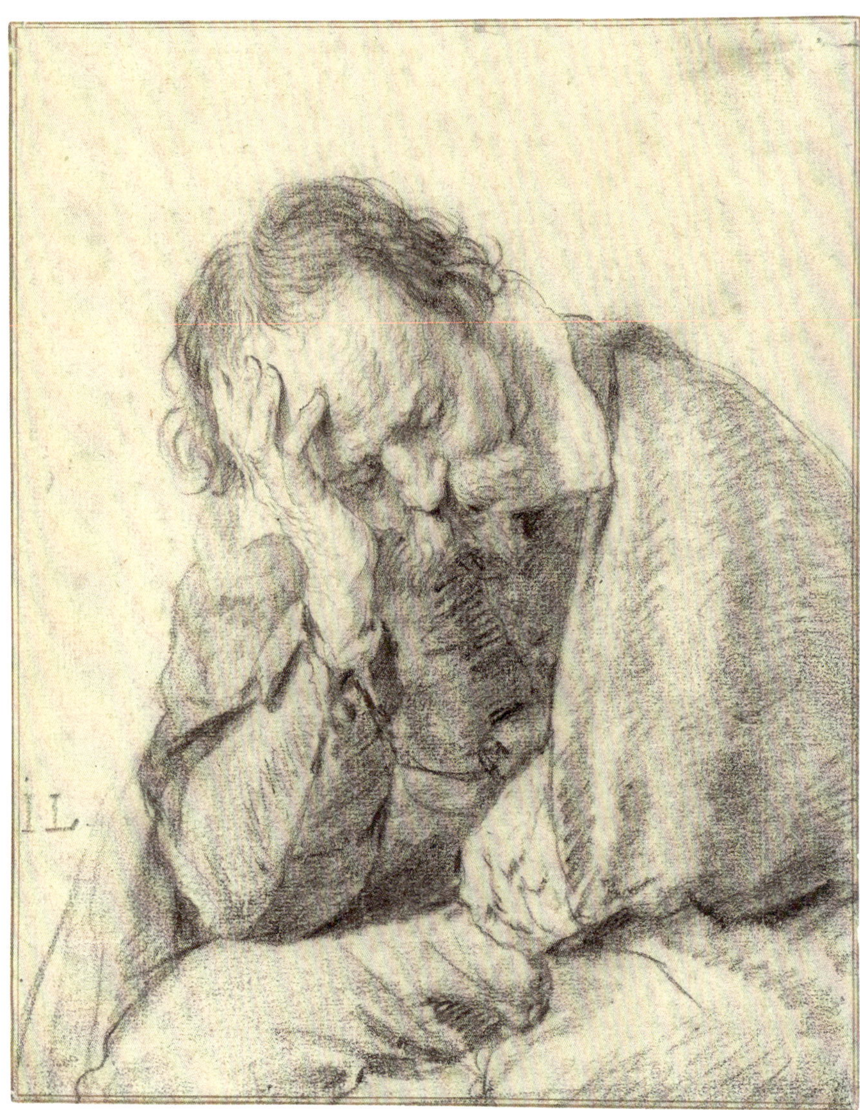

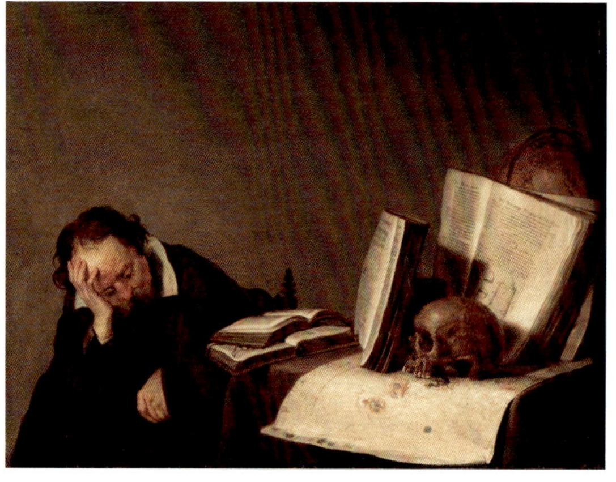

1 | Simon Luttichuys, *A Scholar Resting by a Table with Books*, 1644, oil on panel. Christie's, London, April 7, 1995, no. 1

109 Portrait of Thomas Howard, Earl of Arundel

c. 1643, black and red chalk with stumping, 18 × 14 (7 1/16 × 5 1/2). Staatliche Museen zu Berlin, Kupferstichkabinett (KdZ 5869) *(Milwaukee, Amsterdam)*

Inscription

Top right: IL

Verso, in ink, in an early hand: *d'ouwe Jan Lievense*; and in another hand, in red: *No-97*

Provenance

Adolf von Beckerath; acquired with his collection in 1902

Selected References

Schneider/Ekkart 1973, 203, no. z89 (sitter not identified); Braunschweig 1979, no. 61 (sitter not identified); Keith Andrews, "Letter from Germany," (review of Braunschweig 1979), *Apollo* 110, no. 214 (December 1979), 521, fig. 2 (as *The Earl of Arundel*, c. 1645/1650); Sumowski 1979, 3582, no. 1607 (sitter not identified, c. 1650/1655); Rolf Quednau, "Zu einem Porträt von Jan Lievens," *Zeitschrift für Kunstgeschichte* 43 (1980), 97–104; David Howarth, *Lord Arundel and His Circle* (New Haven, 1985), 207–209, fig. 146

THOMAS HOWARD, 2ND EARL OF Arundel (1585–1646), was the single most important collector of art at the court of the English king Charles I. Initially his interests were focused largely on antiquities, but they later expanded to include paintings and drawings, and he can be considered one of England's first great drawing connoisseurs. Rubens referred to him as "one of the four Evangelists, and the Supporter of our Art,"[1] and depicted him in a number of paintings and drawings. The present drawing had traditionally been described as a study of an unknown man, but in 1979 Keith Andrews recognized it as a portrait of the earl.

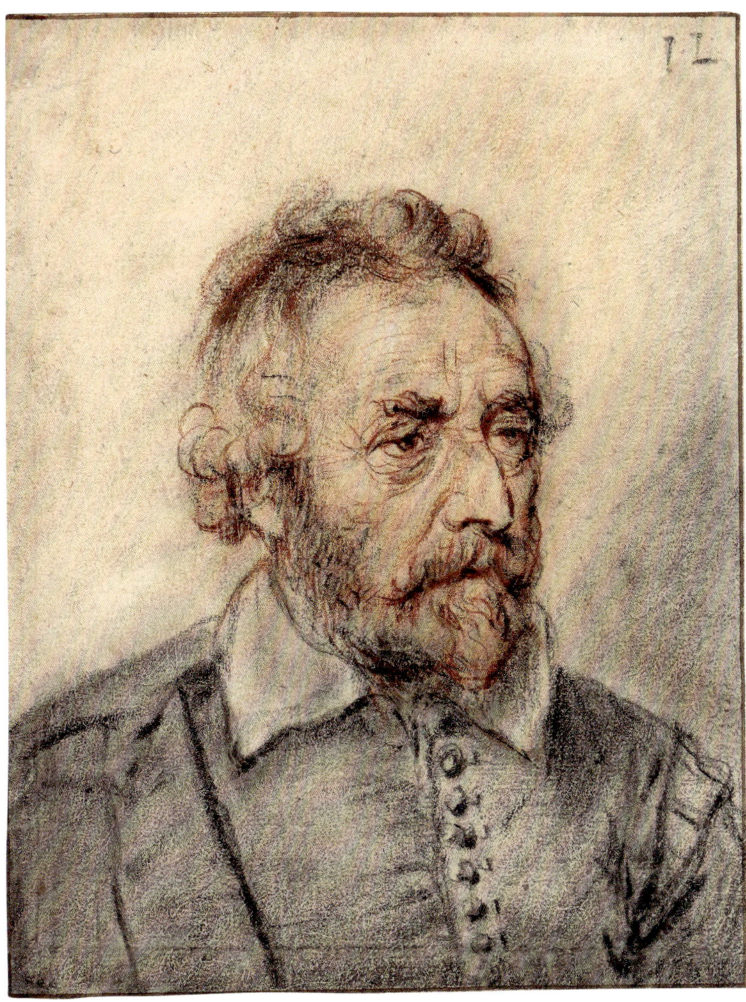

Though Arundel was for many years a highly influential figure, at the very center of English court and political life, his relationship with Charles I was not always smooth. In 1626, shortly after the king's coronation, they came into conflict when Arundel's son, Lord Maltravers, secretly married Lady Elizabeth Stuart, daughter of the Duke of Lenox, for whom the king had other plans. As a result of this, Arundel was imprisoned for a time. On his release, he was fined heavily, which sowed the seeds of financial worries that were to dog him for the remainder of his life.[2] The earl continued to play an important role for much of the 1630s, but by about 1643 his power and influence — and also his financial resources — were greatly diminished, and he was living in exile in Antwerp. This must have been when Lievens made this moving portrait, in which, as David Howarth has observed, Arundel's many problems are written all over his careworn features.[3]

Technically, this drawing is unusual among Lievens' portraits, almost all of which are drawn on larger sheets in pure black chalk. Here, the head is drawn in a combination of red and black chalks reminiscent of some of the artist's earlier drawings, although the handling is softer and more animated, as in other Antwerp-period drawings such as the Vienna *Saint Mark the Evangelist* (see Rubinstein fig. 14) and the black chalk portrait of Constantijn Huygens (cat. 103). The costume is drawn in black chalk with stumping, in a flatter, more tonal way. Lievens may have made this drawing in two stages, starting out with a study of Arundel's striking face, much like the later portrait of Admiral Tromp (cat. 116), and later working it into a more finished portrait by adding the body and costume.

The earl's widow, Aletheia, Countess of Arundel, lived out her final years in Amsterdam, dying there in 1654. Listed in the inventory of pictures still in her possession at the time of her death is one "Drawing of a Head" by Lievens.[4] It seems unthinkable that this should refer to the present drawing, as the subject would surely have been recognized, but the mention is nonetheless intriguing. GMGR

110 Forest Landscape with a Pond

early 1640s, pen and brown ink over black chalk, 21.8 × 35.5 (8 9/16 × 14). Maida and George Abrams Collection, Boston, Massachusetts, on loan and promised gift to Fogg Art Museum, Harvard University (25.1998.113)

Inscription

Verso, in pencil, in a modern hand: *J. Leupen c 1660*

Provenance

Possibly G. van Rossum, Amsterdam; (possibly his sale, Amsterdam, February 8, 1773, no. E393); Henry S. Reitlinger, London (L.2274a); Carl R. Rudolf, London (L.2811b)

Selected References

Schneider/Ekkart 1973, 390, no. SZ429; Sumowski 1979, 3888, no. 1749x

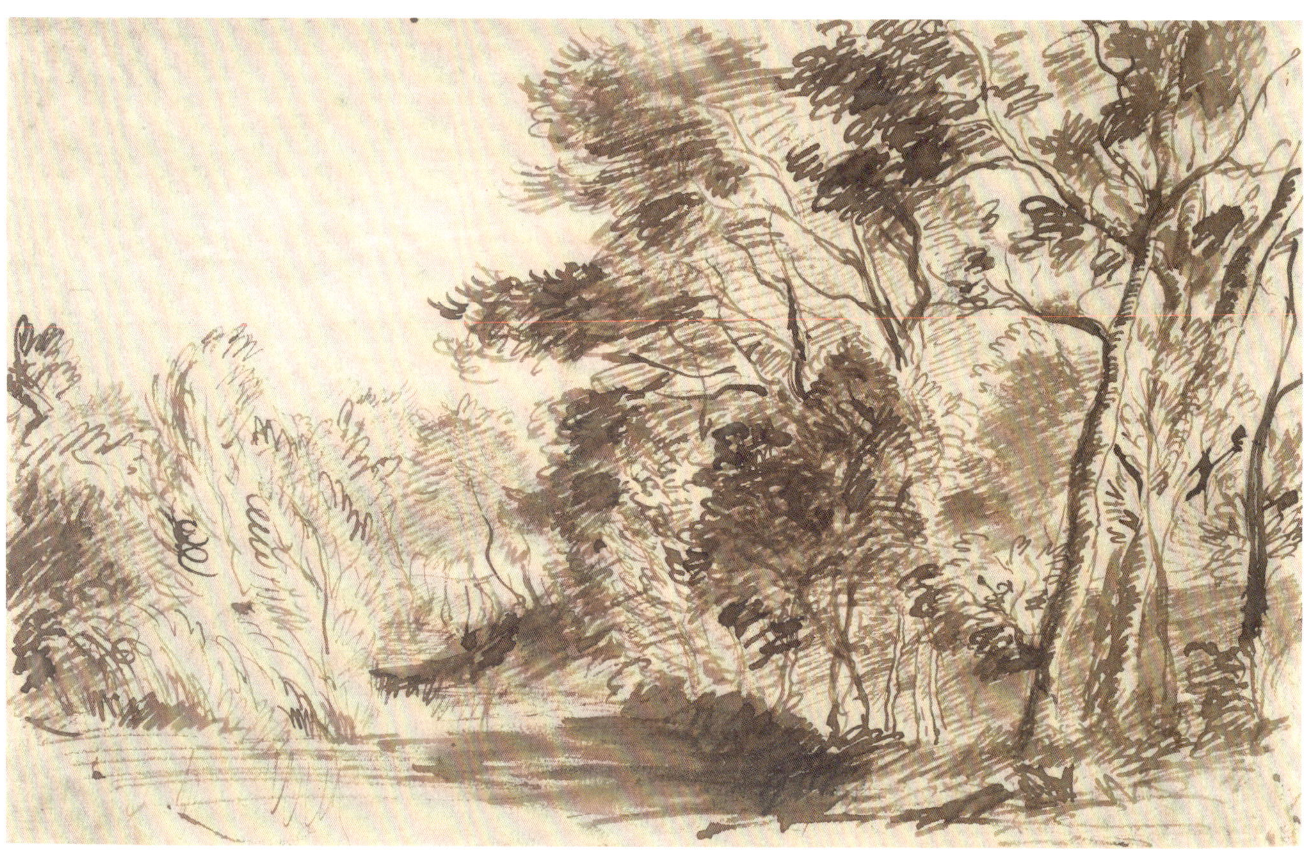

THE ATTEMPT TO ESTABLISH A chronology within Lievens' landscape drawings may ultimately be doomed to failure, but this particularly free and fluid work might provide some pointers.[1] There is an overall sense of harmony and movement here that is different from the impression given by the densely wooded landscapes that would appear to date from later in the artist's career (see cats. 138, 139). This rhythm and tranquility — and indeed the specific, rounded forms of the leaves and trees — are strongly reminiscent of some of the innovative landscape drawings that Van Dyck made during his stay in England, such as *The Edge of a Wood* in Washington,[2] and it might be reasonable to conclude that this drawing dates from Lievens' Antwerp period. It is unfortunate that another Lievens drawing, described in an early nineteenth-century sale catalogue as a "View from Brussels,"[3] is now lost, as it might have provided a valuable indicator of the artist's earlier landscape style. GMGR

111 The Rollerbridge to the Sloterpolder, near Amsterdam

middle to late 1640s(?), reed pen and brown ink with brown and grayish brown wash, on oriental paper, with sketches of trees on the verso, 13.6 × 23.2 (5 3/8 × 9 1/8). Private collection, Germany *(Washington)*

Provenance

Jacob de Vos Jbsz.; (probably his sale, Amsterdam [Roos...], May 22, 1883, in no. 307, with two others, to Thibaudeau); A. Ritter von Franck, Graz; (his sale, Frankfurt am Main, December 4, 1889, no. 118); (sale, Berlin, June 8, 1896, no. 400); Rudolf P. Goldschmidt; (his sale, Frankfurt am Main [Prestel], October 4–5, 1917, no. 340, pl. 45, to Cassirer); Carel Emil Duits, London; (sale, Sotheby's, Amsterdam, November 9, 1999, no. 47)

Selected References

Schneider/Ekkart 1973, 222, 367, no. z216; *Wahre Wunder, Sammler und Sammlungen im Rheinland*, Josef-Haubrich-Kunsthalle, Cologne, 2000–2001, no. c52; Luuk Pijl in Groningen 2005, 202

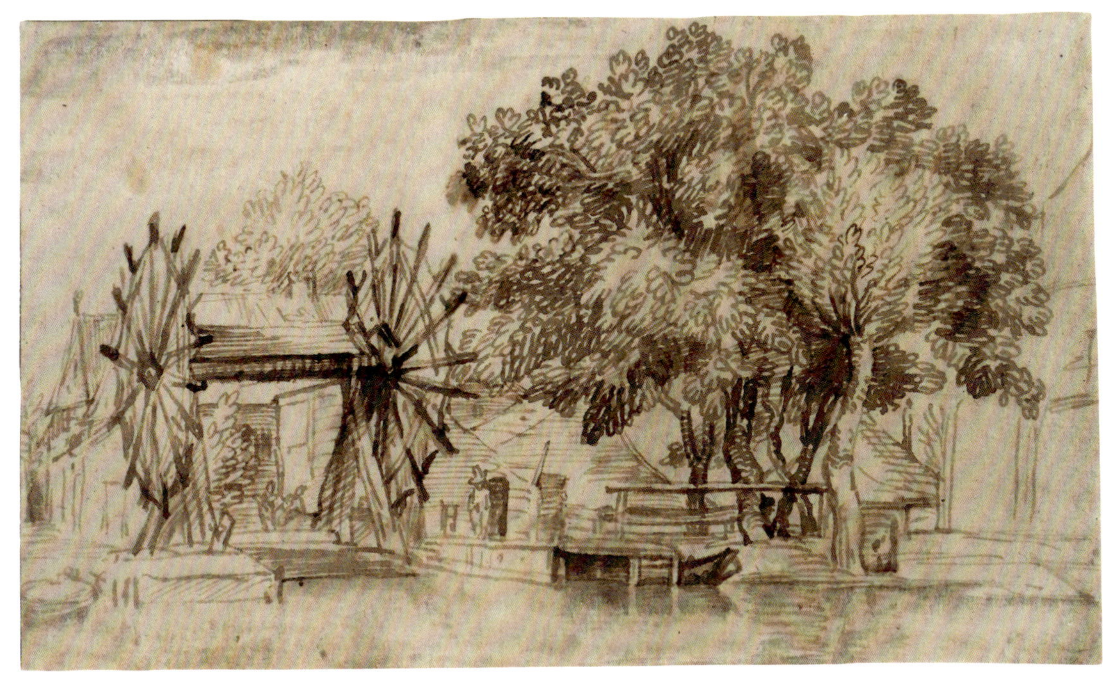

IN THIS DRAWING LIEVENS DEPICTS an *overhaal*, which was a kind of hand-operated escalator or "rollerbridge," employed as a cheap alternative to a lock for raising boats from one water level to another. The *overhaal* seen here lay in the western outskirts of Amsterdam, beside the larger and more celebrated Overtoom that existed until as recently as 1915, allowing boats to pass between the Overtoomseweg canal and the Sloterpolder. This location also appears in the left background of Rembrandt's drawing in Groningen,[1] in a sketch by Jan van Goyen from his sketchbook of 1650–1651,[2] and, most clearly of all, in an etching by Reinier Nooms, called Zeeman (fig. 1).[3]

Although Lievens made a number of other drawings of identifiable Dutch locations (see cats. 124, 130, 131), a view like this of a relatively humble spot on the borders of Amsterdam was unusual for him. These were, however, the kinds of scenes that Rembrandt drew and etched repeatedly in the 1640s and 1650s, and it is tempting to suggest that a drawing such as this provides evidence for some renewed artistic contact between Rembrandt and Lievens following the latter's return to Amsterdam in 1644.

Although the oriental paper that Lievens has used for this drawing is usually associated with the large, finished sheets that he made in the studio, the drawing's spontaneity and small scale suggest that it was a sketch from life. A drawing of comparable size in the Lugt Collection, *Landscape with a Farm at the Water's Edge* — on Western rather than oriental paper — is similar in terms of its compositional balance and treatment of detail.[4]

No larger, more elaborate drawing by Lievens based on this atmospheric study is known, but two copies were made by other hands, one in Lieden and the other in Groningen.[5] GMGR

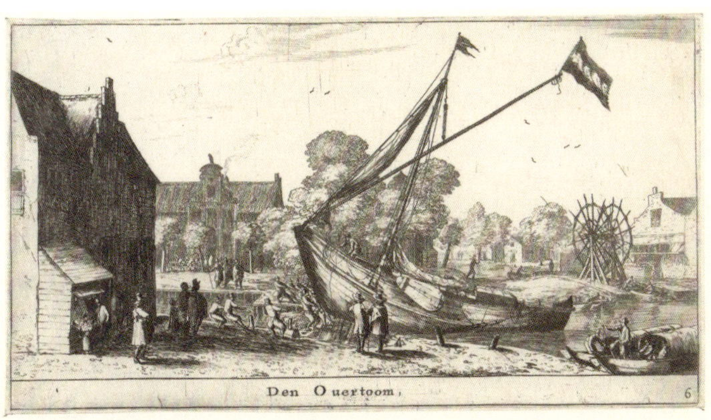

1 | Reinier Nooms, called Zeeman, *The Overtoom (Portage) at Amsterdam*, c. 1655–1660, etching. Rijksmuseum, Amsterdam

112 Portrait of René Descartes

113 Portrait of Caspar Streso

112

1644–1649, black chalk, 24.1 × 20.6 (9 ½ × 8 ⅛). Museum voor Stad en Lande, Groningen (1931-173) *(Amsterdam)*

Inscription

Verso, by an old hand: *Renatus Descartes*

Provenance

A. de Visser, Amsterdam; (sale, Amsterdam, May 16, 1881, no. 488, as Cornelis Visscher); Adalbert, Freiherr von Lanna (L.2773); (his sale, Gutekunst, Stuttgart, May 6, 1910, no. 579, as C. Visscher); Cornelis Hofstede de Groot

Selected References

Bolten 1967, no. 46; Schneider/Ekkart 1973, 195, 361, no. z56; Braunschweig 1979, no. 60; Sumowski 1979, 3698, no. 1660*; Amsterdam 1988, no. 45

FOLLOWING HIS MOVE TO AMSTERDAM in 1644, Lievens embarked on a series of exceptional portrait drawings that have no real parallel in seventeenth-century Dutch art. Some served as studies for prints, while others seem to have been made as finished works. The range of sitters was considerable, including statesmen, writers, poets, and theologians.

The subject of the drawing in Groningen has occasionally been debated, but comparison with the several known portraits of René Descartes (1596–1650) by Frans Hals confirms his identity here.[1] A celebrated, if controversial figure in Holland — especially after 1643, when he wrote an open letter against the Counter-Remonstrant theologian Voetius[2] — Descartes was an eminently suitable subject for an artist seeking to portray the leading cultural figures of his time. Surprisingly, this characteristic portrait was not always attributed to Lievens and was sold on at least two occasions as the work of Cornelis Visscher. Yet it is very comparable in style with the fine signed and dated portrait of the Amsterdam printer and publisher Cornelis Dircksz Cool that Lievens executed in 1649.[3]

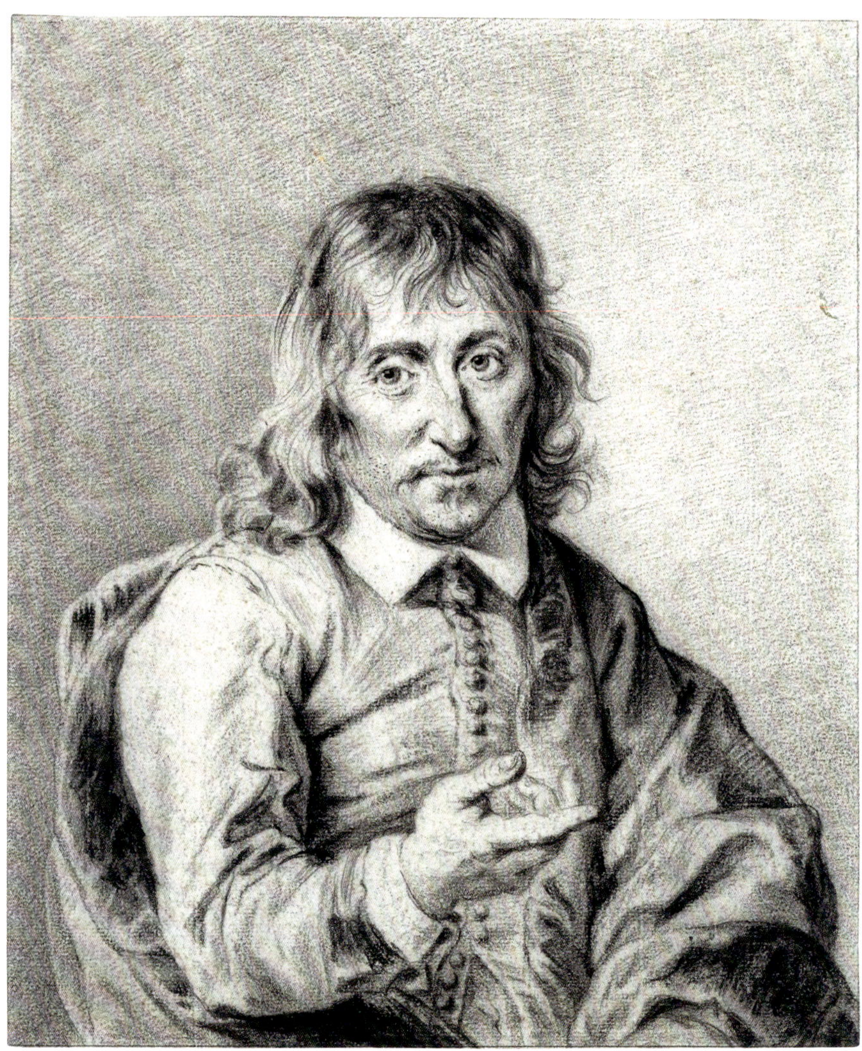

CAT. 112

On the basis of biographical evidence, a similar, or slightly earlier, dating is plausible for the portrait of Descartes. The great French philosopher and mathematician's involvement with the Netherlands was a long one. As early as 1618 he had served Maurits of Nassau during the Thirty Years' War, and although he subsequently lived for some years in Germany and France, he returned to the Dutch Republic in 1628 and remained there until September 1649, when he departed for Stockholm. The portrait must therefore date from the period between Lievens' arrival in Amsterdam in early 1644 and

113

1650s, black chalk, possibly oiled, and stumping, indented for transfer, 22.9 × 19 (9 × 7½). Frits Lugt Collection, Institut Néerlandais, Paris (3461) *(Washington, Milwaukee)*

Inscriptions

Right, near knob on chair back: IL

Verso, in ink (possibly eighteenth century): *domine Str[e]so. predikant in/S gravenhage. door J. Lievensz./na't Leven getekent* [possibly in the same hand as on the verso of cat. 102]

Provenance

Gerrit Schaak; (his sale, Amsterdam [Verkolje... Verkolje], October 28, 1748, portfolio O, no. 13); Cornelis Ploos van Amstel, Amsterdam; (his sale, Amsterdam [van der Schley... Roos], March 3, 1800, portfolio C, no. 15, to van der Schley); James Kerr-Lawson, London; Frits Lugt, Maartensdijk and Paris (L.1028), acquired January 26, 1928

Selected References

Schneider/Ekkart 1973, 66 n. 1, 199, 270, 362, no. Z72; New York and Paris 1977–1978, no.35; Braunschweig 1979, no. 70; Sumowski 1979, 3590, no. 1611; Amsterdam 1988, 72, fig. 48a; Paris and Haarlem 1997–1998, no. 86

Descartes' departure for Sweden, during which time the philosopher was living in Egmond-Binnen.

The portrait of the Calvinist minister Caspar Streso (1603–1664) makes clear that the seventeenth-century Dutch respect for thinkers and writers extended to theologians and clerics. Indeed, unprecedented numbers of portraits of such men survive, and in many cases, as here, these images were etched and disseminated as widely circulated prints. Lievens' print (cat. 86) closely follows the design of the drawing (which has been indented for transfer), but it is more extensive, showing the cleric seated by a table, with his left hand resting on a book and his right hand in his lap. Streso commissioned a second engraved portrait of himself, published in 1654,[4] but it is not certain which of these prints came first.

Caspar Streso was born in Anhalt (in Brandenburg), but from 1638 until his death, he was a Reformed Calvinist minister in The Hague — and by all accounts something of a firebrand, who militantly opposed the more religiously tolerant factions at the Dutch synod of the Reformed Church. To judge by his apparent age in this portrait, it seems likely that the drawing dates from the period when Lievens was also living and working in The Hague (1654–1658). GMGR

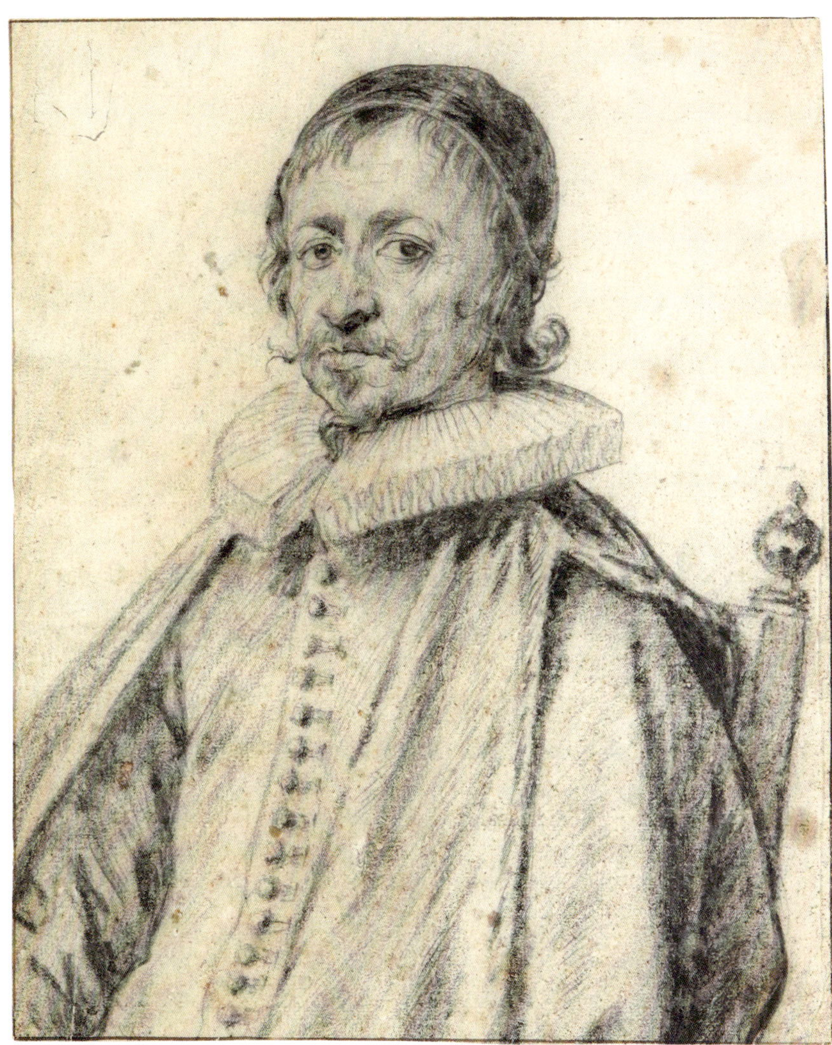

CAT. 113

114 Portrait of Johannes Wtenbogaert

115 Woman Seated in Three-quarter Length, Facing Left

114

1650, black chalk, with touches of pen and brown ink, 32.5 × 26.6 (12 13/16 × 10 1/2). Amsterdams Historisch Museum, Bequest C. J. Fodor (TA 10208) *(Milwaukee, Amsterdam)*

Inscription

Lower right: I.L. / 1650

Verso, in pencil, by a later hand: *De heer Uijtenbogart Ontfanger*

Provenance

Jacob de Vos, Amsterdam; (his sale, Amsterdam, October 30, 1833, portfolio F, no. 7, to Brondgeest); J.G. Baron Verstolk van Soelen, Amsterdam; (his sale, Amsterdam, March 22, 1847, portfolio B, no. 40, to Brondgeest); C.J. Fodor, Amsterdam

Selected References

Schneider/Ekkart 1973, 200, 362, no. z75; S.A.C. Dudok van Heel, "Mr. Johannes Wtenbogaert (1608–1680), een man uit Remonstrants milieu, en Rembrandt van Rijn," in *Jaarboek Amstelodamum* 70 (1978), 146–169; Braunschweig 1979, no. 64; Sumowski 1979, 3576, no. 1604

NOT TO BE CONFUSED WITH THE Remonstrant preacher of the same name, painted by Rembrandt in 1633,[1] this Johannes Wtenbogaert (1608–1680) was a lawyer and "receiver-general" (chief tax collector) for the province of Holland. Rembrandt portrayed this Wtenbogaert as well, in an etching of 1639 generally known as *The Goldweigher*.[2] Like Andries de Graeff, whom Lievens drew in 1657 (cat. 117), Wtenbogaert was a powerful Amsterdam patrician, and these two drawings show that Lievens remained in favor with this group of influential patrons throughout the 1650s.[3]

The sitter's status and self-confidence are abundantly clear in this stylish likeness, one of a particularly accomplished group of portraits that Lievens made in the years around 1650. In contrast with the style of his earlier, Antwerp-period portraits (see cats. 102, 103), the handling here is calmer, and the modeling of draperies subtler and more tonal, which allowed Lievens to convey to perfection Wtenbogaert's authoritative expression.

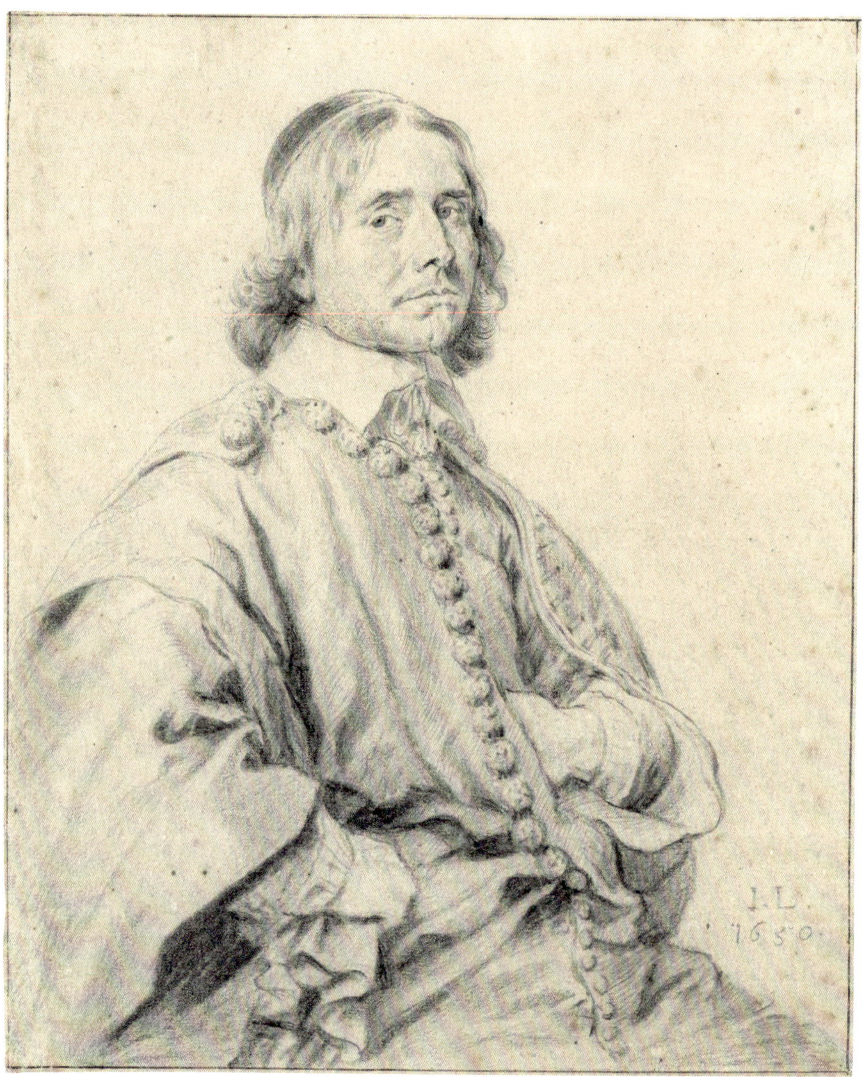

CAT. 114

115

1650, black chalk, 29.9 × 23.8 (11 ¾ × 9 ⅜). Städel Museum, Frankfurt am Main (835) *(Milwaukee, Amsterdam)*

Inscription

Lower left: IL / 1650

Selected References

Schneider/Ekkart 1973, 66 n. 1, 208, no. Z114; Sumowski 1979, 3580, no. 1606

The identity of the sitter in the Frankfurt drawing is not known, although Schneider suggested that this might be the portrait by Lievens of the poet Maria van Bellen, mentioned by Jan Six in a poem of 1651.[4] Although Lievens' earlier figure studies represent men and women in fairly equal numbers, only two of his full-fledged portrait drawings depict female sitters: the present work, and one in Düsseldorf that dates from some years earlier.[5] GMGR

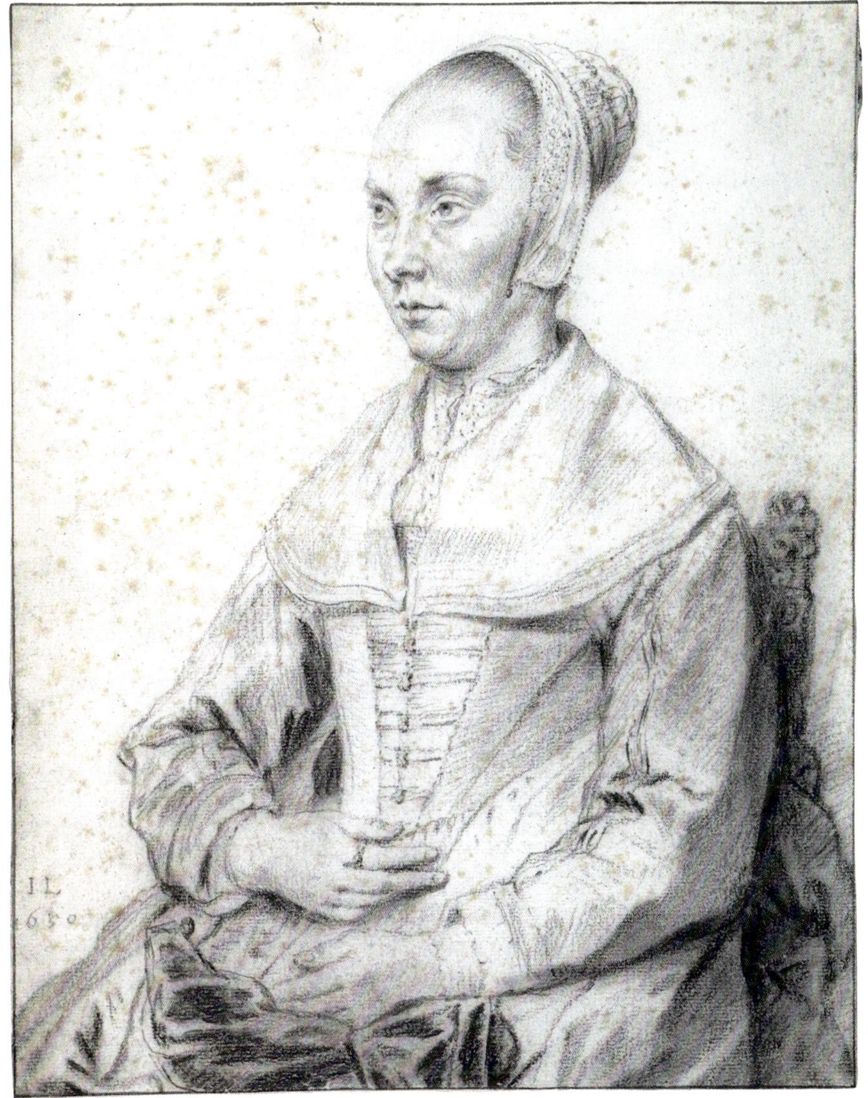

CAT. 115

116 Portrait of Admiral Maerten Harpertsz Tromp

c. 1652, black chalk, 23.4 × 18 (9 3/16 × 7 1/16). The British Museum, London (1836.8.11.344) *(Washington, Amsterdam)*

Inscription

Upper right: IL

Provenance

Johan de Bosch, Amsterdam; (his sale, Amsterdam, October 5, 1767, no. 253); Cornelis Ploos van Amstel, Amsterdam; (his sale, Amsterdam, March 3, 1800, portfolio DDD, no. 12, to Josi); (sale, Amsterdam, March 22, 1802, portfolio 4, no. 46); Sir Francis Baring; John Sheepshanks (L.2333)

Selected References

Schneider/Ekkart 1973, 199, no. Z73; Sumowski 1979, 3586, no. 1609

THIS ENGAGING HEAD STUDY OF the great Dutch naval hero Admiral Maerten Harpertsz Tromp (1598–1653) is unusual among Lievens' portrait drawings, in that all of the others are half- or three-quarter-length images, with the possible exception of the drawing of the Earl of Arundel (cat. 109), which may have started out as a head study. A finished portrait drawing of Tromp, signed with Lievens' initials and dated 1652, is recorded in two nineteenth-century collections,[1] and the present sheet may represent the rapidly sketched life study on which that lost drawing was based. Stylistically, a dating of 1652 seems reasonable for this work.

Admiral Tromp, a legendary figure, was the son of a naval officer. He went to sea with his father at the age of nine and was alongside him when the elder Tromp was killed by English pirates three years later. After his release from captivity in North Africa, the younger Tromp rose to become de facto commander of the Dutch fleet, a position he held more or less continuously from 1637 until his death. Perhaps as a result of his early experiences at the hands of the English, he fought fiercely during the First Anglo-Dutch War of 1652–1653, commanding the Dutch fleet with great success in the battles of Dungeness, Portland, and Scheveningen. In the last of these conflicts, he was killed by an English sharpshooter, an event that ultimately changed the course of Anglo-Dutch relations.

Tromp's passing was greatly mourned. Joost van den Vondel wrote a poem describing the marble monument to the admiral in Delft, and Lievens was commissioned to paint a posthumous portrait, now in the Rijksmuseum.[2] As Sumowski has, however, pointed out the costume in the painting does not correspond with the faint hints of a collar visible in this drawing,[3] which is probably more closely connected with the lost portrait drawing of 1652. GMGR

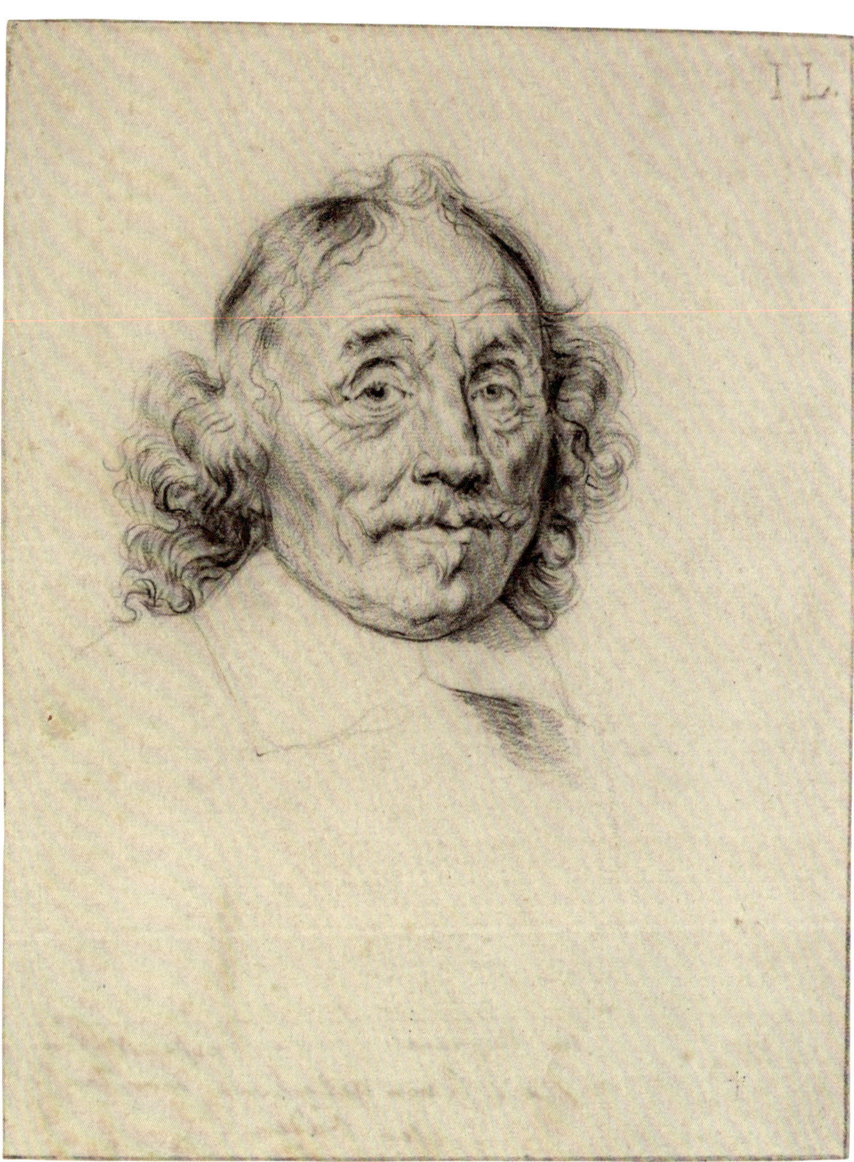

117 Portrait of Andries de Graeff

118 Portrait of Jan Vos

117

1657, black chalk, with traces of white heightening, 42.1 × 31.3 (16 9/16 × 12 5/16). Teylers Museum, Haarlem (portfolio P6) *(Washington, Amsterdam)*

Inscription

Lower right: I.L./1657

Provenance

Possibly Jeronimo de Bosch; (Amsterdam, October 5, 1767, no. 254, as portrait of Constantijn Huygens); possibly Cornelis Ploos van Amstel; (Amsterdam, March 3, 1800, portfolio C, no. 16, as portrait of Constantijn Huygens, to Josi); S. H. de la Sablonière or P. C. Ekama; (Amsterdam, June 30, 1891, no. 140, as portrait of Constantijn Huygens, purchased for the museum)

Selected References

Braunschweig 1979, no. 71 (as portrait of Frans de le Boë Sylvius); Sumowski 1979, 3594, no. 1613 (as portrait of Frans de le Boë Sylvius); Gregor Weber, "Dus left de dapper Graaf, Zu einem Bildnis Andries de Graeffs von Jan Lievens," *Oud Holland* 99 (1985), 44–45 (as portrait of Andries de Graeff); Amsterdam 1988, no. 49; Michiel C. Plomp, *The Dutch Drawings in the Teyler Museum*, vol. 2, *Artists Born between 1575 and 1630* (Haarlem, 1997), 222, no. 237; Haarlem and Paris 2001–2002, no. 73

IN LATER PORTRAIT DRAWINGS Lievens did not keep so rigidly to the compositional formula he had established for the genre beginning around 1650 (see cats. 112–115). The portrait of Andries de Graeff, a leading patrician and mayor of Amsterdam, is formal and highly worked, whereas that of the poet and playwright Jan Vos is more casual, in execution as well as pose, showing the sitter as a thoughtful man of letters.

The Teylers drawing was thought to be a portrait of Constantijn Huygens when it was acquired in 1891.[1] Subsequent identifications have included Gillis Valckenier and the Leiden medical professor Frans de le Boë Sylvius. But Gregor Weber has convincingly argued that it represents Andries de Graeff (1611–1678), based on a marble bust of De Graeff in the Rijksmuseum that bears a striking resemblance to the portrait seen here. It seems likely that Lievens made this drawing to commemorate De Graeff's election as mayor of Amsterdam in 1657. The artist clearly took enormous care over it. With its background allusions to De Graeff's civic status and country estates, the composition is remarkably complete, and the attention the artist paid to the sumptuous costume is also unusual. This was obviously a man whom Lievens wanted to satisfy.

As DeWitt has noted, the patronage of Dutch aristocrats was not always dependable in the changing political landscape of the 1650s, but portraits like this and that of Johannes Wtenbogaert (cat. 114) demonstrate that Lievens was successful in cultivating these important

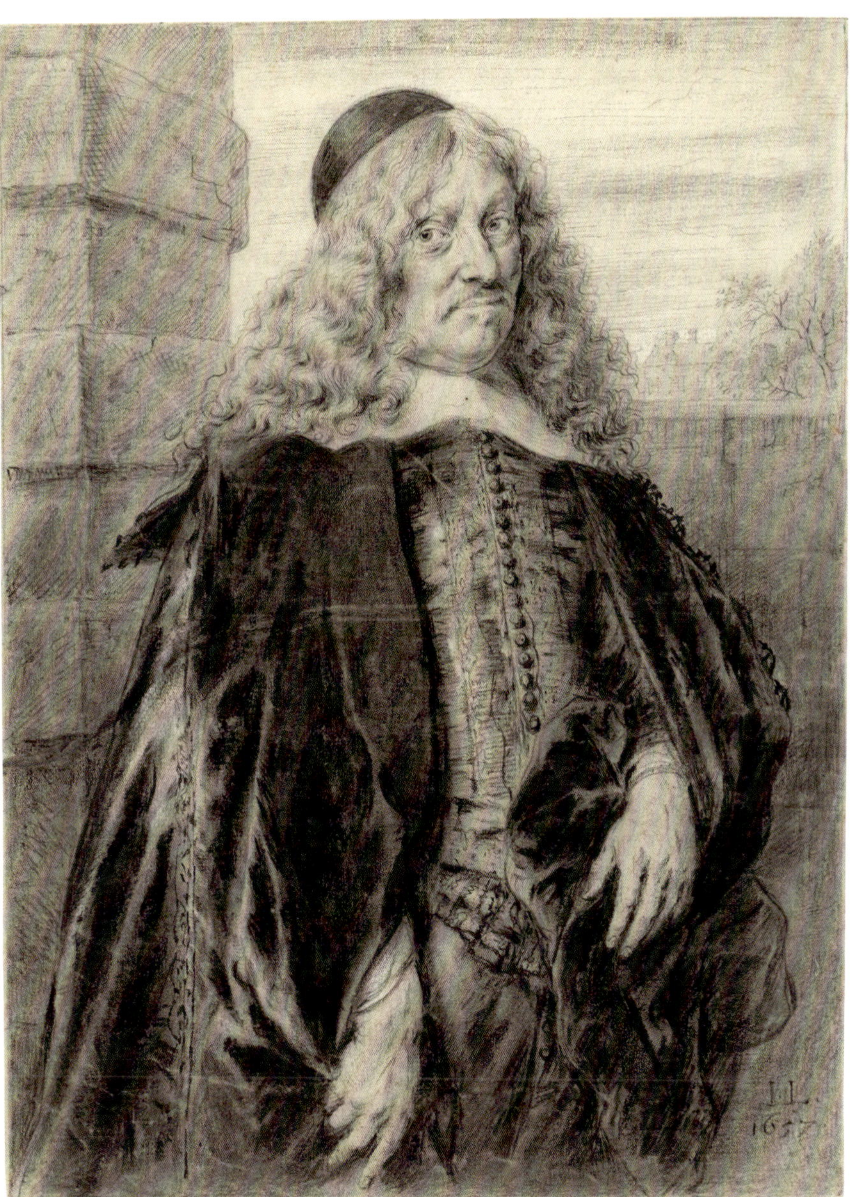

CAT. 117

118

c. 1660, black chalk, 32.5 × 25.6 (12 ¾ × 10 ⅑⁄₁₆). Städel Museum, Frankfurt am Main (836) *(Amsterdam)*

Inscription

Right, above elbow: I.L.

Verso, in an old hand: *Jan Vos door IL naar 't leven tekent*

Provenance

Jeronimo de Bosch; (Amsterdam, October 5, 1767, no. 255); C. Zonne; (Rotterdam, July 20, 1768, portfolio C, no. 20); Cornelis Ploos van Amstel; (Amsterdam, March 3, 1800, portfolio C, no. 14, to Yver)

Selected References

Schneider/Ekkart 1973, 66, 71, 73, 201, 363, no. z78; Sumowski 1979, 3596, no. 1614

relationships.[2] He impressed artists and poets as well, for Jan Vos wrote a short laudatory poem about the portrait of De Graeff, and copies survive of both this portrait and the one Lievens made of Vos.[3]

Jan Vos (1610–1667) was best known as a poet, playwright, and theater director and was a friend of many of Amsterdam's leading families. He must have come into contact with Lievens by the time both were working on the decoration of the new Amsterdam town hall in the 1650s, for Vos was also a glassmaker and provided all the windows for the building, while Lievens was commissioned to produce a major painting.[4] Lievens' portrait of Vos was probably made around 1660, and definitely before the 1662 publication of the poem in its praise.

Sumowski suggests that cursory head studies on both sides of a sheet in the British Museum may be preparatory sketches for this portrait, but the connection is not certain. In contrast to the more formal portrayal of De Graeff, where the clothing in particular is rendered in a tonal, almost sculptural technique, here Lievens has returned to a linearity and hatching similar that used in his earlier drawings, with a corresponding increase in liveliness. At the same time, this engaging image has a strong three-dimensional presence, its visual impact enhanced by Vos' keen, if slightly world-weary, expression. GMGR

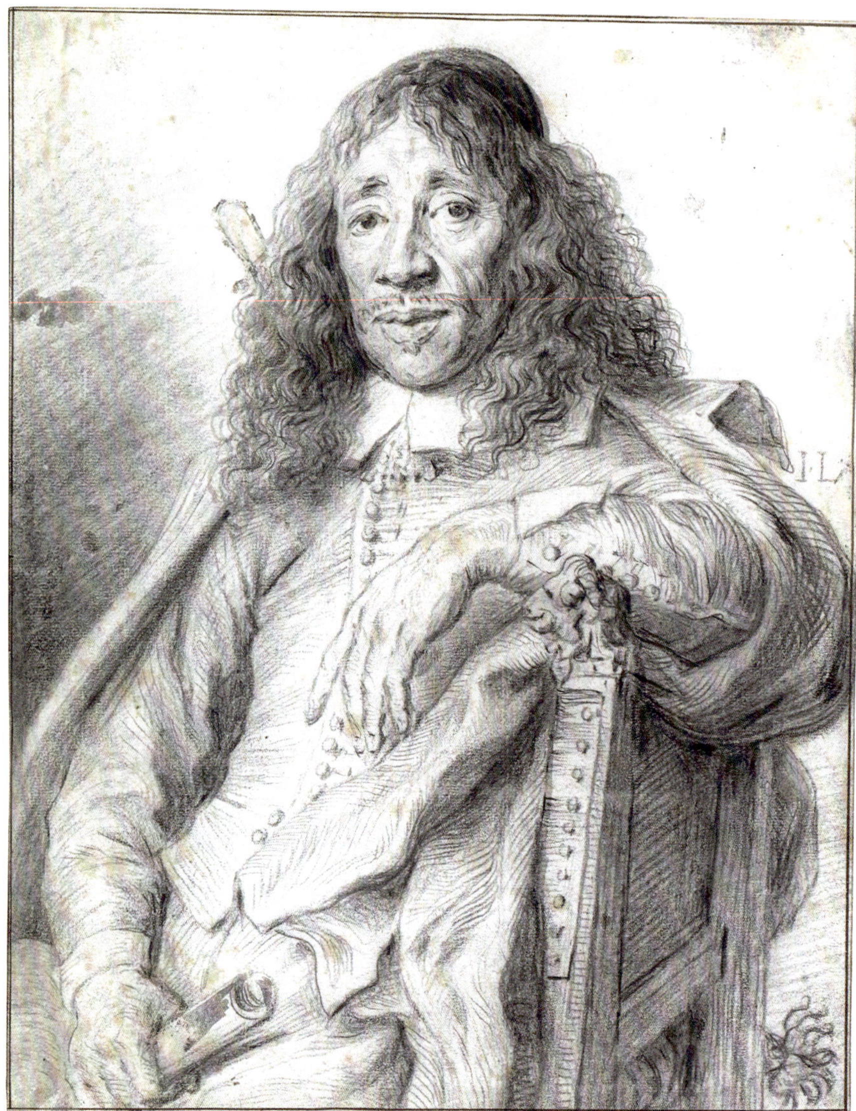

CAT. 118

119 Two Studies of a Man in a Hat

120 Sheet of Studies

119
late 1650s, pen and brown ink, 19.1 × 17.5 (7½ × 6⅞). Staatliche Museen zu Berlin, Kupferstichkabinett (KdZ 2609) *(Washington, Amsterdam)*

Inscriptions
Lower left, in ink: *Caubas* (?); with another illegible word

Lower right: the remains of a further inscription

Selected References
Schneider/Ekkart 1973, 208, no. Z121; Braunschweig 1979, no. 82; Sumowski 1979, 3642, no. 1635[x]

1 | Jan Lievens, *Study Sheet*, after c. 1650, pen and brown ink on buff paper. The British Museum, London

A SMALL BUT INTRIGUING PART of Lievens' drawn oeuvre consists of sheets of studies in pen and brown ink. None of these sketches has ever been linked with any finished works by the artist, thus the problem of dating them is even greater than for his portraits and landscapes.

Following Lievens' departure from Leiden in 1632, his pen-and-ink figure drawings provide very few fixed points on which to construct a chronology for his use of the medium. These consist of one or two portrait drawings from his London and Antwerp years and a signed 1665 drawing of *Saint Jerome in a Landscape* (see Rubinstein figs. 2, 5, 12). A sheet of studies in the British Museum (fig. 1) includes some sketches of trees, and the handling of those elements suggests that the sheet probably dates from c. 1645–1655. These trees are similar to those in landscape drawings from that period, such as the *Ruins of the Castle of Brederode* (cat. 123).

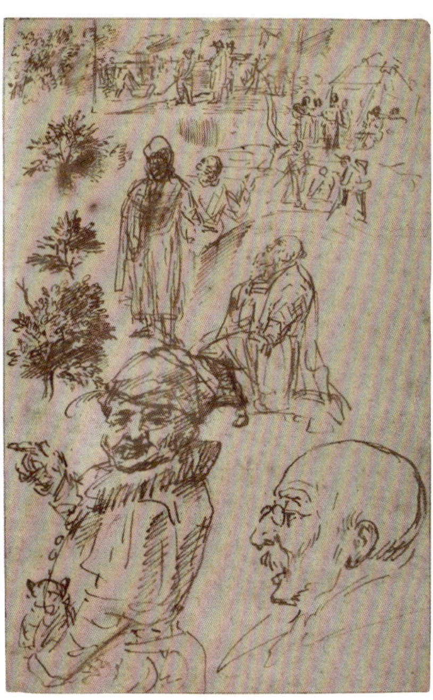

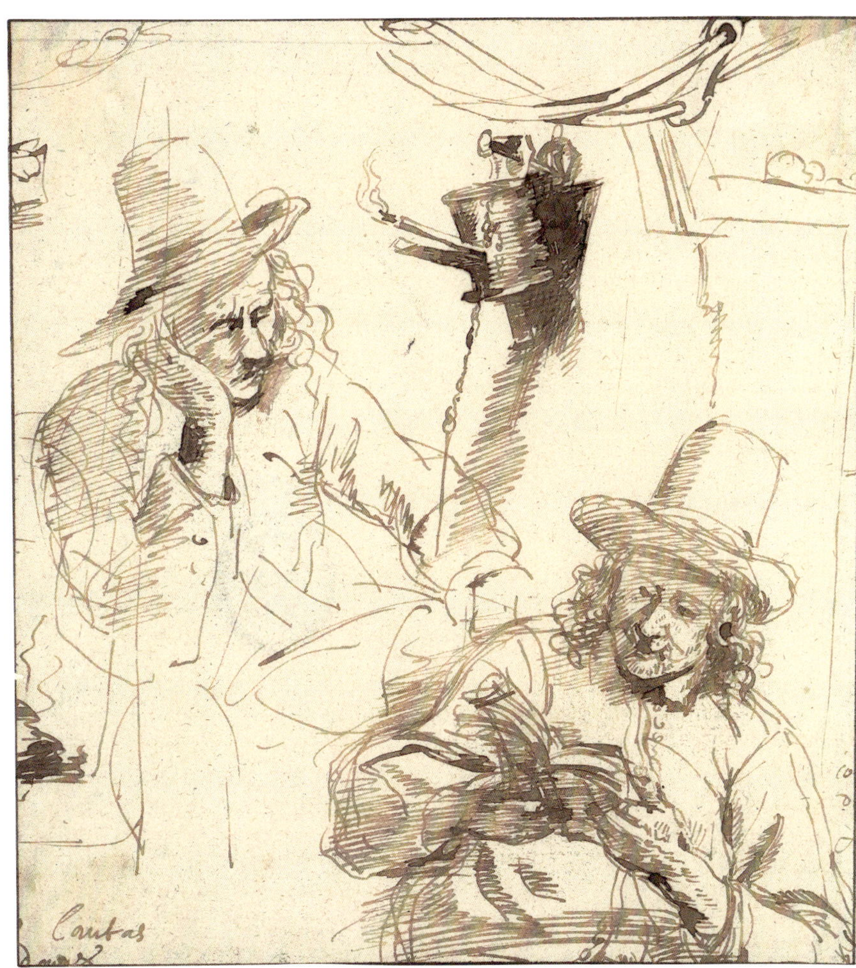

CAT. 119

The faces in the studies from Berlin recall those in the London drawing, but the figures are more thoroughly drawn. Within rapid, sketchy outlines, they are modeled with rhythmic, hatched shading. As a result, the sheet is more pictorial. Schneider described it as depicting a ship's interior, although it actually seems to show two separate studies of the same figure in different poses. Sumowski rightly noted that Lievens' so-called self-portrait

120

1660s, pen and brown ink, 25.6 × 17.6 ($10\frac{1}{16} \times 6\frac{15}{16}$). Kunstmuseum, Düsseldorf (FP 5092) *(not in exhibition)*

Inscriptions

Lower right, in pen: IL

Verso: *1618*

Selected References

Schneider/Ekkart 1973, 209, 365, no. Z125; Braunschweig 1979, no. 81; Sumowski 1979, 3600, no. 1616

in Vienna is the most comparable in style to the Berlin sheet,[1] but the traditional late dating of that drawing to c. 1660 is based entirely on its unconvincing identification as a self-portrait. The sitter's costume in the present drawing has sometimes been dated to 1660–1665, but this assertion remains speculative.[2] Further complicating the dating is the similarity of isolated accents to those in *Seated River Gods* (cat. 105), which dates to c. 1638–1643. On balance, a date in the late 1650s seems the most probable.

The drawing in Düsseldorf is unquestionably more calligraphic than the study sheets in Berlin and London. Sumowski saw parallels with the 1665 *Saint Jerome*, but these studies show much greater fluidity of line.[3] The treatment of anatomy in the seated figure's legs — the very high positioning of the calf muscle, for example, and the exaggerated recession of the little toe — is remininiscent of the unique chalk study of legs on the verso of *Woodland Scene with a Draftsman* in Berlin (see Rubinstein fig. 6), from the mid-1660s.[4]

Such late pen-and-ink figure studies still require much research, but they are works of the greatest originality and interest, with few close parallels in the Dutch art of their time. The drawings have their own clear style, and they add a significant dimension to the corpus of Lievens' surviving works. GMGR

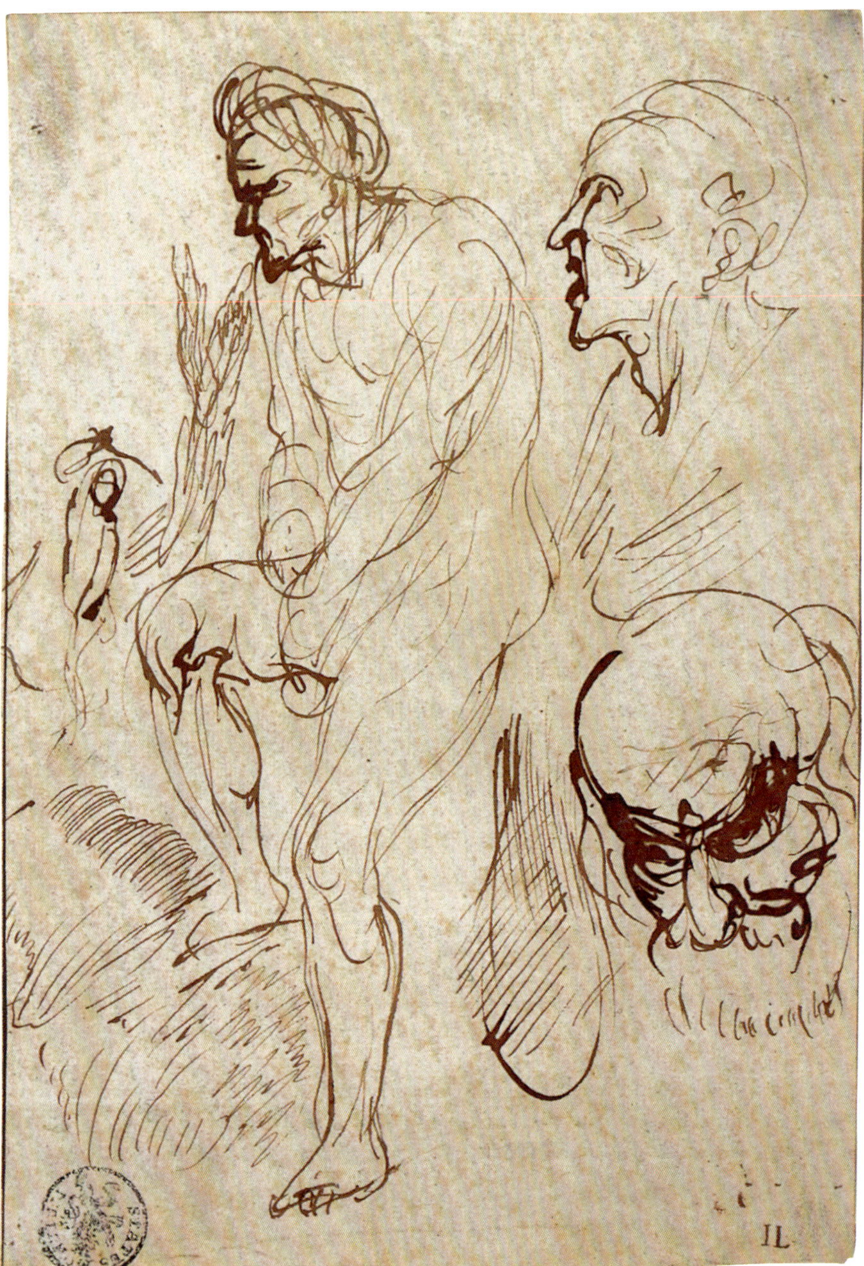

CAT. 120

121 A Path in the Haagse Bos

122 "Het Roomhuis" in the Haagse Bos

121

c. 1654–1658, pen and brown ink on oriental paper, 22.9 × 38.1 (9 × 15). The J. Paul Getty Museum, Los Angeles (2001.13) *(Washington, Amsterdam)*

Inscription

Lower right, indistinct, in pencil: *fl7*

Provenance

William Esdaile, London (L. 2617, partly abraded); Earl Spencer (L. 1532); A.W.M. Mensing; (F. Muller, Amsterdam, April 27, 1937, no. 341); Ernst Goldschmidt, Brussels; (by inheritance until sale, Ader Tajan, Paris, October 28, 1994, no. 38); private collection, New York; (Sotheby's, New York, January 23, 2001, no. 140)

Selected References

Schneider/Ekkart 1973, 390, no. SZ432, fig. 58 (the illustration incorrectly captioned, giving details of no. SZ430); Sumowski 1979, 3740, no. 4, under no. 1679x

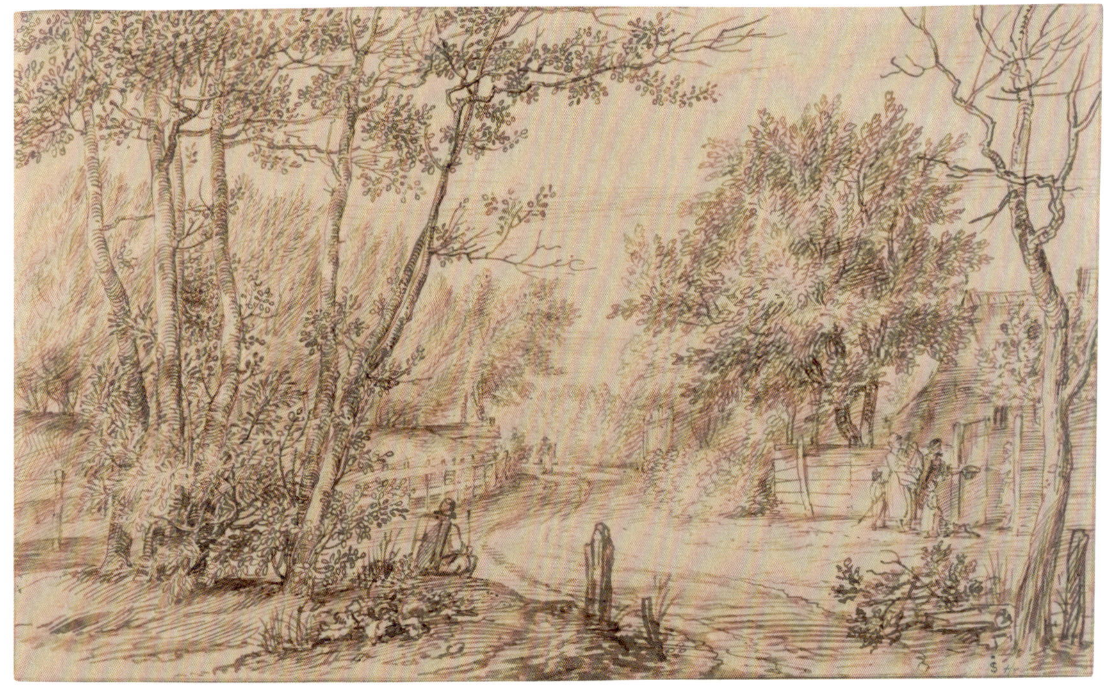

CAT. 121

THESE TWO EXCEPTIONAL EXAMPLES of large, well-preserved studio drawings on oriental paper are more elaborate and elegant than many of Lievens' other landscapes. Apart from Rembrandt, Lievens was the only artist of his time who used oriental papers on a regular basis.[1] This type of paper offers a fine, hard surface on which to draw, but it does not absorb the ink as thoroughly as Western paper, so drawings on this support are much more prone to fading. When Lievens' drawings on oriental paper are still in good condition, as here, they demonstrate a unique surface brilliance and subtlety of handling.

Both of these drawings depict locations in the Haagse Bos, the last remaining section of the great forests that stretched in medieval times from The Hague to Haarlem, which were used for centuries as a royal hunting park. As early as 1576 an act was passed protecting the surviving woods from being sold or cut down, and ever since, the Haagse Bos has been a popular and freely accessible area, widely used by local residents for a range of recreational purposes.[2]

The specific site depicted in the Getty drawing has not been identified, but the sheet in the Lugt Collection shows a well-known spot, also recorded in a drawing by Jan de Bisschop.[3] The building seen here was located by the eastern entrance to the wood and must surely have been the house of one of the park rangers. In the early nineteenth century it was turned into a café called "Het Roomhuis" (The Creamery), the name by which both the location and the Lievens and Bisschop drawings have subsequently been identified.

Lievens is known to have lived and worked in The Hague between 1654 and 1658, and it seems reasonable to date these two superbly accomplished drawings to this period of his career. GMGR

122

c. 1654–1658, pen and brown ink on oriental paper, 22.4 × 36.8 (8¾ × 14½). Frits Lugt Collection, Institut Néerlandais, Paris (1411) *(Milwaukee, Amsterdam)*

Inscriptions

Lower right: *Lievens*; black lead: *coll. H.W.C.* [Campe]

Verso: lower left, in brown ink: *1807 WE P55* [55 changed to 62] *N387* [Esdaile]

Provenance

William Esdaile (L. 2617), acquired in 1807; (Christie's, London, June 18–25, 1840, within nos. 1057–1059); Heinrich Wilhelm Campe, Leipzig (L. 1391); his daughter Luise Vieweg, Braunschweig; (C.G. Boerner, Leipzig, 1918, cat. 37, no. 113); (Bernard Houthakker, Amsterdam); (Sotheby's, London, Sir Kenneth Mackenzie Collection, and others, February 15, 1921, no. 86); (E. Parsons and Sons, London, 1921, cat. 38, no. 159); (Bernard Houthakker, Amsterdam); Frits Lugt, Maartensdijk and Paris, acquired November 26, 1923

Selected References

Brussels, Rotterdam, Paris, Bern 1968–1969, no. 96; Schneider/Ekkart 1973, 73, 123, 365, no. z146; Braunschweig 1979, no. 68; Sumowski 1979, 3720, no. 1670*; Charles Dumas, *Haagse stadsgezichten* (Zwolle, 1991), 177, 180, 185

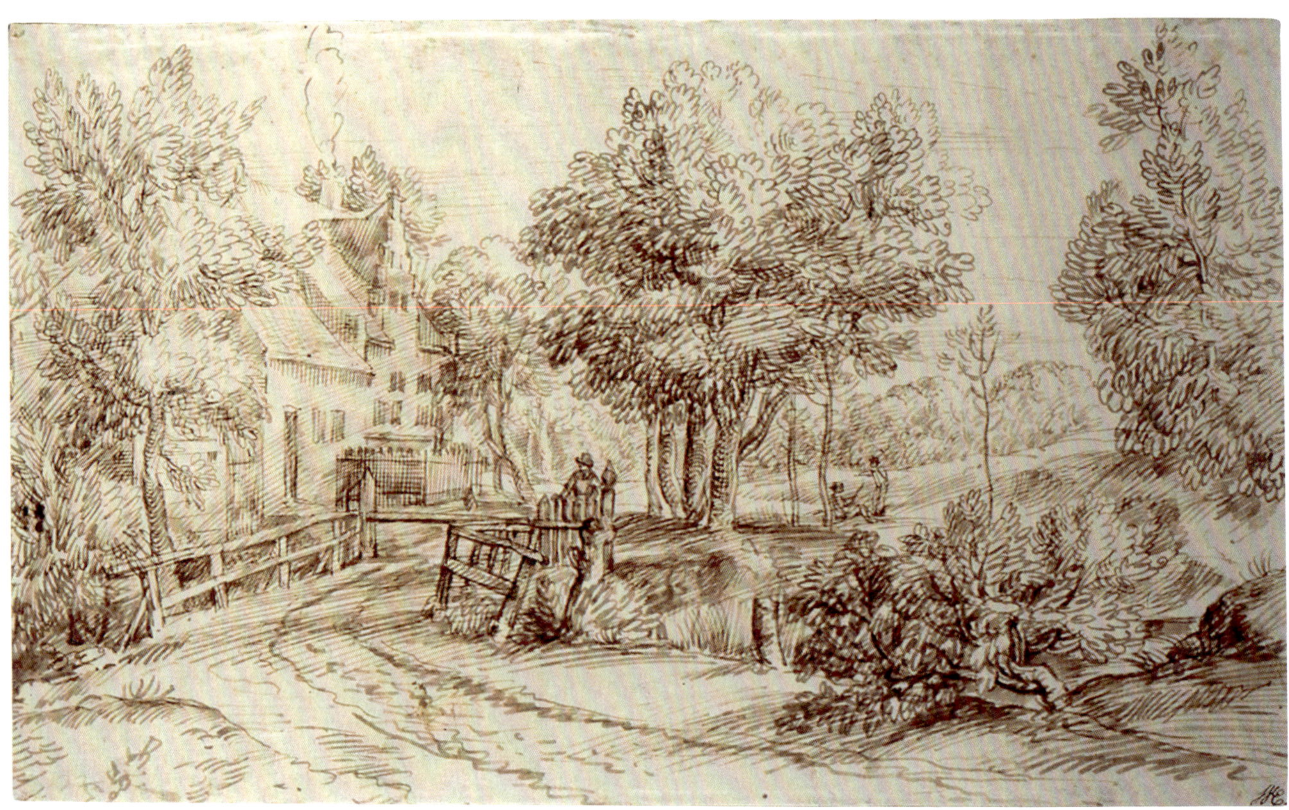

CAT. 122

123 Ruins of the Castle of Brederode

124 Ruins of the Abbey Church at Egmond

123

c. 1645–1655, pen and brown ink and brown wash, 29.2 × 38.3 (11 1/2 × 15 1/16). Peck Collection, Boston *(Washington, Milwaukee)*

Inscriptions

Verso: center right, in brown ink (seventeenth-century): *slot te breederoo 3 guilden*; and lower right, in pencil: *140*

Provenance

H.M. Montauban van Swijndegt (1841–1929), Rotterdam; (his sale, Amsterdam, R.W.P. de Vries, April 5, 1906, no. 115); (sale, Amsterdam, R.W.P. de Vries, March 4, 1930, no. 182); H.C. Valkema Blouw (1883–1953); (his sale, F. Muller, Amsterdam, March 2–4, 1954, no. 266); Bernard Houthakker, Amsterdam (L.1272); (his sale, Sotheby Mak van Waay, Amsterdam, November 17–18, 1975, no. 42); (Theo Laurentius, Voorschooten, 1975); F.W.A. Knight; (his sale, Sotheby Mak van Waay, Amsterdam, October 29, 1979, no. 29); acquired at the sale by Leena and Sheldon Peck

Selected References

Amsterdam 1964, no. 52; Schneider/Ekkart 1973, 218, 366, no. z185; Sumowski 1979, 3872, no. 1741*; Van der Wyck, Kloek, and Niemeijer 1989–1990, 2: 85, fig. 134; Chapel Hill, Ithaca, Worcester 1999–2001, no. 18

A SMALL BUT SIGNIFICANT GROUP of Lievens' landscape drawings depicts ruined castles and abbeys — with apparent topographical accuracy. The widespread destruction that had taken place during the United Provinces' struggle for independence gave rise in the second quarter of the seventeenth century to an entirely new genre in Dutch landscape art: the heroic "ruinscape." During the Twelve Years' Truce between 1609 and 1621, artists began to create paintings, drawings, and prints as a way to record structures that had been damaged during the Dutch revolt. The artists who portrayed such ruins were motivated not only by an appreciation of their picturesque qualities but also by a desire to pay homage to the terrible losses their homeland had suffered and to document for posterity what remained of the country's historic buildings before they deteriorated further. Works of this type form a distinct subsection among drawings of the native Dutch landscape by a number of artists, including Jan Lievens. Particularly noteworthy is the celebrated series of nearly 250 large drawings made by Roelant Roghman in 1646–1647, representing the ruins of many castles and country houses.[1]

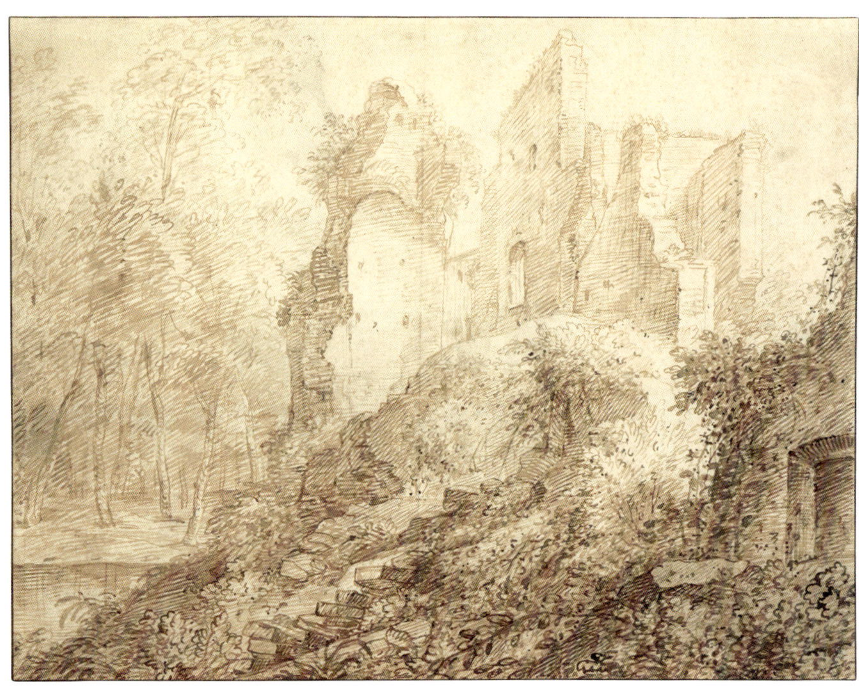

CAT. 123

The castle of Brederode, north of Haarlem, was an important ruin, and it appeared in numerous visual records. The once grand medieval building was damaged in 1351, 1426, and 1491, then was totally destroyed by the Spanish in 1573. Hendrick Goltzius depicted Brederode as early as 1600,[2] followed by Jacob Matham, Jan van de Velde, Willem Buytewech, Hercules Seghers, Simon de Vlieger, Nicolaes Berchem, Jacob van Ruisdael, and others. Lievens made more than one drawing of Brederode.[3]

This view exhibits the rhythmic execution of foliage and hatching seen in the artist's topographical drawings of the middle to late 1640s, such as *The Rollerbridge to the Sloterpolder* (cat. 111). The ruin and the woods beyond are rendered with a dense, almost sculptural fabric of long, repeated pen strokes, which fill most of the sheet, while a broad swath of short, rounded strokes and darker notes in the foreground provides a rich texture of contrasting accents. Lievens here has created a sophisticated scheme of lighting and composition that is atmospheric and evocative — and at the same time almost impenetrable, as befits the romantic grandeur and dereliction of the subject. The watermark in the paper was in use between 1637 and about 1655,[4] which is consistent with a stylistic dating of the drawing in the late 1640s or early 1650s.

Of all the ruins in Holland, the historic seat of the Counts of Egmond near Alkmaar seemed to strike the most resonant chord among Dutch artists. The castle had been occupied by the Spanish during the invasion of 1573–1574, but no sooner had it been liberated than William the Silent, then Lord of Egmond, ordered

124

c. 1655–1665, pen and brown ink, with study of tree trunk on verso, 32 × 41.6 (12 5/8 × 16 3/8). Prentenkabinet der Rijksuniversiteit, Leiden (1622) *(Amsterdam)*

Inscription

Verso, in brown ink (probably seventeenth-century): *abdije van Egmont*

Provenance

Bernardus Hagelis (1680–1762); (his sale, Amsterdam, De Leth, March 8, 1762, no. 635); (sale, Amsterdam, July 17, 1775, no. A65)

Selected References

Schneider/Ekkart 1973, 76, 212, 365, no. Z144; Braunschweig 1979, 182, under no. 87 (as probably a copy); Sumowski 1979, 3832, no. 1722x; Amsterdam 1988, no. 61

Copy

A copy by J. C. Wendel (dates not recorded), almost identical in dimensions, is in the library of the Rijksuniversiteit, Leiden (Boedel Nijenhuis Collection, P303 III, no. 11)

it destroyed to prevent its being retaken by the Spanish invaders. In subsequent decades various artists depicted the remains, notably Jan Lievens, as seen in this expressive drawing (cat. 124), and Jacob van Ruisdael, who made some seven drawings and three paintings incorporating elements based on the ruins of Egmond.[5]

As Schatborn pointed out, the left side of the castle facade (at the right of the present composition) was intact when Roghman drew it in the 1640s but had partly collapsed by the time Lievens made his drawing.[6] Unfortunately, no other images from the second half of the seventeenth century record the building from the same vantage point, so Lievens' work cannot be dated from documentary evidence. Stylistically, the open composition and the rapid — in parts almost cursory — pen work imply a date in the late 1650s or early 1660s. Schneider described this highly atmospheric drawing as "the purest and most beautiful sheet" among the landscapes with an identifiable geographical location.[7] Ekkart thought it no more than a copy, but Sumowski and Schatborn rightly consider it a fine original work by Lievens.[8] A clearly autograph partial study of a tree on the verso further argues for its being by the artist. A second drawing by Lievens of a different part of the ruins, now in Braunschweig,[9] seems earlier in date, suggesting the artist visited the site more than once. GMGR

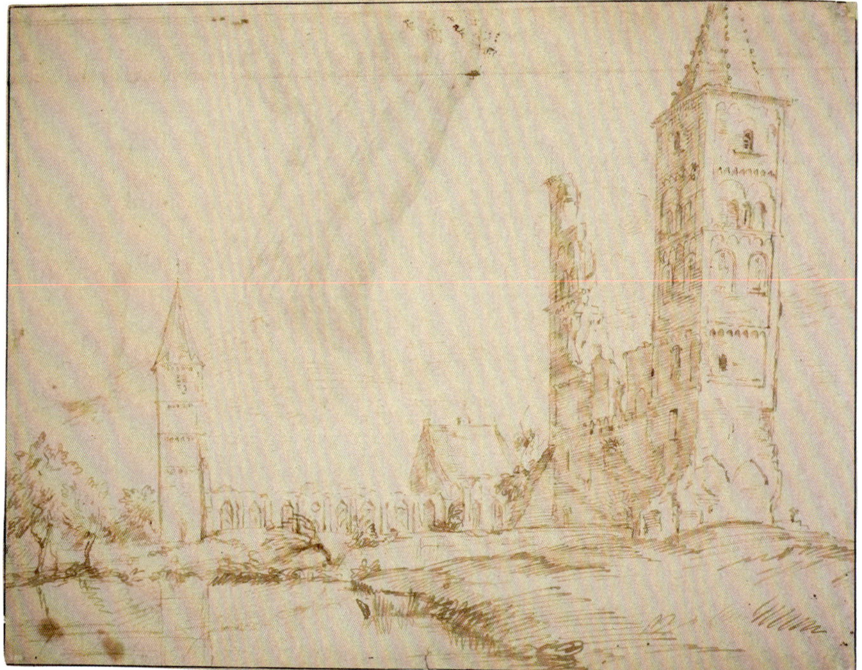

CAT. 124

125 Village Street with a Windmill

1650s(?), pen and brown ink, 25.4 × 40.5 (10 × 15 15/16). The Pierpont Morgan Library, New York, Gift of J. P. Morgan Jr., 1924 (III, 186d) *(Washington)*

Provenance

Charles Fairfax Murray, London and Florence; (Galerie Alexandre Imbert, Rome); acquired in 1909 by Pierpont Morgan, New York; J.P. Morgan Jr., New York

Selected References

Schneider 1932, 247, no. 3 (as an unseen drawing, of undetermined attribution); Schneider/Ekkart 1973, 388, no. SZ423; Washington, Denver, Fort Worth 1977, no. 41; Sumowski 1979, 3798, no. 1706x; Turner 2006, no. 131

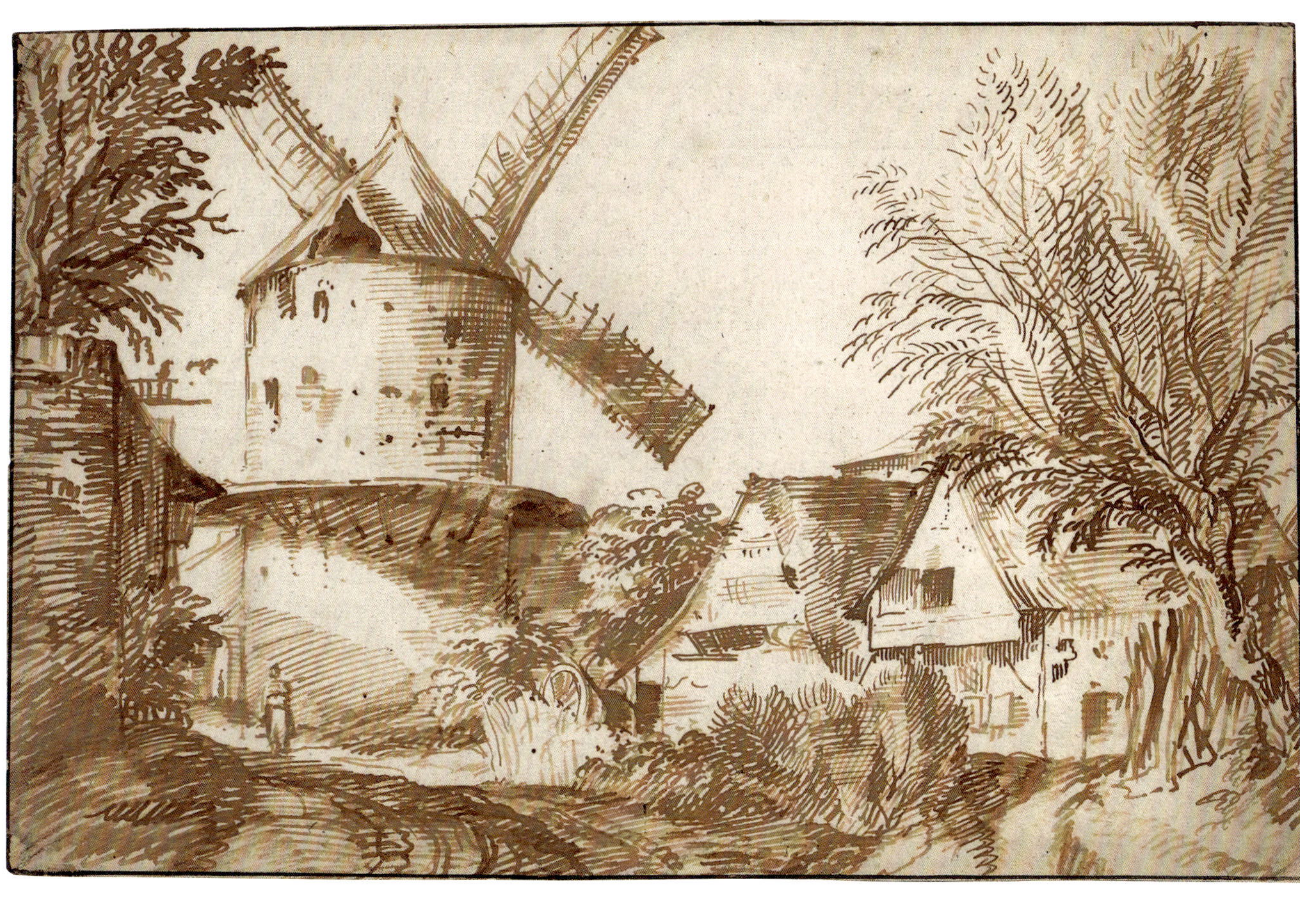

EXTENSIVE PASSAGES IN THIS imposing drawing are rendered with powerful, parallel pen strokes, more typical of Lievens' isolated study sheets than of his landscapes. Yet a few other landscape drawings employ similar strokes in combination with the artist's familiar, looping treatment of foliage. Good examples are in Leiden and Braunschweig, but perhaps the closest in handling is a drawing in Frankfurt, which Hans-Ulrich Beck identified as a view of the Kuhhirtenturm (Cowherds' Tower) in Cleves.[1]

This topographical information is extremely interesting, as Jaap Bolten independently suggested that the Morgan drawing, together with one in Groningen, might depict a town under the authority of the Elector of Brandenburg, for whom Lievens worked in Berlin in 1653–1654.[2] J. Q. van Regteren Altena also independently observed that the windmill shown here is of a German type, possibly from the region of Bentheim.[3] The precise geographical location still cannot be identified with certainty, but it seems highly likely that the town is in Germany and that the drawing can be associated with Lievens' journey to Berlin.

The large scale and compositional completeness of this drawing suggest that it was made in the studio, but it retains a sense of immediacy often seen in studies from life, such as the later *View of Haarlem* (cat. 128). This must largely be due to the unusual boldness of many of the lines, created with a more broadly trimmed pen nib than Lievens ordinarily used.[4] Intermingled with these heavy, dark lines are numerous delicate touches, and the lively and varied contrasts between these pen strokes of differing intensities make this one of Lievens' most impressive landscape drawings. GMGR

126 Homestead in a Forest

127 Wooded Landscape with Shepherds, Flocks, and a Village

126

c. 1654–1658, pen and brown ink with brown wash on oriental paper, 22.2 × 37 (8¾ × 14⁹⁄₁₆). The British Museum, London (1847.3.26.13) *(Washington, Milwaukee)*

Inscription

Verso [by Ploos van Amstel]: *Jan Lievens f / geb. Leiden 1606 / hoog 8¾ dm / br 14¾ d / f22*

Provenance

Cornelis Ploos van Amstel (L. 3002–3003); (possibly Van der Schley... Roos, Amsterdam, March 3, 1800, portfolio N, no. 38 or 39); Jan Gijsbert, Baron Verstolk van Soelen (L. 2490); (De Vries... Roos, Amsterdam, March 22, 1847, no. 307); purchased from Messrs Smith, 1847

Selected References

Schneider/Ekkart 1973, 75, 233, no. Z301; Sumowski 1979, 3752, no. 1685*; Sumowski 1980, 371, pl. 43a; London, Paris, Cambridge, MA, 2002–2003, 144, fig. 1

1 | Jan Lievens, *Homestead in a Forest*, c. 1654–1658, pen and brown ink. The Pierpont Morgan Library, New York

2 | Jan Lievens, *Homestead in a Forest*, c. 1654–1658, pen and brown ink on oriental paper. Maida and George Abrams Collection, Boston, Massachusetts

THESE DRAWINGS SHED CONSIDERABLE light on Lievens' working method as a landscape draftsman and on the complex issues of attribution regarding multiple versions of the same composition. The British Museum drawing turns out to be closely related to one in the Pierpont Morgan Library (fig. 1), which shows the same low building with three trees in front, but from a closer viewpoint, without the large tree and figures to the far left, and with a different view to the right.[1] The Morgan sheet is smaller and simpler in layout—and Sumowski proposed, with some justification, that it may be the sketch from life on which Lievens based the larger, more elaborate studio drawing on oriental paper now in London.

Another version of the London drawing, however, also on oriental paper, is found in the Abrams Collection (fig. 2) and may be, as Robinson has persuasively argued, Lievens' primary version.[2] The sense of space is more convincing in the Abrams drawing, which, significantly, is the only landscape by Lievens to bear an authentic "IL" signature.[3]

In 1932 Schneider listed the London drawing among the best of Lievens' pastoral scenes,[4] but as early as 1915 Hind had already suggested that the work might actually be by Jan Andrea Lievens, rather than his father.[5] Royalton-Kisch supports the latter view but has suggested that the Abrams version might also be by Jan Andrea.[6] The absence of any significant stylistic difference between the drawings does argue for their being by the same hand, but the signature on the Abrams version, in the same ink as the rest of the drawing, proves that the artist was Jan Lievens, not Jan Andrea.

The British Museum/Abrams composition represents a clearly defined type in the corpus of Lievens' finished studio drawings in which rustic buildings are seen through fairly open woodland. While less formal and highly worked than, for example, the views of the Haagse Bos (cats. 121, 122), these drawings are also carefully constructed, as the artist explored ways in which sunlight falls through a canopy of trees onto buildings and figures. The drawings' serenity and sense of harmony is reinforced by the inclusion of pastoral staffage: shepherds and their flocks resting under the trees, or figures playing pipes to each other.

The most pastoral of all is the recently discovered *Wooded Landscape with Shepherds, Flocks, and a Village*, a work of exceptional originality and quality, which is almost Claudian in atmosphere. It is not entirely clear if this drawing is a studio work or an unusually large and elaborate sketch from nature. Its scale and compositional complexity argue for the former, but the spontaneity and freedom of handling, particularly in the figures and animals, suggest the latter. GMGR

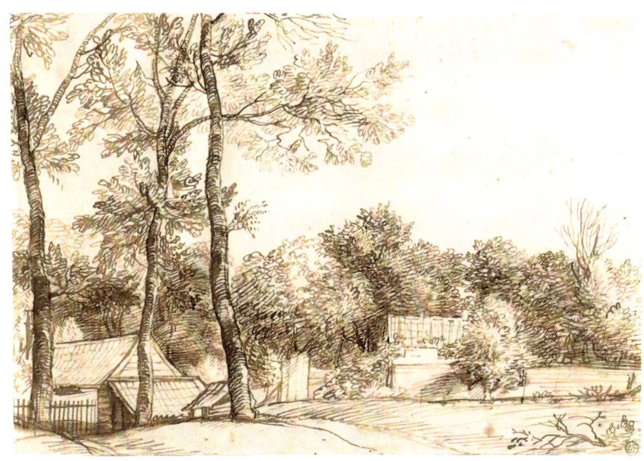

FIG. 1

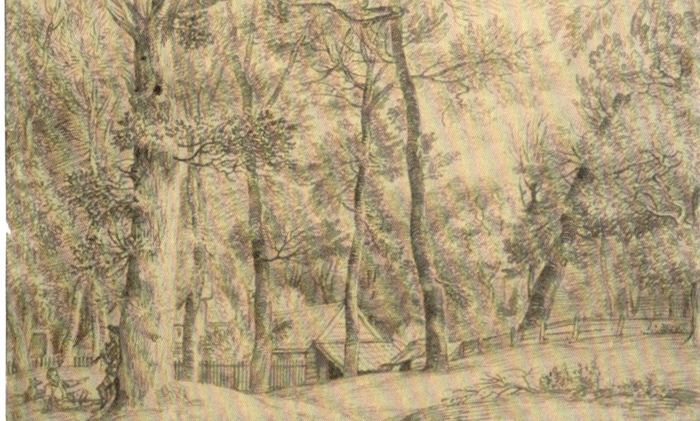

FIG. 2

127

late 1650s(?), pen and brown ink, 25.5 × 36.5 (10 1/16 × 14 3/8). Collection Noro Foundation *(Milwaukee)*

Provenance

Marquet de Vasselot (L. 2499); (Piasa, Paris, March 18, 2005, no. 40)

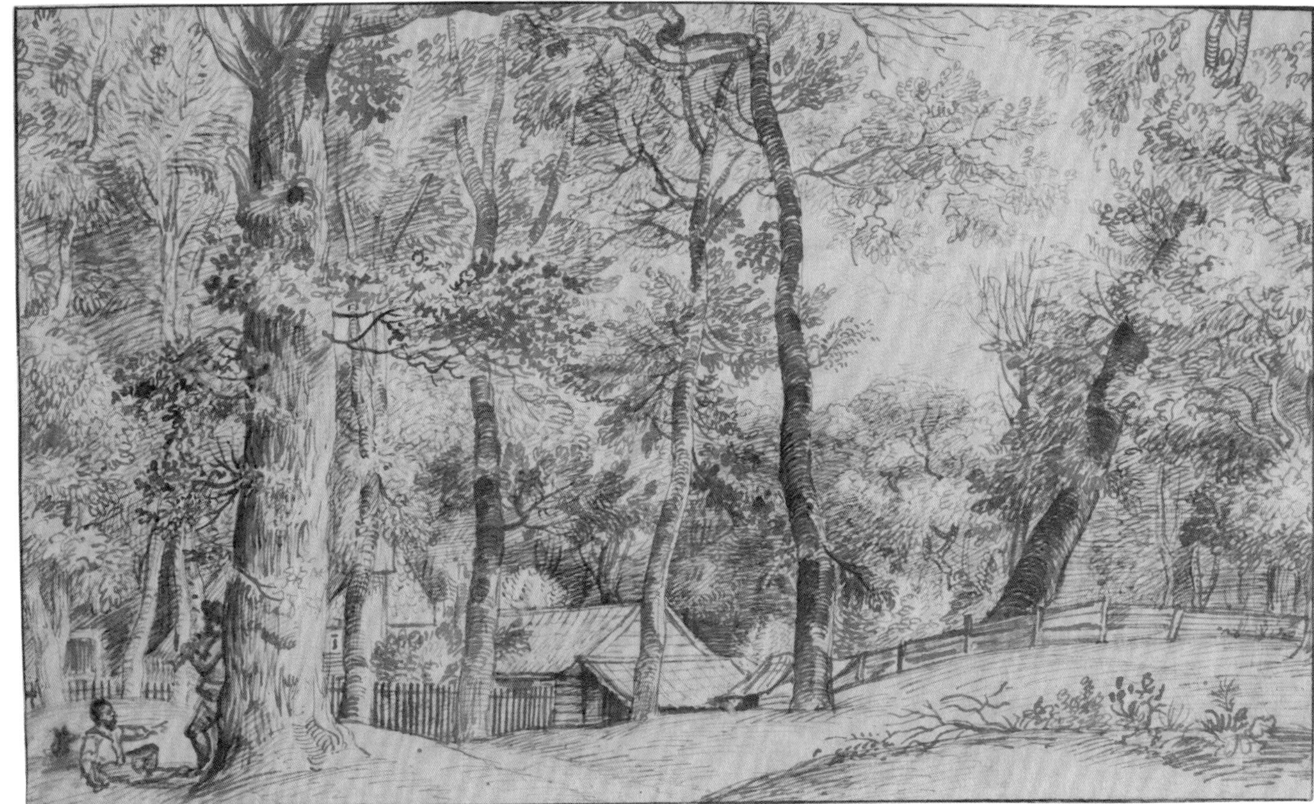

CAT. 126

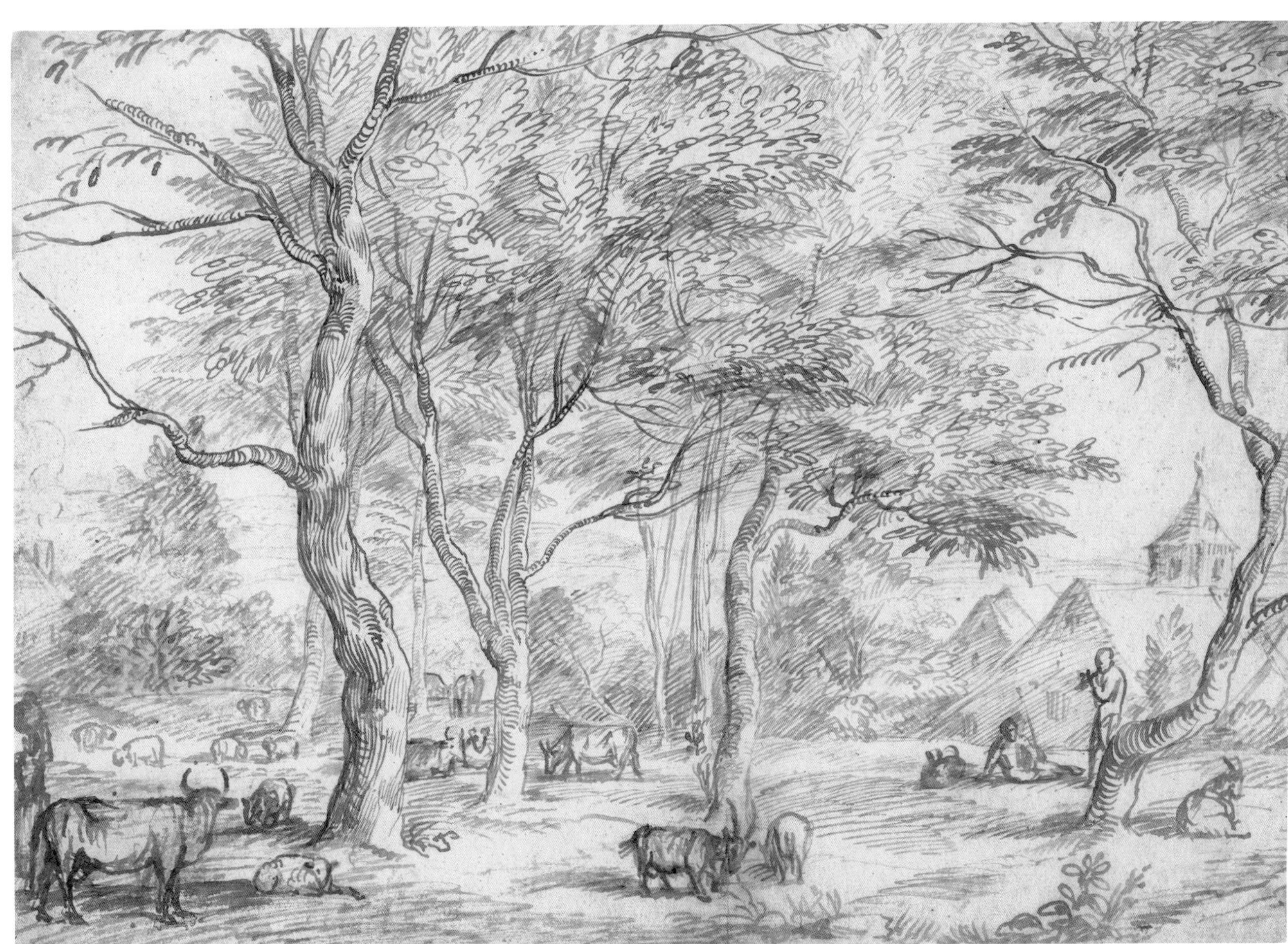

CAT. 127

128 View of Haarlem

129 View of Cleves

128

1650s(?), pen and brown ink, 20.9 × 30.5 (8¼ × 12). Staatliche Museen zu Berlin, Kupferstichkabinett (KdZ 5862) *(Milwaukee, Amsterdam)*

Inscription

Bottom left, in ink, by a later hand: *Jan Lievens Fec.*

Verso: *Gezicht op de Poorte / te Haarlem / door Jan Lievens*

Provenance

Hendrik Busserus, Amsterdam; (Van der Schley… Maarszen, Amsterdam, October 21, 1782, no. 688); (P. van der Schley and D. du Pré, Amsterdam, December 22, 1817, portfolio L, no. 3); Adolf von Beckerath (L. 2504); acquired with his collection in 1902

Selected References

Schneider/Ekkart 1973, 213, no. Z150; Berlin 1974, no. 114; Braunschweig 1979, no. 84; Sumowski 1979, 3876, no. 1743ˣ

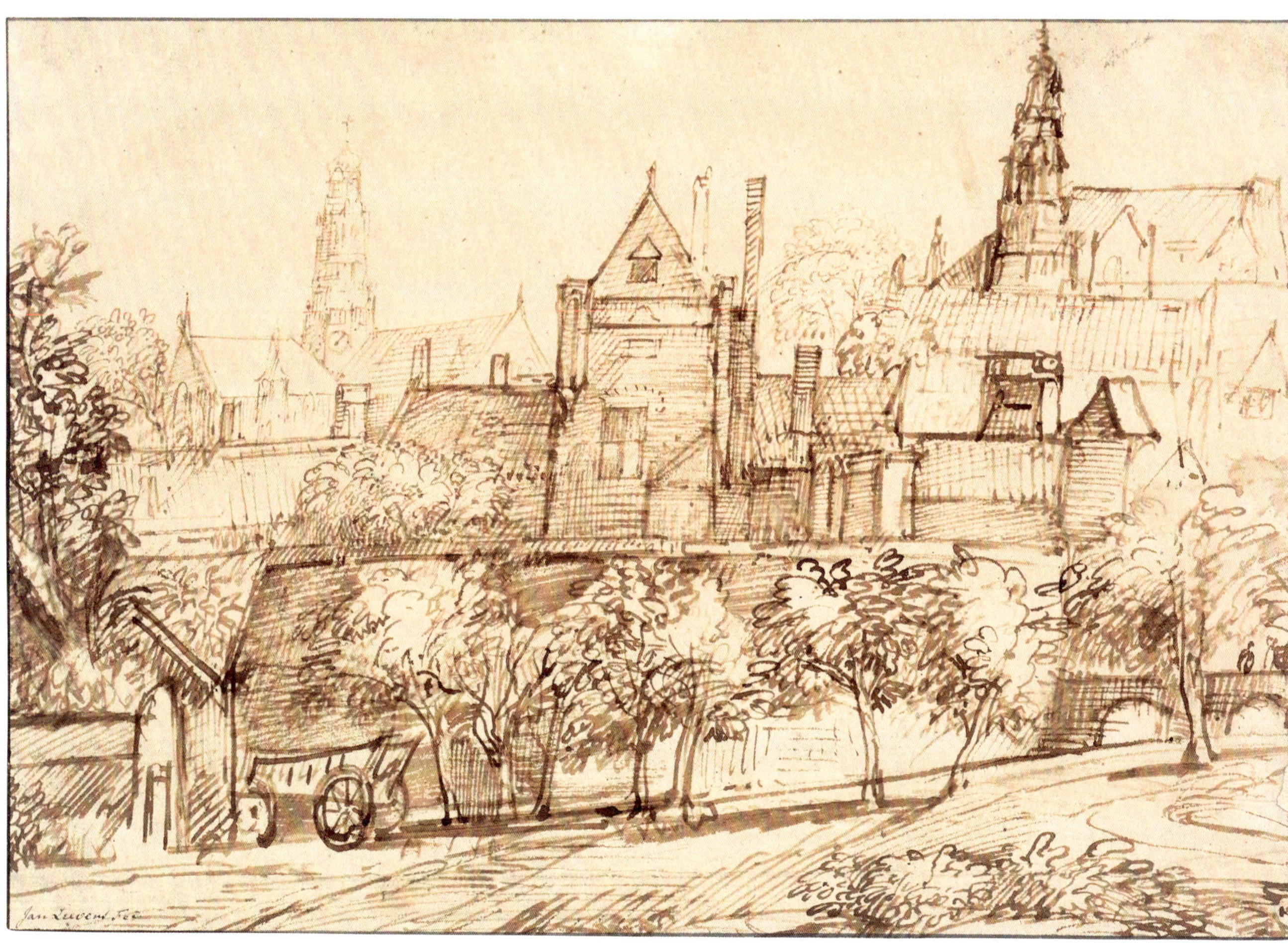

CAT. 128

THESE TWO FINE TOWN VIEWS once again bring into focus the difference between drawings that Lievens made from life and those he created in the studio. His *View of Haarlem* is one of the most substantial and imposing of the former. Drawn with great speed and facility, it is bold and animated, vividly capturing the impression of all the buildings being huddled together within the protection of the city wall. To the right we see the tower of the town hall, while in the distance toward the left the silhouette of Saint Bavo's Cathedral is faintly visible. The canal in the foreground may be the Nieuwe Gracht. The drawing is unusual in combining a rapid, sketchy quality, particularly in the foreground foliage, with a sense of three-dimensionality in the more carefully defined architectural details. A similar approach is apparent in another drawing by Lievens, *The Outer Gate of the Ruins of Brederode Castle.*[1]

The somewhat larger *View of Cleves* is different in atmosphere. The vantage point is farther from the buildings, and the pen strokes, while generally similar in form to those in the Berlin drawing, seem more controlled, giving the drawing a calmer, more monumental feeling. More strictly topographical than his *View of Haarlem*, Lievens' *View of Cleves* shows the Swan Tower standing majestically toward the right, around which other buildings of the old town can also be identified, including the spire of the monastery at the far right.

Lievens referred to a projected trip to Cleves in a letter of June 27, 1664, to Pieter de Graeff.[2] On the basis of this document, drawings by the artist identified as views in that area have often been dated to 1664 or later. But this presupposes that the

129

c. 1655–1665, pen and brown ink with brown wash; touches of pen and black ink and gray wash by a later hand, 24.9 × 39.5 (9 13/16 × 15 9/16). Rijksmuseum, Amsterdam (RP-T-1885-A-482R) *(Washington, Milwaukee)*

Provenance

Abraham de Haas; (De Vries...Roos, Amsterdam, November 8, 1824, portfolio G, in no. 18, to Brondgeest); J.G. Baron Verstolk van Soelen; (Amsterdam, March 22, 1847, portfolio M, no. 490); Jacob de Vos Jbzn. (L. 1450); (Roos...van Gogh, Amsterdam, May 22, 1883, no. 300)

Selected References

Schneider/Ekkart, 212, 365, no. Z142; Braunschweig 1979, no. 67; Sumowski 1979, 3812, no. 1713x; Amsterdam 1988, no. 58

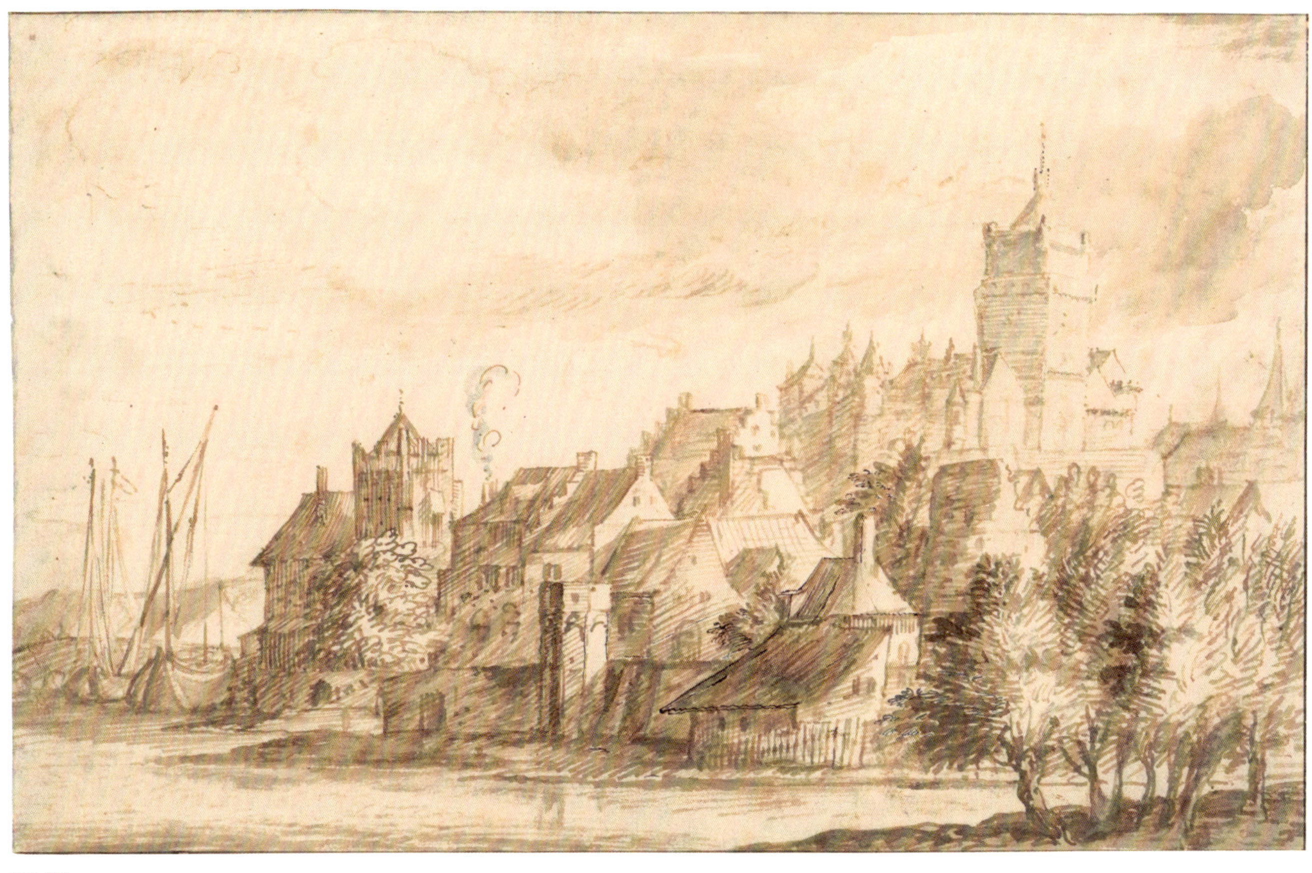

CAT. 129

much-traveled Lievens never otherwise visited the Lower Rhine region, which had attracted streams of Dutch landscape artists for generations.[3] Moreover, it does not take into account the possibility that a finished drawing made in the studio might be based on a sketch made some years earlier. In this instance, one piece of useful topographical evidence is known: the Swan Tower acquired a clock in 1665 that is not visible in Lievens' drawing, indicating at least that Lievens based this *View of Cleves* on a sketch made before that date.

Three such sketches from life of locations in and around Cleves have so far been identified.[4] Although they do not relate directly to the present view, they give some idea of the bold, rather summary studies on which this drawing must have been based. GMGR

130 Distant View of Haarlem

131 Landscape with Peasant Dwelling among Trees

130

c. 1655–1665(?), pen and brown ink, with traces of brown wash and black chalk, 23 × 35.5 (9 1/16 × 14). Maida and George Abrams Collection, Boston, Massachusetts, on loan to Fogg Art Museum, Harvard University (25.1998.66)

Provenance

Jan Six, Amsterdam; (his sale, Amsterdam, October 17, 1928, no. 476); H. E. ten Cate, Oldenzaal; (C. G. Boerner, Düsseldorf, December 1964, no. 62); (sale, Sotheby's, London, July 7, 1966, no. 72); Nathan Chaikin, Crans; acquired in 1966

Selected References

Hanover, Wellesley, Providence, Storrs 1969, no. 53; Schneider/Ekkart 1973, 244, 375, no. z381; Poughkeepsie 1976, no. 30; Sumowski 1979, 3854, no. 1732x (as a view of Alkmaar); Cambridge and Montreal 1988–1989, no. 56; Amsterdam, Vienna, New York, Cambridge, MA, 1991–1992, no. 66; London, Paris, Cambridge, MA, 2002–2003, no. 61

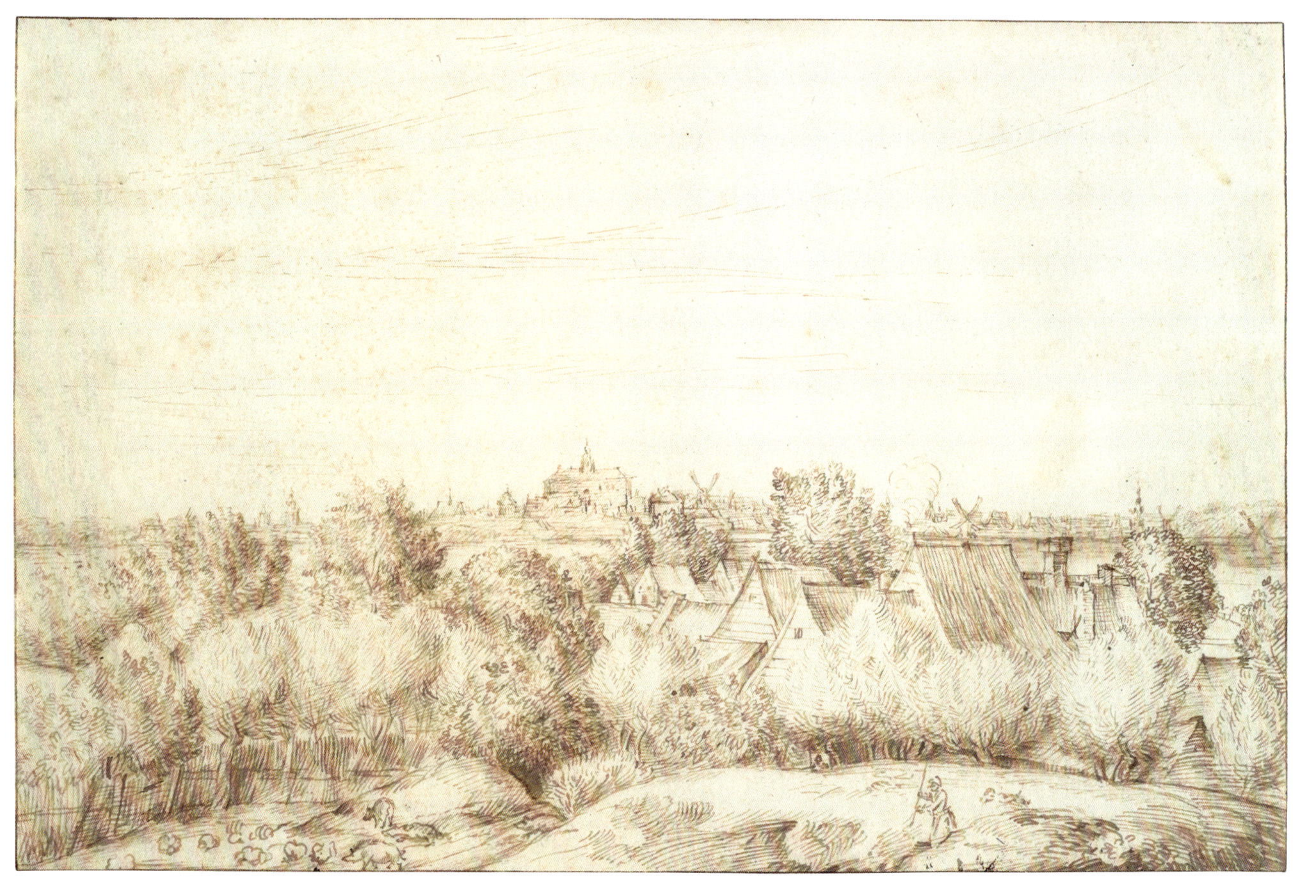

CAT. 130

THESE TWO LARGE AND WELL-preserved drawings are outstanding examples of a type of extensive landscape composition in which Lievens explored the visual possibilities of broad views and subtle variations of light. The refined, confident handling in the two works is generally very similar, although *Distant View of Haarlem* is on Western paper, while *Landscape with Peasant Dwelling among Trees* is on the oriental paper that Lievens used for a significant proportion of his landscapes. It is instructive to compare the different effects Lievens achieved by drawing on these different papers. On Western paper the sophisticated structure of feathery pen lines and the golden tonality of ink create a lively, yet serene look. When similar strokes of the pen are applied to the oriental paper, the appearance is flatter and more uniform, but the surface sheen intrinsic to this paper contributes its own liveliness. Throughout his career as a landscape draftsman, Lievens used both types of paper to striking effect.

The location depicted in the Abrams drawing[1] has been alternately identified as Alkmaar and Haarlem — two of the three Dutch cities whose skylines are dominated by a large cathedral with a central tower (the third is Leiden). The profiles of these cities are indeed similar, but careful comparison with paintings by Gerrit Berckheyde, Jacob van Ruisdael, and others confirms that this drawing and another in the British Museum definitely depict Haarlem.[2] Immediately to the left of the imposing form of Saint Bavo's, other landmarks of that city are clearly visible, including the Klock Huis, the Saint Jans Kerk, and the Bakenesser Kerk. The humbler view seen in the Morgan drawing is not so readily identifiable, although the

131
c. 1655–1665(?), pen and brown ink, on oriental paper, 22.6 × 37.6 (8⅞ × 14$^{13}/_{16}$). The Pierpont Morgan Library, New York (III, 186b) *(Washington, Milwaukee)*

Inscription

Verso, lower left, in brown ink: *de Maas*

Provenance

Charles Fairfax Murray, London and Florence; purchased in 1909 by Pierpont Morgan, New York; J.P. Morgan Jr., New York

Selected References

Schneider 1932, 247, no. 1 (drawings not seen, and attributions unverified); Schneider/Ekkart 1973, 374, under no. Z355 (as probably a copy of the version in Brussels); Sumowski 1979, 3856, no. 1733ˣ (as Lievens); Paris, Antwerp, London, New York 1979–1980, no. 82; Cambridge and Montreal 1988, no. 55; Turner 2006, no. 130

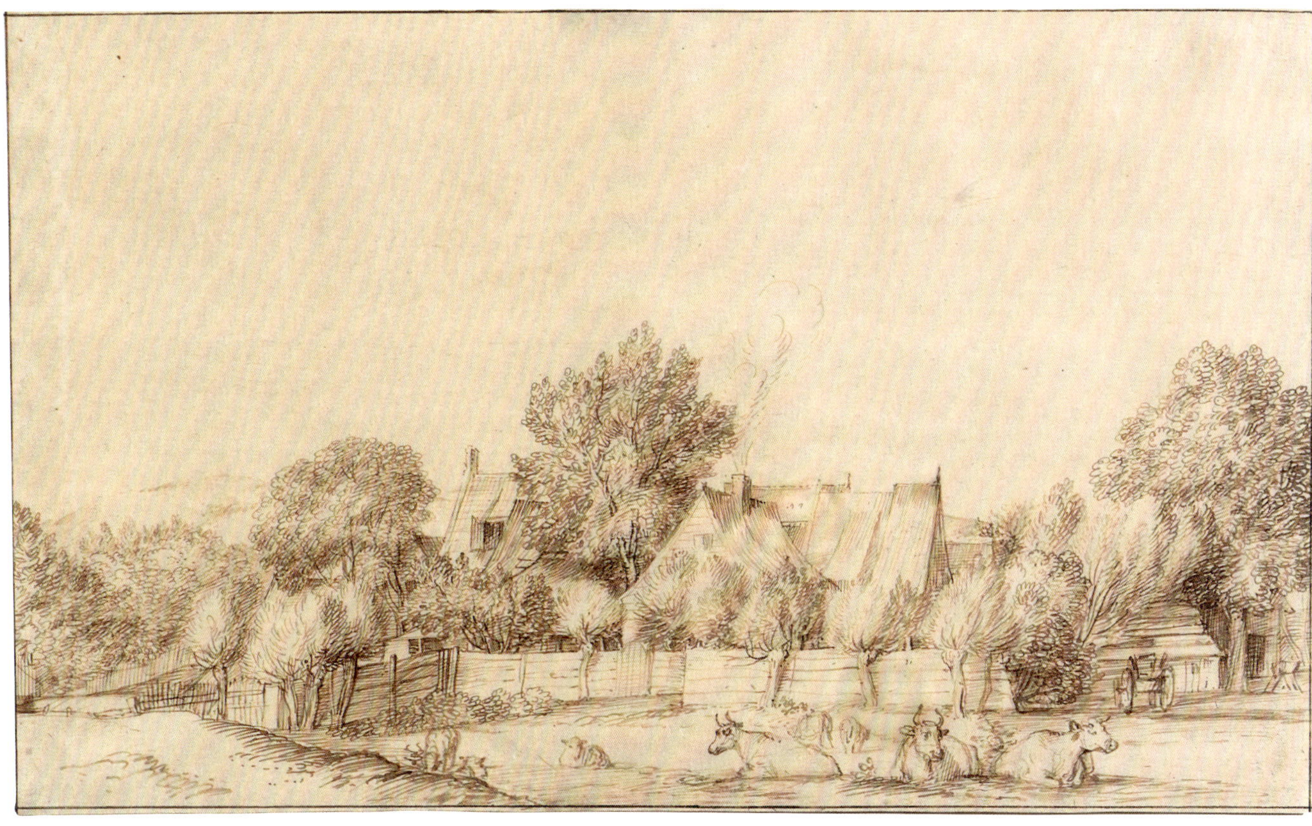

CAT. 131

inscription, "de Maas," on the verso may give a clue as to the location.

A copy of the Morgan drawing is in the De Grez Collection, in Brussels. Ekkart suggested that the latter might be the original, but Sumowski rightly reasserted the primacy of the Morgan sheet. A further copy is in Turin.[3] The existence of these multiple versions raises the question of whether or not some of them might be by Jan Andrea Lievens, rather than his father. Indeed, another drawing very similar to these two, *Village Between Trees* in Vienna, bears the old inscription "Jan Lievensze. de jonge. f. omstreeks a°. 1660," which has been cited as basis for attributing that drawing to Jan Andrea.[4] Schneider and Sumowski both firmly rejected this theory and accepted the Vienna drawing without reservation as being by Jan Lievens himself.

There is, however, no debate about the attribution of the two superb drawings shown here, although their dating does remain uncertain. Both *Distant View of Haarlem* and *Forest Interior with a Draftsman* (cat. 132), also in the Abrams Collection, have watermarks very close to one published by Churchill as dating from 1664,[5] but they seem so different from one another in style that it is hard to see them as dating from the same period of Lievens' career. The Haarlem view seems more structured in composition and handling, without the extravagant, mannered pen work of the late, densely wooded scenes. Yet details such as the pigs in the foreground are comparable to those seen in the British Museum's *Sandpit with Two Sheds* (cat. 136), which probably dates from the 1660s. So perhaps, in the final analysis, these two majestic landscapes are indeed also late works. GMGR

132 Forest Interior with a Draftsman

1660s(?), pen and brown ink and brown wash, 24 × 36.2 (9 7/16 × 14 1/4). Maida and George Abrams Collection, Boston, Massachusetts, on loan to Fogg Art Museum, Harvard University (25.1998.66)

Provenance

Possibly Henri Duval, Liège; (sale, his collection and others, Amsterdam, June 22, 1910, no. 215); Henry Oppenheimer, London; (his sale, Christie's, London, July 10, 1936, no. 264); E. Rosenthal, Munich; (sale, Sotheby Mak van Waay, Amsterdam, April 19, 1982, no. 20); acquired at the sale

Selected References

Schneider/Ekkart 1973, 235, 372, no. Z313; Sumowski 1979, 3732, no. 1675a*; Amsterdam, Vienna, New York, Cambridge, MA, 1991–1992, no. 65; Paris and Haarlem 1997–1998, 196, under no. 87; London, Paris, Cambridge, MA, 2002–2003, no. 60

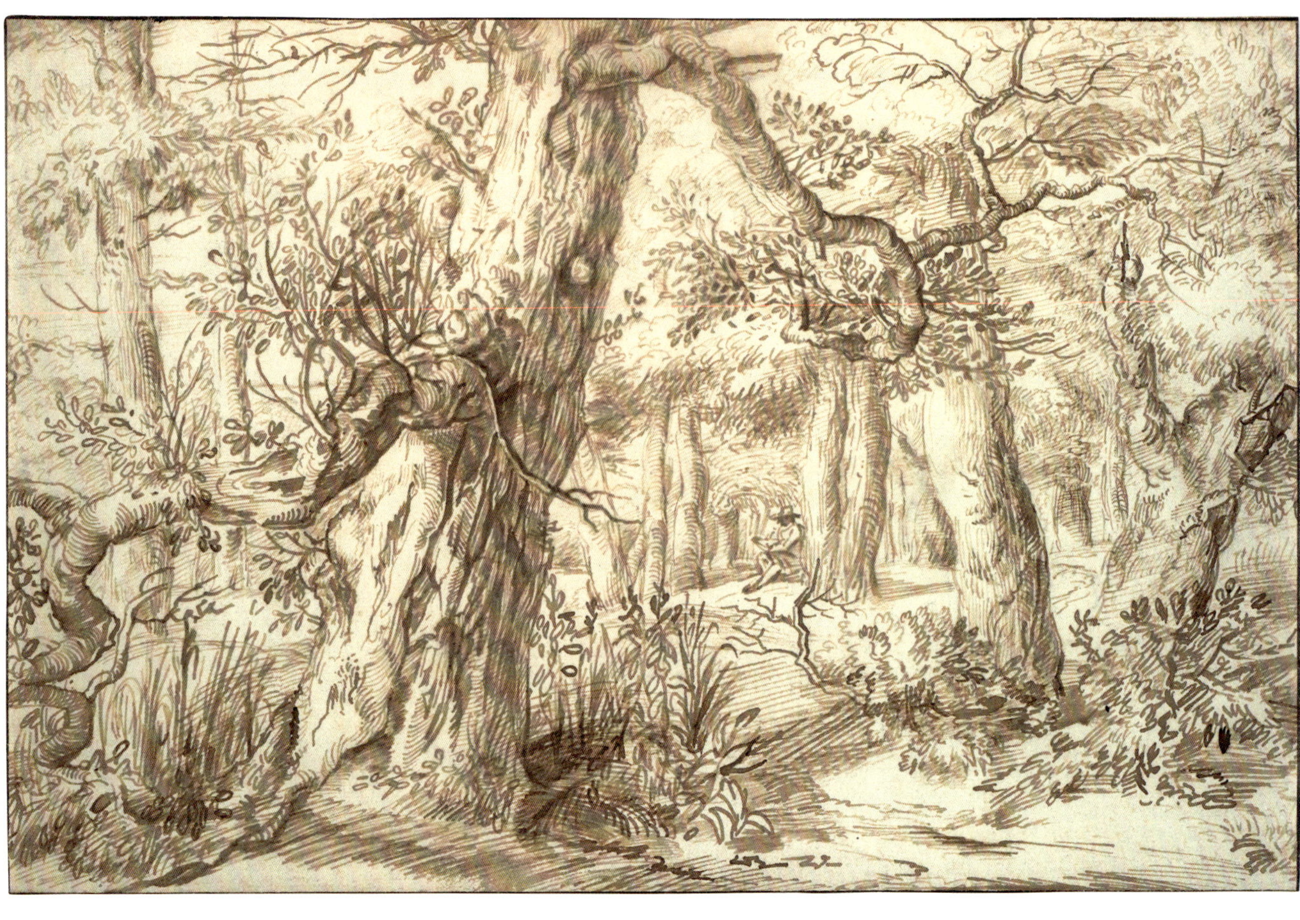

THIS IS ONE OF A NUMBER OF Lievens' landscape drawings of which a second version is known: the other drawing, executed in pen and wash on oriental paper, is in Dresden.[1] Often when two such versions exist, the compositions and dimensions are almost identical, but one drawing is on Western paper, while the other is on the smoother-surfaced and more absorbent oriental ("Japan") paper.

Occasionally, as in the case of the Dresden sketch *Farm under Trees*, and the larger, more fully worked variant of the same scene in the Metropolitan Museum of Art, New York (see Rubinstein figs. 8, 9), the chronological order of the two versions of a composition is obvious. But both the Abrams drawing and its Dresden counterpart must have been drawn in the studio as finished works, probably on the basis of a slighter sketch from nature, so there is no way to establish which was executed first.[2]

Although the dating of Lievens' landscapes remains speculative, the intense, rather agitated draftsmanship seen here does seem to be typical of his late drawings. Long repeated hatchings combine with loops, accents, and jagged bare branches, and the illusion of space and recession almost dissolves amid the welter of bravura surface effects. Some of these dense, late landscapes seem quite abstract, so dominated are they by the pen work. Yet when, as here, the balance between technique and illusion is maintained, the result is a tension and visual excitement rarely seen in Dutch landscape drawings of the second half of the seventeenth century. The watermark, which Churchill dates to 1664, also supports a late dating.[3] GMGR

133 Garden Entrance

c. 1655–1665, pen and brown ink on oriental paper, 22.2 × 37.1 (8¾ × 14⅝). Amsterdams Historisch Museum, Bequest C. J. Fodor (TA 10207) *(Washington, Amsterdam)*

Provenance

W. Baartz; (Lamme, Rotterdam, June 6, 1860, portfolio P, no. 341); C. J. Fodor (L.1036); bequeathed to museum, 1860

Selected References

Schneider/Ekkart 1973, 246, 346, no. Z391; Braunschweig 1979, no. 91; Sumowski 1979, 3848, no. 1729*; Broos, 1981,174–175, no. 49; Amsterdam 1988, no. 55; Cambridge and Montreal 1988, no. 57

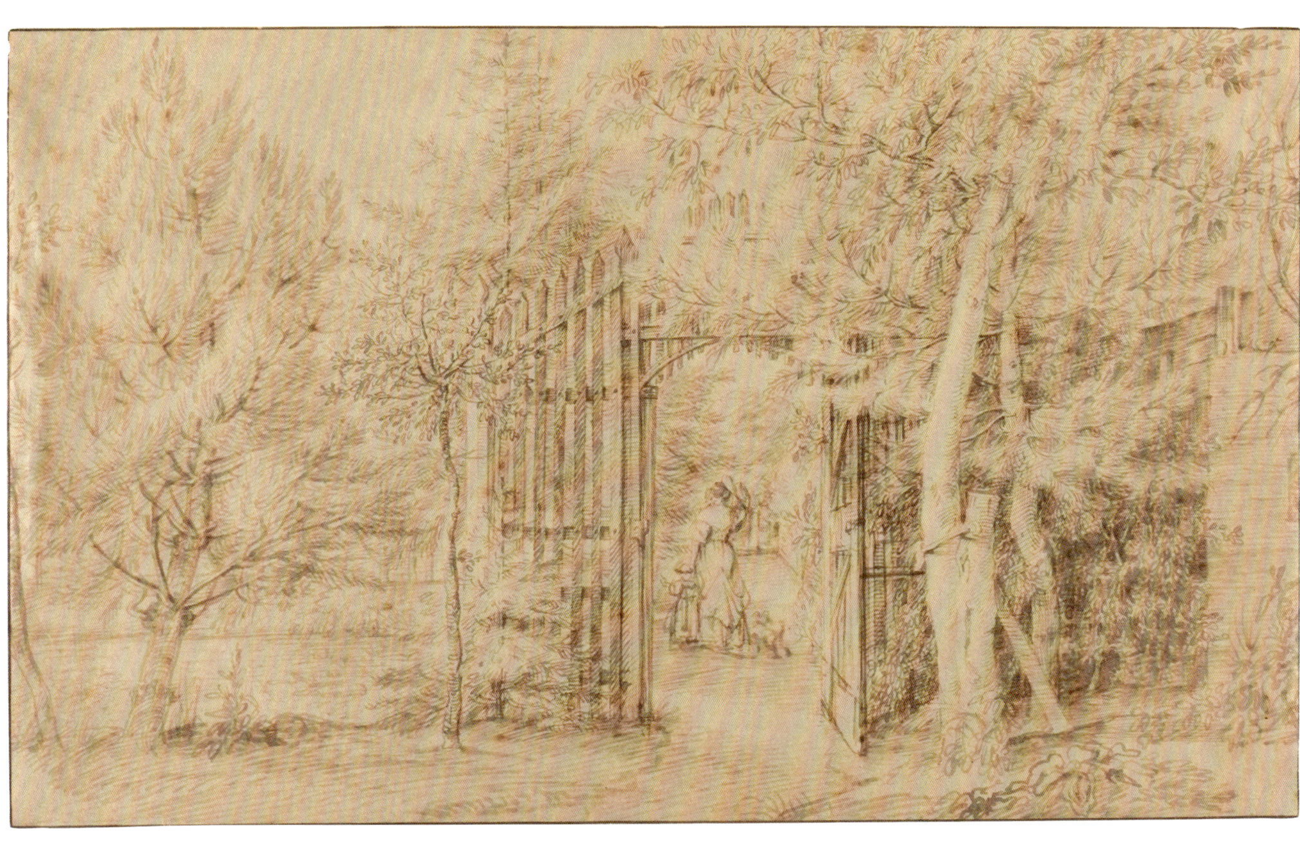

THE COMPOSITION OF THIS POETIC landscape drawing, with the path and figures seen through the flat foreground plane of the gate and surrounding trees, is unusual, not only in Lievens' drawings but also in the broader context of Dutch landscape traditions. Although the elegance of this partly natural, partly man-made scene recalls the views in the Haagse Bos (see cats. 121, 122), the lighting and pen work are here more delicate and refined, resulting in an atmospheric image of great subtlety. Much is made of Lievens' debt to the landscape drawings and prints of Venetian artists such as Domenico and Giulio Campagnola and Titian, which he probably encountered in Antwerp through Rubens and other artists and collectors, and this drawing provides rare visual evidence of such an influence. The feathery, diaphanous leaves of the tree to the left, drawn with light, repeated strokes of the pen, have a distinctly Venetian feel.

Some earlier commentators suggested that this drawing should be dated to Lievens' Antwerp period — not on account of any Venetian associations, but because of a spurious link perceived with certain works by Rubens. Meanwhile, Ekkart and others considered it to date from some thirty years later. Sumowski has proposed more convincingly that it was made during the 1650s.[1] But these widely divergent opinions only serve to illustrate once more how difficult the dating of Lievens' landscape drawings can be. GMGR

134 Decaying Pollard Willow

135 Old Tree Trunk in Front of a Forest

134
c. 1655–1665, pen and brown ink on oriental paper, 37.8 × 22.8 (14⅞ × 9). Kupferstich-Kabinett, Staatliche Kunstsammlungen Dresden (C1898-31) *(Amsterdam)*

Inscriptions
Lower left, in ink [by Zomer]: J.L.

Bottom center, by same hand: *Extra*

Provenance
Jan Pietersz Zomer; D. Vis Blokhuyzen; A. Sträter; (Gutekunst, Stuttgart, May 10–14, 1898, no. 1145)

Selected References
James Byam Shaw, *Old Master Drawings* 4 (1929/1931), 47–48, pl. 50 (as Jan Andries Lievens); Schneider/Ekkart 1973, 227, 283, no. z255; Sumowski 1979, 3786, no. 1700ˣ; Michiel C. Plomp, "Jan Pietersz. Zomer's Inscriptions on Drawings," *Delineavit et Sculpsit* 17 (1997): 19, figs. 14, 14a; Dresden and Vienna 1997–1998, no. 86

PICTURESQUE, GNARLED TREES often appear in Lievens' drawings of densely wooded landscapes (see cats. 138, 139). He also made a few large studies of individual trees, which, despite their size, were probably drawn from life. The way Lievens would have used these studies can be seen in a wooded landscape in Dresden, in which the central motif is a reduced and somewhat altered version of a tree taken from one of his independent studies.[1] Although this is the only instance in which such a direct connection can be established, Lievens must have based many more of his finished landscapes on detailed tree studies.

Given that the two studies shown here are drawn on sheets about as large as any used by Lievens for his completed landscapes, one would expect the trees to be reduced in size when incorporated into more extensive compositions. The outlines of the tree study in the British Museum are, however, partly indented, so it seems that the artist sometimes transferred his models directly, without any such reduction in scale.[2]

Although only a few large, independent studies of trees by Lievens survive, several similar sketches appear on the versos of more complete drawings, including *Ruins of the Abbey Church at Egmond* (cat. 124) and *Wooded Landscape* in the Lugt Collection with a watermark datable to 1664.[3] Such a dating seems plausible for the tree study in London, but *Decaying Pollard Willow* in Dresden may be slightly earlier.

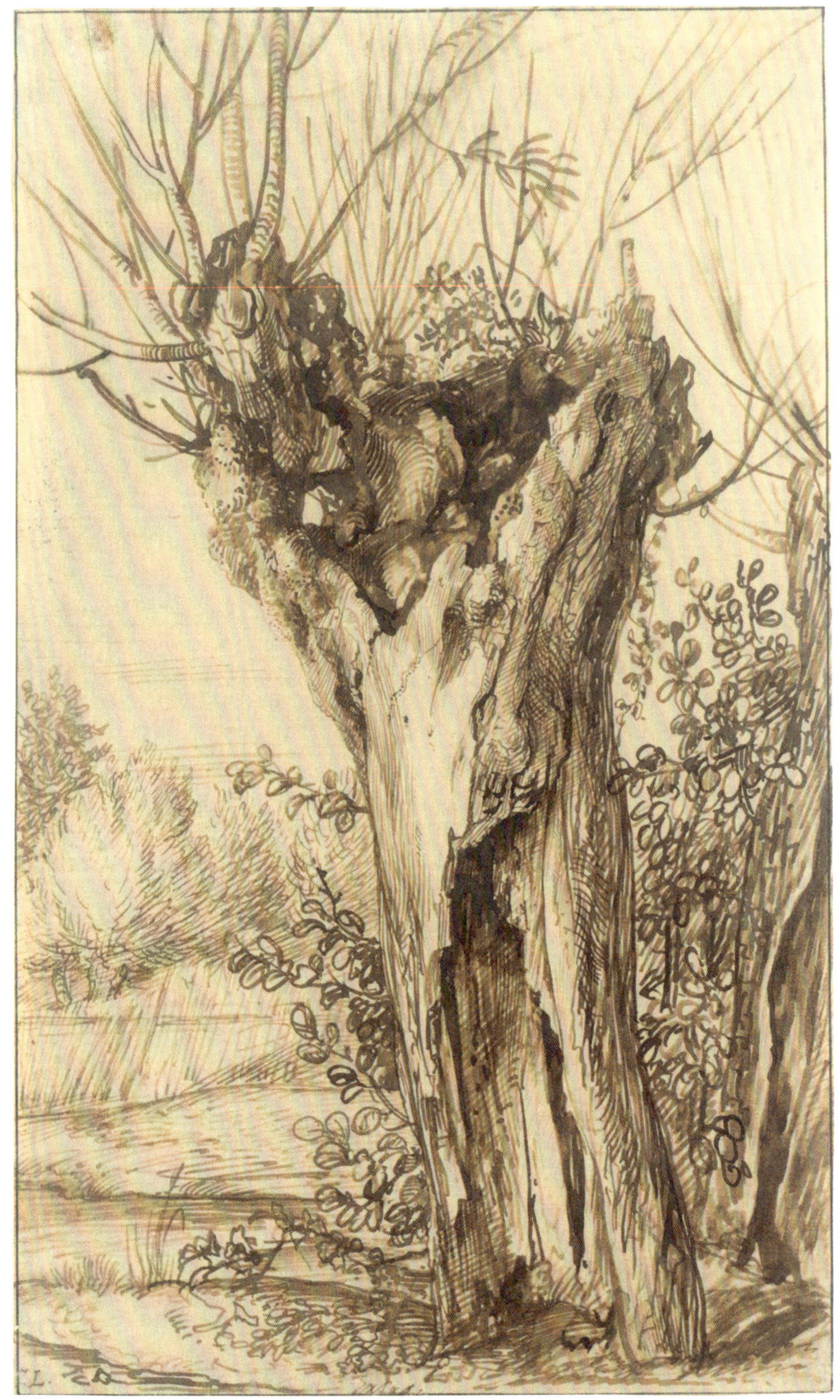

CAT. 134

135

c. 1655–1665, pen and brown ink on oriental paper, the outlines partly indented, 35 × 22.2 (13¾ × 8¾). The British Museum, London (1836.8.11.340) *(Washington, Milwaukee)*

Provenance

John Sheepshanks (L. 2333); purchased with his collection in 1836

Selected References

Schneider/Ekkart 1973, 227, no. Z254; Sumowski 1979, 3788, no. 1701x

Trees like this became increasingly prominent in Lievens' landscape drawings as his career progressed, yet the origins of his interest in the motif can be traced back to his Antwerp period, when he made his only landscape woodcut (cat. 80). Lievens' fascination with richly detailed nature studies places him in a noble Dutch tradition going back to Jacques de Gheyn and Hendrick Goltzius, both of whom made superb studies of trees, sharing a clear sense of joy in capturing the marvels of the natural world.[4]

As Michiel Plomp has recently discovered, the inscriptions on the Dresden drawing are in the hand of the notable Amsterdam dealer and collector Jan Pietersz Zomer; but the significance of the word "Extra," written by Zomer on the bottom of the drawing, remains obscure. GMGR

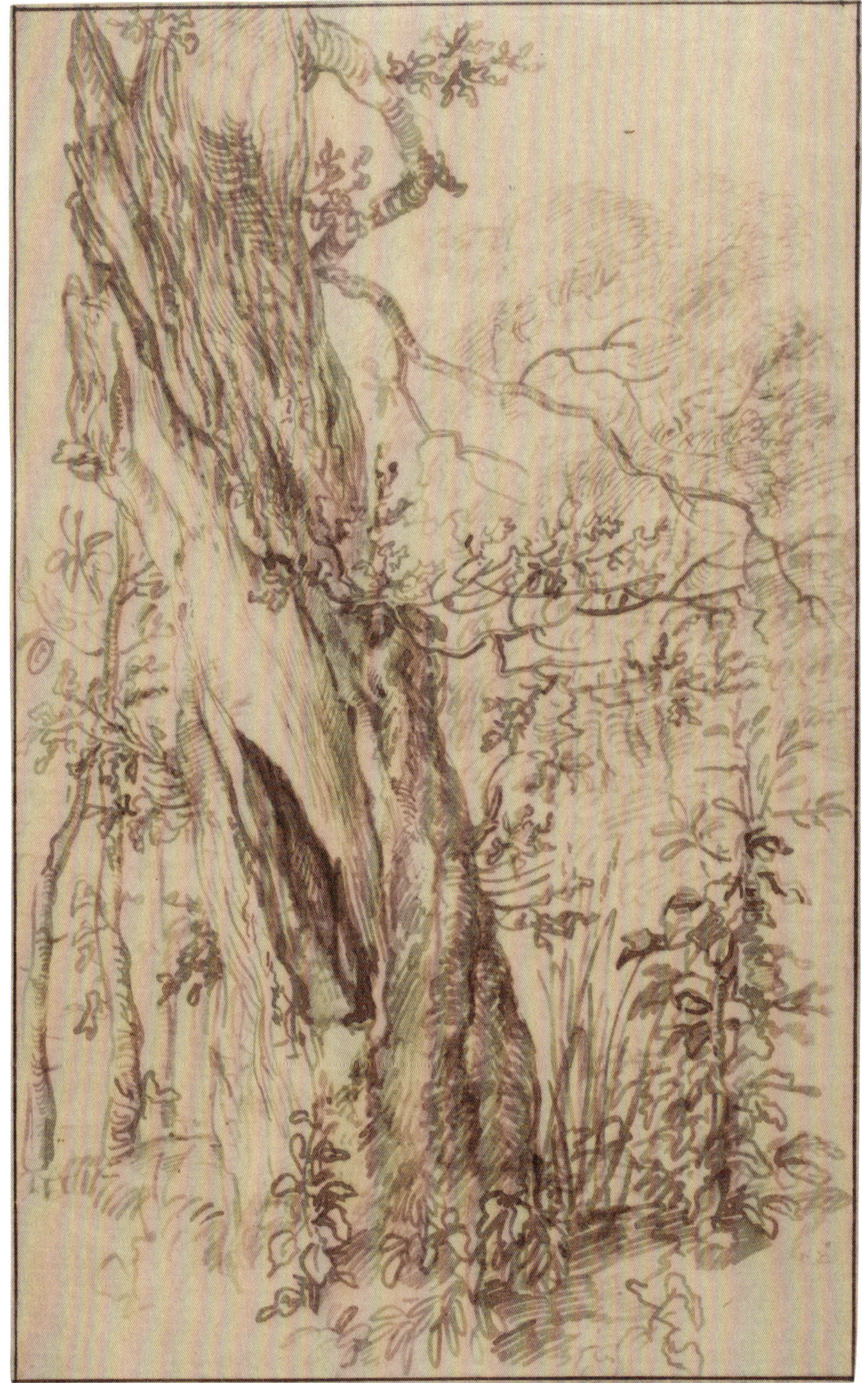

CAT. 135

136 Sandpit with Two Sheds

137 Sandpit with Two Sheds, Pigs in the Foreground

136

c. 1664, pen and brown ink and brown wash; slight sketch of a hill on the verso, 25.7 × 40.5 (10 1/8 × 16). Frits Lugt Collection, Institut Néerlandais, Paris (2477) *(Washington, Milwaukee)*

Inscriptions

Bottom left, in a later hand: *J. Livens*

Verso, in pencil: *182, 60*; and *J. Lievens*

Provenance

Gustav Nebehay, Berlin and Vienna; (C.G. Boerner, Leipzig, November 13, 1924, A. Köster and other collections, no. 266, unsold); (C.G. Boerner, Leipzig and Düsseldorf); Frits Lugt, Maartensdijk and Paris (L. 1028), acquired May 5, 1926

Selected References

Brussels, Rotterdam, Paris, Bern 1968–1969, no. 97; Schneider/Ekkart 1973, 239, 373, no. z341; Braunschweig 1979, no. 78; Sumowski 1979, 3844, no. 1727[x]; Paris and Haarlem 1997–1998, no. 88

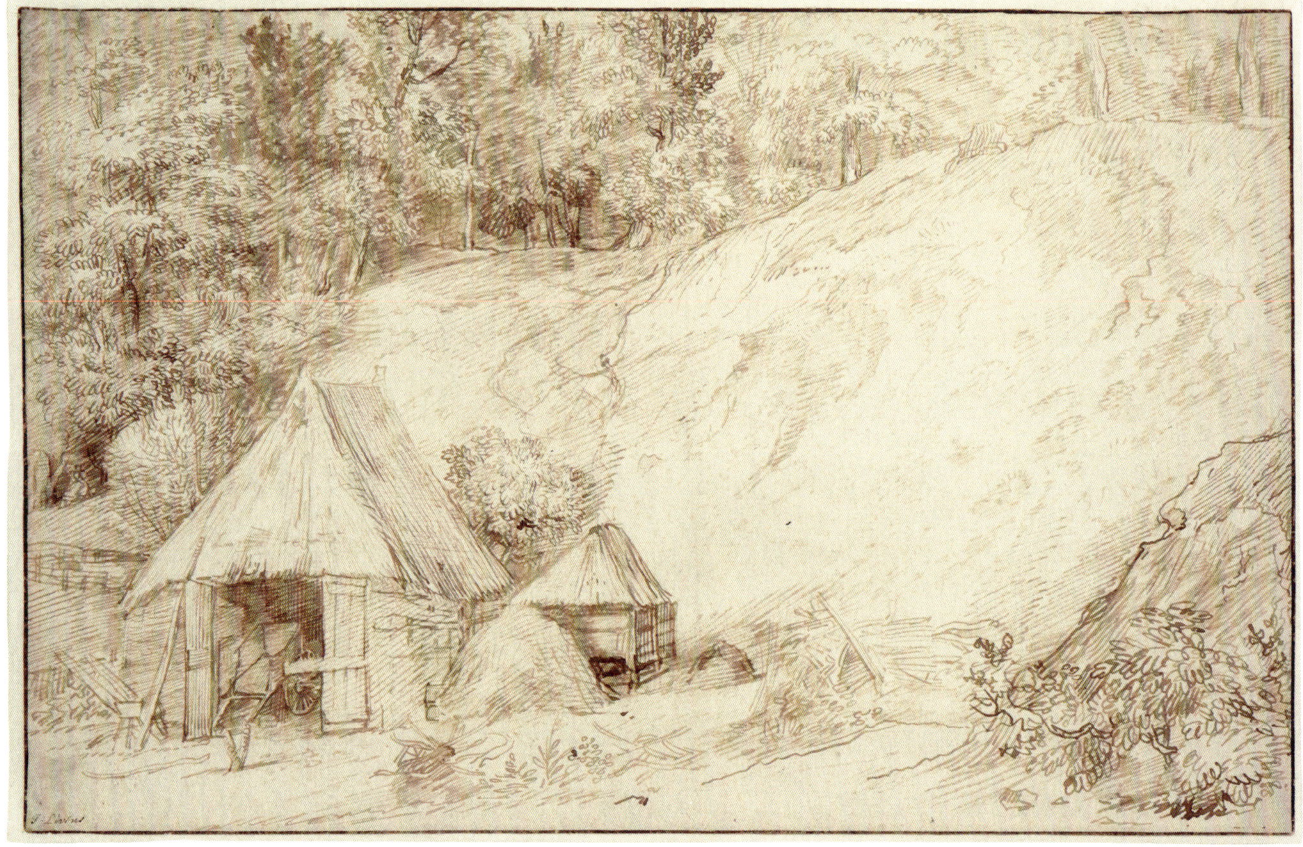

CAT. 136

THE ATTRIBUTION ISSUES RELATING to multiple versions of the same composition discussed in the previous entry are also illustrated by the example of these two drawings. Though both sheets are approximately the same size, the drawing in the British Museum is more extensively worked and includes a number of motifs and figures that are absent from the other version. Despite the animation these figures add to the composition, however, the overall effect is less spontaneous, and it seems reasonable to conclude that the London drawing is a subsequent reworking of the composition in the Lugt Collection. Whether the latter was drawn from nature, or based on a previous sketch, remains unclear.

It has regularly been argued that a less accomplished and less interesting second version, such as the drawing in the British Museum, should be attributed to Jan Lievens' son, Jan Andrea. The fundamental question, however, is whether the stylistic relationship between these two drawings — both differences and similarities — can best be explained if the works are by two different hands, or if they are both by the same artist repeating his own composition. No objective and unequivocal answer is possible. All that can be said with certainty is that stylistically the two sheets resemble one another more closely than they do any securely attributable drawing by Jan Andrea. In addition, although only a small detail, the pigs in the foreground of the British Museum drawing are very distinctive and surely by the same artist as those in the Abrams Collection *Distant View of Haarlem* (cat. 130).

At least two other drawings record this distinctive location, which probably

137
c. 1664, pen and brown ink with brown wash, 25.1 × 41.2 (9⅞ × 16¼). The British Museum, London (1946.7.13.160) *(Washington, Milwaukee)*

Provenance

Count Moritz von Fries (L. 2903); Sir Thomas Lawrence (L. 2445); (Samuel Woodburn); (Christie's, London, June 4, 1860, no. 538, with three others); Sir Thomas Philipps; by inheritance to Thomas Fitzroy Philipps Fenwick; presented by the National Art-Collections Fund, 1946

Selected References

Schneider/Ekkart 1973, 392, no. SZ441; Sumowski 1979, 3846, no. 1728x

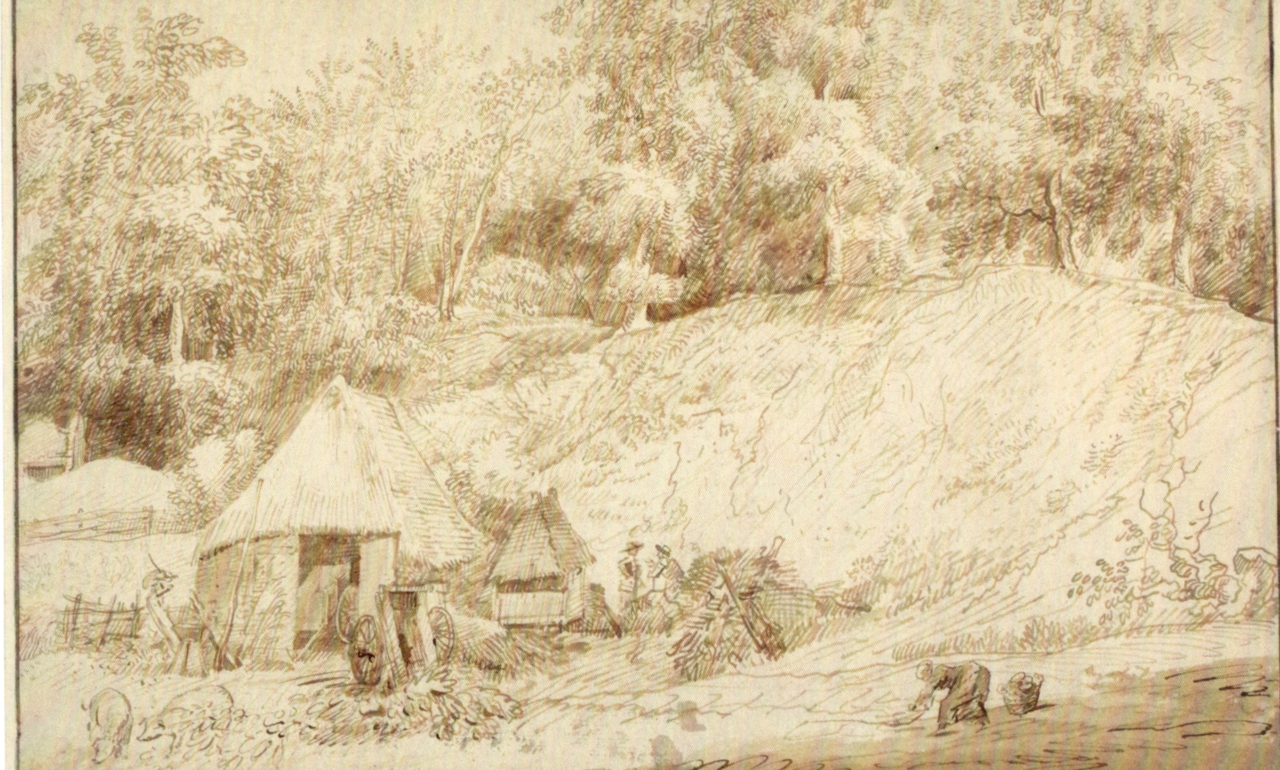

CAT. 137

lay in the sandy region of the Veluwe, not far from Arnhem and Rhenen. One in Amsterdam was formerly attributed to Gerbrand van den Eeckhout but is now given to Jacob Esselens.[1] The second is a signed drawing by Eeckhout now in Munich (fig. 1).[2] Both of these drawings show the shed doors closed rather than open, and there are other minor differences in detail. This seems to contradict the suggestion that the three artists made their drawings on a joint sketching trip. Several drawings by Eeckhout and Esselens do show identical views in the Lower Rhine region,[3] so these two artists may well have traveled together there, but we have no evidence that Lievens joined them.

The drawing in the Lugt Collection is on paper with a watermark datable to 1664[4] — the year when we know that Lievens went to Cleves[5] — and nothing in the style of the drawing would seem to argue against such a date of execution. GMGR

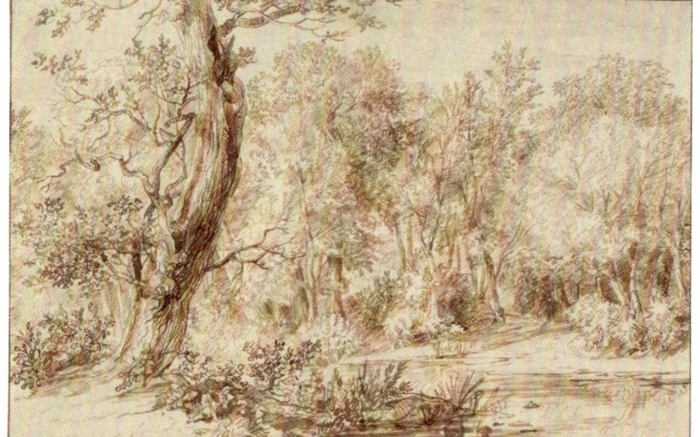

1 | Gerbrand van den Eeckhout, *Sandpit with Two Sheds*, 1660s, pen and brown ink with brown wash. Staatliche Graphische Sammlung, Munich

138 Densely Wooded Landscape with a Pond

139 Densely Wooded Landscape with Deer

138
1660s, pen and brown ink, on oriental paper, 22.9 × 37.4 (9 × 14¾). Katrine Ames, New York

Provenance

(P. & D. Colnaghi, London, 1958); Winslow and Anna Ames, Saunderstown, RI (bears their mark, not in Lugt)

Selected References

Providence, Rhode Island, Museum of Art, *Drawings of the Collection of Mr. and Mrs. Winslow Ames*, 1965, no. 64; Sumowski 1979, 3740, no. 1679*; Sumowski 1980, 371–372, pl. 39; Cambridge and Montreal 1988–1989, no. 53

1 | Jan Lievens, *Wooded Landscape with Pond*, 1660s, pen and brown ink with brown wash. The British Museum, London

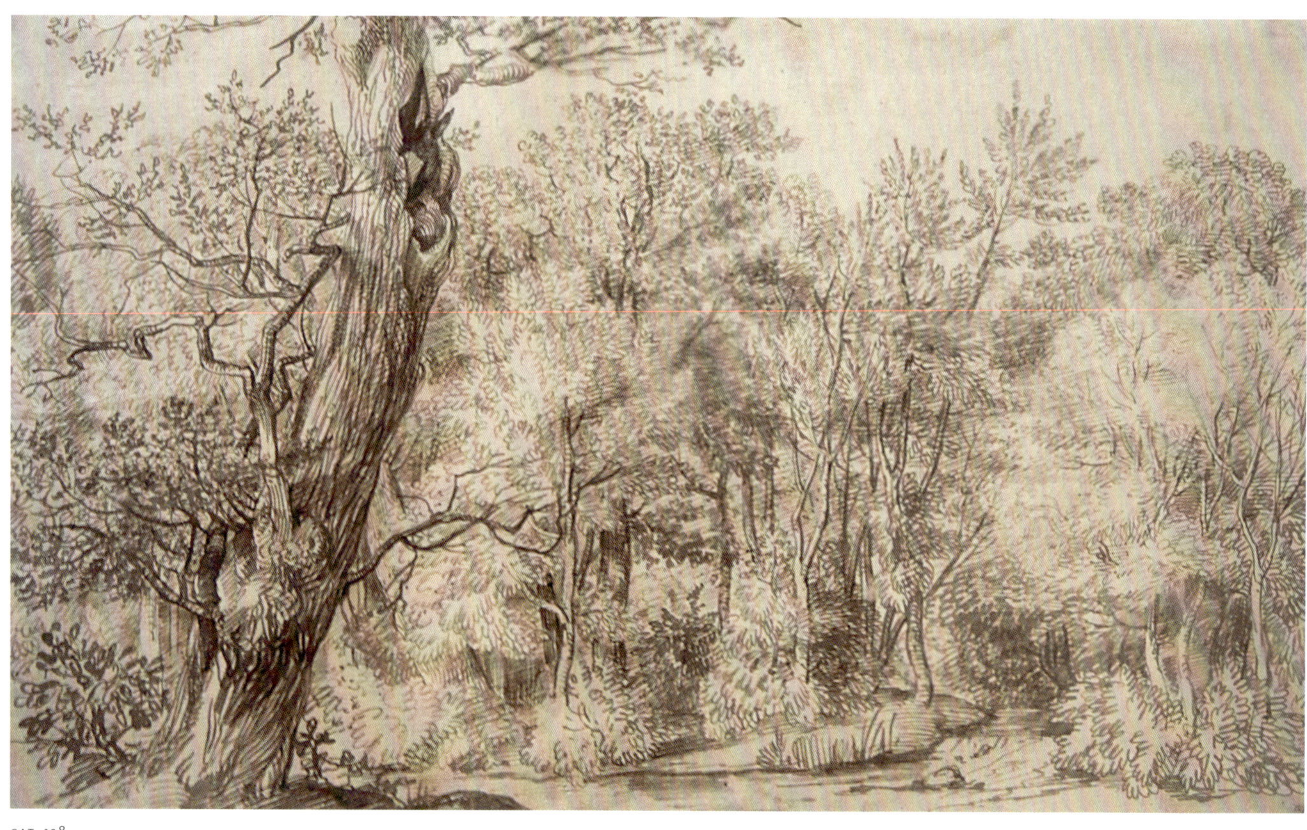

CAT. 138

SOME OF LIEVENS' MOST DISTINCTIVE and original landscape drawings are those that depict particularly dense forests. In contrast to the harmonious atmosphere of drawings such as the views in the Haagse Bos (cats. 121, 122) or other pastoral wooded landscapes (cats. 126, 127), the seemingly impenetrable forests seen here exude a rather forbidding aura, which is reinforced by the occasional figures and animals lurking in the undergrowth. In the Washington drawing, one of a number that include deer,[1] the animals are shown at rest, but one nonetheless feels that at any moment the peace might be shattered by a shot from the undergrowth and the emergence of the hunters who appear in several other such compositions.[2]

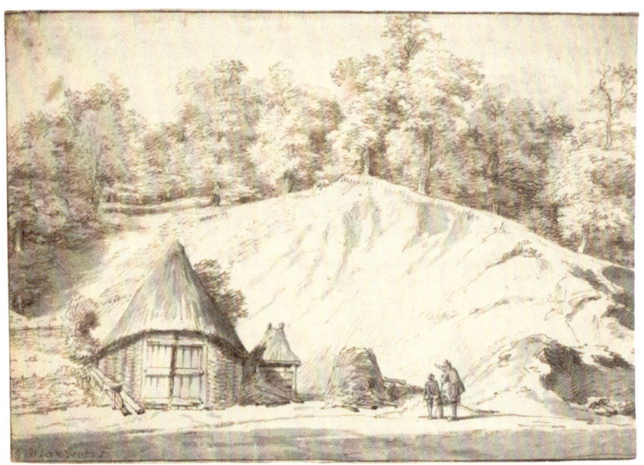

139
1660s, pen and brown ink, 27.6 × 40.5 (10⅞ × 15⅞). National Gallery of Art, Washington, Ailsa Mellon Bruce Fund (1978.19.5) *(Washington, Milwaukee)*

Inscription

Verso, in brown ink, by a later hand: … *de Rembrandt*

Provenance

Count Karl Lanckoronski, Vienna, 1932; Countess Adelheid Lanckoronska; (Christie's, London, March 30, 1971, no. 98)

Selected References

Schneider/Ekkart 1973, 237, 372, no. Z324; Washington, 1978, 59; Sumowski 1979, 3742, no. 11, under no. 1679[x]

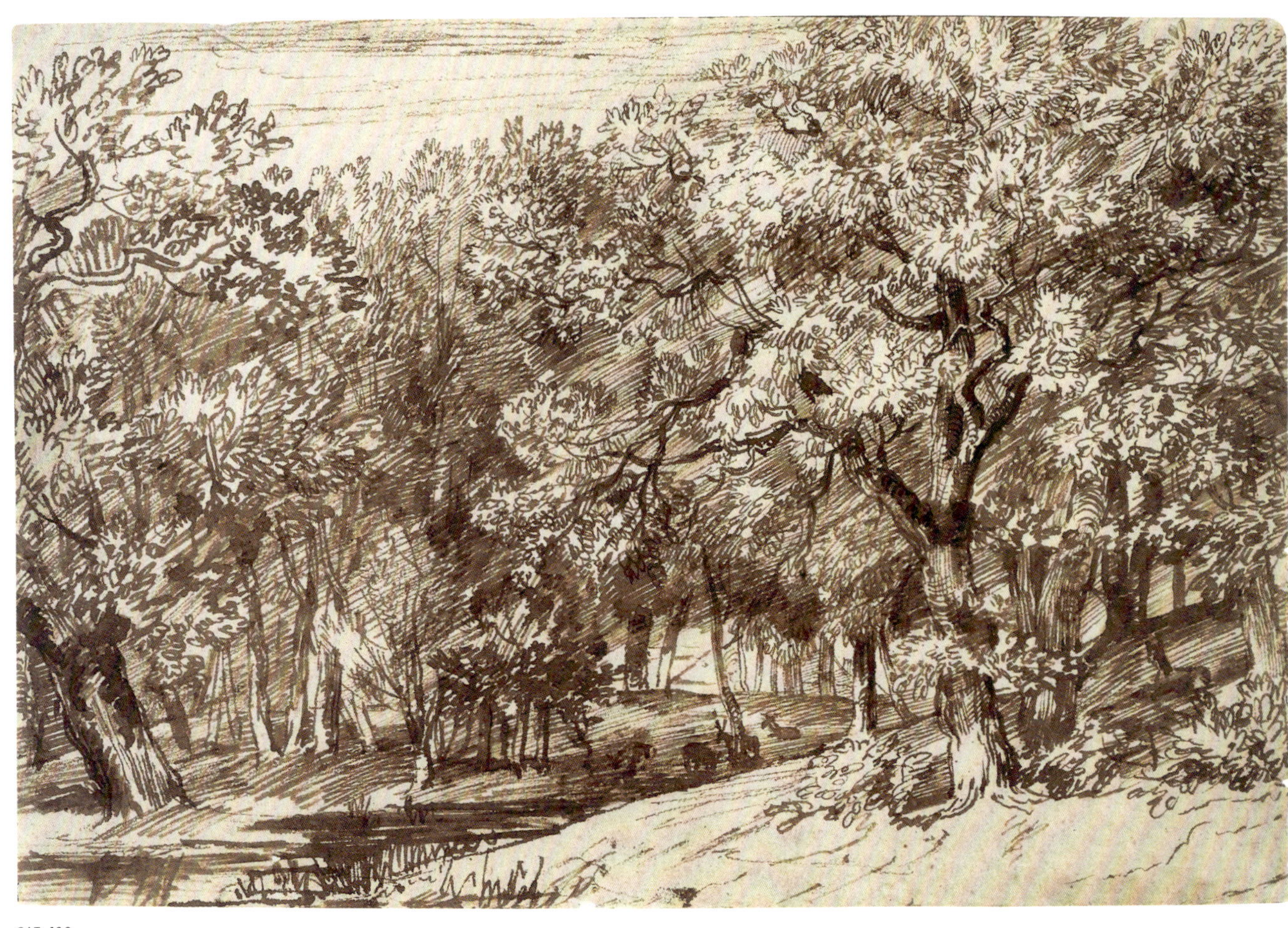

CAT. 139

This sense of unease is exacerbated by the intense, sometimes almost frenzied draftsmanship that characterizes drawings of this type. With this much foliage, Lievens' distinctive way of defining trees and leaves through complementary passages of parallel hatching and rounded loops can appear chaotic. Although no spatial confusion exists in either of these two very fine drawings, in others the sense of recession disappears almost entirely, and the forest virtually dissolves into an abstract mass of lines.[3]

Another version of the Ames drawing is in the British Museum (fig. 1).[4] The former has clearly been cropped at the bottom, and there are a few minor differences of detail, but otherwise the two compositions are identical. The quality of the two drawings is equivalent, and there is no basis for proposing that one sheet has primacy over the other. As Sumowski notes, a variant of the large tree to the left appears in another wooded landscape in Berlin,[5] possibly a study from nature that provided Lievens with a model for this motif in these finished studio drawings. GMGR

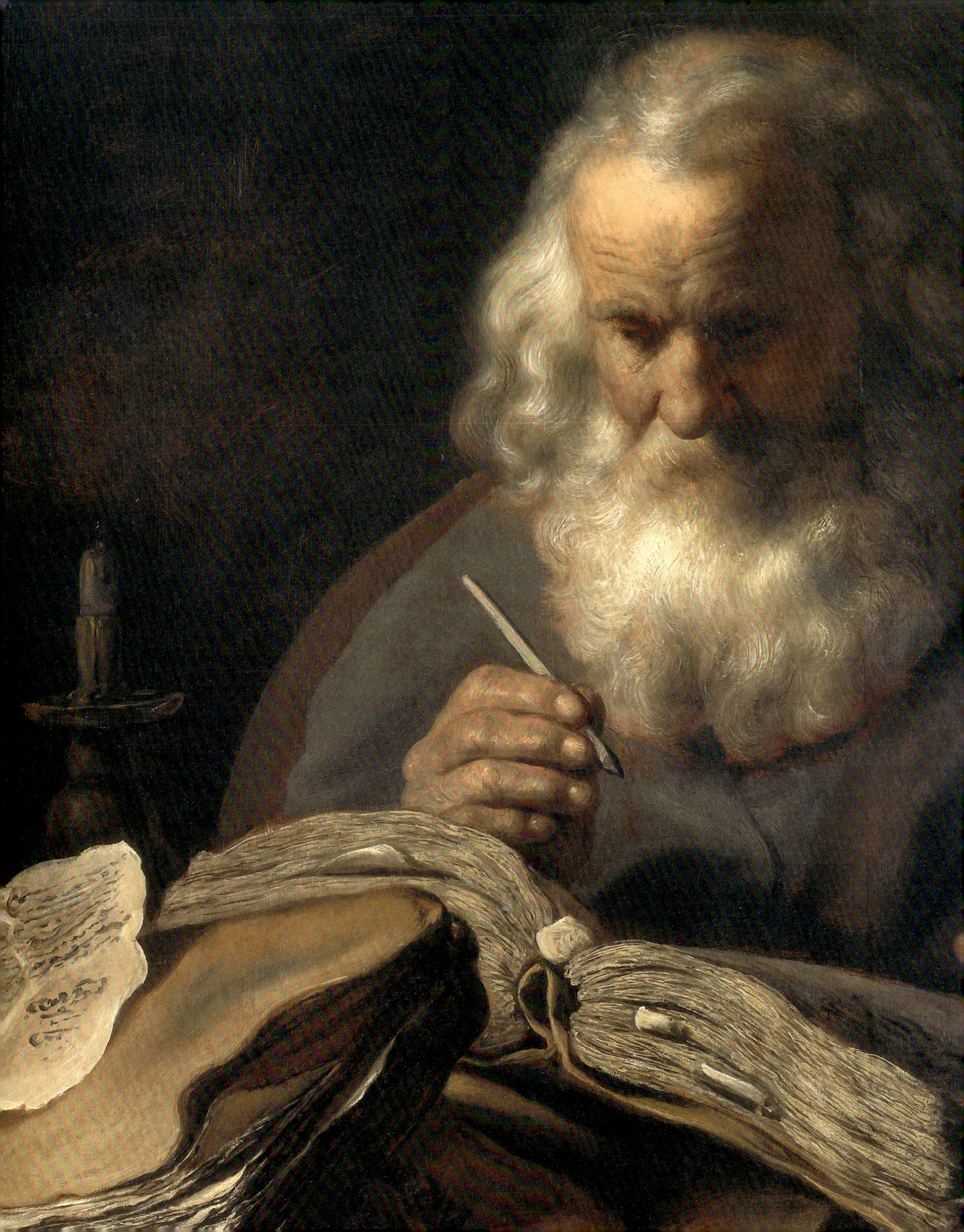

APPENDIX | NOTES TO THE CATALOGUE | SELECT BIBLIOGRAPHY | INDEX

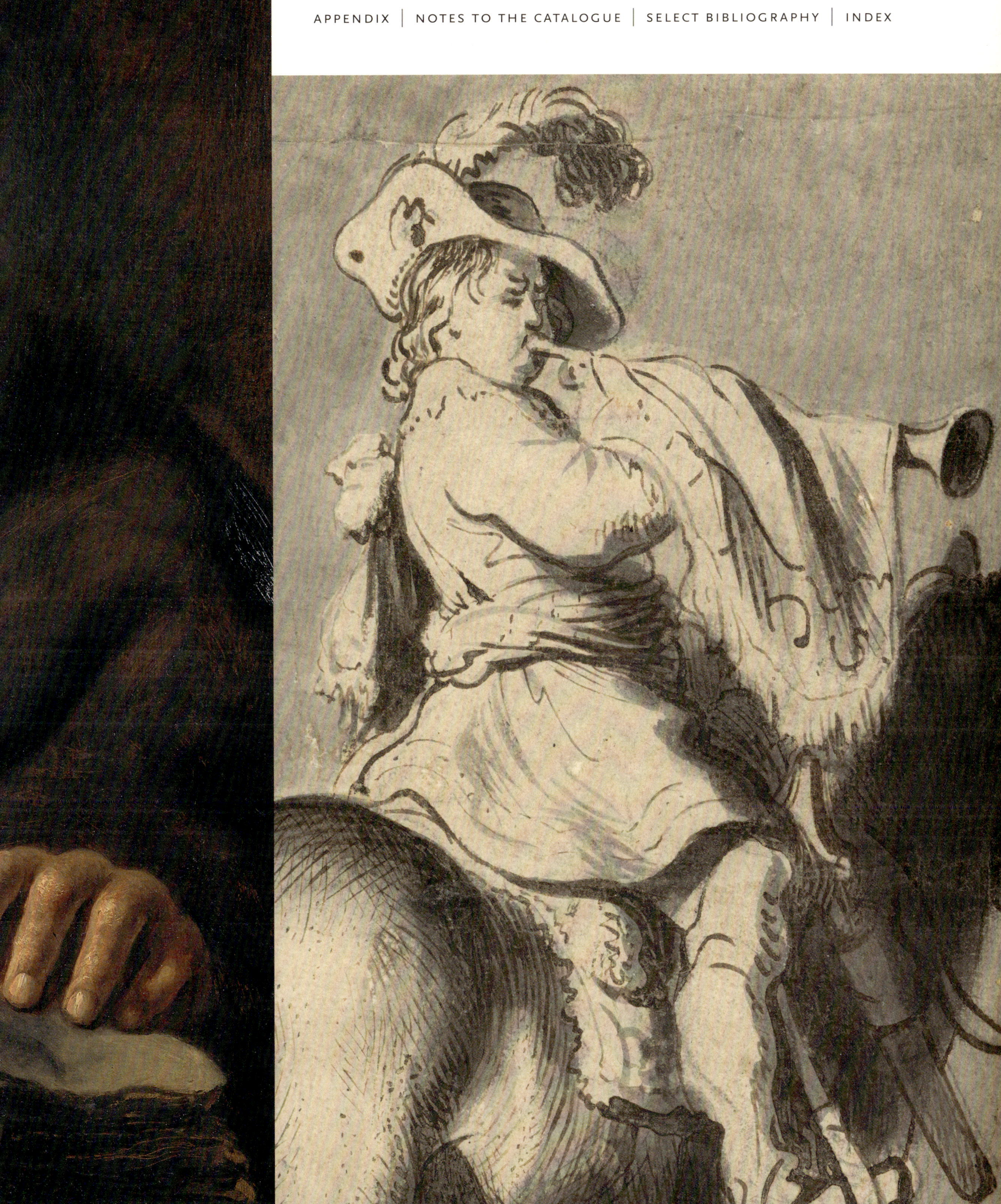

Appendix

"I believe I have already mentioned Lievens' character in passing…" Personality as the Key to the Career and Artistic Vision of Jan Lievens

LLOYD DEWITT

MANY ASPECTS OF JAN LIEVENS' life and career remain obscured. We do not know, for instance, if he shared a studio in Leiden for a time before 1628 with his friend and colleague Rembrandt. We do not know much about what he painted while living in England for three years, whether he converted to Catholicism, or the full extent of his relationships with Rubens and Van Dyck. Lievens did, however, make a strong impression on many contemporaries, and several — among them his patrician neighbor and early patron Jan Jansz Orlers, the stadtholder's secretary Constantijn Huygens, and the English ambassador Sir Robert Kerr — have left written records of their experiences with the artist. So we are well informed regarding his forceful personality, or "character," as Huygens put it. What they observed is visually confirmed in Lievens' own self-portraits, which reveal a precociously talented, vain, supremely confident man.

Another dimension to Lievens' personality is perceptible both in these texts and throughout his work, and that was restiveness, which was manifest in his relentless pursuit and assimilation of styles as he sought to produce what Huygens called the most "magnificent and lofty" results. Moving from one city to another, he was freed from any one local style or market, but by absorbing new stylistic influences that he judged would help him achieve his goal of becoming a court artist, he ultimately isolated himself. By contrast, when Rembrandt moved to Amsterdam, he built upon the style that he had evolved in Leiden with Lievens and continued to cultivate a recognizable artistic identity.

Huygens was likely introduced to Lievens through Orlers, who lived near the Lievens family in Leiden. The two gentlemen must have discussed the young artist with one another, because they describe him in such similar ways. Huygens wrote that Lievens, like Rembrandt, was unusually industrious — "they regard even the most innocent diversions of youth as a waste of time" — and that "compared with his age, the production of the illustrious youth is immense." A decade later Orlers commented in his published history of Leiden that Lievens "applied himself with such industry and diligence to improving his skills that he was oblivious to anything else" and that even the riots of October 1617 had "failed to distract him." Orlers commented that Lievens was small, like a boy (*jongman*), while Huygens called him a "sapling" (*tam tenuis trunci*).

Huygens visited Lievens and Rembrandt in Leiden in 1628, when they were twenty-one and twenty-two years old, respectively, and he gave a detailed report of the meeting in an unpublished autobiographical account that he wrote for his children between May 1629 and April 1631. While praising the talents of both young artists in superlative terms, he expressed reservations about one particular flaw in their characters: their overconfidence. With regard to Lievens, Huygens wrote, "My only objection is his stubbornness, which derives from an excess of self-confidence." Invoking Saint Paul as well as Horace, Huygens found Lievens' vanity and arrogance especially reproachable in one so young. He also noted how poorly Lievens accepted criticism. Though this memoir was a private document, Huygens' admonition is severe. In his opinion, Rembrandt and Lievens were showing overconfidence and "folly" by refusing to visit Italy and "perfect their artistic powers." He finally lamented, "If only these men, born to raise art to the highest pinnacle, knew themselves better!"

Lievens may have felt the need to correct a negative impression he had made on the stadtholder's secretary in this first meeting, for he soon appeared unannounced on the great man's doorstep in The Hague, "seized by the desire" to paint Huygens' portrait. He claimed to have been so obsessed that he could not work or sleep, which, Huygens observed, perhaps sardonically, was "all the more remarkable in view of his customary aversion to being persuaded to portray a person."[1] Because of Huygens' other obligations at the time, the artist could convince him to pose for only a short while, but Lievens was able to finish the clothes and hands in a manner that pleased Huygens, who agreed to have him return the following spring to add the face. The sitter greatly admired the resulting likeness (cat. 16), described the rendering as "contemplative," and acknowledged that he had been distracted by various personal concerns, a state of mind that he felt Lievens had succeeded in conveying through the expression he depicted. In other words, Lievens revealed what Huygens had sought to hide — which the sitter deemed no minor accomplishment. Though Lievens may have been reluctant to make portraits, he seems to have intuitively understood the effectiveness of studied informality. He placed Huygens in a relaxed pose, hands resting quietly in his lap, casually obscured within the darkness of this nearly monochromatic painting.

Huygens' suggestion that Lievens, despite having spent two years training in history painting with Pieter Lastman, should concentrate on portraiture may have been the advice the young man took "in bad spirit." Huygens may also have tried to school Lievens in courtly graces after discovering in him "an acute and profound insight into all kinds of things." Lievens persisted in depicting such grand subjects as *The Raising of Lazarus* and *Christ on the Cross* (cats. 31, 32), but with smaller-scale figures than when Huygens first met him and noted that he tended to paint everything larger than life. Lievens also sought to blend portraiture with history painting in the courtly fashion for *portraits historiés* (cats. 29, 49). These efforts demonstrate Lievens' desire to adapt his style to accommodate an important patron — clinging to his ambition to be a great history painter but trying to combine that with artistic strengths Huygens had recognized.

Huygens, who was trained in classical languages, often emulated canonical Latin texts in his writing,[2] and the comparison he makes between Rembrandt and Lievens and their styles of painting mimics the way Pliny the Elder compared Xeuxis and Parhassius. After extensively praising Rembrandt's history painting *Judas, Repentant, Returning the Thirty Pieces of Silver* (see Wheelock fig. 13), Huygens turned to Lievens: "in painting the human countenance he wreaks miracles," an assertion he supported by referring to his own portrait by the artist. Lievens' portrait of Huygens as well as the pensive and self-absorbed self-portraits he began to produce in the late 1620s have a peculiar quality of detachment. The latter works differ from Rembrandt's self-portraits from about the same time in that they function more like experimental genre portraits, or tronies (cats. 18, 20) — studies in physiognomy, costume, or class — than like explorations of the inner self. Only one unquestioned self-portrait by Lievens survives from after his Leiden period (cat. 48). Painted when he lived in Amsterdam, it shows the same undaunted confidence of his earlier likenesses.[3] He portrays himself in a golden cloak, gazing past the viewer while posing gracefully, an elegant wrist draped over the armrest, asserting his status as a gentleman and court painter. A wry mention of him during this period makes clear that his brash personality had changed very little. Sir Robert Kerr, the English ambassador, whose portrait was painted by Lievens around 1654 (cat. 51), wrote a letter to his son representing the artist's high opinion of himself, in terms similar to those Huygens had used around 1630: "he thinks there is none to be compared with him in all Germany, Holland, nor the rest of the seventeen provinces."[4]

Such drive and self-assurance manifested themselves in the way Lievens met the challenges posed by commissions throughout his career. Beginning in Leiden, he drew ideas from classical and literary sources (see Wheelock figs. 6, 7, and cat. 2), a practice he followed until his later years (see Wheelock fig. 24, and cats. 22, 26, 49, 50). He was also greatly inspired by the prodigious artistic inventiveness of Peter Paul Rubens (cats. 6, 7), the most successful and highly honored artist of his day. By the second half of the 1620s Lievens had begun to model works on Rubens' figural compositions (cats. 19, 32, 36). Later, after moving to Antwerp in the 1635, he also explored several of Rubens' other signature genres — including landscape painting and woodcut prints — resulting in some of his most experimental and startling creations (cats. 37, 81). Then in June 1640, while living in Antwerp, Lievens conveyed the news of Rubens' death to Huygens via the latter's brother-in-law and in almost the same breath offered to complete unfinished paintings left in Rubens' studio[5] — daring to suggest that he thought himself worthy to assume the mantle of this preeminent Flemish master.

Whether or not Lievens ever met Rubens is uncertain, but he was personally acquainted with the other great Flemish painter of the time, Anthony van Dyck, who was in The Hague around 1631/1632. Van Dyck recorded Lievens' proud likeness (see Wheelock fig. 11) for a series of portrait engravings of prominent individuals to be published in his *Iconography*, an honor he did not accord Rembrandt. The caption below the portrait of Lievens identifies him as a painter of "large figures" (*figurarum maiorum*), language similar to that used by Huygens, which suggests that the stadtholder's secretary may have introduced the young artist to Van Dyck.[6] The encounter came at a decisive moment in Lievens' life, as he would soon fulfill long-standing plans to leave Leiden for London, where he seems to have worked in close association with Van Dyck during the early 1630s.[7] Although little survives from Lievens' production in England, the level of patronage he reputedly received there accords with his abilities and ambitions. Perhaps through Huygens or Van Dyck, both of whom had royal connections, he gained access to Charles I as well as the king's family and courtiers (see Dickey fig. 8, Rubinstein fig. 2, and cats. 74, 75). Lievens' first attempts at landscape drawing directly followed examples by Van Dyck (cat. 101), and he eagerly pursued this theme and stylistic approach from the older master for the much of his remaining career.

Lievens remained in contact with Huygens, and probably with Van Dyck, after moving to Antwerp in 1635. Once back on the Continent, he sought to secure commissions for large-scale religious paintings in Jesuit churches, an extraordinary about-face for the son of Calvinists. His monumental *Visitation* for the Jesuits in Brussels (see Wheelock fig. 18) reveals how hard Lievens worked to emulate Flemish models, significantly altering his Dutch style and painting techniques to achieve the resonant color and monumentality that could compete effectively with Rubens and Van Dyck in their own territory.

An important commission for the Leiden town hall lured Lievens back to Holland in 1639. *The Magnanimity of Scipio* became the first public work of art in his native country to be painted in the Flemish manner by a Dutch artist (see Wheelock fig. 19). Flattering mention in two subsequent Leiden publications — by Jan Jansz Orlers in 1641 and Philips Angel in 1642 — must have further encouraged him that a promising career awaited him in the Dutch Republic. Moving to Amsterdam in 1644, he received commissions for prominent projects from various illustrious patrons over the next several decades. His painting of Anna Maria van Schurman (cat. 45) and his portrait prints and drawings of Joost van den Vondel, René Descartes, and Jan Vos (cats. 85, 113, 118) are among numerous testaments to his self-confidence and ease in dealing with the highest echelons of society.

The Flemish-style classicism that Lievens had developed for his history paintings in Antwerp served him well in Holland, and Huygens continued to honor the artist he had championed twenty years earlier. He assigned Lievens one of the paintings in the decorative cycle for the Oranjezaal (see Wheelock fig. 22), a vaulted space in the villa outside The Hague that was turned into a commemorative hall to honor the Prince of Orange after his death in 1647. This project led to painting commissions for Schloss Oranienburg in Bützow, outside Berlin, for the prince's daughter Louise Henriette, who had married the Elector of Brandenburg in 1646. Lievens' allegories for the Brandenburg palace featured goddesses modeled on the princess herself.

When Lievens returned to Amsterdam again in 1654, he quickly secured work in the new Amsterdam town hall because his "Flemish" manner had become a popular and quasi-"official" style. The history paintings he provided, among the most important of his career, proved the durability of his style and reputation. Today his *Brinio Raised on a Shield* of 1660 remains in its original location, whereas Rembrandt's comparable *Conspiracy of Claudius Civilis* was rejected and later reduced in size to enhance its marketability (see Wheelock figs. 25, 26). Lievens was then asked in 1663 to paint *Mars (The Allegory of War)* for the newly constructed Statenzaal, in the Binnenhof in The Hague (see Wheelock fig. 1). Correspondence concerning this commission provides one of the few known instances in which Lievens documented his artistic intentions. Regarding his preliminary oil sketch, Lievens wrote boldly in a letter of April 24, 1664, to the *raadpensionaris* Johan de Witt: "I hope I have met with approval.... I have a great desire to stir up something extraordinary in it, because War is a picturesque subject."[8] As leader of the Dutch Republic, Johan de Witt was also an important private patron of Lievens, having commissioned several portraits of his own and his wife's family and having apparently referred Lievens to Amelis van den Bouckhorst, chair of the Gecommitteerde Raden (executive council) and *dikereeve* (head) of the Rijnland, for other prestigious projects (see Wheelock and Van der Veen essays and cat. 55).

Lievens never established a large and active workshop with assistants and pupils to produce paintings under his direction. Nearly all of his students were either family members or the dilettantes who paid tuition but did not challenge his authority. His only gifted pupil, his son Jan Andrea, seems to have left his employment after a single project (cat. 55). It is possible that Lievens' arrogance and controlling personality blinded him to the potential benefits of attracting and concentrating talent around him, but his restlessness throughout his career also precluded his running such a workshop. Indeed, the frequency with which he changed residences also meant that he did not cultivate a stalwart community of friends and patrons to sustain him in his later years.

Lievens' self-confidence rarely wavered until the end of his life. It expressed itself in a variety of sometimes contradictory ways, but even the artist's late commissions are sophisticated, ambitious, and experimental, and he continued to merit the esteem of critics, colleagues, and patrons. He apparently maintained friendships with Rembrandt and Jan Steen, the latter being related by marriage (see Dickey essay and fig. 15).[9] One of his brothers, Titus, would do small favors, but Lievens was estranged from his son for a time after an open row. And Lievens' itinerancy and restiveness proved to be his Achilles' heel. It was manifested in the occasionally hurried, unresolved, or unfinished quality of some of his later works, an unfortunate corollary to the dashing, adventurous bravura that made his early works so remarkable. Despite his artistic successes, Lievens spent his final years in poverty that he made no attempt to conceal from his prestigious patrons.[10] In the course of one of his last commissions he even tried to board his children in a client's home — causing considerable dismay.[11] Near the end of his life, financial ruin left him unable to lodge his family in Amsterdam. His personal situation was no doubt aggravated by the the French invasion of the Netherlands in 1672, resulting in economic collapse that accounts for the low valuations assigned to the paintings in Lievens' possession at his death in 1674.[12]

The following excerpts from first-hand accounts by Constantijn Huygens (1629–1631) and Jan Jansz Orlers (1641), depict Leivens at two different points in his journey. Huygens gives us a glimpse of the young prodigy at what appeared to be the start of a brilliant career, while Orlers reflects back on Lievens' boyhood and gives us a sense of the artist reaching the height of his powers. Both narratives articulate the promise that the writers saw in this fertile mind and sure, energetic hand, but they also reveal the perils that ambition held for him, and they adumbrate the sad end met by this flawed but astoundingly inventive artist.

Notes

1 This comment suggests that Huygens and Lievens had a disagreement about the artist's aptitude for portraiture.

2 Bialostocki in Braunschweig 1979, 14. Huygens lived the adage "no day without writing" (*nulla dies sine linea*).

3 A panel in the Dulwich Picture Gallery identified as a self-portrait by Lievens in Schneider/Ekkart 1973, no. 247; Sumowski 1983, no. 1287; and others, is in fact a sketch for a self-portrait by the English artist Robert Walker (Sotheby's, London, November 23, 2006, lot 20). Walker used the pose from Van Dyck's *Self-Portrait with a Sunflower* in his own later self-portrait (National Portrait Gallery, London, NPG 753). Lievens and Walker were both closely tied to Van Dyck's manner and practice, and the two may well have known one another.

4 Braunschweig 1979, 113, no. 38.

5 In a subsequent letter the brother-in-law, David de Wilhelm, informed Huygens that Lievens had in the intervening month visited the studio and found the canvas had not even been begun, suggesting that Huygens had sent Lievens to look and perhaps had even acceded to Lievens' request. See Schneider/Ekkart 1973, 292.

6 Both Cornelis Schut and Gaspar de Crayer were each similarly identified in the captions to their portraits in Van Dyck's print series as painters of "figurarum maiorum."

7 *Journaal der Leidsche Schutterij*, April 10, 1629, in Moes 1907, 142–143. See also Schneider/Ekkart 1973, 3, 4.

8 Jan Lievens to Johan de Witt, April 24, 1664. See Schneider/Ekkart 1973, 298.

9 Weyermann 1729, 353. H. Perry Chapman, et al. *Jan Steen: Painter and Storyteller*, exh. cat., National Gallery of Art, Washington, and Rijksmuseum, Amsterdam, 1996, 28, 35 n. 60. The landscape setting of Jan Steen's *Flight into Egypt* has in the past been attributed to Lievens. See Schneider/Ekkart 1973, 99, no. 27.

10 In another letter to Johann de Witt, May 8, 1664, Lievens asks for payment for the *Mars* commission before finishing the hands and landscape, explaining that he is in arrears on his rent. See Schneider/Ekkart 1973, 298. He had delegated his brother Titus to pick up the sketch of *Mars* from Bouchorst, so that he could proceed.

11 Bredius 1915–1922, 210–211.

12 Bredius 1915–1922, 187–189.

Constantijn Huygens on Lievens and Rembrandt

I HAVE DELIBERATELY REFRAINED from mentioning a pair of young and noble painters from Leiden in this parade. Were I to say that they were the only ones who can vie with the absolute geniuses among the aforesaid prodigies [De Gheyn the Elder, Goltzius, Rubens and Van Mierevelt], I would still be underestimating the merits of these two. And were I to say that they will soon surpass those geniuses, I would merely be expressing what their astonishing beginnings have led connoisseurs to expect. Considering their parentage, there is no stronger evidence against the belief that nobility is in the blood. Some people swear by such nobility, but I recall how cleverly they were confuted by the biting satire of Traiano Boccalini, a modern author who writes in a most painstaking and pure style. In a tale about the anatomical dissection of a nobleman's corpse, he relates how all the doctors, after carefully inspecting the veins, declared unanimously that nobility did not dwell in the blood, for there was no difference between this man's blood and that of a commoner or peasant.

One of our two youths was the son of a commoner, an embroiderer, the other a miller's son, but assuredly not of the same grain. Who could help but marvel that two such prodigies of talent and skill should ripen from such humble seeds?

Enquiring as to their childhood teachers, I discover men whose reputation was scarcely known outside the common classes. Due to their parents' straitened circumstances, the youths were compelled to take teachers whose fees were modest. Were these teachers to be confronted with their pupils today, they would feel just as abashed as those teachers who gave Vergil his first lessons in poetry, Cicero in rhetoric, and Archimedes in mathematics. Let it however be said, with due respect for everyone's capacities and without detracting from anyone (for what is it to me?): these two owe nothing to their teachers but everything to their aptitude. Had they never received any tuition but been left to their own devices and suddenly been seized by the urge to paint, I am convinced that they would have risen to the same heights as they indeed have. It would be wrong to think that others have led them to this point.

The first, whom I described as an embroiderer's son, is called Jan Lievens; the other, whose cradle stood in a mill, Rembrandt. Both are still beardless and, going by their faces, more boys than men. I am neither able nor willing to judge each according to his works and application. As in the case of the aforementioned Rubens, I wish these two would draw up an inventory of their works and describe their paintings. Each could supply a modest explanation of his method, going on to indicate how and why (for the admiration and education of all future generations) they had designed, composed, and worked out each painting.

I venture to suggest offhand that Rembrandt is superior to Lievens in his sure touch and liveliness of emotions. Conversely, Lievens is the greater in inventiveness and audacious themes and forms. Everything his young spirit endeavors to capture must be magnificent and lofty. Rather than depicting his subject in its true size, he chooses a larger scale.

Rembrandt, by contrast, devotes all his loving concentration to a small painting, achieving on that modest scale a result which one would seek in vain in the largest pieces of others....

I believe I have already mentioned Lievens' character in passing. He is a young man of great spirit, and great things may be expected of him if he is granted a long enough life. He has an acute and profound insight into all manner of things, riper than a mature man, as I have often had occasion to note in conversations. My only objection is his stubbornness, which derives from an excess of self-confidence. He either roundly rejects all criticism or, if he acknowledges its validity, takes it in bad spirit. This bad habit, harmful at any age, is absolutely pernicious in youth. After all, a little leaven leaveneth the whole lump [1 Corinthians 5:6; Galatians 5:9]. And those ridden with the vice which closely resembles this bad habit "deceive themselves," according to the Holy Scripture [Galations 6:3]. It is a sign of great sagacity to realize that God has given to each man "with a chary hand what is sufficient," in the words of the poet [Horace, *Carmina* 3.16 and 44], but that no man has ever received everything; consequently all men, whoever they be, should be approached with a well-disposed heart and an inquisitive mind, in the belief that there is always something to be learned from everyone.

Compared with his age, the production of the illustrious youth is immense. Seeing the maker beside his paintings, it is scarcely credible that such a meager sapling can put forth so much fruit. In painting the human countenance he wreaks miracles. One would be rendering him good service by endeavoring to curb this vigorous, untamable spirit whose bold ambition is to embrace all nature, and by persuading the brilliant painter to concentrate on that physical part which miraculously combines the essence of the human spirit and body. In what we are accustomed to calling history pieces, the artist, his astonishing talent notwithstanding, is unlikely to match Rembrandt's vivid invention.

In the collection of our Prince is a painting of a man purported to be a Turkish potentate with a Dutchman's head [see cat. 19]; Brouart has a portrait whose face is sere and wrinkled like that of a philosopher. De Gheyn, I believe, has some portraits of youths, and Sohier diverse portraits which the artist painted some time ago, while still a pupil. There are works of inestimable value and unrivaled artistry. May their maker be preserved for us in the length of days.

Allow me to related in passing that once, in the company of my brother, I called on him; he had no prior acquaintance with me at this time. He was seized with the desire to paint my portrait. I assured him that I should be only too pleased to grant him the opportunity if he would come to The Hague and put up at my house for a while. So ardent was his desire that he arrived within a few days, explaining that since seeing me his nights had been restless and his days so troubled that he had been unable to work. My countenance had lodged so firmly in his mind that his eagerness brooked no further delay. This effect on his imaginative powers was all the more remarkable in view of his customary aversion to being persuaded to portray a person. It being winter and the days drawing in, and my own affairs leaving me scant time to pose, he was content to paint my clothes and my bare hands (a task of which he acquitted himself most tastefully) and to postpone the portrayal of my face until the advent of spring. Again, he made his appearance long before the appointed date. So evident in the finished work [see cat. 16] was his enthusiasm that I paid tribute to its excellent maker by allotting it a permanent place amongst my most treasured possessions. Not a day goes by but it is regarded by Van Mierevelt and countless others with the utmost admiration. There are however those who opine that the contemplative rendering of the face detracts from the vivacity of my mind, to which I can but respond that the fault is mine. During this period I was involved in a serious family affair of some importance and, as is only to be expected, the cares which I endeavored to keep to myself were clearly reflected in the expression of my face and eyes.

I do however censure one fault of these celebrated young men, from whom I can scarcely tear myself away in this account. I have already criticized Lievens for his self-confidence, which Rembrandt shares; hitherto, neither has found it necessary to spend a few months traveling through Italy. This is naturally a touch of folly in figures otherwise so brilliant. If only someone could drive it out of their young heads, he would truly contribute the sole element still needed to perfect their artistic powers. How I would welcome their acquaintance with Raphael and Michelangelo, the feasting of their eyes on the creations of such gigantic spirits! How quickly they would surpass them all, giving the Italians due cause to come to Holland. If only these men, born to raise art to the highest pinnacle, knew themselves better!

Let me describe the pretext with which they justify their lack of mobility. They claim to be in the bloom of youth and wish to profit from it; they have no time to waste on foreign travel. Moreover, the best Italian paintings of the genre most appreciated and collected these days by kings and princes north of the Alps are to be found outside Italy. What is scattered around in that country and only to be traced by dint of considerable effort can be found in abundance and even in surfeit here.

The validity of this excuse is a moot point. I feel it incumbent upon myself to state that I have never observed such dedication and persistence in other men, whatever their pursuits or ages. Truly, these youths are redeeming the time [Ephesians 5:16; Colossians 4:5]. That is their sole consideration. Most amazingly, they regard even the most innocent diversions of youth as a waste of time, as if they were already old men burdened with age and long past such follies. Such indefatigable application to diligent labor may well yield great results quickly, but I have often wished that these excellent young men would practise moderation and consider their constitutions, which a sedentary occupation has already rendered less vigorous and robust.

Based on Leiden 1991, 128–134, where the text appears in both Dutch and English.

Jan Jansz Orlers on Lievens

... Jan Lievensz.
Was born in Leiden on October 24, 1607, the son of respectable parents, Master Lieven Hendricxsz, a skilled embroiderer, and Machtelt Jansdr van Noortsant. On observing his son's great love of painting, the father decided that he should acquire the foundations of the art, and apprenticed the eight-year-old boy to the proficient painter Master Joris Verschoten, from whom he learned the principles of both drawing and painting.

When he was about ten years old, and his father saw how eager he was to continue his studies, he consented to send the boy to the celebrated painter Pieter Lastman, a resident of Amsterdam; Jan spent some two years with him and made great progress.

After leaving Lastman he had no further teachers, and started working in his father's house, spending all his time diligently and industriously painting many and varied subjects from life. His consummate skill astounded numerous connoisseurs of art who found it hard to believe that a mere stripling of twelve or scarcely any older could produce such work — usually his own compositions and ideas to boot. During this period he copied two outstanding pieces by the excellent Master Cornelis Ketel of Haarlem, a Democritus and a Heraclitus. He did this so well that those with an understanding of art could not distinguish the originals from the copies. The paintings were sold as originals from the estate of Mr. Boudewijns and sent to Germany.

In 1621, at the age of fourteen, he portrayed his mother so cleverly and with such great skill that everyone was astonished.

He applied himself with such industry and diligence to improving his skills that he was oblivious to anything else. Even the riots of October 4, 1618 [1617], between the Remonstrant forces and the townspeople, during which all the doors and windows were closed and the magistrates were forced to call in the militia to quell the uprising, failed to distract him from drawing prints by "Witty Willem" [Willem Buytewech], for he regarded the love of art as more important than all the upheaval in the world.

In his youth and for some years thereafter, he made a large variety of paintings and portraits which are still regarded as extremely valuable. Some of them are still in the hands of the heirs of Pieter Huygen du Bois: diverse portraits, a Cupid with a satchel of almanacs and, slung round his shoulders, a cask with white hoops, filled with turnips and other vegetables, consummately rendered. Adriaen van Leeuwen has a panel with the Five Senses, Jan van der Graft a Pilate [probably cat. 7], and various other pieces which are too many to enumerate.

A little later he made a life-size painting of a person wearing a round cap, studying near a turf fire, painted with such spirit that His Highness the Prince of Orange caused it to be purchased and presented to the ambassador of the king of England who in turn gave it to his master the king; it can still be seen at Westminster.

On feeling the urge to see another country and other customs, Lievens went to England in 1631, at the age of about 24, where his fine works gained him immediate acclaim. His fame was noted by the king himself, whom he portrayed with his consort the queen, his son the Prince of Wales, his daughter the princess, as well as several great lords. For this he was richly rewarded by the king of England.

After he had spent some three years in England he returned to Calais and thence to Antwerp, where he settled. He painted several excellent pieces for the Jesuit church and other private persons there, works which were greatly admired by connoisseurs. In Antwerp he married the daughter of Michiel Colijns, an excellent and skilled sculptor and stone-dresser. In 1640, for His Highness the Prince of Orange and for the burgomaster of the city of Leiden, he painted two pieces of exceptional quality, the latter of which I have already mentioned in my description [*The Magnanimity of Scipio*, destroyed in a fire at the Leiden town hall; see Wheelock fig. 19]. From my approximate account of Master Jan Lievens of our city of Leiden, anyone with an understanding of art can expect him to paint many more fine pictures.

Based on Leiden 1991, 135–139, where the text appears in both Dutch and English.

Notes to the Catalogue

1 Old Woman Reading

1 See Van Straten 2005, 22–24; DeWitt 2006, 42–44; and Wheelock essay.

2 Of eight surviving children, Jannetgen, the youngest, was baptized on March 2, with her grandmother Margaretha Smuncx as witness. See De Baar 1992, 16.

2 Allegory of the Five Senses

1 No such images had been painted in Leiden prior to this work. Bauch 1960, 114, and Bauch 1967, 161, sought to connect this painting with genre scenes by Haarlem artists, arguing that Lievens was influenced by the Haarlem School early in his career.

2 Gerson 1969, 139, also doubted that it was by Lievens.

3 According to Christiaan Vogelaar (correspondence, October 22, 2007), Adriaan van Leeuwen was married to Maria van Swanenburch, possibly a relative of the painter and notorious burgomaster Isaac van Swanenburch. He was buried in Pieterskerk on March 21, 1645, and his wife was buried there on August 24, 1645. They had two daughters, of whom Johanna Adriana was married to Jacob van der Graft. Orlers noted a Jan van der Graft (perhaps a father or brother) as the owner of *Pilate Washing His Hands* (cat. 7). A sister Catharina remained unmarried but left an immense fortune of 31,500 guilders to Jacob and Johanna (see Regionaal Archief Leiden, Warboek AAAA, fol. 324, dated June 16, 1650), who had two sons, Cornelis and Jacob, both of whom died without heir. Cornelis built an almshouse at Breestraat and at his death on January 4, 1706, left a rich inventory with a number of family portraits.

3 The Cardplayers

1 Judson and Ekkart 1999, 17–19.

2 On the reverse of the painting is a label with the name "Van Honthorst." The first art historians to recognize the correct attribution to Lievens were B.J.A. Renckens and R.E.O. Ekkart in 1976 (letter to then-owner).

3 First suggested by Renckens in letter to then-owner, April 7, 1976.

4 Bernhard Schnackenburg, in the sales catalogue, Sotheby's, Amsterdam, May 8, 2007, no. 77.

4 Saint Paul

1 Suggested in Schwartz 1985, 93, in relation to Rembrandt's slightly later *Two Old Men Disputing* (cat. 20, fig. 1), supporting the identification of the subject as Saints Peter and Paul heralding the New Testament. The idea is given credence by the extinguished candle in Rembrandt's *Presentation in the Temple* (Hamburger Kunsthalle, Hamburg), c. 1627–1628, also marking the superseding of the Old Testament in Christian theology.

2 See Sumowski 1983, 3: 1791, no. 1224.

3 For Rembrandt's *Three Singers* (Collection of W. Baron van Dedem, London), see Corpus 1982–, 1: 399–404, no. B1; concerning its attribution to Rembrandt, see Kassel and Amsterdam 2001–2002, 150–153.

4 See the series in the Historisch Museum De Waag Deventer: Slatkes and Franits 2007, 115–117, no. A26.

5 For Ter Brugghen's *Saint Mark* (private collection, Westphalia), see Slatkes and Franits 2007, 228–230, no. WTBVB3.

6 Van Dyck's *Saint Thomas*, or a copy of it, was in the collection of Henricus Vuylenborch in Utrecht in 1661, and perhaps by 1624; see Washington 1990, 130–134, no. 20. Its influence on Ter Brugghen suggests it was already in Utrecht by 1623.

7 At the synod in Dordrecht in 1618, the principles of the Reformed Church were enshrined in a set of canons; see *Articles of the Synod of Dordt*, trans. Rev. Thomas Scott (Philadelphia, 1841). Articles 1–7, chap. 1, deal with predestination and refer to Paul's letters to the Ephesians (1:4–6, 11; and 2:8) and Romans (8:30).

5 Saint Peter Released from Prison

1 Xander van Eck, "From Doubt to Conviction: Clandestine Catholic Churches as Patrons of Dutch Caravaggesque Painting," *Simiolus* 22 (1993–1994): 230. Van Eck argues that the theme also offered hope that the Catholic Church would once again be the predominant church in the Netherlands.

2 The sections had been reattached by the time the painting was sold at Sotheby's, London, July 6, 2000, no. 63. Mayna Dressner, senior conservator at the Tel Aviv Museum of Art, who prepared the painting for the exhibition, notes that all four edges have been trimmed (correspondence, December 5, 2007). She believes that more was cut off at the bottom, where canvas inserts replacing damaged areas at the lower left appear to come from a missing portion of the original painting.

3 This history was kindly provided by Doron J. Lurie, curator at the Tel Aviv Museum of Art (correspondence, February 26, 2007).

6 The Feast of Esther

1 Raleigh 1998–1999, 165. The profusion of rich fabrics reminds one that Lievens' father was a skilled textile worker.

2 De Baar and Moermann in Leiden 1991, 33, state that "Lievens' father had to leave G[h]ent, most likely when Parma seized the city in 1584, and on these grounds alone should be reckoned as a (Counter-Remonstrant)." See also Israel 1995, 371–372.

3 Jan Jansz Orlers, *Waerachtige beschryvinge en afbeeldinghe van alle de overwinningen* (Leiden, 1619).

4 Israel 1995, 488.

5 See Israel 1995, 441–449, 459; and Schwartz 1985, 36–38. In an effort to unify the Reformed Church and quell civil unrest, the States of Holland under Oldenbarnevelt adopted the "Sharp Resolution" on August 4, 1617. Troops were stationed in the towns to suppress the Calvinist Counter-Remonstrant preachers and protect the Remonstrant congregations. This policy was opposed not only by the Counter-Remonstrants but by the stadtholder Maurits, who saw the action as an "affront to the true Reformed religion and our person." The 1618 synod of Dordrecht decisively resolved the conflict by deciding against the Remonstrants, and this was followed by a "coup d'état" against the States by Prince Maurits that led to the trial of Oldenbarenvelt for treason and the unexpected death sentence that was quickly carried out on May 13, 1619.

6 Schwartz 1985, 37.

7 Bredius/Gerson 1969, no. 531a.

8 Sumowski 1983, 3: 1776.

7 Pilate Washing His Hands

1 For a change in the design of the turban, see Gifford essay.

2 See the discussion by Schnackenburg in Kassel and Amsterdam 2001–2002, 192–195, no. 24.

3 Van Thiel in Washington, Detroit, Amsterdam 1980, 90, relates this fabric to that of the cope of David of Burgundy, bishop of Utrecht from 1456 to 1496, now in the Rijksmuseum Het Catharijneconvent (on loan from the Oud-Katholieke Kerk). See *Bourgondische pracht* [exh. cat., Rijksmuseum] (Amsterdam, 1951), 47, no. 150.

8 Christ at the Column

1 Van der Ploeg et al. 2002, 102.

2 See Sutton 1990, 258; and Hill 2003. There is no evidence, however, that Lievens visited Sir Dudley Carleton in the early to middle 1620s before executing this work.

3 Sutton 1990, 258.

9, 10 The Evangelist Matthew; The Evangelist John

1 Multifigured compositions are found among Lievens' drawings, however; see cat. 90.

2 See Schneider/Ekkart 1973, 324, no. 60.

3 See Slatkes and Franits 2007, 115–117, nos. A24–A27. See also Paul Huys Janssens, *Jan van Bijlert 1597/1598–1671: Catalogue Raisonné* (Amsterdam, 1998), 105–107.

4 Gerson 1978, 754–757. See also Slatkes and Franits 2007, 228–229, nos. WTBVB 2–5.

5 Long attributed to Abraham Bloemaert, then Jacob Backer, the paintings were exhibited as Lievens for the first time in Braunschweig 1979, nos. 10–13. Brown 1979b, 742, expressed reservations about the panels depicting Mark and John.

6 Gutbrod 1996, 190.

7 Cornelis Ketel used fellow artists and collectors as models for his series of Christ and his Apostles. See Van Mander 1604/1618, 276r.

11 Still Life with Books

1 Bauch 1967, 260.

2 Wallert 2006a, 152–153, notes that the identical book appears in the paintings of Saints Mark and Luke (see cat. 9–10, figs. 1, 2).

3 Rijksmuseum 1976, 473, no. A4090, where the painting is assigned to the "milieu of Rembrandt." For the relationship to the still lifes of books painted in Leiden by Jan Davidsz de Heem in the late 1620s, see Amsterdam and Cleveland 1999–2000, 146–147.

4 The x-radiograph also reveals that a female portrait had been painted on the panel before the still life; see Wallert 2006a. Paint analysis confirms that the portrait was finished and varnished before the panel was reused. Dendrochronology indicates that the portrait could have been painted after 1624, which is consistent with the style of the woman's dress.

5 See Haak 1969, 68–69; Schneider/Ekkart 1973, 354; and Wallert 2006a, 146–147. No one has explained how an artist active in Amsterdam would have had access to a still life painted in Leiden.

6 Wouter Kloek and Alan Chong in Amsterdam and Cleveland 1999–2000, 146–148, no. 18.

7 Personal communication, following her examination of the painting in July 2007.

8 The painting is identified as a *vanitas* still life in Leiden 1970, no. 25; but Kloek and Chong in Amsterdam and Cleveland 1999–2000, 146–147, argue that the objects relate to a scholar or artist.

9 Leiden 1976, 18: "een groot inbyten geschildert by Mr Jan Lievens soon."

12 Youth Embracing a Young Woman

1 Lievens' predilection for painting figures larger than life size was noted by Huygens; see Appendix.

2 I would like to thank Brighton Hanson for this observation.

3 See the sales catalogue, Christie's, Amsterdam, May 6, 2003, no. 120.

13 Lute Player

1 As noted in Bowron 1977, unpaginated.

2 The figure in the feathered cap in Rembrandt's *Music Lesson* (see Wheelock fig. 12) is often thought to be Lievens.

3 Bowron 1977, unpaginated. The model may be the same one Lievens used in the newly discovered *Youth Embracing a Young Woman* (cat. 12).

15 Samson and Delilah

1 Though the primary version of this painting was in Rome in the seventeenth-century, Judson and Ekkart 1999, 54–55, no. 10, suggests that Lievens may have known it through a shop copy.

2 See Schnackenburg in Kassel and Amsterdam 2001–2002, no. 27.

16 Portrait of Constantijn Huygens

1 See the Appendix. Schwartz 1985, 73–77, suggests that Orlers arranged for Huygens' introduction to Lievens and Rembrandt on October 15 or 17, 1627, when Huygens was visiting Leiden with his brother. Ekkart in Leiden 1991, 53–56, notes that stylistic evidence points to a visit during the winter of 1628/1629. Huygens was indeed in Leiden in October 1628 and, unusually, in The Hague in the first months of 1629. See Schneider/Ekkart 1973, 309.

2 At the same time, Jacob van Campen wrote Huygens in July 1633 offering to paint a "white" portrait to go with "the black one by Lievens"; see Schwartz 1985, 76 (Held 1991, 664, suggests "black" referred to the mood). Van Campen asked Huygens to send the framed Lievens portrait in a specially built chest with a second slot for Van Campen's finished work, which was to be a token of gratitude for the securing of a hunting license. The painting, executed in 1635, is now lost.

3 The Latin epigram, *In Effigiem meam, manu I. Livij,* appears in Leerintveld 1989, 176. This translation is from Van Straten 2005, 108.

4 Huygens wrote a number paeans to portraits of himself, including *On my portrait, made shortly before my wedding* (August 2, 1627): "Speak, painting, and say how powerful a happiness has raised me up inside, when I feared if I would win the heart of my Star...." Following Emmens 1956, 83–84, Leerintveld 1989, 159–183, argues that this epigram and another written on August 7, *Still about the same one,* refer to Lievens' portrait and that Huygens was worrying about his marriage proposal to Susannah van Baerle (they married in February 1627). See also Schwartz 1985, 81.

5 Van Schendel 1963, 6, 9; Gerson 1971, 148.

18 Self-Portrait

1 The print by Vorsterman was based on a now-lost portrait that Van Dyck made while in The Hague in the winter of 1631/1632. A unique sketchy impression of state 1 at the Institut Néerlandais, Paris, depicts Lievens without a moustache. It seems unlikely, as some have suggested, that the appearance of a moustache in state 2 indicates that Lievens grew it only after Van Dyck had drawn or painted his likeness. Rather, Vosterman probably overlooked the slight growth on Van Dyck's model and made his revisions after Van Dyck had seen the first state.

2 See Braunschweig 1979, 100, no. 32.

3 The dendrochronological examination was undertaken by Peter Klein, Ordinariat für Holzbiologie, Universität Hamburg. For the dating of Rembrandt's painting, see Corpus 1982–, 1: 249–257, no. A24.

4 As early as 1629 Lievens had already indicated that he aspired to move to London (see Wheelock essay).

19 Man in Oriental Costume

1 On April 10, 1629, Lievens told the Leiden militia "that he had intended to leave Leiden soon for England but that at the request of the Prince of Orange he had taken on a painting on which he would be working for about three months, and therefore had to postpone his trip and departure for that time." See Leiden 2005, no. 37. Thus the *terminus post quem* for the present painting is 1629, while the *terminus ante quem* is late 1631, as Lievens departed for England in early 1632.

2 For more on Eastern fashions represented in Dutch art, see Goetz 1938, 280–290; and De Winkel 2006, 255–261.

3 Rembrandt's *Old Man in a Turban,* 1627, in the Kremer Collection is one of the earliest examples. See Van der Ploeg et al. 2002, no. 28.

4 See Schneider/Ekkart 1973, 304.

5 Rubens' image was inspired by a figure in Bernardino di Betto Pinturicchio's fresco in the Biblioteca Piccolomini in Siena, which was based on a drawing by Gentile Bellini or Constanzo da Ferrara, c. 1495 (Musée du Louvre, Paris). See De Winkel 2006, 145. Also noted in Van Straten 2005, 91–92.

6 Liedtke 2007, 2: 556, no. 125; Leiden 2005, no. 37.

7 Orlers inventory, 1640.

8 Liedtke 2007, 2: 560.

20 Bearded Man with a Beret

1 Rembrandt also used this scratching technique around 1630 on comparable tronies of old men.

2 De Winkel 2006, 166.

3 Broos in The Hague and San Francisco 1991, 320.

4 Lievens and Rembrandt shared models commonly referred to as Rembrandt's "mother" and "father" (see cat. 21).

5 Broos in The Hague and San Francisco 1991, 320.

21 Profile Head of an Old Woman

1 Gottwald 2007, 165–250.

2 Jan Lievens, *Old Woman with a Book*, Rijksmuseum, Amsterdam, no. SK-A-4702.

3 Gottwald 2006, 339, questions the validity of evidence provided by Clement de Jonghe's inventory, drafted two years after his death, by a notary.

4 This characterization of Dutch artists was most famously voiced in Fromentin 1948, 108–116.

5 Lievens created a second version c. 1630, which is more thickly painted and exhibits less liveliness and transparency; see Sumowski 1983, 3: 1801, 1901, no. 1262.

22 An Old Man Holding a Skull

1 See Huygens' comments in the Appendix.

2 H. W. Janson, "The Putto with the Death's Head," *Art Bulletin* 19, no. 3 (September 1937): 423–449.

3 See Washington, London, Haarlem 1989, 130–136, 208–211.

4 After appearing in Orlers' inventory, this painting was recorded in the collection of Barton Booth (1681–1733) of England, one of the most famous tragic actors of his day. Among other roles, Booth played Laertes, the Ghost, and Horatio in *Hamlet.* Although no evidence connects Lievens — or any Dutch artist — with Shakespeare's plays, this provenance does suggest some association between *vanitas* imagery in seventeenth-century painting and themes in contemporary theater.

5 See E. Jacobowitz et al., *The Prints of Lucas van Leyden and His Contemporaries* [exh. cat., National Gallery of Art] (Washington, 1983), 197–198.

6 See H. Leeflang et al., *Hendrick Goltzius (1558–1617): Drawings, Prints, and Paintings* [exh. cat., Rijksmuseum] (Amsterdam, 2003), 262–263. Lievens' painting is listed alongside the same subject in Orlers' inventory, and it has been argued that the two could have been pendants.

7 This sitter appears in a number of Lievens' and Rembrandt's early works, among them Lievens' *Tric Trac Players* (cat. 3, fig. 2) and Rembrandt's *Old Man in a Fur Cap* (Tiroler Landesmuseum, Innsbruck).

8 Leiden 1976, 18: "Twe stucken van Mr Jan Lievens soon het een de Coster vant Gasthuys met een Dootshooft inden arm, het ander een Belle blaser, beyde naert leven 48gl."

23 Saint Jerome Meditating in a Grotto

1 See Van de Wetering in Amsterdam and London 2000, 36–63.

24 The Penitent Magdalene

1 See Buchberger 1957–1965, 7:2, col. 39.

2 Da Voragine 1993, 1: 376.

3 The only other candidate would be Mary of Egypt, but she consistently appears with a lion or three loaves of bread. For a Dutch example, see Roethlisberger 1993, 1: 181, no. 198, and 2: fig. 300. The much better known Magdalene, with a widely established pictorial tradition, did not require such specific references to be recognized.

4 The conversation with Titian is reported in Baccio Valori's *Ricordi;* see Tinagli 1997, 181.

5 See Harksen 1976, 31, no. 29, fig. 25.

6 On the impact of the conflict in Leiden, see Dudok van Heel 2006, 195–196.

7 Jan Evertsz Geesteranus' poem, "Tegen 't Geestighdom der Schilder-Konst / Straf-Rymen. / Ofte anders / Idolelenchus," was translated from Latin into Dutch by Dirck Rafaelsz Camphuysen and included in his *Stichtelycke Rymen* (1639), 480–517. Friedrich Samuel Bock, *Historia Antitrinitariorum, maximae Socinianismi et Socinianorum* (Königsberg, 1774), 366–367, reports that the poem was published in an edition of 1632.

8 Lievens later availed himself of a freer climate in Amsterdam, judging from a poem of 1650 by Lambert van den Bos that describes a sumptuously dressed young Magdalene by Lievens in the collection of the Amsterdam dealer Martin Kretzer; see Unger 1884, 118–119.

9 See Sumowski 1983, 3: 1790, 1860, no. 1221.

25 Job in His Misery

1 On the iconographic tradition related to Job, see Nichols 1983, 182–188; Terrien 1996, 187–188; and Pigler 1974, 1: 205.

2 Sumowski 1983, 3: 1803, no. 1269; Schneider/Ekkart 1973, no. SZ.LXXII. Rembrandt depicted the same model in a drawing in Stockholm (Benesch 38).

3 In Cornelis Saftleven's *Job on the Dung Heap* of 1631 (Karlsruhe), Job resembles the stoic Saint Anthony tormented by demons seen in works by Hieronymous Bosch.

4 Lievens followed the erroneous iconography of Job sitting on a stinking dung heap rather than in ashes (Job 1:20 and 2:7, 8), a popular misconception based on a misreading of the text (Nichols 1983, 186, no. 20). The first official translation of the Bible into Dutch appeared only in 1637, correctly translating the term as "asschen."

5 Rubens' painting, commissioned by the musicians' guild in Brussels, was destroyed in 1695. See Stephen Viccio and Lucinda Dukes Edinberg, *The Sweet Uses of Adversity: Images of the Biblical Job* [exh. cat., Elisabeth Myers Mitchell Gallery, St. John's College] (Annapolis, 2002), 59.

6 Braunschweig 1979, 84.

26 Preciosa and Doña Clara

1 The two known copies after this painting do not include the inscription, suggesting that it was added later or was never comprehensible. See photographs at the Netherlands Office for Art History (RKD), The Hague: August Schmetz sale, Berlin, March 14, 1905, no. 52 (as Manner of Ferdinand Bol); and W.A. Hofer, Berlin, in 1937.

2 Lievens follows a Dutch characterization of Spanish nobility owning Moorish slaves. The best-known expression is Sinterklaas arriving from Spain with Zwarte Piet, his black servant.

3 This interpretation was first published in De Witt 1999.

4 Cervantes 1998, 19.

5 The coin is not payment for the palm reading, as first asserted in De Witt 1999, 186. It is a lucky coin, wholly consistent with the tradition for depicting soothsayers.

6 Examples of Frederik Hendrik's taste for obscure themes in history paintings include two depictions by Abraham Bloemaert of scenes out of Heliodorus' *Aethiopica*; see The Hague 1997, 100–107, nos. 2, 3.

7 The first six of Cervantes' novellas (including *The Spanish Gypsy*) were translated by F. de Rosset, the remaining six by a Mr. D'Augidier; they were published in one volume in Paris in 1614 and reprinted six times, attesting to their popularity and wide dissemination. See Hainsworth 1933, 58–74.

8 Miguel de Cervantes Saavedra, *Het Schoone Heydinnetje*, trans. Felix van Sambix (Delft, 1643).

9 Gaskell 1982.

10 De Witt 1999, 185.

11 DeWitt 2006, 112.

12 See also *Vertumnus and Pomona*, c. 1631, in Sumowski 1983, 3: 1779, no. 1188.

13 Staatliche Museen zu Berlin, Kupferstichkabinett; see Plomp 1986, 124–125, no. 33. Like the copies mentioned above (note 1), Bramer's drawing omits the figure of the servant.

27 Bathsheba Receiving King's David Letter

1 Sluijter 2006, 340.

2 Schneider/Ekkert 1973, 95, no. 15; Angel 1996, 242. See also Sluijter 1998, 56, 85.

28 Young Girl in Profile

1 Albert Blankert in Melbourne and Canberra 1997, 216–219, no. 34, referring to Johannes Wtenbogaert's will, dated June 3, 1641: "another *tronigen* of a smiling young girl, also painted by Jan Lievens." This painting had been bequeathed to Wtenbogaert by Jacques de Gheyn III, an artist friend of Constantijn Huygens who must have acquired it before moving from The Hague to Utrecht in 1634.

2 Huygens admired Lievens' ability to capture his contemplative mood in the portrait the artist made of him (cat. 16).

29 Prince Charles Louis with His Tutor

1 See Brown 1979b; Washington, Detroit, Amsterdam 1980, 156.

2 The *portrait historié* was popular in the courts in London and The Hague. Elizabeth's brother Charles I commissioned from Honthorst the grand *Charles I and Henrietta Maria as Apollo and Diana Welcoming the Muses into England* (1627, Hampton Court) as the backdrop to the throne in the banqueting room at Whitehall. On Honthorst's return to Holland in 1627, Frederik Hendrik commissioned from him a closely related work, *Amalia von Solms and Her Entourage as Diana and Her Attendants* (c. 1627, lost). This new genre linked contemporary life to the golden age of classical antiquity. See Wishnevsky 1967, 76.

3 Braunschweig 1979, 14; Kassel and Amsterdam 2001–2002, 331. For other possible competitions between Rembrandt and Lievens, see cat. 32.

4 Wishnevsky 1967, 6; Kassel and Amsterdam 2001–2002, 326–331.

31 The Raising of Lazarus

1 Guratszch 1980, 353. Not only Lastman, but most of the other "Pre-Rembrandtists" — including Jacob Pynas, his brother Jan Pynas, and Jan Tengnagel — follow this model closely.

2 See Guy de Brès' *Confession* to Philip II of 1561 and the catechism commissioned by Frederick III of the Palatinate from Heidelberg theologians Caspar Olevianus and Zacharius Ursinus in 1563, adopted by the synod of the Reformed Church in Dordrecht in 1618 (Articles 5, 7, 22, and 26).

3 Rembrandt based his red chalk copy of Lievens' painting on a print by Jacob Louys of Haarlem, then transformed it into *The Entombment of Christ*. Rembrandt dated his drawing 1630, although most scholars now believe he dated it retroactively, perhaps to make it appear that he and not Lievens invented the composition. See Dickey essay and cat. 73. See also Royalton-Kisch 1991a, 270–272.

32 Christ on the Cross

1 Wheelock in Washington, Detroit, Amsterdam 1980, 138. The commission for the Passion series went to Rembrandt.

2 Bauch 1962, 140, does not once mention Lievens' painting in his discussion of Rembrandt's *Christ on the Cross*.

3 This print is dedicated to Bartolome de los Rios y Alarcon, a priest at the court in Brussels (1624–1641). The painting or drawing after which it was made is now lost, but was akin to Rubens' *Christ Dead on the Cross* (one in Munich, c. 1612; one in Mechlin, c. 1614). See J. Richard Judson, *The Passion of Christ*, Corpus Rubenianum Ludwig Burchard (New York, 2000), 7: 156, 158, 159, nos. 40, 41.

4 Knipping 1974, 1: 216, says the preponderance of the "lonely" Crucifixion may relate to patrons' requests. If executed for Frederik Hendrik, the Catholic imagery in Lievens' painting may appear to have been out of place in the collection of a Protestant ruler; but inventories of his residences in The Hague demonstrate that the stadtholder was not religiously biased when it came to art. See Drossaers and Lunsingh Scheurleer 1974–1976, 1: 179–237.

33 Young Man in Yellow (Self-Portrait?)

1 See Jacob in Braunschweig 1979, no. 31; and Brown 1979b, 742. Van Straten 2005, 92, suggests it represents Jacob de Gheyn III, both a painter and patron of Lievens and Rembrandt, and compares this image to one that Rembrandt painted of De Gheyn in 1632 (Dulwich Picture Gallery, London). De Gheyn's nose and mouth and eyes, however, are very different from those of Lievens.

2 In a smaller full-length self-portrait of about the same time, Rembrandt strikes a similar pose while wearing a comparable oriental costume (*Self-Portrait with a Poodle*, Musée du Petit Palais, Paris). Rembrandt may have been a more sensitive observer of emotions, but he was less persuasive as an actor here.

3 See Braunschweig 1979, 98.

34 Self-Portrait

1 See Raupp 1984, 200–204, 302–304, and esp. 306–308, on the moralizing significance of mirrors in self-portraits. Pieter van Laer used the profile pose to display his oversize nose, c. 1626–1630 (Galleria Pallavicini, Rome), a comic effect very different from what Lievens sought.

2 Wadum 1998a, 193–194. Like this painting, the version now in a private collection in Oslo (formerly Stuttgart: see Schneider/Ekkart 1973, 148; sale, Christie's, Amsterdam, May 9, 2000, no. 87; sale, Munich, Neumeister, March 19, 2003, no. 450) was also stamped on the verso with Antwerp panel maker Guillam Gabron's second mark and Antwerp brand no. 4 between 1626 and 1638.

3 Peter Klein, dendrochronological report dated December 23, 2004, on file in the conservation department, Statens Museum for Kunst, Copenhagen.

4 Melanie Gifford, examination reports dated May 16–17, 2006, and January 15, 2007, on file in the scientific research department, National Gallery of Art, Washington.

35, 36 A Greedy Couple Surprised by Death; Fighting Cardplayers and Death

1 In *Allegory of Gluttony*, from a series of four engravings by Pieter van der Heyden after Pieter Bruegel the Elder published in 1558, Avarice appears as a man in a cask filled with money and fitted with sharp spikes. Despite the torture, he snatches at coins as a demon rolls the barrel toward Hell, the futility of his efforts indicated by the stream of coins that falls out of the cask in his wake.

2 Rubens' drawings after Holbein's Dance of Death series are in Antwerp (Museum Plantin-Moretus and the Stedelijk Prentenkabinet). Hans Lützelburger made woodcuts after Holbein's designs.

3 See Joos van Craesbeeck, *Brawl Outside an Inn*, Museum voor Schone Kunsten, Antwerp, where Death also intrudes.

37 Landscape with Peasants

1 See Klinge in Van der Ploeg et al. 2002, 104–107, no. 22. The latter has the mark of the Antwerp panel makers' guild. It also has an addition to expand the sky, probably applied in the mid-seventeenth century, after Lievens executed the painting. A similar addition to *Landscape with Peasants* was removed in 2001.

2 See Christopher Brown, *Rubens's Landscapes: Making and Meaning* (London, 1996), 59–78.

3 The paint layers are continuous under the figure.

4 A copy of the private collection painting (see fig. 1), without the figures, was sold at Sotheby's, New York, January 24, 2002, no. 230.

5 See Sumowski 1983, 3: no. 1285.

38 Head of an Old Man

1 Bredius 1915–1922, 192; Schneider/Ekkart 1973, 147, no. 241.

39, 40 The Lamentation of Christ (*modello*); The Lamentation of Christ

1 See Hubert Thurston, "Crown of Thorns," *The Catholic Encyclopedia*, vol. 4, *Clandestinity-Diocesan Chancery*, 1913 (online edition; accessed February 2008).

2 An unusual fifteenth-century wood Pietà with the Virgin holding the dead Christ in her lap and the crown of thorns in her left hand in the Klooster Gasthuiszusters Augustinessen, Antwerp, may relate to the existence of such a relic in that religious organization. See Joanna E. Ziegler, *Sculpture of Compassion: The Pietà and the Beguines in the Southern Low Countries c. 1300–c. 1600* (Brussels and Rome, 1992), 209, no. 2.

3 Brown 1979b, 745, was particularly critical of Lievens' efforts to paint in Van Dyck's manner.

4 See Braunschweig 1979, 110 (as a copy or replica); Sumowski 1983, 3: 1784 (as a copy).

41 The Sacrifice of Isaac

1 See David Rosand and Michelangelo Muraro, *Titian and the Venetian Woodcut* [exh. cat., National Gallery of Art] (Washington, 1976), 55–69.

2 Kristin Lohse Belkin, *Rubens* (London, 1998), 165–166, notes that Rubens paired *The Sacrifice of Isaac* with *The Raising of the Cross*.

3 Flavius Josephus (c. 37–100) embellished Old Testament stories with extensive dialogues that evoke the psychological states of the participants in relation to unfolding events. This painting must have been similar to Lievens' *Abraham and Isaac*, c. 1637 (see Wheelock fig. 17). See Christian Tümpel, "Die Rezeption der Jüdischen Altertümer des Flavius Josephus in den holländishen Historiendarstellungen des 16. und 17. Jahrhunderts," in Herman Vekeman and Justus Müller Hofstede, eds., *Wort und Bild in der niederländischen Kunst und Literatur des 16. und 17. Jarhunderts* (Erfstadt, 1984), 173–204.

4 Angel 1996, 246–247, mentions a now-lost grisaille of Abraham and Isaac embracing after "God had stayed Abraham's hand." This episode, not described in the Bible, appears in Josephus' narrative.

5 William Whiston, trans., *The Genuine Works of Flavius Josephus*, 4 vols. (London, 1755), 1: 47: "so he went immediately to the altar to be sacrificed."

6 Broos 1972, 141–142, discussing the version in the Galleria Doria Pamphilj (see note 8 below), argued that Lievens' painting preceded and influenced Rembrandt's painting of 1635. But Marcus Dekiert, *Rembrandt. Die Opferung Isaaks* (Munich, 2004), 83, proposed a date of c. 1640.

7 See Washington 1990, 201–203, no. 46. Van Dyck painted this altarpiece (Koninklijk Museum voor Schone Kunsten, Antwerp) in 1628 for the Church of Saint Augustine in Antwerp.

8 Sumowski 1983, 3: 1782, no. 1194. See also Ettore Sestieri, *Catalogo della Galleria Ex-Fidecommissaria Doria-Pamphili* (Rome, 1942), 240, no. 343. The work is slightly larger than the version exhibited here (250 × 176 cm) and has a spurious Titian signature; early Doria Pamphilj inventories attribute the work to Titian.

9 Little is known about Lievens' workshop, but documents indicate that he accepted Hans van den Wijngaerde as a pupil in Antwerp in 1636 (see Wheelock essay).

42 Landscape with Willows

1 The exception is *Panoramic Landscape* (Norton Simon Museum of Art), inscribed "IL: fecit: 1640"; see Schneider 1990, 155–157. This painting, which neither Schneider/Ekkart 1973 nor Sumowski 1983 accept as by Lievens, is probably autograph, though its technique and panoramic vista differ from other landscapes attributed to him. The stylistic difference may be explained by Lievens' trip to Leiden in 1639, when he must have seen some of Rembrandt's fanciful landscape paintings. Many of Lievens' landscapes were formerly attributed to Adriaen Brouwer. See Larson 1960.

2 Melanie Gifford, examination report dated October 2, 2006, on file in the scientific research department, National Gallery of Art, Washington.

3 The Venetian effects in this landscape are noted by Hans Buijs in The Hague 2002, 118.

4 This date conforms to that proposed by most authors. Buijs in The Hague 2002, 116–119, however, defines a broader time frame, c. 1640–1650, noting that Lievens continued to work in his Antwerp style once he moved to Amsterdam.

5 This Antwerp inventory (dated March 28–April 10, 1691), lists as no. 158: "Een lantschapken met slaepende boerken van Lievens." See The Hague 2002, 209 n. 2.

43 Dune Landscape with Trees

1 One Dutch landscape artist who seems to have responded to Lievens' bold manner of painting woodland scenes, albeit in a larger scale, was Philips Koninck. See the Jacques Goudstikker collection sale, Christie's, New York, April 19, 2007, no. 38.

2 Braunschweig 1979, 132, no. 46, dates the painting c. 1650. Sumowski 1983, 3: 1812, no. 1302, dates it to the second half of the 1630s.

3 Strauss and Van der Meulen 1979, 349–388, records three Lievens landscapes (nos. 18, 19, 22) in Rembrandt's inventory of 1656; while Postma 1988 lists five in Becker's inventory of 1678. See also Bredius 1915–1922, 1:186–227. For an Antwerp inventory with a Lievens landscape, see cat. 42, n. 5. Schneider/Ekkart 1973, 57, notes that no fewer than sixteen had appeared in inventories or poems by 1700.

44 Portrait of Adriaen Trip

1 See H. J. Trip, *De Familie Trip* (Groningen, 1883), 81–89.

2 In drawing up the marriage contract, the bridegroom was assisted by his mother, his guardian, and his brothers-in-law Balthasar and Joseph Coymans; the bride by her two brothers and several other family members. Stadsarchief Amsterdam, notary J. van Zwieten, Notarial Archive 874, fol. 91–92v, October 10, 1645.

3 Corpus 1982–, 3: nos. A131, A132. The portraits of the Coymans-Trip couple are dated 1645; a portrait of Sophia Trip (probably after Bartholomeus van der Helst) appeared at Sotheby's, London, July 12, 1988, no. 102.

45 Portrait of Anna Maria van Schurman

1 *Alba amicorum* (friendship books) bound together blank pages that the owner would have friends inscribe. Popular in academic circles, this may be what Van Schurman has before her, though her book is larger than extant examples, which are octavos and only two centimeters thick. See Van Leeuwen 2006, 102.

2 Born in Cologne in 1607, Van Schurman moved to the Northern Netherlands with her family between 1613 and 1615, eventually settling in Utrecht. See further De Baar 1996 and Franeker 2007.

3 De Baar 1996, 59, 65.

4 See Baker/Henry 2001, 380. Van Schurman's self-portrait, 1640, is the first pastel known from the Northern Netherlands; see De Baar 1996, 42.

5 For Lievens' *Iconography*, see DeWitt 2006, 186–187.

6 The *Galerie des Illustres* in the Château de Beauregard includes portraits of princes and famous personages; see The Hague 1997, 44, fig. 13. This possibility was suggested by Arthur Wheelock.

46 Jacob Receiving Joseph's Bloody Coat

1 See Tümpel in Münster 1994, 41–47.

2 Joost van den Vondel, *De Volledige werken van Joost van den Vondel*, ed. Hendr. C. Diferee, vol. 3 (Utrecht, 1930), 143.

3 Plomp 1986, 123–124.

4 Postma 1988, 17. The inventory lists "Een bloedige rock van Joseph van Jan Lievense" as being in the back room.

5 See Maria A. Schenkeveld, *Dutch Literature in the Age of Rembrandt: Themes and Ideas* (Amsterdam and Philadelphia, 1991), 120–121. See also Wheelock essay.

6 Schneider/Ekkart 1973, 54, 93, no. 9; Sumowski 1983, 3: 1784, no. 1203.

47 Gideon's Sacrifice

1 Werner Sumowski, written communication to the present owner, December 3, 2005.

2 For the two paintings in Castle Howard and the Herzog Anton Ulrich-Museum, Braunschweig, see Sumowski 1983, 3: 1782, 1783, nos. 1195, 1199.

3 Sumowski 1983, 3: 1786, 1816, nos. 1209, 1311.

4 Compare J. van Gent and G. Pastoor in Amsterdam 1991, 67–68.

5 The connection between this painting and Herman Becker (c. 1617–1678, originally from Riga in Latvia) was first suggested by Sumowski; see note 1.

6 Mentioned in Schneider/Ekkart 1973, 94, no. 11. See also Postma 1988, 6.

7 For Becker's financial dealings with artists, and his collection of paintings, Postma 1988, 8–9, app. 2 (with a complete list of his painting collection). Jan Lievens the Younger was presumably Jan Andrea Lievens.

48 Self-Portrait

1 On the emergence of male dress *à la negligence*, see De Winkel 2006, 126–130.

2 De Winkel (correspondence, December 12, 2007), notes comparable ribbons in portraits by Simon and Isaack Luttichuys.

3 Sumowski 1983, 3: 1809, no. 1292. See particularly the screen of tree trunks backlit by the setting sun and the feathery impasto used to depict foliage.

4 See Washington 1990, 162, no. 31. The portrait is in the Herzog Anton Ulrich-Museum, Braunschweig.

5 Rembrandt attended the Van Uffel auction and was influenced by a number of portraits sold there, including works by Van Dyck, Raphael, and Titian.

49 Triumph of Peace

1 This work is less elaborate and specific to the Treaty of Münster than the allegories by Jacob Jordaens (1654, Oslo) and Adriaen van Nieulandt (1650, Amsterdam).

2 In the 1743 inventory of Schloss Oranienburg the chimneypiece was listed as: "die Künste über den Krieg triumphiren"; see Bartoscheck 1978, 14. As that painting was installed c. 1653–1655 and listed in the 1699 inventory, it cannot be the work in Lievens' inventory at his death.

3 First suggested in Bredius 1915–1922, 187.

4 Braunschweig 1979, 111–112; Münster and Osnabrück 1998, 401. For portraits of Louise Henriette, see Pieter Nason's double portrait of 1666 in Potsdam 1988, 31. See also cat. 50, fig. 1.

50 Mars and Venus

1 Lievens was one of several Dutch painters, including Honthorst, Govaert Flinck, and Jan Mijtens, that the Elector and his wife invited to execute paintings for their palace.

2 The original format was revealed in 1953 when the painting was restored. Two later additions were removed from the upper left and right corners that had transformed the painting into a rectangular shape. See Börsch-Supan 1964, 90.

3 Lievens may also have executed *The Triumph of Peace* for the Schloss Oranienburg, but it remained in his possession until his death. See cat. 49, n. 2.

4 The Hague 1997, 40.

5 Similarly, Rubens' allegorical portraits of Marie de' Medici as Juno in *The Meeting of Marie de' Medici and Henry IV at Lyons* and in *The Felicity of the Regency* depict her with one bared breast.

51 Sir Robert Kerr, First Earl of Ancram

1 See Braunschweig 1979, 113.

2 The Earl of Ancram was Charles I's emissary at the funeral of Frederick Henry, son of the Winter King and Queen who resided in The Hague. He was probably introduced to Lievens and Rembrandt by Constantijn Huygens.

3 *Self-Portrait with Cap and Chain* (Walker Art Gallery, Liverpool) and *Head of an Old Woman* (Royal Collection, Windsor) were listed as by Rembrandt in Van der Doort's 1639 inventory of Charles I's collection. The painting at Windsor is now thought to be by Lievens. See Sumowski 1983, 6: 3970, no. 2360. See also Van Straten 2005, 131–132.

4 The earl may have purchased *Capuchin Monk Praying* directly from Lievens, as it still resides in the collection of his descendents. See also Wheelock essay, n. 41.

5 Lievens' talent in this area was noted by Huygens early in the artist's career (cat. 16).

52 Christ and the Centurion

1 See Huys Janssen in The Hague 1992, 224, fig. 28d.

2 DeWitt 2006, 228.

53 Portrait of Jacob Junius

1 Sumowski 1983, 3: 1810, no. 1295, believes the portrait dates from the mid-1650s. David De Witt dates it to c. 1658 (and kindly shared with me his draft text on the painting).

2 She bequeathed "een con[trefeytsel] van Pieter Leenaerts voornoemt, geschildert door Jan…" (August 26, 1680); the surname of the portraitist has been burned in this document, but Lievens is the most likely candidate. An earlier will (April 11, 1679) mentioned portraits of Pieter Lenaerts the Elder, his wife Elisabeth van Outen, and their son Pieter, without giving the name of the painter. See the Stadsarchief Amsterdam, Notarial Archive 2663.

3 See Van der Veen essay, n. 9.

54 Brinio Raised on a Shield

1 Tacitus 1995 (4:15, 219) describes Brinio as a "foolish desperado," who secured his position because he came from a "distinguished family." His tribe, the Cannenefates, joined forces with the Frisians and overran two Roman outposts.

2 Fremantle 1959, 49–50.

3 In *De antiquitate Reipublicae Batavicae* (1610), Hugo Grotius argued that the Batavians had never been subject to monarchical or princely authority but had always been ruled by a government made up of the community's most eminent citizens. Grotius' grounding of an essentially oligarchic model of government in the ancient past, together with his assertion of an essential continuity between the Batavians and the contemporary Dutch, buttressed Amsterdam's ideological objections to the office of the stadtholderate. As noted in Kossmann 2000, 32, however, Grotius wrote in 1646 that he had been too assertive in his earlier opinions. According to Weber 1992, 44, Albert Blankert related Lievens' depiction of Brinio to efforts during the stadtholderless period to abolish the position of a permanent captaincy-general (lecture held in Braunschweig in 1979).

4 For the complex issues related to the position of the Prince of Orange within the political structure of the Netherlands, particularly in relation to Amsterdam, see Carroll 1986.

5 For poems in celebration of the town hall, see Spies 1993, 15–33.

6 See, in particular, Fremantle 1959 and Goossens 1996.

7 Bredius 1915–1922, 1: 199–200. Jacob Jordaens was given the commission for two of the other lunettes, and the following year Rembrandt was given the other one. Rembrandt's painting, *The Conspiracy of Claudius Civilis*, 1662, was removed shortly after it was installed. For more on the circumstances surrounding these paintings, see Van de Waal 1952, 228–232; Fremantle 1959, 48–54; Van de Waal 1974; Schwartz 1985, 318–320; Carroll 1986; Goossens 1996, 61–63.

8 For Flinck's drawing (Hamburg, Kunsthalle), see Sumowski 1979, 9, no. 2086[x].

9 As noted in Weber 1992, 48.

10 Melanie Gifford generously shared her observations about Lievens' painting techniques in this work.

56 Saint John the Evangelist on Patmos

Daulby 23, D., Rov., B. 4, Holl. 9

1 Some early sources (e.g., Eusebius, c. 325) date John's exile to around AD 95, at the end of a very long life, but Northern artists usually depicted him as a young man.

2 See Martin Schongauer, engraving, c. 1469–1474, copied by Israhel van Meckenem (Holl. 60, 363); Hans Wechtlin, woodcut, 1516 (B. VII.484); Pieter Lastman, 1613, Museum Boijmans Van Beuningen, Rotterdam (Amsterdam 1991, no. 4). Lievens depicted Saint John again, with the eagle clutching his inkwell, for a series of small etchings of the Four Evangelists (Holl. 10–13; see also cat. 82).

3 Several authors have suggested that this may be Lievens' earliest etching (Leiden 1976, 63; Braunschweig 1979, 194). *The Circumcision* was attributed to Rembrandt by Von Seidlitz (no. 398); the attribution to Lievens in Van Straten 2002 and Van Straten 2005, 36–38, 291–299, has not been accepted. For Lievens' *Saint John* and Rembrandt, see Burchard 1917, 90–92; Van der Coelen in Amsterdam 1996, 20; White 1999, 20–22; and Hinterding in Amsterdam and London 2000, 82–84, no. 1.

4 The calligraphy of the Berendrecht inscription on Rembrandt's *Circumcision* is different, suggesting that the publisher acquired the plates at different times, rather than together as usually supposed (see Amsterdam 1988, 25; Leiden 1991, 60–63; Amsterdam and London 2000, 13; Van Straten 2002). On Berendrecht's activities, see Wyckoff 1998, 157–158 (Rembrandt and Lievens). See also cat. 57 and Dickey essay.

57 Jacob Anointing the Stone

D. 8, Rov., B. 9, Holl. 4

1 In medieval manuscripts and frescoes from England, Germany, and Italy, Jacob's dream of the ladder and anointing of the stone were shown together; see Denny 1977, 57, 60, esp. fig. 22 (psalter, twelfth century, Kupferstichkabinett, Berlin, 78.a.46, fol. 4v). Lievens' subject was not immediately identified by connoisseurs; Daulby, Linck, and Rovinski call this print "Kneeling Man," and Linck 1859, 272, mentions that it was sometimes called "Gideon's Sacrifice."

2 Pelikan 1968, 5: 251–265; Steinmetz 1986; John Calvin, *Institutes of Christian Religion,* bk. 4, chap. 13:5. The allusion to tithing refers to an Old Testament practice that has long been contentiously debated among Protestant factions.

3 Defoer 1977, 17–18; Amsterdam 1988, 24. The robed, kneeling figure in a landscape appears in a number of prints by and after Willem Buytewech, including Jan van de Velde, *Saint Francis of Assisi* (Holl. 17).

58 Mercury Lulls Argus to Sleep

Daulby 64, D., Rov., B. 10, Holl. 18

1 Van Mander 1604/1618, V 55h; Miedema 1973, 1: 172–173, 2: 484.

2 Lievens may have consulted precedents by Goltzius (see Holl. 47 or 138; pl. 17 from a suite of fifty-two illustrations of Ovid's *Metamorphoses*).

59 Young Girl with Long Hair

D., Rov., B. 25, Holl. 43

1 See, for example, B.347; Amsterdam 1988, 54.

2 There are probably three states rather than two as defined by Hollstein. In the earliest impressions Lievens' initials appear as a thin outline only, and there is less work in the hair so that an ornamental band can be seen behind the girl's ear (see an example in the Teylers Museum, Haarlem). Rovinski describes a state between 1 and 2 with Van den Wijngaerde's address but before reworking the costume and hair. This seems consistent with an impression in the British Museum, London (no. S73).

60 Young Woman in a Cap

D., Rov., B. 27; Holl. 45

1 An impression of state 1 is in the British Museum, London (no. 1848.0708.125). State 3 with Van den Wijngaerde's address is recorded in Linck 1859, 275, indicating that this etching, like many of Lievens' tronies, was reissued in Antwerp.

61 Profile Head of an Old Woman

D., Rov., B. 30, Holl. 49

1 Simon Luttichuys, *Vanitas Still Life* (Danzig); Van Straten 2005, 324–336; Gersaint 1752, 183.

2 Holl. 61 (7.7 × 6.3 cm).

62 Young Man in a Fur Cap

D., Rov., B. 51, Holl. 72

1 Rembrandt made several etchings of himself c. 1630 wearing similar headgear: see B. 12, 16 (dated 1631), 24, 316; see also B. 366.

2 Daulby 1796, 315, no. 66, links the title page with a group of "seven busts of men and women" but this figure with "Diverse Tronikens" (see cat. 63–66; Rovinski 1894, 31). Amsterdam 1988, 13, ties the print to "Variae Effigies." Linck 1859, 278, lists a final state with the initials of Franciscus van den Wijngaerde.

63–66 Tronikens: Character Heads

D., Rov., B. 39, 41, 42, 45, Holl. 60, 62, 63, 66

1 Daulby 1796, 307, describes this figure as "a Morisco woman"; see also Braunschweig 1979, 86. In the painting of *The Raising of Lazarus* (cat. 31), the woman's skin is dark.

2 Daulby 1796, 317, no. 79, counts seven heads in the series, including three of the four shown here; see also Schatborn in Amsterdam 1988, 20 nn. 4, 5, remarking that the series was published in Antwerp and the cross-hatching identifies the state published by Martinus van den Enden. Rovinski 1894, under no. 29, says the Robert-Dumesnil catalogue of 1835 cited a suite of eighteen prints and the collection of Friedrich August II (Dresden) contained state 2 of the title page with the address of Van den Enden; under no. B. 38, Rovinski lists his nos. B. 38–51 as belonging to the series. Hollstein (based on Dutuit, 5: 124) assigns eighteen prints (D. 38–55, Holl. 59–77) to the series, but not all have the cross-hatched background.

3 A number of Netherlandish artists made prints after Leonardo's grotesques; see Muylle 1994, 2001, 2002.

67–70 A Series of Character Studies

Daulby 34, D., Rov., B. 17, Holl. 34

Gersaint 8, Daulby 8; D., Rov., B. 18, Holl. 35

Daulby 28, D., Rov., B. 22, Holl. 40

Gersaint 10, Daulby 11, D., Rov., B. 21, Holl. 36

1 See Amsterdam 1996, 50–52, no. 5.

2 In many late impressions, the name of De Baillù has clearly been rubbed out and Van den Wijngaerde's initials inserted. See Dickey essay as well as Antwerp and Amsterdam 1999, 366 (De Baillù), 390 (Van den Wijngaerde).

3 According to Linck 1859, 274, B. 22III, cat. 70 was republished in Amsterdam by Salomon Savery, who also published *Old Man in Profile, Facing Right* (Holl. 75). *Old Man with a Large White Beard*, state 1 inscribed "IL. S. Savery excut" (Holl. 78), was probably etched by Savery after a painting by Lievens.

4 See Salomon Koninck, *Man in a Turban*, 1638 (Holl. 2), in Boston 1981, no. 89. For Castiglione, see Dickey essay.

5 For Rembrandt's four prints, B. 286–289, based on Lievens (Holl. 35, 36, 39, 44), see Boston 1981, 141; White 1999, 263 n. 63; Amsterdam and London 2000, 149–151.

71 Seated Hermit

Gersaint 2, Daulby 2 (19?), D., Rov., B. 6, Holl. 17

1 D., Rov. (as an anchorite monk), B. 7, Holl. 16; Daulby 1796, 311, no. 26 (as Saint Jerome), two states, 12.2 × 9 cm.

2 Identified as Saint Francis by Gersaint, Daulby, Linck, Rovinski. Similarly, Willem Buytewech's *Saint Francis* (Holl. 9) was inscribed in state 1 as Saint Jerome.

3 The sequence of states as described by Rovinski and Hollstein requires clarification (see also Schatborn in Amsterdam 1988, 39–40). The plate was cut down to 20.8 × 14.6 cm (in state 7?) and finally to 20 × 14 cm.

72 Saint Jerome Meditating in a Grotto

Gersaint 4, Daulby 4, D., Rov., B. 5, Holl. 15

1 Rembrandt's first etching of Saint Jerome (see Dickey fig. 2) probably predates Lievens' but was unsuccessful; for later versions, see B. 100–105. Van Vliet's etching after a lost painting of Saint Jerome by Rembrandt is dated 1631 (Holl. 13); see Amsterdam 1996, 46–47, no. 3.

2 Compare Rembrandt's red chalk drawing of the seated old man, Kupferstichkabinett, Berlin (Amsterdam 1988, 41, no. 16). See also the etching B. 291.

3 B. 44; Boston 1981, 129, no. 80; White 1999, 264 n. 29; Amsterdam and London 2000, 129–131, no. 21.

4 Ferdinand Bol's *Saint Jerome in Penitence*, 1644 (Holl. 3), owes more to Lievens than to Rembrandt; see Boston 1981, 149, no. 96.

5 Ackley in Boston 1981, 129. A unique impression before state 1, with less background detail, is in the Albertina, Vienna; Boston 1981, 129; see Munich 1982, no. 89a, pl. 84; Amsterdam 1988, 46.

73 The Raising of Lazarus

Gersaint 1, Daulby 1, D., Rov., B. 3, Holl. 7

1 For Rembrandt's versions, see also cat. 31; for comparative iconography, see also Stechow 1973, 6–11; Guratzsch

1980, 1: 144–151; Halewood 1982, 36–48; Los Angeles 1991–1992; Royalton-Kisch in London 1992, 62; Schama 1999, 259.

2 Royalton-Kisch in London 1992, 62–63, no. 11. The print by Louys (Holl. 1) was already mentioned in Daulby 1796, 301.

74 Portrait of an Elderly Man

D. 70, Rov. 75a, Holl. 28

1 An impression of state 2 in Munich is labeled in ink, "Lord Digby" (Munich 1982, no. 90, fig. 85), and an impression of state 1 in Rotterdam (BdH 20838) is inscribed in pencil, "Charles Digby" (Linck 1859, 281; Boston 1981, 145; Munich 1982, 119; Amsterdam 1988, 58, no. 36).

2 State 1, Institut Néerlandais, Paris (no. 3385), inscribed "Jacques Pern [?]. Musicien du Roy d'Angleterre."

3 Matham (who published state 6 of cat. 85) may be the subject of two portrait drawings by Lievens in the British Museum (Sumowski 1979, 3568–3571, nos. 1600–1601; see Dickey 2004, 133.

4 Neither Gersaint nor Daulby gives it to Lievens. Linck 1859, 281, no. 167, notes that Bartsch (2: 108, no. 25) calls it "style of Rembrandt." Rovinski 1894, no. 25, repeats this but accepts it as Lievens (no. 75a); Schneider/Ekkart 1973, 270, cites Rovinski's comment that he would have attributed the plate to Salomon Koninck without the identifying inscriptions.

5 See Jost Amman, *Portrait of Hans Sachs*, 1576 (*The Illustrated Bartsch*, vol. 20, pt. 2, no. 19 [363]); Lucas Cranach, *Portrait of Philip Melanchthon*, 1560 (Holl. 49), both dating from the year of the subjects' deaths, Sachs at eighty-two, and Melanchthon at sixty-three. For old age as a theme in Netherlandish prints, see Janssen 2007.

6 For state 1 (Albertina, Vienna), see Linck 1859, 281; Schneider/Ekkart 1973, 270; Boston 1981, 145. For an impression possibly between states 1 and 2, with reworking in the face and hair (Kupferstichkabinett, Berlin, no. 954/13), see Braunschweig 1979, 206, 209, no. 107.

75 Portrait of Jacques Gaultier

Gersaint 11, Daulby 12, D., Rov., B. 59, Holl. 23

1 For the portrait of Lanier, see Dickey fig. 8.

2 See *The Burwell Lute Tutor* (c. 1670; repr., Leeds, 1974), fol. 68. For the lute's construction, see Thomas Mace, *Musick's Monument* (London, 1676), 32, fig. 20. Owing to the reversal that occurs in printing, the bass strings appear in Lievens' etching on the treble side.

3 Spink 1964; Jacobs 2001/2002; Spring 2004.

4 Thanks to Anthony D'Elia for the translation: "John Lievens dedicated this image etched on bronze from his easel as a sign of faithful friendship to Jacques Gaultier, musician of the Lydian, Dorian, and Phrygian lute and first of the players among the royal Orpheians and Amphions of Great Britain."

76 Virgin and Child with a Pear

Daulby 17, D., Rov., B. 1, Holl. 8

1 See Van Dyck's *Rest on the Flight into Egypt*, c. 1630–1632 (Royal Collection, London) in Barnes et al. 2004, no. III.10. Both Van Dyck and Lievens may have drawn inspiration from Italian prints; see *The Illustrated Bartsch* 39, pt. 2, no. 002, B. 3 [20], C2, C3, and no. 012, B. 31[56], C3.

2 See Dürer's *Madonna of the Pear*, 1512 (Kunsthistorisches Museum, Vienna), as well as engravings from 1511 and 1513 (B. 35, 41). For Italian examples, see Levi d'Ancona 1997, 296–299.

3 Schneider/Ekkart 1973, 99, 261, no. 28 ("Maria handing a small apple to the child," owned by Valerius Röver in Delft before 1750 and lost during the Napoleonic wars), and no. 28a.

4 The others are *Saint Anthony* (Holl. 1411; see under cat. 77), and *Jacques Gaultier* (cat. 75). Lievens made etchings after his own paintings on at least two other occasions (see cats. 31 and 73 and cats. 36 and 78).

77 Bust of a Capuchin Monk

Gersaint 12, Daulby 13, D., Rov., B. 14, Holl. 27

1 A Capuchin convent was founded in Antwerp in 1583, and there were fifty-five communities in Flanders by the mid-seventeenth century; see Châtellier 1997, 20–21. A notation in ink on an impression in the British Museum, London (no. S49), led erroneously to Hollstein's identification of the model as the Italian artist Giovanni Benedetto Castiglione; Gersaint and Daulby already describe the figure as a Capuchin.

2 Compare first states from *Iconography* such as Van Dyck's *Portrait of Jan Snellincx* or Pieter de Jode II after Van Dyck's *Portrait of Anton Triest* (M.-H. 10, 13), in Antwerp and Amsterdam 1999, 136–139, 209–213, nos. 14 and 29a.

3 Holl. 14 (26.5 × 20.3 cm), four states, listing Lievens as publisher in state 2 and Van den Wijngaerde in state 3; see Schneider/Ekkart 1973, 262 (c. 1635–1636); Braunschweig 1979, 207, 211, no. 110.

78 Fighting Cardplayers and Death

Daulby 21, D., Rov., B. 11, Holl. 19

1 Anthony D'Elia and Pierre Tuynman assisted with the translation. See also Munich 1982, 120; Saxton 1994, 423.

2 See Van Craesbeeck's *Brawl Outside an Inn* (Museum voor Schone Kunsten, Antwerp), where Death also intervenes; De Clippel 2006, 1: 243–247, no. A102; and 2: fig. 102.

3 For the Antwerp print trade, see Antwerp and Amsterdam 1999; Luijten 2001, 45; Manfred Sellink in Antwerp and Quebec 2004, 150–155. For prints after Brouwer, see Scholz 1985.

79 Portrait of Daniel Heinsius

Daulby 65, D. 57, Rov., B. 58, Holl. 22

1 See Ekkart 1974.

2 The drawing of Heinsius was last recorded in a sale catalogue in 1810; Schneider/Ekkart 1973, 196, no. Z58; Ekkart 1974, 60.

3 Holl. 163 (26.5 × 20.5 cm), inscribed with a Latin eulogy by Daniel Heinsius' son, Nicholas. State 1 was published by Van den Enden, state 2 by Joannes Meyssens.

4 "Daniel Heinsius Knight and Counsellor to the Most Serene King of the Swedes. This is that famous son of Heinsius, whom Apelles alone can paint, of whom Apollo alone can fittingly speak, whom Ghent, mother of gods, was alone worthy to bear, and mother Leiden alone could nurture in her bosom." Thanks to Anthony D'Elia for the translation.

5 Ekkart 1974, 46, 52. For Heinsius' activities, see Sellin 1968.

6 An impression of state 1 in the Dutuit Collection, Paris (no. 5732), is worked up with gray wash on the vertical creases of drapery, the jowl beneath the chin, and the lower contours of the arms. For examples of this procedure in Van Dyck's *Iconography*, see Antwerp and Amsterdam 1999.

7 M.-H. 75. Based on a painting of c. 1628–1629 in the Kunsthistorisches Museum, Vienna (see Barnes et al. 2004, no. III.74), and more closely on a drawing in chalk and wash annotated 1634 in the Louvre, Paris (see Vey 1962, no. 273; and Washington 1990, no. 69). Van den Enden was engaged in publishing the *Iconography* from 1636 to 1644.

80 Landscape with a Group of Trees

Daulby 20, D. 62, Rov., B. 63, Holl. 100

1 See Strauss 1973; Boston 1981, nos. 14, 15, 27; Amsterdam and Cleveland 1992.

2 See Berlin 1970, 45, no. 7. The motif of a large, picturesque tree became popular in Dutch landscape etchings of the 1640s by artists such as Jan van Goyen and Jacob van Ruisdael (see Holl. 6), anticipated by Hercules Seghers (Boston 1981, 191, no. 68).

3 Bredius 1915–1922, 1: 186–189, item 27, "10 Stuckx houte plaaten."

81 Cain Slaying Abel

D. 71, Rov. 67, B. 73, Holl. 99

1 The motif appears as a stone sculpture above the figure of Eve on the interior of the altarpiece (Saint Bavo, Ghent).

2 For Lastman's painting, c. 1625 (Museum Het Rembrandthuis, Amsterdam), see Amsterdam 1991, no. 15.

3 For Goltzius (Holl. 373), see Amsterdam and Cleveland 1992, no. 25. For Buytewech after a painting by Rubens (Holl. 1), see Rotterdam and Paris 1974, no. 110; Braunschweig 1979, 214; Amsterdam 1996, 68.

4 Hind 1913, 235; Schneider/Ekkart 1973, 84–85; Ackley in Boston 1981, 142; Schama 1999, 332. For Jegher and Rubens, see Myers 1966/1967; Antwerp and Quebec 2004, 92–107, esp. 96–97 and 99.

5 See Washington 1983, no. 124. See also Lucas van Leyden (Holl. 12, 13).

6 J. Andries, *Necessaria ad salutem scientia* (Antwerp, 1654); see Schneider/Ekkart 1973, 268; and Braunschweig 1979, 214.

82 Man in a Cap Facing Left

Rov. 69, Holl. 105

1 For The Four Evangelists drawings in the Albertina, Vienna (Holl. 10–13), 27.8 × 21.1 cm, see Chicago 1969, 250, no. 192, attributing all four prints to La Hyre; Schneider/Ekkart 1973, no. Z21, fig. 40; and Sumowski 1979, 3: 3692–3693, no. 1657[x].

2 For Baldung's woodcut *Portrait of Caspar Hedio*, 1543 (Holl. 268), and Cranach's *Margrave Christoph I von Baden*, 1511 (B. 59), see Bartrum 1995, nos. 59, 68. Compare also Dickey fig. 13 and cat. 84.

83 A Seated Cleric

Gersaint 7, Daulby 7, D. 60, Rov., B. 61, Holl. 102

1 Gersaint 1752, 182; Hind 1913, 237. For seventeenth-century clerical dress, see *Caeremoniale Episcoporum* (1600), app. 1, and entries in *The Catholic Encyclopedia* (1913).

2 Hind 1913, 236–237; see also Haverkamp-Begemann and Logan in Chicago 1969, 197–198; Braunschweig 1979, no. 57; Ackley in Boston 1981, 142–143; Amsterdam and Cleveland 1992, 204, 235.

3 See British Museum, London, no. 1895.0122.1183; no. S134; and no. 1868.0822.705; and Städel Museum, Frankfurt, no. 6161 (touched with ink and black chalk).

84 Bust of a Man Facing Forward

Daulby 3 and 28, Rov., B. 70, Holl. 106

1 Bialler in Amsterdam and Cleveland 1992, 235, contrasts Lievens' approach with the more complex method of Christoffel Jegher. A precedent for both is Goltzius—for instance, *Portrait of Gillis van Breen*, c. 1588 (Holl. 375).

2 British Museum, London (no. D.8.95); Daulby 1796, 321; Hind 1913; Schneider/Ekkart 1973, 86–88; Strauss 1973, 342; Sumowski 1983, 6: 3560.

3 For Dieussart see Charles Avery, "François Dieussart," *Grove Art Online*, *www.groveart.com* (accessed October 26, 2007).

85 Portrait of Joost van den Vondel

Daulby 14 (as after Lievens), D. 56, Rov., B. 57, Holl. 21

1 "Mother Cologne gave Vondel his birth, father Amsterdam his seat, a Belgian muse his fame, and the old religion, custodian and messenger of truth, opened the road by which a just old man seeks the stars." With thanks to Anthony D'Elia for the English translation. See also Amsterdam 1988, 70.

2 For Vondel and his portraits, see Sterck 1930; Porteman 1979; Dickey 2004, 135–137.

3 *Poëzy* (Amsterdam, 1650), title page and 189; see Porteman 1979, 109; Amsterdam 1988, 70; Dickey 2004, 135.

4 For state 1, Rijksmuseum, Amsterdam (OB12852), see Amsterdam 1988, 70–71, fig. 47a. The British Museum holds an impression (without chalk) that represents an undescribed state between 2 and 3: the background has been added but lacks the final layer of linework visible in state 3 (no. S122, inscribed in pen and ink in lower margin: "Joost vander Vondel Celebre poëte hollandaise. No.7. duS. Gravé par J. Livens"). In Amsterdam 1988, 70, that impression is confused with the one shown here, touched with chalk.

5 For touched proofs from Van Dyck's *Iconography*, see Antwerp and Amsterdam 1999. For a touched proof by Paulus Pontius in collaboration with Lievens, see Dickey fig. 119.

86 Portrait of Caspar Streso

D. 67, Rov. 76, B. 67, Holl. 24

1 Nieuw Nederlands Biografisch Woordenboek 1937, vol. 10, col. 984; Grell 1989, 180, 222, 290.

2 Cited in Frijhoff and Spies 2004, 355–356.

3 Vermij 2003, 282–285.

4 British Museum D.8.67. The impression of state 3 in the Bibliothèque Nationale, Paris, is so far unique. It is touched up with brown ink on the coat.

87 Portrait of Ephraim Bueno

Gersaint 14, Daulby 15, D. 55, Rov., B. 56, Holl. 20

1 Amsterdam 1986, 52; Nadler 1999, 89; Zell 2002, 20–21; Nadler 2003, 66; Dickey 2004, 137–138. I am grateful to Anthony D'Elia and Steven Nadler for consultation on the translation: "A second Avenzoar according to a great judge, a distinguished physician, and disciple of a distinguished father."

2 Paris 2007, 200.

3 Nadler 2003, 66.

4 Clement de Jonghe dealt frequently in secondhand plates, including many acquired from Rembrandt. For the private circulation of portrait prints (including Rembrandt's works from the 1650s), see Amsterdam 1986 and Dickey 2004; see also cat. 83. The commission probably began with a preparatory drawing, possibly the one listed in the collection of C. Josi in 1821; see Schneider/Ekkart 1973, no. Z52.

88 The Stoning of Saint Paul at Lystra

1 Bauch 1939, 241, 244, fig. 162

2 See Sumowski 1979, 3612, for the full previous literature and attribution history.

3 Bredius/Gerson 1969, no. 531.

4 Sale, Amsterdam, June 16, 1732, nos. Q54–56. See Sumowski 1979, 3907–3909, nos. 12–21, for fuller descriptions of the subjects. For information on Ten Kate, see Plomp 2001, 58–60.

89 Mercury Lulls Argus to Sleep

1 Some slight indentations visible under raking light could be vestiges of the transfer process, but if the sheet was ever indented in the traditional manner, it has been so flattened that little trace of this remains.

2 Amsterdam 1988, 11, 22, fig. 1.

3 Two other comparable sheets are in Sumowski 1979 (nos. 1619^{x}–1620^{x} and 1621^{x}): the first a double-sided drawing in Dresden, which has *Sleeping Satyr in a Landscape* on one side and an unidentified historical scene on the other; the second *The Circumcision*. Neither is so close in style to the present drawing that the attribution is totally certain.

90 Mucius Scaevola and Porsenna

1 Bauch 1960, 213.

2 Leiden 1991, 139.

3 Sumowski 1979, nos. 1624^{x}, 1627^{x}–1629^{x}.

4 Corpus 1982–, 1: nos. A6, A9.

5 Sumowski 1979, 3614.

6 Christopher White, "Rembrandt Exhibitions in Holland," *Burlington Magazine* 98, no. 642 (September, 1956): 323.

91, 92 Trumpeter on Horseback; Christ Praying in the Garden of Gethsemane

1 Werner Sumowski, "Bemerkungen zu Otto Beneschs Corpus der Rembrandt-Zeichnungen I," *Wissenschaftliche Zeitschrift der Humbold-Universität zu Berlin* 7, no. 4 (1956–1957): 259.

2 Kunstmuseum, Basel; Corpus 1982–, 1: no. A9.

3 Amsterdam 1991, no. 20.

4 Amsterdam 1988, 31.

5 *Mercury Lulls Argus to Sleep* and *The Feast of Esther* (cats. 89, 93) were recorded in the Dresden collection in 1738. They were probably acquired in Leipzig, either from the Wagner Collection in 1728 or M. G. Wiedemann in 1723; Thomas Ketelsen believes the latter more likely. *Christ Praying in the Garden of Gethsemane* was probably acquired at the same time.

93 The Feast of Esther

1 Benesch 1954–1957, no. 154.

2 Sumowski 1979, no. 2138^{xx}; and Sumowski 1983, 3: nos. 1721, 1727, 1749.

94 Old Man Reading

1 Benesch 1954–1957, no. 15; Kassel and Amsterdam 2001–2002, no. 85.

95 Head of an Old Woman

1 Amsterdam 1991, nos. 30–36.

2 Benesch 1954–1957, no. 7.

3 National Gallery of Victoria, Melbourne; Corpus 1982–, 1: no. A13.

4 Private collection; Amsterdam 1988, no. 12.

5 Martin Royalton-Kisch, while still believing *Head of an Old Woman* to be by Lievens, now thinks *Bust of an Old Man* may be an early Rembrandt after all, along with another similarly executed drawing of a reclining horse, now in the British Museum, which he had previously published as Lievens. See Royalton-Kisch 1991b.

6 Leiden 2005.

7 A rare example of a work that seems to show the same sitter, but in native Dutch costume, is a drawing in Frankfurt, which has also sometimes been attributed to Lievens: Schneider/Ekkart 1973, no. Z112 (Lievens); Sumowski 1979, no. 532 (G. Dou); Leiden 2005, no. 13 (Lievens).

96 Old Woman in Half-Length Profile

1 Amsterdam 1988, nos. 21–27, 32, 33.

2 Benesch 1954–1957, no. 55; Amsterdam 1988, no. 10.

3 Benesch 1954–1957, no. 22; Kassel and Amsterdam 2001–2002, no. 46.

4 Sale, London, Sotheby's, July 5, 1993, no. 206; Sumowski 1979, no. 1641^{x}.

5 Amsterdam 1988, no. 33.

97 Moorish Man with Turban

1 Museum het Catharijneconvent, Utrecht; Corpus 1982–, 1: no. A5.

98 Bearded Old Man in Profile

1 Sumowski 1979, no. 1643x.

100 Hermit in Contemplation

1 Most comparable in style are *Seated Old Man*, signed with monogram and dated 1631 (private collection); *Old Man in an Armchair*, signed with monogram and dated 1631 (Teylers Museum, Haarlem); and *Seated Old Man with Folded Hands*, c. 1631 (Kupferstichkabinett, Berlin). See Benesch 1954–1957, nos. 20, 40, 41.

2 Sumowski 1979, no. 1632x.

3 Sumowski 1983, 3: nos. 1191, 1242 (Holl. 15).

101 View of London

1 Barnes et al. 2004, 459–461, no. IV.45. Van Dyck's painting shows the same buildings from a position farther to the right.

2 Malcolm Warner, *The Image of London* [exh. cat., Barbican Art Gallery] (London, 1987), 107, no. 20. Hollar's etching shows the buildings from farther to the left.

3 Royalton-Kisch 1998, 621, fig. 36. The crosses, however, are also missing from the gable end of Westminster in the background of Van Dyck's portrait of Charles I and his family, 1632.

102 Portrait of Adriaen Brouwer

1 Both in the British Museum, London; Sumowski 1979, nos. 1651x, 1652x.

2 Sumowski 1979, nos. 1657x, 1595, respectively.

103 Portrait of Constantijn Huygens

1 Sumowski 1983, 3: no. 1286.

2 Some lines show hints of indentation, but because the outlines were drawn with an extremely hard, sharp chalk, it is not clear whether this feature derives from the medium used or from the drawing's being indented for transfer to the engraver's plate.

104,105 River God with an Eagle; Seated River Gods

1 Hans Mielke and Matthias Winner, *Peter Paul Rubens, Kritischer katalog der Zeichnungen. Die Zeichnungen Alter Meister im Berliner Kupferstichkabinett* (Berlin, 1977), no. 42 Kr.

2 An entire exhibition has recently been devoted to this subject, from which Lievens was surprisingly omitted; see Rotterdam and Frankfurt 1999–2000.

106 A Painter's Studio

1 *Kitchen Scene*, present location unknown, pen and brown ink with wash, 42.1 × 27.9 cm; see Sumowski 1979, 3904–3905, no. 1757xx.

2 Ovid, *Metamorphoses* 11: 146–193. The subject of the painting has elsewhere been described as Apollo and Marsyas, which involved a similar musical contest. Though the figure in the foreground does seem to be playing the flute (like Marsyas), rather than Pan's characteristic syrinx, the presence of King Midas in the center of the composition leaves no doubt as to which subject Lievens actually intended to depict.

3 Amsterdam 1988, 67.

107 Scholar Sitting in His Studio

1 Sumowski 1979, 3558, no. 1595 (also the study for an etching).

108 Man with Moustache and Goatee

1 Sale, Christie's, London, April 7, 1995, no. 1. I am most grateful to Holm Bevers for bringing this painting to my attention.

2 Bernd Ebert most generously shared this information, to be included in his forthcoming monograph on Isaac and Simon Luttichuys, and also pointed out the fascinating possibility of a link between the still-life and *vanitas* compositions of Lievens and Luttichuys.

109 Thomas Howard, Earl of Arundel

1 Mary F.S. Hervey, *The Life, Correspondence and Collections of Thomas Howard, Earl of Arundel* (Cambridge, 1921), 174.

2 Howarth 1985, 192.

3 Howarth 1985, 207. What a contrast to his younger and more confident appearance in Rubens' drawing of c. 1629 (Ashmolean Museum, Oxford, no. WA 1994.27).

4 Hervey 1921, 483.

110 Forest Landscape with Pond

1 Schneider/Ekkart 1973, 390, suggested, for reasons that are not explained, that the present drawing might be the same as no. Z269 in the original Schneider 1932 publication, with the provenance dating back to G. van Rossum's sale in 1773.

2 National Gallery of Art, Washington (1970.14.1); see New York and Fort Worth 1991, no. 88.

3 Sale, Amsterdam, April 29, 1817, no. L20; Schneider/Ekkart 1973, no. Z141.

111 The Rollerbridge to the Sloterpolder

1 Bolten 1967, no. 69.

2 Hans-Ulrich Beck, *Jan van Goyen* (Amsterdam, 1972), 1: no. 847/139.

3 Holl. 58. See also Amsterdam and Paris 1998–1999, 309–311.

4 Lugt Collection, no. 6029; Paris and Haarlem 1997–1998, no. 80 (as Philips Koninck?). The Lugt drawing bears an inscription on the reverse, "P koningk f. 1669," in what has usually been thought to be the hand of the artist Philips Koninck, the name under which Frits Lugt acquired it. But it had been sold more than once in the nineteenth century as by Lievens, and more recently Peter Schatborn has justifiably restored it to that artist's oeuvre.

5 University of Leiden Printroom (no. 1624) and Groninger Museum voor Stad en Lande, Hofstede de Groot Collection (no. 1931–174); see Bolten 1967, no. 48.

112, 113 Portrait of René Descartes; Portrait of Caspar Streso

1 Washington, London, Haarlem 1989, 314–316.

2 DeWitt 2006, 244.

3 Sumowski 1979, no. 1603.

4 Engraved by Theodor Matham after a drawing by the little-known Maerten Lengele (Holl. 11: no. 138; Paris and Haarlem 1997–1998, 194).

114, 115 Portrait of Johannes Wtenbogaert; Woman Seated in Three-quarter Length

1 Rijksmuseum, Amsterdam; Corpus 1982–, 1: no. A80.

2 Bartsch 281.

3 DeWitt 2006, 217.

4 Schneider/Ekkart 1973, 194, under no. Z48.

5 Sumowski 1979, no. 1654x.

116 Admiral Maerten Harpertsz Tromp

1 The drawing was recorded in the William Mayor collection in 1875, and in the sale of the R. P. Roupell Collection, Frankfurt, December 6, 1888, no. 66 (see Schneider/Ekkart 1973, 200, 362, no. Z74).

2 Sumowski 1983, 3: no. 1296.

3 Sumowski 1979, 3586.

117, 118 Portrait of Andries de Graeff; Portrait of Jan Vos

1 H. J. Scholten's 1904 catalogue of the French and Dutch drawings in the Teylers Museum stated that this drawing was the same as the Lievens portrait of Huygens in the De Bosch and Ploos van Amstel sales. Plomp 1997 has, however, pointed out that the drawing does not bear Ploos' collector's mark and characteristic inscriptions, so the provenance remains uncertain.

2 DeWitt 2006, 217.

3 Weber 1985, 49–50, proposes that the poem by Vos—"door Jan Lievens geschildert" (painted by Jan Lievens)—was actually in praise of this drawing, rather than a painting. Vos' collected writings, published in 1662, contained no fewer than four laudatory verses concerning works by Lievens: in addition to the portrait of De Graeff, he praised Lievens' painting *Quintus Fabius Maximus* for the Amsterdam town hall, his lost portrait of the burgomaster

Joan Huydecoper II, and the portrait drawing of the poet himself shown here ("Myn afbeelding door Jan Lievensen geteekent"). See DeWitt 2006, 220, 245, 250. Copies of the De Graeff portrait are in the British Museum, and formerly on the Paris art market. A copy of the Jan Vos is in the Rijksmuseum. See Sumowski 1979, 3594, 3596, under nos. 1613, 1614. Unlike Lievens' landscapes, no multiple autograph versions of his portraits are known, only relatively weak copies.

4 For this and further biographical information, see S.A.C. Dudok van Heel, "Jan Vos (1610–1667)," in *Jaarboek Amstelodamum* (1980): 23–43.

119, 120 Two Studies of a Man in a Hat; Sheet of Studies

1 Sumowski 1979, 3598–3599, no. 1615.

2 Braunschweig 1979, no. 82.

3 In this respect, the drawing is more similar to the earlier pen-and-ink portraits in Paris and Bayonne. Sumowski 1979, 3554–3555, 3656–3657, nos. 1593, 1640x.

4 Sumowski 1979, 3850–3851, no. 1730x, the verso reproduced 3942, fig. 97.

121, 122 A Path in the Haagse Bos; "Het Roomhuis" in the Haagse Bos

1 For a further discussion of these papers, see Rubinstein essay and cat. 130–131.

2 Dumas 1991, 177–187.

3 Also in the Lugt Collection (no. 4971); Brussels, Rotterdam, Paris, Bern 1968–1969, 14–15, no. 15, pl. 143.

123, 124 Ruins of the Castle of Brederode; Ruins of the Abbey Church at Egmond

1 Reznicek 1961, no. 391.

2 Sumowski 1979, no. 1742x; formerly John and Alice Steiner Collection, sold, Sotheby's, New York, January 25, 2006, no. 21.

3 Chapel Hill, Ithaca, Worcester 1999–2001.

4 See Van der Wyck, Kloek, and Niemeijer 1989–1990. The earliest inventory of these drawings (1708) lists 247 sheets, of which some 220 are known today. For one of Egmond, see Kupferstichkabinett, Berlin, SMPK (no. 12230).

5 Slive 2001, 43.

6 Amsterdam 1988, 85.

7 Schneider/Ekkart 1973, 76.

8 Schneider/Ekkart 1973, 365; Sumowski 1979, 3832; Schatborn in Amsterdam 1988, 85.

9 Braunschweig 1979, no. 87.

125 Village Street with a Windmill

1 Sumowski 1979, nos. 1714x, 1715x, 1709x.

2 Bolten 1967, 83.

3 Note from 1958 in the Pierpont Morgan Library curatorial files. Although Lievens' mill differs from a typical Dutch mill, as seen in many of Rembrandt's drawings, it is similar in form to the mill at Wijk bij Duurstede, depicted in Ruisdael's painting in the Rijksmuseum (Slive 2001, no. 81).

4 Turner 2006, 100.

126, 127 Homestead in a Forest; Wooded Landscape with Shepherds, Flocks, and a Village

1 Sumowski 1979, 3754, no. 1686x; Turner 2006, 98, no. 127.

2 London, Paris, Cambridge, MA, 2002–2003, 144, under no. 59.

3 I am grateful to William W. Robinson and the conservation staff of the Fogg Art Museum for reexamining the drawing recently with infrared light of various wavelengths. This examination revealed no observable difference between the ink of the signature and that of the rest of the drawing. A third related drawing, again in the Morgan Library, is a weaker repetition of the composition and seems to be a straightforward copy after the version in the British Museum. Turner 2006, 101, no. 133.

4 Schneider 1932, 75–76.

5 Hind 1915, 88, no. 23.

6 Martin Royalton-Kisch very generously shared his draft entry on the drawing from his forthcoming catalogue of drawings by Rembrandt and his school in the British Museum. See also Royalton-Kisch 1998, 622.

128, 129 View of Haarlem; View of Cleves

1 Sale, New York [Sotheby's], January 25, 2006, no. 21; Sumowski 1979, 3874–3875, no. 1742x.

2 Schneider 1932, 300.

3 Heinrich Dattenberg, *Niederrheinansichten holländischer Künstler des 17. Jahrhuhnderts* (Düsseldorf, 1967); Friedrich Gorissen, *Conspectus Cliviae. Die klevische Residenz in der Kunst des 17. Jahrhunderts* (Cleves, 1964).

4 Sumowski 1979, 3796–3797, 3804–3805, 3810–3811, nos. 1705x, 1709x, 1712x. The locations depicted in the first and third of these were identified by Peter Schatborn (see Amsterdam 1988, 82); that in the second was identified by Hans-Ulrich Beck.

130, 131 Distant View of Haarlem; Landscape with Peasant Dwelling

1 Robinson in Amsterdam, Vienna, New York, Cambridge, MA, 1991–1992, 150 n. 3, suggests that this drawing may correspond with one of the two listed by Schneider under no. Z151, with the following early provenance: D. Smith; (sale, Amsterdam, July 13, 1761, portfolio G, no. 459); (sale, Amsterdam, November 16, 1778, no. 176).

2 London, Paris, Cambridge, MA, 2002–2003, 148, under no. 61.

3 Schneider/Ekkart 1973, no. Z355; Sumowski 1979, 3856.

4 Sumowski 1979, no. 1737x.

5 Churchill 1967, no. 423.

132 Forest Interior with a Draftsman

1 Sumowski 1979, no. 1689x.

2 A further complication is that the condition of the Dresden drawing is so much worse, and its quality is therefore harder to judge.

3 Watermark HIS, PB below, similar to Churchill 1967, no. 423.

133 Garden Entrance

1 Sumowski 1979, 3848; Schneider/Ekkart 1973, 376, no. Z391.

134, 135 Decaying Pollard Willow; Old Tree Trunk in Front of a Forest

1 Both drawings are in the Kupferstich-Kabinett, Dresden. For both the tree study (no. C1436) and the wooded landscape (no. C1896–30), see Sumowski 1979, 3768–3769, 3770–3771, nos. 1692x, 1693x.

2 I am most grateful to Martin Royalton-Kisch for bringing the indentation to my attention and for sharing his draft entry from his forthcoming catalogue of drawings by Rembrandt and his school in the British Museum.

3 Paris and Haarlem 1997–1998, 194–198, no. 87.

4 John Oliver Hand, *The Age of Bruegel: Netherlandish Drawings in the Sixteenth Century* [exh. cat., National Gallery of Art] (Washington, 1986), 146–148, 174–175, nos. 51, 62.

136, 137 Sandpit with Two Sheds; Sandpit with Two Sheds, Pigs in the Foreground

1 Rijksmuseum, Amsterdam (no. A315). See M.D. Henkel, *Catalogus van de nederlandsche teekeningen in het Rijksmuseum te Amsterdam*, vol. 1, *Teekeningen van Rembrandt en zijn school* ('s-Gravenhage, 1942), 79, no. 20, pl. 129.

2 See Sumowski 1979, 1460–1461, no. 675.

3 Sumowski 1979, 1490–1491, no. 690.

4 Paris and Haarlem 1997–1998, 200, under no. 88.

5 Amsterdam 1988, 82.

138, 139 Densely Wooded Landscape with a Pond; Densely Wooded Landscape with Deer

1 See Sumowski 1979, 3740–3744, nos. 1, 9, 14 (under no. 1679x).

2 See Sumowski 1979, 3744–3745, 3774–3775, nos. 1681x, 1695x.

3 See the background of *Wooded Landscape with Shepherd Playing a Flute* in Budapest (Sumowski 1979, 3764–3765, no. 1690x).

4 British Museum, London (no. 1895.9.15.1198); see Sumowski 1979, 3742–3743, no. 1680x.

5 Sumowski 1979, 3868–3869, no. 1739x. See also cat. 134–135, regarding Lievens' studies of trees.

Select Bibliography

EXHIBITIONS

Amsterdam 1956 *De verzameling van Dr. A. Welcker.* Rijksprentenkabinet.

Amsterdam 1964 *De verzameling van Bernard Houthakker.* Rijksprentenkabinet (catalogue by J. W. Niemeijer).

Amsterdam 1986 *Face to Face with the Sitters for Rembrandt's Etched Portraits.* Museum Het Rembrandthuis (catalogue by Rudolf E. O. Ekkart and Eva Ornstein-van Slooten).

Amsterdam 1988 *Jan Lievens, 1607–1674. Prenten en tekeningen.* Museum Het Rembrandthuis (catalogue by Peter Schatborn).

Amsterdam 1991 *Pieter Lastman. Leermeester van Rembrandt/The Man Who Taught Rembrandt.* Museum Het Rembrandthuis (catalogue by Astrid Tümpel and Peter Schatborn).

Amsterdam 1993 *Tekeningen van oude meesters. De verzamling Jacobus A. Klaver.* Rijksprentenkabinet (catalogue by Marijn Schapelhouman and Peter Schatborn).

Amsterdam 1996 *Rembrandt and Van Vliet: A Collaboration on Copper.* Museum Het Rembrandthuis (catalogue by Christiaan Schuckman et al.).

Amsterdam 1998 *Buiten tekenen in Rembrandts tijd.* Museum Het Rembrandthuis (catalogue by Bob van den Boogert et al.).

Amsterdam 2002–2003 *Kopstukken. Amsterdammers geportretteerd, 1600–1800.* Amsterdams Historisch Museum.

Amsterdam and Cleveland 1992 *Chiaroscuro Woodcuts: Hendrick Goltzius (1558–1617) and His Time.* Rijksmuseum; Cleveland Museum of Art (catalogue by Nancy Bialler).

Amsterdam and Cleveland 1999–2000 *Still-Life Painting from the Netherlands, 1550–1720.* Rijksmuseum; Cleveland Museum of Art (catalogue by Alan Chong and Wouter Kloek).

Amsterdam and London 2000 *Rembrandt the Printmaker.* Rijksmuseum; British Museum (catalogue by Erik Hinterding, Ger Luijten, and Martin Royalton-Kisch).

Amsterdam and Paris 1998–1999 *Landscapes of Rembrandt: His Favourite Walks.* Gemeentearchief; Institut Néerlandais (catalogue by Boudewijn Bakker et al.).

Amsterdam and Rotterdam 1956 *Rembrandt tentoonstelling ter herdenking van de geboorte van Rembrandt op 16 juli 1606.* Rijksmuseum; Museum Boijmans Van Beuningen.

Amsterdam, Vienna, New York, Cambridge, MA, 1991–1992 *Seventeenth-Century Dutch Drawings: A Selection from the Maida and George Abrams Collection.* Rijksprentenkabinet et al. (catalogue by William W. Robinson).

Antwerp and Amsterdam 1999 *Anthony van Dyck as a Printmaker.* Museum Plantin-Moretus; Rijksmuseum (catalogue by Carl Depauw and Ger Luijten).

Antwerp and Quebec 2004 *Copyright Rubens. Rubens en de grafiek.* Museum voor Schone Kunsten; Musée Nationale des Beaux-Arts (catalogue by Nico van Hout et al.).

Berlin 1970 *Tizian und sein Kreis. 50 venezianische Holzschnitte aus dem Berliner Kupferstichkabinett Staatliche Museen Preussischer Kulturbesitz.* Kupferstichkabinett (catalogue by Peter Dreyer).

Berlin, Amsterdam, London 1991–1992 *Rembrandt, the Master and His Workshop: Drawings and Etchings.* Kupferstichkabinett; Rijksmuseum; National Gallery (catalogue by Holm Bevers, Peter Schatborn, and Barbara Welzel).

Boston 1981 *Printmaking in the Age of Rembrandt.* Museum of Fine Arts (catalogue by Clifford S. Ackley).

Braunschweig 1978 *Die Sprache der Bilder. Realität und Bedeutung in der niederländischen Malerei des 17. Jahrhunderts.* Herzog Anton Ulrich-Museum (catalogue by Rüdiger Klessman et al.).

Braunschweig 1979 *Jan Lievens, ein Maler im Schatten Rembrandts.* Herzog Anton Ulrich-Museum (catalogue by Rudolf E. O. Ekkart, Sabine Jacob, and Rüdiger Klessmann).

Braunschweig 2004 *Peter Paul Rubens. Barocke Leidenschaften.* Herzog Anton Ulrich-Museum (catalogue by Nils Büttner and Ulrich Heinen).

Brussels, Rotterdam, Paris, Bern 1968–1969 *Dessins de paysagistes hollandais du XVIIe siècle, de la collection particulière conservée à l'Institut Néerlandais de Paris.* Bibliothèque Albert Ier et al.

Cambridge, MA, and Montreal 1988–1989 *Landscape in Perspective: Drawings by Rembrandt and His Contemporaries.* Harvard University Art Museums; Montreal Museum of Fine Arts (catalogue by Frederik J. Duparc).

Chapel Hill, Ithaca, Worcester 1999–2001 *Fresh Woods and Pastures New: Seventeenth-Century Dutch Landscape Drawings from the Peck Collection.* Ackland Art Museum, University of North Carolina at Chapel Hill, et al. (catalogue by Franklin W. Robinson and Sheldon Peck).

Chicago 1969 *Rembrandt after Three Hundred Years: An Exhibition of Rembrandt and His Followers.* Art Institute of Chicago (catalogue by J. Richard Judson).

Copenhagen 2006 *Rembrandt? The Master and His Workshop.* Statens Museum for Kunst (catalogue by Lene Bøgh Rønberg and Eva de la Fuente Pedersen).

Dresden and Paris 2004–2006 *Rembrandt. Die Dresdener Zeichnungen 2004.* Residenzschloss, 2004; *Rembrandt. Les dessins de Dresden.* Institut Néerlandais, 2006 (catalogue by Christian Dittrich and Thomas Ketelsen).

Dresden and Vienna 1997–1998 *Van Eyck, Bruegel, Rembrandt. Niederländische Zeichnungen des 15. bis 17. Jahrhunderts aus dem Kupferstich-Kabinett Dresden.* Kupferstich-Kabinett; Kunstforum (catalogue by Christian Dittrich).

Edinburgh and London 2001 *Rembrandt's Women.* National Gallery of Scotland; Royal Academy of Arts (catalogue by Julia Lloyd Williams).

Epinal 2003 *Rembrandt et les peintres-graveurs italiens de Castiglione à Tiepolo.* Musée départemental d'art ancien et contemporain (catalogue by Matthieu Gilles, Bozena Anna Kowalczyk, and Jaco Rutgers).

Franeker 2007 *Vrouw van de Wereld. Het Leven van Anna Maria van Schurmann.* Museum Martena (catalogue by Marjan Brouwer).

Groningen 2005 *Van Cuyp tot Rembrandt. De verzameling Cornelius Hofstede de Groot.* Groninger Museum (catalogue by Luuk Pijl et al.).

Haarlem 1986 *Portretten van echt en trouw. Huwelijk en gezin in de Nederlandse kunst van de zeventiende eeuw.* Frans Halsmuseum (catalogue by E. de Jongh).

Haarlem and Paris 2001–2002 *Hartstochtelijk Verzameld. Beroemde tekeningen in 18de-eeuwse Hollandse collecties.* Teylers Museum; Institut Néerlandais (catalogue by Mària van Berge-Gerbaud et al.).

The Hague 1992 *The Hoogsteder Exhibition of Rembrandt's Academy.* Hoogsteder and Hoogsteder (catalogue by Paul Huys Janssen and Werner Sumowski).

The Hague 1997 *Princely Patrons: The Collection of Frederick Henry of Orange and Amalia of Solms in The Hague.* Mauritshuis (catalogue by Peter van der Ploeg and Carola Vermeeren with Ben Broos et al.).

The Hague 2002 *A Choice Collection: Seventeenth-Century Dutch Paintings from the Frits Lugt Collection.* Mauritshuis (catalogue by Quentin Buvelot and Hans Buijs).

The Hague and San Francisco 1991 *Great Dutch Paintings from America.* Mauritshuis; Fine Arts Museums of San Francisco (catalogue by Ben Broos with Edwin Buijsen et al.).

Hanover, Wellesley, Providence, Storrs 1969 *The Collection of Dutch Drawings of Maida and George Abrams.* Hopkins Center Art Galleries et al. (catalogue by Franklin W. Robinson).

Kassel and Amsterdam 2001–2002 *The Mystery of the Young Rembrandt.* Staatliche Museen Kassel; Museum Het Rembrandthuis (catalogue by Ernst van de Wetering and Bernhard Schnackenburg).

Kingston 1996–1997 *Wisdom, Knowledge, and Magic: The Image of the Scholar in Dutch Seventeenth-Century Art.* Agnes Etherington Art Centre (catalogue by Volker Manuth et al.).

Krefeld, Oranienburg, Apeldoorn 1999 *Onder den Oranje boom. Niederländische Kunst und Kultur im 17. und 18. Jahrhundert an deutschen Fürstenhöfen.* Kaiser Wilhelm-Museum; Schloss Oranienburg; Palais Het Loo (catalogue by Markus Schacht).

Leiden 1948–1949 *Honderd Tekeningen uit de verzameling van Dr. A. Welcker.* Stedelijk Museum De Lakenhal.

Leiden 1970 *IJdelheid der ijdelheden. Hollandse Vanitas-voorstellingen uit de zeventiende eeuw.* Stedelijk Museum De Lakenhal (catalogue by I. Bergstrom and M. L. Wurfbain).

Leiden 1976 *Geschildert tot Leyden anno 1626.* Stedelijk Museum De Lakenhal.

Leiden 1991 *Rembrandt and Lievens in Leiden.* Stedelijk Museum De Lakenhal (catalogue by Christiaan Vogelaar et al.).

Leiden 2005 *Rembrandt's Mother: Myth and Reality.* Stedelijk Museum De Lakenhal (catalogue by Christiaan Vogelaar and Gerbrand Korevaar).

Leiden and Kassel 2006 *Rembrandt's Landscapes.* Stedelijk Museum De Lakenhal; Staatliche Museen Kassel (catalogue by Christiaan Vogelaar et al.).

London 1992 *Drawings by Rembrandt and His Circle in the British Museum.* British Museum (catalogue by Martin Royalton-Kisch).

London 1996 *Landmarks in Print Collecting: Connoisseurs and Donors at the British Museum since 1753.* British Museum (catalogue by Antony Griffiths).

London 1998 *The Print in Stuart Britain 1603–1669.* British Museum (catalogue by Antony Griffiths).

London and Amsterdam 2006 *Uylenburgh and Son: Art and Commerce from Rembrandt to De Lairesse, 1625–1675.* Dulwich Picture Gallery; Museum Het Rembrandthuis (catalogue by Friso Lammertse and Jaap van der Veen).

London and The Hague 2007–2008 *Dutch Portraits: The Age of Rembrandt and Frans Hals.* National Gallery; Mauritshuis (catalogue by Rudolf E. O. Ekkart et al.).

London, Paris, Cambridge, MA, 2002–2003 *From Bruegel to Rembrandt: Dutch and Flemish Drawings from the Maida and George Abrams Collection.* British Museum; Institut Néerlandais; Fogg Art Museum (catalogue by William W. Robinson).

Los Angeles 1991–1992 *"The Raising of Lazarus" by Rembrandt. Masterpieces in Focus.* Los Angeles County Museum of Art (catalogue by Richard Rand).

Melbourne and Canberra 1997 *Rembrandt: A Genius and His Impact.* National Gallery of Victoria; National Gallery of Australia (catalogue by Albert Blankert et al.).

Milwaukee 1989 *The Detective's Eye: Investigating the Old Masters.* Milwaukee Art Museum (catalogue by Alfred and Isabel Bader).

Munich 1982 *Graphik in Holland. Esaias und Jan van de Velde, Rembrandt, Ostade und ihr Kreis; Radierung, Kupferstich, Schabkunst.* Staatliche Graphische Sammlung München (catalogue by Konrad Renger).

Münster 1994 *Im Lichte Rembrandts. Das Alte Testament im Goldenen Zeitalter der niederländischen Kunst.* Westfälisches Landesmuseum (catalogue by Christian Tümpel).

Münster and Osnabrück 1998 *1648: War and Peace in Europe.* Westfälisches Landesmuseum (catalogue editors, Klaus Bussmann and Heinz Schilling).

New Orleans 1997 *In the Eye of the Beholder: Northern Baroque Paintings from the Collection of Henry H. Weldon.* New Orleans Museum of Art (catalogue by Nancy T. Minty).

New York and Fort Worth 1991 *Van Dyck Drawings.* Pierpont Morgan Library; Kimbell Art Museum (catalogue by Christopher Brown).

New York and Fort Worth 1995 *Drawings from the Albertina: Landscape in the Age of Rembrandt.* Drawing Center; Kimbell Art Museum (catalogue by Marian Bisanz-Prakken; preface by Konrad Oberhuber).

New York and Paris 1977–1978 *Rembrandt and His Century: Dutch Drawings of the Seventeenth Century from the Collection of Frits Lugt, Institut Néerlandais, Paris.* Pierpont Morgan Library; Institut Néerlandais (catalogue by Carlos van Hasselt).

Paris 1983 *Reflets du siècle d'or. Tableaux hollandaise du dix-septième siècle.* Institut Néerlandais (catalogue by Saskia Nihom-Nijstad).

Paris 2007 *Rembrandt et la nouvelle Jérusalem. Juifs et chrétiens à Amsterdam au siècle d'or.* Musée d'art et d'histoire du Judaïsme (catalogue by Laurence Sigal-Klagsbald and Alexis Merle du Bourg).

Paris, Antwerp, London, New York 1979–1980 *Rubens and Rembrandt in Their Century: Flemish and Dutch Drawings of the 17th Century from the Pierpont Morgan Library.* Institut Néerlandais et al. (catalogue by Felice Stampfle).

Paris and Haarlem 1997–1998 *Rembrandt et son école. Dessins de la collection Frits Lugt.* Institut Néerlandais; Teylers Museum (catalogue by Mària van Berge-Gerbaud).

Potsdam 1988 *Der Grosse Kurfürst (1620–1688). Sammler, Bauherr, Mäzen.* Neues Palais (catalogue by Hans-Joachim Giersberg et al.).

Poughkeepsie 1976 *Seventeenth-Century Dutch Landscape Drawings and Selected Prints from American Collections.* Vassar College Art Gallery (catalogue by Curtis O. Baer).

Raleigh 1998–1999 *Sinners and Saints, Darkness and Light: Caravaggio and His Dutch and Flemish Followers.* North Carolina Museum of Art; Milwaukee Art Museum; Dayton Art Institute (catalogue by Dennis P. Weller et al.).

Rome 1951 *Mostra di incisioni e disegni di Rembrandt* (catalogue by I. Q. van Regteren Altena).

Rotterdam 1988 *Een gloeiend palet. Schilderijen van Rembrandt en zijn school.* Museum Boijmans Van Beuningen.

Rotterdam 2006a *Prenten in de Gouden Eeuw. Van Kunst tot Kastpapier.* Museum Boijmans Van Beuningen (catalogue by J. van de Waal et al.).

Rotterdam 2006b *Rembrandts passie. Het Nieuwe Testament in de Nederlandse prentkunst van de zestiende en zeventiende eeuw.* Museum Boijmans Van Beuningen (catalogue by Peter van der Coelen).

Rotterdam and Frankfurt 1999–2000 *Dutch Classicism in Seventeenth-Century Painting.* Museum Boijmans Van Beuningen; Städel Museum (catalogue by Albert Blankert et al.).

Rotterdam and Paris 1974 *Willem Buytewech, 1591–1624.* Museum Boijmans Van Beuningen; Institut Néerlandais.

San Francisco, Baltimore, London 1997 *Masters of Light: Dutch Painters in Utrecht during the Golden Age.* Fine Arts Museums of San Francisco; Walters Art Museum; National Gallery (catalogue by Lynn Federle Orr and Joaneath A. Spicer).

Stockholm 1992 *Rembrandt och hans tid, människan i centrum* [Rembrandt and his age, focus on man]. En utställning ingående i Nationalmuseums 200-årsjubileum (catalogue editor, Görel Cavalli-Björkman).

Stockholm 2005 *Holländsk guldålder. Rembrandt, Frans Hals, och deras samtida.* Nationalmuseum (catalogue by Görel Cavalli-Björkman).

Tel Aviv 1997 *Jan Lievens: "The Sacrifice of Isaac."* Tel Aviv Museum of Art (catalogue by Doron J. Lurie).

Tokyo 2003 *Rembrandt and the Rembrandt School.* National Museum of Western Art (catalogue by Akira Kofuku).

Washington 1978 *Master Drawings: Selections from the National Gallery of Art Collection and Promised Gifts.* National Gallery of Art.

Washington 1983 *Prints of Lucas van Leyden and His Contemporaries.* National Gallery of Art (catalogue by Ellen Jacobowitz et al.).

Washington 1990 *Anthony van Dyck.* National Gallery of Art (catalogue by Arthur K. Wheelock Jr., Susan J. Barnes, and Julius S. Held).

Washington 1996 *Jan Steen: Painter and Storyteller.* National Gallery of Art (catalogue by H. Perry Chapman et al.).

Washington, Denver, Fort Worth 1977 *Seventeenth-Century Dutch Drawings from American Collections.* National Gallery of Art; Denver Art Museum; Kimbell Art Museum (catalogue by Frank Robinson).

Washington, Detroit, Amsterdam 1980 *Gods, Saints, and Heroes: Dutch Painting in the Age of Rembrandt.* National Gallery of Art; Detroit Institute of Arts; Rijksmuseum (catalogue by Albert Blankert et al.).

Washington, London, Haarlem 1989 *Frans Hals.* National Gallery of Art; Royal Academy of Arts; Frans Halsmuseum (catalogue by Seymour Slive et al.).

Washington, London, The Hague 2000 *Gerrit Dou, 1613–1675.* National Gallery of Art; Dulwich Picture Gallery; Mauritshuis (catalogue by Ronnie Baer et al.).

Washington and Los Angeles 2005 *Rembrandt's Late Religious Portraits.* National Gallery of Art; J. Paul Getty Museum (catalogue by Arthur K. Wheelock Jr. et al.)

LITERATURE

Angel 1642 Angel, Philips. *Lof der schilder-konst.* Leiden, 1642. Facsimile ed., Utrecht, 1969.

Angel 1996 Angel, Philips. "Praise of Painting." Translated by Michael Hoyle, introduction by Hessel Miedema. *Simiolus* 24 (1996): 227–258.

De Baar 1996 De Baar, Mirjam. *Choosing the Better Part: Anna Maria van Schurman (1607–1678).* Dordrecht, 1996.

De Baar 1992 De Baar, P.J.M. *De Leidse Verwanten van Rembrandt van Rijn en hun Leidse afstammelingen tot heden.* Leiden, 1992.

Bader 1995 Bader, Alfred. *Adventures of a Chemist Collector.* London, 1995.

Baker/Henry 2001 Baker, Christopher, and Tom Henry. *The National Gallery Complete Illustrated Catalogue.* London, 2001.

Bangs and Breugelmans 2006 Bangs, J. D., and R. Breugelmans. "Two New Rembrandt Etchings, 1632." *Quaerendo* 36 (2006): 158–186.

Barnes et al. 2004 Barnes, Susan J., et al. *Van Dyck. A Complete Catalogue of the Paintings.* New Haven and London, 2004.

Bartoscheck 1978 Bartoscheck, Gerd. *Gemälde aus Schloß Oranienburg,* Oranienburg, 1978.

Bartsch Bartsch, Adam von. *Le peintre graveur.* 21 vols. Leipzig, 1818–1876.

Bartrum 1995 Bartrum, Giulia. *German Renaissance Prints, 1490–1550.* London, 1995.

Bauch 1939 Bauch, Kurt. "Rembrandt und Lievens." *Wallraf-Richartz-Jahrbuch* 11 (1939): 239–268.

Bauch 1960 Bauch, Kurt. *Der frühe Rembrandt und seine Zeit. Studien zur geschichtlichen Bedeutung seines Frühstils.* Berlin, 1960.

Bauch 1962 Bauch, Kurt. "Rembrandt's *Christus am Kreuz.*" *Pantheon* 20 (1962): 137–144.

Bauch 1967 Bauch, Kurt. "Zum Werk des Jan Lievens (I–II)." *Pantheon* 25 (1967): 160–170, 259–269.

Benesch 1954–1957 Benesch, Otto. *The Drawings of Rembrandt.* 6 vols. London, 1954–1957.

Białostocki 1966 Bialostocki, Jan. "Puer sufflans ignes." In *Arte in Europa. Scritti di storia dell'arte in onore di Edoardo Arslan,* 591–595. Milan, 1966.

Białostocki 1988 Bialostocki, Jan. *Message of Images: Studies in the History of Art.* Vienna, 1988.

De Bie 1661 De Bie, Cornelis. *Het Gulden Cabinet van de edel vry Schilderconst.* Antwerp, 1661. Reprint, Soest, 1971.

Von Bode 1883 Von Bode, Wilhelm. *Studien zur Geschichte der holländischen Malerei.* Braunschweig, 1883.

Böhmer 1940 Böhmer, Günter. *Der Landschafter Adriaen Brouwer.* Munich, 1940.

Bolten 1967 Bolten, Jaap. *Dutch Drawings from the Collection of Dr. C. Hofstede de Groot.* Utrecht, 1967.

Börsch-Supan 1964 Börsch-Supan, H. *Die Gemälde im Jagdschloss Grunewald.* Berlin, 1964.

Börsch-Supan 1992 Börsch-Supan, H. *450 Jahre Jagdschloss Grunewald, 1524–1992.* Berlin, 1992.

Bowron 1977 Bowron, Edgar Peters. "Two Rembrandtesque Paintings." *The Walters Art Gallery Bulletin* 29 (1977): unpaginated.

Van den Branden 1883 Van den Branden, F. Jos. *Geschiedenis der Antwerpsche Schilderschool.* Antwerp, 1883.

Bredius 1915–1922 Bredius, Abraham. *Künstler-Inventare.* 8 vols. The Hague, 1915–1922.

Bredius/Gerson 1969 Bredius, Abraham. *Rembrandt: The Complete Edition of His Paintings.* Revised by Horst Gerson. London, 1969.

Brière-Misme 1936 Brière-Misme, Clotilde. "Un portrait retrouvé de Constantijn Huygens." *Oud Holland* 53 (1936): 193–201.

Broos 1972 Broos, Ben. "Rembrandt. Verandert. En overgeschildert." *De Kroniek van het Rembrandthuis* 26 (1972): 137–152.

Broos 1981 Broos, Ben. *Oude tekeningen in het bezit van de Gemeentemusea van Amsterdam waaronder de collectie Fodor.* Vol. 3, *Rembrandt en tekenaars uit zijn omgeving.* Amsterdam, 1981.

Brown 1979a Brown, Christopher. *Dutch Landscape Painting.* London, 1979.

Brown 1979b Brown, Christopher. "Jan Lievens at Brunswick." *Burlington Magazine* 121 (1979): 741–746.

Brown 1983 Brown, Christopher. "Jan Lievens in Leiden and London." *Burlington Magazine* 125 (1983): 663–671.

Brown 1992 Brown, Christopher. "Lastman, Lievens, and Bredius: Amsterdam, Leiden, and The Hague." *Burlington Magazine* 134 (1992): 268–272.

Buchberger 1957–1965 Buchberger, Michael. *Lexikon für Theologie und Kirche.* 2nd ed. Freiburg, 1957–1965.

Buijsen 1998 Buijsen, Edwin. *Haagse Schilders in de Gouden Eeuw. Het Hoogsteder Lexicon van alle schilders werkzaam in Den Haag, 1600–1700.* The Hague and Zwolle, 1998.

Burchard 1917 Burchard, Ludwig. *Die Holländischen Radierer vor Rembrandt. Mit beschreibenden Verzeichnissen und biographischen Übersichten.* Berlin, 1917.

Carroll 1986 Carroll, Margaret Deutsch. "Civic Ideology and Its Subversion: Rembrandt's *Oath of Claudius Civilis.*" *Art History* 9 (1986): 10–35.

Casteels 1961 Casteels, Marguerite. *De Beeldhouwers de Nole te Kamerijk, te Utrecht en te Antwerp.* Brussels, 1961.

Cervantes 1998 Cervantes Saavedra, Miguel de. "The Little Spanish Gypsy." In *Exemplary Stories.* Translated by L. Lipson. Oxford and New York, 1998.

Châtellier 1997 Châtellier, Louis. *The Religion of the Poor: Rural Missions in Europe and the Formation of Modern Catholicism, c. 1500–1800.* Cambridge, 1997.

Churchill 1967 Churchill, W. A. *Watermarks in Paper in Holland, England, France, etc. in the XVII and XVIII Centuries and Their Interconnection.* Amsterdam, 1967.

De Clippel 2003 De Clippel, Karolien. "Brouwer, Portrait Painter: New Identifications and an Iconographic Novelty." *Simiolus* 30 (2003): 196–216.

De Clippel 2006 De Clippel, Karolien. *Joos van Craesbeeck (1605/1606–c. 1660). Een Brabants Genreschilder.* Turnhout, 2006.

Colie 1956 Colie, Rosalie L. *"Some thankfulnesse to Constantine": A Study of English Influence upon the Early Works of Constantijn Huygens.* The Hague, 1956.

Corbett and Norton 1964 Corbett, Margery, and Michael Norton. *Engraving in England in the Sixteenth and Seventeenth Centuries: A Descriptive Catalogue with Introductions.* Pt. 3, *The Reign of Charles I.* Cambridge, 1964.

Corpus 1982– Bruyn, Josua, et al. *A Corpus of Rembrandt Paintings.* 4 vols. The Hague, Boston, and London, 1982–.

Van Damme 1990 Van Damme, J. "De Antwerpse tafereelmakers en hun merken. Identificatie en betekenis." *Jaarboek van het Koninklijk Museum voor Schone Kunsten Antwerpen* (1990): 193–237.

Daulby 1796 Daulby, Daniel. *A descriptive catalogue of the works of Rembrandt, and of his scholars, Bol, Livens, and Van Vliet, compiled from the original etchings, and from the catalogues of De Burgy, Gersaint, Helle and Glomy, Marcus, and Yver.* Liverpool, 1796.

Defoer 1977 Defoer, H.L.M. "Rembrandt van Rijn. De Doop van de Kamerling." *Oud Holland* 91 (1977): 2–26.

Denny 1977 Denny, Don. "Notes on the Lambeth Bible." *Gesta* 16, no. 2 (1977): 57–60.

Descamps 1753–1763 Descamps, Jean-Baptiste. *La vie des peintres flamands, allemands, et hollandais. Avec des portraits gravés en taille-douce, une indication de leurs principaux ouvrages, et des réflexions sur leurs différéntes manieres.* 4 vols. Paris, 1753–1763.

Dickey 2001 Dickey, Stephanie. "Van Dyck in Holland: The *Iconography* and Its Impact on Rembrandt and Jan Lievens." In Vlieghe 2001, 289–303.

Dickey 2004 Dickey, Stephanie. *Rembrandt: Portraits in Print.* Philadelphia, 2004.

Drossaers and Lunsingh Scheurleer 1974–1976 Drossaers, S.W.A., and Th. H. Lunsingh Scheurleer. *Inventarissen van de inboedels in de verblijven van de Oranjes en daarmede gelijk te stellen stukken, 1567–1795.* 3 vols. The Hague, 1974–1976.

Dudok van Heel 1983 Dudok van Heel, S.A.C. "In Presentie van de Heer Gerard ter Borgh." In *Essays in Northern European Art Presented to Egbert Haverkamp-Begemann,* 66–71. Doornspijk 1983.

Dudok van Heel 2006 Dudok van Heel, S.A.C. *De jonge Rembrandt onder tijdgenoten. Godsdienst en schilderkunst in Leiden en Amsterdam.* Nijmegen, 2006.

Dumas 1991 Dumas, Charles. *Haagse Stadsgezichten, 1550–1800. Topografische Schilderijen van het Haags Historisch Museum.* Zwolle, 1991.

Dutuit Dutuit, Eugène. *Manuel de l'amateur d'estampes.* 5 vols. Paris, 1881–1888. Reprint, Amsterdam, 1970–1972.

Van Eijnden and Van der Willigen 1816 Van Eijnden, Roeland, and Adriaan van der Willigen. *Geschiedenis der vaderlandsche schilderkunst, sedert de helft der XVIII eeuw.* 3 vols. Haarlem, 1816.

Ekkart 1974 Ekkart, Rudolf E. O. "Portraits in Leiden University Library." *Quaerendo* 5 (1974): 52–65.

Ekkart 1991 Ekkart, Rudolf E. O. "Rembrandt, Lievens, en Constantijn Huygens." In Leiden 1991, 48–59.

Elen 1982 Elen, A. J. "De restauratie van de gevel van het pand Breestraat 84 'van outs genaemt de Vergulde Druyff' doch tegenwoordig bekend als 'In den Verguldden Turck.'" *Leids Jaarboekje* 74 (1982): 86–112.

Emmens 1956 Emmens, Jan Ameling. "Ay Rembrandt, maal Cornelis stem." *Nederlands Kunsthistorisch Jaarboek* 7 (1956).

Filedt Kok 1996 Filedt Kok, J. P. "Artists Portrayed by Their Friends: Goltzius and His Circle." *Simiolus* 24 (1996): 161–181.

Fremantle 1959 Fremantle, Katharine. *The Baroque Town Hall of Amsterdam.* Utrecht, 1959.

Frijhoff and Spies 2004 Frijhoff, Willem, and Marijke Spies. *Dutch Culture in a European Perspective.* Vol. 1, *1650: Hard-Won Unity.* Assen, 2004.

Fromentin 1948 Fromentin, Eugène. *The Masters of Past Time, or, Criticism on the Old Dutch and Flemish Painters.* Ithaca, 1948. Translation of *Les maîtres d'autrefois. Belgique-Hollande.* Paris, 1877.

Fruin/Japikse 1919–1922 Fruin, R., and N. Japikse. *Brieven van Johan de Witt, 1648–1672.* 2 vols. Amsterdam 1919–1922.

Fruin/Kernkamp 1906–1913 Fruin, R., and G. W. Kernkamp. *Brieven van Johan de Witt.* 4 vols. Amsterdam 1906–1913.

Garff 1998 Garff, Jan. "'Mr Lievens, I presume': On Some Hitherto Unnamed Portraits by Rembrandt." *Statens Museum for Kunst Journal* (1998): 67–85.

Gaskell 1982 Gaskell, Ivan. "Transformations of Cervantes' 'La Gitanilla' in Dutch Art." *Journal of the Warburg and Courtauld Institutes* 45 (1982): 263–270.

Van Gelder 1948–1949 Van Gelder, J. G. "De Schilders van de Oranjezaal." *Nederlands Kunsthistorisch Jaarboek* 2 (1948–1949): 119–164.

Van Gent 1998 Van Gent, J. "Portretten van Jan Jacobsz Hinlopen en zijn familie door Gabriël Metsu en Bartholomeus van der Helst." *Oud Holland* 112 (1998): 127–138.

Gersaint 1752 Gersaint, Edme François. *A catalogue and description of the etchings of Rembrandt van-Rhyn, with some account of his life. To which is added, a list of the best pieces of this master for the use of those who would make a select collection of his works.* London, 1752.

Gerson 1954 Gerson, Horst. "Twee vroege studies van Jan Lievens." *Oud Holland* 69 (1954): 179–180.

Gerson 1969 Gerson, Horst. "Rembrandt en de schilderkunst in Haarlem." In *Miscellanea I. Q. van Regteren Altena,* 138–142. Amsterdam, 1969.

Gerson 1971 Gerson, Horst. Review of *Le siècle de Rembrandt,* Petit Palais, Paris, 1970–1971. *Kunstchronik* 24 (1971): 145–153.

Gerson 1978 Gerson, Horst. "An Unknown Evangelist Series by Terbrugghen." *Burlington Magazine* 120 (November 1978): 754–755.

Gifford 1985 Gifford, E. Melanie. "*The Lute Player* by Jan Lievens: A Technical and Stylistic Study." In *The American Institute for Conservation of Historic and Artistic Works, Preprints of Papers Presented at the 13th Annual Meeting, Washington, DC, May 22–26, 1985,* 58–67.

Goetz 1938 Goetz, Herman. "Persians and Persian Costumes in Dutch Painting of the Seventeenth Century." *Art Bulletin* 20 (1938): 280–290.

Goossens 1996 Goossens, Eymert-Jan. *Treasure Wrought by Chisel and Brush: The Town Hall of Amsterdam in the Golden Age.* Zwolle, 1996.

Gottwald 2006 Gottwald, Franziska. Review of *Rembrandt's Mother: Myth and Reality,* Stedelijk Museum de Lakenhal, Leiden, 2005. *Kunstchronik* 7 (July 2006): 354–339.

Gottwald 2007 Gottwald, Franziska. "Das *tronie.* Versatzstück, Übungsfeld, und Meisterwerk. Die Genese einer Gattung der Malerei vom 15. Jahrhundert bis zu Rembrandt." PhD diss., Freie Universität, Berlin, 2007.

Grell 1989 Grell, Olle Peter. *Dutch Calvinists in Early Stuart London: The Dutch Church in Austi Friars, 1603–1642.* Leiden and New York, 1989.

Guratzsch 1980 Guratzsch, Herwig. *Die Auferweckung des Lazarus in der niederländischen Kunst von 1400 bis 1700. Ikonographie und Ikonologie.* 2 vols. Kortrijk, 1980.

Gutbrod 1996 Gutbrod, Helga. *Lievens und Rembrandt. Studien zum Verhältnis ihrer Kunst.* Frankfurt am Main, 1996.

Haak 1969 Haak, Bob. *Rembrandt: His Life, His Work, His Time.* Translated by Elizabeth Willems-Treeman. New York, 1969.

Haak 1984 Haak, Bob. *The Golden Age: Dutch Painters of the Seventeenth Century.* New York, 1984.

Haeger 1997 Haeger, Barbara. "Rubens' *Adoration of the Magi* and the Program for the High Altar of St. Michael's Abbey in Antwerp." *Simiolus* 25 (1997): 45–71.

Hainsworth 1933 Hainsworth, G. *Les "Novelas exemplares" de Cervantes en France au XVIIe siècle.* Paris, 1933.

Halewood 1982 Halewood, William H. *Six Subjects of Reformation Art: A Preface to Rembrandt.* Toronto, 1982.

Harksen 1976 Harksen, J. *Schloss Mosigkau. Alter Gemäldebestand.* Dessau–Mosigkau, 1976.

Haverkamp Begemann 1959 Haverkamp Begemann, Egbert. *Willem Buytewech.* Amsterdam, 1959.

Held 1991 Held, J. S. "Constantijn Huygens and Susannah van Baerle: A Hitherto Unknown Portrait."" *Art Bulletin* 73 (1991): 653–655.

Hermens 1998 *Looking Through Paintings: The Study of Painting Techniques and Materials in Support of Art Historical Research.* Edited by Erma Hermens et al. *Leids Kunsthistorisch Jaarboek* 11 (1998).

Heuscher 1738 Von Heuscher, Johann H. "Consignation en détail de tous les tomes d'estampes du Salon d'Estampes de Sa. Maj. Le Roi de Pol. Elect. De Saxe, Dresden 1738." MS, Kupferstich-Kabinett, Archives, Staatliche Kunstsammlungen Dresden.

Hill 2003 Hill, Robert. "Sir Dudley Carleton and His Relations with Dutch Artists, 1616–1632." *Leids Kunsthistorisch Jaarboek* 13 (2003): 255–274.

Hind 1913 Hind, A. M. "The Woodcut Portraits of Jan Lievens and Dirk de Bray." *The Imprint* 1 (1913): 233–239.

Hind 1915 Hind, A. M. *Catalogue of Dutch and Flemish drawings preserved in the department of prints and drawings in the British Museum.* Vol. 1, *Rembrandt and His School.* London, 1915.

Hirschfelder 2000 Hirschfelder, Dagmar. "Portrait or Character Head? The Term *Tronie* and Its Meaning in the Seventeenth Century." In Kassel and Amsterdam 2001–2002, 82–90.

Hofstede de Groot 1907–1927 Hofstede de Groot, Cornelis. *A Catalogue raisonné of the works of the most eminent Dutch painters of the seventeenth century, based on the work of John Smith….* 8 vols. London, 1907–1927. Translation of *Beschreibendes und kritisches Verzeichnis der Werke der hervorragendsten holländischen Maler des XVII. Jahrhunderts.* 10 vols. Esslingen and Paris, 1907–1927.

Hollstein 1949– Hollstein, F.W.H. *Dutch and Flemish Etchings, Engravings, and Woodcuts, c. 1450–1700.* 71 vols. Amsterdam, 1949–.

Hoogstraten 1678 Hoogstraten, Samuel van. *De Inleyding tot de Hooge Schoole der Schilderkonst anders de Zichtbaere Werelt.* Rotterdam, 1678.

Hottle 2004 Hottle, Andrew David. "Peter Paul Rubens and the Dedicated Print: Strategies in the Marketing of an Early Modern Master." PhD diss., Temple University, Philadelphia, 2004.

Houbraken 1753 Houbraken, Arnold. *De groote schouburgh der Nederlantsche konstschilders en schilderessen.* The Hague, 1753. Reprint, Amsterdam, 1980.

Van Hout 1998 Van Hout, Nico. "Meaning and Development of the Ground Layer in Seventeenth-Century Painting." In Hermens 1998, 99–225.

Howarth 1995 Howarth, David. *Lord Arundel and His Circle.* New Haven, 1995.

Huygens/Worp 1891 Worp, J. A. "Constantijn Huygens over de schilders van zijn tijd." *Oud Holland* 9 (1891): 106–136.

Huygens/Heesakkers 1994 *Mijn jeugd/Constantijn Huygens.* Translated by C. L. Heesakkers. Amsterdam, 1994.

Israel 1995 Israel, Jonathan I. *The Dutch Republic: Its Rise, Greatness, and Fall, 1477–1806.* Oxford, 1995.

Jacobs 2001/2002 Jacobs, Fred. "Jacques Gaultier, 'koninklijk luitspeler.' Naar aanleiding van zijn portret door Jan Lievens." *Kroniek van het Rembrandthuis* 1–2 (2001/2002): 24–31.

Janssen 2007 Janssen, Anouk. *Grijsaards in zwart-wit. De verbeelding van de ouderdom in de Nederlandse prentkunst (1550–1650).* Zutphen, 2007.

De Jager 1990 De Jager, Ronald. "Meester, leerjongen, leertijd. Een analyse van 17de-eeuwse Noord-Nederlandse leerlingcontracten van kunstschilders, goud- en zilversmeden." *Oud Holland* 104 (1990): 69–111.

James 1999 James, Susan E. "The Model as Catalyst: Nicholas Lanier and Margaret Lemon." *Jaarboek der Koninklijke Museum voor Schone Kunsten Antwerpen* (1999): 70–89.

Judson and Ekkart 1999 Judson, J. Richard, and Rudolf E. O. Ekkart. *Gerrit van Honthorst, 1592–1656.* Doornspijk, 1999.

Kan 1946 Kan, A. H. *De jeugd van Constantijn Huygens: Door hemzelf beschreven.* Rotterdam, 1946.

Kernkamp 1897 Kernkamp, G. W. *H. Bontemantel. De Regeeringe van Amsterdam, 1653–1672.* 2 vols. The Hague, 1897.

Kirby 1999 Kirby, Jo. "The Painter's Trade in the Seventeenth Century: Theory and Practice." *National Gallery Technical Bulletin* 20 (1999): 5–49.

Klessmann 1996 Klessmann, Rüdiger. "Jan Lievens und die Utrechter Caravaggisten." *Bulletin du Musée National de Varsovie* 37, no. 3–4 (1996): 181–198.

Klessmann and Keiser 1983 Klessmann, Rüdiger, and Bernd-Peter Keiser. *Die holländischen Gemälde. kritisches Verzeichnis mit 485 Abbildungen.* Braunschweig, 1983.

Knipping 1974 Knipping, John B. *Iconography of the Counter Reformation in the Netherlands: Heaven on Earth.* Nieuwkoop, 1974.

Köhne 1932 Köhne, Carl Ernst. *Studien zur Graphik von Ferdinand Bol und Jan Lievens.* Bottrop, 1932.

Kooijmans 1997 Kooijmans, L. *Vriendschap en de kunst van het overleven in de zeventiende eeuw en achttiende eeuw.* Amsterdam, 1997.

Kossmann 2000 Kossmann, E. H. *Political Thought in the Dutch Republic: Three Studies.* Amsterdam, 2000.

Larsen 1960 Larsen, Erik. "Brouwer ou Lievens. Etude d'un problème dans le paysage flamand." *Revue Belge d'archéologie et d'histoire de l'art* 29 (1960): 37–48.

Leerintveld 1989 Leerintveld, A.M.H. "'T'quam soo wel te pass.' Huygens' portretbijschriften en de datering van zijn portret geschilderd door Jan Lievens." *Leids Kunsthistorisch Jaarboek* 8 (1989): 159–183.

Van Leeuwen 2006 Van Leeuwen, Jan Storm. *Dutch Decorated Bookbinding in the Eighteenth Century.* 't Goy-Houten, 2006.

Lehmann-Haupt 1977 Lehmann-Haupt, Hellmut. *Introduction to the Woodcut of the Seventeenth Century.* New York, 1977.

Leupe 1874 Leupe, P. "De schilder Jan Lievensz. en de portretten van de Bickers, 1663–1664." *De Nederlandsche Spectator* (1874): 122–123.

Levi d'Ancona 1997 Levi d'Ancona, Mirella. *The Garden of the Renaissance Botanical Symbolism in Italian Painting.* Florence, 1997.

Liedtke 2007 Liedtke, Walter. *Dutch Paintings in the Metropolitan Museum of Art.* 2 vols. New York, 2007.

Linck 1859 Linck, J. F. "Bemerkungen und Zusätze zu dem Verzeichnisse von A. Bartsch über die Radierungen und Holzschnitte des Jan Lievens." *Archiv für die Zeichnende Künste* 5 (1859): 269–284.

Luijten 1989 Luijten, Ger. "Jan Lievens." *Print Quarterly* 6 (1989): 334–337.

Luijten 2001 Luijten, Ger. "Seventeenth-Century Flemish Painters and Their Prints." In *Rubens, Jordaens, Van Dyck, and Their Circle: Flemish Drawings from the Museum Boymans van Beuningen,* 41–47, by A.W.F.M. Meij et al. Rotterdam, 2001.

MacLaren 1960 Maclaren, Neil. *The Dutch School.* London, 1960.

MacLaren and Brown 1991 MacLaren, Neil, and Christopher Brown. *The Dutch School: 1600–1900.* London, 1991.

Magurn 1955 Magurn, Ruth Saunders. *The Letters of Peter Paul Rubens.* Cambridge, 1955.

Van Mander 1604/1618 Van Mander, Karel. *Het Schilder-Boeck.* Haarlem, 1604. 2nd ed. Amsterdam, 1618.

M.-H. Mauquoy-Hendrickx, Marie. *L'Iconographie d'Antoine van Dyck. Catalogue Raisonné.* Brussels, 1956.

Miedema 1973 Miedema, Hessel, ed. and trans. *Karel van Mander. Den Grondt der Edel vry Schilder-const.* 2 vols. Utrecht, 1973.

Millar 1960 Millar, Oliver, ed. "Abraham van der Doort's Catalogue of the Collections of Charles I." *Walpole Society* 37 (1960).

Moes 1907 Moes, A. W. "Jan Lievens." *Leids Jaarboekje* 4 (1907): 136–164.

Muller 1853 Muller, Frederik. *Beschrijvende catalogus van 7000 portretten, van Nederlanders, en van buitenlanders, tot Nederland in betrekking staande, afkomstig uit de collectiën. De Burlett, Verstolk van Soelen, Lamberts, enz.* Amsterdam, 1853.

Muylle 1994 Muylle, Jan. "Groteske koppen van Quinten Metsijs, Hieronymus Cock en Hans Liefrinck naar Leonardo da Vinci." *Zeventiende eeuw* 10, no. 2 (1994): 252–265.

Muylle 2001 Muylle, Jan. "Tronies toegeschreven aan Pieter Bruegel. Fysionomie en expressie." *Zeventiende eeuw* 17, no. 2 (2001): 174–204.

Muylle 2002 Muylle, Jan. "Tronies toegeschreven aan Pieter Bruegel. Fysionomie en expressie (2)." *Zeventiende eeuw* 18, no. 2 (2002): 118–148.

Myers 1966/1967 Myers, Mary L. "Rubens and the Woodcuts of Christoffel Jegher." *Metropolitan Museum of Art Bulletin* 25 (1966/1967): 7–23.

Nadler 1999 Nadler, Steven. *Spinoza: A Life.* New York, 1999.

Nadler 2003 Nadler, Steven. *Rembrandt's Jews.* Chicago, 2003.

Nichols 1983 Nichols, Lawrence W. "Job in Distress, a Newly Discovered Painting by Hendrick Goltzius." *Simiolus* 13 (1983): 182–188.

Orlers 1641 Orlers, Jan Jansz. *Beschrijvinge der Stadt Leyden.* Leiden, 1641.

Pappe 1925 Pappe, A. "Nachtrag zu dem Brustbild eines alten Mannes von Jan Lievens in der Eremitage." *Oud Holland* 42 (1925): 277.

Pelikan 1968 Pelikan, Jaroslav, ed. *Luther's Works.* Vol. 5, *Lectures on Genesis Chapters 26–30.* Saint Louis, 1968.

Pelinck 1941 Pelinck, E. *Jaarboekje voor Geschiedenis en Oudheidkunde van Leiden en Rijnland* 33 (1941): 198.

Peter-Raupp 1980 Peter-Raupp, Hanna. *Die Ikonographie des Oranjezaal.* Hildesheim and New York, 1980.

Pigler 1974 Pigler, Andor. *Barockthemen.* Vol. 1. Budapest, 1974.

Van der Ploeg et al. 2002 Van der Ploeg, Peter, Epco Runia, and Ariane van Suchtelen. *Dutch and Flemish Masters from the Kremer Collection.* The Hague, 2002.

Plomp 1986 Plomp, Michiel C. "'Een merkwaardige verzameling teekeningen' door Leonaert Bramer." *Oud Holland* 100 (1986): 81–153.

Plomp 1997 Plomp, Michiel C. *The Dutch Drawings in the Teylers Museum*. Vol. 2, *Artists Born between 1575 and 1630*. Haarlem, 1997.

Plomp 2001 Plomp, Michiel C. *Hartstochtelijk Verzameld. 18de-eeuwse Hollandse verzamelaars van tekeningen en hun collecties*. Bussum, 2001.

Porteman 1979 Porteman, K. "Vondel en de schilderkunst." *Vlaanderen Tielt* 28, no. 172 (1979): 299–305.

Postma 1988 Postma, Hugo J. "De Amsterdamse verzamelaar Herman Becker (c. 1617–1678). Nieuwe gegevens over een geldschieter van Rembrandt." *Oud Holland* 102 (1988): 1–21.

Van Raay, Spies, and Van Zoest 1987 Van Raay, S. B., W. P. Spies, and R. van Zoest. *"Tot hun Contentement gemaeckt." Het kunstbezit van het Hoogheemraadschap van Rijnland*. Amsterdam, 1987.

Raupp 1984 Raupp, Hans-Joachim. *Untersuchungen zu Künstlerbildnis und Künstlerdarstellung in den Niederlanden im 17. Jahrhundert*. Hildesheim, Zürich, New York, 1984.

Van Regteren Altena and Van Thiel 1964 Van Regteren Altena, I. Q., and Pieter J. J. van Thiel. *De portret-galerij van de Universiteit van Amsterdam en haar stichter Gerard van Papenbroeck, 1673–1743. In opdracht van de Historische Commissie der Universiteit*. Amsterdam, 1964.

Reznicek 1961 Reznicek, E.K.J. *Die Zeichnungen von Hendrick Goltzius mit einem beschreibenden Katalog*. 2 vols. Utrecht, 1961.

Rijksmuseum 1976 Van Thiel, Pieter J. J., et al. *All the Paintings of the Rijksmuseum in Amsterdam: A Completely Illustrated Catalogue*. Amsterdam, 1976.

Roethlisberger 1993 Roethlisberger, Marcel. *Abraham Bloemaert and His Sons: Paintings and Prints*. 2 vols. Doornspijk, 1993.

Rovinski 1894 Rovinski, Dmitri. *L'oeuvre gravé des élèves de Rembrandt et des maîtres qui ont gravé dans son goût*. Saint Petersburg, 1894.

Roy 1999 Roy, Ashok. "The National Gallery Van Dycks: Technique and Development." *National Gallery Technical Bulletin* 20 (1999): 50–83.

Royalton-Kisch 1991a Royalton-Kisch, Martin. "Rembrandt's Drawing of *The Entombment of Christ* over the *Raising of Lazarus*." *Master Drawings* 29, no. 2 (1991): 263–283.

Royalton-Kisch 1991b Royalton-Kisch, Martin. "An Early Drawing by Jan Lievens." *Master Drawings* 29, no. 4 (1991): 410–415.

Royalton-Kisch 1998 Royalton-Kisch, Martin. "The Lugt Drawings by Rembrandt and His School." *Burlington Magazine* 140 (1998): 618–622.

Saxton 1994 Saxton, J. "Lievens." *Print Quarterly* 11 (1994): 423–424.

Schama 1999 Schama, Simon. *Rembrandt's Eyes*. New York, 1999.

Van Schendel 1963 Van Schendel, A. "Het Portret van Constantijn Huygens door Jan Lievens." *Bulletin van het Rijksmuseum* 11 (1963): 5–10.

Schnackenburg 2004 Schnackenburg, Bernhard. "*Knabe im Atelier* und *Bücherstilleben*, zwei frühe Gemälde von Jan Lievens und ihr Leidener Kontext. Rembrandt, Jan Davidz. de Heem, Pieter Codde." *Oud Holland* 117 (2004): 33–47.

Schnackenburg 2007 Schnackenburg, Bernhard. "Jan Lievens und Pieter de Grebber." *Wallraf-Richartz Jahrbuch* 68 (2007): 181–218.

Schneider 1990 Schneider, Cynthia P. *Rembrandt's Landscapes*. New Haven, 1990.

Schneider 1929 Schneider, Hans. "Jan Lievens." *Thieme-Becker* 23 (1929): 214–215.

Schneider 1932 Schneider, Hans. *Jan Lievens, sein Leben und seine Werke*. Amsterdam, 1932.

Schneider/Ekkart 1973 Schneider, Hans. *Jan Lievens, sein Leben und seine Werke*. Supplement by Rudolf E. O. Ekkart. Amsterdam, 1973.

Scholten 2006 Scholten, F. "Quellinus's Burgomasters: A Portrait Gallery of Amsterdam Republicanism." *Simiolus* 32 (2006): 87–125.

Scholz 1985 Scholz, Horst. *Brouwer invenit. Druckgraphische Reproduktionen des 17.–19. Jahrhunderts nach Gemälden und Zeichnungen Adriaen Brouwers*. Marburg, 1985.

Schwartz 1985 Schwartz, Gary. *Rembrandt: His Life, His Paintings*. New York, 1985.

Sellin 1968 Sellin, Paul R. *Daniel Heinsius and Stuart England*. Leiden and London, 1968.

Silver 2003 Silver, Larry. "The Face Is Familiar: German Renaissance Portrait Multiples and Medals." *Word and Image* 19 (2003): 6–21.

Slatkes 1965 Slatkes, Leonard. *Dirck van Baburen (c. 1595–1624): A Dutch Painter in Utrecht and Rome*. Utrecht, 1965.

Slatkes and Franits 2007 Slatkes, Leonard J., and Wayne Franits. *The Paintings of Hendrick ter Brugghen, 1588–1629*. Amsterdam, 2007.

Slive 2001 Slive, Seymour. *Jacob van Ruisdael: A Complete Catalogue of His Paintings, Drawings, and Etchings*. New Haven and London, 2001.

Sluijter 1998 Sluijter, Eric Jan. "Rembrandt's *Bathsheba* and the Conventions of a Seductive Theme." In *Bathsheba Reading King David's Letter*, 145–169. Edited by Ann Jensen Adams. Cambridge and New York, 1998.

Sluijter 2006 Sluijter, Eric Jan. *Rembrandt and the Female Nude*. Amsterdam, 2006.

Smith 1829–1842 Smith, John. *A catalogue raisonné of the works of the most eminent Dutch, Flemish and French painters*. 9 vols. 1829–1842.

Van Someren 1888–1891 Van Someren, Jan Frederik. *Beschrijvende catalogus van gegraveerde portretten van Nederlanders. Vervolg op Frederik Mullers catalogus van 7000 portretten van Nederlanders*. 3 vols. Amsterdam, 1888–1891.

Spies 1993 Spies, Marijke. "Minerva's commentaar. Gedichten rond het Amsterdamse stadhuis." *De zeventiende eeuw* 9 (1993): 15–33.

Spink 1964 Spink, Ian. "Another Gaultier Affair." *Music and Letters* 45, no. 4 (1964): 345–347.

Spring 2004 Spring, Matthew. "Gaultier, Jacques (fl. 1617–1652)." *Oxford Dictionary of National Biography*. Oxford, 2004. *www.oxforddnb.com/view/article/11164*, accessed September 20, 2007.

Stechow 1973 Stechow, Wolfgang. "Rembrandt's Representations of the *Raising of Lazarus*." *Los Angeles County Museum Bulletin* 19 (1973): 7–11.

Steinmetz 1986 Steinmetz, David C. "Luther and the Ascent of Jacob's Ladder." *Church History* 55:2 (June 1986): 179–192.

Sterck 1930 Sterck, Johannes Franciscus Maria. *De werken van Vondel*. Amsterdam, 1930.

Stewart 1990 Stewart, J. Douglas. "Before Rembrandt's 'Shadow' Fell: Lievens, Van Dyck, and Rubens — Some Reconsiderations." *The Hoogsteder Mercury* 11 (1990): 42–47.

Stewart 2004 Stewart, J. Douglas. "Crossing the 'North-South Divide': The Young Lievens, Van Dyck, Rubens, and Rembrandt — Connections and Influences." In Volker Manuth and Axel Rüger, eds. *Collected Opinions: Essays on Netherlandish Art in Honour of Alfred Bader*, 188–201. London, 2004.

Stolow et al. 1969 Stolow, Nathan, James F. Hanlan, Raymond Boyer. "Element Distribution in Cross Sections of Paintings Studied by the X-ray Macroprobe." *Studies in Conservation* 14 (1969): 146–150.

Van Straten 2002 Van Straten, Roelof. "Rembrandt's 'Earliest Prints' Reconsidered." *Artibus et historiae* 45 (2002): 167–177.

Van Straten 2005 Van Straten, Roelof. *Young Rembrandt: The Leiden Years, 1606–1632*. Leiden, 2005.

Strauss 1973 Strauss, Walter. *Chiaroscuro: The Clair-Obscur Woodcuts by the German and Netherlandish Masters of the XVIth and XVIIth Centuries*. London, 1973.

Strauss and Van der Meulen 1979 Strauss, Walter L., and Marjon van der Meulen. *The Rembrandt Documents*. New York, 1979.

Sumowski 1979 Sumowski, Werner. *Drawings of the Rembrandt School*. Vol. 7. Edited and translated by Walter L. Strauss. New York, 1979.

Sumowski 1980 Sumowski, Werner. "Observations on Jan Lievens' Landscape Drawings." *Master Drawings* 18 (1980): 370–373, 430–439.

Sumowski 1983 Sumowski, Werner. *Gemälde der Rembrandt-Schüler*. Vols. 3 and 6. Landau, 1983.

Sutton 1990 Sutton, Peter. *Northern European Painting in the Philadelphia Museum of Art*. Philadelphia, 1990.

Tacitus 1995 Cornelius Tacitus. *The Histories*. Translated by Kenneth Wellesley. London, 1995.

Taylor 1998 Taylor, Paul. "The Glow in Late Sixteenth and Seventeenth Century Dutch Paintings." *Oud Holland* 114 (2000): 159–178.

Terrien 1996 Terrien, Samuel. *The Iconography of Job through the Centuries*. University Park, PA, 1996.

Terwen and Ottenheym 1993 Terwen, J. J., and K. A. Ottenheym. *Pieter Post (1608–1669)*. Zutphen, 1993.

Van Thiel 1978 Van Thiel, Pieter J. J. "Houtsneden van Werner van den Valckert en Mozes van Uyttenbroeck." *Oud Holland* 92 (1978): 7–42.

Tinagli 1997 Tinagli, Paola. *Women in Italian Renaissance Art*. Manchester, 1997.

Turner 2006 Turner, Jane Shoaf. *Dutch Drawings in the Pierpont Morgan Library. Seventeenth to Nineteenth Centuries*. 2 vols. New York, 2006.

Unger 1884 Unger, J.H.W. "Vondeliana II. Vondel's Handschriften." *Oud Holland* 2 (1884): 13–33, 111–134, 225–232, 293–308.

Vermij 2003 Vermij, Rienk. *The Calvinist Copernicans: The Reception of the New Astronomy in the Dutch Republic, 1575–1750*. Amsterdam, 2003.

Vey 1962 Vey, Horst. *Die Zeichnungen Anton van Dycks*. Brussels, 1962.

Vlieghe 2001 *Van Dyck, 1599–1999: Conjectures and Refutations*. Edited by Hans Vlieghe. Turnhout, 2001.

Vogelaar 2003 Vogelaar, Christiaan. "Schilderen en bouwen voor burgerij en stad." In R. C. J. van Maanen, ed. *Leiden. De Geschiedenis van een Hollandse Stad*, 149–171. Vol. 2, ed. S. Groenveld. Leiden, 2003.

Vogelaar 2008 Vogelaar, Christiaan. "'Ars longa, vita brevis.' Het boek in de Leidse schilderkunst van de gouden eeuw." In *Stad van Boeken. Handschrift en Druk in Leiden 1260–2000*, 269–287. Leiden, 2008.

Da Voragine 1993 Da Voragine, Jacobus. *The Golden Legend: Readings on the Saints*. 2 vols. Translated by William Granger Ryan. Princeton, 1993.

Vos 1662 Vos, Jan. *Alle de Gedichten*. Amsterdam, 1662.

Waagen 1857 Waagen, Gustav Friedrich. *Galleries and Cabinets of Art in Great Britain*. London, 1857.

Van de Waal 1940 Van de Waal, H. "De Hollandsche houtsneden der zeventiende eeuw. I: Landschappen van Hendrick Goltzius; II: Werner van den Valckert en Jan Lievens." *Halcyon* (1940): 1–16.

Van de Waal 1952 Van de Waal, H. *Drie eeuwen vaderlandsche geschied-uitbeelding 1500–1800. Een iconologische studie*. 2 vols. The Hague, 1952.

Van de Waal 1974 Van de Waal, H. "The Iconographical Background to Rembrandt's *Civilis*." In *Steps Toward Rembrandt: Collected Articles 1937–1972*, 28–43. Amsterdam and London, 1974.

Wadum 1998a Wadum, Jørgen. "The Antwerp Brand on Paintings on Panel." In Hermens 1998, 179–198.

Wadum 1998b Wadum, Jørgen. "Historical Overview of Panel-Making Techniques in the Northern Countries." In *The Structural Conservation of Panel Paintings*, 149–177. Edited by Kathleen Dardes and Andrea Rothe. Los Angeles, 1998.

Wallert 2006a Wallert, Arie. "Drie halen, één betalen." *Bulletijn van het Rijksmuseum*, 54 (2006): 144–153, 220–221.

Wallert 2006b Wallert, Arie. "Een onopgelost probleem. Samson en Delila." *Bulletin van het Rijksmuseum* 54 (2006): 157–161, 221–222.

Weber 1985 Weber, Gregor J. M. "*Dus leeft de dappre Graaf.* Zu einem Bildnis Andries de Graeffs von Jan Lievens (1607–1674)." *Oud Holland* 99 (1985): 44–56.

Weber 1992 Weber, Gregor J. M. "Jan Lievens's *The Shield-Raising of Brinio*: A Second Oil Sketch." *The Hoogsteder Mercury* 13–14 (1992): 44–50.

Van de Wetering 2000 Van de Wetering, Ernst. *Rembrandt: The Painter at Work*. Amsterdam, 2000.

Weyerman 1729 Weyerman, Jacob Campo. *De levens-beschryvingen der nederlandsche konstschilders en konstschilderessen*. Vol. 1. The Hague, 1729.

White 1999 White, Christopher. *Rembrandt as an Etcher: A Study of the Artist at Work*. New Haven, 1999.

Wilson 1994 Wilson, Michael I. *Nicholas Lanier, Master of the King's Musick*. Aldershot and Brookfield, 1994.

De Winkel 2006 De Winkel, Marieke. *Fashion and Fancy: Dress and Meaning in Rembrandt's Paintings*. Amsterdam, 2006.

Wishnevsky 1967 Wishnevsky, Rose. "Studien zum *Portrait Historiée* in den Niederlanden." PhD diss., Ludwig-Maximilians-Universität, Munich, 1967.

De Witt 1999 De Witt, David. "A Scene from Cervantes in the Stadholder's Collection." *Oud Holland* 113 (1999): 181–186.

DeWitt 2006 DeWitt, Lloyd. "Evolution and Ambition in the Career of Jan Lievens, 1607–1674." PhD diss., University of Maryland, College Park, 2006.

Wood 2003 Wood, Jeremy. "Nicholas Lanier (1588–1666) and the Origins of Drawings Collecting in Stuart England." In *Collecting Prints and Drawings in Europe, c. 1500–1750*, 85–122. Edited by Christopher Baker et al. Aldershot and Burlington, 2003.

Worp 1892–1899 Worp, J. A. *De Gedichten van Constantijn Huygens*. Groningen, 1892–1899.

Worp 1897 Worp, J. A. "Fragment eener autobiographie van Constantijn Huygens." *Bijdragen en Medeelingen van het Historisch Genootschap* 18 (1897): 1–121.

Wurfbain 1997 Wurfbain, M. L. "The *Soothsayer* by Jan Lievens in Berlin: An Attempt at an Interpretation." In *Rembrandt, Rubens, and the Art of Their Time: Recent Perspectives*, 224–233. Papers in Art History from the Pennsylvania State University 11. University Park, PA, 1997.

Van der Wyck, Kloek, and Niemeijer 1989–1990 Van der Wyck, H.W.M, Wouter Th. Kloek, and J. W. Niemeijer. *De kasteeltekeningen van Roelant Roghman*. 2 vols. Alphen aan den Rijn, 1989–1990.

Wyckoff 1998 Wyckoff, Elizabeth. "Innovation and Popularization: Printmaking and Print Publishing in Haarlem during the 1620s." PhD diss., Columbia University, 1998.

Zell 2002 Zell, Michael. "The Gift among Friends: Rembrandt's Art in the Network of his Patronal and Social Relations." In *Rethinking Rembrandt*, 173–194. Edited by Alan Chong and Michael Zell. Zwolle, 2002.

Index

Note: Page numbers in **bold** type indicate illustrations.

Credits

FRONT COVER

Stedelijk Museum De Lakenhal, Leiden, The Netherlands

COLORPLATES

Bildarchiv Preussischer Kulturbesitz / Art Resource, NY: *back cover and cats. 26, 61–66, 68, 73, 77, 79, 108, 109, 119, 128* (Volker H. Schneider, photographer)

Collection Groninger Museum: *cat. 112* (John Stoel, photographer)

© President and Fellows of Harvard College: *cats. 96, 110* (Imaging Department), *cat. 130* (Allan Macintyre, photographer), *cat. 132* (Katya Kallsen, photographer)

Paul Litherland, photographer: *cat. 4*

Musée des Beaux-Arts, Nancy: *cat. 32* (G. Mangin, photographer)

Photographs © 2008 Museum of Fine Arts, Boston: *cats. 72, 75, 82, 84*

© The National Gallery, London: *cats. 45, 48*

Images courtesy of the Board of Trustees, National Gallery of Art, Washington: *cats. 20, 87, 104* (Lorene Emerson, photographer), *cats. 98, 139* (Dean Beasom, photographer)

Photograph © National Gallery of Canada: *cat. 25*

Palace of Westminster Collection: *cat. 101*

Prudence Cuming Associates Limited: *cat. 36*

Réunion des Musées Nationaux / Art Resource, NY: *cat. 94* (Madeleine Coursaget, photographer)

© Rijksmuseum, Amsterdam: *cats. 15, 16*

Reproduced with the kind permission of the Royal Pavillion and Museums (Brighton and Hove), United Kingdom: *cat. 31*

The Pierpont Morgan Library, New York: *cat. 125*

Stedelijk Museum De Lakenhal, Leiden, The Netherlands: *cats. 7, 25*

Photograph © The Walters Art Museum, Baltimore: *cat. 13*

COMPARATIVE ILLUSTRATIONS

Anonymous owner: *Gifford fig. 10* (x-radiograph)

Art Resource, NY: *Wheelock fig. 26* (Erich Lessing, photographer)

Bildarchiv Preussischer Kulturbesitz / Art Resource, NY: *Dickey fig. 14; Rubinstein figs. 6, 10, 13; cat. 11 (fig. 1), cat. 28 (fig. 1), cat. 37 (fig. 2), cat. 80 (fig. 1), cat. 95 (fig. 1)*

Herbert Boswank, photographer: *Rubinstein fig. 8*

© The British Museum: *Dickey figs. 5, 8–11; Rubinstein fig. 11; cat. 15 (fig. 3), cat. 31 (fig. 2), cat. 32 (fig. 3), cat. 71 (fig. 2), cat. 81 (fig. 2), cat. 119–120 (fig. 1), cat. 138–139 (fig. 1)*

© Christie's Images Ltd: *cat. 108 (fig. 1)*

© The Cleveland Museum of Art: *cat. 15 (fig. 1)*

© Eglise du Mas d'Agenais, France / Giraudon / The Bridgeman Art Library: *cat. 32 (fig. 1)*

Details and photomacrographs by Melanie Gifford: *Gifford figs. 1, 2, 4, 5, 8, 9, 12, 14, 17*

© President and Fellows of Harvard College: *cat. 126–127 (fig. 2)*

Photograph © 1998 LACMA / Museum Associates: *cat. 31 (fig. 3)*

LWL-Landesmuseum für Kunst und Kulturgeschichte Münster: *cat. 9–10 (fig. 3)* (Sabine Ahlbrand-Dornseif and Rudolf Wakonigg, photographers)

© Lukas-Art in Flanders: *cat. 39–40 (fig. 1)*

Images © The Metropolitan Museum of Art: *Wheelock fig. 14; Rubinstein fig. 9* (Malcolm Varon, photographer)

© Museum Martena, Franeker: *cat. 45 (fig. 1)*

© Museumlandschaft Hessen Kassel: *Wheelock figs. 6, 7; cat. 7 (fig. 1)*

Images courtesy of the Board of Trustees, National Gallery of Art, Washington: *Van der Veen figs. 1, 4; Dickey fig. 12; cat. 22 (fig. 1), cat. 81 (fig. 1)*

Netherlands Institute for Art History (RKD): *Wheelock fig. 9*

Courtesy of the Philadelphia Museum of Art: *Gifford fig. 1* (photomicrograph of paint cross section); *Gifford fig. 2* (x-radiograph)

© The Pierpont Morgan Library, New York. 2007: *cat. 101 (fig. 1)*

Réunion des Musées Nationaux / Art Resource, NY: *Wheelock fig. 18; cat. 32 (fig. 2)*

© Rijksmuseum, Amsterdam: *Wheelock figs. 10, 12; Dickey figs. 1–4, 6, 7; cat. 2 (fig. 1), cat. 19 (fig. 1), cat. 25 (fig. 2), cat. 67–70 (figs. 1, 2), cat. 71 (fig. 1), cat. 73 (fig. 1), cat. 81 (fig. 1), cat. 87 (fig. 1), cat. 111 (fig. 1)*

© The Saint Louis Art Museum: *cat. 12 (fig. 1)*

© SPSG, Verwendung nur mit Genehmigung und Quellenangabe: *cat. 50 (fig. 1)*

© Staatliche Graphische Sammlung München: *cat. 136–137 (fig. 1)*

© Stichting Koninklijk Paleis te Amsterdam: *Wheelock fig. 25*

© Stichting RKD; IRR assembly by Melanie Gifford: *Gifford fig. 3* (infrared reflectogram)

© Uffizi, Florence — Gabinetto Disegni e Stampe / Photo VASARI, Rome: *Rubinstein fig. 1*

Courtesy of The Walters Art Museum: *Gifford fig. 5* (photomicrograph of paint cross section); *Gifford fig. 6* (x-radiograph)

Joseph Zehavi, photographer, 2008: *cat. 126–127 (fig. 1)*

DETAILS AT SECTION OPENINGS

All works by Jan Lievens

pages i–ii: *Self-Portrait*, c. 1629–1630, oil on panel (cat. 18). Private collection

page vi: *Bearded Man with a Beret*, c. 1630, oil on panel (cat. 20). National Gallery of Art, Washington, Gift (Partial and Promised) of the Kaufman Americana Foundation in honor of George M. and Linda H. Kaufman

page xii: *Prince Charles Louis with His Tutor, as the Young Alexander Instructed by Aristotle*, 1631, oil on canvas (cat. 29). The J. Paul Getty Museum, Los Angeles

page 1: *Cain Slaying Abel*, c. 1640–1644, woodcut, only state (cat. 81). Rijksmuseum, Amsterdam

pages 28–29: *Portrait of Adriaen Trip*, 1644, oil on canvas (cat. 44). Museum Het Rembrandthuis, Amsterdam, on loan from a private collection

page 29: *Portrait of Andries de Graeff*, 1657, black chalk, with traces of white heightening (cat. 117). Teylers Museum, Haarlem

page 40–41: *Portrait of Rembrandt*, c. 1629, oil on panel (cat. 17). Rijksmuseum, Amsterdam, on loan from a private collection

page 41: *Landscape with Peasants* (figures added by David Teniers II), c. 1638, oil on canvas (cat. 37). Kremer Collection

pages 54–55: *Fighting Cardplayers and Death*, c. 1638, etching, state 3 (cat. 78). Städel Museum, Frankfurt am Main

page 55: *Bust of a Man Facing Forward*, c. 1640–1644, chiaroscuro woodcut, only state (cat. 84). Museum of Fine Arts, Boston, Bequest of W. G. Russell Allen

pages 68–69: *The Feast of Esther*, c. 1625–1628, pen and brush with chalk and gouache (cat. 93). Kupferstich-Kabinet, Staatliche Kunstsammlungen Dresden

page 69: *Forest Interior with a Draftsman*, 1660s(?), pen and brown ink and brown wash (cat. 132). Maida and George Abrams Collection, Boston, Massachusetts, on loan to Fogg Art Museum, Harvard University

pages 80–81: *Job in His Misery*, 1631, oil on canvas (cat. 25). National Gallery of Canada, Ottawa, Gift of the National Art Collections Fund of Great Britain, 1933

page 81: *Seated Hermit*, c. 1630, etching and engraving, state 1, with pen and brown ink (cat. 71). The British Museum, London

pages 280–281: *Saint Paul*, c. 1624–1625, oil on panel (cat. 4). Agnes Etherington Art Centre, Kingston, Gift of Alfred and Isabel Bader, 2006

page 281: *Trumpeter on Horseback*, c. 1625–1628, pen and brown ink with gray wash, over black chalk (cat. 91). Rijksmuseum, Amsterdam

Art

A Dutch Master Rediscovered

ROGER KIMBALL

IN his classic essay "Of the Standard of Taste," David Hume asked how we could tell whether a given work was a masterpiece. "Durable admiration" was the criterion he offered. Which is to say, it's not so much *our* judgment as the judgment of the ages that does the sifting. Faced with the work of our contemporaries, we can announce our likes and dislikes, but we must wait upon the dispassionate adjudications of time to arrive at any authoritative discriminations. When it came to matters of aesthetic judgment, authority, for Hume, was largely a posthumous energy.

I thought about Hume's thesis as I made my way through one of this season's most engaging exhibitions: "Jan Lievens: A Dutch Master Rediscovered." I saw the show twice, once at the National Gallery in Washington and once at the Milwaukee Art Museum, where it is on view in Santiago Calatrava's dramatic building until April 26.

My guess is that, unless you are an expert in 17th-century Dutch painting, you have never heard of Lievens (1607–74). I hadn't, or if I had, I promptly forgot the name. Yet during his lifetime, Lievens was widely considered the equal if not the superior of his friend and fellow Leiden-born artist Rembrandt. The diplomat and cultural impresario Constantijn Huygens, who met them both in 1628, decided that Rembrandt was "superior to Lievens in his sure touch and liveliness of emotions" but that Lievens displayed "greater . . . inventiveness and audacious themes and forms."

This exhibition of some 140 paintings, etchings, and drawings aims to promote Lievens from his tenancy among the footnotes of art history to an honored place in the main text. Even a quick look at Lievens's work shows that some such corrective is long overdue. The temptation of course lies in overstating the case. This is something that the curators by and large avoid. Their goal is to rescue Lievens from unjust obscurity, not to elevate him beyond his deserts.

The story of Lievens's reputation offers a fascinating study in the vicissitudes of popular taste. A year younger than Rembrandt, Lievens was clearly the more precocious of the two. Indeed, Lievens began his career as a sort of Mozart of the art world, setting up shop at the age of 12. By 14, he was producing virtuoso works. By 16, he was capable of paintings like *The Cardplayers*, a work of considerable psychological penetration—the loser's cuirass cannot defend him against the assaults of bad luck—as well as astonishing technical command. (The smiling chap with the blue sash and pipe, by the way, is almost certainly Rembrandt.)

In the scheme of things, the 1620s were not so long ago. But obscurity colludes with the voracious amnesia of time. Our knowledge of Lievens's life and career consists of a dozen visible milestones interspersed by numerous question marks. We know the basic itinerary. A notable debut in Leiden. To London when he was 24: another brilliant performance, with commissions from Charles I and the Earl of Arundel. Lievens learned a lot about portraiture from Anthony van Dyck (b. 1599), who included him (but not Rembrandt) in the *Iconography*, his famous visual chrestomathy of notable artists.

The word "peripatetic" occurs frequently in discussions of Lievens. In 1635, he went to Antwerp, where he developed a more cosmopolitan style—what the curators refer to as an "international style"—absorbing something of the drama of Rubens, the elegance of Titian. The year 1644 found Lievens in Amsterdam, where Rembrandt's star had risen and, following the death of his wife Saskia, was beginning to fade. He went to The Hague in 1654, back to Amsterdam in 1659, and then back to Leiden.

Lievens never achieved the celebrity or the riches that Rembrandt enjoyed at the apogee of his career, but like Rembrandt he died in poverty. In 1674, in his late sixties, he went back to Amsterdam with all his worldly goods in tow. His landlord refused to let him in without a deposit. He died in June, halfway to the obscurity that awaited him. *Vita brevis*, and *ars* only sometimes *longa*.

History's radar is not usually precise

Mr. Kimball is publisher of Encounter Books, and co-editor and publisher of The New Criterion.

about figures such as Lievens. We know he was born of (as a contemporary patron put it) "respectable parents"—his father was a moderately successful embroiderer—in Leiden. We know he studied with Pieter Lastman, who was also Rembrandt's teacher. We know that he and Rembrandt were friendly rivals. Did they briefly share a studio in Leiden? We aren't sure. But their friendship shows itself in Lievens's sympathetic portrait of Rembrandt (1629), and in the frequency with which he included him in his early canvases. The rivalry peeks out in other ways. At the instigation of Huygens, Lievens and Rembrandt painted several paintings on the same themes: the raising of Lazarus, for example. Rembrandt admired Lievens's treatment sufficiently to acquire the canvas for his own collection. But Rembrandt was not above backdating some of his own work, presumably to suggest that he had pioneered rather than followed in the exploration of certain themes and modes of painting.

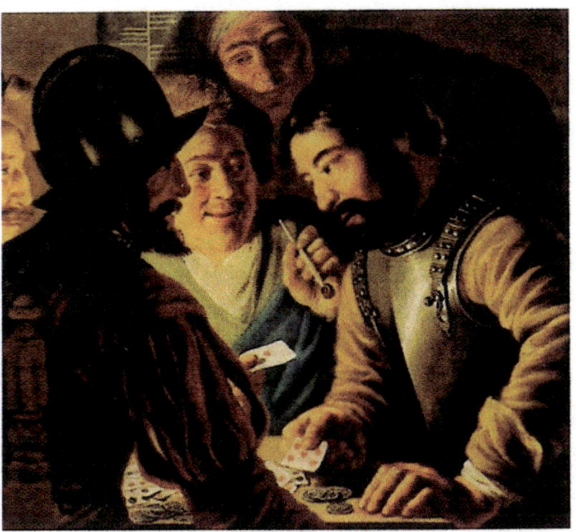

The Cardplayers, *ca. 1623–24*

NATIONAL GALLERY OF ART/MILWAUKEE ART MUSEUM

You cannot walk through this exhibition without acknowledging what the curators set out to teach you: that Jan Lievens was an extraordinary artist whose work encompassed history painting, Biblical allegory, landscape, and portraiture. Portraiture, in fact, was Lievens's special strength. He had a knack for animating faces with character, and this exhibition features several memorable portraits. A drawing of René Descartes (mid-1640s), for example, depicts a more vulnerable, less stately personage than the famous oil portrait of the philosopher by Frans Hals, while Lievens's portrait of Anna Maria van Schurman (1649), the first woman to attend university in the Netherlands and herself an accomplished artist, is a study in warmth and delicacy.

Is Lievens set to become a household name like Rembrandt, Rubens, Titian, and van Dyck? No. In his excellent introductory essay for the catalogue, Arthur Wheelock remarks: "The cruel irony is that Lievens's artistic achievement, whether in assessment of individual works or his entire oeuvre, has come to be considered almost exclusively in relation to Rembrandt during his early Leiden years." This exhibition both underscores that irony and inspires a new appreciation for the wisdom of tradition.

Wheelock offers several reasons for Lievens's failure to enter the canon as conspicuously as Rembrandt. He was a Dutch artist who rarely painted in the Dutch style. He exuded brio, but not clarity or precision. He was adept at creating effects, but Wheelock is right about a "labored" quality to his modeling and sometimes "muddy" paint handling.

Lievens was good at inveigling commissions from the great and influential. He endeavored mightily to give them what they wanted, which helps account for his immediate success. He was less skilled at inveigling a consistent artistic vision from himself. He was something of a chameleon, not in the sense of changing frequently—though he did that as well—but in the sense of absorbing influences promiscuously. The word "Rembrandt" adumbrates a mood, a quality of perception, as well as a particular artist. There is no correlative sensibility that we can attach to Jan Lievens. He was too miscellaneous in his achievement.

His technical mastery was dazzling, and always brash. Constantijn Huygens accused both Lievens and Rembrandt of "stubbornness" and an excess of "self-confidence." But Rembrandt negotiated that final hurdle to greatness that Lievens never managed: He matured into himself. Lievens never quite stopped being precocious, which means that there always remained something penultimate about his development. He was bursting with talent, fired by ambition, buoyed by that self-confidence that Huygens registered. But there was an omnivorousness about Lievens that impeded him from evolving from the propaedeutic activity of mastering styles to the consummate achievement of creating one. Arthur Wheelock and his colleagues have done yeoman's service recovering Lievens from the margins of art history. **NR**

Travel

The Hills Are Alive

JAY NORDLINGER

Augusta, Ga.

I WOULD be embarrassed to admit how big a part the Masters has played in my life: in my mental life, and, to a degree, my writing life. I'm talking, of course, about the tournament held every April at the Augusta National Golf Club.

Over the years, on practice ranges far and wide, I have "played" holes at Augusta National. This relieves the tedium of practice. I take the clubs I believe will be necessary on each hole. For example, I'll take a 6-iron on 16 tee—aiming for the traditional Sunday pin position. And, at night, I compete in the Masters, as I'm drifting off to sleep. Often, I'm head to head with Tiger. Strangely, he loses.

I am not alone in this, by the way—this Masters fantasizing. In fact, it is a pretty common condition. I can introduce you to many others who suffer from it, or rather, enjoy it.

Like them, I have watched the Masters on television from an early age. I remember the tournaments more than I do Christmases, and probably as much as I do presidential elections. Seve slashing his way around the course. Mize chipping in on Norman. Lyle coming out of the bunker. Floyd hitting it into the water on 11. And, above all, Nicklaus winning the tournament in 1986, at the age of 46. (He was the oldest Masters champion ever.) I will never forget watching the final round unfold, as I sat in my dorm room. That was an afternoon of utter amazement and jubilation.

The next Sunday, in the same room, on the same television, I watched Horowitz return to Russia, for the first time in over 60 years. I was extremely nervous as he played—as I had been when Nicklaus played. But, like Jack, he triumphed. A couple weekends later, Willie Shoemaker